THE HUMAN VENTURE
The Globe Encompassed

THE
HUMAN
VENTURE

The Globe Encompassed

A World History since 1500

Anthony Esler

College of William and Mary

Prentice-Hall, Inc., Englewood Cliffs, New Jersey 07632

For Jamie Arthur Esler
who did the history of the world
on one page
many years ago

Library of Congress Cataloging in Publication Data

Esler, Anthony.
    The human venture.

    Includes bibliographies and index.
    1. History, Modern.   I. Title.
D209.E75   1986   909   85-9405
ISBN 0-13-447855-X

Editorial supervision: Serena Hoffman
Interior design: Levavi & Levavi
Cover design: Dawn Stanley
Manufacturing buyer: Barbara Kelly Kittle

PRINTED IN THE UNITED STATES OF AMERICA

10 9 8 7 6 5 4

ISBN 0-13-447855-X 01

PRENTICE-HALL INTERNATIONAL (UK) LIMITED, *London*
PRENTICE-HALL OF AUSTRALIA PTY. LIMITED, *Sydney*
EDITORA PRENTICE-HALL DO BRASIL, LTDA., *Rio de Janeiro*
PRENTICE-HALL CANADA INC., *Toronto*
PRENTICE-HALL HISPANOAMERICANA, S.A., *Mexico*
PRENTICE-HALL OF INDIA PRIVATE LIMITED, *New Delhi*
PRENTICE-HALL OF JAPAN, INC., *Tokyo*
PRENTICE-HALL OF SOUTHEAST ASIA PTE. LTD., *Singapore*
WHITEHALL BOOKS LIMITED, *Wellington, New Zealand*

Contents

Preface

This attempt at a history of the world aims at global perspective and breadth of coverage, as any world history should. It also seeks to personalize the past by giving *people* the place they deserve in it. Above all, it attempts to tell history like it is—as a story going somewhere.

Global perspective means, in the first instance, a book that is not Western- or Europe-centered—not a history of Western civilization with chapters on "other cultures" pasted in here and there. This world history also tries not to be Eurasian-centered, by giving due attention to the emergence of civilizations in Africa and the Americas as well. All continents do not get equal coverage, but the goal was to start from the pole and follow history where it led.

Breadth of coverage here means more than geographical sweep, however. It means going beyond the frontiers of all historic civilizations to spend some time at least with preurban peoples, from Eurasian steppe nomads to Australian Bushmen. It means concern with the female half of humankind, both in terms of outstanding individuals and the broad social roles played by women over the centuries. It means a special focus on "high culture"—the art and ideas of each age and people—since ideas constitute our most enduring legacy from the global past.

The *humanizing of history* seems to the author no more than its due. A history that is entirely given over to trends and movements, classes, institutions, statistics, and other abstractions is, for many readers, no history at all. Writing human beings back into global history would seem to be of particular importance, given the abstract quality the rest of the world already has for most of us. By illuminating the Chinese, Indian, or African past with the characters and deeds of Huang-ti, Asoka, Mansa Musa, Buddha, and Confucius (their Washingtons, Napoleons, and Christs) we may recapture the pasts of other peoples with some of the same richness and fullness we feel toward our own.

Finally, the *strong narrative line* that the book attempts to maintain reflects two convictions on the author's part. The first is that history is, by its very nature, a matter of movement, of change, of development or degeneration, but in any case, of human affairs on the move through time. The second and more controversial assumption here is that global history is going somewhere, that it is the story of the coming together of all the peoples of the world. To what final end, only the future can say.

So hefty a labor as this has inevitably accumulated many pleasant debts.

I would like to thank Dan Pellow of Prentice-Hall's sales department for asking what my next writing plans were—and for taking the outlandish answer seriously. I would particularly like to thank Steve Dalphin, the history editor at Prentice-Hall, for seeing possibilities beneath my exuberant explanations of the project, dispatched to him during my wanderings from Cambridge, Provence, and Greece. Thanks also to Steve for providing just the right amount of prodding, for ignoring my suggestions that we defer a deadline or two, and for general encouragement with this enterprise.

I would like to express my gratitude to the History Department at the College of William and Mary for providing time, occasional travel money, and unlimited Xeroxing privileges (which must have taken rather more of a chunk out of the budget than anybody expected). I would also like to thank the William and Mary Developing Nations Seminar (Judy Ewell, director) for listening to pieces of the work-in-progress and offering cogent criticisms.

Thanks to Serena Hoffman, my production editor, for seeing both volumes through the exhausting final phases, and for dropping in a heartening word just when it was needed most. My appreciation also to Prentice-Hall's highly professional copy editor, Bruce Fulton, for close reading, excellent suggestions, and understanding on those occasions when I stubbornly refused to take the advice offered.

My very real gratitude goes to the traditionally anonymous scholarly readers commissioned by the publisher for their hard work, insights, objections, and advice. The finished product owes much to their criticisms—though all surviving errors are, of course, my own responsibility. My thanks to Joe Gowaskie, Rider College; John Voll, University of New Hampshire; Penny S. Gold, Knox College; Walter S. Hanchett, SUNY/Cortland; Donald L. Layton, Indiana State University; Melvin E. Page, Murray State University; Susan Fitzpatrick, Lindenwood College; and Frank A. Kierman, Jr.

Extravagant thanks must go to the colleagues and friends who listened, argued, answered my endless questions, and generally made this book possible. I cannot possibly list all the tolerant scholars who put up with my intrusions over the three years in which the project was officially in progress. Among those I badgered most incessantly and unconscionably, however, let me at least take this chance to thank once more Professors Ismail Abdalla, Craig Canning, Tom Chang, Ed Crapol, Carol Clemeau Esler, Judy Ewell, Pat Lewis, Gil McArthur, Rich Sigwalt, John Voll, Cam Walker, and Jeanne Zeidler.

For scholarly help and encouragement from a distance, I would like to thank especially: Marjorie W. Bingham, of Women in World Area Studies; Steve Brush, for Peru when things were much too exciting to be saddled with a guest as well; Chris Drake, for showing me how to look at the land; Carol Clemeau Esler, for all the village-level sojourns in Europe; Marcia Davidson Field, for her insights into Latin America over many years; Richard Goff, who went through the manuscript first and took time out from the Atlantic to provide caustic comment and sage council; Professor Isaria N. Kimambo, of the University of Dar es Salaam; Professor Dong Leshan, of the Chinese Academy of Social Sciences; Don Meyer, for Nairobi, Lamu, and the border roads of India; and Professor Jerry Weiner, for running a tight ship from Abidjan to Zanzibar.

Anthony Esler
College of William and Mary

Introduction

THE GLOBAL VENTURE

THE VOYAGE OF THE *VICTORIA*

On September 20, 1519, Ferdinand Magellan sailed from San Lucar in Spain on a voyage intended, like Columbus's voyages of a quarter century before, to reach the East Indies by sailing west. Magellan had five ships and 240 men under his command.

On the three-year voyage that followed, the Iberian mariners faced the storms around Cape Horn, three months without supplies or fresh water on the wide Pacific, combat with South Sea islanders, the monsoon winds of the Indian Ocean, and heavy going around the Cape of Good Hope. They deserted, mutinied, ate rats and sawdust, starved and died in large numbers. Four ships vanished one by one—sunk, burned, deserted. Magellan himself was killed in a petty tribal skirmish in the Philippines. Only a single vessel and eighteen men completed the voyage. But Captain Sebastian del Cano and the seventeen surviving crewmen who tacked the battered, barnacle-heavy *Victoria* back into the harbor of San Lucar on September 6, 1522, were the first human beings to circumnavigate the globe.

The voyage of the *Victoria* and the brutal, insubordinate, mostly illiterate men who sailed her was more than an epic of the sea. It stood for a much larger historic fact: the encompassing of the globe by European arms, technology, fanaticism, greed, and daring. It was the beginning of something even larger—five centuries of the slow and frequently painful coming together of all the peoples of the world.

This volume is an attempt to trace the slow stages and convoluted paths of that historic movement.

PERILOUS VENTURE

The human adventure we call history, as was suggested in the first volume of this book, has always been a perilous one. Nor has its outcome ever been assured.

Dangers of all sorts have menaced every human culture, bedeviled every significant human endeavor down the centuries. Nature itself has been the source of many of these threats, from the advance of the glaciers to the Black Death. Human enemies have also done their share to fill the world with danger, threatening us with tyranny or anarchy, with foreign invasion or domestic dictatorship. Perilous as many of the world's borderlands—and the streets of some of our own cities—may be today, they were considerably more dangerous in the not-too-distant past.

The outcome, too, has always been in doubt, as it is today. Whole species of our hominid line died out over the long evolutionary road to the present. In more recent times, entire cultures have collapsed under the buffetings of history, from Mohenjodaro in ancient India to most of the Amerindian societies who once owned the North American continent. As far as historians, archaeologists, and other students of the human past can tell, we have been given no title to this planet. There seems to be no intrinsic reason why we should not pass like the dodo or the dinosaur when our turn comes.

Yet human beings never seem to accept such a verdict in their hearts for long. We take our risks, accept the odds against success—and forge ahead with truly astonishing enterprises. We have peopled the earth in greater numbers than any other mammal. We have invented tools and language, agriculture, art, religion, science. And still we move onward, generation after remarkable generation, adventuring further into history.

We may not really know where we are going—though we often think we do—and the chances of survival for any given culture are not high. But we are the most purposive of creatures, and we will undoubtedly keep on trying.

The greatest enterprise of the whole human venture has been the building of the far-reaching and immensely complex cultures we call civilizations. And the climax of this great enterprise may well be the global venture upon which we have been embarked for the past five centuries.

THE GREATEST ENTERPRISE

The unique form of human society we call civilization first appeared on earth more than five thousand years ago. It has been with us, in one form or another, in one place or another, ever since.

Civilization is a hard term to define. Historians tend to see its beginnings among the first people who learned to build cities, work metals, read and write. Civilization is also commonly defined in terms of segregation into nations and social classes, the establishment of bureaucratic government, conquest and empire building, and some form of organized exchange of goods over long distances. More debatably, civilizations are credited with increasingly complex religions and philosophies, more subtle and more splendid arts.

All of these things began to happen in some semblance of harmony around 3500 B.C. in the Middle East.

Over the millennia that followed, a number of different civilizations grew up in Asia, Africa, Europe, and the Americas. From these centers, the skills necessary for city life, advancing technology, and social complexity spread over large portions of the globe.

From our vantage point, it may appear to us that the growth of urban-imperial culture in the world was somehow inevitable. But in fact, the rise of civilization was a perilous enterprise from the beginning.

Culture Areas of the World about 1500

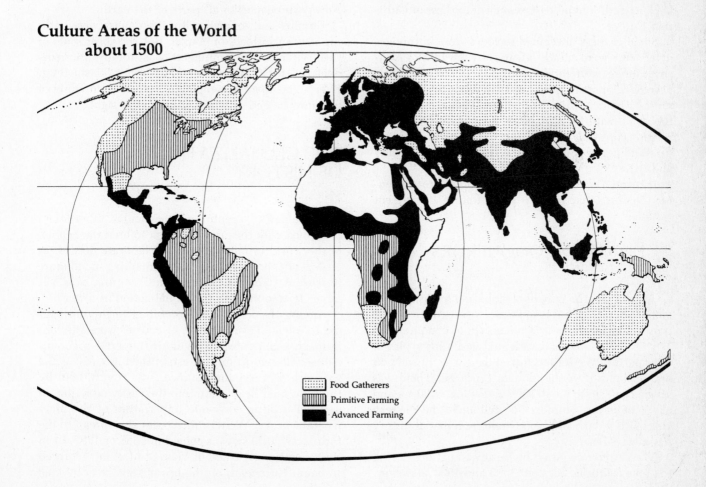

Food Gatherers
Primitive Farming
Advanced Farming

Much of humankind stuck to the old ways of preurban societies, hunting, fishing, farming in tiny villages, or wandering the world's marginal lands as tenders of flocks and herds. Early civilizations suffered from the depredations of these latter in particular, pastoral nomads who repeatedly reduced great cities to smoldering ruins. The developed cultures themselves were frequently at odds with one another—for example, the Greeks and Persians of ancient times and the Muslims and Christians of the Middle Ages. Finally, civilizations often collapsed into savage civil strife, including even such relatively stable traditional societies as China and India.

Yet a number of civilizations did survive both themselves and their rivals. They were here when modern history began.

In 1519, while Magellan and his crews poked their way around the globe, Incas ruled the Andes, the Ming emperors governed China, the Moguls were embarked upon their conquest and reunification of India, and sculptors in the West African kingdom of Benin were already producing their splendid bronze figures of the odd European intruders from overseas. All of these and other developed cultures could look back to traditions at least as ancient as those of Christian Europe.

Some of these developed societies were in contact, or at least were faintly aware of each other's existence; others were totally unaware. In modern times, developed societies would learn to relate to each other more intimately than ever before. They would girdle the globe with an ever more complex web of interrelationships—of mutual understanding and misunderstanding, of political and economic ties, of enmity and strife.

It is the story of this last and perhaps greatest human venture that remains to be told in the present volume.

THE WORLD CONQUERORS

As we will see, the growth of global consciousness and global interaction has taken many forms. Much of that growth, however, is a familiar tale of conquest and exploitation. Greed, fanaticism, and vanity played their parts as Westerners forced their way into all seas and all lands over the modern centuries. There was savagery to spare on all sides as hapless villagers and arrogant empire builders alike fell under the Western yoke. It is a dark and bloody tale, as imperial history has always been.

The empires acquired by European nations during the four centuries between 1500 and 1900, however, were something special. In the first place they were immensely large, many times larger than the European states who founded them. In the sixteenth century, Spain brought most of continental South America, all of Central America, and part of North America under a single government in Madrid. In the nineteenth century, a quarter of the inhabited globe acknowledged the authority of the British crown. By main force, a single culture—that of western Europe—imposed its unifying control on almost all the other major and minor cultures of the world.

For much of the period of European colonial hegemony, however, Western influence remained rather shallow over most of the world. The majority of the peoples whose rulers submitted to European overlordship lived pretty much as they always had. But Western power did bring about some critical structural changes in the non-Western world from the beginning. European invaders toppled empires in the Americas, transported millions of Africans to the New World to serve them as slave labor, and drove the Arabs from the sea lanes of the Indian Ocean—all as early as the sixteenth century. In later centuries, European domination continued to transform the political, economic, social, and intellectual lives of non-European peoples in all parts of the earth.

Empires and zones of cultural influence were nothing new in history, of course. But the sheer scale of the Western predominance was totally unprecedented. And it led to something even more startling. It brought about a complex mixing and mingling of cultures the end of which is not yet in sight.

THE GLOBALIZATION OF HISTORY

Over the past two centuries in particular, other forces combined with the great conquest to bind the peoples of the world in more and more elaborate nets of interdependence. The result was something much more important than another conquest empire, however large. It amounted to the globalization of history.

Among the forces that combined to produce this unprecedented event, some, of course, were Western influences generated by Western imperial predominance. The world market established as early as the sixteenth century, for instance, was transformed by the Industrial Revolution into the vastly more potent and penetrating economic imperialism of the nineteenth century. Western ideologies also spread to the far places, until slogans coined in 1688 or 1789, or in the revolutionary tracts of Marx or Mazzini, returned to haunt Europeans on the lips of rebellious colonial peoples.

In the twentieth century particularly, however, intercontinental influences began to flow the other way in an increasingly interrelated world. Japanese militarism in the 1930s and Japanese industrial growth in the 1980s, price manipulation by a cartel of Third World oil-producing nations in the 1970s, revolutionary doctrines produced by Mahatma Gandhi or Fidel Castro—all these could send tremors through the West as great as those that Western deeds and thoughts once stirred across the non-Western world.

Institutional ties also emerged in a world already linked economically and ideologically. International organizations, many of them global in scope, have proliferated over the past hundred years. Some of these have failed ignominiously, as did the League of Nations between the two world wars. Others, such as the United Nations, have proved less effective than many had hoped. But some multinational organizations have made quite a difference in the lives of the world's peoples. Without the Common Market, Europe's history since World War II would surely have been vastly different. Without the World Bank and the International Monetary Fund, for all their faults, development in the Third World would have been much more difficult.

Common perils, finally, unite all of us in the great global venture of modern times. Pollution, overpopulation, and the substantial possibility of a nuclear holocaust are problems for all the world's peoples. History remains today, as it was for the first builders of civilization five thousand and more years ago, as it was for their human and prehuman predecessors over the preceding five million years, a most dangerous game.

Nevertheless, it is a game that we all must play. The lives of all the peoples of the earth are now linked as never before. A war in the Middle East, a revolution in Latin America, a fall on the New York stock exchange, a dispute between politicians in Washington and Moscow—each can change the futures of all of us. The history we are living today is one more risky stage in the great human venture—though the stakes are perhaps a little higher in our times.

This volume will attempt to trace the journey from Magellan's day to our own. It will try to explain how we got where we are today. And it will hazard a guess or two about where we may be this time next year, next century, in the next step on the long road from the Paleolithic caves.

We travel around the world routinely now, and we have seen the earth from space, rising grandly over the mountains of the moon. Yet we are no less predatory, no less shortsighted, no less dangerous to ourselves and others than our predecessors were. So our children's children may jet to Peking in half the time it takes us to fly to London now. Or they may grub for root crops in the forests of a new Dark Age.

We cannot know. But we do know one thing that our ancestors did not. We know that whatever happens now, it will be global in its scope. Whatever new order emerges in the new millennium that will begin in the year 2000, it will be a genuine world order.

There have been duller times to live in than the age of the global venture.

SUGGESTED READING

BARRACLOUGH, G., ed. *The Times Atlas of World History*. London: Times Books, 1978. The basic geographical reference for global history, with emphasis on relationships and dynamic elements.

CURTIN, P. D. *Cross-cultural Trade in World History*. Cambridge: Cambridge University Press, 1984. Long-distance trade and the resulting "trade diasporas" as factors in human history.

JONES, E. L. *The European Miracle: Environments, Economics, and Geopolitics in the History of Europe and Asia*. Cambridge: Cambridge University Press, 1981. Europe's advantages at the beginning of the modern age, from climate and coastline to governments that fostered economic development.

LANGER, W. L. *An Encyclopedia of World History*. Boston: Houghton Mifflin, 1972. Standard chronological reference.

STAVRIANOS, L. S. *The Global Rift: The Third World Comes of Age*. New York: William Morrow, 1981. Five centuries of the history of Asia, Africa, and Latin America, with emphasis on the economic impact of the First World on the Third, especially since World War II.

—— *The World Since 1500: A Global History*. Englewood Cliffs, N.J.: Prentice-Hall, 1982. Second volume of Stavrianos's readable and informed text.

THOMAS, H. *A History of the World*. New York: Harper & Row, Pub., 1979. Emphasis on technology and material culture. Two-thirds of the book deals with the period since 1500.

UNESCO History of Mankind (6 vols). New York: Harper & Row, Pub., 1963. Multiauthor, multivolume survey of world cultures, drawing more widely on non-Western scholars and scholarship than some.

WOLF, E. R. *Europe and the People Without History*. Berkeley: University of California Press, 1983. An anthropologist's eye and Marxist economic analysis of the global impact of capitalist imperialism on non-Western peoples since the fourteenth century.

Overview I

The World in Balance

Modern world history is the story of the merging of the histories of the world's diverse peoples into a single human story. In 1500, however, that globalization of history lay in the unthinkable future still.

The world of the fifteenth and sixteenth centuries remained a world of separate zones of culture. Regional societies, great empires, and some of the most impressive civilizations the world has seen shared the earth at the beginning of the modern period. In the first six chapters we will explore each of these zones of culture in turn.

In so doing, we will try to firmly establish a sense of the geographical, historical, and cultural identity of each of the main regions and powers. Such a sense of the major cultural zones will be essential when, in later chapters, the global nature of our modern history compels us to skip about rather casually among the continents and cultures.

We will begin, then, with the comparatively familiar continent of Europe around 1500—the tidy little world from which Columbus sailed, and da Gama, and Magellan. It is a colorful, half-legendary time for Western people, an age of Renaissance art and swashbuckling cavaliers, of queens in jeweled gowns and popes in splendor. Between Columbus's first voyage in 1492 and Magellan's departure in 1519, Leonardo da Vinci painted the *Mona Lisa*, Isabella of Castile and Ferdinand of Aragon completed the unification of Spain, Henry VIII became king of England, and Martin Luther nailed his Ninety-five Theses on the church door at Wittenberg. This Europe, the Western world of the centuries around 1500, will be our starting point.

We will then proceed eastward across the double continent of Eurasia—four fifths of which is Asia—into much less familiar realms. First there will be the great Islamic empires of the Muslim center of Eurasia. By 1500 the faith of Muhammad the Prophet, starting six centuries later, had spread much farther than Christianity had. Mosques were built, the *Koran* read, and the Muslim Law obeyed from West Africa to Southeast Asia. But the jewels of the Islamic world in the early sixteenth century were the three wealthy and powerful central Eurasian empires of Ottoman Turkey, Safavid Persia, and Mogul India. The achievements of this Muslim heartland must, then, concern us here.

Farther still to the east, we will encounter the ancient, immense empire of China and the dynamic island nation of Japan. The Chinese emperors ruled by far the largest country in the world, whose population was many times that of any European nation. They had been doing so, at least intermittently, since well before the time of Christ. Chinese civilization, with its Confucian philosophy and its centralized government of scholar-bureaucrats, had shaped the cultures of much of the rest of East Asia as well. Of these satellite cultures, vigorously evolving Japan—the Japan of the warlord shoguns—will particularly concern us.

Civilization, however, had also grown up outside the world island of Eurasia. There were impressive kingdoms on the grasslands of West Africa and even in the dense forests of the Guinea Coast. On the other side of the continent, trading states flourished along the East African coast, part of the network of trade that bound the nations around the Indian Ocean into a single community of commerce. We will therefore spend some time with the famous Benin bronzes and poke through the bazaars of Timbuktu and the mysterious ruins of Zimbabwe.

The New World—as the Europeans called it—also had its highly developed societies in 1500. When Columbus and his successors reached those shores, the most impressive of all Latin American empires had recently emerged: the Aztec predominance in Mexico and the Inca Empire of Peru. We will look at those American empires as they were before the Europeans fell upon them with fire and sword. A glimpse of the canals and pyramids of Aztec Tenochtitlan, or the golden temples of Inca Cuzco, was enough to convince even the rude Spanish conquistadores that high culture was not a European monopoly.

Civilization itself, finally, was not the only viable human option at the beginning of the modern age. As the preceding volume of this book tried to emphasize, the majority of the world's peoples have lived through most of history in tiny agricultural villages, or have survived by herding cattle or sheep or by hunting, fishing, and gathering vegetable food from nature's bounty. Most of the earth's inhabited land was still populated by these peoples in 1500, including the better part of Africa, the Americas, and Australia. The accomplishments of these preurban cultures deserve our attention here as much as the more flamboyant achievements of the builders of cities and empires.

The varied world of many cultures and civilizations of 1500 was thus something none of us has ever seen. It was a world in balance.

For a last few centuries around 1500, genuine cultural pluralism prevailed. Many civilizations, many cultures lived together on the surface of the globe in a rough equilibrium. Let us take a last, long look, then, at this world of separate cultures and regional hegemonies, the world all our forebears knew back to the beginning of history. That roughly balanced world deserves our attention for the sake of its own accomplishments. And it was out of this pluralistic world that our own astonishing five-hundred-year epoch of world history evolved— the period of the birth of global culture.

Chapter · 1

THE WEST REBORN

FOUNDATIONS
OF MONEY POWER

Remember the Splendors

The folk memory of a people is a strange thing. It filters, distorts, obliterates, remembers what it will, and expunges what it wants to forget. Much of what folk memory preserves it transmutes into fiction—anecdotes, folk tales and songs, romantic plays and novels, and, most recently, film. The result is a communal dream of the past, a golden age of handsome pasteboard men and beautiful unreal women living fairytale lives in a world far more interesting and exciting than our own. Nobody, popular myth-history assures us, ever went to bed bored for lack of a date in Good Queen Bess's glorious days.

From the Renaissance, the first age of modern Western history, we remember the splendors.

We remember Henry VIII—"Bluff Prince Hal"—wassailing in his banquet hall, or Queen Elizabeth's thousand gowns, each more gorgeous than the last. The names that have survived from those vanished centuries conjure up a glittering time—names such as Lorenzo the Magnificent, who ruled Florence when that city was the queen of the Italian Renaissance . . . Ferdinand and Isabella of Spain, who unified their country and sent Columbus on his famous voyages . . . or Francis I, with his long, aristocratic nose and many mistresses, the champagne king of France.

We remember the artistic splendor that survives from the Renaissance—Leonardo's battered but still deeply moving *Last Supper*, Michelangelo's panorama of the creation of the world on the ceiling of the Sistine Chapel in Rome, or Cellini's dazzling golden salt cellar, an amazing sculptural group fit to grace an emperor's table. French schoolchildren remember the heroism of the Cavalier Bayard, who was "without fear and without reproach," as the English do the colorful deeds of such rapier-fighting gentry as Drake and Raleigh. We remember the moral splendor of Martin Luther defying authority for his religious beliefs—"Here I stand!"—or Thomas More dying for his quite different convictions.

We are less likely to know the source of the money that bought the thousand gowns or paid for Cellini's splendid salt cellar. The faceless clerks and bureaucrats who ran Lorenzo the Magnificent's banks or translated King Henry's imperious will into action have faded from the collective memory. Few today can cite the theological arguments behind Luther's ringing declaration, or even name the wars in which the famous heroes fought and so many thousands died in those gory centuries.

We will try here to preserve the memory of the banners and the trumpets. But we must look also at more pedestrian aspects of the life of that Western reawakening that goes by the twin labels of Renaissance and Reformation.

Lands and Peoples

By most definitions, the Western world today encompasses not only a widespread Atlantic community of nations including most of Europe and North America, but also allied countries as far afield as Israel and Australia. Five hundred years ago, however, the West was Europe only, a cramped little cluster of nations occupying the western one fifth of Eurasia. It was

London in Shakespeare's day. London Bridge, old St. Paul's cathedral, and other landmarks show in this view, which is centered on the Thames itself—heart of the city's busy commercial life. The Globe Theater, where Shakespeare's plays were performed, shows in the lower left, on the near side of the river. (Library of Congress)

neither the oldest nor the most impressive of world civilizations.

Geographically, Europe was divided by mountains and rivers, its margins chopped up into peninsulas and islands. The Ural and Caucasus mountains and the Black Sea cut it off from Asia, the Mediterranean from Africa. The Atlantic Ocean lay between Europe and the Americas, the very existence of which was unknown to Europeans before 1492.

Some of the major modern states had already assumed a rough approximation of today's boundaries by 1500. England and France, Spain and Portugal, even Poland and a truncated version of Russia were all there. Some other areas that would later become unified nations were still disunited regions. Germany was "the Germanies," Italy "the Italian states," the Netherlands a loose confederation, and Switzerland a collection of cantons. Austria presided loosely over the Holy Roman Empire, meaning mostly the three-hundred-odd German states. The Scandinavian countries of Sweden, Norway, and Denmark, on the other hand, were temporarily united in 1500. The Ottoman Empire of the Turks included among its provinces many of today's Balkan countries as well as chunks of southern Russia.

This half-familiar collection of countries was inhabited mostly by pale-skinned Caucasian peoples speaking Indo-European languages of the Romance, Germanic, or Slavic varieties. Almost all Europeans were Christians, Roman Catholic in the west and Greek Orthodox in eastern Europe. The monarchs who governed all the larger states claimed to rule by divine right, and the immense Christian religious establishment generally supported this claim.

The society over which these secular and religious authorities presided was as strictly hierarchical as any in the civilized world. A landowning, militarily trained aristocracy dominated the countryside and collected as courtiers and counselors around the princes of Europe. A secondary elite of merchants and leading craft guildsmen ran the many cities of the continent. Most Europeans, however, like most people everywhere, were peasant farmers living in small villages in the countryside. They ranged in legal status from abject serfs—in bondage to the land—in much of central and eastern Europe to relatively prosperous tenants and freeholders in western Europe. All, however, were subordinate to the landed aristocracy who constituted Europe's most prestigious social class.

The lands and peoples of Europe had two thousand years of recorded history behind them in 1500. Western civilization, one of the last Eurasian urban cultures to emerge, had first taken shape in the city-states of ancient Greece, then had swollen to imperial scale in the days of the Roman *imperium*. Europe's Mediterranean phase had ended with the period of internal decay and nomadic invasions that brought Rome down in the fifth century A.D. A new European culture had developed, however, rooted in barbarian vigor and Christian faith. Its political center was north of the Alps, in England, France, and the Germanies. This medieval culture had reached its apogee in the twelfth and thirteenth centuries, the age of the cathedral builders. It was the collapse of this second European civilization that opened the way for the emergence of a third—the vigorous new culture of the modern West.

The Golden Network

Europe around 1500 was engaged in pulling itself out of the deep trough occasioned by the crumbling of the Christian Middle Ages during the preceding couple of centuries. The great fourteenth-century plague called the Black Death and the depopulation and long economic depression that resulted had been major causes of the medieval collapse. So had the Mongol conquest of Russia, the Hundred Years' War between France and England, the Turkish seizure of Constantinople and invasion of southern Europe, and the civil wars that wracked a number of European nations. The temporary division and spiritual decay of the Roman papacy had put the cap on this continent-wide catastrophe.

The worst period ran from the middle 1300s to the mid 1400s. Thereafter the long recovery was clearly under way. But it had been a major disaster in Europe's history.

A few figures may clarify the scope of the debacle and the strength of the recovery that began modern European history. The population of Europe was more than 70 million in 1300, at the height of the commerical revolution of the High Middle Ages. The Black Death struck for the first time in 1347, and by 1400 the population had tumbled to some 45 million. By 1500, however, there were again almost 70 million Europeans, and by 1600, as Europe paused on the brink of the great population explosion of modern times, almost 90 million.

As a result of this revived demand and the expanded supply of labor to meet that demand, the economy of Europe began to grow once more in the fifteenth and sixteenth centuries. Agriculture expanded as more mouths to feed led to a renewed assault upon waste and marginal lands. Much more soil was brought under the plow than at any time since the High Middle Ages. Improved mining technology, particularly in the extraction of precious metals, significantly increased the amount of silver and gold available for coinage. This in turn put more money in circulation and contributed to both economic growth and inflation.

With coins again available and demand high, trade and handicraft industry boomed once more. Renewed economic growth began in the Mediterranean trading cities of Italy, which enjoyed access to the luxury products of Asia. The commercial cities of the German Hanseatic League, the manufacturing and trading towns of the Netherlands, and great European metropolises such as Paris and London were soon reintegrated into the golden network of commercial exchange.

Between them the medieval commercial revolution of the twelfth and thirteenth centuries and the Renaissance economic revival of the fifteenth and sixteenth laid the foundations of modern capitalism in the West. Key characteristics of the modern capitalist economy include private ownership of the means of production (as opposed to feudal landholding in return for military service), production for the market (rather than for mere subsistence, as on the medieval manor), and widespread use of money and credit (by contrast to simple bartering of goods). Other important elements of early capitalism were the development of business law, larger economic organizations, and freedom of economic choice by the individual.

Among the technical innovations that advanced the system from the eleventh to the sixteenth century were expanded minting of coins, double-entry bookkeeping, loans at interest, maritime insurance, bank checks and letters of credit, and above all the joint-stock company, which pooled the capital of many businessmen in a single venture.

Cities were the center of all this business activity. Florence, the most famous of Renaissance cities, had in 1472 some 270 wool merchants' shops, 84 cabinetmakers' establishments, 54 stonecutters' workshops, 44 goldsmiths' shops, and 33 banks. It was not a large city by Asian standards—less than two and a half square miles, with a population of between 50 and 70 thousand. But it was a bustling, vital metropolis, straddling the Arno River in the hills of northern Italy. Woolen cloth, banking, and finance were the core of its prosperity, and the Florentine florin was a gold coin good anywhere in Europe, the dollar of its day. Run by an oligarchy of business wealth, beautified by churches, and distinguished by the palaces of its great financial and commercial families, Florence became the first center of Renaissance art as well as a center of the revived Renaissance economy.

Lorenzo and Isabella

The moneyed aristocracy were among the greatest names of this fifteenth- and sixteenth-century economic revival. There were towering self-made men among them, such as the French tycoon Jacques Coeur, who in his prime negotiated with princes as an equal—and then died broke. There were business dynasties such as the plutocratic Fugger family of Austria, who published an international business newsletter for the far-flung branches of the family firm that was a precursor of today's financial press. Most famous of all, however, was the Medici banking family of Florence.

Generations of the Medici built the family fortune during the fifteenth century, Florence's Renaissance prime. At its height, Medici enterprises included branches in all the major Italian cities—Rome, Milan, Venice, and others—as well as beyond the Alps, in London, Bruges, Lübeck, Avignon, and elsewhere. The Medici were primarily bankers, processors of woolen cloth, and manufacturers of silk, but they dealt also in sugar and cotton, spices, tapestries, rare manuscripts, and they even provided singers from all over Europe for the papal choir.

As the richest bankers in Florence, the Medici soon became the uncrowned political bosses of the city. As the acknowledged rulers of the Florentine Republic, they manipulated the Italian balance of power to keep peace among all the other independent states of the peninsula. In the sixteenth century they became dukes of Florence, popes of Rome, and queens of France—a glittering dynasty of titles and power built on Renaissance money.

The spirit of Western business enterprise is vividly embodied in this portrait of a banker of the early 1500s by the Flemish painter Jan Gossaert. The watchful eyes, tightly pursed lips, quick pen, and the soberly expensive clothes all reflect the character of the age that forged the first truly global market in the history of the world. (National Gallery of Art, Washington, D.C. Alisa Mellon Bruce Fund 1968)

As early as the fifteenth century, furthermore, the Medici millions had been put at the service of Renaissance art and culture. The most famous of the clan, Lorenzo the Magnificent (1449–1492) was also the family's most renowned patron of the arts. Under Lorenzo de' Medici, poets like Angelo Poliziano and philosophers like Marsilio Ficino graced the halls of the Medici palace. Artists like Michelangelo learned their craft by sketching in the Medici gardens. Lorenzo was himself a poet, whose carnival songs are still anthologized in collections of Italian verse.

Self-made men like Jacques Coeur and self-made families like the Medici showed how far brains and ambition could carry a person in the Renaissance business world. Lorenzo the Magnificent—millionnaire, political leader, poet and patron of the arts—also illustrates the multifaceted type we call the Renaissance man.

But there were Renaissance women too.

The condition of upper-class Renaissance women at least seems to have been considerably better than that of their medieval predecessors. A few medieval ladies may have been idealized and loved from afar. But some Renaissance ladies were educated and highly cultured, and the admiration they engendered seems to have been based on these genuine accomplishments rather than on the hazy mystique of troubadour romanticism.

Many aristocratic Renaissance women studied Latin, read ancient religious writings, and plunged eagerly into the literary classics of ancient Rome that were the heart of Renaissance intellectual life. Ladies such as Michelangelo's platonic friend Vittoria Colonna, the talented Este sisters, and the famous daughters of Sir Thomas More were widely admired for their learning. There were celebrated women poets, such as Christine de Pisan and Louise Labé in France, and women painters, such as Artemisia Gentileschi.

One of the most famous of Italian Renaissance women was Isabella d'Este, "the first lady of the world." Raised in her father's cultivated court at Ferrara, she was married young to the hunting-and-fighting duke of Mantua. She ruled the court at Mantua with grace, firmness, and discriminating culture while her husband enjoyed ruder pleasures elsewhere. Learned in Latin and Greek, a lover of Vergil and other Roman poets, Isabella became a major collector of ancient sculpture, vases, bronzes, coins, and medals. She had her walls decorated with paintings by living Renaissance artists, and she patronized Renaissance poets. Like Lorenzo de' Medici and other patrons of her day, Isabella d'Este thus channeled significant portions of the wealth of the age into the culture that would earn that era its distinctive place in the history books.

THE NEW RULERS

Behind the Thousand Gowns

During the European Dark Ages following the fall of Rome—roughly the period 500–1000—most of the genuine power in medieval Christendom was in the hands of the feudal baronage whose forts, keeps, and finally castles provided what protection there was in an anarchic age. Many of the kings from whom they nominally held their vast estates were do-nothing rulers with little actual authority.

However, during the High Middle Ages—the eleventh, twelfth, and thirteenth centuries—strong kings emerged once more in Europe. Monarchs such as William the Conqueror of England and Philip Augustus of France strove to convert the fiction of royal power into a reality. For a time, at the apogee of medieval civilization, they had in fact tamed if not broken their barons. They had also expanded the territories under their own direct rule and begun the slow process of reassembling administrative machinery to govern their nations.

The medieval collapse of the fourteenth and earlier fifteenth centuries had brutally interrupted this slow evolution of the European nation-states. In the later fifteenth and sixteenth centuries, however, strong rulers took up the task of their medieval predecessors once more. Europe would remain a divided region, unlike such contemporary areas as Ming China and Mogul India. But some of the separate European nation-states would become aggressive political powers capable of challenging their larger imperial rivals around the world.

The new rulers who made this possible were the royal monopolists of power of the later 1400s and the 1500s, the "new monarchs" of the Renaissance.

Like the strong rulers of the Middle Ages, the new monarchs suppressed rebellions and brought ambitious barons—"overmighty subjects," as they called them—sharply to heel. They sought to smother local autonomy under a blanket of nationwide royal power, exercised through centralized bureaucracies and hired armies of mercenaries. They asserted with renewed passion their medieval divine right to rule, and bolstered it by comparing their authority to that of ancient Roman emperors.

The new monarchs found support for these efforts in the commercial cities that were the heart of the contemporary economic revival. As in the Middle Ages, the business communities of the towns believed that only centralized royal power could provide the peace and order within which business could flourish. Townsmen were therefore willing to pay taxes (within reason), provide trained officials, give legal recognition of royal authority, and generally underwrite the growth of central government once more.

Several generations of strong kings and queens were involved in this restoration of royal power in the major European nations. In England, there were two Henrys and Elizabeth; in France, a Louis, Francis, and Henry, the first Bourbon; in Spain, Ferdinand and Isabella, Charles, and the greatest of the Philips—to limit ourselves only to the most successful.

There were differences from country to country, as the following pages will indicate. In each case, however, the basic pattern was the same. All these nations experienced a rebuilding of centralized national political institutions under the aegis of royal claims to sovereignty. There was more behind Elizabeth's dazzling thousand gowns than the national wealth that paid for them. There was the political power that they represented—and that their shrewd display enhanced—as well.

The Spider and the Knight

The road to the restoration of royal power in France began, properly speaking, when Joan of Arc set the crown on the head of Charles VII at Reims in 1429. The Hundred Years' War dragged on for another quarter of a century, however, and it was not till the accession of Louis XI (1461–1483) that royal authority really began to grow once more in the ravaged French nation.

King Louis, nicknamed "the Spider" for his Machiavellian intrigues, took up in the later fifteenth century the centralizing labors begun by Philip Augustus and Saint Louis in the thirteenth. Louis was superstitious, conniving, merciless, and so totally unchivalrous that he preferred bribing his enemies to besting them in the field. Nevertheless, he left France more powerful, wealthy, and unified than she had been since the High Middle Ages.

Louis's most famous struggle was with that archetypal overmighty subject, the chivalrous duke of Burgundy, Charles the Bold. Duke Charles was killed in battle by the Swiss, who were subsidized by the French king. By the end of his reign, King Louis had brought almost all the major regions of modern France to heel.

Louis ignored other centers of power, such as the *parlements* (regional law courts) and the Estates General, France's embryonic Parliament, while laboring assiduously to make the central administration ever more efficient. Within his growing realm, he actively sought the support of the burghers of the towns by encouraging foreign trade and new industries and by appointing bourgeois advisers. The augmented wealth of the land filled the royal treasuries and paid for an expanded royal standing army, another source of strength for the monarchy.

No one wept when Louis the Spider died. But he left France strong enough to survive the crises that almost immediately confronted the nation.

The first of these problems was the long series of foreign wars that began in the 1490s and lasted through the 1550s. The great national enemy during this period was the powerful Austrian house of Habsburg—Holy Roman Emperors of the Germanies, rulers of the Netherlands, kings of Spain, and a power in the Italian states. France's most celebrated royal champion in the half-century struggle that followed was Francis I (1515–1547), the most brilliant, knightly, and mercurial of French Renaissance rulers.

The dashing Francis fought four wars with the immensely powerful Habsburg Charles V, mostly over the wealth of Renaissance Italy, where both had dynastic claims. The wars cost both sides dearly in lives and treasure. But they did preserve France from encirclement by Habsburg power and established the basic frontiers of the French nation.

When he was not leading his armies on the battlefield or dallying with his mistresses, Francis I also directed the continued strengthening of France's central government. A natural autocrat, he increased the power of his royal council and centralized the royal revenues under a single treasury. By so doing, he helped prepare France for an even more brutal challenge than the Habsburg wars: the bloody religious civil wars of the second half of the century.

The wars of religion in France that raged from the 1560s through the 1590s were partly the result of sectarian passions unleashed by the Protestant Reformation, which triggered the initial clashes between the French Protestant sect called the Huguenots and the Catholic League. Rivalry for the tottering throne of France, however, led two ambitious noble houses to assume leadership of the two factions—the Guises of the Catholic extremists and the Bourbons of the Huguenots. Half a dozen civil wars laid the nation waste through the later sixteenth century.

A strong hand took control once more at the end of the sixteenth century when Henry IV restored the authority of the monarchy and founded the powerful Bourbon line. But the Bourbons had something to build on—the foundations of modern French power laid by Louis the Spider and Francis I.

Siglo de Oro

Ferdinand and Isabella are best known to Americans as the sovereigns who financed Columbus. In Spanish history, however, they are the rulers who expelled the last of the Moorish conquerors of Spain, unified the country, and made the new kingdom one of the great powers of Europe.

The marriage of Ferdinand of Aragon and Isabella of Castile in 1469 led to the unification of the two largest portions of Spain, to which lesser territories were added by conquest during their reigns. By driving the last Muslims from Granada and using the notorious Spanish Inquistion to expel all Jews from the country, the "Catholic Kings," as they were called, further strengthened the new nation by religious uniformity. By asserting Italian territorial claims, negotiating a French alliance, and marrying their children into the royal houses of England and the Holy Roman Empire, the founders of Spanish unity made their country perhaps the most powerful in Europe. And when, after long negotiations with Queen Isabella, Columbus sailed in 1492, he laid the foundations for a Spanish New World empire that would grow in the following century into the largest in the world.

The *siglo de oro* ("golden century"), as the sixteenth is called in Spanish history, owed much of its glitter to that American empire. But subsequent Spanish monarchs Charles V (grandson of Ferdinand and Isabella) during the first half of the century and his son Philip II during the second half played central roles in European affairs as well.

Charles V (1516–1556), Holy Roman Emperor as well as king of Spain and lord of the Netherlands and large parts of Italy, Mexico, Peru, and other lands beyond the seas, was easily the most powerful of European rulers. His armies fought Turks, Protestants, and American Indians as well as his bitter rival Francis I of France. In pursuing his ambitious foreign policy, he strained the resources of even his vast empire.

Still, Charles further strengthened the unity of Spain. Building on the royal council established by Ferdinand and Isabella, he created a structure of governing councils, which would grow to twelve in number under Philip II. All these Spanish sovereigns were hard-working rulers: they read reports, presided over councils, and decided government policies themselves rather than delegating authority to ministers of state. The policies they chose—especially their war policies—were not always wise. But Spain was more united and more rigorously governed for their labors.

Philip II (1556–1598) harbored even vaster ambitions. A fervent Catholic, he made Spain the sword and shield of the Counter-Reformation. He was also an autocrat by instinct, determined to impress his will on the enormous Spanish domains. The Spain of Philip II had the best armies in Europe and the largest revenues, especially from the Netherlands and the Americas. With the Spanish colossus towering over the West, it looked to rival rulers as if one of the European kings might at last lay a single hegemony upon the whole Western world.

It did not happen, however. The Protestant powers—the England of Elizabeth, the Huguenots in France, and Spain's rebellious Netherlands—allied themselves against Spain in a cause that was as much political as religious. Philip won some great victories, such as the naval battle of Lepanto against the Ottoman Turks, but his greatest military efforts led to defeats. His most famous naval expedition was the attempted invasion of England that climaxed in the humiliating destruction of the Spanish Armada in 1588. His attempt to crush the Protestant revolt in the Netherlands ended, after forty years of bloodshed, in the independence of the Dutch Republic in 1609.

The result of these long wars, furthermore, was to reduce the immensely wealthy Spanish Empire to poverty, to turn her ascendancy into decline. Spain's golden century ended, and from the seventeenth century on, the nation of Ferdinand and Isabella, Charles V, and Philip II was to be an apathetic backwater.

Gloriana

Tudor England would become for later generations of English-speaking people the very incarnation of "merrie England." Bluff Prince Hal and Good Queen Bess—Henry VIII and Elizabeth I—are perhaps the best known of all British sovereigns. And for such homely things: everyone knows that Henry VIII had six wives and threw chicken bones on the floor, that Queen Elizabeth's courtiers spread expensive capes over mud puddles for her, and that the queen herself wore a bright orange wig! The travails of nations and the achievements of sovereigns are so easily replaced by trivia in the folk memory of peoples.

One of the most successful of the Tudors was the founder of the line, Henry VII (1485–1509)—about whom fewer folk memories survive. Shakespeare brought him on at the end of *Richard III* to bring a happy ending to the Wars of the Roses, England's late medieval civil war, by defeating his arch-villain King Richard. In the light of later scholarship, Richard III looks less like a villain, and Henry less a military hero and much more the architect of Tudor England's domestic tranquility and prosperity.

After his victory at Bosworth in 1485, the first Tudor monarch determinedly avoided further military adventures. Instead, he signed trade treaties advancing the cause of English commerce. He furthered domestic peace—and defended the Tudor dynasty—by firmly suppressing a number of rather inefficient conspiracies aimed at reopening the Wars of the Roses. In general, he maintained the "splendid isolation" from European entanglements that was to become England's peacetime trademark.

Henry VII, like the new monarchs elsewhere in Europe, strengthened royal power, using a large royal council and a system of local magistrates called justices of the peace to govern the country. His parliaments were amenable to royal influence, and Henry was his own first minister. When he died, he left the treasury full, the nation at peace, and a popular prince to rule after him as Henry VIII.

Henry VIII (1509–1547), far more famous than his father, is seen by many historians as rather less successful as a ruler. He gave over his earlier years to fun and frolic, hunting, wenching, and an occasional war. He left the real affairs of government during those youthful years to one of the most powerful royal ministers in English history, the intelligent and arrogant Cardinal Wolsey. The latter half of the reign was filled with more serious business for the aging monarch: more wars, the Reformation, and an increasingly desperate effort to provide an heir for the English throne. The wars were, as always, costly. The decision to take Reformation England out of the Roman church—because the pope refused to grant the king a politically necessary divorce—divided the nation religiously. And Henry's six marriages not only failed to produce a healthy male heir but were almost all personal disasters as well.

Yet Henry VIII lived in English memory as a powerful and even admired ruler. This was partly due to the labors of others. Wolsey in the first half of the reign managed affairs with some success. An innovative official named Thomas Cromwell strengthened and professionalized the royal bureaucracy during the 1530s. But Henry VIII himself contributed to the growth of central government by making use of Parliament as often as he could, especially when he was establishing his authority as head of the Protestant church in England. The Parliament, a bicameral assembly of burghers, gentry, and noblemen, was traditionally summoned to vote on taxes. But Parliament also passed laws and sought to influence royal policies—a practice that would have crucial consequences in the next century.

Queen Elizabeth I (1558–1603), finally, was the new monarch par excellence, arguably the most successful of all Renaissance rulers. Of all periods of Eng-

Queen Elizabeth I, looking every inch the Renaissance monarch—something she did very well. This famous "Armada Portrait" by Marcus Gheeraerts is dense with the symbols of the great queen's wealth (jewels, lace, and velvet), royal power (the crown at the left, her hand resting on the great globe itself), and historic accomplishment (the sinking of the Spanish Armada, shown in the picture, upper right). (Cooper-Bridgeman Library, Collection Thyssen-Bornemiszo)

lish history, the Elizabethan Age still kindles the warmest feelings in English hearts.

Princess Elizabeth, a slender, athletic, extremely intelligent young woman, received an ideal Renaissance education in Latin, Greek, and modern languages, in history and Scripture. As Henry VIII's second eldest child, shunted back to third in line for the throne by the complex politics of the period, she also had a very practical education in political intrigue—and the fine art of political survival. She came in 1558 to a royal throne shaken by a decade of misgovernment, religious fanaticism, and economic problems. She proceeded to give England forty-five years of strong government, moderate religious policies, and unexampled prosperity.

Elizabeth was a prudent ruler, avoiding costly wars, seeking religious compromise rather than religious crusades, working through her appointed ministers, and dealing firmly with an increasingly vociferous Parliament. She was well served by lifelong royal counselors such as Lord Treasurer Burgh-

ley and veteran warriors such as Sir Francis Drake. She was less well supported by dashing younger cavaliers such as the Earl of Essex and Sir Walter Raleigh, whose ardent ambitions got in the way of common sense. Elizabeth herself preferred guile to force. She was a past mistress of public relations, alternately charming and terrifying her friends and her enemies, her ministers, courtiers, and subjects.

The later years of Elizabeth's long reign were graced by a scintillating galaxy of poets and playwrights, of whom Shakespeare was only the best known. But these years—the 1580s and 1590s—also saw increasing political intrigue at court. Moreover, religious extremism, both Protestant and Catholic, emerged in the nation, and the exhausting conflict with Philip II at last drew England into the wars of religion.

Religious extremists found Elizabeth hard to live with, and young men eager for war called her timid. But they called her Gloriana to her face. The whole nation was dazzled by her thousand jewel-encrusted gowns and cowed by the stamp of an indignant royal foot. And she has been Good Queen Bess ever since— England's greatest and best-loved ruler.

THE REBIRTH OF WESTERN ART

Heritage

Genuine golden ages are often times of violent conflict; the age of Confucius was also the age of the Warring States in ancient China, and the Periclean Greeks seem to have been almost constantly at war. Golden ages are also not infrequently materialistic times, much concerned with getting and spending the wealth that pays for their culture. Nor are ethical standards always at their highest during such periods, as our own artistically and scientifically brilliant yet morally bewildered century makes clear.

The European Renaissance was as violent, materialistic, and morally questionable as any of the above. But it did leave a cultural legacy that would shape the intellectual and artistic life of the West for the next three centuries at least.

The word *renaissance* means "rebirth," and the age was so called by its own leading intellectual lights, the classical scholars of Renaissance Italy. They thought of their era as one of cultural rebirth, a revival of the wisdom and art of what was for them Europe's greatest age—the ancient world of Periclean Greece and Augustan Rome. The legacy of ancient Rome especially enthralled them. They did a splendid job of imbuing Renaissance culture with Latin literature and Roman history and mythology. Indeed, it is almost impossible to read Renaissance literature or look at Renaissance art without some knowledge of ancient Rome.

The study of classical culture, in contrast with the study of things divine, was known in the Renaissance as *humanism*. The men who began to read the Latin classics seriously again after a thousand years were called humanists. They were a varied lot of classical scholars—teachers and writers, poets and philosophers, pious Christians and libertines. The first of them, the fourteenth-century Italian poet Petrarch, wrote Renaissance love poems and medieval meditations on death with equal enthusiasm. The most famous sixteenth-century humanist, Erasmus, was equally admired for his editions of the New Testament and for his worldly satires on every aspect of Renaissance life, including the sins of organized religion.

The humanists as a group performed one great service for the modern West. They recovered much of our Western heritage of ancient Greek and Latin literature, lost and moldering in forgotten corners of obscure monastic libraries, unhonored and unread. They also attempted, with more modest success, to "civilize" the sword-swinging medieval baronage by a strong infusion of ancient culture. They did not produce the race of Platonic philosopher-kings they hoped for. But they did produce the first really literate aristocracy Europe had had for ten centuries—a first step at least toward matching the more cultivated courtier classes of the Muslim East or China's Confucian scholar-bureaucrats.

Perhaps the most celebrated product of humanist studies was Niccolo Machiavelli, the founder of modern political thought. Machiavelli, well read in Latin literature and history, was also an experienced Florentine diplomat. He fused his knowledge of past and present statecraft in one of the most famous of Renaissance books: *The Prince*. This shrewd, cynical, and brutally realistic commentary on the political style of Renaissance rulers has made the name Machiavelli synonymous with devious political intrigue ever since.

The Most Famous Painting

In some areas, Renaissance culture was neither a rebirth nor a revival, but an original creation of the highest order. Among these areas of artistic innovation, Renaissance painting stands out—particularly when we compare it with the brilliant but clearly derivative development of Renaissance architecture and sculpture.

Renaissance Italian architecture was strongly influenced by the Roman ruins that seemed to be everywhere. The architects had no use for the barbarous style of architecture they were the first to call "Gothic." Instead, Brunelleschi's fifteenth-century dome on the cathedral at Florence and Michelangelo's sixteenth-century one on Saint Peter's in Rome are both modeled on the dome of the Roman Pantheon built by the Caesars.

Renaissance sculpture also showed powerful classical influences. Michelangelo, who called himself a sculptor, learned his trade from Roman statuary, and his own early works included Bacchuses and satyrs. His mature statues of *David* and *Moses*—big-boned, heavy-muscled, with strong features hacked out of the marble—are Old Testament figures, but they look more like Greek or Roman heroes than medieval saints.

Renaissance painting, however, was unique to the age that produced it. No doubt this is partly because there was simply no ancient painting available for copying at that time. But Renaissance painting was also an expression of the creativity of that turbulent

Michelangelo's famous David, *looking as much like a hero of classical myth as like a Biblical shepherd boy. Michelangelo's Renaissance immersion in the Greco-Roman tradition, his sixteenth-century spirituality, and his awesome skill with a chisel all show in this gigantic statue. (Art Resource)*

time. The epoch that discovered new continents, initiated the Scientific Revolution, and spawned the Reformation was almost bound to produce some striking breakthroughs in the arts as well.

The essence of the Renaissance revolution in the graphic arts was what Renaissance painters themselves frequently called *life-likeness*. Fidelity to nature, or Renaissance naturalism, meant reproducing what the eye actually saw as convincingly as possible. To this end, the artists of the time developed new techniques that would become standard in art schools from that day on. Detailed sketches from nature, study of shadows and highlights, attention to pose, costume, and setting, concealing of brushstrokes, revealing character—all were part of the new approach. The science of perspective became a mania with some Renaissance artists. And anatomically accurate figure drawing—the special achievement of Renaissance painting—became a necessity.

Yet each Renaissance painter had his own distinctive style. They were towering individualists all, and it is their uniquenesses and eccentricities of treatment that define their greatness.

Leonardo da Vinci, the eternally restless, many-sided Renaissance mind, was as interested in science and mechanical inventions as he was in art. Experimenting endlessly with everything from pigments to composition, he has left us only a handful of finished paintings. Leonardo's mural of *The Last Supper* is a ruin today, but the subtle poses of the disciples are still there. They turn toward each other, hands, features, angle of head and trunk expressing their horror as the terrible question runs round the table: "Is it *I* who will betray my Lord?" His portrait of a distinguished patron's wife, the *Mona Lisa*, is perhaps the most famous Western painting in existence. The endlessly debated Mona Lisa smile illustrates one of Leonardo's most delicate and distinctive techniques, the use of "smoky" shadows to define the subtle modeling of the lady's cheeks.

Michelangelo Buonarotti may have thought of himself as a shaper of stone above all, but his paintings on the ceiling of the Sistine Chapel in the Vatican have earned him a place among the greatest painters as well. These scenes from Genesis, running from the creation of the world to the story of the flood, are a long parade of heroic Renaissance figures, their heavy limbs and bulging muscles far larger than life size. The most famous of all these scenes is the moment when a white-bearded Jehovah reaches out to pass the gift of life into the limp finger of a just-created Adam—a figure handsome enough to double for Apollo in any classical fresco. That moment in pigment on the Sistine ceiling, combining ancient and medieval inspirations in a uniquely Renaissance way, has for centuries defined the creation of the race in the imagination of Western humanity.

Raphael's seraphic Madonnas and Titian's Renaissance portraits, many of them with the burnished, copper-colored "Titian hair," are also part of our artistic legacy from the Renaissance in Italy. The meticulous bourgeois realism of the Dutch school of Jan and Hubert van Eyck, who produced thoroughly believable portraits of thoroughly believable businessmen, belongs to the artistic heritage of those centuries too. So do Peter Paul Rubens's lush pink goddesses and swirling composition, and the Spanish paintings of El Greco, with their flamelike elongated heads and sour colors.

For the next three hundred years, from 1600 to

1900, Western artists would accept the standards and imitate the techniques of the Renaissance masters. Even on a global scale, the work these masters produced at the dawn of modern history is fit to stand with that of any age and continent.

Not for an Age

The innovative, creative spirit that infused Renaissance art shaped Renaissance literature as well.

Literature in the living languages of modern Europe appeared in substantial quantities for the first time during these centuries. The influence of Latin literary forms, Roman mythology, and even the ideas and styles of ancient writers was present in these Italian, French, English, and other literatures. But new forms, new stylistic devices, and great writers of daunting originality flourished in these Renaissance national literatures as well.

Italy, which led Europe into the new age in so many other areas, also had its share of literary pioneers. Francesco Petrarch, the first humanist, was one of the early masters of poetry in the Italian tongue. His collection of love poems, collected as *Sonnets to Laura*, was set to music and sung in Italian taverns during his own lifetime and influenced Renaissance poetry in a number of languages for two hundred years thereafter. His fourteenth-century contemporary Giovanni Boccaccio produced in the *Decameron* perhaps the most famous short-story collection in Western history. In particular the bawdy tales among them were read, enjoyed, and imitated throughout Europe.

Sixteenth-century France produced a number of famous writers in the French language, but none so celebrated as the risqué Rabelais and the profound and skeptical Montaigne. François Rabelais, a former monk, wrote a single unique work of fiction, the multivolume adventures of the most famous of giants, *Gargantua*, and his son *Pantagruel*. Their raw and gaudy adventures satirized all aspects of Renaissance life, including the monasteries from which the author had fled. Michel de Montaigne, a cultivated Renaissance gentleman of the later sixteenth century, invented a whole new literary form to express his thoughts on life and the world—the essay. His three volumes of *Essays* on everything from friendship and education to cannibals and coaches were full of quotes from the wise ancients, but fuller still of the coolly penetrating insights of Michel de Montaigne.

A final flowering of Renaissance literature came in the last two decades of the sixteenth century and the early years of the century that followed, in the England of Elizabeth. The "nest of singing birds" of later Elizabethan times included poets and playwrights such as Edmund Spenser, Sir Philip Sidney, Christopher Marlowe, and of course William Shakespeare.

Spenser's long epic poem *The Faerie Queene* and Sidney's "novel" *Arcadia* mixed medieval knights, classical mythology, magic, adventure, love, and deeper allegorical and symbolic meaning in uniquely Renaissance literary productions. Kit Marlowe, the Elizabethan bohemian who died young in a tavern brawl, wrote the most admired English plays before Shakespeare. His *Tamburlaine the Great*, *Doctor Faustus*, and other heroes are all giants of ambition, aspiring to more than human achievements—and struck down like their creator for their arrogant presumption.

William Shakespeare is generally regarded as the most prodigious talent ever to write in English. His three dozen plays—*Richard III*, *A Midsummer Night's Dream*, *Romeo and Juliet*, *Julius Caesar*, *Macbeth*, *Hamlet*, *King Lear*, *The Tempest*, and the rest—have enriched the Western imagination with a galaxy of living characters. And if you are asked to identify a "familiar quotation," guess Shakespeare and the odds are you will be right, for his poetry has become part of the language. His plots are borrowed, his ideas seldom original, but his words are often perfect, and his characters are still the greatest challenge any actor can face. Will Shakespeare's work, said his friend and fellow playwright Ben Jonson, was "not of an age, but for all time!"[1] So far this estimate has proved accurate; more than three and a half centuries after his death, Shakespeare's plays are still on view any night of the year in the great cities of the English-speaking world.

THE REFORMATION OF RELIGION

A Stench in the Nostrils of the Pious

The Renaissance began in the fourteenth century and ended somewhere in the sixteenth. But during the sixteenth century it overlapped with another major subdivision of Western history, the Reformation. This great upheaval in the Christian church began not in Italy but in Germany, and spread rapidly across northern Europe. The Protestant revolt produced some powerful religious ideas, kindled a great Catholic Counter-Reformation, and led to a wave of terrible religious wars. It is sometimes referred to as Europe's last great age of faith—the last time Western

---

[1] Ben Jonson, "To . . . Mr. William Shakespeare: And what he hath left us," in Shakespeare's *Complete Works*, ed. Hardin Craig (Chicago: Scott, Foresman and Company, 1961), p. 48.

Martin Luther, in a picture by the celebrated German artist Lucas Cranach. Something of the warmth and geniality of Luther's later years show here, but there is still the haunted look of the young Luther about the eyes, a hint of the spiritual torment in which the Protestant Reformation was born. (New York Public Library Picture Collection)

people were willing to die, and to kill, in large numbers for their religious beliefs.

The powerful personality of Martin Luther, the German monk who started it all, looms over the Reformation. Yet it is sometimes said that if Martin Luther had never lived, some sort of reformation of religion must nevertheless have taken place. For the Roman Catholic church was in deep need of reform long before Luther nailed his Ninety-five Theses to the church door in Wittenberg in 1517.

The Roman church was still wallowing in the aftermath of her great late-medieval collapse as the sixteenth century began. The Babylonian Captivity—the period when the popes lived at Avignon and were widely regarded as tools of the French kings—and the Great Schism—which produced two and then three claimants to Saint Peter's seat—had left the papacy badly demoralized. The popes of the later fifteenth and early sixteenth centuries were more concerned with Renaissance art, humanistic literature, Italian politics, and luxurious living than they were with religion. They were members of worldly, ambitious families such as the Florentine Medici and the Span-ish Borgias. The Borgia pope Alexander VI, and especially his son Cesare and his daughter Lucrezia, made the papacy a springboard for a series of military campaigns, intrigues, and even murders that shocked Europe. The Medici pope Leo X, a son of Lorenzo the Magnificent, is reputed to have greeted the news of his accession with an exultant "God has given us the papacy—let us enjoy it!"[2]

Worldliness and corruption seemed to many to have infected all levels of the church. Simony (buying and selling of offices), nepotism (appointment of relatives to office), clerical concubinage, clerical ignorance, pleasure-loving monks, and high-living cardinals all made ecclesiastical corruption a byword in Europe—and a stench in the nostrils of the pious.

This decadence had stimulated a number of revolts during the century before Luther came on the scene. Jan Hus in the Holy Roman Empire, John Wycliffe in England, Girolamo Savonarola in Italy, and other popular preachers and reformers had defied the church in the fifteenth century. All had been stigmatized as heretics; all had died for their beliefs.

Then came Luther.

Here I Stand

Martin Luther (1483–1546) was a disturbed young man when he entered the Augustinian order of monks in the summer of 1505. Raised by pious middle-class German parents in the duchy of Saxony, he turned his back on law school and entered the cloisters in the grip of a full-fledged religious crisis.

Like other deeply believing Christians of his time, young Luther was convinced that he was a sinner, hated by God, doomed to hellfire. The church taught that two things earned a person salvation: faith in Christ and a life of Christian good works. Luther tried a number of Christian works. Entering a monastery was a great work of Christian commitment. He also confessed his sins repeatedly, mortified the flesh with fasting and flagellation, and undertook a pilgrimage to Rome, where he was duly horrified by the worldliness of the papal court and cardinals. He remained, however, convinced of his own sinfulness, his own damnation.

Seeking a deeper understanding of Christian faith, the unhappy monk had meanwhile become a professor of theology, lecturing on Scripture at the University of Wittenberg. He found himself increasingly dissatisfied not only with the official doctrine of salvation through faith *and* works, but with such church practices as worship of the relics of saints and the sale

[2]S. Harrison Thompson, *Europe in Renaissance and Reformation* (New York: Harcourt, Brace, and World, 1963), p. 453.

of indulgences—papal pardons for sins—to raise money for the church's good works.

In the mid 1510s Martin Luther's rebellious spirit boiled over. While preparing lectures on Saint Paul, he at last found certainty of his own salvation in a new doctrine: belief in salvation through *faith alone*, rather than faith and works. This belief became the cornerstone of Protestantism. Then in 1517, Luther launched the Reformation itself by publicly proposing ninety-five theses (arguments) against the efficacy of purchased indulgences.

The rest of Luther's tumultuous life grew from these two challenges to orthodoxy. He developed other radical doctrines. The only certain source of religious truth, he said, was the Bible—not the Bible plus the accumulated wisdom of popes, church councils, and church tradition. Priests had no special powers: all true believers were priests, and had as much direct access to God as clergymen could claim. The Roman pope, he finally dared to declare, had no control over him or anyone else: the pope had usurped power; he was, in fact, the Antichrist foretold of old.

When defenders of the orthodox faith spoke or wrote against him, Luther confuted them in print or in public debate. When Pope Leo X at last excommunicated the troublesome German monk, the rebel publicly burned the bull of excommunication. When a council called at Worms by the Holy Roman Emperor Charles V outlawed him, Luther answered that he could not oppose his conscience: "Here I stand—I cannot do otherwise."[3]

It was a road of defiance taken by more than one doomed heretic before him. But Luther found many supporters for his rebellion—not all of them impelled by purely religious motives. There were German princes eager to get their hands on the wealth of the German church. There were those who sought to use Luther's crusade to justify their own revolt against the Holy Roman Emperor. There were nationalistic noblemen and knights, angry that German money was building Roman churches or lining the pockets of Italian churchmen. There were peasants who used Luther's name to support their insurrections against the out-of-date manorial exactions imposed upon them by their lords.

Luther accepted the support of German princes and noblemen, rejected that of peasants, and miraculously came through unscathed. Lutheran churches were set up in many North German states, then in Scandinavia. Henry VIII, after authoring an early tract against the Lutheran heresy, took England's religious establishment out of the Roman church for po-

[3]Roland H. Bainton, *Here I Stand: A Life of Martin Luther* (New York: New American Library, 1950), p. 144.

litical reasons—and made himself its head. Religious turmoil spread through Europe, and it looked for a while as though all Roman Catholic Christendom might revolt against the pope.

The mature Luther was a barrel of a man, the gaunt cheeks of his tortured youth comfortably padded by the solid German meals prepared by the nun he married. Earthy and eloquent, equally skillful at writing hymns, theological treatises, polemical invective against his foes, and translations of Holy Writ, he was a powerful propagandist for his cause. Absolutely convinced of his own rightness and righteousness, he epitomized the ideological true believer of modern times. Like Robespierre in the French Revolution or Lenin in the Russian one, Luther made his ideas a force in modern history.

Building the New Jerusalem

The most famous reformer of the generation after Luther was John Calvin of Geneva (1509–1564), who rose to eminence in the 1530s. Calvin was a very different sort of person from Martin Luther. A cultivated Frenchman, trained in humanism and law as well as theology, Calvin was more famous for his lucid logic and shrewd organizing mind than for eloquence or passion. With his thin face, hollow eyes, and long goat beard, he came much closer to the popular image of the religious fanatic than the hearty German monk did.

In the city-state of Geneva in the Swiss Alps, Calvin set up a Protestant theocracy and preached a militant faith that inspired Protestants all over Europe. His doctrines differed from Luther's more in emphasis than in substance. Calvin put special stress on the omnipotence of God. He set the predestination of each human soul to heaven or hell at the center of his theology. His theocratic state of Geneva was dominated by the Calvinist pastors, and the pastors in turn by the iron will of John Calvin. His great book, the *Institutes of the Christian Religion*, was read by Protestants everywhere, and his Geneva became the sixteenth-century Protestant ideal of a Christian community.

Life in Geneva was rigorous, filled with sermons and narrowly restricted by puritanical moral legislation. Calvin's theology was inflexible, a grim vision of a world divided into the saved and the damned, with the pope as antichrist and Calvinist Protestants as the builders of a new Jerusalem on earth. This view, and the fervor it produced, became the crusading faith of religious revolutionaries all across Europe. It spread to the Huguenots in France and to the Dutch Reformed church in the rebellious Netherlands, to English Puritans and Scottish Presbyterians.

It would leave a mark as deep as Luther's on Protestantism, both in northern Europe and in the New England colonies of America.

The long-range impact of Calvinism extended even beyond the sphere of religion. Calvinism may have inspired the taut, rigorous drive that made Calvinist Huguenots and Puritans the most successful businessmen in France and England, respectively. Calvinist religiosity may thus have been an important cause of the growth of capitalism in the West.

Because of their opposition to popes, archbishops, and bishops in the church, Calvinists frequently opposed hierarchy in the state as well. Calvinism could thus be seen as an influence on the emergence of democracy in the Netherlands, in England, and in the New England colonies. Through colonial town meetings and elected assemblies, Calvinism may even have contributed to the birth of the American republic two centuries later.

In his own time, however, John Calvin was a prophet of religious revolt, and it is as such that he looms largest in Western history.

Renewed Fervor for the Fray

The Roman Catholic church, meanwhile, had mounted a massive Reformation of its own. Led by a pious new breed of pope, the church launched a powerful counterattack against the Protestant revolt that had already carried the North German states, England, and Scandinavia out of the Roman fold.

The organizer of the Counter-Reformation was Pope Paul III (1534–1549). During his pontificate the papal court was reformed and Catholic reformers gained commanding positions in the church, from which they were able to guide the Catholic Reformation for the rest of the century.

To deal with the Protestant threat more directly, Pope Paul refurbished the medieval Inquisition and established the board of censors known as the Index of Forbidden Books. He also recognized a militant new order, the Society of Jesus. This order of friars was organized in 1540 by a former Spanish knight—and future saint—named Ignatius Loyola. The Jesuits, as the friars were known, were to become the church's most militant agents, the shock troops of the Counter-Reformation, as well as one of the greatest missionary orders in church history.

Pope Paul also called the Council of Trent, one of the most important of all church councils, which met off and on for twenty years during the 1540s, 1550s, and 1560s. The Council of Trent carried the reforming impulse from the papal center to the Catholic church as a whole. Decrees of the council provided

St. Peter's cathedral in Rome, looking much as it does today, in a painting by Giovanni Panini. The Counter-Reformation attempt to awe Christians into a renewal of faith in the Roman Catholic church by the sheer splendor of its architecture is nowhere better illustrated than in St. Peter's. (National Gallery of Art, Washington, D.C. Alisa Mellon Bruce Fund 1967)

stiff penalities for immorality and corruption among the clergy. The council founded new seminaries in order to create a better-educated priesthood. Trent also reaffirmed the traditional Catholic views on all the theological points the Protestants had challenged. From Trent, then, the Roman church entered the second half of the century better prepared for battle and full of renewed fervor for the fray.

Wars, Atrocities, Assassinations. . .

The result of the clash of religious sects was a bloody period in European history. These wars of religion brought the age of the Reformation to a violent climax.

Europe's religious wars began in the early 1500s with revolts such as the Protestant Peasants' War in Germany and the Catholic Pilgrimage of Grace in Henry VIII's England. They petered out in the early 1600s in the Thirty Years' War in central Europe and the English Puritan Revolution. The height of violence occurred from the 1560s to the early 1600s. During this period, the Dutch Revolt pitted Calvinist Protestants against Spanish Catholics, the wars of religion in France set Huguenots against the Catholic League, and the Anglo-Spanish naval war swept from

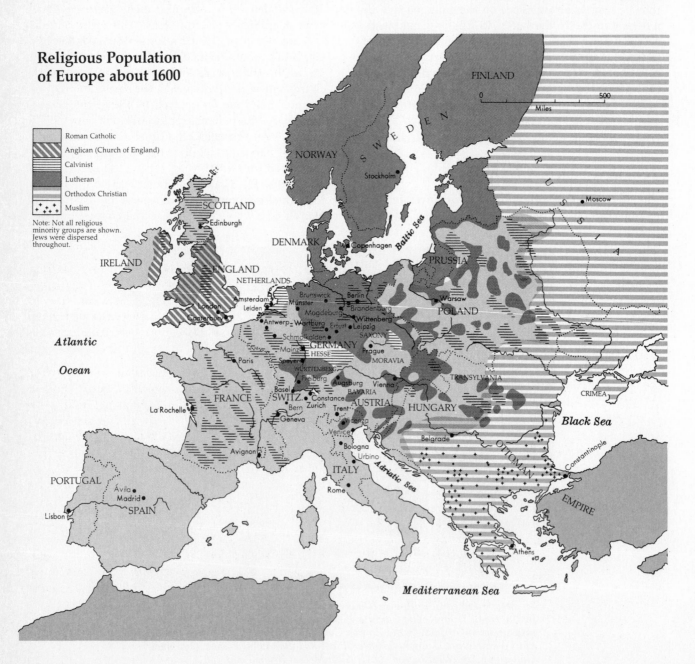

Religious Population of Europe about 1600

Roman Catholic
Anglican (Church of England)
Calvinist
Lutheran
Orthodox Christian
Muslim

Note: Not all religious minority groups are shown. Jews were dispersed throughout.

the English Channel to the Spanish colonies in the New World.

During the great religious wars of the latter half of the sixteenth century, the religious passions of Luther's and Calvin's day exploded in decades of propaganda broadsides, revolutions, wars, atrocities, and assassinations. Protestant mobs vandalized and sometimes looted Catholic cathedrals. The Inquisition broke and burned human bodies. Luther was willing to execute Anabaptists—the lunatic fringe of the Protestant movement—and Calvin to martyr the religious eccentric Servetus. But Protestant violence was more than matched by the long-established repressive machinery of the Roman church.

By the early 1600s on the continent and the middle of the century in Puritan England, the fires of religious zeal kindled by Luther a century before had burned themselves out. Europeans turned from fruitless crusades to secular state building and modern science. The second half of the seventeenth century would be the Age of Louis XIV—and of Isaac Newton.

The World Had a Problem

The age of the Renaissance and Reformation—to give it its full name—was a tumultuous time for Europeans. Europe, recovered from the collapse of late medieval times, was wealthy—and hungering for more. The kingdoms of the West were strong, contentious, armed and dangerous. The reformations, Protestant and Catholic, had rekindled the crusading Christian faith of the High Middle Ages.

The rest of the world, blissfully unaware of the powerhouse that was building up at the western end of Eurasia, went on with its own getting and spending, its own wars and politics, its own artistic and religious impulses. But by 1500 the West was already reaching out. The Europeans were already appearing among other peoples around the globe. They offered their goods for sale on the rialtos of western India. They thrust deeper into the islands and forests of the New World, swords in one hand and crosses in the other. The world, though it did not know it yet, had a problem on its hands.

SUMMARY

Money, politics, art, and religion all exhibited a renewed dynamism in the Europe of the Renaissance and Reformation.

During the fourteenth and fifteenth centuries in Italy, the later fifteenth and sixteenth centuries in Europe north of the Alps, the European commercial economy bloomed once more. Recovering from the wars, plagues, and depression of later medieval times, Renaissance trade made immense fortunes for business families like the Medici of Florence. The Renaissance business revival also completed the work of the commercial revolution of the High Middle Ages in laying the foundations of the dynamic capitalist economy of modern Europe.

Royal power also revived during these early modern centuries. Italian Renaissance despots and the "new monarchs" of other European nations took up the work of building strong central governments for the major European powers. Louis the Spider and chivalric Francis I in France, Ferdinand and Isabella and Philip II in Spain, Henry VII, Henry VIII, and Queen Elizabeth in England all helped build powerful nations in western Eurasia.

Renaissance art and literature established cultural patterns that would influence Western culture through most of modern history. From da Vinci to Shakespeare, they would provide models and inspirations for painters and poets for the next four hundred years.

The Protestant Reformation and the Catholic Counter-Reformation, finally, revitalized Western Christianity, though at considerable cost in Western lives. Militant Protestant reformers like Luther and rigorous Puritans like Calvin successfully challenged the accumulated abuses of the Catholic church. The popes responded by reforms—and a renewed militance—of their own. The religious conflicts that resulted ravaged Europe through the later sixteenth century and left Western Christendom divided between a Catholic south and a Protestant north.

All told, this brilliant, bloody age generated a renewed European vitality that contributed powerfully to the wave of overseas empire building that also began during this era of Western rebirth.

SUGGESTED READING

BAINTON, R. H. *Here I Stand: A Life of Martin Luther*. New York: New American Library, 1978. Standard, scholarly, clearly written, with a strong sense of the times.

—— *Women of the Reformation in Germany and Italy*. Boston: Beacon Press, 1977. By an authority on the Reformation; less knowledgeable on women's history. See also his *Women of the Reformation in France and England* (Boston: Beacon Press, 1973) and *Women of the Reformation from Spain to Scandinavia* (Minneapolis: Augsburg Press, 1977).

BERENSON, B. *The Italian Painters of the Renaissance*. Ithaca, N.Y.: Cornell University Press, 1980. Seminal studies by the founder of modern connoisseurship. For a more recent overview, see J. Beck, *Italian Painting of the Renaissance* (New York: Harper & Row, Pub., 1981).

BRAUDEL, F. *Capitalism and Material Life, 1400–1800*. New York: Harper & Row, Pub., 1973. A trailblazing French historian's stimulating account of the economic realities of the earlier modern West.

BRUCKER, G. A. *Renaissance Florence*, rev. ed. Berkeley: University of California Press, 1983. Government, politics, and the social order. See also H. Baron's classic study of the relations between Renaissance humanism and politics, *The Crisis of the Early Italian Renaissance: Civic Humanism and Republican Liberty in the Age of Classicism and Tyranny* (Princeton: Princeton University Press, 1966).

DAVIES, R. T. *The Golden Century of Spain, 1501–1621*. New York: Macmillan, 1954. Old but standard history of Spain when she was the greatest power in the Western world. For the best picture of Spain in 1500, see J. H. Mariéjol, *The Spain of Ferdinand and Isabella*, trans. B. Keen (New Brunswick, N.J.: Rutgers University Press, 1961).

DICKENS, A. G. *The Counter-Reformation*. New York: Norton, 1979. Solid, vividly illustrated survey.

EISENSTEIN, E. L. *The Printing Press as an Agent of Change in Early Modern Europe* (2 vols.). Cambridge: Cambridge University Press, 1980. Challenging assertion of the larger cultural impact of printing.

ELTON, G. R. *The Tudor Revolution in Government*. Cambridge: Cambridge University Press, 1959. Much debated, pioneering study of governmental changes in one of the most important of the "new monarchies."

HOGREFE, P. *Tudor Women: Commoners and Queens*. Ames, Iowa: Iowa State University Press, 1975. Profiles of women of the English Renaissance, from the guilds to the court.

KRISTELLER, P. O. *Renaissance Thought: The Classic, Scholastic, and Humanist Strains*. New York: Harper & Row, Pub., 1961. One of a number of collections of papers by a leading authority on Renaissance intellectual history.

MATTINGLY, G. *Renaissance Diplomacy*. Baltimore: Penguin, 1964. Standard account of the evolution of interstate relations in Europe at the beginning of modern history.

MONTAIGNE, M. *Selections from the Essays*, trans. D. M. Frame. Arlington Heights, Ill.: Harlan Davidson, 1973. A chance to browse through one of the finest minds of the Renaissance.

NEALE, J. E. *Queen Elizabeth I*. New York: Doubleday, 1957. Still the best life of Britain's most famous ruler.

SHAKESPEARE, W. *The Complete Works of Shakespeare*, ed. Hardin Craig. Chicago: Scott, Foresman, 1961. The finest writer in English brings the beginning of the modern age to life. His Renaissance men and women, even when they are disguised as ancient Romans or medieval kings, speak with the lusty voices of his age.

Chapter · 2

THE MUSLIM CENTER

THE ABODE OF ISLAM

From Timbuktu to Malacca

Europe in 1500 had a truly amazing future. But the present, and indeed the immediate future as well, belonged to Europe's far more powerful neighbor, the vast Muslim center of the Old World.[1]

The Arab prophet Muhammad (570?–632) had called himself the Messenger of God. The message he preached of salvation through submission (*Islam* in Arabic) to the will of God (*Allah*) had spread far across Eurasia and Africa by 1500. The mosque and the minaret, the Koran, the Muslim Law, and mystic Sufi holy men were found everywhere from West Africa to Southeast Asia, from the steppes of Russia to the Indian Ocean. It was a vast terrain, almost four times as far from end to end as Europe was, and well worth a brief geographical survey before we turn to its history.

The heart of the Islamic world was in the Middle East, where civilization itself had been born. The chief Muslim holy city was Mecca, in Arabia, where Muhammad had first preached. The splendid capitals of the medieval Arab Empire had been Damascus and Baghdad, the capitals of Syria and Iraq today. The mountains and plateaus of Turkey, Iran, and Afghanistan were Muslim too, and the dry steppes of central Asia. Much of the history of Islam before and after 1500 took place in this area of desert and oases, chilly uplands and stubbly grasslands.

[1] I borrow this usage from the innovative Tufts University world history program, and from Professor Lynda Schaffer, from whom I first heard it.

In Africa, ancient Egypt, the fertile strip along the Mediterranean shore, and the sun-bleached Sahara were all Muslim. So were the grasslands of the Western Sudan and the trading cities along the East African coast. In Europe, Islamic armies had overrun most of the Balkan states and pushed up into southern Russia. Farther to the east, they had traversed the snowy passes of the Hindu Kush and flooded down into northern India. Muslim merchants and Sufi missionaries had penetrated even the tropical islands of Southeast Asia—mostly Indonesia today—and carried the word of the Prophet as far east as the Philippines.

The range and diversity of the Islamic world was thus far greater than those of Christendom. Arabs, Berbers, and black Africans, Turks and Persians, Slavs, Mongols, Indians, and Southeast Asians all heard the call to prayer five times a day and prostrated themselves toward Mecca.

The great cities of the Islamic sphere dazzled European visitors. From the gold marts of Timbuktu to the silk and spice bazaars of Malacca, from the imperial Constantinople of the Ottomans to the dawning splendor of Mogul India, sixteenth-century Islamic culture matched that of any in the world.

A Transregional Hegemony

Islam in 1500 was thus not merely a regional culture, like Christian Europe or China's East Asian sphere of influence. It was a transregional culture, a truly hemispherical civilization, encompassing portions of three continents. It must qualify as one of the very few transregional hegemonies before the rise of Western imperialism.

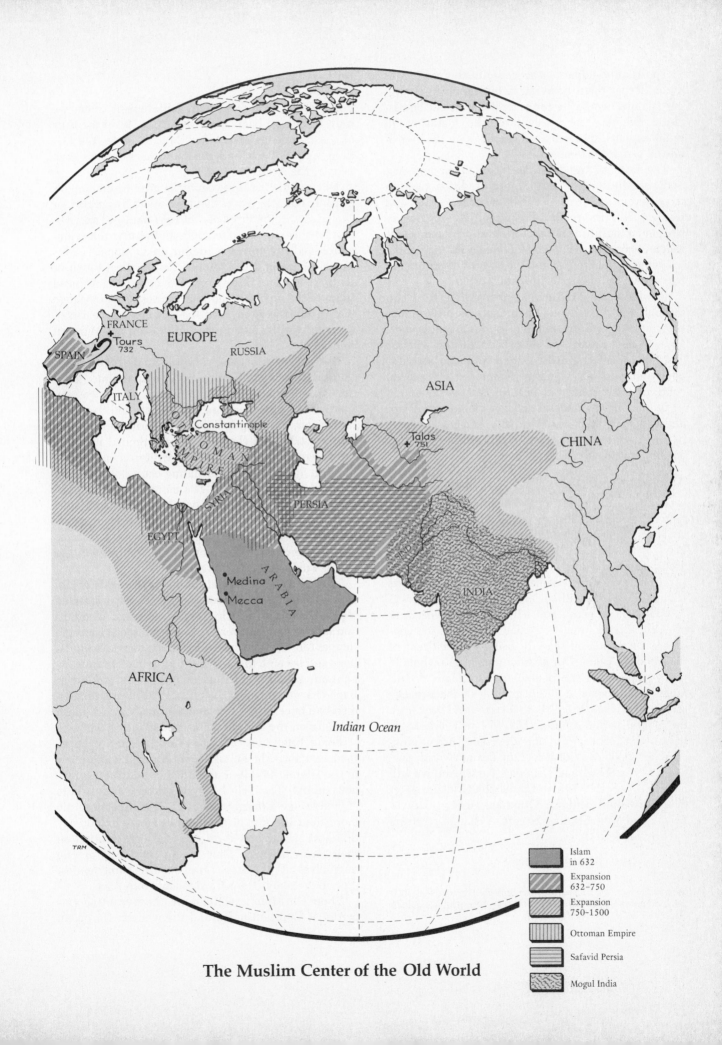

FRANCE
+ Tours
732
SPAIN
EUROPE
ITALY
RUSSIA
ASIA
CHINA
O
T
T
O
M
A
N
Constantinople
E
M
P
I
R
E
+ Talas
751
SYRIA
PERSIA
EGYPT
SIND
ARABIA
• Medina
• Mecca
INDIA
AFRICA
Indian Ocean
TRM

Islam
in 632

Expansion
632–750

Expansion
750–1500

Ottoman Empire

Safavid Persia

Mogul India

The Muslim Center of the Old World

The Islamic impact on its zone, furthermore, was much deeper than the Western impact on its emerging colonies would be for several centuries. The Islamic religion—the youngest of the major world religions—had imposed itself deeply upon the lives of all the peoples it touched.

The faith of the Muslims included an immense body of Muslim law and Islamic tradition that affected every aspect of life. Political organization and business dealings, relations between the sexes, family life, and a multitude of other matters were matters of religious concern. All were regulated according to the teachings of the Prophet and the body of tradition that had grown up about his life and work.

Conquest by Muslims or conversion to Islam through the influence of merchants or missionaries brought other cultural influences into a community. As each new region was absorbed, Muslim scholars and Sufi preachers, artists, architects, and artisans, poets and musicians would be summoned to grace the courts of newly converted local rulers. Mosques would be built, Sufi centers and colleges would spring up, and *Qadis* (judges) would sit in every marketplace, settling disputes and decreeing punishment for crimes on the basis of the Muslim Law.

Nor were these merely scattered islands of Islamic civilization. They were bound by ties of commercial exchange to all the rest of the Muslim zone. Muslim merchants carried luxury goods along the caravan trails of Eurasia and northern Africa, plied the sea lanes of the Indian Ocean and the Southeast Asian archipelago. Muslim holy men, scholars, and administrators traveled these same routes, seeing large parts of the Old World without ever leaving Islam. It was "a cohesive, growing, and self-replenishing network of cultural communication" that created "a self-conscious, cosmopolitan sense of being loyal citizens of the Abode of Islam (*Dar al-Islam*) taken as a whole."[2]

To understand the power and brilliance of this huge Muslim zone at the beginning of modern history, we will have to look both forward and back from the pivotal period around 1500. We will have to go back several centuries to note the emergence of powerful new peoples as leaders of the Islamic world, particularly the Seljuk and Ottoman Turks. And we will have to survey the history of three great Muslim states in the sixteenth century: Ottoman Turkey, Safavid Persia, and Mogul India, the core of Islamic greatness in early modern times.

[2]Ross E. Dunn, "The Challenge of Hemispheric History (1000–1500 A.D.)." Paper presented before the American Historical Association (San Francisco: December 28, 1983).

The Realm Divided

For a clear vision of Muslim achievement, then, we must briefly go back as far as A.D. 1000, to the time of the decadence of the first Muslim state, the far-flung empire built and ruled by the Prophet's own people, the Arabs.

During the first three centuries after Muhammad's death in 632, the Arabs had been ruled by *caliphs*, or "successors to the Prophet," of the Omayyad and Abbasid dynasties. These religious and secular rulers had established an impressive Islamic predominance across North Africa and the Middle East, with a touch of southern Europe thrown in. The culture of Abbasid Islam in the ninth and tenth centuries easily outshone that of Christendom, and the power and wealth of the caliphs of Baghdad dwarfed those of any Western ruler.

By the eleventh century, however, the political authority of the Arab Empire had collapsed into disorder from Spain to Afghanistan. The western subdivisions of the empire, located around the Mediterranean, had largely seceded to form independent Muslim states. Of these, Egypt dominated much of the Levantine east end of the Mediterranean, while Moorish Spain was a scintillating center of medieval culture at the other end. The eastern regions of the Arab Empire, still nominally ruled by the Abbasids, in fact disintegrated into a series of hegemonies established by marauding nomad converts to the faith. The most important and long-lasting of these were the Seljuk Turks and the Mongols.

The Seljuks were herders of the steppes, mongoloid peoples speaking an Altaic language that originated somewhere north of China. Led by tribal chieftans and military adventurers, they drifted south from the steppes into the Muslim Middle East, converted to Islam, and became the new military arm of Islamic expansion. By 1000, officers of the Turkish guard at Baghdad were making caliphs, as Praetorian guardsmen had once made Roman emperors, while Turkish chiefs ruled the Persian countryside.

For a brief two centuries—less in some parts of their domain—the Seljuk Turks brought some unity to the Islamic Middle East. But it was at best a tenuous unity. The Seljuks were soldiers and tribute gatherers, not administrators. Their regime was little more than the sort of traditional tribal confederacy that was the highest form of social organization on their native steppes. They fought constantly among themselves. At the same time, enemies came against them repeatedly, from Europe and from Asia.

Their Christian enemies were the Byzantine emperors at Constantinople and the western European

Crusaders. In their prime, Seljuk armies conquered Palestine and administered shattering defeats to the hitherto strong Byzantine armies, Christendom's easternmost bastion against Asian conquest. But they were unable to conquer Constantinople, and Europe remained beyond their reach. A major counterattack came in the eleventh and twelfth centuries in the form of the Crusades. Worried by Turkish victories over Constantinople and angered by high-handed treatment of Christian pilgrims in Jerusalem, crusading armies of medieval barons seized Jerusalem and held it for a century. The famous Seljuk prince Saladin recaptured the city. But the Seljuk predominance was already weakening, and in the thirteenth century an immensely more powerful enemy appeared out of Asia.

The Mongols of Genghis Khan surged out of the east in the 1200s, built the world's largest empire up to that time, and as quickly faded from the scene. In their glory, however, they were unstoppable. The Mongol cavalry crushed the Seljuks in the 1240s, took and pillaged Baghdad in the 1250s, killing the last figurehead Arab caliph in the process. For a hundred years, the Mongol Ilkhans ruled the Muslim Middle East. Even less skilled at the art of government than the Seljuks, however, they brought no more real unity to Islam. They too feuded among themselves, levied tribute, and kept fear of the conqueror alive in the hearts of the conquered.

Through these troubled late-medieval centuries of secession and conquest, however, Islamic culture survived, persevered, and prospered. The Seljuks encouraged the further development of the Muslim legal system, especially the essential local authority of the *Qadi*. In the end even the Mongol Ilkhans accepted conversion to Islam. And the cosmopolitan cultural and commercial links endured, binding the farthest ends of this politically divided realm.

THE GRAND TURK, THE SOPHY, AND THE MOGULS

Resurgence

Political unity was never to come again for the immense and still-growing expanse of Muslim lands. Like the Christian world, Islam was to be fragmented into many nations. But at the beginning of the modern period, the Islamic peoples enjoyed a sudden dazzling resurgence of power.

This revival of Muslim greatness stretched through the sixteenth century, much of the seventeenth, and even beyond in some places. It was led and dominated by three great Muslim empires—those of the Ottoman Turks around the Mediterranean, the Safavids in Persia, and the Mogul dynasty of northern India. All were peoples of Turkish or Mongol background. All were great empire builders and presided over opulent and cultured courts. All three stand out in the history of Islam.

Around these three empires, Muslim steppe nomads in central Asia, Muslim kingdoms in West Africa, and Muslim enclaves in Southeast Asia made a formidable Islamic presence. Together, they make Islam central—and not only in a geographical sense—to the history of the time.

The Ghazi Princes

The Ottoman Turks, like the Seljuks before them, were nomadic clans from the steppes who had drifted down into the Middle East, converted to Islam, and become militant champions of their new faith. They became military captains and petty princes, carving out little principalities for themselves along the borders of the medieval Byzantine Empire. They were thus lords of the marches on the frontier between Islam and Orthodox Christianity.

Osman (or Othman) I, the founder of the Ottoman dynasty, became prominent early in the fourteenth century. He was a *ghazi*, a fighting frontier lord, the Muslim equivalent of a Christian Crusader. He won victories, and eager swords from all across the Muslim world flocked to join him in his repeated attacks on what was left of Byzantine power in the Middle East.

Whatever defeats they sustained elsewhere in their long history, the Byzantines had always been able to fall back behind the huge walls of Constantinople, "the city protected by God," and ride out the storm. On Constantinople, therefore, the Ottomans fixed their eyes. It took them a hundred and fifty years from the days of Osman the *ghazi*, but in the end they succeeded where all others had failed.

They first gobbled up all that remained of the Byzantine lands on both sides of the straits that divided Europe from Asia. Then, in the 1450s, Muhammad II—the Conqueror, as he came to be called—moved against Constantinople itself.

Muhammad mounted the biggest cannon in the world against the impregnable walls. He portaged a whole fleet overland to gain a strategic advantage on the Byzantine fleet in the Golden Horn, the harbor of Constantinople. In the spring of 1453 the Turks broke through. The last Christian emperor of Byzantium—the eightieth in the line since Constantine—died on the walls. Sultan Muhammad rode in triumph into the city that had been the eastern frontier of Christendom for a thousand years.

Under Muhammad and his immediate successors, especially Selim the Grim in the early sixteenth century, the power of the Ottomans spread far across the Muslim center and into Christian Europe. Like the other empire-builders of the age, they utilized the new technology of gun-powder and artillery with devastating effect. Their fluttering pennons and flashing scimitars drove deep into the Balkans and swung north above the Black Sea into the Ukraine. Southward from Constantinople (now Istanbul) they imposed unity by force upon Mesopotamia and parts of Persia, the Levant, Arabia. They conquered even Egypt, whose military ruling class, the Mamelukes, had once stopped even the Mongols in their tracks.

By 1500, then, the former *ghazi* princes ruled a considerable swath of territory, extending from southeastern Europe around the eastern end of the Mediterranean, from their capital at Istanbul. It was to this tradition and this heritage that Suleiman the

Magnificent, the most renowned of all the Ottomans, was born at the beginning of the sixteenth century.

I Am God's Slave and Sultan of This World

Under Suleiman the Magnificent (1520–1566), the Ottoman Empire became a world power. The Ottomans absorbed new territories in Europe, Asia, and Africa. They put fleets to sea from the Mediterranean to the Indian Ocean. They played the game of power politics with the leading European rulers and dominated the Muslim center as no one had since the Arab caliphs of Baghdad.

Suleiman himself fought a dozen major campaigns, spent a total of ten years in the field, and died in his seventies at the head of his troops. He reclaimed most of the old Omayyad lands along the coast of North Africa and conquered more of western Persia. He advanced still further into eastern Europe, over-

An Ottoman Sultan on horseback and richly garbed. Grudging Western admiration for this formidable Islamic realm is clearly reflected in such pictures. (New York Public Library Picture Collection)

running Hungary, invading Austria, and besieging but barely failing to take Vienna, the capital of the Holy Roman Empire.

Suleiman's commanders on the Mediterranean raided the southern coasts of Italy and France and fought the Spanish fleet to a standstill. In the Indian Ocean, Ottoman squadrons battled the Portuguese on the sea routes to India. On the sea as on land, Ottoman power dominated the heart of the Old World.

By the time he died, Suleiman the Magnificent ruled all or part of what is today Hungary, Yugoslavia, Greece, Albania, Romania, Bulgaria, and southern Russia; Turkey, Iran, Iraq, Syria, Lebanon, Jordan, and Israel; Saudi Arabia, Egypt, Lybia, Tunisia, and Algeria—among others. Unlike the Seljuks and the Mongols, furthermore, the Ottoman sultan really ruled his immense realm. The Ottoman Empire of Suleiman—Suleiman the Lawgiver, as his own people called him—was a far cry from the loose confederations of *ghazi* times. It was a centralized state with an administrative system second to none in that half of the Old World.

Sultan Suleiman's empire did not draw its administrative personnel from a single social class, like the European *bourgeoisie* or China's gentry of scholar-bureaucrats. The Ottoman administrative system built upon three groups who already had important functions in society: the *Qadis*, the *Timariots*, and the *ghulam* system.

The *Qadis*, the traditional Islamic judges, had been assigned administrative functions at the village level as far back as the Arab Empire, and they fulfilled similar functions under the Ottomans. The *timariots* were the old *ghazi* cavalry. Rewarded for their military service by tax revenues from recently conquered villages, they also provided police power and protection for these towns. The *ghulam* system was the Turkish practice of appointing men who were nominally slaves to high positions of civil and military authority in the land. Delegating power to slaves avoided any problems of insubordination, since slaves had no rights against their masters. Christian converts to Islam were incorporated into this system in the fifteenth century, becoming the famous Janissary Corps of elite soldiers and civil servants.

These three groups staffed an impressive administrative structure. At its head was the grand vizier, nominally a slave, but in fact the sultan's right hand. The vizier presided over the royal council, or *divan*, with its many secretaries, scribes, and subordinate bureaus. The provinces of the empire were run by local governors called *pashas* in the cities, *begs* in the countryside. At the local level, *Qadis* and *timariots* performed their traditional functions. Janissaries were seeded through the whole system in key administrative and military posts from the capital to the farthest border provinces.

Sophisticated European visitors much admired the empire of Suleiman the Magnificent. Official merit was recognized and corruption punished, they said, as they were not in Europe. Public charity cared for the needy, schools prospered, and the sultan's armies were ever victorious. It was an idealized picture, but there was much truth in it.

Suleiman himself had a clear picture of his own place in the world. "I am God's slave," he caused to be inscribed on a public monument, "and sultan of this world."[3] Ruling in splendor from Istanbul on the Golden Horn, the Grand Turk, as Westerners called him, was the most powerful of Muslim rulers and more powerful than almost any Christian king.

The Shah of Isfahan

Persia, the Muslim power due east of the Ottoman Empire, was no upstart *ghazi* state. In 1500 the Persians already had two thousand years of history behind them. Many dynasties had ruled there since Cyrus the Great founded the first Persian empire in the sixth century B.C. Since the Arab conquest in the seventh century A.D., Persia had become in many ways the cultural heart of Islam, producing theologians, scholars, and poets in profusion as well as leading schools of art.

She had also managed to civilize—and Islamicize—one after another of her subsequent conquerors and foreign rulers. The Seljuk Turks in the eleventh century, the Mongols in the thirteenth, and the terrible Tamerlane and his descendants in the fifteenth had all been schooled in ancient Persian ways. Politically, however, Persia had remained weak and often fragmented among her conquerors.

Persians had not entirely lost control of their own destiny. Turks and Mongols might conquer, but cultivated Persian viziers did much of the governing for them. Persian taste guided one rude warrior after another into magnificent building, lavish patronage of the arts, and even Islamic piety. Then, in 1500, a native Persian dynasty seized power once more and set Persian history on an odd new path.

Ismail (1500–1524), the first of the Safavids, was thirteen years old when his devoted religious followers, the *Kizilbashi* ("Red Caps") swept him into power. He reunified Persia and gave the nation a Persian ruling house, initiated a great age in Persian history—and fueled a religious rift in the Islamic world that persists to the present day.

[3]Halil Inalcik, *The Ottoman Empire: The Classical Age, 1300–1600*, trans. Norman Itzkowitz and Colin Imber (New York: Praeger, 1973), p. 41.

The Safavids were Shiites, members of Islam's largest minority sect. Regarded as heretics by the Sunnite majority of Islam, the Shiites rejected the traditional leadership of the caliphs, the acknowledged successors to the Prophet. Shiites insisted that only someone directly related to Muhammad—that is, a descendant of the third official caliph, Ali, who had been Muhammad's cousin and son-in-law—could be the true head of Islam. Such a rightful heir to the Prophet, furthermore, would be an *imam*, a real spiritual head of the faithful—not a mere secular ruler, as most caliphs had increasingly tended to be.

Shiites had been martyred for this heterodox faith for centuries. In Safavid Persia they found a homeland at last.

Suleiman the Magnificent's great victory over the Hungarians at the Battle of Mohacs in 1526—here shown in a Muslim miniature—carried Turkish power into the heart of Europe. Combined with Muslim pressure in the Mediterranean and Suleiman's siege of Vienna three years after Mohacs, these Ottoman warriors brought Islam as close as it ever came to conquering the West. (New York Public Library Picture Collection)

Young Ismail, surrounded by Sufi holy men, swept to power on a wave of religious enthusiasm. He was hailed as shah—secular ruler—and *imam* in Tabriz, the red caps of his supporters thronging about him. By seizing power in Persia, however, Ismail drove a wedge into the heart of Islam. To the east and north lay the Sunnite Muslims of India and central Asia; to the west and south, those of Ottoman Turkey, Arabia, Egypt, and North Africa. Even more dangerous, Shiite Persia, with its *imam* emperor and its crusading zeal, exerted a powerful attraction on Shiite minorities elsewhere in the Middle East.

As in Reformation Europe at the same time, the sixteenth century saw savage persecutions and wars of religion in the Muslim Middle East. The Sunnite champion was the Ottoman colossus, Persia's neighbor to the west. The Safavids compelled Persian Sunnites—who were actually in the majority in the early days—to accept Shiite formulations of the faith on pain of death. The Ottomans martyred Shiites, whom they saw as potential rebels, in large numbers. And the armies of the Safavid shah and the Ottoman sultan met repeatedly on the battlefield throughout the century.

In the early days especially, the Ottomans generally had the better of it, adding substantial chunks of Persian territory to their already swollen empire. This is perhaps not surprising, since Ottoman armies were early equipped with firearms and artillery, while Ismail's soldiers were capable of charging bare-chested into battle, calling upon the sanctity of the *imam* to protect them. Around 1600, however, the Safavids produced a ruler who would have considerably more success—the great Shah Abbas.

Abbas I (1587–1629) is in fact generally considered the greatest of all the Safavids. A dark-complected, masterful, immensely energetic man, Abbas, like Ismail before him, came to the throne young, at seventeen. But he reigned much longer than Ismail, and his forty-odd years in power were one of Persia's golden ages.

Shah Abbas came to a throne threatened by encroachment from both sides—by Ottomans occupying western provinces and Uzbek peoples pressing down from central Asia. He made a temporary peace with the Turks, drove the Uzbeks out of the northeast—and then began to prepare for war on better terms with the Ottomans. By the turn of the century, he had replaced an army of religious enthusiasts with a new military arm composed of paid soldiers trained in the European style. He even armed his new troops with artillery made by English cannon founders he had welcomed for the purpose. Thus equipped, he pushed the Ottoman Turks back out of his western provinces at last.

Shah Abbas also streamlined the royal administration along Western lines. He gladly received European traders and opened diplomatic relations with Western nations. He used these Western contacts for his own purposes, however, as when he cooperated with a British naval squadron in forcing the Portuguese out of the strategic island of Hormuz at the mouth of the Persian Gulf.

For his own people, the greatest of the Safavids built roads, dug canals, erected caravansaries to encourage trade. He imported skilled artisans from other lands to expand Persia's ancient store of handicraft manufacturing industries. He fostered the pilgrim trade in Persia by building shrines. But he also distanced himself from the Shiite fanaticism of the *Kizilbashi* and was far more tolerant of other faiths than Ismail had been.

The jewel of Shah Abbas's Persia was the new capital he built at Isfahan. This ancient town, centrally located for administrative purposes and closer to the Persian Gulf for trade, was soon humming with new industry as Abbas imported artisans and built huge bazaars. Isfahan grew in time to a city of half a million souls, with 160 mosques, 50 religious colleges, 275 public baths—and 1800 caravansaries! The shah's palace, the imperial mosque, the roofed bazaars, the royal gardens within and outside of the city were things of beauty. Wealthy homes had lovely gardens of their own, and the poor found public charities ready to hand.

Like many masterful men, Abbas could tolerate no rivals, not even potential successors. His failure to prepare his heirs left Persia with a series of much less capable rulers after his passing. But during the four decades of his reign, the nation prospered, art and culture flourished, and even European travelers admired the Sophy, as they called him, as much as they did the Grand Turk.

Through the Afghan Passes

A journey eastward from Safavid Persia would have brought a sixteenth-century traveler into the third of the great Islamic empires—the realm of the Moguls, comprising most of what is today Pakistan, northern India, and Bangladesh. Mogul India, like Safavid Persia and Ottoman Turkey, was a major exemplar of the transnational, transregional civilization of early-modern Islam.

Two towering individuals shaped the Mogul achievement: Babur, the founder, and Akbar the Great, the true architect of the empire. They were in a sense the Ismail and Shah Abbas of sixteenth-century India.

Like Ismail, Babur (1483–1530) came to precarious power as a youth. He was only eleven when he inherited the throne of the unstable central Asian kingdom of Ferghana, north and west of India. Half Turk, half Mongol, Babur claimed descent from Tamerlane, who had himself sacked Delhi around 1400.

Babur turned to the conquest of northern India only when the fortunes of war and politics had deprived him of hope for a central Asian empire. In the middle 1520s, when he was already in his forties, he and his Mogul tribesmen descended through the Afghan passes of the Hindu Kush, India's ancient invasion route along the Northwest Frontier.

He was an exceptional man. Athlete, warrior, poet, and composer of his own memoirs, Babur was relatively humane in an age of massacres. He was also capable of extraordinary heroism, of diabolical practical jokes, and, in the last fateful decision of his life, of remarkable self-sacrifice.

The small army he led down into the Punjab was a typical rabble of central Asian adventurers. But Babur also trundled artillery along in his train, with Turkish gun crews and a mounted force trained in Turkish cavalry tactics. The Mogul realm, like that of the Ottomans, would be a "gunpowder empire." And Babur, like other famous conquerors, earned at least half his victories through skillful preparation.

The India Babur entered was, like Persia, one of the world's oldest civilizations. Highly developed urban culture had existed for perhaps four thousand years in the Indus and Punjab valleys, where the ancient cities of Harappa and Mohenjodaro rose and fell many centuries before Athens or Rome were dreamed of. The Indian subcontinent as a whole had developed a cohesive culture based on the Hindu religion and the caste system. It was a land of highly developed arts and crafts, many rich commercial cities, and countless peasant villages.

Political unity, however, had been rare in India. Only under the Mauryas (322–185 B.C.) and the Guptas (A.D. 320–540) had a single centralized political order been imposed on most of the vast triangular land mass between the Himalayas and Ceylon (Sri Lanka). Even when there was political power in India, it focused where the Moguls would build theirs—along the wide, brown, sacred river Ganges in the north.

In Babur's time, India had collapsed into a particularly messy period of political division. An earlier Muslim regime in the north, the Delhi sultanate, had crumbled away. Many petty *rajas* vied for power in the resulting vacuum, imposing extortionate taxes on the people and allowing their armies to live off the land. Lesser princes and nobles felt no loyalty to greater ones. The villagers, who had seen so many invaders stream down from the mountains, remained indifferent to the outcome of any war.

Babur thus arrived at an auspicious time. His artillery, cavalry, and personal heroics combined with this disunity and widespread apathy to give him a series of astonishing victories over larger hosts. Neither the traditional Indian elephant cavalry nor the famous chivalry of the Rajput princes could stop the invader from the north. His first great victory at Panipat in 1526 gave him a kingdom in India. Subsequent triumphs expanded it into a brief and glittering empire.

Then suddenly, still in his forties, worn out by a lifetime of struggle, Babur was dead. According to a perhaps apocryphal account, his oldest and best-beloved son had fallen deathly ill, and Babur offered Allah his own life for that of the young man. In a few months, the youth was healthy once more and the emperor had passed away.

The Lives of Akbar the Great

For the next half century Babur's newly won empire struggled to survive. Then, in Babur's grandson Akbar, the true builder of the Mogul order came at last.

Akbar the Great (1556–1605) reigned for half a century and became for later generations in northern India a figure of legendary benevolence and accomplishment. The greatest and strangest of the Moguls, he lived three very different lives, one after another, each stranger than the last.

Yet another young heir to an unsteady throne, Akbar led an irregular, self-willed life of hunting and revelry during his youth, leaving the conduct of affairs to an overbearing but loyal minister of state. So petulantly pleasure-loving was the young Akbar, and so irregular was his style of life, that he apparently refused to trouble himself even to learn to read. In fact he remained unlettered all his life, an illiterate wise man at the center of one of Islam's most sophisticated courts.

Outbreaks of anarchic violence reaching even into his court finally jolted the young emperor into an awareness of his duties. He reportedly hurled the aristocratic murderer of a royal minister from the battlements of the palace with his own hands—and plunged straightaway into his second life, that of a leader of armies and a rebuilder of empire.

Akbar was an aggressive general, famous for incredibly rapid marches that repeatedly caught his enemies off guard. He aimed not only to reassemble the fragments of the empire his grandfather had won, but to achieve a predominant position in all India. He reconquered the north, going well beyond Babur's conquest to rule from Gujarat in the west to Bengal in the east, from the mountains of Kashmir in the north down into the Deccan, the triangular peninsula

of southern India. He thus made the Muslim Moguls heirs of the Hindu Guptas and the Buddhist Mauryas as unifiers of India.

But Akbar was more than a conqueror: he was a pacifier and a conciliator. He humbled the fierce Rajput *rajas* and then made them his vassals and partners in rule, even going as far as to marry a Rajput princess. He launched a Hindu policy, offering equal rights to the Hindu majority among his subjects and opening up high places in his government to high-caste Indians.

He provided, finally, for a centralized administrative system superior to anything northern India had seen since Gupta times a thousand years before. He divided his realm into a dozen provinces and appointed governors for each. He chose provincial officials from all classes and castes, organized them in thirty-three graded ranks, paid them in cash, and promoted them on a merit basis. He organized the crucial land tax efficiently, fixing a system that lasted for hundreds of years.

Meanwhile, a middle-aged Akbar had undergone another crisis and entered the third of his lives—that of a religious mystic and founder of a new faith. He had listened for many years to the discussions of holy men of various faiths at his court—Muslims and Hindus, Buddhists, Jains, and even Jesuit Christian fathers. By 1580 he had abandoned orthodox Islam in favor of a new cult, an attempt at a universal religion with himself as its prophet. He called it the Divine Faith.

There was a practical side to Akbar's new religion, since the cult transcended the divisive pull of Islam and Hinduism and focused religious veneration upon the head of the state. But we may grant him a higher sincerity too when he preached his universal religion:

> O God, in every temple I see people that seek Thee; in every language I hear spoken, people praise Thee; if it be a mosque, people murmur the holy prayer; if it be a Christian church, they ring the bell for love of Thee. . . . it is Thou whom I seek from temple to temple.[4]

Akbar's Divine Faith did not extend far beyond official circles, nor did it long outlast his lifetime. But its overarching tolerance for all religions contrasted strikingly with the bloodshed of Protestant–Catholic and Shiite–Sunnite wars in other parts of Eurasia in early-modern times.

Akbar was a great builder and patron of the arts, a man of broad intellectual and spiritual concerns, and a powerful organizer of empire. Like Asoka in ancient India, he comes as close as any earthly mon-

[4]Steven Warshaw and C. David Bromwell, with A. J. Tudisco, *India Emerges* (Berkeley: Diablo Press, 1974), p. 60.

arch to meeting Plato's criteria for a true philosopher-king.

The City, the Village, and the Face behind the Veil

The wealth of the Grand Turk, the Sophy of Persia, and the Moguls of India was proverbial in Europe. When they were not fighting, they traded with each other and with the Christian West. All three of the empires of the Muslim center, as we have seen, encouraged crafts and manufacturing. By establishing peace and order, they maximized the potential for all economic endeavor.

In Islamic Asia, as in Christian Europe, wealth gravitated to the cities. Istanbul, Isfahan, and Delhi were among the great cities of the world.

The metropolises of the Muslim Middle East and of Muslim-controlled India were divided by occupation and by religion. As in Europe, artisans and merchants were organized into guilds, and all practitioners of the same trade had their shops in the same section of the city. There were more likely to be devotees of other religions in the Muslim city than in the West, however: Jews and Christians in Middle Eastern cities, Hindus, Jains, Sikhs, and others in Indian ones. The sects also kept to their own quarters of the city. There might also be a foreign quarter for merchants from other places. In India, the many Hindu castes, which were also occupational and religious groupings, were firmly segregated by ancient Indian custom.

The governors, judges, and police commanders who ruled the city, however, were almost always Muslims. In the teachings of the Prophet, they could usually find warrant for a religious forbearance that Christian Europeans sadly lacked. The bloody feuds of Shiite and Sunnite were thus rather the exception than the norm in the Islamic world. Even the intermittent wars with Christians or Rajputs were affairs of high policy or wild border raiders—not of civilized city dwellers. In the Muslim metropolis, the Christian merchants had their quarter, the Hindu administrator his high place in government. In the polyglot middle parts of Asia, diversity was simply a fact of life.

The village was much more likely to be homogeneous, however. Villages in the Middle East and in South Asia were physically like villages everywhere: small collections mostly of stone- or mud-walled huts, surrounded by scanty croplands or pasturage. Since Middle Eastern land was less fertile than much of Europe, farm animals were often lean and hungry, and the people burned dung rather than wood. Monsoon India was much wetter, and the Ganges and other streams from the Himalayas provided ample irriga-

tion in the north. Yet villages were meager places, dusty and muddy by turns, and usually poor, even in the subcontinent.

The typical Muslim village was solidly patriarchal. It was run by a headman, and each large household was headed by the father of the family. The authorities expected the headman to keep his village peaceful and productive, the heads of families to be responsible for all their kin. In a period of imperial order, royal armies or authorities from nearby cities would control the lives of villagers. In less orderly times, roving bands of nomads in the Middle East or warring local *rajas* in India would be their masters.

The condition of women also had its distinctive features in Islamic lands. Muhammad had allowed polygamy for those who could afford more than one wife, and sixteenth-century Islam was as thoroughly male-dominated as any section of the globe. Muslim women were generally required to wear the veil and to live their lives in a world of women, cut off from the larger world of men by screens, curtains, and high walls. Bare-faced European women, particularly those wearing the low-cut gowns of Renaissance and later times, seemed shockingly immodest to Muslims.

On the other hand, women in the Islamic world enjoyed property rights, control of their own income, and the right to divorce their husband—none of which was possible, except in exceptional cases, in Christian Europe. Women in the Middle East especially made substantial contributions to the economy, performing farm labor or supervising it on their husband's land, herding flocks, or weaving many of the famous Persian rugs that found such a large market in the West.

In Islamic countries as elsewhere, finally, there were women who wielded great power. This was most commonly done from behind the scenes: it is much harder to find famous female rulers in the Muslim center than in either Christian Europe or Confucian China. But through political intrigue, especially in the intricate and often critical politics of the royal harem, Muslim women could exert immense influence upon the course of events from "behind the veil."

THE GARDEN OF OMAR KHAYYÁM

A Book of Verses

A Book of Verses underneath the Bough,
A Jug of Wine, A Loaf of Bread—and Thou
   Beside me singing in the Wilderness—
Oh, Wilderness were Paradise enow![5]

[5] *The Rubáiyát of Omar Khayyám*, trans. Edward Fitzgerald (New York: Three Sirens Press, n.d.), p. 175.

A Persian miniature dating from around 1600. The subject is the archetypal father-son combat of Sohrab and Rustem, based on a tenth-century epic poem, the Shah Nameh of Firdusi. The integration of martial figures, flowery setting, and script in a charming composition is typical of the elegant Muslim art of miniature painting. (The Metropolitan Museum of Art, Gift of Alexander Smith Coderan, 1913)

These, among the more commonly quoted lines of English verse, are actually a translation from the twelfth-century Persian poet and astronomer Omar Khayyám. Through such poetry, we have direct access to a very different side of Islamic society, a world of sophisticated skepticism rather than religious devotion. *The Rubáiyát of Omar Khayyám* introduces us to a seductive Middle Eastern world where fine wine warms the spirit in spite of the Prophet's prohibition of alcohol, and where all women do not lead secluded lives behind veils and screens.

If the Ottoman Empire was the most powerful of the Islamic states at the beginning of the modern age, Persia was still the cultural heart of the Muslim world. Persian literature, Persian painting, Persian dress and manners, and the Persian language were common among cultured Muslims from Istanbul to Delhi. What Italy was to Renaissance Europe, Persia was to the Muslim center—the predominant force in literature and the life of the mind.

Paradoxically, Persia's own major contributions to literary culture in particular came not under the Safavids, but under the Turkish and Mongol rulers of the later medieval centuries. The Mongol Ilkhanate of the thirteenth and fourteenth centuries produced Persia's most celebrated historical writing, as well as eminent works in astronomy, botany, medicine, philosophy, and of course theology. This earlier period also produced a vital literature of Sufi mysticism and romantic poetry. Omar Khayyám wrote under the Seljuks, but the Mongol period saw the writing of Sadi of Shiraz, widely admired as Persia's greatest poet as well as a famous Sufi. Under the descendants of Tamerlane in the fifteenth century, Hafiz, also of Shiraz, revived something of Omar's spirit in his odes to springtime and rose gardens, wine and youth, blending Muslim mysticism with a melancholy skepticism that Omar would have understood.

Persian literature of the Safavid sixteenth century, by contrast, was far less vital and original. The puritanical narrowness of the Shiite clerics smothered both the passionate mysticism of the Sufis and the worldly lyricism of the poets. Safavid scholarship had little originality. Safavid poetry sank into a morass of elaborate "poetic diction" and complex verse forms, more a challenge to the professional writer than a pleasure to the reader.

At this time, however, Persian influence spread east and west across the Muslim heartland of Eurasia.

The Ottomans took their theology from the Arabs and borrowed geographical ideas from Europe, but they reserved their highest respect for the history and poetry of their mortal enemies in Safavid Persia. Ottoman scholars wrote exhaustive commentaries on the Persian classics, and Ottoman poets copied them, both in the Persian language and in Turkish. Thus the distinctive mixture of mysticism and romanticism that had taken shape in Persia lived on, in the writing of her greatest foe.

Persian culture was also massively transplanted to India under the Moguls, especially Akbar the Great. Persian architecture and painting, language and literature, spread not only across heavily Muslim northern India but down into the Hindu south as well. Educated Rajput princes spoke Persian in polite society, dressed in the Persian style, lounged in Persian gardens. Persian poetry was read in the summer palaces of Indian Kashmir as enthusiastically as it was on the Golden Horn at Istanbul. It was probably read in both places with more appreciation than it could any longer command in the puritanical Persia of the *Kizilbashi*. But then, Omar Khayyám of Khorasan had scarcely expected immortality:

> Ah, my Beloved, fill the Cup that clears
> Today of past Regrets and future Fears:
>   *Tomorrow*—Why, Tomorrow I may be
> Myself with Yesterday's Sev'n thousand Years.[6]

The Luminous Power of Art

No Muslim nation has left us sculpture or painting like that of Renaissance Europe—living human beings, ready to step down from their pedestals or out of their great gilt frames. The artistic genius of Islam lay elsewhere—in Arabic calligraphy and the decorative arts, in glass, ceramics, and textiles, in the exquisite art of the miniature, and perhaps above all, in architecture, the art of mosques and palaces.

Painting of human or divine figures was frowned upon by Islamic theology as conducive to idolatry, or as an attempt to usurp God's creative function. Yet some lovely figure painting was done in the Ottoman,

Safavid, and Mogul empires—on a small scale and for private consumption.

The art of miniature painting flourished first in Persia—naturally—and spread from there to the neighboring Turkish and Indian realms. Small in size (Indian miniatures average less than a foot square), these works usually depicted group scenes—famous victories, royal courts, popular festivals—or illustrated well-known myths or famous poems. Simply drawn, delicately colored figures often move against a flat background of trees and flowers. At the court of Akbar, Mogul painters did some striking portraiture: lightly shaded, oddly luminous likenesses of shahs and Muslim saints in silks and turbans. But the classic Persian miniature depicted legendary heroes in action, royal weddings, or emperors in splendor against abstract backgrounds of bright verdure or arched gates and rectangular walls, all glowing like jewels with color and exquisite detail.

The Muslim world's most admired graphic art, however, was calligraphy. Since the days of the Arab caliphates Arabic script has been widely used to decorate mosques, ceramics, metalwork, and textiles, as well as in gorgeous copies of the Koran. Indeed, the universal use of Arabic lettering for religious, commercial, and other purposes helped to bind Muslims of all nations into a single cosmopolitan community.

The decorative potential of Arabic script filled much of the gap created by the taboo on pictures or sculpture in public places. Verses from the Koran mingled with interwoven abstract patterns to produce a peculiarly Muslim blend of aesthetic pleasure and religious piety. The living word of Allah and the luminous power of art thus mingled in the work of the skilled Arabic calligrapher.

The Most Beautiful Building in the World

But in the days of the Muslim resurgence, as in the original golden age of the Arab Empire, architecture was the most dazzling triumph of Islamic art.

The rulers of the three great Islamic empires lived in a style suitable to the proverbial Oriental potentate. Some of the palaces they built as settings for their elaborate court life survive as evidence of those splendors.

The Topkapi Palace in Istanbul—now a museum—is the example most familiar to travelers. Its sumptuous interiors, polychrome or dazzling blue in color, are brilliant with beautifully woven carpets and glazed tiles in floral or leaf designs. Equally splendid, however, are the palaces of the Mogul rulers of India, particularly the Red Forts of Delhi and Agra and the great Akbar's palaces at Fatehpur Sikri. The Fateh-

[6]Ibid., p. 177.

The Taj Mahal at Agra, built by the Mogul emperor Shah Jahan in the early 1600s in memory of his favorite wife, the Mumtaz Mahal. Exquisite in design and setting, the Taj Mahal is one of the jewels of Mogul—and of Islamic—architecture. (Library of Congress)

pur Sikri complex, built of white marble and red sandstone, enclosed by multi-level galleries and arcades with rows of bell-topped towers in mingled Muslim and Hindu styles, epitomizes the splendid lives of the Moguls. The pleasure gardens of Shalimar in Calcutta and Kashmir, in the foothills of the Himalayas, remind us that these sophisticated Muslim monarchs were only a few generations removed from the open steppes and still enjoyed life in the out-of-doors.

Religion, however, remained central to the life of Islam, as the great mosques built during these centuries testify. The first mosques had been in the open style of the Arabs—a large courtyard, a prayer hall with a decorated *mihrab* (alcove) facing Mecca, and tall, slender towers called minarets from which the faithful were daily called to prayer. Two new styles in particular emerged in later times, retaining the basic elements but clothing them in striking new forms.

One of these was the "four-*ivan*" style developed in Persia, featuring four open-ended vaulted halls focusing on a central court or prayer hall. The huge Mosque of Shah Abbas in Isfahan illustrates this form on a colossal scale, its intricately vaulted surfaces rich with tilework and mosaic. Sumptuous carpets, hanging lamps, and ornate *mihrabs* made such imperial mosques fitting sanctuaries for the God who had smiled upon Islam.

It was the Ottoman Turks, however, who developed the more familiar style of huge domes and slender minarets that most Westerners associate with the architecture of the mosque. The dome does go farther back, beginning with the earliest of Islamic monuments—the gold-sheathed Dome of the Rock, built by the Arabs in Jerusalem. But it was the Ottomans, impressed by such awesome Roman domes as that over Hagia Sophia in Constantinople, who made the central dome the core of the architectural design of the mosque.

After surrounding Hagia Sophia itself with minarets, Ottoman architects proceeded to erect similar buildings of their own. These included such wonders as the Mosque of Sultan Suleiman in Istanbul and the Mosque of Selim at Adrianople. These mountainous accumulations of domes and half domes had multi-galleried minarets at all four corners and vast courtyards filled with trees and walks, hospitals, caravansaries, the tombs of saints, and other pious structures. They broadcast the greatness of their builders—and their faith in Allah—to the world.

A final brief word must be reserved for the last resting places of the saints and potentates of the Islamic world—for the artistry of Muslim tombs.

There was nothing gloomy about these monuments to the mighty dead, beautifully domed and often set in flowering gardens. The azure dome of Tamerlane's mausoleum at Samarkand looms over walls and towers of exquisite glazed brick and carved marble. The garden where Omar Khayyám lies buried—in the shadow of the tomb of a Muslim saint—blooms with a profusion of blossoms that would have brought a smile to the poet's lips. And the blue reflecting pools, the dazzling white domes and minarets of the tomb built by the Mogul Shah Jahan for his empress in the early 1600s make the Taj Mahal at Agra quite possibly the most hauntingly beautiful building in the world.

SUMMARY

The Muslim center of the Old World included parts of all three continents of this half of the inhabited globe. North Africa, Balkan Europe, the Middle East, South and Southeast Asia were among the regions dominated by followers of the teachings of Muhammad around 1500.

The Arab Empire that had established this Islamic hegemony during the earlier Middle Ages had declined and fragmented in later medieval times. First the Seljuk Turks and then the Mongols had replaced the original followers of the Prophet as the predominant people in the central portions of this sprawling

Islamic world. Whether ruled by Arabs, Persians, Seljuks, Mongols, or the array of African kings and South and Southeast Asian rajas, these Muslim peoples enjoyed a powerful cultural, commercial, and religious unity.

Around 1500, finally, three new empires rose to power in the heart of this Muslim zone.

The Ottoman Turks conquered the Byzantine Empire and the Arab states of the Near East and North Africa. The Ottoman sultan, Suleiman the Magnificent, was the most powerful ruler in the western half of the Old World, revered among his own people and respected in Christendom. To the east, meanwhile, the new Safavid dynasty seized power in Persia. Safavid Persia became the militant center of Shiite Islam, a

sect as divisive in the Muslim world as Protestantism was in Western Christendom.

Still further to the east, the Muslim Moguls conquered northern India. Under Akbar the Great, Mogul wealth, administration, and culture gave India another golden age—her last before the coming of the Europeans.

During the centuries of shifting rule in Islam, Muslim culture produced beautiful poetry, painting, Arabic calligraphy, and religious architecture. Persia was the recognized cultural center of the Muslim zone. But the mosques of the Ottoman sultans and the Taj Mahal in Mogul India also revealed the artistic brilliance of the Islamic world at the beginning of modern history.

SUGGESTED READING

ARNOLD, T. W. *The Preaching of Islam*. London: Luzac, 1935. Old survey of twelve centuries of Muslim expansion.

AZIZ AHMAD. *Studies in Islamic Culture in the Indian Environment*. Oxford: Clarendon Press, 1964. Includes studies of Mogul times.

BABUR, Z. M. *Memoirs of Babur* (2 vols.). Oxford: Oxford University Press, 1921. The Mogul founder's own extraordinary account of his life.

Cambridge History of Iran (7 vols.). Cambridge: Cambridge University Press, 1983. Includes both later Abbasid and Safavid times, presented in the thorough and scholarly style of all the Cambridge histories.

GRUBE, E. J. *The World of Islam*. New York: McGraw-Hill, n. d. A beautiful collection of photographs of all forms of Muslim art, from calligraphy to mosques.

HODGSON, M. G. S. *The Venture of Islam: Conscience and History in a World Civilization* (3 vols.). Chicago: University of Chicago Press, 1974. An interpretive account of Islamic history and beliefs. For a briefer introduction, see H. A. Gibb, *Mohammedanism: An Historical Survey* (New York: Oxford University Press, 1970).

INALCIK, H. *The Ottoman Empire: The Classic Age, 1300–1600*. London: Weidenfeld and Nicolson, 1972. Rise

of the Ottoman power through the century of Suleiman the Magnificent.

PARRY, V. J. "The Middle East, 1453–1574," in D. Johnson, ed., *The Making of the Modern World*. London: Ernest Ben, 1971. Brief account of the Ottoman realm around 1500.

PICKTHALL, M. M. *The Meaning of the Glorious Koran*. New York: New American Library, 1953. Readable translation of the Muslim holy book.

SAUNDERS, J. J., ed. *The Moslem World on the Eve of European Expansion*. Englewood Cliffs, N.J.: Prentice-Hall, 1966. Primary sources on the Muslim center.

SMITH, V. *Akbar the Great Mogul*, 2nd ed. Oxford: Clarendon Press, 1927. Still the standard biography.

SPEAR, P. *A History of India*. Baltimore: Penguin, 1965. A solid survey of Indian history, with sections on the reigns of the Moguls.

WADDY, C. *Women in Muslim History*. London: Longman, 1980. An overview, somewhat thin on the early modern period. The first chapter of S. H. Mirza's *Muslim Women's Role in the Pakistan Movement* (Research Society of Pakistan, Punjab University, 1969) includes some discussion of women poets and other leading spirits of the Mogul period.

Chapter · 3

THE EAST ASIAN WORLD

THE CONFUCIAN SPHERE

The World beyond the Mountains

The hardy, not to say foolhardy, sixteenth-century traveler who wanted to go beyond the Muslim center of Eurasia into the farthest East would have found the last leg of his journey much harder than anything before. Trade routes were no longer what they had been in the Classic Age of the Roman and Han Chinese empires, or even in the more recent period of Mongol rule across Eurasia, when Marco Polo had made the trip. And basic geography had always cut East Asia off from the rest of the double continent.

The lands and peoples of East Asia were isolated from the world by some of the most formidable barriers in nature. To the north lay barren deserts and the forbidding steppes of Siberia. In the west, the mountains of the Pamir Knot, the Tibetan Plateau, and the five-mile-high wall of the Himalayas barred the way. Southward, the mountains and dense jungles of mainland Southeast Asia were all but impenetrable. Still farther to the east the Pacific Ocean stretched—forever, as it must have seemed in 1500. In addition, the sheer size and wildly varied geography of China itself, with its huge river valleys—especially the Yellow River in the north and the Yangtze in central China—made the Middle Kingdom an impossible country to know.

Within these protecting and isolating barriers, an almost entirely mongoloid population had created a number of centers of civilization over the preceding three thousand years. But by far the largest and oldest civilization in the Far East was that of imperial China.

The unity of the East Asian world, then, was not like that of either the reborn West or the Muslim center. East Asia was not a system of feuding states with a rough parity of power, like the great powers of Europe. Nor did a common religion, producing cultural similarities among its adherents, bind this part of the globe as it did the Muslim zone. It was rather the historic predominance of a single great nation, warping the history and shaping the culture of all her neighbors, that made the East Asian world a distinct region of Eurasian civilization.

China in 1500 was the largest country in the world, larger in area and population than all of Europe. The very presence of this colossus, with its impressive Confucian civilization and its unified bureaucratic government, had awed the other peoples of the Far East since before the time of Christ. China, vast in its power and influential in its culture, was the great historic fact that imposed cultural unity on the East Asian world.

The Centrality of China

China's sphere of influence included a considerable number of peoples around her far frontiers. There were steppe nomads to the north, beyond the Great Wall, in Mongolia, Manchuria, and elsewhere, sometimes half Sinicized but always a military threat. There were the two peninsular societies of Korea to the northeast and Vietnam to the south, both significantly shaped in China's image by 1500. And there was the island kingdom of Japan, which had been accepting some Chinese influences and rejecting others for more than a thousand years.

Chinese influence has in fact waxed and waned

over all her huge area of cultural and political predominance down the centuries. When powerful, aggressively expansionist dynasties ruled in China, her influence was all but inescapable. This had been the case particularly after the Ch'in unification, during the Han (206 B.C.–A.D. 220), and again after the Sui reunification, during the T'ang (618–906). Over the half-dozen centuries before 1500, however, China's influence had declined, especially under the embattled Sung dynasty (960–1279) and during the century of Mongol rule (1264–1368).

By that time, however, the pervasive impact of Chinese civilization had been felt everywhere in East Asia. The Chinese language and its characters, the classical writings attributed to Confucius, and some Chinese-style central government had appeared in a number of neighboring lands. Buddhism, originating in India, had reached China first and been passed on in Chinese forms to Korea, Japan, and elsewhere. Whether they paid formal tribute to the Son of Heaven in Peking or not, the peoples of East Asia owed a great deal to the land her own people called the Middle Kingdom and thought of—understandably—as the true center of the world.

At the beginning of the modern period, a good case could certainly be made for the superiority of China's historic accomplishment. In Europe, Marco Polo's admiring descriptions of the China of Kublai Khan were still read. It was golden dreams of the wealth of Cathay and Cipango (Japan), as well as of India and the Spice Islands, that drew the Europeans across the oceans. It should be remembered, after all, that it was the West that felt the need of the East: East Asia seems to have been satisfied with what it had of wealth and culture.

A look at the East Asian world, then, will illustrate again the plurality of successful civilizations that prevailed around the world on the eve of the Western predominance. And it will demonstrate once more how unlikely the emergence of such a single predominant power in a world of many impressive cultures really was.

LAND OF THE MANDARINS

The Pig-Faced Founder of the Ming

The Chinese Empire, the vast central expanse of East Asia, had been unified off and on since Ch'in and Han times, contemporaneous with ancient Rome in the West. But the Roman Empire fell, never to rise again, and Europe has never been unified since. The Han dynasty in China, by contrast, was by no means the

The Yung-lo Emperor, perhaps the greatest of the Mings. The huge armadas he sent south across the China Seas and west across the Indian Ocean preceded European expansion by more than half a century. (New York Public Library Picture Collection)

last to rule a united China. In fact, a regular pattern of the rise and fall of central government in China had established itself in the so-called dynastic cycle.

According to this pattern, recognized by Chinese historians before the time of Christ, a particular dynasty ruled China only as long as it enjoyed the Mandate of Heaven, the Chinese equivalent of what was called divine right in Europe (or the will of Allah in Muslim lands). When a regime became corrupt, neglected the ceremonial worship of ancestors and the gods, and oppressed the people, Heaven withdrew the mandate to rule. Divine displeasure was manifested through weak and divided government, flood, famine, rebellion, and foreign invasion, climaxing in the overthrow of the regime and the rise to power of a new dynasty. The latter stages of this cycle were clearly manifested in the fall of the Mongols and the rise of the Ming dynasty in the later 1300s.

The inefficiency and internecine strife of the later Mongol Khans had left dikes untended, the realm ill-governed. In the resulting storm of natural catastrophes and civil discord, the dynasty foundered and fled northward, to the Mongolian steppes from which they had come. The immense expanse of China, as so often before in her history, was surrendered to marauding bandits, rebellious peasants, secret societies, and feuding warlords struggling to see which of them would be granted the divine mandate.

But thoughtful Chinese had long since decided that peace, prosperity, and order required political unity under a duly certified Son of Heaven. In the end, then, autocratic order did emerge from anarchy. There was a winner, and once his supremacy was demonstrated, the nation accepted the new dynasty with gratitude for the end of the crisis. Thus began a new cycle in the seemingly endless history of China.

The founder of the Ming dynasty (1368–1644) must have seemed an unpromising beginning to the cultured gentry and scholarly Confucian bureaucrats who ran the provinces and staffed the new government, as they had done for many centuries. Chu Yüan-chang (1368–1398) was, to put it mildly, a man of the people.

Born of dirt-poor peasant parents, Chu had been successively a novice in a Buddhist monastery (where he learned to read and write), a beggar, a bandit, and finally a rebel leader. He had a swinish face—he was called the Pig Emperor in later chronicles—was paranoically suspicious, and could be extremely cruel, especially in his later years. But he also had a great capacity for organization, decision making, and plain hard work. He called his dynasty Ming, meaning "brilliant"—and he did his best to make it so.

Chu Yüan-chang inaugurated a more rigorous personal autocracy than China had seen before. Building on the foundations laid down by the Mongols—who, as foreign rulers, had also had to rule by fiat—Chu took as much actual power as possible into his own hands. A workaholic, he plowed through piles of official memorials every day. At court, disloyal or inefficient officials were beaten publicly with bamboo as examples to their peers. In the countryside, a system of neighborhood responsibility for labor service and security set neighbors to watching neighbors. Part of the founder's legacy to the Ming dynasty was thus an unprecedented degree of imperial power.

But Chu's thirty-year reign also saw a number of more positive accomplishments. He provided some economic relief for the peasants after the devastation of the civil wars and introduced a more efficient system of taxation. He constructed many schools; reinstituted the civil-service examinations, which had been virtually ignored by the Mongols; and restored Confucianism—the closest thing to a state religion the secular Chinese have ever had—as the nation's official philosophy.

The Ming founder built on a grand scale, especially at his capital at Nanking, which he made perhaps the largest walled city in the world. While medieval Europe sank into the chaos of the Black Death, the papal schism, and the Hundred Years' War, China thus found unity under a strong dynasty once more.

The Precious Ships

A strong founder has normally been essential to dynastic success in China. Equally important, however, has been the part frequently played by a powerful successor as consolidator and sustainer of the newly established regime. Chu Yüan-chang was followed on the dragon throne—after a brief power struggle—by perhaps the most powerful of the Ming rulers: the Yung-lo emperor (1403–1424).[1]

As the consolidator of the Ming, Yung-lo embarked upon such sizable public works as the renovation of the Grand Canal linking central and North China. He moved whole populations into war-devastated areas to develop these regions once more. He built more schools, honored at least the letter of Confucian doctrine, and commissioned huge scholarly projects for the preservation of Chinese literary culture.

Yung-lo also moved the capital back to Peking, the ruined Mongol capital, in North China. He rebuilt the city on a still grander scale, ringing it with fourteen miles of forty-foot walls. The new Peking was centered in the administrative section called the Imperial City and the red-walled Forbidden City, where the emperors were to live thereafter in a paradise of palaces and gardens.

Yung-lo's most startling enterprise, however, was the launching of an unprecedented series of overseas expeditions. These were the voyages of the Precious Ships, as they are called in Chinese history.

Between 1405 and 1433, a total of seven great fleets of seagoing junks carrying tens of thousands of men sailed from China to explore southern and western seas. Under the command of a shrewd Muslim court eunuch named Cheng Ho (1371–1433), these huge armadas nosed their way through the islands of Southeast Asia, touching at the rich seaports of western India. They went on to the Persian Gulf and Arabia, up the Red Sea, and down the coast of East Africa. Giraffes, ostriches, and zebras were brought back from Africa. The kings of Ceylon and Sumatra were brought to Peking in chains. Tributary relations were established with scores of nations. Then, less than sixty years before Columbus inaugurated the great age of

---

[1]Reign names like "Yung-lo" (he was born Ch'eng-tsu) are commonly used by western historians as if they were personal names, and will often be so used here.

European expansion, China's overseas expeditions ceased as abruptly as they had begun.

They were the largest maritime ventures in human history up to that time, some of them involving more than sixty great ships and almost thirty thousand men and traversing thousands of miles of distant seas. The Precious Ships that were the backbone of the fleets were up to four hundred feet long and featured four decks, watertight compartments, and the seaworthiness for which the junk has always been known. They navigated with the help of compasses and detailed sailing instructions accumulated over the centuries in South Chinese trading ports such as Canton. They were an impressive demonstration of the scale on which China might have operated at sea if this had been her chosen field of endeavor.

But the great maritime ventures of Yung-lo were also extremely costly. In addition, they were the special project of the court eunuchs, and hence were opposed by the scholar-bureaucrats, who were the eunuchs' great rivals in Peking. Furthermore, China's land frontiers soon preoccupied the Ming emperors. It is also probably fair to say that the emperors of China, with their vast heartland empire, had little sense of the potential importance of seapower in the world.

Ink Brushes, Rice Paddies, and Bound Feet

The majority of later Ming emperors were competent men; the latest did not even attain that level. But for two centuries after the founder and the sustainer of the dynasty, the Chinese system of government carried even mediocre rulers, giving China the domestic tranquility all nations crave. A look at Chinese government in general, and at the Chinese economy and society in early-modern times, is thus more important here than more names and dates of emperors.

Despite the augmented, sometimes arbitrary powers of the emperor, the organization chart of Chinese government looks much the same under the Ming as it had for centuries previous. Central government fell traditionally into three main divisions: civil administration, the military, and the board of censors. Civil government was carried out through the ancient six ministries for defense and justice, revenues and public works, personnel matters and religious rites. The imperial army, consisting of almost five hundred guards and garrison units of more than five thousand men each, sounded more impressive than it was: in an unwarlike society, under an unaggressive dynasty, the troops got comparatively little practice. The censors, finally, were young officials chosen for integrity and courage, who inspected all bureaus and subdivisions of government and reported corruption and treason directly to the palace.

Ming China, a nation the size of the United States today, was divided into 15 provinces, approximately 160 prefectures, 235 subprefectures, and 1200 counties. Each province had civil and military administrators, each lower subdivision its prefect, subprefect, or county magistrate, plus a few clerks to carry out the paperwork.

The backbone of this administrative system were the scholar-bureaucrats, or *mandarins*, as Europeans came to call them. Chosen by a graded system of nationwide examinations on the Confucian classics, this highly educated ruling class came largely from the landowning gentry. There were problems, of course. The civil service could do little about weak emperors or feuds between officials and court eunuchs. Nevertheless, it seems fair to say that the Chinese government was the closest approximation of a real meritocracy to be found anywhere in the world in 1500.

Much local government was still undertaken on a voluntary basis by prestigious local gentry, especially degree holders, who had passed at least some of the Confucian examinations. These educated landed families organized everything from repairing roads and irrigation ditches to maintaining local schools and temples. Demands upon the peasant masses were limited, consisting of land taxes at harvest time and a variety of compulsory labor.

The Ming centuries were a prosperous time economically. North China, ravaged by the Mongols—who turned large parts of it into hunting parks—was restored to agricultural use under the Ming. Central China, especially the fertile Yangtze valley, produced a prodigious rice crop and flourishing commercial cities such as Nanking and Hangchow. The south, finally, remained the most populous and prosperous section of the country, and trade became highly developed at ports such as Canton. From the political capital at Peking in the north to the economic heartland in the south, from the rice bowl of the Yangtze valley to the endless chilly plains of Sinkiang in China's Far West, the Middle Kingdom of the sixteenth century flourished on a scale unmatched elsewhere.

In many ways, Chinese society under the Ming looked rather like the China of 1900—the China into which Mao Tse-tung, China's great twentieth-century leader, was born.

At the top of Ming Chinese society were the landholding classes, though they were more likely to be middle-rank gentry than the huge landholders of earlier centuries. The nation's recognized leaders were the holders of the chief offices of state, with their titles and protocol, their silken robes, ink brushes, long, thin beards, and long fingernails. At the bottom of

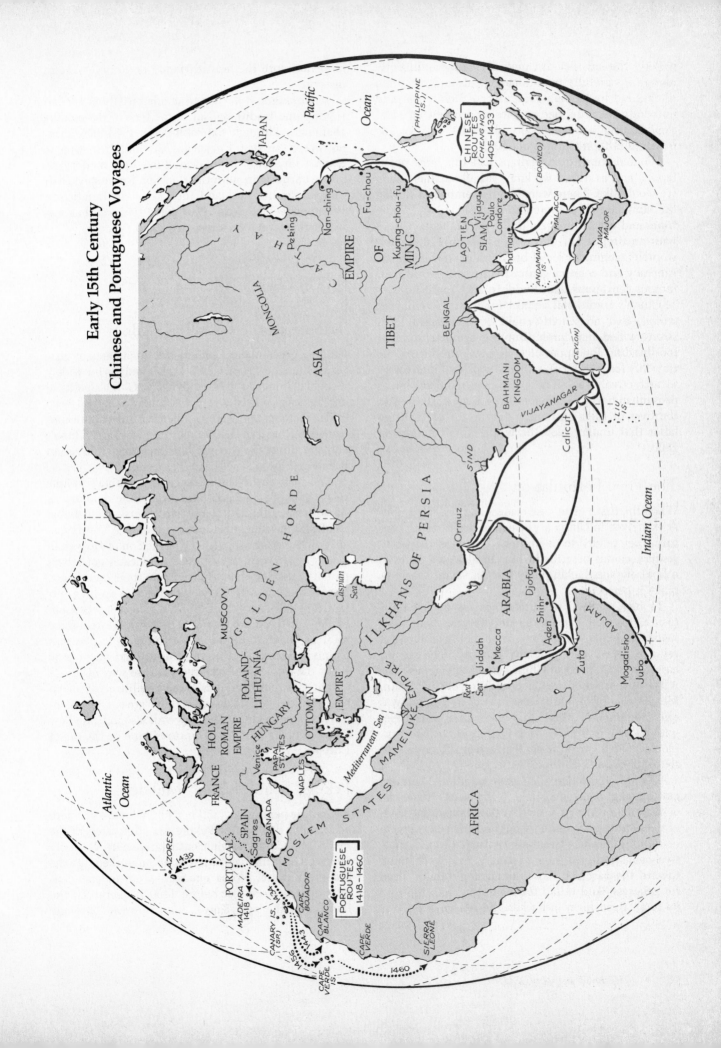

Early 15th Century
Chinese and Portuguese Voyages

Atlantic Ocean

Pacific Ocean

Indian Ocean

(PHILIPPINE IS.)

CHINESE ROUTES (CHENG HO) 1405-1433

(BORNEO)

JAPAN

CATHAY

EMPIRE OF MING

Nan-ching

Peking

Fu-chou

Kuang-chou-fu

MONGOLIA

ASIA

TIBET

BENGAL

LAO-TIEN

SIAM Vijaya

Poulo Condore

Sharnau

ANDAMAN IS.

MALACCA

JAVA MAJOR

(CEYLON)

BAHMANI KINGDOM

VIJAYANAGAR

Calicut

LIU IS.

MUSCOVY

GOLDEN HORDE

ILKHANS OF PERSIA

SIND

Caspian Sea

POLAND-LITHUANIA

HOLY ROMAN EMPIRE

FRANCE

HUNGARY

Venice

PAPAL STATES

NAPLES

OTTOMAN

EMPIRE

Mediterranean Sea

MAMELUKE EMPIRE

Ormuz

ARABIA

Djofar

Shihr

Aden

Mecca

Jiddah

Red Sea

ADJAM

Zuta

Mogadisho

Jubo

AFRICA

MOSLEM STATES

SPAIN

PORTUGAL

Sagres

GRANADA

AZORES

1439

MADEIRA 1418

CANARY IS. (SP.)

1434

1456

CAPE BOJADOR

CAPE BLANCO

CAPE VERDE

CAPE VERDE IS.

1443

PORTUGUESE ROUTES 1418-1460

SIERRA LEONE

1460

society, the vast peasant majority worked diligently along the carefully maintained canals and irrigation ditches fed by China's great rivers. Rich black mud and dully gleaming rice paddies, wide straw hats and slow-moving water buffalo filled the days of the hundred million Chinese of 1500.

Women constituted perhaps half this huge population, and as usual, we know less about them than we would like. There were no great empresses during the Ming period, as there had been in Han and T'ang times and would be again under the Manchus. There was an important minority of highly educated women, ranging in social background from court aristocracy and country gentry to imperial concubines, famous courtesans, and Buddhist and Taoist nuns.

China's traditional respect for mothers remained strong, and households could be dominated by a strong-willed matriarch. But the brutal custom of foot-binding for upper-class women, producing the tiny "lily feet" and stiff, swaying walk that men found so attractive, was already common. And the great peasant majority of women lived lives as limited as the lives of their husbands—the life of unremitting labor that undergirded the wealth of all nations in 1500.

The Final Formulation

When the first Portuguese traders and Jesuit missionaries arrived in China at the end of the sixteenth century, they tended to be impressed by what they saw. Jesuit accounts described China in idealized terms as a land of sages lacking only the Christian Gospel to make it perfect.

In fact, under the Ming emperors of the fourteenth, fifteenth, and sixteenth centuries China enjoyed another enviably long spell of political stability, relative peace, and general prosperity. The secular cast of mind typical of China spared the Chinese the religious tumults of the Christian West or the Muslim Middle East. The nation's economic well-being was quite comparable even to that of Renaissance Europe, with its new prosperity. And China's central government avoided the endemic warfare of fifteenth- and sixteenth-century Europe.

The Ming period actually gave traditional Chinese culture what became its final formulation. It was the civilization of Ming China that the Manchu invaders of the seventeenth century would inherit and carry on down into the early twentieth century. It was a massively conservative system of society, heavily oriented toward the past and more famous for stability than for progress. And it had the misfortune to settle into its final, fixed form just when the reborn West was launching into the most dynamic period of Western history.

In hindsight it is easy to condemn China for her rigidity and traditionalism in the face of the coming challenge. Through sixteenth-century Chinese eyes, however, the first Europeans to find their way to South China must have seemed like only moderately subtle barbarians, with their passion for money, their rampant militarism, and their religious fanaticism. What, indeed, did the West have to offer that was better than stability, prosperity, and peace?

SATELLITE CIVILIZATIONS

Tribute to the Middle Kingdom

Chinese preeminence, one of the great facts of East Asian life since Han times, continued to be widely recognized under the Ming dynasty. China's political and military power was not as great as it had been under the Han and T'ang emperors. But tribute continued to flow into the Middle Kingdom, and China's cultural influence was perhaps greater in 1500 than it had ever been.

The tributary system exemplified China's unique relationship to the East Asian world she dominated. As tributary states, lesser Asian rulers—from tribal chieftains in Manchuria to the emperor of Vietnam—acknowledged the supremacy of the Son of Heaven in Peking. In return, these lesser potentates got letters patent certifying their right to rule their own lands, a seal to use on official documents, and an intermittent flow of pious exhortations to rule in a true Confucian spirit. More important, perhaps, they got some military protection, the right to trade in the vast Chinese market, and permission to send missions to study the immensely admired Chinese way of life.

Three or four examples of the satellite civilizations that resulted will make clear how great China's influence was. Such an overview will also indicate how vigorous other East Asian cultures were on the eve of European intrusion.

Peking, Seoul, Hanoi, Mukden

Korea, the peninsular land north of China—or, more accurately, due east of Peking—is often cited as the model of a Chinese-style Confucian society. Partially Sinicized in earlier centuries, briefly absorbed into the Mongol Empire, Korea emerged as an independent nation once more just before 1400. General Yi, the founder of the new Korea, was, however, strongly pro-Chinese. Yi quickly dispatched the obligatory tribute to the new Ming dynasty, and under his descendants, Korea proceeded once again to import Confucian culture, ideals, and governmental structures wholesale.

Korea was soon divided administratively into provinces and smaller subdivisions on the Chinese model. China's six ministries and board of censors blossomed in miniature in the new Korean capital at Seoul. The Chinese system of Confucian education and state examinations for civil-service posts became still more firmly rooted. Indeed, the fifteenth century was actually a golden age of Confucian scholarship—in the neighboring tributary nation of Korea.

Vietnam, the peninsular country south of China, had a rather rougher long-term relationship with the Middle Kingdom. In the end, however, China's influence played a crucial part here too.

Governed as part of South China for nearly a thousand years, from Han times till the collapse of the T'ang, Vietnam gained its political independence in the tenth century—and at once proceeded to send formal tribute to the Son of Heaven to the north. In the centuries that followed, the Vietnamese bitterly resisted Chinese attempts to reimpose their rule by force of arms, fighting off both the Mongols and the Mings. At the same time, however, the Sinification of Vietnam continued apace.

During the fifteenth century especially, the Le dynasty modeled Vietnamese government very closely on that of Ming China. The southern nation was divided into thirteen provinces and subdivided into prefectures, counties, and smaller units. A graded system of bureaucratic government, centered in the new Vietnamese capital at Hanoi, was imposed on the land. Chinese culture, dress, and styles of life were cultivated at the court in Hanoi, and the royal chronicles of Vietnam were dutifully compiled in the Chinese style—and in the Chinese language.

This pervasive Chinese influence in Vietnamese ruling circles did have the unfortunate effect of cutting the monarchs off from the masses, who retained their traditional Southeast Asian codes and folkways. But the Chinese model also gave Vietnam a government concerned with public works, the patronage of culture, and other valuable features of the Chinese way in 1500.

Northeast of China, another and rather less likely example of the transforming impact of Chinese influence appeared somewhat later, in the sixteenth century. This was the militarized Manchurian state that was to play such a significant part in China's future.

Southern Manchuria, northeast of Peking, had been part of China under the Han, and the Ming dynasty exercised a loose suzerainty over the area. Chinese emperors sent certificates of authority and honorific awards to Manchu tribal chiefs and accepted their daughters into the imperial harem. Chinese settlers moved into Manchuria, establishing Chinese towns among the seminomadic tribes and exerting a slowly growing cultural influence on their leaders.

But Manchuria lay north of the Great Wall, China's main line of defense against restless steppe invaders. In this no-man's-land beyond the Wall, the unaggressive Ming emperors found the Manchu difficult to control. Then, in the later 1500s, a leader arose who was able to unify the tribes into a roughly centralized state—which suddenly became a threat to China itself.

The new leader in the north was a restless chieftain named Nurhachi. Nurhachi built state power in Manchuria through a combination of negotiation and warfare, strategic marriages and tribal alliances. He converted the region from a clan-based society to a bureaucratic state by means of a system of military units called *banners* run by appointed commanders. But he also drew heavily on Chinese models and Chinese personnel. China's six ministries were soon duplicated at the Manchurian capital of Mukden, and literate Chinese-settler administrators were recruited to run the Manchu banners.

In the next century, the Middle Kingdom would regret the strength and order its cultural exports had given to the new Manchurian state. In the 1600s, the Manchu banners would break through the Great Wall itself and come flooding south to overwhelm the ancient civilization that had been their teacher. The establishment of what became China's last historic dynasty was surely facilitated by the influence of Chinese culture on the society of the Manchus before the conquest.

Samurai and Shogun

The island empire of Japan, stretching northeastward from the coast of Korea, some 120 miles off shore, had absorbed the Chinese model early in her history. A unified Japanese government had first emerged in the sixth century, with a capital at what is today Kyoto in southern Honshu, the large central island of the group. During the formative centuries that followed, Japan had gone to school—like so many others—to the great T'ang empire. Japan had copied T'ang government institutions, learned the Chinese written language, accepted Chinese Buddhism and Chinese costume and customs.

When the T'ang empire fell, shortly after 900,

A Japanese Buddhist temple complex. The turned-up pagoda roof lines and the giant statue of the Buddha meditating behind the tree on the right recall Chinese influences in earlier centuries. (New York Public Library Picture Collection)

however, Japan had turned inward to shape over the centuries a distinctively Japanese life style and society.

What actually developed were two cultures. At the imperial capital, the Heian culture flourished. Political power slipped away from the imperial government and into the hands of feuding court families. At the same time, however, these courtly Japanese aristocrats cultivated a unique elegance and sensitivity in their personal lives. They developed in their pavilions and palaces a delicate, sensual, and highly aesthetic style of living, delighting in poetry, sophisticated fiction, and the fine art of love.

In the Japanese countryside, however, another culture entirely was growing up. This was the virile, violent life style of the *bushi*, the warrior, with his *bushido* code of Japanese chivalry. From about 1200 on, the bushi—under the more familiar label of *samurai*, "one who serves"—became the real arbiters of Japan's destiny.

From the thirteenth century through the sixteenth, then, Japan underwent a progressive political disintegration. At the top, this process was precipitated by the rise of a military commander called the *shogun*. Appointed by the emperors, nominally as military leaders against barbarian invasion from the northern islands, the shoguns in fact became the feudal overlords of the samurai—and much closer to the true rulers of Japan than the emperors were.

The two early shogunates were those of Kamakura and of the Ashikaga family. The Kamakura shogunate (1185–1333) dominated Japan from a separate court at the city of Kamakura in central Honshu, far to the east of the imperial capital at Kyoto. The Ashikaga shogunate (1336–1603) saw the warriors move into Kyoto itself while the feudal lords of the countryside filled the land with war.

Even at their strongest, the shoguns of these medieval centuries were only paramount feudal lords, never wielders of centralized state power. And even at the top there was conflict—between shoguns and emperors who tried to assert their own long-dormant authority, between rivals for the imperial throne in Kyoto or for the shogunate itself. With central authority thus in disarray, actual power devolved increasingly upon the greatest of the warrior barons, landed magnates called *daimyo*, or "big names."

In the fourteenth century—about the time that Europe's medieval synthesis was collapsing—Japan's "centralized feudalism" also slid over the brink into the anarchy of the Japanese dark age. For two and a half centuries, central political authority was almost totally lacking in Japan.

Political breakdown, however, was not accompanied by economic decline. Japanese agriculture actually became more productive during these centuries. New strains of rice, new farm tools, and more farm animals helped increase Japanese population. Trade expanded, especially with Ming China. The Chinese, however, let very few Japanese into the Middle Kingdom, largely because of the reputation of the Japanese as pirates and brawlers.

By 1500 Japan had thus drifted far from the Chinese model of earlier centuries. While centralized government run by scholarly bureaucrats prevailed on the mainland, the island kingdom had fallen into hopeless anarchy, ravaged by soldiers whose power extended only a short distance beyond their castle walls.

The contrast between the Confucian mandarin of China and the feudal samurai of Japan could scarcely have been greater. The Japanese equivalent of Europe's medieval knights had their code of chivalry too, prescribing such ancient warrior virtues as courage, pride, and loyalty to one's overlord. The samurai was expected to reject wealth, live a hard, strenuous life on the battlefield, and be prepared for death at any moment. Defeat meant certain death by decapitation. Dishonored, the samurai was expected to commit suicide like an antique Roman, by disemboweling himself with his sword in the ritual of *seppuku*. The shogun, as supreme military commander, was expected to be the perfect embodiment of these warrior virtues.

They were inspiring qualities for "those who served" in a war-torn age. The samurai, it was said, let go of his life as easily as a cherry blossom falls from the branch in spring. This oddly poetic warrior ideal would live on long after the age that engendered it had passed away. The militant spirit of the age of samurai predominance, from the thirteenth through the sixteenth centuries, would survive and impose itself upon much of the history of modern Japan.

The Europeans who appeared in Japanese waters in the sixteenth century would find their muskets much more welcome than their missionaries. In the nineteenth and twentieth centuries, they would discover that Japan's bushido tradition, equipped with big guns and battleships, could be a formidable rival indeed.

A TALE OF TWO CULTURES

The Difference between Them

A central feature of East Asian history in later modern times would be the conflict between China and Japan. In the nineteenth and twentieth centuries particularly, China's majestic preeminence in East Asia would be challenged by the vigorous, adaptable Japanese. Some of the crucial differences between these two great peoples go back to the cultures that had evolved in China and Japan by 1500, the very beginnings of modern times.

In China, as we have seen, the Ming period saw a final reformulation of the ancient cultural patterns that would survive through the Manchu centuries into the present one. In Japan, whose civilization had begun to emerge more recently, the period of the Kamakura and Ashikaga shogunates saw the first formulation of much of the ethos and artistic tradition that would dominate the modern Japanese spirit. This final section, then, will concentrate on the culture of these two pivotal East Asian nations at the beginning of the modern age.

The most striking thing about the two is the range of differences between them.

Ming China remained, like the China of earlier centuries, an astonishingly secular society, especially by contrast with the religious bent of Hindu India, the Muslim center of Eurasia, or Europe in the Reformation. China was also distinguished by its passion for the culture of the word. It was as profoundly literary a society as any in history, as the intellectual developments of the Ming period make clear.

Japan, by contrast, was as devoted to religion, especially to various forms of Buddhism, as the Hindu, Muslim, or Christian cultures further to the west. The other major aspect of Japanese culture between 1200 and 1600, however—the ethic, art, and literature of the samurai military tradition—makes an equally striking contrast with the literary culture of China—a contrast between sword and pen that is also to be found within the Muslim and Christian worlds.

In stressing these differences, one runs the risk of undermining the larger notion of a single East Asian civilization shaped primarily by the pervasive influence of the Middle Kingdom. In reading what follows, then, it will be useful to remember how much of Japanese culture, from Buddhism to painting to written language, was, after all, derived from China. We may also ask ourselves if there is not a distinct, if ill-defined, East Asian flavor even to the differences between the two national cultures. The samurai and the mandarin may have their parallels in other cultures, but both are distinctive products of the East Asian world.

Ink-Bamboo and Monkey

Ming China was firmly committed to the Neo-Confucian philosophy that had taken shape during the Sung dynasty. Buddhism, once so influential in China, was banished to the provinces by Ming times. Under the Ming, hundreds of Confucian schools sprang up to train local collections of scholars and students. And the great Hanlin Academy was established at the capital to undertake, under imperial patronage, truly staggering scholarly projects in the tradition of the Confucian sages. An often cited example is the great *Encyclopedia* produced around 1400 under the most famous of the Mings, Yung-lo. This immense collection of major Chinese works of the past on history and geography, government and ethics, occupied the labors of 2000 scholars and ran to more than 1100 volumes!

The most influential Confucian philosopher of the period was Wang Yang-ming, a learned official and military commander who experienced a moment of philosophical enlightenment like that of a Buddhist saint. Wang urged self-cultivation as the road to sagehood, but stressed particularly the close relation between right knowledge and moral action. We do not really *understand* the doctrine of reverence for elders and ancestors, he urged, unless we are so convinced of it that we do *in fact* revere them. Knowing and doing are one.

The most famous Ming painters—nature artists in the great Sung tradition—blended literary skills into their painting. These "literati" of China's Southern school were poets as much as they were painters, and they frequently added a clearly literary dimension to pictorial art.

Executed in the ancient Chinese way, with brushes and ink on hanging or hand scrolls made of paper or silk, these pictures project a sense of reality that would have impressed a contemporary Renaissance artist. Ch'iu Ying's *Fisherman's Flute Heard over the Lake* vibrates with the reality of leaves and bark, rock and water, a tree-shrouded house on the near shore and misty mountains far off beyond the lake. T'ang Yin's *Ink-Bamboo* projects the same sense of reality in the simple shadow of a bamboo branch seen across a window. Other Ming painters went beyond realism, manipulating nature to suit their personal aesthetic canons. They turned mountains into startling architectural forms, or trees into abstract patterns against the sky.

Ming drama also combined art forms and stressed authorial artistry. Here again there was a Southern style, reflecting the increasing importance of the prosperous and populous South in Chinese history.

Ming dramatists produced plays composed of dozens of scenes, highlighted by flute music and songs. The most famous Ming playwright, T'ang Hsien-tsu, created a series of dream plays. His *Dream of Han Tan*, for instance, is the story of a young man who dreams an entire future life for himself and awakens vividly aware of the brevity of this earthly existence—a popular Renaissance European theme as well. These subtle dramas, many of them written by scholarly men, were intended to win the plaudits of fellow sophisticates rather than the cheers of a mass audience.

There was, however, a large popular readership for the stories and novels of the period. Printed on the wood-block press and read by a growing audience of literate common folk, these Ming fictions drew on both history and fantasy for their subjects.

Some of the most famous of Chinese novels date from this period. The universally popular *Romance of the Three Kingdoms* fictionizes the struggles of three rivals for the throne of the dying Han dynasty, and *All Men Are Brothers* recounts the exploits of a band of Robin Hood bandits in the closing years of the Northern Sung. *Monkey*, by contrast, is the story of the pilgrimage of a real Chinese Buddhist monk to India—accompanied in this version by a mischievous, magical monkey hero assigned by Buddha himself to protect the holy man in his wanderings. *The Golden Lotus*, finally, is a thoroughly erotic novel, still hard to find in English without asterisks!

It is a range as wide and human as the age itself. On a smaller scale, the same may be said of the short stories of writers such as Ling Meng-ch'i. Ling's tales of Chinese kings and generals, scandalous Buddhist monks and Taoist sages, strange lands, demons and ghosts, comic incidents, exotic revenges, and properly filial offspring bring the whole of the Ming to life.

Cherry Blossoms

The thought and art of contemporary Japan focused rather more starkly on two dominant themes: religion and war. But the Japanese expressions of these two ancient concerns of the human race are as rich and vivid as the whole broad spectrum of life revealed in Chinese culture.

Religion in Japan still meant, in part, reverence for the ancient spirits of nature worshiped at simple Shinto shrines. But the shrines were presided over by shamans who were also frequently Buddhist monks. And two forms of Buddhism were even more widespread in Japan than they had been in the preceding Heian period: the Pure Land sect and Zen meditation.

Believers in the Pure Land—the Western Paradise or heaven of popular Buddhism—believed like many Christians that simply to call with a believing heart upon the Enlightened One was to find salvation. Zen Buddhism, by contrast, required a rigorous monastic life and a personal quest through daily meditation, and only serious adepts were likely to take it up. Masses of common people flocked to the Pure Land and other sects in those violent times. Samurai and great nobles were drawn to the demanding self-discipline of Zen.

Intense vitality and astonishing anatomical realism are main features of Japanese Buddhist sculpture during these centuries. Buddha figures such as the fifty-

This detail from a Japanese silk screen painting done around 1600 exemplifies the realistic painting of everyday sixteenth-century life that was popular at the time. These are the architecture and costumes that early European merchants and missionaries saw in Japan on the eve of the Tokugawa unification. (The Metropolitan Museum of Art, Rogers Fund)

foot meditating *Buddha of Kamakura* retain traditional poses and proportions, the calm round face and lowered lids, the conventionalized swooping folds of the robe. But the ferocious figures of temple guardians at holy places are carved or cast in metal with an almost supernatural realism. The bulging lifelike muscles and swollen tendons, the menacing gestures, the snarling mouth, bared teeth, and glaring eyes have a ferocity that reflects the savage side of that age of endemic warfare and samurai supremacy. These figures also, incidentally, reflect a mastery of human anatomy that no Renaissance European sculptor could better.

Religious and military themes mingle also in the literature of the early shogunates.

Courtly literature in prose and poetry continued to weave its delicate spell even at the court of figurehead emperors. But now the *Confessions of Lady Nijo*, after detailing her love affairs, conclude with her retirement to a Buddhist convent and a life of chanted prayers and religious rites. The most uniquely Japanese literary development of the period, the No drama, reveals a deep sense of the mystery of life behind the gorgeous No costumes, the masks, the stylized gestures and choral songs. The typical No play features gods and demons, warriors, women—and lunatics.

Warrior tales of the Kamakura period hail the great battles, ingenious ruses, and famous victories of heroes such as the celebrated Yoshitsune, the most famous samurai of them all. But even the great Yoshitsune came to a tragic end, betrayed and driven to ritual suicide by his own brother. Even in their hero tales, the Japanese of the age of the bushido code never forgot the brevity of life and honored above all things the warrior's willingness to cast his own life away.

It was a strange culture and a strange age, at least from a Western perspective. It was an era of seemingly endless warfare, of severed heads and *seppuku*. It was also the period that developed the delicate formality of the traditional Zen tea ceremony, the rich symbolism of Japanese flower arrangement, and the austere beauty of the sand and stone gardens of old Kyoto. The samurai spirit of blazing temple-guardian eyes and flashing swords also found expression in the stillness of Zen meditation and the calm formality of pouring a cup of tea.

The greatness of China was recognized across East Asia in 1500, and even Europeans had heard of the wonders of Cathay. The formidable talents of the Japanese would be a few centuries yet in emerging to the astonished gaze of Western people.

SUMMARY

The ancient Middle Kingdom of China continued to dominate East Asia as the modern age began. Cut off from the rest of the Old World by formidable geographical barriers, the world's largest nation exercised a degree of preeminence at her end of Eurasia unmatched by any state in either the Muslim or the Christian zones.

Under the Ming dynasty, China recovered thoroughly from the Mongol conquest of the Later Middle Ages. The powerful fifteenth-century Ming emperor Yung-lo even sent out fleets of junks across island Southeast Asia and the Indian Ocean to the Middle East and East Africa more than half a century before the Portuguese crossed the Indian Ocean the other way. Un-

der the less spectacular later Mings of the sixteenth century, China's unique Confucian administrative system and prosperous society took on the forms that would prevail in the Middle Kingdom until the Europeans at last forced their way into China hundreds of years later.

The scattered satellite cultures around the Middle Kingdom were closely modeled on Ming China. These sister civilizations in 1500 included the Koreans, the Vietnamese, and even the half-settled Manchurians, who in the seventeenth century would become China's last conquerors before the Europeans came. But the most dynamic of China's neighbors, the island kingdom of Japan, which had owed so much to China in earlier times, developed along contrasting lines in the later medieval and early modern centuries. In Japan, not scholar-bureaucrats but soldiers (samurai) were the leading social class. And strong central government came to Japan in 1600, not through a divine-right monarchy, but through the victory of the samurai overlord, the shogun.

Chinese culture during the Ming period featured a continuing national commitment to Confucianism, as well as exquisite landscape painting and a range of popular literature from drama to romance. In Japan, Zen and Pure-Land Buddhism flourished, and the bushido warrior code of the samurai found its natural home in a war-torn age.

SUGGESTED READING

BARY, W. T., et al. *Sources of Chinese Tradition.* New York: Columbia University Press, 1960. Useful collection of primary source materials, ancient and modern.

BUCK, P., trans. *All Men Are Brothers* (2 vols.). London: Methuen, 1957. Translation of the classic Ming novel. See also A. Waley's *Monkey,* an abridged version of *Journey to the West* (London: Allen and Unwin, 1942.)

CAHILL, J. *Parting at the Shore: Chinese Painting of the Early and Middle Ming Dynasty, 1368–1580.* New York: Weatherhill, 1978. Ming art, continuing the great tradition of the T'ang and Sung.

COOPER, M., ed. *They Came to Japan—An Anthology of European Reports on Japan.* Berkeley: University of California Press, 1965. Outsiders' views of Japan starting from the sixteenth century.

FAIRBANK, J. K. *East Asia: Tradition and Transformation.* Cambridge, Mass.: Harvard University Press, 1973. The best one-volume account of the history of China, Japan, Vietnam, and Korea.

GALLAGHER, L. J., trans. *China in the Sixteenth Century: The Journals of Matteo Ricci.* New York: Random House, 1953. A European view of Ming China.

HALL, J. W., and T. TAKESHI, eds. *Japan in the Muromachi Age.* Berkeley: Univerity of California Press, 1977. Highly praised collection of papers on all aspects of Japan in the Ashikaga shogunate, from politics and economics to religion and culture.

HUCKER, C. H. *The Traditional Chinese State in Ming Times, 1368–1644.* Tucson: University of Arizona Press, 1961. Brief but highly recommended analysis. See also Hucker, ed., *Chinese Government in Ming Times: Seven Studies* (New York: Columbia University Press, 1969) and, on the Confucian examination system, I. Miyazaki, *China's Examination Hell: The Civil Service Examinations of Imperial China,* trans. C. Schirokauer (New York: Weatherhill, 1976).

KEENE, D., ed. *Twenty Plays of the Nō Theater.* New York: Columbia University Press, 1970. Collection of classic Japanese drama, with drawings to illustrate this highly visual art form.

NEEDHAM, J. *Science and Civilization in China.* Cambridge: Cambridge University Press, 1954– . A multivolume work still in progress. Volume 4 discusses the Precious Ships, Ming marine design, and technology generally.

REISCHAUER, E. O. *Japan: The Story of a Nation,* rev. ed. New York: Knopf, 1970. Excellent one-volume account by a leading authority and former ambassador to Japan.

SANSOM, G. *The Western World and Japan.* New York: Knopf, 1950. A good and readable survey of relations between Japan and Europe.

SCHIROKAUER, C. *A Brief History of Chinese and Japanese Civilizations.* New York: Harcourt Brace Jovanovich, Inc., 1978. Particularly good on the cultural history of the two great powers of East Asia.

SIMKIN, C. G. F. *The Traditional Trade of Asia.* London: Oxford University Press, 1968. Includes the westward probes of Yung-lo.

TSUNODA, R., et al., eds. *Sources of the Japanese Tradition.* New York: Columbia University Press, 1960. Valuable collection of materials.

YANG, L. "Female Rulers in Imperial China," *Harvard Journal of Asiatic Studies,* 23 (1960–1961). Suggestive discussion of the institution and functions of the dowager empress as ruler. On the more traditional place of women, see R. Willier, "Confucian Ideal of Womanhood," *Journal of the China Society,* 13 (1976).

Chapter · 4

KINGDOMS OF AFRICA

KINGS OF GOLD AND IVORY

Terra Incognita

Much closer to Europe than the far reaches of Asia lay the third part of the Old World and the second largest of continents—Africa. And yet, surprisingly, Europeans were just beginning to make contact with many African peoples as the modern period began.

The history of some parts of Africa had been closely interwoven with that of Europe and Asia for many centuries. Africa had been linked by trade and cultural exchange to the Middle East since Egypt and Mesopotamia were the only two centers of civilization in the world. North Africa had interacted with southern Europe since Carthage battled Greece and then Rome for mastery of the western Mediterranean. East Africa had long been part of the Indian Ocean commercial community: African coastal cities exchanged goods with India, Southeast Asia, and even China, usually through Arab or Indian intermediaries.

But neither Europeans nor Asians had much knowledge of what lay behind the coastal lands of Africa. The whole interior of the continent was *terra incognita*—"unknown land"—on traders' maps. European charts sometimes showed Africa breaking off abruptly somewhere around the equator, or curving round to the east to link up with southern India, making the Indian Ocean an inland sea like the Mediterranean.

The reality was a great, roughly tapered continent traversed by broad climatic bands running east to west: the green Mediterranean coastal belt, the Sahara Desert, the open, lightly wooded grasslands of the Sudan, the dense rain forests of the Guinea Coast and the Congo, then more grassy savannas, more deserts, and the plains and hills of South Africa. Broadly speaking, it was Africa south of the Sahara—black Africa—that was unknown to outsiders. And it was over the wide expanses of this region that political growth and development were mushrooming in the centuries around 1500.

The Portuguese, who in the later fifteenth century first sailed around Africa, found a number of highly developed states on the far side of the continent. The most impressive of them were the empires of the Western Sudan and the trading cities of East Africa. Some of the antecedents of these kingdoms and city-states went back to the tenth century and before. But there were newer kingdoms in the rain forests of the Guinea Coast and even the Congo River basin too. New names thus began to appear on European maps: Songhai, Benin, Ife, Kilwa, the kingdom of Kongo, and, centuries later, the most mysterious of them all—Great Zimbabwe, "where the stone houses are."

In 1500, then, Africa south of the great desert was a world unto itself, living by its own rhythms, growing according to its own patterns of social evolution. A look at some of the emerging states of sixteenth-century Africa will reveal striking similarities with Eurasian civilizations—and striking differences as well.

The Fortunes of Songhai

The Sudanic belt—grasslands dotted with trees—just south of the Sahara had produced a number of African nations during Europe's Middle Ages. Among these, the Kanem-Bornu states went back to the tenth century, the Hausa city-states to the twelfth. The

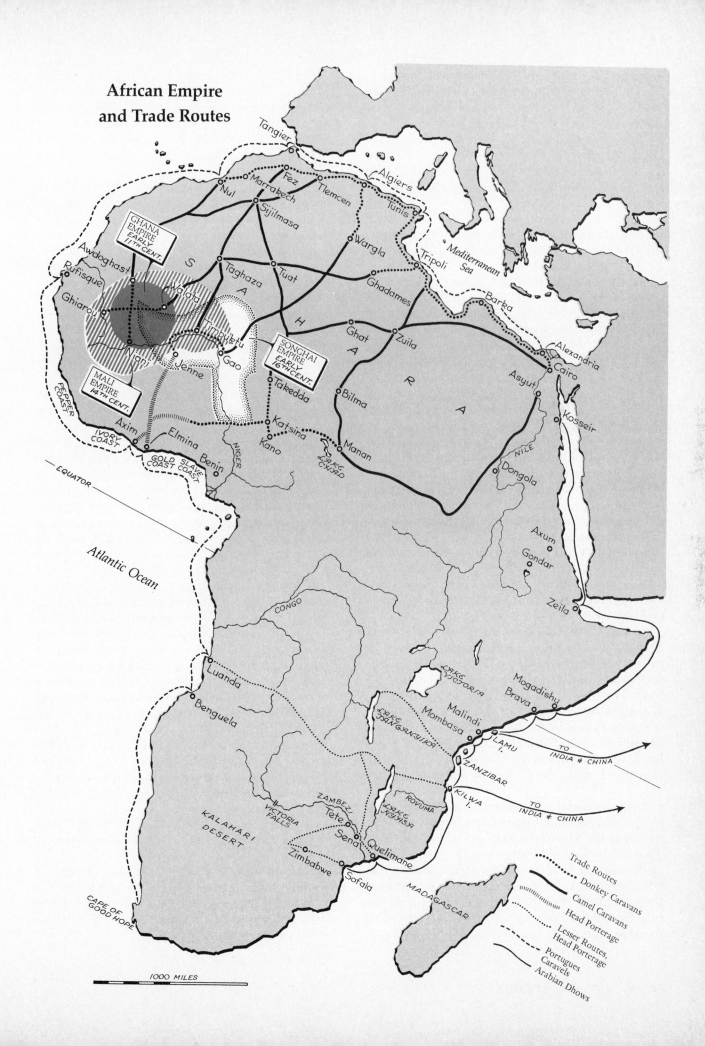

African Empire
and Trade Routes

Tangier

Fez
Nul
Marrakech
Algiers
Sijilmasa
Tlemcen
Tunis
Awdoghast
GHANA
EMPIRE
EARLY
11TH CENT.
S
Wargla
Taghaza
Tuat
Mediterranean
Sea
Rufisque
Walata
A
Tripoli
Ghadames
Barka
Ghiarou
Timbuktu
H
Ghat
Zuila
Alexandria
Nani
Jenne
Gao
SONGHAI
EMPIRE
EARLY
16TH CENT.
A
Asyut
Cairo
MALI
EMPIRE
14TH CENT.
Takedda
Bilma
R
A
Kosseir
PEPPER COAST
Axim
Katsina
Manan
NILE
Elmina Benin
Kano
Dongola
IVORY COAST
GOLD SLAVE
COAST COAST
NIGER
LAKE CHAD
EQUATOR

Axum
Gondar

Zeila

CONGO

Atlantic Ocean

Luanda
LAKE VICTORIA
Mogadishu
Brava
Benguela
LAKE TANGANYIKA
Malindi
Mombasa
LAMU I.
TO INDIA & CHINA
ZANZIBAR
ZAMBEZI
ROVUMA
KILWA I.
TO INDIA & CHINA
KALAHARI DESERT
VICTORIA FALLS
Tete
LAKE NYASA
Zimbabwe
Senai
Quelimane
Sofala
CAPE OF
GOOD HOPE
MADAGASCAR

.... Trade Routes
━━━━━━ Donkey Caravans
──────── Camel Caravans
::::::::: Head Porterage
·········· Lesser Routes,
          Head Porterage
- - - - - Portugues
          Caravels
────── Arabian Dhows

1000 MILES

westernmost portions of the Sudan had, however, been most prolific in new nations between 1000 and 1500. The most important of these kingdoms were Ghana, Mali, and finally Songhai.

Ghana and Mali had developed successively as the largest kingdoms of the Western Sudan in the centuries before 1500. The kings of these states had built their power on the villages of the grasslands. But their wealth had come from trade. Muslim merchants from north of the Sahara had brought salt, manufactured goods, and other things to exchange for gold and slaves from the forest lands south of the Sudan. The Sudanic kings of Ghana and Mali had been the middlemen, managers of the marketplaces of West Africa's commercial cities between the desert and the forest.

Typical Sudanic trading states had thus developed. They were hereditary monarchies with black elites of the powerful Mande people—known later in the West as the Mandingo—and resident communities of Muslim Arabs and Berber merchants. Appointed officials and standing armies held these states together. Differences of religion and culture divided them: Mande elites became increasingly Islamicized and lived in walled capitals and trading cities such as Timbuktu, while the majority of the people remained animists and lived in agricultural and pastoral communities scattered across the grasslands. There were also feuds over the royal succession and endemic rebelliousness among conquered peoples—problems in imperial cultures everywhere.

In the latter part of the fifteenth century, the third and greatest of this West African succession of empires emerged: the kingdom of Songhai.

In the days of Mali's greatness, the Songhai peoples dominated the Niger River between its big bend and its juncture with the Benue River in what is today Nigeria. They were farmers and river boatmen. As river navigators, they provided a vital link between the Malian heartland and the empire's eastern provinces. Though subjects of the kings of Mali, the rulers of Songhai—whose capital of Gao was a great trading city too—chafed under foreign domination. In the second half of the fifteenth century, the royal Sonni line of Songhai produced a ruler who could focus this resentment and make it pay: the soldier-king Sonni Ali (1464–1492).

The kingdom of Mali had grown weak and weary by the later fifteenth century. Her kings wasted the wealth of the land and could not hold the provinces against rebellion and foreign invasion. In his nearly thirty years on the throne of Songhai, Sonni Ali battered Mali, the erstwhile superpower of the Western Sudan, into a second-class nation, a petty Sudanese state that soon became part of an even larger Songhai Empire.

The founder of Songhai power was a hard man. He looted Timbuktu and was particularly harsh with resident foreigners, the Berbers and Arabs from north of the Sahara. His followers were drawn from the animist majority of the population, and though he was a nominal Muslim himself, Sonni Ali had little respect for mosques and Islamic scholars.

By the time of his death—in 1492, the year Columbus sailed—Sonni Ali's empire controlled the economic heart of West African commerce—the three great trading centers of Timbuktu, Gao, and Jenne. Under his successors, Songhai grew until it commanded the largest sweep of West Africa ever ruled by a Sudanic kingdom.

The most effective of those who followed Sonni Ali was the man who destroyed the ancient Sonni dynasty. He also restored what was in essence the old Muslim Mande elite of Ghanaian and Malian times. His name was Askia Muhammad (1493–1528), popularly known as the Great.

Askia Muhammad had been one of Sonni Ali's generals. He rebelled against the old man's heir, however, and established his own dynasty at the end of the fifteenth century. Like Sonni, he was a fighter and an empire builder, and he completed the edifice of Songhai power that his predecessor had begun. He was also an administrative reformer, dividing the enlarged empire into a number of provinces for more efficient governance. He spread the fame of Songhai farther abroad by making a triumphant royal pilgrimage to Mecca and establishing closer relations with the Muslim states of North Africa and the Middle East.

Askia Muhammad's seizure of the throne meant the return to power of the urban elite of Islamicized Mande and northern merchants who had dominated Ghana and Mali. These wealthy, sophisticated communities provided the Songhai Empire with most of its administrators, generals, traders, and thinkers, as they had done for the earlier Sudanic powers. They gave continuity to this succession of West African empires for more than five hundred years.

Under Askia the Great, Muslim culture flourished as never before in West Africa. He encouraged the building of mosques and schools. Muslim universities at Timbuktu and Jenne drew scholars and poets from distant places. Under Askia, Songhai was thoroughly integrated into the cosmopolitan world of Islamic peoples that stretched from West Africa to Southeast Asia.

The fortunes of Songhai, the greatest of West African kingdoms, never stood higher than in the days of Askia Muhammad. But worse days were coming for the empire of the grasslands—indeed, before the end of the great king's reign.

Blind in his old age, Askia was deposed in 1528 by his own rebellious sons. His successors strove to carry on in his tradition and that of Sonni Ali, but the second half of the century saw rebellion and invasion by neighboring princes sweep over Songhai. And in 1590, the rulers of Songhai faced an invasion unlike anything they had ever confronted before.

The new invaders were Moroccans who had successfully crossed the Saharan barrier into the Sudan in force. They were armed with muskets and artillery, and the bow-and-arrow soldiers of Songhai soon learned that such weapons introduced a new and chilling dimension into the ancient art of empire building.

The Moroccan invaders, fresh from victories over the Portuguese along the shores of the Mediterranean, crushed the armies of Songhai also in the field. Like the Almoravids of earlier centuries, however, they did not succeed in establishing their own power south of the Sahara. They merely plunged the Western Sudan into prolonged chaos, a condition from which West Africa would scarcely emerge before the coming of the Europeans in much greater force centuries later.

The Rise of the Forest Peoples

South of the Songhai Empire lay the rain forests of the Guinea Coast. The forest peoples who dwelt there had learned agriculture and ironworking centuries earlier, at the time of the great Bantu migrations. But the culture of the forest remained one of agricultural villages, loosely linked by clan and tribal ties, until the last few centuries before 1500. Then larger states appeared there too, in the deep woods and mangrove forests between the grasslands and the sea.

Little is known about the states of the Guinea Coast of West Africa—Ife, Oyo, Benin, and others—in these early years. They kept no written records themselves, and few Muslims from the north or Europeans coming by sea penetrated the dense rain forests. From oral traditions, scattered European accounts, and some archaeological remains, it is possible, however, to piece together something of this new zone of state building and even urban culture.

The forest peoples of West Africa may have been significantly influenced by more sophisticated societies not in the Western but the Eastern Sudan. Egyptian influences on the powerful Yoruba people of what is today Nigeria, for example, have been suggested. The source of the wealth to support the new cities of the Guinea Coast is also open to conjecture. Probably, however, it came primarily from trade in such forest products as pepper, ivory, and, later, especially slaves.

Limited by the thick jungles, the kingdoms of the forest belt tended to be smaller than those of the open savannas, over which conquering armies could sweep with ease. They may, however, have been commensurately tightly knit and well organized. The Guinea kingdoms were the work of true Negro peoples, who are generally described as stockier and more robust than the Mande of the Sudan. These peoples were

The walled city of Benin shows in the distance behind two subjects of the oba in this picture by a Dutch artist. A sense of African plenty and of foreign exoticism is conveyed by the costumes, especially the headgear, and by the tropical products and vegetation. (Library of Congress)

skilled in arts and crafts, immensely self-confident, and particularly talented at political organization. Certainly their achievements in these areas were impressive when the Europeans first encountered them in the late 1400s.

Perhaps the most famous of the Guinea Coast states was the kingdom of Benin, located in what is today Nigeria, at the great inner angle of Africa.

Benin was probably an offshoot of the earlier Ife culture. Ife produced some of the continent's most beautiful terra-cotta and bronze sculpture as early as the twelfth and thirteenth centuries but is otherwise little known. Benin seems to have taken shape sometime in the fourteenth century and to have been flourishing in the fifteenth, when the first Europeans arrived.

They found a kingdom 250 miles across lying just west of the mouth of the Niger. The city of Benin was a walled metropolis three miles long with broad avenues and houses in tidy rows, very unlike the close-pressing huts of many African villages. There was a huge palace with many courtyards and long galleries decorated with brass plaques and statues.

Crops grew luxuriantly in the cleared land around the city. Prosperous Benin merchants traded as far away as the Sudan. Benin's carvers of ivory and wood and casters of brass were as famous as those of Ife had been.

The political system was a complex one centering in a political and religious leader, the *oba* (king). But a good deal of power was also dispersed among the *Iyoba* (queen mother), the crown prince, a group of leading noblemen or palace chiefs, and the town chiefs outside the capital. The kingdom was divided into provinces with appointed governors, and there was a standing army with a supreme commander and an enviable reputation for winning.

Ewuare the Great (ca. 1440–1473) was busy building an empire of his own when Portuguese ships first touched at his main port of Gwatto in the 1470s. Ewuare was reputed to have added more than two hundred villages to his domain. Yet he and the other *obas* of Benin had a reputation for mild and beneficent rule, to which European observers would testify in the centuries that followed—even as they themselves proved less than benevolent intruders into African affairs.

The Kingdom of Kongo

The rain forest of Africa flows east along the Guinea Coast, then south and east again across the endless Congo River basin. Just south of the mouth of that jungle river, fifteenth-century Portuguese explorers found a flourishing African nation—the kingdom of Kongo.

The Congo River winds some 2700 miles through the deep forests of modern Zaire, draining the whole central portion of Africa. It is one of the continent's greatest rivers, comparable in importance to the Nile and the Niger, the Senegal and the Zambesi. The Portuguese, exploring slowly down the western side of Africa in preparation for da Gama's voyage to India fifteen years later, reached the mouth of the Congo in the 1480s. Africans who came down to the river to trade told the foreigners that the king of all that region lived a week's journey to the south. On a later voyage, the Europeans made the journey.

What they saw when they emerged from the footpath through the jungle, with its rich green trees, scarlet birds, and savage mosquitoes, did not impress them as Benin had, or as Timbuktu had impressed Arab travelers. Mbanza, the capital of Kongo, was a dusty African town of straw houses built around a central square. The gates of the royal enclosure were guarded by armed men and trumpeters. There was a great baobab tree where the king of Kongo meted out traditional justice to his people, as King Alfred or Saint Louis had done in Europe centuries before.

Yet from this simple center, a kingdom the size of Belgium or the Netherlands was effectively governed.

Kongo was a developed agricultural society, depending most heavily on a variety of palm trees from which the people made oil, wine, bread, and the fibers they used for everything from clothing to the roofs of houses. The people of Kongo were also stock raisers and worked both iron and copper.

The political organization of this country lost in the rain forest and elephant grass of central Africa was based on the immemorial village, but was articulated all the way up to the national level. Each village had its head, chosen locally on a matrilineal basis, headship descending through the female side. Villages were grouped into districts, each run by an official appointed from above. The districts in turn were grouped into the six large provinces that constituted the nation of Kongo.

The king was in theory an absolute monarch, governing according to traditional law through a small but centralized bureaucracy in Mbanza. Unlike the rulers of West Africa, the king of Kongo had no standing army, depending instead upon a universal military-service obligation to rally all the men of the kingdom at need. Taxes and tribute were collected by provincial governors, and cowrie shells from an island off the coast were used as coinage. The throne was not directly hereditary: the ruler was chosen by a board of electors, like the Holy Roman Emperor of the Germans.

Kongo was only one of a number of central African countries emerging about this time, but it was more strongly centralized than most. It was an awkward time to be emerging, just as the imperial expansion of the West was getting under way. Like Japan in later centuries, however, Kongo responded positively, even enthusiastically to the coming of the Europeans. The people of Kongo absorbed some European technology, and Christianity spread among the elite.

After the technicians and the missionaries, however, would come the slavers, and with them a considerable decline in the popularity of things European.

The Mystery of Great Zimbabwe

On archaeological maps of the African interior there is a blob-shaped area, inland from the coastal cities of East Africa, north of the Limpopo River and south of the Zambesi, usually labeled "Stone Buildings" or "Where the Stone Works Are." Much of this area is in the modern state of Zimbabwe, and the heart of it is the ruined city known today as Great Zimbabwe, for which the new nation is named.

Great Zimbabwe is one of the mysteries of the African past—"perhaps," says one authority, "the greatest riddle in the whole of African history."[1]

It was an impressive stone city, stretching over rocky hilltops and the valley below. There were huge

[1]Roland Oliver, "The Riddle of Zimbabwe," in Roland Oliver, ed., *The Dawn of African History* (London: Oxford University Press, 1961), p. 53.

walls, a sprawling palace, conical towers, and a looming fort and temple on the hill beyond. It is a remarkable sight—so remarkable that the first Europeans to see it, in the nineteenth century, assumed it to be the work of ancient Phoenician traders, or perhaps even King Solomon's famous African mines.

Instead it was almost certainly the capital of an African trading empire linked to the commercial cities of East Africa. Bits of Chinese porcelain and glass beads that came from India or Southeast Asia show that this great city of the African interior was linked by commerce to the trading community of the Indian Ocean. When the Portuguese sailed up the distant coast around 1500, there were Arab traders in Sofala, probably the main port for Zimbabwe, and in the interior also. But Great Zimbabwe itself, much of it built perhaps two to five hundred years earlier, was no longer an imperial capital in 1500: its great days were already shrouded in the past.

The empire of the Bantu-speaking Karanga people whom the Portuguese discovered in that part of East Africa in the sixteenth century may have been an offshoot of the earlier Zimbabwe empire. The Karanga kingdom of Zimbabwe was a remarkable state in itself, probably larger than today's Zimbabwe. It had a traditional god-king with a huge court, a powerful queen mother, and nine main wives, all of whom had their own courts. A centralized bureaucracy ruled the nearer districts; appointed governors ran the farther provinces. This government hierarchy maintained order among a diversity of tribes, collected tribute for

Stonework at Great Zimbabwe, now crumbling and overgrown with forest. This mystery city of East Africa was a flourishing metropolis centuries before Europeans arrived. (New York Public Library Picture Collection)

the royal coffers and conscripts for the royal army. The people cropped the land, herded cattle, made fine textiles, mined and smelted gold. They also traded gold and ivory for luxuries from India and China.

But the capital of the Karanga empire, two hundred miles to the north of Great Zimbabwe, was built of wood and thatch. The splendors of their precursors, the builders of the earliest stone city in the south, can only be guessed at now.

Queens of the Marketplace

African society south of the Sahara was thus evolving rapidly beyond—or away from—village culture as the modern age began. From the grasslands to the rain forests, kingdoms were springing up across the second largest continent. Royal councils, appointed governors, hierarchies of officials much like those of Eurasia appeared. Though many of these administrations lacked the key Eurasian element of literacy and written records, they were able to govern countries as large as the nations of Europe quite effectively.

Structured societies containing an established nobility and an important, sometimes Muslim, merchant class developed above the older village organization. Villages still based their social structure on family and clan, age groups, and traditional sex roles. But the court of the East African Karanga people, with its aristocracy and its concubines, its powerful official class and its even more powerful queen mother, had more in common with the courts of Europe or Asia than it did with the African villages it ruled.

The many roles of women in this Africa of emerging nation-states illustrates vividly the nature of those changing times.

Women were at least as important as men in the subsistence economy of the African village, for they dominated the traditional hoe culture on which many villages depended. Women were important in the political and social organization of village Africa too. Leaders of women's age-set organizations were also the recognized authorities on such aspects of village life as peacemaking and price scales. Women held important religious positions as mediums, diviners, and faith healers.

But women also participated significantly in the new political and economic hierarchy of the evolving kingdoms of Africa. They shared power as queens, queen mothers who were co-rulers, chiefs, and sub-chiefs. They were sometimes the recognized magistrates of their districts. In the economic sphere, the famous West African women's trading network was probably already emerging. This pattern of female domination is still to be found in West Africa, where powerful women merchants reign as queens of the marketplace.

By 1500, however, some of these high-status positions were being undercut by the spread of Islam in Africa. Women's religious roles were undermined by the more limited part granted women in the new religion. Still later, women's political roles would frequently be ignored by Europeans who were unused to the complexity of African political organization and sought a single "chief" with whom to exchange gifts and negotiate trade treaties.

Altogether, then, the varied roles played by African women exemplify the transitions that Africa was undergoing in 1500—and the changes that were still to come.

The emerging Africa of five hundred years ago, like the modernizing African states of today, already had an impressive cultural achievement to show. The balance of this chapter will therefore deal with African culture on the eve of the European intrusion—the inner lives of Africans before the rise of the West began to change the lives of peoples everywhere.

THE WEALTH OF THE AFRICAN SPIRIT

The Life of Timbuktu

The very names of some towns have the power to stir wanderlust in any red-blooded reader, names like Samarkand and Zanzibar . . . and Timbuktu. During its heyday, from the thirteenth to the sixteenth century, Timbuktu would certainly have repaid the effort necessary for a visit.

Timbuktu today is a dusty little market town in the state of Mali. It still enjoys the location that once made it great, on the southern edge of the Sahara and only eight or nine miles north of the big bend of the Niger. But it is hard to imagine it as the splendid center of trade and culture it was in the days of the Mali and Songhai empires.

Fortunately, we do not have to depend on imagination. We have archaeological remains, as well as the vivid descriptions of Timbuktu as it looked to such experienced Muslim travelers as Ibn Batuta in the fourteenth century and Leo Africanus in the sixteenth. And the reconstitution of the life and spirit of this city perhaps more than any other brings us in contact with the courtly culture of the Sudanic kingdoms.

Around 1500, Timbuktu was a walled city of perhaps 25,000 people, a mixed population of Muslim and animist, black Sudanese, Berber, and Arab. In the market squares of Timbuktu, salt from the Sahara and copper, cloth, and metal weapons and tools from the Mediterranean and Europe were all on sale. They were exchanged for the products of the south—ivory, ebony, ostrich plumes and cola nuts, black slaves and gold.

Leo Africanus paints a vivid picture of the city in the days of Askia the Great. Then as now, market women dominated the food marts. And since the desert had not pressed as far south five hundred years ago as it has today, there was plenty of food grown around Timbuktu, a region of cattle and grain and sweet well water. The merchants, Leo assures us, were all very rich, and skilled artisans wove excellent linen and cotton cloth. The houses were unimpressive, thatched roofs on whitewashed wattle-and-daub walls. But there were some impressive brick mosques, and the old stone palace of Mansa Musa, the most famous of Malian kings, was still there.

Askia the Great, the sixteenth-century patron of Muslim culture, surrounded himself with scholars, doctors, *qadis* (judges), and *imams* (holy men) of his faith. The Sankoré mosque, with its typically pyramidal West African tower, was the center of the most famous university in the Sudan, where learned men taught Muslim law and medicine, Islamic religion, philosophy, and government. The king supported many of these scholars, both native-born and foreign, from his own purse. Manuscripts and books in Arabic, the universal language of the Muslim world, were imported from the Mediterranean. Books, said Leo Africanus, fetched a better price in the markets of Timbuktu than any other merchandise.

The spirit of this city of merchants and mosques, courtiers and scholars was the open, cosmopolitan spirit of a wider Islamic world. But there were other aspects of the culture of the new African kingdoms that were distinctively their own. None of these achievements of African genius has aroused more admiration than the art of one of the forest peoples to the south of Songhai—the famous Benin bronzes.

The Bronzes of Benin

The widely used term *Benin bronzes* is in fact a bit of a misnomer. For one thing, they originated not in Benin but in Ife to the north. Benin sculpture also includes ivory carving and terra-cotta objects as well as metalwork—and the metal in question is actually brass, not bronze. An artistic phenomenon, however, this art of the West African forests truly is.

Ife was the religious center of a whole section of the Guinea Coast, its famous oracle consulted by many Yoruba peoples. The earliest of all the organized forest states appeared at Ife, probably around

Bronzework from Benin. Attention to intricate detail and a combination of smooth and carefully worked surfaces distinguish this vivid image of a Bini warrior. (New York Public Library Picture Collection)

1050. Perhaps as early as the twelfth century, a uniquely naturalistic style of sculpture began to be produced there.

Most African sculpture, like that of most Amerindian peoples, was abstract and symbolic. It made little effort to depict human beings or animals realistically, as Greco-Roman or East Asian Buddhist art frequently did. But the Ife heads, most of them brass or terra-cotta, were strikingly lifelike. The patterns of parallel grooves running over some of the faces may represent ritual scarification, but they also heighten the sense of form and contour brilliantly. There is a lofty serenity to some of these idealized but thoroughly convincing African heads that no later African work could match.

Nevertheless, the techniques of metal casting and other sculptural skills did pass to neighboring peoples, including the new kingdom of Benin. And in Benin especially, the result was an array of carved ivory and cast brass that has impressed the world since it first went on display in the West in the present century.

It was perhaps the technical facility revealed by the "bronzes" in particular that first stirred Western viewers. These works were first produced as early as the twelfth century, though their great period is dated from the sixteenth—just in time for the Portuguese to be properly impressed. The castings were made by the classical lost-wax process and are extremely delicate work, no more than two or three millimeters thick. "Cellini himself could not have molded better," as one European authority asserts, "nor anybody else before or after him."[2]

But once more, as in the art of so many lands, it is the work itself that moves us in the end. A metal rooster, fat and strutting, displays an elegantly formalized patterning of feathers that may remind us of the scales of ancient Chinese dragons. A famous sixteenth-century ivory mask, once part of the royal regalia of a king of Benin, stares at us with deep, liquid eyes beneath heavy lids out of the yellowed bone.

In Benin sculpture the naturalism of Ife has been replaced by an exaggerated emphasis on lips and nose and by an increasing stylization, especially of ears, eyes, costume. Yet the life of the people who made them glows from the dark metal of an ancestral head, the smooth skin contrasting with the royal cap and choker of coral beads, the strong features radiating vitality. One is reminded of something even older than Chinese dragons—of the bronze head, cast more than 2000 years before Christ, of Sargon of Akkad, the first of the historic empire builders. This *oba* of West Africa, whose likeness once stood on the altar of a temple in Benin City, was a builder of nations too.

Dancing the Mask

Africa is a huge continent with many and diverse populations, and generalizations about an African world view are as dubious as generalizations about a European or an Asian view of the world. Nevertheless, efforts have been made to summarize the religious views in particular that predominated in the African villages south of the Sahara before the two great world religions of Islam and Christianity reached them. We will close this overview of Africa at the beginning of modern history with such an attempt.

Recent studies of the indigenous religious life of Africa tend to focus on a profound sense of unity in African life. They stress the continuity of nature and humanity, land and people, the individual and the group, the living and the dead. More commonly than not, this faith is called *animism*—a religion that sees a common *life* in all things.

There is, African animists seem to feel, a spiritual vitality in everything around them. Mountains, streams, wells, trees, the animals they kill and the plants they grow all live as people do, and may communicate with them as people do with each other. Africans and the world they inhabit are thus, in a deep spiritual sense, one.

The individual is also one with the group, or groups, of which he or she is a part. The family and the clan, the age group into which one is born, the village community as a whole form a living network of relationships. This network absorbs people at birth, nurtures them all their lives, and determines their destinies. The individual is part of the community, as he or she is of nature.

There are, finally, fundamental ties binding the generations, living and dead. The spirits of ancestors are with the living still, to guide, warn, or haunt them as their actions warrant. Past and present, life and what we call death thus merge in the mind of the African animist into a seamless web of spirituality surrounding us all.

Much African art seems to focus on this fundamentally religious vision of the world. It is an art made for religious purposes—an art of fetishes and nature spirits, ancestor worship and magic. Like the art of the medieval cathedral, it has no other object but to enhance the numinous experience of being in the presence of the divine.

The African mask, perhaps the most successful African sculptural form, expresses these spiritual themes with unsurpassed intensity. African masks clearly illustrate the continuity of the clan and the people. They are made according to strict tribal traditions, and every West African can tell a Senufo from a Mande mask, the shaman's mask from that of the men's secret society. Carved in wood, painted, decorated with raffia, cowrie shells, and colorful beads, these masks have a life of their own—the vivid, sometimes fearful life of the spirit they personify.

It may look like a finished art product, strikingly carved and intricately decorated, hanging on the wall of a museum. But an African mask is never really experienced until it is seen in motion—in performance—worn by an African dancer as part of the ceremonial activity it was made for.

The art and ritual of "dancing the mask" is still taught over long periods of secret initiation in sacred groves around small villages in the interior of Africa. Dancing the mask still expresses the deep African feeling of oneness, of identity among the dancer, the mask he wears, and its indwelling spirit. It is this spiritual presence that possesses the dancer when he presses the wood against his face, feels the leather thongs behind his head and the raffia mane spreading over his shoul-

[2]Felix von Luschen, *Die Altertümer von Benin*, in Ladislas Segy, *African Sculpture Speaks*, 4th ed. (New York: Da Capo Press, 1975), p. 190.

ders. And it is this spiritual presence that possesses him as he sees through narrow slits the familiar village faces, the hard-packed earth of the dancing place, as they appear in the distorting and exalting vision of the spirit of the mask.

SUMMARY

Kingdoms had sprung up in many parts of Africa south of the Sahara by 1500. On the grasslands of the Western Sudan, the Songhai kingdom of Sonni Ali and Askia Muhammad followed in the imperial tradition of Ghana and Mali. In the rain forests of the Guinea Coast, Benin and other kingdoms sprang up, impressing the first European mariners as the empires of the Sudan had earlier Arab caravans. The institutional complexities of the kingdom of Kongo in central Africa were less visible to early European visitors. And the civilization of Great Zimbabwe had largely faded by the time outsiders came to marvel at its mysterious stone ruins.

Much of Africa had thus moved beyond village culture by the time Europeans began to sail regularly along its shores. The complexity of evolving African society south of the Sahara was well illustrated by the varied roles played by women in the society: from faith-healer to subsistence agriculturalist, from queen-mother to queen of the marketplace.

African culture flourished during the centuries around 1500. Cities like Timbuktu shared in the cosmopolitan interregional culture of the Muslim world, with its mosques, scholars, sophisticated courts, and merchant wealth. Among the most impressive artistic accomplishments of the age are the Benin bronzes and the more naturalistic—but not more artistically impressive—sculpture of Ife.

The achievements of Timbuktu and Benin are those of urban-imperial cultures; however, the village culture of Africa survived everywhere and produced its own popular expressions in art and thought. This indigenous African traditional culture focused on animistic religion. It produced such moving folk art as the wide variety of ceremonial masks that played a central part in the life of the African spirit on the eve of first contact with the Europeans.

SUGGESTED READING

AJAYI, J. F. A., and I. ESPIE, eds. *A Thousand Years of West African History*. Ibadan: Ibadan University Press, 1965. A scholarly Nigerian view. See also J. D. Fage, *An Introduction to the History of West Africa*, 3rd ed. (Cambridge: Cambridge University Press, 1962).

BALANDIER, G. *Daily Life in the Kingdom of the Congo: From the Sixteenth to the Eighteenth Century*. New York: Meridian Books, 1968. Good on family life and social customs.

BOVILL, E. W. *The Golden Trade of the Moors*. London: Oxford University Press, 1958. The commercial side of the important northern influence on West Africa. For the religious impact, see Trimmingham, below.

CATON-THOMPSON, G. *The Zimbabwe Culture: Ruins and Reactions*. London: Oxford University Press, 1931. A classic study of the archaeology of Zimbabwe. For a more colorful treatment, see R. Summers, *Zimbabwe: A Rhodesian Mystery* (New York: Tri-Ocean Books, 1963).

CHITTICK, N. "Kilwa and the Arab Settlement of the East African Coast," *Journal of African History*, 1, no. 1 (1960). On the trading emporium of East Africa.

DAVIDSON, B. *The African Past: Chronicles from Antiquity to Modern Times*. Boston: Little, Brown, 1964. Primary sources.

EGHAREUBA, J. *Short History of Benin*, 3rd ed. Ibadan: Ibadan University Press, 1960. A handy survey of the most celebrated of the kingdoms of the West African forest peoples. See also R. E. Bradbury, *The Benin Kingdom and the Edo Speaking Peoples of Southwestern Nigeria* (London: Oxford University Press, 1957).

GIBB, H. A. R., ed. and trans. *Ibn Battuta: Travels in Asia and Africa* (2 vols.). New York: Cambridge University Press, 1958–1962. Famous Arab traveler and his observations on the western Sudan. See also Leo Africanus, *The History and Description of Africa* (3 vols.) (London: Hakluyt Society, 1896).

HUNWICK, J. O. "Songhay, Bornu, and Hausaland in the Sixteenth Century," in J. F. A. Ajayi and M. Crowder, eds., *History of West Africa* (New York: Columbia University Press, 1972). A brief, scholarly survey.

LEBEUF, A. "The Role of Women in the Political Organization of African Societies," in D. Paulme, ed., *Women in Tropical Africa* (Berkeley: University of California Press, 1960). Female power on all levels, from African queens and queen mothers to the village level, with a historical dimension.

OLIVER, R., and J. D. FAGE, eds. *The Cambridge History of Africa* (8 vols.). Cambridge: Cambridge University Press, 1975. Solid and scholarly. For a shorter treatment by these two leading authorities, see Oliver and Fage, *A Short History of Africa* (Baltimore: Penguin, 1962).

OLIVER, R., and G. MATHEWS, eds. *History of East Africa.* Oxford: Clarendon Press, 1963. Includes essays on the period before European intrusion began. For an archaeological perspective, see J. S. Kirkman, *Men and Monuments on the East African Coast* (London: Lutterworth Press, 1964).

SEGY, L. *African Sculpture Speaks*, 4th ed. New York: Da Capo Press, 1975. Excellent overview, with emphasis on religious purposes and regional styles. For a subtler aesthetic analysis, see D. Williams, *Icon and Image: A Study of Sacred and Secular Forms of African Classical Art* (New York: New York University Press, 1974).

SUDARKASA, N. *Where Women Work: A Study of Yoruba Women in the Marketplace and in the Home.* Ann Arbor: University of Michigan Anthropological Papers, 1973. Good study of West African market women, with some account of the historical evolution of their role.

VANSINA, J. *Kingdoms of the Savanna.* Madison: University of Wisconsin Press, 1966. By a leading American Africanist.

Chapter · 5

AMERICAN EMPIRES

KINGDOMS BEYOND THE SEAS

A Separate World

East Asia and Africa south of the Sahara were comparatively isolated patches of the Old World, sundered by distance and geographical barriers from other developed societies. All of the Old World, however, was totally cut off from an even more isolated zone of habitation: the linked continents of the Americas. It is to the remarkable political and cultural achievements of the New World that we must turn in order to complete our survey of the globe the Europeans scarcely knew as modern history began.

Geographically, it was a separate world indeed. The two huge continents of North and South America, the narrow isthmus of Central America between, and the archipelagoes of the Caribbean contained all the geographical forms of the world of Eurasia and Africa. The Rockies and the Andes were the New World equivalents of the Alps and the Himalayas. The great plains of western North America and the Argentine pampas matched the savannas and steppes of Africa and Asia. The deserts of Chile and the American Southwest were as forbidding as any Sahara or Gobi. Nor were the Niger, the Danube, and the Yangtze more impressive rivers than the Mississippi and the Amazon.

The differences were cultural ones. For there were striking differences, as well as impressive similarities, in the ways people lived on opposite sides of the globe. The Atlantic and Pacific oceans were far more cultural than geographical barriers in 1492.

Twenty Centuries of History

Culturally, it seems fair to say, the range of development was much greater in the New World than it was over most of the Old. The closest parallel is perhaps with Africa. In Africa, as in the Americas, some people lived in cities, paid taxes and tribute, and organized their lives according to the will of distant governments. Many others in both places, however, still lived and died in isolated villages, obeying only the traditional mores and taboos of the tribe, clan, and village elders.

We will be concerned here only with the Amerindian kingdoms of the Incas and the Aztecs as they were around 1500. But the fact that a vast spectrum of preurban cultures also flourished in the Americas should not be forgotten. These preurban cultures may explain some features of the Mexican and Peruvian empires. They certainly explain much of the attitude of superiority Europeans developed from the beginning toward pre-Columbian Americans.

In fact, civilization had emerged in the New World as early as it had on the mainland of Europe, in Mycenean Greece—in the first millennium B.C. The huge and astonishingly realistic Olmec stone heads of Mexico were as old as the golden mask of Agamemnon. Highly developed cultures, built around religious ceremonial centers rather than true urban areas, had been rising and falling in Middle and South America for two thousand years before Columbus came. Larger political states—kingdoms and conquest empires—had also emerged, though this is harder to demonstrate because of the general lack of written records over most of the Americas. But of the artistic brilliance of cultures like that of the Teotihuacán in

Gulf of Mexico

Atlantic Ocean

Querétaro
Oxitipan
Tuxpan
Tenochtitlán
TLAXCALA
Coatza-
coalco
Petlatlán
Acapulco
Oaxaca
Mitla
Chiapa
Comitán
Ayotlán
*INDEFINITE
EASTERN
FRONTIER*

TARASCANS

MAYAS

Chichén Itzá
Uxmal
Tikal
Copan

Caribbean Sea

APPROXIMATE AREA OF THE AZTEC EMPIRE	

THE
CHIBCHAS

Orinoco R.

– EQUATOR –

Pasto
Manta
Quito
Tumbez

Moyobamba

Cajamarca
Chimu
Huanuco

Amazon R.

SOUTH AMERICA

Machu Picchu
INCAS
Cuzco
L. TITICACA
Tiahuanaco
Cochabamba
Arequipa

CHINCHAS

APPROXIMATE AREA OF THE INCA EMPIRE	

Pacific Ocean

Iquique

Tarija

Atacama

Copiapó

Tucumán
Catamarca

Coquimpu

*MAULE
R.*

ARAUCANIANS

**Amerindian Empires
on the Eve of the Spanish Conquest**

1000 MILES

Mexico (ca. 200 B.C.–A.D. 700) and the Mochica in Peru (A.D. 300–700), and of the intellectual brilliance of the Classical Maya of Middle America (A.D. 300–900), there can be no doubt.

It was on a foundation of twenty centuries of cultural evolution, then, that the great civilizations of the Aztecs in Mexico and the Incas in Peru were built—both, as it happens, not long before 1500. These were the American empires the European conquerors found, and the ones to be dealt with in the pages that follow.

WARRIOR LORDS OF MEXICO

Lord of the Dawn House

Of all the ancient gods of Mexico, none aroused more reverence and awe in the hearts of Mesoamericans than that incarnation of the numinous they called Quetzalcóatl, the feathered serpent. The god of merchants, god of priests and learning, lord of the wind, lord of the "dawn house" (the planet Venus), the once and future god who sailed off across the sea promising to return, he held a high place in the pantheon of many Indian cultures.

This hybrid divinity, a plumed serpent, often bearded, having the fangs of a great cat, was worshiped far back in the history of civilization in Middle America. Gargoylelike, barbarically abstract heads of the plumed serpent projected from the walls of the Temple of the Sun at Teotihuacán as early as the first or second century A.D. In the 900s, Quetzalcóatl in human form led the famous Toltecs into the lands of the Maya, where temples were built to him under the name of Kukulcan. And in the 1500s, he was so revered among the Aztecs that when the Spanish appeared out of the east in the very month foretold for his return, Moctezuma's armies refrained from the violence with which they would otherwise have greeted such an invasion, lest they raise their hands against divinity.

Quetzalcóatl was many things to many peoples, yet a core of identity persists in the plumed serpent for perhaps fifteen hundred years. In this core of continuity and these multiple meanings of the god of the merchants, god of the wind, god of the dawn house, we have a vivid symbol of the unity within multiplicity that characterizes the whole sweep of Mesoamerican history. In the following sections, we will look first at the common core of this unified Mesoamerican culture. Thereafter, we will turn to the last and by far the best-known of the many distinctive cultures that have risen and fallen here under the vol-

canoes of Mexico: the brilliant, blood-colored splendor of the Aztecs.

Mesoamerican Culture

Geographically, Mesoamerica is a chain of upland valleys and mountains running between strips of coastal lowlands from Mexico down the length of Central America. Here, by the first millennium B.C., civilization in the New World had begun with the development of maize and other food crops and the resulting growth in population density and social sophistication. Olmec culture, the mother culture of Mesoamerica, had taken shape in the Caribbean lowlands, and the most renowned of Middle American societies, that of the Mayans, had also flourished there. But the influence of both had extended into the high plateaus between the mountains also. With the emergence of the metropolis of Teotihuacán in the upland plateau of central Mexico, the Mesoamerican cultural heartland shifted to the high valleys, and Mexico, at the northwestern end of the isthmus, became its power center.

By the year 1000 of the Christian calendar, the classical Mesoamerican civilizations of the Mayans and of the great city of Teotihuacán had passed away. But the cycles of civilization continued in the area now occupied by Mexico, Guatemala, Honduras, and neighboring states. A well-developed Mesoamerican culture had clearly emerged, one with a capacity for recovering from periodic disasters and for absorbing conquerors apparently comparable to that of India or China.

Mesoamerican culture was built on an agricultural base of maize, beans, chilis, and squash, which supported a comparatively dense population of several million people. Mesoamerican societies were as hierarchical as any in the Old World. Besides the farming majority, they supported many sorts of artisans, a powerful priesthood presiding over large ceremonial religious centers, a fierce warrior caste, and merchants who circulated goods over hundreds of miles. Mesoamericans also had elaborate mythologies and cosmological theories, mathematics and astronomy, and, in some places, forms of writing.

Amerindians in this part of the New World were learning the art of effectively governing large empires. They continued to conduct human sacrifices—a fading practice elsewhere on the globe. They also suffered periodic influxes of less-settled, skin-clad Indians from the north, attracted as Goths were to Roman Europe or Mongols to China by the seductive charms of civilization.

The most successful of these earlier northern barbarian invaders were the Toltecs, who came to be revered in later days as a race of golden-age heroes. But there was an even more formidable name yet to come down from the north: the Aztecs, future conquerors of all Mexico.

The Halls of Moctezuma

Aztec codices (folded scrolls of picture writing) and information collected by the Spaniards after the conquest tell us a great deal about the history of this last of Mesoamerican Indian civilizations. These sources chronicle, reign by reign, the rise and transformation of a half-savage people into great conquerors and rulers during the two centuries preceding the descent of the Europeans upon their coasts. They also explain, in grisly detail, how it was that perhaps a thousand Spanish soldiers were able to topple an empire of several millions.

As late as the fourteenth century, the Aztecs were a small, warlike people, one of the many uncultivated Nahuatl-speaking groups to drift down into Mexico from what is today the United States. They had been nomadic for centuries, following their priests and their god Huitzilopochtli in search of a vaguely promised land in the south. They found it on a muddy island in Lake Texcoco in the high Valley of Mexico, where around 1325 they began to build the city that became Tenochtitlán, the amazing Aztec capital the Spanish found when they arrived in their turn in 1519.

In the early days, the Aztecs were a rude folk, living largely by hunting, by gathering lake creatures, and by trading with the more developed peoples around them. They were said to be given to stealing the daughters of their neighbors for wives, as the most ancient Romans had done, and to forms of human sacrifice that even the sacrifice-prone Mesoamericans found disgusting. Small in numbers and regarded as primitive, the Aztec clans were at first oppressed by their civilized neighbors and generally looked down upon.

But the rich mud of their island home and the environing shores produced lavish quantities of corn, beans, and chilis, and the Aztecs managed to acquire enough brides to produce a rapid growth in their population. They were also fierce warriors, in demand as mercenaries and allies in the frequent wars of the Mexican uplands. And they seem to have been very quick learners indeed, picking up techniques of Machiavellian intrigue, alliance making, and empire building from the developed zone of urban culture in which they had settled.

Their resulting rise was as rapid as any we have recorded. Wielding bows and arrows—the Toltec had apparently fought primarily with the atlatl, or spear-thrower—and swinging wooden swords edged with razor-sharp obsidian, the Aztecs stepped into the power vacuum left by the disintegration of the older Toltec hegemony.

They began by freeing themselves from persecution by their neighbors in the Valley of Mexico and ended by conquering them. Under kings with names like Izcoatl (Obsidian Serpent) and Moctezuma (Angry Lord) I, they made warfare a paying proposition, imposing their will by force and collecting tribute over a sphere that extended far beyond the valley of central Mexico. Under more philosophically inclined leaders such as Netzahualcóyotl and his son Netzahualpilli in the fifteenth and early sixteenth centuries, they reared great temples, palaces, and gardens, cultivated such arts as astronomy and eloquence, and ruled severely but impartially over a wide swath of Mexico.

The Aztecs made much of their alleged descent from the legendary Toltecs, and they certainly learned a good deal from the surviving Mayan city-states they conquered in Yucatán. But the hegemony they established in the fifteenth century bore the unique mark of their own society and temperament.

Aztec society was dominated by priests and warriors. Most people were now settled farmers, but all men were liable for the military service necessary to keep subject peoples in awe. Though they did not have money, the Aztecs developed a system of market exchange, even in small provincial cities, that was superior to that of the Mayans. Food flowed into the huge market squares of Tenochtitlán from a hundred miles around. Jade, gold, and silver, feathers and skins, honey, cacao, and other valued luxury items came in tribute from an empire of five million people settled over much of the area of modern Mexico.

Like the contemporary West African kingdoms, the Aztecs had succession problems. Their kings too were not directly hereditary, but were chosen from the males of the more prestigious lineages. The Aztecs compensated for this, however, by considering their monarchs not only as essential intermediaries between the people and their gods, but increasingly as gods themselves, like the pharaohs of ancient Egypt.

As rulers, Aztec kings were able to impose a system of enforced alliances or appointed governors on some sixty provinces and subject peoples. A large scribal bureaucracy kept records of the flow of tributes and the endless wars. Warfare was necessary to maintain Aztec supremacy—and to supply prisoners of war for sacrifice to Huitzilopochtli at his gigantic pyramid temple in Tenochtitlán.

Aztec nobles, high priests, and kings lived in spacious stone houses built in the Mesoamerican style. These flat-roofed buildings were doorless—rigorous laws made thievery rare—and had cool patios and

Moctezuma, emperor of the Aztecs, is shown here in an idealized European rendering. Unrealistic combinations of Western artistic taste, hazy traditions about the New World (feathers!), and a vaguely conceived Aztec city reveal a European sense of the impressive New World culture they were destroying. (Library of Congress)

gardens filled with flowers, fruit trees, and pools. The fabled halls of Emperor Moctezuma impressed even the European conquerors with their size, cleanliness, and grandeur.

The average Aztec family had little share in such splendors. Like peasants the world around, they were taught to keep their places and respect their betters. The new order required not only military service but payments to the state in produce and labor. Some peasants were serfs; others were slaves.

Most Mesoamericans, however, lived under the Aztecs as their ancestors had before the conquest. Men worked in the fields, using simple wood and stone tools. They had no beasts of burden to help, since no large domesticatable animals had survived the hunting stage in Middle America.

Women spun and wove cloth made of cotton and other vegetable fibers into the short pants and long mantels or capes worn by men and the long skirts and blouses the women themselves wore. The women also spent many hours a day—as many Indian women still do—grinding corn by hand to make the tortillas that, with beans and chili, were the mainstay of the Mesoamerican diet.

It is hard to associate the sturdy, broad-faced, hardworking people of the surviving codices and paintings with the splendors—and the horrors—of the priestly-military elite who ruled over them, or with the towering, blood-drenched pyramid on the great plaza of Tenochtitlán.

THE EMPIRE OF THE ANDES

A Land and People Divided

The Andes change color through the day. Driving down through the mountains toward the coast, you crawl like an insect among ridges and peaks that are dark blue in the morning, gray slashed with green and ocher in the dry cold noon, and red in the sunset, sliding through violet and purple toward the dark. The precipitous surge and fall of that miles-high world of angled rock, plunging gorges, and bare, isolated valleys far above the timberline make hard enough driving on a narrow modern road. The thought of traveling through this world before the age of modern transport—let alone living and building here—can kindle an impulse of respect in the most cynical modern spirit.

To unify such a realm in any but the loosest cultural sense would require both immense labor and a kind of genius rare in history. As far as we know, it happened only once before the coming of the conquistadores—in the days of the Sapa Incas, rulers of the largest empire in the history of pre-Columbian America.

Pan-Andean cultural unity was of course achieved long before the Incas conquered the Andes. As in Mesoamerica, the Amerindians of what is today Peru and portions of neighboring nations had perfected a thoroughly workable style of life, with sophisticated forms of art and social organization, centuries and even millennia earlier.

Agriculture was widely practiced. Potatoes were the upland staple, though corn, beans, and various squashes were common here as in Mexico. Hills and mountainsides were terraced, irrigation canals and ditches spread water over arid lowland valleys, and fertilizing was common. Ceremonial centers and even some true cities featured large stone temples and palaces. Many crafts were practiced, including the ancient ceramic and textile industries and more metal working than in Middle America. Society was acquiring the habits of specialization and hierarchical class divisions characteristic of urban civilization everywhere.

But the Andes divided and subdivided Peru and the peoples who lived there as the mountains and the high central plateaus divided Mexico. If anything, the world's longest mountain range did a more thorough job of breaking up the western side of South America. Peru's rocky spine effectively separated the tropical rain forests of the interior from the coastal deserts along the Pacific. Ecologically, these three zones—jungle, mountains, arid coastland—contrasted as sharply as any in the world. In addition, the ridges and jagged crests subdivided the uplands and the coastal lowlands into many narrow valleys—and separate valley societies—with only the most difficult communication between them.

The economy reflected these geographical and ecological divisions. Llama and alpaca herds were pastured, and potatoes cultivated, in the higher altitudes. Corn was raised in the hills below. Fish were taken mostly from the sea, while coca and other tropical products came from the other side of the mountains, where the rain forests of the Amazon basin began. Each separate people, scattered among mountains or hills or forests, also had its unique traditional patterns of ceramic and textile design. Each had a style of life that suited its ecology and its traditions.

To overcome some of these problems rooted in environmental differences, Andean peoples had long since learned to trade with one another, exchanging the produce of one region for that of another. Another solution was to send out "colonies" for seasonal harvesting in a different zone, or even for permanent exploitation of crops available only in a neighboring area. Thus whole regions of this rugged corner of the world attained at least a degree of economic unity. In some cases, as among the areas conquered by the Mochica, there was regional political unity as well.

There had been significant efforts to impose hegemony over even larger tracts of pre-Columbian Peru. During the second half of the first millennium A.D., several sizable empires had divided most of Peru among them. These were the conquest empires of Huari in the north and Tiahuanaco in the south, both flourishing from approximately 600 to 1000, and the Chimu state, which flowered somewhat later in the northwestern coastal areas earlier organized by the Mochica.

As in Mesoamerica, a key factor behind the rise of these larger political units was the increase in population caused by improved agricultural techniques. The people seem to have needed some higher authority than the usual clan and family structure to deal with the more complex problems of life in their overcrowded valleys. Arguments over water use, landownership, and the conflicting traditional rights of neighboring villages could most effectively be settled by a superior governmental power. And there was never a shortage of ambitious chiefs, priests, and warriors eager to establish such a higher power.

But there was more to come than the successful regional empires of Huari, Tiahuanaco, and Chimu. There was pre-Columbian America's most impressive political achievement—the pan-Andean imperium of the Incas.

The Kingdom of the Sun

The Incas were the ruling house of a small kingdom that rose in the upland mountain-ringed valley of Cuzco perhaps as early as 1200 A.D. It was not until 250 years later, however, that a great conqueror came to the throne and became the real founder of the Inca Empire.

The historically significant rulers of Inca Peru thus number no more than half a dozen, from the emergence of the empire around 1450 to its fall to the Spanish in 1532. And the greatest of these Inca empire builders was the first, the famous Pachacuti.

Pachacuti Inca (1438–1471) seized power during a disastrous war with a powerful neighboring people. He first overthrew his father, who had retreated before the enemy, and then executed his brother, who had been so successful against the foe as to seem a threat to Pachacuti's authority. In the process of achieving and assuring his throne, the new ruler also defeated the foreign enemy who had made his rise possible. He then capped his achievement by enlisting his defeated neighbor's armies for a great campaign of conquest up and down the Andes and across the coastal lowlands as well. Pachacuti Inca and his highly competent heir Topa Inca extended their domain north into what is today Ecuador, south as far as the middle of Chile, and inland to include half of Bolivia and even a corner of Argentina.

Topa Inca's successor added little to the empire, and two of Topa's grandsons fought a civil war over the throne, a conflict that was just ending when Pizarro appeared. But the Incas had already earned their place in history. The empire they had assembled was the most impressive—and, among scholars of a later age, the most controversial—in the New World.

The peoples who lived under the Inca emperors found their lives changed significantly by their new rulers. For in their comparatively short tenure of power, the Incas demonstrated an unsurpassed skill at social and political organization.

The Inca Empire stretched for 2500 miles down the western side of South America, over some of the most difficult terrain in the world. The population may have run as high as six or eight million. To unite this realm and the divided peoples who lived there, the Inca rulers established an awesome hierarchy of officials.

The empire was divided into quarters, each of which was further divided into provinces. There was an appointed or hereditary *curaca*, or leader, for every 10 families, and again for every 50, 100, 500, 1000, 5000, and 10,000. There were appointed governors for each of the quarters. There were officials in the central government in Cuzco charged with special functions, from transportation to the military. And all this vast bureaucracy was run by people whose most complicated record-keeping device was the *quipu*, a tangle of knotted strings that served as an all-purpose aid to memorizing both statistics and events!

The great king, or Sapa Inca, at the top of this society lived in splendor in Cuzco. He never wore the same elaborate royal regalia twice, was carried about in a golden litter to a chanting of hymns, and was generally believed to be descended from the Sun, who was one of the chief gods in the Inca pantheon.

The millions of Inca subjects were expected to provide tribute in produce and were compelled to perform long hours of labor for the state. They were regulated by government edict in everything from care of crops and herds, craftwork, and construction to marriage and religion. In return, the Inca government attempted to provide defense, justice, transportation and communication facilities, food distribution from government granaries in times of scarcity, and at least minimal care for widows and orphans, the old and the sick.

To some scholars this sort of governmental intervention right down to the village level looks like benevolent welfare-state socialism. To others, it smacks of nothing more than modern totalitarianism. It was neither, of course. The Incas had neither the ideology nor the modern administrative machinery for such ventures. What they did do was provide rigorous government and vigorous prosperity at a cost of rigid regulation, compulsory labor, and occasional military intervention or deportation, sometimes moving whole peoples from one part of the empire to another.

In the context of the times, the price was perhaps not as high as it might seem to a later age. And the Incas, as we shall see, used their power for some of the more impressive works left by our predecessors on this planet.

TENOCHTITLÁN AND CUZCO

Common Base, Parallel Evolution

Like the civilizations of China and Japan, those of the Incas and Aztecs were very different from each other. The Incas, like the Chinese, demonstrated remark-

able skills in the arts of social organization, whereas both the warlike Aztecs and the Japanese of the age of the samurai made martial vigor central to their societies.

As with the cultures of China and Japan in the centuries around 1500, we will therefore note more differences than similarities between the Aztecs and the Incas. Yet these Amerindian civilizations will turn out to have much in common. From sun worship and temple pyramids to a highly developed social morality, Mexico and Peru reveal a distinctive substratum of shared ideas, attitudes, and cultural forms.

Since there is no evidence of cultural contact of any significance between them, however, these similarities are not a matter of cultural diffusion—the influence of one society upon another. They must instead reflect parallel evolution out of a common American cultural base. Such parallel evolution accounts for a substantial proportion of the basic similarities among peoples around the world as different cultures find their way to similar solutions to the problems they all share.

Hearts for the Gods of Mexico

Tenochtitlán was the center of the Aztec world, and its great central square the ideological core of Aztec life. It is to that vast plaza with its looming temples that we must go, then, if we would understand the source of the throbbing energy and the grim rigor of spirit that made the Aztec achievement possible.

In their later years at least, the once barbaric Aztecs mastered many of the traditional Mesoamerican arts and sciences. They possessed considerable knowledge of astronomy, mathematics, and a form of picture writing. They also had great skill in engineering, architecture, and sculpture in stone, and a distinctive style of painting featuring flat colors, heavy outlines, and lively cartoonlike figures. As the ancient Romans learned from the Greeks, or the Arabs from the peoples they conquered, so the Aztecs acquired a sophisticated high culture from their predecessors.

The uniqueness of the Aztecs lay not in art or science, however, but in the rigor of their morality and the extravagance of their religion.

Aztec children were taught from their earliest years to fear the gods, respect their elders, stand firm in battle. They learned to avoid vice and injustice, work hard, and accept punishment with humility. Courage, self-discipline, justice, and piety were preeminent Aztec virtues. Both parents and a widespread system of village education taught all children these virtues, as well as a trade and the necessary military skills. An equally widespread system of law courts punished misdeeds so rigorously—death for stealing

The Pyramid of the Sun dominates the ceremonial site at Teotihuacán, near Mexico City. Many pyramids of ancient Mexico matched those of Egypt in size and exceeded them in numbers.

more than four ears of corn—that crime seems to have been all but eliminated among the Aztecs.

Infusing this system of values, finally, were the powerful religious beliefs of the Aztec people. Aztecs, like other Mesoamerican peoples, were animists, feeling the closeness of the supernatural in earth and rain, the stars and the forests, the sharp edge of the obsidian blade and the burning of the fire. They personified these felt presences in anthropomorphic gods and goddesses, whom they often depicted as hybrid combinations of animals, such as Quetzalcóatl, the feathered serpent with a jaguar's teeth. There were two sorts of divinities: nature gods worshiped by farmers—for example, "your lordship, the corn"—and the great gods of the state, headed by the ancient Aztec sun god, Huitzilopochtli.

In the measured judgment of most historians, it was an intensely felt need to placate the great Huitzilopochtli, the all-devouring Mexican sun, that drove the whole brilliant, brutal machinery of the Aztec state.

Human sacrifice has been practiced at one time or another almost everywhere, usually in order to acquire supernatural powers—or to placate them. The Aztecs believed that the sun above, source of all life, required constant feeding on human hearts. Their unending wars, their stoic warrior ethic, the empire itself was from this perspective but an elaborate way of gathering food for the sun. As long as blood continued to darken the pyramidal temple of Huitzilo-

pochtli on the great plaza—as long as fresh-plucked hearts were held up to the sky—so long would the sun shine, the crops flourish, and the Aztecs rule.

The conquistadores were vastly impressed by the lake city of Tenochtitlán, the Venice of the New World, with its "great towers and . . . buildings rising from the water, and all built of masonry,"[1] with green jungles and purple volcanoes behind it. Five square miles in area, its population perhaps as high as 100,000, it was larger than Renaissance Florence. The streets were swept clean daily; even human waste was thriftily hauled away by canoe to be used as fertilizer. The temples, plazas, palaces, and market squares, the sculptured walls, pleasant gardens, and aromatic trees were like something out of a fairy tale.

And then they saw the racks of skulls, thousands upon thousands of them, at the foot of the temple stairs. The Spaniards, who burned people alive in their own country to please their God, were, of course, unconvincing champions of humanitarianism. We can lament the destruction of that Venice of the Americas, all gone today beneath the hum and roar of Mexico City. But it is hard to regret the cessation of the rise and fall of that razor-edged obsidian blade, the swiftly probing hand, and the still-pumping lump of flesh thrust up against the sun.

[1]Bernal Díaz del Castillo, *The Discovery and Conquest of Mexico*, trans. Irving A. Leonard (New York: Grove Press, 1950), p. 190.

The King's Highway

But there was another way of worshiping the great central fire, and another kind of culture to be built upon this primal human religion. Two thousand miles south and east, the Inca way evolved, producing its own uniquely American cultural forms.

The Incas and their subjects, like most peoples in history, were polytheistic. They believed in a creator god, Viracocha, who had made all things in heaven and earth, including human beings fully equipped with their tribal languages, traditional music, and textile patterns. Viracocha, however, did not rule the universe: he left that to his chief assistant, Inti, the sun, who was believed to be the ancestor of all the Incas.

The moon, various stars, and Mother Earth were also gods and had earthly responsibilities as patrons of crops, herds, and trades. Numinous power also clustered about many earthbound objects, from the tombs of ancestors to the boundary stones of fields. Even a heap of rocks along the road might be worth a prayer, and might give strength to the traveler.

Religion was as well organized as everything else in the empire of the Incas. There were shrines and temples at the village and provincial-city level as well as at the mountain capital of Cuzco. Priests and priestesses—the latter among the best-educated and -trained women in the empire—performed rituals and sacrifices punctually. The sacrifices, unlike those in Mesoamerica, were normally guinea pigs or llamas.

The subjects of the Incas were not as advanced in mathematics and had not invented writing, as Mayans and Aztecs had. But they had made some practical advances. They had domesticated the llama as a beast of burden—a considerable advantage, even though a llama could carry no more than a hundred pounds. They had also learned a good deal more about working metals, edging and pointing their tools with bronze instead of with hard stones such as obsidian.

Women in Inca Peru spun and men wove gorgeous textiles out of cotton (on the coast) or alpaca and llama wool (in the highlands), using almost two hundred different dyes. Ceramicists crafted amazing pots in the Mochica and Chimu traditions, some shaped like animals or gods, some sculptured to resemble particular individuals—a striking form of pot portraiture. They worked in bronze and copper, silver and gold, using gold especially for jewelry, for dishes for noble tables, and for idols and the decoration of temples.

These crafts, like so much else in Inca society, were also organized for large-scale production. Textiles and ceramics especially were mass-produced according to standard patterns in sizable workshops.

But it is in their great public works that this most organized of New World societies excelled. The Incas were above all else great builders.

Inca stonework was probably the best in the Americas, despite the greater flamboyance of Mesoamerican architecture. Inca workmen cut, polished, beveled, and fitted stones with an unexcelled precision. Much of their best work was done at Cuzco, where royal palaces, noble mansions, and the great Temple of the Sun provided a challenge suited to their talents.

The Inca capital was a huge city, containing an estimated 100,000 to 300,000 people. The population of Cuzco represented all the varied populations of the empire, and each was required to wear his or her own brightly colored native costume. The palaces of the Incas and of the noble heads of great clans were complexes of low buildings built around many courtyards, with gardens and storehouses for the clan treasures. There was a great public square for religious ceremonies. And there was the Coricancha, the Temple of the Sun, some of whose walls may be seen today serving as foundations for a Spanish colonial church.

The greatest of all Inca engineering feats, however, was the famous royal highway through the Andes. There were apparently almost 9500 miles of it, up and down and across one of the world's highest mountain ranges. The roadway was graded, smoothed, frequently paved with stone and walled where it ran along the edge of a precipice. There were hostels and way stations for the runners who carried the royal post. There were hundreds of bridges over gorges and rivers. All of it was built, cared for, cleaned of falling rock, and repaired when heavier slides carried whole sections away, by the corvée labor of the peasants. Amazingly, much of this royal road was kept up by local villagers long after the fall of the Incas who built it, so strong a sense of social responsibility had the Inca regime instilled in its people.

To see Inca building today, one must go by train, bus, and foot up to Machu Picchu, the famous "lost city" in the clouds north of Cuzco. Here, framed by mist-draped crags high above the valley floor, yellow grass sprouts among the beveled stones, and the characteristic trapezoidal doors open on roofless rooms. The labor, the skill, and the organizing will that shaped this masonry and set it in its place so perfectly that a knife blade still cannot be inserted between the blocks testify to the unique genius of the Incas.

It is perhaps easy to discount the cultural achievements of the Aztecs and the Incas. They would fall so easily, so rapidly, to handfuls of European adventurers. They were the first great victims of the Western imperialism that is in so many ways the defining feature of our era. And their accomplishments are so completely gone today, so totally a matter of artifacts in museum cases and lonely ruins in distant jungles or mountain peaks.

The same, however, might be said of ancient Egypt and Mesopotamia, of medieval Byzantium or old Baghdad, yet we do not revere these splendid cultures less for having fallen to the universal fate. The canals of Tenochtitlán and the royal highway of the Incas were among the most impressive of human achievements in 1500. They are further evidence of the rich variety, the breadth and depth of the world's many civilizations at the beginning of the modern period of history.

SUMMARY

In the Americas, as in Africa, urban cultures had emerged much earlier than we are used to thinking. This was so in two areas in particular: Mesoamerica and the Peruvian Andes. Here many of the arts of civilization had been practiced for two thousand years when the first Europeans broke in upon this independent stream of social evolution shortly after 1500.

In both Mexico and Peru, techniques of imperial government were evolving rapidly. In the northern zone of civilization, the vigorous and militaristic Aztecs fought their way to power among the peoples of the high valleys of central Mexico in the fourteenth and fifteenth centuries. Initially regarded as northern barbarians, the Aztecs rapidly mastered a range of traditional Mexican skills, from settled agriculture and city building to diplomacy and bureaucratic administration. By 1500 they governed the largest empire in Mesoamerican history.

The largest of all pre-Columbian American empires, however, was that of the Incas, which emerged in the fifteenth century in Peru. Pachacuti Inca, the founder of Inca power, demonstrated amazing skill at imposing centralized authority on the historically and geographically divided peoples of northwestern South America. Over a realm of high mountains, coastal plains, and interior jungles, a structured government exacted labor and obedience and provided services ranging from defense to social welfare.

In both of these highly developed urban-imperial societies of the New World, arts and ideas flourished. They shared a variety of common elements, from sun worship and temple pyramids to a strong sense of social morality. There were, however, striking differences between them.

The Aztecs enforced rigorous moral standards and martial vigor. Their central religious ceremony, human sacrifice on the altar of the sun, was believed necessary to guarantee continued prosperity to the empire. The Incas, though neither literate nor as mathematically inclined as the Mesoamerican peoples, developed other skills. They worked metals on a larger scale and were probably the most expert builders with stone in the Americas. The astonishing Inca royal road through the Andes was one of the great feats of engineering—and social discipline—of the age.

SUGGESTED READING

ANTON, F. *Women in Pre-Columbian America*. New York: Abner Schram, 1973. Good pictures, thorough commentary on Amerindian women before the Europeans came.

DAVID, N. *The Aztecs: A History*. New York: Putnam, 1974. A good recent account.

DE LA VEGA, G. *Royal Commentaries of the Incas and General History of Peru* (2 vols.), trans. H. V. Livermore. Austin: University of Texas Press, 1966. Primary source, perhaps too sympathetic to the Incas.

DRIVER, H. E., ed. *The Americas on the Eve of Discovery*. Englewood Cliffs, N.J.: Prentice-Hall, 1964. Useful book of readings, including the developed urban-imperial cultures of the New World.

FURST, J. L., and P. T. FURST. *Pre-Columbian Art of Mexico*. New York: Abbeville Press, 1980. Large format, impressive photographs.

LÉON-PORTILLA, M. *Aztec Thought and Culture: A Study of the Ancient Nahuatl Mind*. Norman, Okla.: University of Oklahoma Press, 1963. Cultural history of a people often considered—like the ancient Romans—less cultured than some of those they conquered.

MCADAMS, R. *The Evolution of Urban Society: Early Mesopotamia, Prehistoric Mexico*. Chicago: University of

Chicago Press, 1965. Illuminating example of comparative history and of the cultural evolutionist analysis that prevails among students of pre-Columbian America.

MÉTRAUX, A. *History of the Incas.* New York: Pantheon, 1969. Scholarly summary.

NASH, J. "Aztec Women: The Transition from Status to Class in Empire and Colony," in M. Etienne and E. Leacock, eds., *Women and Colonization: Anthropological Perspectives.* New York: Praeger, 1980. Marriage and work before and after the conquest.

SAHAGÚN, B. DE. *General History of the Things of New Spain* (12 vols.), trans. and ed. A. O. J. Anderson and C. E. Dibble. Santa Fe: School of American Research, 1950–1969. Basic primary source for the Aztecs.

SILVERBLATT, I. "Andean Women in the Inca Empire," *Feminist Studies,* 4, no. 3 (1978), 36–61. Social status and labor contribution of women in the Inca Empire.

SOUSTELLE, J. *The Daily Life of the Aztecs on the Eve of the Conquest,* trans. P. O'Brian. New York: Macmillan, 1962. Social history.

VON HAGEN, V. W. *The Aztec, Man and Tribe.* New York: New American Library, 1958. Older, but by a leading authority on pre-Columbian American civilization.

—— *The Incas: People of the Sun.* Cleveland: World Pub. Co., 1961. Well-written description of the society of this most impressive of Andean empires.

WOLF, E. J. *Sons of the Shaking Earth.* Chicago: University of Chicago Press, 1959. Evocative portrait of pre-conquest Mexico.

Chapter · 6

FROM THE POLES TO THE BURNING LINE

THE PREURBAN WORLD

Beastmen and Anthropophagi

Europe was only one among many highly developed cultures at the beginning of modern history. There were polities in the Muslim center of Eurasia, in the Far East, in Africa, and the Americas that rivaled the European nations in power, wealth, or splendor, in artistic brilliance or spiritual profundity. Islam had spread much farther than Christianity in half the time. China had united a population larger than all Europe's under a central government—something Europe has not managed to this day. No Western monarch could point to a road like the royal highway of the Incas. The Western sense of superiority was thus little more than an ethnocentric illusion in 1500.

But there was more to the non-European world than Istanbul and Isfahan and Delhi, Peking and Kyoto, Timbuktu and Cuzco and Tenochtitlán. There was a *pre*urban world out there too. To this world, where cities, kingdoms, and empires had not yet appeared, all urban-imperial peoples felt immensely and intrinsically superior. And always had.

Muslims called them pagans, Chinese called them barbarians. To sixteenth-century Europeans, these peoples who had neither cities nor countries, written laws nor visible religious institutions, were only marginally human. They called such people savages, beastmen, or even anthropophagi, a reference to their allegedly common proclivity for cannibalism.

As recently as the earlier part of the present century, we were still calling them backward and primitive, barbarous and heathen. Today we use words such as *underdeveloped, developing,* and *preurban—* and still too often tend to mean *precivilized.*

What they were in fact were people who for a variety of reasons, including their own free choice, had not followed the same lines of cultural evolution as their cousins within the city walls. A closer look at this preurban—or nonurban—world will complete this overview of the earth's peoples at the beginning of modern history.

Levels of Culture

The following survey will be couched in terms of levels of culture. It is important at the outset to assert clearly that this terminology refers to *chronological order* of development and is not intended to impute superior value to more recent cultural developments.

Recent anthropological and archaeological research indicates that people like those who scavenge the barren wilderness of the Kalahari may get a more than adequate diet. They get it furthermore, by working about half as many hours per day as a farmer or a factory worker does, and they do not have to pay taxes or serve in anybody's army. They also do not have modern medicine, social security, books, television sets, or Saint Peter's cathedral—but these are, after all, in considerable part a matter of taste.

Without implying any superiority to the urban civilizations we have examined thus far, then, let us remind ourselves of the other chronological levels of cultural development that shared the world with the urban-imperial peoples in 1500.

The oldest existing culture, it will be recalled, was that of the hunting and gathering peoples who had evolved with the race over several million years of prehistory. Because hunting and gathering could feed only small populations, and because these peoples' technological sophistication was not great, they had retreated before later comers, into the cold north, the deep forest, or deserts such as the Kalahari. Yet large parts of several continents were still populated, however thinly, by such peoples at the beginning of the sixteenth century.

The most recent basic way of life to emerge, the nomadic-herding mode, had developed only a few thousand years before. Nomadism evolved when peoples too weak to claim a share of good agricultural land—or disdaining the hard work involved—retreated to the fringes. On deserts or steppes, they found food and water sufficient to feed animals as long as the herds were kept on the move. In their endless migratory round, many of the nomad peoples had become tough, well-organized, highly mobile—and historically a serious threat to the more settled peoples around them.

The most widespread preurban style of life, however, was that of the agricultural village. The Neolithic Revolution, which had begun around 8000 B.C., had spread slowly around the world, bringing with it agriculture, the domestication of animals, ceramics, weaving, and many other skills. It was from the settled villages that larger towns, walled cities, and empires slowly developed.

The city, however, proved a Frankenstein's monster to the village culture that had spawned it. Urban centers turned neighboring villages into a hinterland, more distant ones into provinces. They put once free peasants to work on irrigation canals, temples, palaces, pyramids, and the Great Wall of China. But there were a great many farming villages in the world, and in 1500 many of them remained unabsorbed by the urban-imperial peoples of the earth.

The following sections, then, will offer a brief montage of hunter-gatherers, nomadic herders, and agricultural-village societies around the world. Masters of much of Asia, Africa, and South America and all of North America and Australia, these preurban peoples still owned a very large tract of the globe at the beginning of the modern period.

MEN WHOSE HEADS DO GROW BENEATH THEIR SHOULDERS

Europe's Steppe Frontier

The Old World, for all its ancient cities, had its share of preurban societies too in 1500. Europe, Asia, and Africa were by no means entirely parceled out among the kingdoms we have examined in earlier chapters.

Europe, one of the smallest of continents, had few hunters and gatherers outside of a handful of reindeer hunters in northern Scandinavia. It would have been hard to find agricultural villages that were not integrated one way or another into the European system of landed estates, urban markets, and national economies. But there were still migratory populations in Europe, sheepherders who made the rounds of southern Italy or moved back and forth between France and Spain. There were, above all, the nomads of eastern Europe's steppe frontier.

Nomadic herders of cattle and horses, sheep and goats had been drifting into Europe from central and East Asia for thousands of years. Indeed, the settled populations of the European nations—Greeks and Romans, Celts, Slavs, Germans—were Indo-European nomads who had come that way. The most recent waves, however, were mongoloid peoples such as the Golden Horde that had conquered Russia in the thirteenth century. For a time, Russia had been a khanate of the Mongol Empire, and the rest of eastern Europe, with the Ottoman Turks pressing up from the south, looked very much at risk.

The Mongols, at least, had ceased to be a serious threat by 1500. The Golden Horde was gone, and the mongoloid nomads who remained on the southern steppes of Russia were capable of destructive raids but no longer of permanent conquests. Europe's steppe frontier was in fact on its way to pacification and eventual absorption by the growing Russian state.

The Borderlands of Asia

Asia, the largest of all the continents, had also developed some of the largest civilized states. The Persian Empire at its height, India during its periods of unity, and above all China brought many millions of Asians within the purview of urban-imperial civilization. Smaller trading states had developed in southern India and Southeast Asia, and clones of the Chinese Empire in Korea, Vietnam, and elsewhere. But there were still large tracts of Asia in which the older ways of life survived.

There were hunting-and-fishing peoples in the islands of Southeast Asia and in northeastern Asia as well, from Kamchatka to the Bering Strait. There were villages of hunter-gatherers in the hills of India, animists still, living entirely outside the ancient Indian system of caste, cities, and major religions. Once more, however, the nomads of the Eurasian steppes were the most important remaining representatives of the preurban world.

China, India, and Persia, like Europe, had suffered repeatedly from nomadic invasions launched from the sparse grasslands and barren deserts north of their frontiers. Indo-European barbarians called Aryans had conquered India in ancient times. The Mongols had overwhelmed and ruled all China, as they had Russia, in more recent centuries. Huns and Hsiung-nu, Kushans, Turks, Tatars, and many others, they had been a clear and present danger for many centuries. And they were there still in 1500.

The whole vast sweep of northern Asia—the region constituting most of the Soviet Union today—was given over to pastoralism wherever the land would support it. Living north of the empires of southern Asia, subject only to their own transient confederations, these steppe nomads still loomed as a threat to the urban cultures of the warmer south. Even China, the world's largest urban-imperial state, was to undergo one more barbarian conquest.

Africa farther South

Africa south of the Sahara had its share of cities and kingdoms in 1500, as we have seen. The northern coasts had long since been integrated into the civilization of the Mediterranean, the east-coast ports into that of the Indian Ocean. Now the Sudanic empires and the kingdoms of the Guinea Coast, the Congo, and elsewhere were evolving rapidly. Most of the second-largest continent, however, was still occupied by hunter-gatherers, nomadic pastoralists, and unaffiliated village agriculturalists at the beginning of the modern period.

The Sahara, from the Atlantic across to the Red Sea, belonged to the bedouin and the camel. Cattle herders occupied much of the Sudanic belt, and many of them acknowledged none of the new kings who had risen among them. Cattle raisers also moved on the plains of East Africa, from the Nile almost to the Cape.

Agricultural villages unaffiliated with any of the new kingdoms were common in the rain forests of West and central Africa. Hoe culture and root crops were more likely to be the heart of their economy, rather than the plowed fields and grains that predominated in Eurasia. Hand cultivation could not support the population that plowed lands could, and so there were fewer cities in Africa. And the lack of cities meant a simpler style of life.

Simplest of all, of course, were the lives of Africa's hunter-gatherers, mostly Pygmies and Bushmen. These primordial peoples were still to be found in the forests of central Africa and on the dry southern sa-

vannas and the Kalahari Desert of southwest Africa. Grubbers in the arid earth or killers of elephants in the steaming rain forest, these peoples preserved humankind's oldest life style in its pristine state.

These preurban African majorities were organized into societies based on tribe, clan, and family, like preurban peoples in other parts of the world. Traditional sex roles and age groups with assigned responsibilities further structured the world of the villagers, the herders, and the hunters. A common language group and cultural pattern strengthened felt relationships between some villages, but had not yet crystallized into kingdoms or empires. Animists, tellers of tales, producers of some haunting "primitive" art, they lived by local taboos, worshiped local gods.

Big, however, is not necessarily beautiful, and there is no way at all to tell whether these small peoples of unorganized Africa were more or less happy than peasant farmers who paid taxes to the Yung-lo Emperor or to Queen Elizabeth.

Naked as Adam and Eve

Europeans, whe knew so little about the most impressive empires that had grown up around the world, knew next to nothing about these cultures of the marginal grasslands, the deserts, and the deep woods of the Old World. For knowledge they substituted legend and fantasy derived from dubious Roman sources and medieval travelers' tales. The geography of 1500 was mostly tall tales, pure and simple.

From these, Westerners learned that Finland—in northern Europe—was full of witches and monsters. They were informed that in Africa lived Cyclops, noble savages (called Ethiopians), dwarfs, sorcerers, and tribes of hairy women who had no mates. Asia had an even vaster array of wonderful peoples to offer— races of Amazons and noble philosophers (called brahmans), cannibals and the khan of Cathay and people whose heads did grow beneath their shoulders, their faces in their chests.

In the southern parts of the world, readers of this myth-history were assured, people often went naked as Adam and Eve because of the heat. But in the north, where it was very cold, there were people whose ears were so large that they wrapped them around themselves like a coat.

All these unlikely denizens of the far places of the earth were located on a map that showed only half of the globe as we know it today—the Old World half. But there was another world out there too, unknown to Europeans in 1500. And in this other hemisphere, the predominance of the older cultures over the urban-imperial mode was even greater. Needless to say, Europeans would soon be peopling these lands too with imaginary Amazons, anthropophagi, and exotic peoples "deformed against the kind . . . of man or of beast or of anything else. . . . "[1]

HERE BE CANNIBALS

The Rest of Latin America

In all of the Americas in 1500, there were only two great empires: the Aztec Empire in Middle America and that of the Incas running down the west coast of South America. Legend would fill both continents with El Dorados, but the facts were otherwise. All the rest of what would become Latin America belonged to isolated agricultural villages, hunter-gatherer peoples, and peoples who combined these sources of sustenance in varying proportions.

Agriculture predominated in Central America and the Caribbean islands and in the tropical forests of Brazil. On the Central American isthmus and in the Caribbean, maize—Indian corn—and manioc fed most people. In the isolated villages of the Amazon rain forests, manioc and other root crops, cultivated by hand, were the main means of subsistence.

Hunting and food gathering were common in eastern Brazil and down the long sweep of Argentina. Here the life style of the earliest humans flourished undiluted by cultivation of the soil or domestication of animals. People hunted game, fished the sea and the rivers, gathered nuts, berries, roots, and shellfish, as all their ancestors had done since the first mongoloid migrations from the north.

These Amerindian populations of Central and South America included some chiefdoms, hereditary rule without any of the other paraphernalia of an urban-imperial culture. But most were much more loosely organized socially. Most of these peoples apportioned responsibilities by age and sex and claimed ties by virtue of family and clan relationships and vaguer tribal affinities. Here as in Africa, common language and culture had not yet led to any more rigid political organization outside the empires discussed above.

A more rigid political order was coming, of course. The Portuguese came among them offering axes for brazilwood, and the Spanish in their iron shirts and

[1]Sir John Mandeville, *The Travels of Sir John Mandeville* (London: Macmillan, 1915), p. 32.

helmets pressed down the rivers looking for El Dorado.

Stone Age North America

North America in 1500 had no urban societies at all: the entire continent was given over to preurban forms of social organization. Metal was worked here and there, but mostly for articles of adornment rather than for tools. Hoes, axes, arrowheads, fishhooks, knives were all still made of stone or bone, the shafts of spears, bows, and other long tools out of wood. To all intents and purposes, it was a Stone Age world.

This is not to say that a monotonous sameness prevailed across the immensities of what are today two of the world's largest nations, the United States and Canada.

It looks simple enough on a map. Across the thickly wooded eastern two thirds of the United States and southern Canada, a modest village hoe-culture prevailed. Down the Pacific coast from Alaska to California and eastward across the great plains of the United States and northern Canada, hunting and fishing outweighed all other means of subsistence. Nowhere were true cities or organized kingdoms yet to be found.

Yet even in this preurban world, there was a considerable variety of cultural forms. The famous Pueblo Indian culture was rearing its multistory "apartment houses" against the red cliffs of the American Southwest—as close to towns as you can get without the marketplace and municipal institutions. In the East, the mound-building societies of the Mississippi culture were erecting their temple-mounds, trading over large sections of the country, and probably creating chiefdoms that combined a number of neighboring villages. Before the sixteenth century was over, the celebrated Iroquois Confederacy would link half a dozen great North American tribes by a "covenant chain" of agreements, a central council, and a central sacred fire in a political association that pushed deceptively close to true empire.

In differing degrees, this range of social forms prevailed all across the New World. Nevertheless, beyond Mesoamerica and the Andean highlands, the Americas were still entirely in the hands of preurban peoples.

Once more, these were not inferior peoples. The English settlers who first established Britain's claim to the New World, at Jamestown Island in Virginia in 1607, were helpless in the wilderness. Half of them died the first year, and the rest survived only on the charity of the Indians, who offered maize and fish

A stockaded Amerindian village in what became Virginia, as it looked to the English artist John White in the late sixteenth century. (New York Public Library)

and a little technological help for their future conquerors.

To the Antipodes

There is a romantic aura about some of these peoples of the jungles, grasslands, and the sea, at least when seen from a Western perspective. And nowhere did the Western imagination create a more romantic image for the preurban peoples of other parts of the globe than in the far Pacific.

Western people did not actually begin to penetrate Australia and the Pacific islands until rather well along in their unprecedented imperial expansion—not in any numbers until the eighteenth century. Before that, these unknown watery regions were spattered with hypothetical islands on the maps—islands often grimly labeled, like Asia and Africa on older maps, "Here Be Cannibals."

Oceania, comprising the continent of Australia and the scattered island groups of Melanesia, Micronesia, and Polynesia, was in fact the last refuge of European dreamers as recently as the present century. Who indeed has not dreamed of a South Sea island in the sun? Books, films, travel posters spread the image to this day.

There was in fact some truth to both these mythic images of the South Seas. There were certainly many islands in the sun. And there were some cannibals too.

The great migrations that peopled the islands of the South Pacific were over well before 1500. Many of the small atolls—ring-shaped islands surrounding a central lagoon—were inhabited by then. So were most of the mountainous, tropically forested volcanic islands, such as Tahiti and Hawaii. From New Guinea and New Zealand to Hawaii and Easter Island, millions of square miles of ocean had been occupied and settled by preurban peoples centuries before the Europeans came.

The people of the islands lived by fishing and by cultivating root crops and tree crops, especially the ubiquitous coconut. Though their great migrations were over, they were still famous seafarers, the "Vikings of the Pacific." Their long double canoes could navigate hundreds of miles of ocean between one island group and another to exchange goods, either as gifts or on a commercial basis. There were hereditary chiefdoms on some of the islands, and even tributary relationships that, once more, verged on more complex political structures.

And on the continent of Australia, some of the least developed of human societies flourished, apparently quite happily, as they had for thirty thousand years.

The australoid Aborigines were Old Stone Age hunters and gatherers, like many Indians of North America, in 1500. Theirs was the oldest of preurban cultures—the migratory life of people who lived off game and fish, fruits, roots, and nuts in their seasons—and the entire continent was given over to it. They had no higher form of social organization than the hunting band of two or three dozen, no arts more complex than body paint, no theologies more elaborate than the myths and legends of the Dream Time before history began. They had no villages, no houses, no clothes.

Yet the Aborigines had already survived in this minimalist mode for something like six times as long as the oldest of urban-imperial societies. Some of them still live that way today, literally and quite cheerfully hand to mouth.

There was a darker side to the preurban paradise of Oceania on the eve of European conquest, of course. Australian Aborigines and Polynesian islanders both fought wars as bloody—in proportion to their numbers—as those of more developed societies. And there was ritual cannibalism in some of these islands in the sun.

Three-Quarters of the Earth

Europeans had learned from Arab legend that the equator was a "burning line"—so hot that the sea boiled, ship's tar melted, and sails and rigging caught fire under the blazing sun. Green weed would foul your hull there, and crocodiles as big as whales rolled in the waves, waiting to devour you. The burning line was one of many barriers, like the ice of the polar north or the unmeasured expanse of the Ocean Sea itself, that penned Western people into their narrow end of Eurasia.

In 1500, Europeans were just embarking upon an unparalleled expansion, a drive toward all horizons that would breach all barriers, real or imagined. From the poles to the burning line, the whole earth suddenly lay open to them.

Three-quarters of the land surface of that earth was populated by animists, makers of stone tools, societies based on family, clan, and scattered chiefdoms. When the grim-faced men with iron helmets and firearms, sailing ships and military discipline came among such peoples, they would have little chance.

Isolation, tropical diseases, or the sheer fact that they had little that the Westerners wanted would protect them for a long time. They would fight for the lands they inhabited, however thinly. And an Apache or a Zulu could easily be the equal of a conquistador or a redcoat, man for man. But the society of the hunter, the herder, the village tiller of a meager earth was not equal in strength to the society of the invader.

Three quarters of the earth belonged to the preurban peoples in 1500. Almost none of it belongs to them today.

SUMMARY

Most of the population of the earth had been brought under centralized government and integrated, however loosely, into the urban-imperial culture by 1500. Geographically speaking, however, most of the planet was still inhabited by practitioners of earlier forms of social organization. Agricultural villagers, pastoral nomads, and hunting-and-gathering peoples were still thinly scattered over all of Australia and North Amer-

ica, most of Latin America and Africa, and parts of Asia and Europe as well.

In the Old World, Europe still had its pastoral herders who moved with the seasons, as well as a broad steppe frontier to the east. All of northern Asia was inhabited by such pastoral nomads, and there were pockets of hunter-gatherers here and there as well. In

Africa, desert bedouins survived on the inhospitable Sahara, nomadic cattle-herders were common in East Africa, and Pygmy and Bushman hunter-gatherers were still to be found in rain forests and in the far south. In addition, many African agricultural villages still remained free of higher governmental jurisdiction.

In the New World, Latin America's two urban-imperial cultures alone represented the more complex social forms. Preurban agricultural villages were common in Central America and the Caribbean, in western Brazil, and in the eastern United States and Canada. Hunting, fishing, and the seasonal gathering of vegetable foods fed the populations of northern and western North America, of eastern Brazil, and the Argentine stem of South America.

In Oceania, finally, the peoples of the islands and the isolated continent of Australia did without cities and empires entirely. Islanders farmed and fished, Australian aborigines hunted and gathered as their ancestors had done.

These hunters, herders, village farmers—historically looked down on by peoples who had built cities and empires—had nevertheless survived for five thousand years, since the first cities rose in Mesopotamia. In the centuries after 1500, however, these older cultures would be largely absorbed or destroyed by the most successful of all urban-imperial cultures, that of the imperialistic West.

SUGGESTED READING

BERNAL, I. *Mexico before Cortez: Art, History, Legend.* Garden City, N.Y.: Doubleday, 1963. Amerindians of the Valley of Mexico; illustrated.

BERNDT, R. M., and C. H. BERNDT. *The World of the First Australians: An Introduction to the Traditional Life of the Australian Aborigines.* Chicago: University of Chicago Press, 1964. A good study of this much studied preurban—and preagricultural—people of the Australian outback.

COON, C. S. *Caravan: The Story of the Middle East,* rev. ed. New York: Holt, Rinehart & Winston, 1961. Ecological frame and cultural forms of pastoral societies from North Africa to Pakistan.

DENEVAN, W. M., ed. *The Native Population of the Americas in 1492.* Madison: University of Wisconsin Press, 1976. Balanced estimate of Native American populations.

DOCKSTADER, F. J. *Indian Art in America: The Arts and Crafts of the North American Indian,* 3rd ed. Greenwich, Conn.: New York Graphic Society, 1966. Useful introduction to the rich variety of Amerindian art in the northern continent.

DRIVER, H. E., ed. *The Americas on the Eve of Discovery.* Englewood Cliffs, N.J.: Prentice-Hall, 1964. Useful collection of readings on pre-Columbian North and South America.

—— *Indians of North America,* 2nd ed. Chicago: University of Chicago Press, 1969. Topical survey of all aspects of Native American culture, from horticulture and crafts to marriage and religion.

ELKIN, A. P. *The Australian Aborigines,* 3rd ed. Garden City, N.Y.: Anchor, 1964. An older but still solid account.

FAGE, J. D., and R. OLIVER, eds. *Cambridge History of Africa: Vol. III, 1050–1600.* New York: Cambridge University Press, 1975. Includes preurban populations as well as the African empires, kingdoms, and city-states.

HALLET, R. *Africa to 1875: A Modern History.* Ann Arbor: University of Michigan Press, 1970. Excellent general history, with coverage of this period.

KRADER, L. *Social Organization of the Mongol-Turkic Pastoral Nomads.* The Hague: Mouton, 1963. Historic Mongols and other steppe-dwelling nomads are discussed.

OLIVER, R. A. *The African Middle Ages: 1400–1800.* New York: Cambridge University Press, 1981. Regional organization; by a leading authority.

STEWARD, J. H., ed. *Handbook of South American Indians* (7 vols.). Washington, D.C.: Bureau of American Ethnology, 1946–1959. A standard source.

—— *Theory of Culture Change.* Urbana: University of Illinois Press, 1955. Old but standard formulation of the theory of local evolution of culture, requiring no influences from more "developed" cultures to bring about change. Applied here to Latin America, but also applicable to many societies outside Eurasia.

WAUCHOPE, R., ed. *Handbook of Middle American Indians* (15 vols.). Austin: University of Texas Press, 1964–1975. Authoritative.

Overview II

The World of Intercontinental Empires

The world had seen empires before, but never empires like these.

Empire building goes back to the dawn age of human civilization. The city-states of ancient Mesopotamia spawned several empires large enough to encompass the entire Tigris-Euphrates valley, and Egypt for a time extended its power around the southeastern corner of the Mediterranean. During the classic age that followed, empires established in Roman Europe, the Persian Middle East, northern India, and Han China linked all Eurasia commercially. Later periods saw the emergence of other empires across Eurasia, as well as in parts of Africa, Middle America, and South America. Empire building has thus been a basic pattern of territorial organization from the beginning.

During the centuries immediately preceding the great age of European conquests, there were two particularly astounding waves of interregional empire building in the Old World. The expansion of Islam, beginning in the seventh century, created a loose religious and cultural hegemony that stretched from Spain to Southeast Asia and reached well down into Africa as well. And the amazing conquests of the Mongols in the thirteenth century absorbed most of Eurasia, from Russia to China, into a single vast empire, the largest the world had ever seen.

The Mongols had fallen away by 1492. Islam, though still expanding, had long since fragmented into a number of feuding nations no more politically united than Christian Europe. But a third great surge of interregional empire building began just before 1500—the rise of the West.

Western imperialism would be similar to earlier waves of imperial outreach in the past in some fundamental ways. Like earlier empire builders, Europeans frequently employed military force to impose their will upon other peoples. Like earlier empires, Europe's imperial predominance also commonly took on a political form, converting formerly independent peoples into colonies ruled by Europeans. As in the past, Western political and military power led to economic exploitation, ranging from favorable trade agreements to the massive extraction of natural resources, exploitation of cheap local labor, and large-scale investment—all of greater benefit to Westerners than to indigenous populations. As had frequently happened in the past, finally, military, political, and economic hegemony led to a growing intellectual and social influence by Western society on non-Western societies, a process frequently described as "cultural imperialism."

All these features of Western imperial expansion would have been familiar enough to anyone aware of Persian, Roman, Indian, Chinese, Islamic, West African, Peruvian, Mexican, and many other forms of imperialism. But there were unique elements in this new wave as well.

One essential feature was the medium upon which Western imperialism depended from the beginning: sea power, and the resulting mastery of the world's oceans.

This led in turn to a second distinguishing characteristic: the intercontinental reach of the new European empires. By bridging the oceans, European empires brought continents and peoples thousands of miles apart under common Western rule.

A third crucial feature, manifested especially during the last century of European predominance, was the global impact of Europe's Industrial Revolution, ideological development, and social evolution. All of these combined to transform the life ways and world views of non-Western peoples as well.

The greatest consequence of Western imperialism, finally, may have been to trigger a genuinely global interaction for the first time in human history. The European intercontinental empires, by bringing all the peoples of the world into much closer contact than ever before, fostered an increasing amount of mutual interaction—cultural, economic, demographic, even ecological—including as much influence of the conquered on the conquerors as the other way around.

The next few chapters, then, will deal with the history of the world in the age of European intercontinental empires—roughly the four hundred years from the sixteenth through the nineteenth centuries. European imperialism is only one of the main strands of modern global history, yet it runs like the proverbial scarlet thread through the history of these centuries, affecting all the other strands.

European global expansion began around 1500 with the Spanish *conquista* of South and Central America and the Portuguese commercial penetration of Brazil, the coasts of Africa, India, and points farther east. The great conquest continued after 1600 when the North Atlantic powers—Britain, France, and the Netherlands—began to carve out overseas empires for themselves, especially in North America and the Caribbean, in India and Southeast Asia. After 1700 came a series of significant imperial adjustments, including the ebbing of Dutch imperial vigor and a duel between Britain and France that ended in the 1760s with Britain's emergence as the greatest of global empire builders.

The nineteenth century, finally, climaxed with the New Imperialism that began around 1870. In a few decades thereafter, European empire builders, making use of the new technology of the Industrial Revolution, reduced almost all of Africa to colonial status and transformed much of Asia into protectorates or spheres of influence. By 1900, the Western hegemony of the world was essentially complete.

For most of this period, however, there was another history besides that made by European soldiers, traders, missionaries, and proconsuls of empire. The great conquest is the unifying factor, but it was by no means the whole story of the four centuries between 1500 and 1900.

In the Far East, China was conquered by the Manchus and the last of the Chinese dynasties was established in Peking during the seventeenth century. During the 1600s also, feudal Japan fell under the centralizing Tokugawa shoguns, who dominated her history until the nineteenth century. Much of Asian history, however, especially during the latter part of this period, is a story of decline, withdrawal, and turning inward. Tokugawa, Manchu, Mogul, and Ottoman emperors were soon past their first vigor, no match for the Western onslaught.

In the Americas and in Australia, conquered and colonized by Europeans, these centuries saw a double transformation. These three continents evolved politically from dependencies of European imperial powers into a number of independent nations. But they were nations ruled and increasingly populated by Western peoples, and the resulting process of Westernization continued apace after political independence. By the end of the nineteenth century, then, Australia and both the Americas had been dramatically transformed along essentially Western lines.

Europe itself, finally, underwent remarkable changes during the seventeenth, eighteenth, and nineteenth centuries. The powers of the royal rulers of European nation-states grew during the age of absolutism that began in the 1600s. The wealth of the European economies increased amazingly, particularly with the coming of the Industrial Revolution in the later 1700s. New ideas spread through the West in these centuries, particularly the ideas of the Scientific Revolution and the social and political views of the Enlightenment. During the 1700s and the 1800s, science contributed fundamentally to the industrial development of Europe, while the ideologies spawned by the Enlightenment led to an astounding series of political revolutions across the Western world. By 1900, then, technological advance, democratic institutions, social reform, and nationalistic foreign policies had swept Europe to the brink of what is in many ways the most astonishing of centuries—our own.

The age of intercontinental empires was therefore a time of great changes in the global picture. It saw the rise to genuinely worldwide predominance of one of the world's major cultures, an event unprecedented in history. It saw the decay of great empires, the transformation of whole continents. It saw the establishment and spread of radical new ideas and the creation of a technological capacity unparalleled in human experience.

Granted, many peoples—in the interiors of Africa, central Asia, and South America, for instance—remained unaffected and even unaware of these phenomenal changes. But in the century that began in 1900, they too would feel the impact of the new conditions for world history that had been laid down in the earlier modern centuries. By that time, too, the greatest change of all was clearly discernible, even in its earlier stages: the birth of a genuinely global community, a world order that reached far beyond Western hegemony and pointed toward even more astonishing changes still to come.

Chapter · 7

THE GREAT CONQUEST BEGINS

THE FAR PLACES OF THE EARTH

Ships

There was an explosion of white foam under a ship's bow, a scream of gulls overhead, and the gliding shadow of a great fish beneath a sliding wave. Above all, there would be the buffeting of the wind about Chinese, Arab, European cheeks, about bare brown Polynesian shoulders or the frozen beards of Vikings. The sea and sea creatures, the push of the wind, and the voyagers who roamed the oceans of the world are all essential elements to the now half-forgotten romance of the sea. But the key to this daring chapter in the long human venture is the ship itself, and to ships we must turn as we begin the story of the farthest voyagers of all.

Boats of papyrus and balsa wood, triremes and double canoes, Venetian galleys, Viking dragon ships, Arab dhows, and Chinese junks have all carried human beings to violent adventure, dazzling wealth, or the loneliest of deaths on the vast blue reach that covers most of the surface of the globe. We who have so easily conquered the air in a single century must make an effort of the imagination to empathize with those of our ancestors who at such cost learned to ride freely on the waters.

Europeans were not the first to venture out upon the oceans of the world. But between the fifteenth and the nineteenth centuries Western humankind mastered the seas as no other peoples had. And by mastering the sea, they opened a watery road to the conquest of all the mainlands and islands of the earth.

The European sailing ships of Columbus's time were not the largest vessels in the world. Any of the huge seagoing junks that China's Yung-lo Emperor sent east across the Indian Ocean could have carried all the crews of the four ships of Vasco da Gama that crossed the Indian Ocean the other way sixty-five years later. But the Portuguese caravels of the years around 1500—and the Spanish galleons of the later sixteenth century—had advantages that no other vessels could match. And in the seventeenth century, Europeans began to build huge trading vessels themselves. These "East Indiamen," intended for the round trip to the Far East, could carry 1600 tons of cargo and as many as a thousand passengers and crew.

It was not size, however, that primarily distinguished Western ships of the age of sail. A major innovation was a new combination of the sails themselves. This mix of medieval European square sails and Arab lateen (triangular) ones made it possible for Europeans to develop unprecedented skill at tacking—sailing across or even into the wind. European ships thus became the most maneuverable of sailing vessels, ideally suited for exploring—or for fighting.

European vessels also employed an impressive array of navigational aids for their time. Some of these devices were borrowed, like the magnetic compass, developed first by the Chinese. Some were ancient instruments, like the astrolabe, used for measuring the altitude of the sun above the horizon, and hence the ship's latitude north or south of the equator. There were sand glasses for measuring time, sounding leads for assessing the depth of the water, and the original "log"—a piece of wood flung over the stern at the end of a knotted cord—for estimating speed at sea, and hence longitude east or west.

Improvements in map making also gave Europeans an advantage. Many of the detailed coastal charts drawn by explorers and traders were extremely accurate. The technique of the Mercator projection made it possible to represent the curved surface of the earth on a flat map—a valuable aid for a people embarking on what became a global venture. By the end of the sixteenth century, only a hundred years into the great conquest, Europeans had charted the coasts of all the continents except Australia, which was added more slowly over the next two centuries.

To excellent ships and unexcelled navigational equipment, finally, Western overseas venturers added a range of weaponry that gave them a powerful advantage wherever they went. The cannon and firearms of European infantry—harquebuses, muskets, and larger powder-and-shot weapons, gave Western soldiers the edge over even the best non-Western troops not so equipped. Above all, the broad spectrum of artillery mounted on European ships made them likely victors in any naval conflict. With rows of cannon lining gun decks and firing in unison to produce devastating broadsides, the ships of European countries soon became the acknowledged rulers of the waves.

It was with these ships that the European empire builders advanced against the world. During the centuries of the so-called Old Imperialism—from the later 1400s to the later 1700s—they imposed their will

Vasco da Gama's flagship, the Sao Gabriel, led the little fleet that carried the first Europeans to India by sea in 1498. Western vessels like this, with their combination of square and lateen sails, their artillery and increasingly sophisticated navigational equipment, would soon be seen on all the oceans of the world. (New York Public Library Picture Collection)

on peoples of distant continents in an unprecedented manner.

God, Gold, and Glory

The means for this first stage of the great conquest were thus clearly there by the time Columbus began to importune Queen Isabella to invest in an attempt to reach the East by sailing west. The motives also had developed among these restless, aggressive peoples of Eurasia's western fringe. Columbus's own dreams embodied most of them.

Wealth was certainly the primary motive for many, as it was one of Columbus's great bargaining points with the king and queen of Spain. Gold and silver, silks and spices, and later the valuable products that could be grown (like sugar) or caught (like furs or fish) in foreign parts all drew the makers of the Old Imperialism to far places.

And they made money too. Columbus may have died a disillusioned man, but the silver and gold that Spain extracted from the Americas over the next century made her Europe's richest and most powerful nation. Vasco da Gama brought home spices enough from India to pay for his long voyage many times over. Many a Dutch or English fortune was founded on a timely investment in the East India Company of Holland or Britain.

Gold was clearly a prime cause of the Old Imperialism. But God also inspired many of these world conquerors. Christopher Columbus himself, after all, claimed that he—like Saint Christopher—was carrying the Light of the World across the water.

The Iberian nations were old Crusaders; Ferdinand and Isabella had in fact just expelled the last of the Moors from Spain when the great overseas conquest began. The sixteenth century was also the century of the Protestant Reformation and the Catholic Counter-Reformation. It was a religiously charged time that saw Jesuits set out to save souls in China and South America as well as in Protestant lands. Seventeenth-century English Puritans and Dutch Protestants were heavy investors in overseas expansion, and their objectives also included the spread of Christianity as well as the extraction of profits from the heathen.

Gold, God, and, dubious as it may seem, glory stand as the three main causes of European empire building in the early centuries. The glory sought was the sort of public adulation and eternal fame that champions of European chivalry had fought and died for on European battlefields for centuries. The conquistadores of all Western nations were soldiers of a society where soldiering was the most respected of professions, honor the greatest virtue. They wanted crowds to cheer them, crowned heads to honor them with knighthoods and titles, poets and historians to immortalize them. For such insubstantial honors, men such as Hernando Cortes and Sir Walter Raleigh would risk their lives—and sometimes get their hearts' desires.

Money and what it would buy, converts for the Christian God, and a meed of glory to warm a soldier's heart—these were the taut springs that drove the men who manned the remarkable ships of the Western world.

All of these motives, in one form or another, could be found among others of the world's peoples. But in Europe there was a competitive diversity of peoples that perhaps stimulated these passions beyond the normal. There was a freedom for merchant investors, filibustering soldiers, missionary orders, and ambitious princes that was not so common in the centralized empires of the East. Even the most autocratic European rulers, such as the kings of Spain or France's Louis XIV, allowed much of the exploring, trading, and conquering overseas to be done by ambitious private citizens, thereby multiplying the impact by the number of competitors.

China's vast armadas of Precious Ships were an imperial venture and could be stopped forever by a memorial from the Son of Heaven. It is hard to imagine any force powerful enough to restrain the motley hordes of Western conquerors, lusting after golden idols and cargoes of spices, converts beyond the burning line, and immortal glory when they sailed home again.

The Farthest Voyagers

The beginning of this great conquest is sometimes called the Age of Discovery. Literally, of course, it was nothing of the sort. Europeans were not scaling Mount Everest, reaching the North Pole, or otherwise going where no human ever had before. Most of the lands they reached were thoroughly inhabited, possessing ancient cultures of their own. But these voyagers did run risks, suffer hardships, and accomplish feats of seamanship and exploration deserving all the honor that posterity has heaped upon them. Storm-swept or becalmed, wracked by hunger and thirst, scurvy and malaria, beset by foreign foes, rival merchants, and the priesthoods of other peoples' faiths, they plunged with desperate courage into perils few of us can clearly imagine.

Many of these men were also brutal, treacherous, blind with greed and prejudice. They were, after all, the aggressors, the invaders, and as savage as intruders into other peoples' lands have always been. But savagery and treachery, avarice and prejudice have never been rare on this earth. The courage, ingenuity, and accomplishment of these travelers of distant seas have been in rather shorter supply.

With both sides of the picture clearly in mind, then, let us proceed to a brief overview of some of the more famous voyages and conquests of the three centuries between 1492 and 1776—the centuries of the Old Imperialism.

The Portuguese were the pioneers, pushing methodically down the coast of Africa until Vasco da Gama's epochal voyage of 1497–1499 from Lisbon around the Cape of Good Hope and on to the Malabar Coast of India and back. Thereafter, Portuguese and later Dutch merchants thrust still farther east, through Southeast Asia and around to South China. Portugal thus became the first European nation to push her way into the East, shoulder Arab traders aside, and establish a Western trading empire in Asia.

The Spanish were later into the game, though Christopher Columbus sailed five years before da Gama's climactic Portuguese voyage. Columbus sailed four times to Middle America and the Caribbean and died probably believing he too had reached the East, though Spain had little profit to show for it. But he blazed a trail that more martial Spanish captains followed. Vasco de Balboa crossed the Isthmus of Panama and looked on the Pacific in 1513. In the years 1519–1521, Ferdinand Magellan, sailing under the Spanish flag, commanded an expedition that crossed the Atlantic, the Pacific, and the Indian oceans, circumnavigating the globe for the first time in human history.

Hernando Cortes discovered and conquered Aztec Mexico in the 1520s and Francisco Pizarro did the same to Inca Peru in the 1530s. The Portuguese Cabral had stumbled upon the eastward bulge of Brazil in 1500 and claimed this vast region for his king. But the rest of the continent was circumnavigated, crisscrossed, and claimed by Spanish conquistadores during the sixteenth century. The Amazon was traced from its Andean headwaters to its Atlantic mouth, and in the far south Cape Horn was rounded. Spanish missionaries and explorers traversed the deserts of the southwestern United States and worked their way up the California coast. Spain's huge settlement empire in the Americas thus came to encompass much of South and Central America, the Caribbean, and part of the northern continent as well.

Most of North America, however, was explored by French and English seekers, mostly after 1600. The French settled thinly across eastern Canada and probed down the Mississippi to its mouth. The British settled thirteen colonies down the east coast, from New England and New York to Virginia, the Carolinas, and Georgia. The French, the English, and the

Dutch as well soon established profitable sugar colonies in the Caribbean. The Dutch were also for a time established in eastern North America, from Hudson's Bay in Canada down to New Amsterdam—New York after the British came.

But it was the British and the French who dominated eastern North America and profited most from the West Indies. It was they who, in the middle 1700s, dueled for mastery of the area. And it was English-speaking people who, during the 1800s, would complete the exploration and conquest of the North American continent.

Australia alone remained, its first postaboriginal discoverers lost in the uncertainties of late-medieval and early-modern history. Chinese voyagers may have touched its shores several hundred years before the first European could have. But its northern and western coasts were charted by Dutch mariners in the seventeenth century, and the famous captain James Cook explored its eastern margins in the eighteenth. Cook and the gallant French explorer Antoine de Bougainville also explored many of the island groups of Oceania, including such paradises as Tahiti and Hawaii.

During the seventeenth and eighteenth centuries also, the three northern European powers had followed the Iberians into Asia. The British and the French replaced the Portuguese as the chief traders in India, and began to interfere in the politics of the Moguls. The Dutch became the paramount European power in the Southeast Asian trade. All three powers had begun to jostle impatiently for more of the South China trade by the end of the eighteenth century.

They were everywhere. Their dead-pale, sweaty faces showed at the courts of East Asian emperors and the *maharajas* of India, around the smoky campfires of Indian *sachems* along the Mississippi, and at the dark slave pens of West Africa. Their little vessels were dwarfed by the great rivers—the Congo, the Amazon, the Mississippi, and the Ganges—and all but vanished in the vastness of the three oceans. Their numbers were swallowed up in the teeming cities of Asia or lost in the barren deserts, deep woods, or triple-canopy rain forests of Africa, Australia, and the Americas. But they were everywhere nonetheless. And they would not go home.

EMPIRES BEYOND THE SEAS

Three Centuries of Conquest

It was the crash of their great guns that a startled world most vividly remembered. The Chinese had developed gunpowder weapons long before the Euro-

peans did. In 1453, the Ottoman Turks mounted the largest cannon in the world against the walls of Constantinople. But Western gunnery had distanced that of all other peoples by 1500, and Western ships were thereafter converted into floating gun platforms lined with huge "ship-killing" artillery. "They have guns with a noise like thunder," a Ceylonese source wrote of the first Portuguese to come that way, "and a ball from one of them, after traversing a league, will break a castle of marble."[1]

Explorers, missionaries, merchants, soldiers all played important parts in the establishment of the European predominance. But the final arbiter was always military force.

The first three hundred years of the conquest that resulted, from the end of the fifteenth century through most of the eighteenth, will be outlined in the sections that follow. The climactic phase of Western imperialism—the nineteenth century—will be dealt with in a later chapter.

Century by century, the pattern was something like this. The sixteenth century was the age of Iberian overseas expansion. During this period, the Portuguese set up a primarily commercial empire in the East that encompassed trading posts in Africa, India, and Southeast Asia, an outpost in South China, and a huge territory in Brazil. Spanish power established an even vaster settlement empire in the West, centering in Middle and South America and the Caribbean and extending into North America and across the Pacific to the Philippines.

The seventeenth century was the century of the interlopers, the age in which the North Atlantic powers challenged the monopoly of intercontinental empire enjoyed by the Iberian nations. This was the golden age of the Netherlands, when Dutch traders drove into the Far East, South Africa, and North America. France in the age of Louis XIV established an elaborate edifice of colonies, commercial relations, and mercantilist policies especially in Canada, the Caribbean, and India. The British staked their claims to colonies in what would become the eastern United States, and in the Caribbean and India also.

There were thus five European powers with holdings on four other continents and many islands by the end of the seventeenth century. In the eighteenth there came a settling out, and a global duel for imperial supremacy. The Dutch gave ground, as the Spanish and Portuguese had before them. And the British shouldered the French aside to emerge as the greatest of European empire builders.

Let us look now in a little more detail at the in-

[1]C. M. Cipolla, *Guns, Sails and Empires: Technological Innovation and the Early Phases of European Expansion, 1400–1700* (New York: Pantheon Books, 1966), p. 107.

yepolinhã mexica

The last Aztec ruler surrenders to Cortes in 1521. If trade was the object of European penetration of the Far East, in the New World, the pattern was one of military conquest pure and simple. The Aztecs, a warlike people themselves, met their match in the conquistadores from Spain. (New York Public Library)

tercontinental empires established by each of the European imperial powers in these centuries, and at the struggle for empire that climaxed the period of the Old Imperialism.

Portugal! Portugal!

When Vasco da Gama reached Calicut on the Malabar Coast of India in 1498, the Arab merchants who were already established there sneered at the goods he laid out for sale. "They spat on the ground," he reported, "saying, 'Portugal, Portugal!'"[2] It was war from the beginning between the Portuguese invaders and the Arabs who had dominated the trade of the Indian Ocean for centuries. The architect of Portuguese victory, and of the Portuguese commercial empire that resulted, was one of the greatest of the European empire builders, Affonso de Albuquerque.

Albuquerque, governor-general of the Portuguese Indies in the early sixteenth century, seems to have

[2]E. G. Ravenstein, ed., *A Journal of the First Voyage of Vasco da Gama* (London: Hakluyt Society, 1898), p. 68.

been a man with an intuitive understanding of the proper deployment and use of sea power to seize and defend key points in Portugal's monopoly of Eastern trade. Instead of basing his operation in far-off Lisbon, Albuquerque captured the wealthy and readily defended island city of Goa off India's west coast to serve as his headquarters. He established a series of lesser bases down the western side of India and others on islands at the entrances to the Red Sea and the Persian Gulf. With Portugal's bases in East Africa, what had once been the Arabian Sea thus became a Portuguese lake.

At the same time, Albuquerque pushed on into Southeast and even East Asia. He seized the rich Southeast Asian commercial center of Malacca on the strait between Malaya and Sumatra through which all Asian trade had to pass. And he dispatched other Portuguese vessels north and still further east to set up a trading port at Macao in South China, just downriver from the great Chinese entrepôt of Canton.

Portugal thus bestrode crucial waterways and coastlines from East Africa to South China. The profits in silks and spices that had once gone to Arab middlemen now lined the purses of Portuguese merchants. And the little medieval kingdom of Portugal stood taller than ever before in the affairs of Europe.

The Portuguese crown defended this monopoly with savage rigor. European vessels that dared intrude were sunk, their crews thrown into the sea. Muslim spice ships—and sometimes Muslim pilgrim ships bound for Mecca—shared a similar fate. Arab dhows were gutted to the waterline, Arab traders swallowed up by the sea that had once been theirs—brutal evidence of a policy of frightfulness unsurpassed by any Mongol horde or Aryan conqueror of the past.

For a time, at least, it worked. In the later sixteenth century, however, the Portuguese monopoly crumbled. Portugal's failure to establish close ties with local *rajas* and her increasingly rigorous policy of religious repression in Goa and elsewhere weakened her position. The smallness of Portugal itself and the comparatively few people Lisbon could put into the Far East further limited Portuguese strength. When the North Atlantic powers—the Dutch, French, and English—burst onto the eastern seas in force around 1600, Portuguese power dwindled rapidly.

New Spain

The conquistadores of Spain followed a different path to a very different empire. These military adventurers first occupied the Caribbean islands, including the large central island of Cuba. They then probed westward to the mainland of Mexico, south to Peru and beyond, and north to the American Southwest, the Gulf Coast, and Florida. Both the conquest and the organization of Spanish America were models of the vigor—and the cruelty—of the great conquest.

The conquest of Aztec Mexico in the 1520s by Cortes and a few hundred ambitious, out-at-elbows swordsmen is one of the bloodiest epics of the *conquista*. Cortes burned his ships behind him, followed the rumors of a great city on a lake in a high valley beyond the coastal jungles—and found his El Dorado. The Spanish first occupied Tenochtitlán as Emperor Moctezuma's guests. When they converted him into a puppet ruler, the Aztecs revolted and drove them from the city, killing a third of their number in one terrible night. Reinforced at the coast, and supported by a number of other Amerindian peoples who had suffered under the Aztecs, Cortes returned to Tenochtitlán, captured it, and destroyed it. Aztec power was broken; Spanish rule soon replaced it.

Francisco Pizarro's seizure of the still larger Inca Empire in Peru was an even more unlikely—and equally brutal—feat of arms. Pizarro followed his rumors to Peru with less than two hundred men. But the Inca Empire was just emerging from a bloody civil war, and the Spanish capture of the Inca Atahualpa himself further demoralized the ruling elite. The story of that ambush in the village square at Cajamarca, and of the subsequent ransoming and murder of Atahualpa, is another of the gory romantic legends of the New World conquest.

The Europeans had profited from the fact that the realms of the Aztecs and the Incas were both conquest empires that had earned the resentment of their subject peoples. The Europeans, however, wreaked far greater havoc among the Amerindians than any native conquest ever had. Spain had conquered the most heavily populated areas in the Americas. But Western weapons, forced labor in fields and mines, unfamiliar diseases to which the Indians had no immunities, and plain cruelty reduced the population drastically. It was, in fact, to replace declining Indian labor forces—and to prevent further decimation of their numbers—that African labor began to be imported soon after the conquest.

Few of the conquistadores enjoyed the fruits of their victories for long. Balboa was executed for treason. Pizarro was killed in a power struggle with his own lieutenants. Cortes was called back to Spain, heaped with honors—and firmly deprived of his New World kingdom.

Instead, Spanish lawyers and bureaucrats were sent out to govern the new Spanish Empire in the king's name. The aging conquistadores grudgingly settled down to raise cattle and run gold or silver mines with Indian slave labor. Their descendants would run plantations worked by black slaves from Africa. But the colonial cities that grew up on the ruins of Tenochtitlán and Cuzco were dominated by the new imperial bureaucracy, the paper-shuffling administrators of New Spain (Mexico), New Granada (Peru), and the other divisions and subdivisions of the huge Spanish settlement empire in the Americas.

The Dutch Golden Age

The sixteenth century belonged to the empire builders of Spain and Portugal. The most successful European overseas empire of the seventeenth century, however, was that of the Netherlands. In some ways, indeed, the Dutch seaborne commercial empire was the most efficient of all those established during the period of the Old Imperialism.

The architects and operators of the Dutch Empire

were not soldiers like Cortes and Pizarro, or even royal administrators like Albuquerque. They were the solid, stolid Dutch burghers who stare unsmilingly out of their Rembrandt portraits at us. A dull and unromantic lot, one might think—certainly not given to burning their ships behind them or following rumors of El Dorado. But in the seventeenth century, the Dutch East and West India companies dominated trade with the Far East and siphoned off much of the commercial profit from other European colonies in the New World as well.

The Dutch brought to their far-flung trading empire centuries of business experience, manufacturing skills, and accumulated capital. Their ships and their seamanship were acknowledged to be the best. Their trade goods were carefully selected to suit their customers—sultans and *rajas* in Asia, European colonists in the Americas. At need, they could be as ruthless and unscrupulous as any in the great imperialist venture. For a hundred years, they profited exceedingly in the global marketplace that they themselves did so much to create.

The Dutch East India Company shouldered its way into the Spice Islands of Southeast Asia around 1600, expelling first the Portuguese and then the fledgling British East India Company. They paid much more attention than the Portuguese had to the local sultans, giving them the goods they wanted, signing treaties with them, avoiding both rank piracy and religious persecution. From the company's capital at Batavia in Java, they soon controlled not only the European spice trade but much of the profitable regional commerce of Southeast Asia as well.

The Dutch West India Company, meanwhile, set up its trading posts in the Caribbean and in North America, especially along the Hudson River in what would be New York State. Settlers from French, English, and Spanish colonies often preferred trading illegally with the Dutch at New Amsterdam—later New York City—or Curaçao to dealing with their own more expensive and less efficient compatriots.

For a golden century, hardheaded Dutch merchants handled most of Europe's imperial carrying trade, coasted Australia, settled in South Africa, and took their profits home to build tall houses in Amsterdam and commission Rembrandt or Vermeer to paint their pictures. Then sheer lack of numbers caught up with them, as it had with the Portuguese. Exhausting foreign wars further weakened them. The British expelled them from North America in the later seventeenth century. Dutch predominance survived in the East Indies, but the center of European imperial activity in Asia shifted to the richer pickings of India, where England and France were the prime contenders.

The Organizing Mind of Colbert

The French were the great organizers of empire. The foremost European exemplars of royal absolutism in politics and mercantilism—government regulation—in economics, seventeenth-century France also took the lead in royal supervision of colonies overseas. It was, as will be evident, a mixed blessing.

In the earlier seventeenth century, French overseas adventures were largely undertaken by daring individuals or by groups outside royal control. Like Spanish conquistadores or Dutch merchants, French fur traders and Jesuit missionaries in Canada, French plantation owners in the West Indies, and French East India Company traders in India had to depend on their own resources and work closely with indigenous peoples. Jesuits, trappers, and traders in the Great Lakes region of North America were better than any other Europeans at living and working with the Native American tribes, learning their languages, marrying and settling among them. In India the French, like the Dutch and English, depended on treaties with and the protection of Indian princes.

In the second half of the seventeenth century, however, the all-encompassing power of Louis XIV and the tidy organizing mind of his first minister, Colbert, reorganized France's overseas holdings. Mercantilistic policies, which most early-modern European governments followed, involved official encouragement and regulation of all branches of the economy—agriculture, handicraft industry, domestic and foreign trade. Under Colbert's direction colonies overseas became a crucial element in developed French mercantilism.

Colonies provided tropical and other products unavailable in France. They offered a market for French manufactured goods. And they were expected to give plenty of carrying trade to the French merchant marine. Colbert undertook to increase the population of New World settlements and to establish military strongholds there to strengthen French colonies against their English rivals. The French East India Company was heavily financed by the French crown.

By the early 1700s, then, there were French trading and settlement colonies in eastern Canada, their capital at Quebec; in Louisiana at the mouth of the Mississippi, and in West Indian islands such as Martinique and Guadeloupe. There was also a growing French commercial presence in India, headquartered at Pondichéry on the southeastern coast of the subcontinent. France, the most powerful nation in Europe under Louis XIV, was determined to take a leading role in the building of intercontinental empire as well.

English Enterprise

The second man to circumnavigate the globe was an Englishman. Sir Francis Drake with a single ship, the *Golden Hind,* accomplished the feat in 1578–1580, sixty years after Magellan's expedition. Drake's vessel sailed up the Thames laden to the gunwales with stolen treasure and golden memories. He spent six hours telling Queen Elizabeth about it:

So the voyage lived again, more wonderful than the jewels and bullion in the room. . . . the worst storm since Noah, the giant Indians, the flying fish which the dolphins had hunted . . . the sophisticated rajahs of the Spice Islands—the wonders and perils of the world, its seas so much wider than the great Columbus had believed, its lands so rich in the surprising inventions of the Almighty.[3]

Queen Elizabeth's swashbuckling soldiers and sea dogs, men such as Sir Francis Drake, Sir John Hawkins, and Sir Walter Raleigh, founded no lasting colonies for England. But their raids on Spanish holdings and their dreams of English empire launched Great Britain on what became the most extravagantly successful career of imperial conquest in world history.

British empire building in the next century laid the groundwork at least for the great English venture into intercontinental power.

The beginnings were not promising. Britain's first surviving American colony in Virginia suffered from the climate and their own helplessness in the wilderness, then from Indian massacres, and for years from financial losses before the colonists discovered in tobacco a crop that would pay. The Dutch ousted early English traders from Southeast Asia, so that they had to fall back on the then less profitable Indian trade.

But English merchants were thirsty for profits. English political history in the revolutionary seventeenth century produced religious exiles in need of new lands to settle in. And the English kings after mid-century proved more willing to encourage colonial development. By the early 1700s, then, Britain's overseas holdings were as widely dispersed as those of the Netherlands or France.

Great Britain's major settlement colonies were across the Atlantic in North America and the Carib-

bean. These included colonies inhabited by Puritan nonconformists in New England, planter settlements in Virginia and surrounding territories, and the plantations of the Lesser Antilles, Jamaica, and the Bahamas. Typically, these colonies were founded by commercial companies having little royal support. In time, however, royal governors were appointed and mercantilistic regulations imposed on England's growing American empire.

The British East India Company was also a private venture. It never had the government support accorded its French and even its Dutch rivals. In the early eighteenth century, however, British traders were well established on the coast of India, having developed bases at Bombay in the northwest, Calcutta in the northeast, and Madras on the southeastern shores of peninsular India.

The English had good relations with the Mogul emperors and were protected by them. As the Mogul Empire declined, however, the British East India Company found it increasingly necessary to fight its own battles. In the middle 1700s, the company would do just that—with spectacular results.

Duel for Empire

By 1700, then, the Dutch, with too small and embattled a base at home, were losing momentum everywhere to their larger rivals. Spain and Portugal were rapidly declining into backwaters, their overseas empires no longer expanding and much less profitable. In the 1740s, 1750s, and 1760s, therefore, Britain and France fought each other across two oceans and three continents for imperial supremacy.

The War of the Austrian Succession in the 1740s and the Seven Years' War in the 1750s and 1760s, in both of which England and France chose opposite sides, provided occasions for conflict between the two nations overseas. Hostilities raged in North America and India, as well as in the Caribbean and on the west coast of Africa. The Indian and American encounters, however, determined the outcome of the struggle.

In India, the French had the advantage in the early years; they even temporarily overran the English settlement at Madras. Thereafter, however, the conflict resolved itself into a feud between the two extraordinary governors of the French and British East India companies, Joseph Dupleix and Robert Clive. Dupleix, by extending judicious French military support to local princes in southern India, had the English base at Madras once more surrounded and in imminent danger of extinction. But Clive, who had worked

[3]George Malcolm Thomson, *Sir Francis Drake* (London: Futura Publications, 1972), p. 154.

his way up from genteel destitution through the British East India Company, was both a skilled military commander and a superior politician. Instead of Madras, it was the French capital at Pondichéry that fell, and with it all serious hope for a French empire in India.

In North America also, the French began strongly, thanks again to close ties with the indigenous population. With the help of Indian allies, they pushed down the Mississippi Valley, seeking to link up their Canadian colonies with Louisiana. They might thus box the British in against the Atlantic shore and at the same time lay out a mid-American empire for themselves. An expedition sent to dislodge them—in which a Virginia colonist named George Washington warned the British commander that French-and-Indian tactics were superior—was cut to pieces in the forest.

But a new English prime minister came to power: William Pitt, one of Britain's most famous war leaders. His grand strategy, his choices of leaders and targets all seemed to work like a charm. Clive swept to victory in India. French settlements in West Africa and the West Indies fell to British forces. And in Canada, British armies captured Quebec high on its impregnable bluffs overlooking the St. Lawrence, and then Montreal. All French Canada fell into British hands.

With Britain's victories in India and Canada, English supremacy was unquestionable. Britain had taken a great step forward on the phenomenal march to world empire that would distinguish her history in the following century.

In 1763, when a peace signed at Paris settled the fate of Native Americans and East Indians who had never heard of the City of Light, European power was entrenched around the world. Europeans held as much of North and South America as they had yet had time to occupy, and the rest was pretty clearly theirs for the taking. They had bases and ports around the coasts of Africa south of the Sahara, though they had as yet scarcely penetrated inland. They had a number of ports on both coasts of India and had compelled or bought profitable alliances with *rajas* all across the subcontinent. They owned the Caribbean and were masters of the island portion of Southeast Asia.

They had been rudely repulsed from Japan, had made little progress in China, and were only beginning to explore Australia and Oceania. Huge expanses of the interiors of Asia, Africa, and the Americas—protected by difficult geography, diseases to which Europeans had no immunity, and other factors—remained to be penetrated. But they would be penetrated in time. A beginning had thus been made in the greatest conquest the world had ever seen.

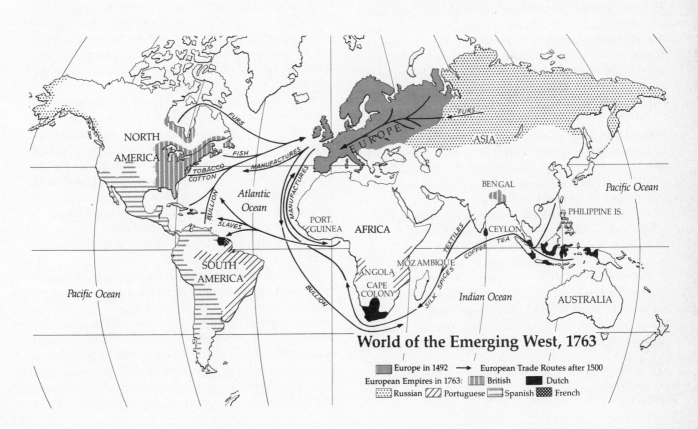

World of the Emerging West, 1763

Europe in 1492 → European Trade Routes after 1500
European Empires in 1763: British Dutch
Russian Portuguese Spanish French

Codfish, Pepper, Slaves, and Gold

There were pious missionaries eager for converts and young men mad for glory among these Western imperialists. But there were probably more who went out to the far places of the earth, as a chronicler who marched with Cortes put it, "to grow rich as all men desire to do."[4] And like empire builders from one end of history to the other, Europeans brought home many things from conquered lands. Asia, Africa, North and South America all paid their tithes to Europe during the early-modern centuries.

Asia was the first objective, and the first to pay. The original goal of the Western voyagers had been to find a sea route to the spices and luxury goods of the Far East that would be cheaper and surer than the overland routes controlled by other peoples. First the Portuguese, then the Dutch, French, and English broke into the trade of the Indian Ocean and Southeast Asia, and soon they were its masters.

In the holds of caravels and lumbering East Indiamen, Europeans brought home silk, tea, porcelain, and spices such as pepper, cloves, and cinnamon from China; cottons and precious stones from India; coffee from Arabia and the Middle East; drugs, saltpeter for gunpowder, indigo dye—the list is almost endless. Europe's consumption of pepper doubled in the first half of the sixteenth century. In the seventeenth, coffee and tea became national drinks in Europe. Indian cotton would spawn a whole new industry in Britain and trigger the Industrial Revolution. The long-range consequences of Asian imports are even more incalculable than their immediate impact.

On the way to Asia, European vessels had to sail around the second-largest continent—Africa. They found profitable commodities here too: pepper and cloves, gold and ivory—and, above all, slaves. Cheap labor became Africa's primary contribution to the burgeoning wealth of the West.

Perhaps twelve million Africans were bought from slave-raiding African peoples—who of course redoubled their activities once they realized they could get a good price from the Europeans. The victims were transported not to Europe but to the Americas, where they made a very substantial contribution to the labor force of the New World. They became part of the famous triangular trade route linking Europe, Africa, and the Americas: manufactured goods to Africa, slaves to the Americas, and agricultural products such as sugar, molasses, and rum back to Europe.

All the imperial European nations were involved one way or another in the grisly trade. All must live with the memory of creaky little ships with upwards of two hundred human beings crammed belowdecks. All made the same calm commercial calculation of a 10 to 25 percent death rate on the long voyage from the West African slave pens to the auction blocks, fields, and mines of the American colonies.

The North American colonies paid tribute to their European rulers in such commercial goods as ships' stores and timber, furs, codfish, tobacco, and sugar. French fur trappers in the sun-dappled quiet of Canadian forests, English fishing vessels laboring in heavy seas off New England or the Newfoundland banks, sweating slaves bending under the watchful eyes of European overseers in the tobacco fields of Virginia or the sugar plantations of the West Indies were also profitable parts of these sprawling European intercontinental empires.

Timber, furs, sugar, fish—it was a stodgy and unromantic contribution compared with the spices and precious stones from the East or the black gold from Africa. Yet by 1776 the North American and Caribbean settlements were probably the most profitable of all the European colonies around the world.

The simplest and most avidly sought form of profit from conquered lands overseas, however, was the silver and gold of Middle and South America. First as booty ripped from the walls of Inca temples, later as ore from mines in Mexico, Bolivia, and elsewhere, hundreds of tons of gold and thousands of tons of silver were shipped across the Atlantic.

All of it was originally destined for the coffers of Spain, but much of it ended up in other hands. Some of it was seized by English or French pirates and privateers. More flooded out over Europe as payment for Spain's huge debts or in salaries and supplies for the armies of Europe's greatest power in the sixteenth century. Much of it, finally, was siphoned off to more industrious peoples like the Dutch, who produced all the good things that Spanish *caballeros*—officers and gentlemen all—were too proud to soil their hands in manufacturing for themselves.

The flood of silver and gold replenished a continent poor in precious metals. It also led to a century of inflation, doubling or tripling prices over the 1500s in various parts of Europe. The new wealth—and the accompanying inflation—benefited the commercial classes, who profited from high prices. But inflation hurt the old nobility who lived on fixed revenues from land. It also hurt the peasantry, many of whom were expelled from their farms to make way for more prof-

[4]Bernal Díaz, quoted in Robert Knecht, "The Discoveries," in Douglas Johnson, ed., *The Making of the Modern World*, Vol. I (New York: Barnes and Noble, 1971), p. 14.

itable sheepwalks as their landlords strove to keep up with inflation.

The great influx of precious metals also left Europe with its most enduring memories of that first great surge of intercontinental empire building—memories of real-life El Dorados found beyond the burning line.

Global Impact

In the long run, however, the broader global impact of Europe's intercontinental imperialism would prove even greater than its commercial value to Europe. During the period of the Old Imperialism, there began a great reshuffling of plants, animals, and peoples, a series of economic and political realignments, that would truly transform the world.

Basic ecological changes were initiated by Europeans eager to exploit their new overseas holdings to the maximum. Europeans transplanted such profitable plants as sugar and coffee and cotton, as well as basic grains such as wheat and large domesticated animals such as horses, cattle, and sheep, from Europe and Asia to the Americas. From the New World they carried potatoes, corn, tobacco, and other crops to the Old. Native American food crops alone would come to feed as much as half the world's population in centuries to come.

Populations also began a shift more dramatic than any since the great prehistoric migrations that had peopled the continents tens and hundreds of thousands of years before. The major population changes in these early centuries of the Western hegemony came in North and South America. Here the original exclusively mongoloid population descended from prehistoric Asian immigrants began its long decline, decimated by European weapons, work discipline, diseases, and brutality. At the same time, millions of caucasoid European settlers and negroid slaves from Africa poured into the Americas, creating the most diverse population pattern anywhere in the world. It was a diversity that would grow even more in later centuries.

The profitable exchanges of goods undertaken by Europeans during these centuries had a larger economic impact too. They created the first genuinely worldwide market in human history, inaugurated a global division of labor, and pointed toward the global economic integration and interdependence of later centuries.

Europe contributed manufactured goods to this emerging global economy, Asia contributed luxury exports, Africa labor, and North and South America raw materials and plantation products.

The heaviest flow of goods was across the Atlantic, between Europe and the Americas, where Europeans settled in large numbers and were soon producing the things that Europeans at home wanted. Africa, in return for a large drain in labor, got more European manufactured goods than she had had before and, perhaps most important, American agricultural imports, including Indian corn, which was soon growing all over Africa.

The meagerest exchange was between Europe and her ancient trading partner, Asia—due, as in ancient times, to the fact that Europe produced little that the highly developed civilizations of Asia wanted or needed. This too would change, however, for in later centuries the European Industrial Revolution would flood the Far East, like the rest of the world, with Western manufactured goods.

The global power balance, finally, shifted dramatically between 1500 and 1800. In 1500 the most powerful nation in the world was certainly China. The most dynamic expanding culture was probably that of the Muslim center of Eurasia. In Africa and the Americas, independent centers of empire were developing in the Western Sudan, Mexico, and Peru. Pluralism prevailed, and Europe was by no means the greatest of world civilizations.

As 1800 approached, all this had clearly changed. European power had destroyed the American empires, and the African kingdoms had declined in a welter of internecine conflict. The Western nations, meanwhile, had repulsed and outflanked the Islamic lands, transformed the Indian Ocean from a Muslim to a European lake, replaced Muslim power in Southeast Asia with European power. The rulers of India were being slowly sucked into the maw of European dependency. Everywhere except the Far East, the weight of Western political predominance was being felt as the eighteenth century drew to a close.

The famous philosopher Voltaire, perhaps the most alert of all eighteenth-century observers of his own time, stated a great truth very casually in his "Remarks on History" of the middle 1700s:

> The silver on which we take our meals, our furniture, our needs, our new pleasures, all these remind us every day that America and the Great Indies, and consequently all the parts of the whole world have been reunited for almost two and a half centuries by the labors of our fathers.[5]

Few people outside the Western world—indeed, few Westerners—could have estimated so accurately

[5]François Marie Arouet de Voltaire, "Remarques sur l'histoire," *Oeuvres historiques*, ed. René Pomeau (Paris: Gallimard, 1957), p. 44.

the dimensions of the European predominance. That predominance was growing, warping the old world of many cultures into a new shape and placing the West at the world's center. Since the world had never had a single political, economic, or cultural center before, this represented a very significant change indeed.

SUMMARY

The Western conquest of the world that began around 1500 is a saga of adventure and brutality, raw greed and raw courage, to match any that history has seen.

The ships, navigational aids, and weapons the European peoples deployed in these opening centuries of the great conquest were among the most advanced of their time. Their motives, however, were not new: a thirst for gold, for converts to their religion, and for the military honor that could only be earned in war. These were old ambitions, though particularly developed in the West at the beginning of modern history. Southern Europeans—Spanish and Portuguese, often with Italian navigators—set the pace in the sixteenth century. In the seventeenth, northern European nations—England, France, and the Netherlands—took the lead in empire building. By the eighteenth century, Britain emerged as the greatest Western imperial power of all.

The Portuguese, led by daring commanders like da Gama and the brilliant imperial organizer Albuquerque, pushed eastward to India, Southeast Asia, and beyond. They established a cruelly enforced monopoly over the sea trade of the Indian Ocean. The Spanish probed westward. Columbus discovered a "New World," and Cortes, Pizarro, and their fellows conquered much of South and Middle America, looted the realms of the Aztecs and Incas, and established a continental empire.

The Dutch were the most successful of all the seventeenth-century empire builders. They established trading posts in North America, the Caribbean, South Africa, Southeast Asia, and even East Asia. By the eighteenth century, however, British and French commercial enclaves in India and settlement empires in North America and the Caribbean made them the prime contenders. After the wars of the middle 1700s, British triumphs in India and Canada made her master of the greatest of overseas empires.

From their overseas holdings, Europeans brought home spices, silk, cottons, slaves, gold and silver, codfish, sugar, tobacco, and much more. The impact of the so-called Old Imperialism was, however, even greater on the rest of the world. Plants, animals, and human populations were shuffled around the globe on the little European sailing ships. The beginnings of a genuine global economy emerged, and the world power balance began decisively to tilt toward the West.

SUGGESTED READING

BANNON, J. F., ed. *The Spanish Conquistadors: Men or Devils?* New York: Holt, Rinehart & Winston, 1960. A book of essays on the "black legend" of Spanish cruelty in the Americas.

BOXER, C. R. *The Christian Century in Japan, 1549–1650.* Berkeley: University of California Press, 1967. The impact of Western religion on samurai Japan, by a leading authority on the Old Imperialism.

—— *The Dutch Seaborne Empire, 1600–1800.* New York: Knopf, 1965. The Dutch golden age overseas, and their relative decline thereafter.

—— *The Portuguese Seaborne Empire, 1415–1825.* New York: Knopf, 1969. An outstanding account of the oldest of the European intercontinental empires.

CARRINGTON, C. E. *The British Overseas: Exploits of a Nation of Shopkeepers.* Cambridge: Cambridge University Press, 1950. Uncritical but still useful survey of the history of the British Empire.

CIPOLLA, C. M. *Guns, Sails, and Empires.* New York: Minerva Press, 1965. Material explanations of the great conquest.

CURTIN, P. D. *The Atlantic Slave Trade: A Census.* Madison: University of Wisconsin Press, 1969. The impact of the trade on Africa, by an authoritative Africanist and an expert on intercontinental trade.

FRANKE, W. *China and the West.* Oxford: Blackwell, 1967. Interaction between the Western world and the most isolated of Eurasian civilizations. See also G. F. Hudson, *Europe and China: A Study of Their Relations from Earliest Times to 1800* (Boston: Beacon Press, 1961).

HAMILTON, E. *American Treasure and the Price Revolution in Spain, 1501–1650.* Cambridge, Mass.: Harvard University Press, 1934. Seminal study of one of the major consequences of the Old Imperialism.

LACH, D. F. *Asia in the Making of Europe.* Chicago: University of Chicago Press, 1965. Early relations between East and West, and their impact on the latter.

LÉON-PORTILLA, M. ed. *The Broken Spears: The Aztec Account of the Conquest of Mexico,* trans. L. Kemp. Boston: Beacon, 1961. The other side of Cortes's victory. For an eyewitness account by a Spaniard, see B. Diaz del Castillo, *The Discovery and Conquest of Mexico,* trans. A. P. Maudslay (New York: Grove Press, 1956).

LEVENSON, J. R., ed. *European Expansion and the Counter-Example of Asia, 1300–1600.* Englewood Cliffs, N.J.: Prentice-Hall, 1967. Approaches the question of why European imperialism took place by looking at Asia, which did not reach out to other continents.

MORISON, S. E. *Admiral of the Ocean Sea: A Life of the Admiral Christopher Columbus* (2 vols.). Boston: Little, Brown, 1942. Still the standard life of Columbus, with vivid detail and a seaman's appreciation.

PANIKKAR, K. M. *Asia and Western Dominance.* New York: Harper & Row, Pub., 1954. An Indian perspective on the great conquest.

PARRY, J. H. *The Age of Reconnaissance: Discovery, Exploration and Settlement, 1450–1650.* New York: New American Library, 1963. Excellent standard work on the most active years of the Old Imperialism. See also Parry's collection of source materials, *European Reconnaissance: Selected Documents* (New York: Harper & Row, Pub., 1968).

—— *The Spanish Seaborne Empire.* New York: Knopf, 1966. Another standard work by a leading interpretor of the great conquest.

—— *Trade and Dominion: The Overseas European Empires in the Eighteenth Century.* New York: Praeger, 1971. Survey and analysis of the first imperial system fully assembled.

PRIESTLY, H. I. *France Overseas Through the Old Regime: A Study of European Expansion.* Englewood Cliffs N.J.: Prentice-Hall, 1939. Old but still valuable overview.

Chapter · 8

THE POWER OF EUROPEAN THRONES

THE INCARNATION
OF SOVEREIGNTY

Periwigs, Palaces—
and a Philosophic Smile

From a broad overview of the world of intercontinental empire, we turn now to a closer look at some of the major regions of the globe in the centuries before 1900. We begin, because of its significance as well as its familiarity, with the Western world.

Europe in the seventeenth and eighteenth centuries conjures a pleasantly homogeneous collection of images. Periwigs and knee breeches come to mind, or low-cut gowns and lace. Carriages, chandeliers, stately homes, and baroque palaces. Playing fountains, elegant facades—and the Hall of Mirrors at Versailles. We have to think a minute to call up beggars and the plague years, women hanged for witchcraft, debtors' prisons, and Hogarth's vivid depiction of the London slums, *Gin Lane*—all as much a part of the seventeenth and eighteenth centuries in Europe as green lawns and the stately homes of England.

In many ways, it was an in-between period for Europe. It was the climax of the age of kings and queens, hereditary aristocrats, and the power of churchmen if not of religion. It was also, however, a transition to a startling new age of popular ideological revolutions, unprecedented industrial growth, and the predominance of Europe's middle classes over the old aristocracy.

We are dealing in this chapter, then, with the middle period of modern Western history. During the Renaissance and Reformation, Europe had reabsorbed its classical past, survived its medieval religious hangover, and moved on into modern history. Over the next two centuries, from 1600 to the late 1700s, the earlier modern period came to a climax and the seeds of later modern history were planted. The seventeenth and eighteenth centuries saw a continent that was already imposing its will on so much of the world evolve politically, economically, and culturally toward the revolutionary crises that would impose new directions on the West—and thus on the world—in the decades around 1800.

Seen as a part of global history, this middle period of modern European history accomplished two things. It significantly strengthened the power of Europeans to impose their will upon the rest of the world. It also saw the development of ideas and trends that, exported to the world at large over the following two centuries, would drastically transform the way many other peoples thought and lived.

With this larger impact as background, the pages that follow will outline the increasing power of European thrones in the age of Louis XIV and Peter the Great. They will also examine the expanding wealth of the West in the days of the Dutch burghers we have already met and the Bank of England that will be with us from this time onward. Finally we will explore intellectual currents, which played an equally important role, from the Scientific Revolution to the Enlightenment.

To many contemporaries, the splendor of Louis XIV's great palace at Versailles was the ultimate symbol of that age of royal triumph. But the mocking smile on the lips of the liberal philosopher Voltaire—or the legendary apple that fell in Isaac Newton's garden—may in the long run have done more to shape the history of centuries to come.

Louis XIV's huge royal palace at Versailles, outside Paris. This contemporary engraving gives a rather modest impression of the palace that could house 10,000 people. (Réunion des Musées Nationaux)

A Balance of Powers

There were five great powers in Europe during the 1600s and 1700s. Three of them—Britain, France, and Austria—were established states with roots deep in the Middle Ages. The other two, Prussia and Russia, were new monarchies shouldering their way to the fore. Much of the history of this age was made by these powerful nation-states and the competitive dynasties that ruled them.

The most powerful and admired of European nations was France, particularly during the long reign of Louis XIV, in the latter half of the seventeenth and the early eighteenth centuries. Enjoying a balanced agricultural, commercial, and industrial economy, a large population, a strong royal government, and a high culture that was the most imitated in Europe, Bourbon France was by common consent the greatest of European states.

The other great power of western Europe was the empire-building island kingdom of Great Britain. Britain was on its way to commercial, naval, and imperial preeminence during these centuries. Wracked by a long revolution in the seventeenth century, she emerged after 1688 as Europe's major liberal power, the possessor of a strong Parliament and a constitutionally limited monarchy.

The long-standing power of central Europe was the Holy Roman Empire, centered in Austria and ruled by the oldest of European dynasties, the Habsburgs. Because the Austrian Habsburgs had never been able

to convert their feudal suzerainty over several hundred central European principalities, duchies, free cities, and other units into a modern centralized monarchy, their authority outside Austria was sometimes shadowy. Austria's eighteenth-century enlightened despots would strengthen that power, however, and the Habsburgs would continue to govern a large multinational realm, including Slavic, Italian, Magyar, and other peoples, as well as the German states.

The second power in central Europe was the aggressive new state of Brandenburg-Prussia. This divided principality in North Germany, partially incorporated in the Holy Roman Empire, was actually on its way to replacing Austria as the greatest of the German states. The ambitious Hohenzollern dynasty depended on Prussia's hardworking Junker aristocracy to staff the highly efficient Prussian civil service and to officer the redoubtable Prussian army. Frederick the Great would do much for both these institutions in the eighteenth century, and both would carry the Hohenzollerns and their country far in centuries to come.

The largest power in eastern Europe, and on the continent as a whole, was Russia. Unfortunately, Romanov Russia was also the most underdeveloped of all the major European powers. Cut off from the rest of the continent by the vast East European plain, by Byzantine influences, and by two centuries of Mongol rule, Russia had not shared in early modern Europe's dynamic growth. The Romanov czars expanded their territorial holdings far across Asia and shoved their way determinedly into European affairs during the seventeenth and eighteenth centuries. But Russia remained a poverty-stricken land of serfs and ill-disciplined ancient nobility despite all that heavy-handed eighteenth-century autocrats like Peter the Great and more subtle ones like Catherine the Great could do.

There were other large nations and many smaller ones in this politically fragmented continent. The Mediterranean states that had played central roles in the fifteenth and sixteenth centuries—Renaissance Italy and the Iberian empire builders, Spain and Portugal—had declined to sleepy backwaters. The Netherlands, as we have seen, enjoyed a golden century of commercial and imperial power in the 1600s, only to settle for well-scrubbed but second-class-power status thereafter. In northern Europe, Sweden was the strongest of the Scandinavian states, taking a leading part in the Thirty Years' War and fighting a long duel with Peter the Great's Russia before sinking back into comparative obscurity. Poland, large and powerful enough to march on Moscow in the early seventeenth century, was partitioned off the map of Europe by more powerful neighbors in the later eighteenth.

Five powerful nations and dozens of lesser states thus continued to divide the western end of Eurasia among them. Their traditional rivalry bred a series of bloody wars, including the Thirty Years' War (1618–1648), the four wars of Louis XIV (1667–1714), and the mid-eighteenth-century cluster of wars centering in the War of the Austrian Succession and the Seven Years' War (1740–1763).

European rulers fought one another for dynastic rights and territory in Europe and for commercial rights and colonies overseas. They fought to maintain—or to upset—the balance of power, the rough parity in war-making potential that alone guaranteed that no one power would ever come to dominate all Europe politically. The West thus jealously defended the political divisiveness that made Europeans among the most fiercely competitive of the world's peoples. If unity has eluded Europeans down the centuries, it is at least partly because they have resisted it tooth and nail throughout their history.

Absolutism and Enlightenment

The royal rulers of seventeenth-century Europe acquired more power over their peoples than their medieval or Renaissance predecessors had ever exerted. Governing through larger and more efficient bureaucracies than Europe had known since ancient times, these seventeenth-century monarchs came to be known as *absolute* rulers, so unquestioned was their authority. The absolutists of the seventeenth century in fact elevated hereditary monarchical government to a peak of power and paved the way for the even stronger republican governments of more recent centuries. The most powerful of all the power brokers of the 1600s were perhaps Prussia's Great Elector, Frederick William; Russia's most powerful czar, Peter the Great; and above all Louis XIV, the Sun King of France.

The seventeenth century was thus a time of hard-driving nation builders, brutal wars, and royal splendor. European kings and queens in the eighteenth century retained the expanded authority and the enlarged administrative systems of their absolutist predecessors. But some of them added an ostentatious new concern with the welfare of their subjects that earned for these monarchs the label *enlightened*. This concern was sometimes genuine, at least with regard to selected afflictions of their subjects. It was also sometimes a cloak for increased state revenues or a means of decreasing the likelihood of popular rebellion. And it was sometimes merely a matter of royal vanity. But the eighteenth-century "enlightened despots" were at least a straw in the great wind blowing toward the democracies and welfare states of later centuries. Among the most celebrated examples of enlightened despotism were Frederick the Great of Prussia, Catherine the Great of Russia, and Maria Theresa and her son Joseph II of the Holy Roman Empire.

A look at Europe's great powers under the absolute monarchs of the seventeenth century and the enlightened despots of the eighteenth follows.

Nations of Soldiers and Bureaucrats

Frederick William (1640–1688) pulled his new nation of Brandenburg-Prussia together out of the ashes of the Thirty Years' War, Europe's bloodiest seventeenth-century war, which centered in the German states. This sanguinary conflict began as a last flare-up of the European wars of religion and ended as a struggle for territory involving England, France, Spain, the Holy Roman Empire, and a number of other powers. Perhaps a third of the population of the German states was killed, wolves prowled the streets of deserted villages, and German development was retarded for generations. It is perhaps not surprising, then, that Frederick William chose to base the new power he built from the rubble on what must have seemed the prime essential of his violent age: military strength.

The Great Elector's twin goals—and those of his successors in Brandenburg-Prussia—were to link up the scattered Hohenzollern holdings into a united block of territory stretching across North Germany, and to impose the royal will upon the resulting nation. The Prussian army won him powerful allies, as well as more territory. The army also helped bring his new lands to heel, imposing royal authority upon free cities and the medieval assemblies of his expanding realm.

Frederick William found a second ally in the Prussian nobility, the hardheaded Junkers. Unlike aristocrats in many countries, the Prussian Junkers cast their lot with royal absolutism. They staffed the Hohenzollern bureaucracy and made it arguably the best in Europe. They officered the army. They ran their landed estates efficiently too, thus building the country's agricultural wealth. From Frederick William's day to Bismarck's, the Junkers would be synonymous with Prussian power.

Frederick II the Great (1740–1786) was Prussia's greatest enlightened despot—and her greatest royal general. He ended up, in fact, with a greater reputation as a war-maker than as a reformer. A Frenchified lad who resisted Hohenzollern militarism and loved poetry and playing the flute, Frederick hardened in later years into Prussia's most brilliant military commander.

As an enlightened despot, he wrote volumes of philosophy and history, sponsored reforms of the judicial system, and encouraged religious toleration. He called himself the "first servant" of the state and seems genuinely to have believed that only absolute power in royal hands could bring a better life for his people.

He most captured the imagination of Europe in a more typically Hohenzollern role, however: as a general and a state builder. He fought a long duel with the Habsburg empress Maria Theresa and her allies during the mid-century surge of violence called the War of the Austrian Succession and the Seven Years' War. While England and France were using these wars to fight for colonies overseas, Prussia and Austria battled for territory in central Europe. And in the end, by inspired generalship and at considerable cost to his beleaguered homeland, Frederick did detach a sizable chunk from Austria and attach it to the Kingdom of Prussia.

Maria Theresa (1740–1765) and her son Joseph II (1765–1790), rulers of Europe's oldest great power, were the most dedicated enlightened innovators of all rulers of major powers. A pious Catholic, Maria Theresa nevertheless forced reforms upon her church. A firm believer in the Habsburg dynasty's power and destiny, she nonetheless drastically reformed both the central and provincial administration of the empire.

Her son Joseph, even more ambitious, sponsored legal reform, religious toleration, and comparative freedom of the press. Above all, he worked to improve the lot of the peasants by introducing tax reforms for them and eliminating vestiges of serfdom.

Unfortunately, Joseph's autocratic style of implementing these innovations alienated his subjects so thoroughly that little was actually accomplished.

Soldiers and bureaucrats were thus the keys to central European power in the seventeenth and eighteenth centuries—and particularly to the rise of Prussia, the core of what would become modern Germany.

A Window on the West

In Russia, on Europe's eastern frontier, Peter the Great and Catherine the Great faced problems of modernization rather than of unification. But they, like Frederick William and Frederick the Great, depended on royal absolutism and military force to achieve their objectives.

Peter I the Great (1682–1725) built on the centralizing efforts of earlier Russian rulers such as Ivan the Great in the fifteenth century and Ivan the Terrible in the sixteenth. Ivan III the Great had reduced the other Russian princes who had survived the reign of the Mongols to vassal status under Muscovy in the 1400s. Ivan IV the Terrible had imposed a rough form of central government by terror on the growing east-

Russia's most famous state-builder, Peter the Great, complete with sword, canon, and map of future conquests. Some sense of Peter's vigor and driving sense of purpose is apparent in this painting. (Library of Congress)

ern European nation in the 1500s. Peter the Great, the most colorful and autocratic of all the czars, sought to turn his still medieval country into an up-to-date absolutist regime by sheer energy and ham-fisted force of will in the decades around 1700.

Six feet four inches tall and massively built, given to violent rages and symbolic gestures such as chopping the old-fashioned beards off his noblemen with his own hands, Peter was the stuff of which legends are made. His determination to redesign Russia on the model of western Europe divided his country between Westernizers and Slavophiles—admirers of the West and lovers of old Russian ways—for the next two centuries. But he did make Russia a great power—and the most rigidly autocratic of all European states.

Under Peter I, royal power was felt more heavily by more people than ever before in Russian history. A new structure of civil-service nobility, in which one's title depended on service in the bureaucracy or the army, gradually superseded the anarchistic old *boyar* aristocracy. The Russian Orthodox church was taken over by a royal appointee, its ancient monasteries confiscated to fill the royal treasuries. Taxes, military conscription, and forced labor were heaped on the Russian peasantry, and serfdom actually increased in Russia in the eighteenth century.

Peter's accomplishments, however, were as prodigious as his tyrannies. He built the huge bureaucracy that would be Europe's largest, both in czarist and communist times. He created a powerful army, founded the Russian navy, and fought long wars with the Turks in the south and the Swedes in the north. The latter conflict won a slice of Baltic seacoast that gave the largely landlocked country a crucial "window on the West" through which trade and Western influences would flow henceforth. Peter made himself an emperor and built himself a great new capital on this conquered land—St. Petersburg, the Leningrad of today.

Peter the Great found his country hopelessly medieval and only half European. He left it, if not modern or yet Westernized, at least a recognized great power and more rigorously centralized than it had ever been before.

Catherine the Great (1762–1796), Russia's most celebrated enlightened despot, was actually not Russian at all. She was a German princess married to an ineffectual young czar who soon died, leaving the throne to his shrewd young widow. Catherine brought the reforming ideas of the European Enlightenment with her to the endless steppes and dark forests of Russia. She also proved to be another of Russia's most colorful rulers, entertaining her court indiscriminately with philosophical letters from Voltaire and her long line of stalwart lovers.

Reforming ideas, unfortunately, did not find a congenial environment in Europe's most unbending autocracy. The Legislative Commission Catherine convened produced no enlightened legislation. Her Charter of Nobility merely strengthened the nobles' control over their serfs. In the end, she made more of a mark in history by crushing a famous peasant uprising—Pugachev's Rebellion—by acquiring Russia's share of Poland in the partitioning of that unfortunate state, and by conquering more lands from the Turks.

By the end of the eighteenth century, then, Russia had thrust her way into the councils of Europe's great powers—and had laid the foundations of the global power of the Soviet Union of today.

L'État, C'est Moi

No ruler of the age, however, embodied the spirit of royal absolutism as did Louis XIV (1643–1715), for

Catherine the Great—German by birth, Russian by royal marriage, French by cultural preference—epitomized the cosmopolitan spirit of the Enlightenment. The sophisticated empress looks appealingly human in this picture. (New York Public Library Picture Collection)

whom the age is sometimes named. Who but the Sun King, the Grand Monarch, could have interrupted a diplomat's pompous references to the French state with an impatient but quite accurate *"l'état, c'est moi"*—*"I am the state"*—and have historians nodding sagely ever since?

Louis erected his edifice of power on the state-building efforts of powerful French rulers of the first half of the seventeenth century. Henry IV, the chivalric and cynical White Plume of Navarre, had ended France's long religious civil wars and established the Bourbon dynasty on the throne. The powerful and thoroughly secular Cardinal Richelieu had strengthened royal power and laid the foundations of Louis's new structure of administration. But it was Louis himself, during his reign of more than seventy years, who supervised the building of that structure.

Building royal power meant undermining local and regional power centers, and this Louis did with a will. The old independent-minded French aristocrats were turned into tame courtiers at Louis's court. Town officials became royal appointees. Royal regulations were imposed upon medieval guilds. Provincial courts called *parlements* were compelled to rubber-stamp royal decrees. The Estates General, France's embryonic Parliament, became a dead letter by virtue of never being summoned to meet during Louis's long reign.

In place of medieval regional autonomy, absolutist royal institutions grew up. Central councils presided over by the king formulated government policies. Powerful royal ministers such as the Marquis de Louvois, minister of war, and Jean Baptiste Colbert, chief minister for finances and many other matters, elaborated and applied these policies. A centralized administrative system of agents called *intendants* then implemented them in the provinces, collecting taxes and army conscripts, regulating the economy, and providing at least some government protection in the countryside.

Perhaps the most impressive achievement of absolutism under Louis XIV, however, was the elaborate system of mercantilist regulation of the national economy developed by Colbert. The traditional goals of mercantilism were to increase national production, secure a favorable balance of trade in the goods produced, and thus guarantee a flow of payments in gold and silver bullion into the country. Bullion, in the mercantilist view, constituted true national wealth. It could also be readily taxed by the state—an additional incentive not lost on Louis's administrators.

Under Colbert, then, an intricate structure of monopolies, chartered companies, protective tariffs, controls on wages, prices, and product quality, and colonial regulations was established to achieve these ends. All major powers practiced mercantilistic regulation of their economies. But few did so as efficiently and wholeheartedly as Louis and his first minister, Colbert.

Louis's war minister, Louvois, presided over the worst fruit of royal absolutism: the four wars fought during Louis's long reign.

They were clearly dynastic wars fought to secure lands Louis claimed for his wife (the Spanish Netherlands—Belgium today), for his grandson (Spain itself), or in his own right (the Rhineland). Louis's immense power and matching ambition elevated France to the position—enjoyed by Spain a century earlier during her *siglo de oro*—of Europe's greatest power, threatening to impose her predominance upon the continent.

The result—as in Philip II's day—was a series of alliances against Louis XIV. Most of them were led by William of Orange, ruler first of the Netherlands and then of Great Britain, a comparatively liberal ruler in an age of absolutism. Louis's ambitions were finally frustrated in the early 1700s, when a Europe-wide conflict called the War of the Spanish Succession prevented the Sun King from uniting the throne of France with that of Spain and all her possessions overseas.

The symbol of Louis's predominance was the biggest palace in Europe, built at Versailles, outside Paris. Versailles provided a regal setting for the most admired of absolute monarchs, a world of formal gardens, glittering fountains, and acres of stately baroque architecture. Here Louis and his ministers, mistresses, and courtiers paraded in their ermines and velvets, living in a style befitting the Grand Monarch, the incarnation of sovereignty whose only fitting symbol was the Sun.

England's Century of Revolution

Most of Europe's seventeenth- and eighteenth-century monarchs, enlightened or not, were dedicated absolutists. But there was another line of political development to be detected in the 1600s and 1700s. This was the much rarer liberal line of governmental evolution best illustrated by the rise of Parliament and constitutional monarchy in Great Britain. And if royal absolutism pointed ahead to the more authoritarian governments to come, constitutional monarchy would lead in time to the mass democracies of more recent centuries.

There were other comparatively liberal governments in this period, most importantly that of the Netherlands. But Britain would be the primary proving ground for democracy in the West, and her Par-

The Sun King himself, Louis XIV, posed in seventeenth-century splendor, from huge wig to high red heels, against an appropriately Roman backdrop. Hyacinth Rigaud's portrait catches much of the magnificence of Europe's absolute monarchs in what has been called the Splendid Century. (Louvre, Paris)

liament the mother of representative institutions around the world.

The seventeenth century was England's century of revolution.

A series of foreign rulers—the Scottish Stuarts—who tried to impose absolute monarchy on England without understanding English traditions undoubtedly helped to precipitate the English Revolution. So did the survival of the strong Tudor Parliament, which served as a rallying point for the enemies of absolutism. So, finally, did unfinished business from the previous century: unresolved Reformation tensions, simmering discontent with the autocratic Tudor style of governance, and the rise of a prosperous and self-confident English gentry class and a merchant middle class ready to defend its interests.

In the seventeenth century, then, resistance to the crown developed among several groups of English people. Puritan Protestants opposed immorality at the royal court and feared creeping Catholicism in the Anglican church. Thrifty merchants resented courtly extravagance and high taxes. Above all, solid country squires rebelled at favoritism shown to a handful of royal courtiers, at the abridgment of their own rights in Parliament, and at the high-handedness of James I and his successors in the Stuart line.

Through the first half of the century, this opposition took the form of famous court cases and courtly scandals, running battles in Parliament, and finally armed revolt. A Puritan country squire named Oliver Cromwell defeated the royal armies in battle, beheaded the second Stuart king, Charles I, in 1649, and ruled the country as Lord Protector for the next decade. Charles II was restored to power in 1660, but his successor, James II, was expelled for good in 1688. A parliamentary faction then imported a new king from the Netherlands: William of Orange, strong Protestant and archenemy of royal absolutism, who became England's first constitutional monarch.

The Glorious Revolution of 1688 gave Parliament a large share in governing the country, including the power to control royal revenues and the rights to free elections and debate. The eighteenth century saw the slow evolution of parliamentary power, especially the authority of the elected House of Commons, though the hereditary House of Lords remained powerful too.

In the 1700s, the cabinet system and the office of prime minister both emerged. The chief royal advisers and heads of the royal administration became a cabinet, or council of leading members of Parliament. They were led by a prime (first) minister, who was the head of the majority party in the House of Commons. Parties themselves also took shape: a conservative Tory faction and a more liberal Whig party. Each group was bound by ties of political interest, governmental principles, and family connection. And the competition of these parties of elected politicians determined to an increasing degree the policies of England.

Elections were still far from democratic: only a handful voted, usually on the basis of property ownership. The kings remained very powerful. But a start had been made on a road that would lead over the next two centuries to genuine democracy in Britain.

THE WORLD OF THE RISING MIDDLE CLASSES

The Bourgeoisie on the Brink

If the politics of the age of absolutism and enlightened despotism was still dominated by the old aristocracy, the economics of these centuries remained solidly in the hands of the middle classes. Much of the present section, on the economic and social trends of the age, will thus be concerned with that famous historical cliché, the rising middle classes, now closing rapidly in on their blue-blooded rivals.

In much of Europe, the closeness of the contest was by no means apparent in the 1600s and 1700s. In many places, the dominant aristocracy seemed to establish a lock on high places in royal courts and royal governments, in churches, armies, the diplomatic corps, and other top spots in European society. In central and eastern Europe especially, aristocrats bought increased authority over the peasant majority of the population in return for acknowledging the absolute power of the monarchy over the nation as a whole. Since the middle classes in middle and eastern Europe tended to be servants of the state rather than independent merchants, there was really no contest. Aristocratic social prestige remained high all over Europe, and the social-climbing tradesman, or "bourgeois gentleman"—a contradiction in terms—remained an object of satire.

In western Europe, however, the middle classes were actually doing very well indeed. Thriving on the commercial and imperial expansion of the Atlantic powers, the upper bourgeoisie grew wealthier than ever before. In government, middle-class administrators such as Colbert did much of the work of absolutist government. Merchants ran the government of the Netherlands and sat in the increasingly powerful Parliament of Britain. And despite the jeers of their betters, bourgeois citizens were also increasingly well-educated, self-confident—and willing to criticize the fecklessness and unearned privileges of their traditional social superiors.

The great upheavals that were about to transform Europe—the French Revolution of 1789 and the Industrial Revolution that would begin in Britain about 1760—would further enhance the fortunes of the bourgeoisie. But those fortunes were already well advanced. Thanks to a great surge of money power in the 1600s and 1700s, western Europe's middle classes were strongly positioned to take advantage of what was to come as this middle period of modern European history drew to a close.

Prosperity

The prosperity of the commercial middle classes took different forms in different parts of western Europe. Dutch burghers and shipmasters built on a tradition of trade and seamanship that went back to the Middle Ages. In the seventeenth century, the Netherlands dominated the carrying trade of all Europe and was a leading producer of manufactured goods, as well as

perhaps the most successful of the new empire builders. In the eighteenth century, British merchants profited from Europe's largest free-trade zone after the union of England and Scotland. They also benefited from the West's solidest financial institution, the Bank of England, as well as from extensive foreign trade and Britain's own triumphant empire. French merchants had western Europe's largest population to supply. They also had the West's most elaborate mercantile system, and a sizable empire too, at least until France's imperial duel with England ended in 1763.

In western European countries especially, capitalist institutions and governmental supports were thus widespread. Joint-stock companies pooled capital for large-scale commercial projects, and stock exchanges facilitated investment. Mercantilistic governments provided subsidies, monopolies, protective tariffs, and other forms of encouragement for business. Europe's bourgeoisie might be mere tradesmen to the old aristocracy, but they were among the world's richest businessmen too.

Industrial production remained largely in the hands of city guilds or peasants engaged in cottage industry. Peasants spun and wove wool into cloth, made wine, and otherwise processed the fruits of their

The solid middle classes who continued to guide Europe's economic expansion during the middle-modern centuries challenged the skills of painters like Jan Vermeer. His picture of a Woman Holding a Balance *reveals some of the calm strength and dignity of this woman and her class. (National Gallery of Art, Washington, D.C. Widener Collection 1942)*

lands and labors. Guild artisans still made most of the useful objects Europeans needed, from shoes and barrels to books and jewelry. Some of the heavier industries—mining and metallurgy, shipbuilding, cannon foundries, and printing presses—used elaborate machinery containing intricate combinations of pulleys, screws, and other mechanisms for multiplying force. Waterpower and windpower, however, remained all that the West—and the world at large—could muster beyond the labor of animals and human backs to do the world's work.

Numbers

The demographic history of Europe took an astonishing and decisive turn around the middle of this period. After stalling in the seventeenth century, population growth turned decisively upward in the middle decades of the eighteenth. We must rely largely on estimates for most of this period, but Europe's total population may have risen by as much as 80 percent between 1730 and 1830. It was, in fact, the beginning of the greatest population explosion in the history of the world.

Explanations for this initial take-off are complex and sometimes contradictory. One likely cause for the new numbers, however, is clearly the agricultural revolution of the early 1700s.

Agricultural improvements in the eighteenth century included advances in fertilizer and the rotation of crops to increase production, and stock breeding to develop heavier beef cattle or pigs. Enclosure of village lands and advanced techniques of land management helped make such improvements possible. These agricultural developments came in areas where there were already large enough concentrations of population to make worthwhile the work involved and the cost of the improvements. Thus the new agricultural revolution was initially limited to parts of England and France, to the Netherlands, the Rhineland, and northern Italy—all of which were areas with several large cities to be fed.

Once the agricultural revolution was in train, however, it contributed substantially to further population growth. More food could feed more people. Life expectancies therefore increased, more people lived to reproduce, and a cycle was set in motion that would multiply the population in the next few centuries.

Most Europeans were still desperately poor. Serfs in central and eastern Europe and tenants in western Europe were at the mercy of their landlords or masters. Even free peasants who owned their own land, which many of them did in France or England, still lived within reach of starvation in years of bad harvest. Excess rural population, no longer needed on more efficient farms, clogged the cities seeking nonexistent work. Living on black bread and little else in the best of times, sinking easily into total destitution, crime, or the endemic violence stimulated by cheap rum and gin, these early generations of the population boom had little to be grateful for. They too, however, would have their part to play in the history of Europe's next period, the impending age of revolutions.

The Conditions of Women

Women, as usual, played many parts in this period. At one end of the scale, there were poverty-stricken peasant women even in such prosperous countries as France. Bent and wizened, made old and ugly by years of field labor and a level of childbearing "close," as the demographers say, "to the biological maximum," such women could look sixty—and be in their twenties. At the other extreme, there were the court ladies, the salon hostesses, royal mistresses such as mesdames de Pompadour or du Barry, charming or regal in their velvets and laces, their high-piled wigs and winking diamonds. In between there were many middle-class women, well if not ostentatiously dressed, thoroughly respectable, managers of households or businesses, readers of novels as well as Scripture.

Scattered generalizations may be made about these women of the Age of Reason. They were normally married (as were most men), and married by their parents with property and other material considerations in mind—though this may be as good a recipe for a happy union as marrying a man for the way his eyes crinkle or a woman for the way she fills a sweater. Within the family, women remained at least formally subordinate to their husbands, perhaps most notably so in the more puritanical Protestant households. All married women were much preoccupied with the bearing and rearing of children, who were still valued, both as potential free laborers and as a form of old-age insurance for their parents. In addition, women of the peasant, servant, and other working classes had hard physical labor to do all their lives.

Nevertheless, there does seem to have been some improvement in the feminine condition, particularly during the eighteenth century. There were a number of successful women rulers, including Queen Anne of Great Britain, the empresses Maria Theresa and Catherine the Great, and two other Russian rulers. Managing a great house or even a solid middle-class home, with its many servants and other supernumeraries, was a challenge as it had always been. There were celebrated women novelists such as Mademoiselle de

Scudéry in the seventeenth century and women paint-ers such as the famous portraitists Elizabeth Vigée-Le Brun and Adelaide Labille-Guyard at the court of Marie Antoinette. Extraordinary women shone in the salons; ordinary women, in western Europe at least, found it easier to move freely in society and felt less stigma in remaining "spinsters."

Laws still limited the legal rights of women; wom-en's education was still distinctly limited; and mar-riage and family were still the required careers of most. But social and cultural areas formally closed to women were beginning to open up to them. Like other unprivileged groups in Western society, women were on the verge of at least a beginning of emancipation by 1800.

THE TRIUMPH OF REASON

Mr. Newton's World

The cultural life of this middle period of modern Eu-ropean history has a distinctly cerebral cast. The bub-bling creativity of the Renaissance, on the one hand, and the passion of Romanticism, on the other, bracket Europe's great Age of Reason. It was a period of sci-entific discovery and social philosophizing, of both courtly and bourgeois art and literature, of academic training, classical influences, dry wit, and stinging satire.

The Scientific Revolution of the sixteenth and sev-enteenth centuries provided the intellectual under-pinnings for much of the cultural life of this age of triumphant rationality.

The physical sciences, as we have seen, flourished in many cultures, including those of China, India, the Islamic center of Eurasia, and the Mayans in the New World. Europe's last significant contribution had come among the ancient Greeks. Hundreds of years before Christ, Greek thinkers reasoned their way to the globular shape of the earth, calculated the dis-tances of the sun and the moon mathematically, de-veloped Archimedean physics and Euclidean geo-metry. They also classified biological organisms and at least urged an empirical approach to medicine.

The ancient Greeks, however, left one great error to bedevil later scientific understanding: the astron-omer Ptolemy's geocentric (earth-centered) theory of the structure of the universe. It was in correcting this error that the sixteenth-century astronomer Coper-nicus launched the Scientific Revolution.

Nicolaus Copernicus, a Polish churchman who made astronomy his hobby, first propounded the he-liocentric (sun-centered) theory in a book *On the Revolutions of the Heavenly Spheres* in 1543. In Co-pernicus's view, the sun is the center, the earth merely one of a number of planets. The earth, he said, spins around the sun and rotates on its own axis at the same time, giving the illusion that the universe itself is moving around us. Copernicus retained some of the creaky old machinery of the Ptolemaic system, in-cluding circular orbits, "eccentrics," and "epicycles" to explain anomalies of planetary motion, and a "sphere of the fixed stars" beyond that of the farthest planet. But the Polish astronomer had made the great breakthrough: the Scientific Revolution is sometimes called the Copernican Revolution in his honor.

Scientists of many lands built on his foundations over the century and a half after 1543. The German mathematician Johannes Kepler proposed the three laws of planetary motion—including the key recog-nition that planets move around the sun in elipses rather than circles. The famous Italian astronomer and physicist Galileo Galilei built the first astronom-ical telescope and observed for the first time the mountains on the moon, sunspots, the rings of Saturn, the moons of Jupiter, and the stellar composition of the Milky Way. Galileo is also celebrated for such ter-restrial discoveries as the law of the acceleration of falling bodies and the principle of the pendulum.

The mind that tied all this into a coherent scientific picture of the universe was that of the English math-ematician Sir Isaac Newton. The linchpin of New-ton's theory was the law of universal gravitation: every particle of matter in the universe, from planets in their orbits to falling bodies here on earth, attracts every other particle of matter with a force called gravity. This gravitational force, Newton declared in his *Mathematical Principles* of 1687, varies directly with the sum of their masses and inversely with the square of the distance between them.

Copernicus, Galileo, Newton, and the other mak-ers of the Scientific Revolution gave the West—and the world—a new technical language and a new ap-proach to truth. Empirical observation and mathe-matical calculation replaced ancient authority and abstract logic as the road to understanding the world. Science and its jargon became the new cult of the West.

During the seventeenth and eighteenth centuries scientific explanations, based on empirical observa-tion or experiment and on mathematical analysis of the results, gained wide acceptance in Europe. Sim-plified layman's explanations of the world according to Newton popularized the new discoveries and the empirical-mathematical approach to truth that had produced them. Scientific societies were organized in England, France, Italy, and elsewhere. In the En-lightenment of the eighteenth century, amateur dabbling in science acquired the sort of prestige among the aristocracy and even the middle classes that dabbling in literature and art had enjoyed in the Renaissance.

The Scientific Revolution was the beginning of several centuries of progress in pure and applied science that would dwarf all earlier scientific advances. It was also the basis for the equally revolutionary social thought that began during these centuries.

The Radical Critique

"My trade," the eighteenth century's most famous intellectual is supposed to have said, "is to say what I think."[1] Voltaire was a philosophe, one of the intellectual leaders of the French Enlightenment, the climax of the Europe-wide Age of Reason. A writer of poetry, fiction, drama, history, popular science, political philosophy, and much, much more, François-Marie Arouet, known as Voltaire (1694–1778), was celebrated as much for his radical critique of the society of his time as for his literary brilliance. Of his many books, none is more widely known and imitated than *Candide* (1759), a picaresque, satirical novel about a naive young man who manages to encounter hypocrisy, injustice, and folly in every country and every class of eighteenth-century society.

Voltaire's contemporary, Jean Jacques Rousseau (1712–1778), was a wild man among the coolly witty philosophes, stressing emotional sincerity rather than satirical wit and urging the superiority of the natural world to artificial modern society. Rousseau was given to passionate declarations like "Man was born free, and everywhere he is in chains," which influenced such later revolutionaries as Robespierre.[2]

The French *Encyclopedia*, edited by Denis Diderot and Jean d'Alembert, used this apparently neutral form as a cloak for more subtle attacks on the "old regime," the society of his own age. The influence of such works, particularly in the hands of the educated French bourgeoisie, was inexorably subversive, undermining faith in the major social institutions of the time.

Enlightened philosophes were thus not system builders, like Aristotle or Thomas Aquinas; they were social critics, the most vigorous Europe had known for centuries. Voltaire and his colleagues attacked the churches of their day—Catholic and Protestant—as nests of superstition, fanaticism, and useless logic-chopping. They condemned the European aristocracy

[1]Evelyn Beatrice Hall, *Life of Voltaire*, 3rd ed. (New York: G. P. Putnam, 1926), p. 145.
[2]Jean Jacques Rousseau, *The Social Contract*, trans. Maurice Cranstan (Baltimore: Penguin Books, 1968), p. 49.

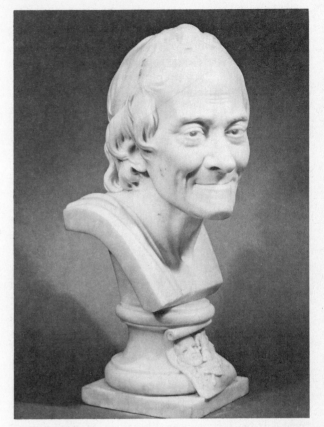

The most celebrated mind of the Enlightenment was that of Voltaire, shown here in a bust by Jean Antoine Houdon. The skeptical, satiric spirit of the age perhaps shows best in the hooded eyes of the king of the philosophes. (The Fine Arts Museums of San Francisco. Gift of Mrs. Rose F. Magnin)

as mere decorations rather than pillars of society, daring to suggest that merit might be more important in determining a person's true value than inherited social position. And if kings and queens were less vigorously assaulted, it was primarily because the philosophes hoped to work through duly enlightened despots to build a more rational and more just world.

On the positive side, these same often satirical social critics found hope in the Scientific Revolution that a better society was possible once human reason was set to solving social problems. They pointed out that before Copernicus, Galileo, and Newton began to probe, the natural world had seemed as confused and unsystematic as the social world still did in the eighteenth century. Another century or two of determined *social*-scientific inquiry, they believed, would uncover "natural laws" as valid in society as the laws of planetary motion or the law of gravity were in the material world.

Indeed, such natural laws of history and society seemed to come to light before the end of the Age of Reason itself. John Locke, a British political thinker writing at the time of the English Revolution of 1688, insisted that all people have natural rights, including liberty, equality, and property. In the middle 1700s, the Baron de Montesquieu's monumental *Spirit of the Laws* argued that within governing institutions there were political principles such as "checks and balances" that, properly applied, would guarantee just and virtuous government. And in 1776 Adam Smith, the father of modern economics, declared in his *Wealth of Nations* that the road to prosperity lies in accepting the law of supply and demand as it functioned naturally in the free, unregulated market economy.

It was a period of revolutionary social thought that seemed to shed a dazzling new light on the way human society works. This Enlightenment critique challenged such ancient social principles as divine-right monarchy, the alliance between church and state, and the hierarchy of unequal classes on which developed societies had been built since ancient Babylon. In the shorter term, the subversive attacks of the philosophes fueled the fires of the impending American and French revolutions. In the longer run, Enlightenment confidence in the possibility of building a better society on the basis of radical social theories spawned all the revolutionary ideologies of the next two centuries, from Jeffersonian liberalism to Leninist socialism. This Enlightenment faith in reason underlies the social engineering and big government, as well as the more revolutionary creeds, of our own time.

From Baroque to Bourgeois

By and large, literature and the arts during the 1600s and 1700s tended to suit the tastes of the two most prominent elements in the society of those two centuries: the courtly aristocracy and the rising bourgeoisie.

Courtly art produced baroque and classical styles rooted in the art of the Renaissance and the Catholic Counter-Reformation, as well as in the traditional culture of ancient Greece and Rome.

The baroque style emerged first as Catholic church art, intended to awe the faithful into acceptance of religion through the sheer grandeur of churches such as the new Saint Peter's in Rome. But secular rulers of the seventeenth century soon saw that the same baroque qualities of rich color, vitality and movement, gilt, glass, light, and sheer scale could awe their subjects into submission to absolute monarchy also. Louis XIV's Versailles, Peter the Great's new capital at St. Petersburg, and many a palace, church, and monastery in between were built with these religious or political ends in view.

The classical style in art went back to the Renaissance, which had emphasized classical Greek and especially Roman models. The more restrained classical approach in painting, architecture, and sculpture differed from the baroque in many ways. It stressed balance, not movement; drawing, not color; simplicity, not complexity. In literature this approach resulted in the French classical drama at the court of Louis XIV, where writers such as Racine and Corneille shaped powerful emotions to the formal precision of hexameter verse.

In all areas, classical art and literature sought guidance in rules and in models. Rules for painting, writing, even acting were made available in books and taught in academies. The models were provided by the "old masters"—Greek, Roman, and Renaissance—in every art.

Aristocratic taste responded to the dry wit and worldly wisdom of La Rochefoucauld's maxims or the poetry of Alexander Pope. Phrases like "A little learning is a dangerous thing," "Fools rush in where angels fear to tread," and "We are so accustomed to disguising ourselves before others that we end by disguising ourselves from ourselves" became part of the temper of the times.

Aristocrats also loved the romantic novels of Mademoiselle de Scudéry, who earned wealth and fame and in the process created a national rage for her delicate mapping of the "tender passions." And the comedies of Molière, France's greatest comic dramatist, showed the court of the Sun King how to laugh at all the pretensions of their age.

Gentlemen and gentlewomen with classical educations and a part to play at royal courts felt right at home with classical art and baroque magnificence. But solid Dutch burghers, aggressive French bourgeois citizens, and middle-class merchants in England had entirely different tastes in art. These middle-class tastes also found expression in the arts of the 1600s and 1700s.

Painters such as Rembrandt van Rijn could depict the merchant oligarchs of the Netherlands—*The Syndics of the Cloth Guild,* say—with the sober dignity and seriousness of purpose they saw as their own great virtues. The French artist Jean Baptiste Chardin could paint a Parisian housewife cutting bread, or a family offering *Grace before Meat* with a simple strength that universalized these aspects of everyday bourgeois life.

In England, the most striking manifestation of middle-class taste was the development of the English novel. In Daniel Defoe's *Robinson Crusoe,* for instance, the bourgeois virtues of industry, ingenuity, common sense, perseverance, and piety that enable Robinson to conquer his island are often regarded as the virtues with which middle-class Europeans were mastering the material world of their own time. Samuel Richardson's early novel *Pamela* deals in a realistic if sentimental way with so commonplace if reprehensible an event as the attempted seduction of a servant girl. It also focuses on Pamela's concern with her proper place in society, with marriage and the security it brings, and with such old-fashioned virtues as chastity and honor—a psychologically realistic portrait that the different values of a later age should not obscure.

A cynical Voltairian aristocrat might sneer at the subtitle of *Pamela*—*Virtue Rewarded*. For the Protestant or Catholic middle ranks of society, however, God still did reward staunch adherence to the middle-class virtues. Art in such novels, such paintings, was merely mirroring life as these middle-class people saw it.

Hostesses to Genius

The center of the cultural life of the Enlightenment was a unique social institution known as the *salon*. A word or two on this living heart of the Age of Reason will serve to close this look at Europe in the middle of the modern period. In particular, the preeminent part played by women in the salon deserves special attention here.

The salon of the seventeenth and eighteenth centuries was not so much a place—an elegant drawing room—as it was a social occasion. The typical salon was a weekly "at home" bringing together witty, cultured people in the drawing room of a witty, cultured, and fashionable hostess. Seventeenth-century salons such as that of the Marquise de Rambouillet

featured literary people in particular; eighteenth-century gatherings such as those at Madame Necker's or *chez* Julie d'Espinasse added science, philosophy, and even political reform to the intellectual fare. In both centuries, the salon brought the aristocratic ruling class and the leading intellectual lights of the age together, advancing intellectual careers and civilizing the aristocracy in the process.

The central role in the salon was of course that of the hostess. Salon hostesses of the 1600s tended to be more aristocratic, like the Marquise de Rambouillet, who designed her own mansion and entertained the literary giants of her day in almost regal splendor. In the 1700s, the social tone became at least marginally less aristocratic—Madame Necker's husband was a mere banker, after all, though for a short time first minister to Louis XVI. But most of the hostesses had some things in common. They tended to be well off if not overwhelmingly wealthy; to be older rather than young; to be single, separated, or widowed rather than married; and to have a large talent for getting people to talk well.

Intellectually, the salon hostess cultivated range more than depth. She had to know enough to guide conversations on everything from the latest play in Paris to German philosophy, from Newton to political reform. She also had to develop such managerial skills as the ability to curtail the bore, encourage the timid, and cut off the potentially explosive argument. She moved with ease and confidence among the best minds of her age, creating among the chandeliers and mirrors an island of intellectuality where ideas could grow, pass from mind to mind, and produce the unique culture of the Age of Reason.

SUMMARY

Politically, Europe was dominated during the seventeenth and eighteenth centuries by its powerful monarchs. In the long run, however, the rise of bourgeois money power and the intellectual breakthrough of the Enlightenment would prove even more important in Western history.

Five great powers and dozens of smaller states divided Europe among them during the 1600s and 1700s. The first of these centuries saw the great strengthening of governmental power under royal absolutists like Louis XIV. The following century saw the rationale for royal government shift from simple divine right toward public service and enlightened rule.

Two German-speaking nations, Prussia and Austria, dominated central Europe. Austria was old and es-

tablished; under Maria Theresa and Francis Joseph it was the most enlightened of European monarchies. Prussia was aggressive, efficient, militaristic; under rulers like Frederick the Great it was the most rapidly growing of the great powers.

Russia, the sprawling backward giant of eastern Europe, emerged as a major power for the first time under Peter the Great and Catherine the Great. France under Louis XIV was the seventeenth-century model of a modern absolutist state, his court at Versailles the ultimate symbol of royal power. And Britain, after a century of revolutionary turmoil and overseas empire building, emerged as the wave of Europe's future: constitutional government with a strong commercial base.

The rise of Europe's commercial bourgeoisie was another major trend of these centuries. In western Europe particularly, middle-class merchants and handicraft manufacturers dominated the economy and, supported by mercantilistic governments, developed the wealth of the continent. In the eighteenth century, the population also took off, beginning the greatest demographic expansion in history.

The intellectual life of the West was shaped by the Scientific Revolution of the sixteenth and seventeenth centuries and by the Enlightenment of the eighteenth. Scientists from Copernicus to Newton began the great modern expansion of our understanding of the material universe. Philosophes like Voltaire and Rousseau turned the resulting confidence in human reason toward a critique of traditional society that called all inherited institutions into question and proposed the creation of a brave new world.

The arts of the time reflected both courtly and bourgeois cultures. Baroque splendor and the classical emphasis on rule and order suited the ruling aristocracy. Dutch painting and the English novel appealed to middle-class audiences with their solid morality and their comfortable middle-class subjects. Presiding over the exciting cultural and intellectual life of these two centuries, the salon hostess epitomized the age as a whole: cultivated, witty, autocratic, forward-looking, and elegant.

More violent times were coming as the eighteenth century drew to a close.

SUGGESTED READING

ANDERSON, M. S. *Europe in the Eighteenth Century, 1713–1783.* London: Longmans, Green, 1976. An excellent introduction.

COLE, C. W. *Colbert and a Century of French Mercantilism.* Hamden, Conn.: Archon, 1964. Scholarly analysis of the policies of the most famous of mercantilists. See also E. F. Heckscher's interpretive and controversial *Mercantilism,* 2nd ed. (New York: Macmillan, 1962).

CRAIG, G. *The Politics of the Prussian Army, 1640–1945.* Oxford: Oxford University Press, 1964. Enlightening account, putting this key element in Prussia's emergence as a great power in the broader context of modern German history.

CRANKSHAW, E. *Maria Theresa.* New York: Viking, 1969. Life of one of the more enlightened of the enlightened despots.

FRASER, A. *The Weaker Vessel: Woman's Lot in Seventeenth-Century England.* New York: Knopf, 1984. Vignettes from top to bottom of society.

GAY, P. *The Enlightenment.* New York: Simon & Schuster, 1974. Authoritative and insightful. See also the thoughtful analysis by one of Europe's most admired intellectual historians, E. Cassirer, *The Philosophy of the Enlightenment* (Princeton: Princeton University Press, 1951). For samples, see C. Brinton, *The Portable Age of Reason Reader* (New York: Viking, 1956).

HELD, J., and D. POSNER. *Seventeenth and Eighteenth Century Art.* Englewood Cliffs, N.J.: Prentice-Hall, 1972. Well-illustrated survey. See also G. Bazin's provocative volume on *The Baroque* (New York: Norton, 1978).

HILL, C. *The Century of Revolution, 1603–1714.* New York: Norton, 1982. Survey of British history in the century of the Puritan Revolution by a leading authority, with a socioeconomic slant.

—— *God's Englishman.* New York: Harper & Row, Pub., 1972. Oliver Cromwell, flinty revolutionary, military dictator, and ideologue. See also C. V. Wedgewood's highly readable *Oliver Cromwell,* 2nd ed. (London: Duckworth, 1973).

KRIEGER, L. *Kings and Philosophers, 1689–1789.* New York: Norton, 1970. Useful survey of enlightened despotism, from the English Revolution to the French one.

MADARIAGA, I. DE. *Russia in the Age of Catherine the Great.* New Haven: Yale University Press, 1981. Recent and authoritative, with a range that goes beyond standard political treatments to economic, social, and intellectual developments.

MASSIE, R. K. *Peter the Great: His Life and World.* New York: Knopf, 1981. Up-to-date account, stressing the role of Peter's dominating personality in shaping the history of his time. For a range of views on the controversial emperor, see M. Raeff, ed., *Peter the Great Changes Russia* (Lexington, Mass.: Heath, 1972).

RAGNILD, H. H. *Europe in the Age of Louis XIV.* New York: Norton, 1979. Good overview of main currents of French and European history in the age of the French predominance.

RITTER, G. *Frederick the Great.* Berkeley: University of California Press, 1968. Scholarly studies of Prussia's most intriguing eighteenth-century ruler.

SOREL, A. *Europe Under the Old Regime.* New York: Harper & Row, Pub., 1964. Stimulating brief interpretation of Europe before the French Revolution.

WOLF, J. *Louis XIV.* New York: Norton, 1968. Thorough political biography.

Chapter · 9

THE DECLINE OF THE EAST

119

THE CENTER FAILS

The End of Asian Preeminence

While Westerners were exploding in all directions out of their end of Eurasia, the eastern four-fifths of the double continent was undergoing a very different process. While Europe was dynamic, aggressive, and expansionist, much of Asia sank into lethargy and decline or simply turned inward, away from the perils of the new age. It was a startling reversal of what had been the norm more often than not: the preeminence of the East in Eurasian history.

Europe had only twice matched the cultural achievements of the major Asian civilizations over the five thousand years of premodern history. During Greek and Roman times (roughly 500 B.C.–A.D. 500) Europe had been one of the great global centers of urban culture. The same had been true during the High Middle Ages (approximately 1100–1350). For most of the rest of the time, however, Asia had clearly led in the building of complex societies, large empires, civilized arts and ideas.

Evidence for Asian preeminence is not hard to find. History and civilization began in the Near East. All the Eurasian world religions originated in Asia, rather than in the European countries. All but one of the greatest Eurasian empires before 1500 were built in Asia. Trade between East and West almost always drained gold out of Europe because Asians disdained European manufactured items as inferior, while Europeans continually coveted the superior workmanship of the East.

At the beginning of modern times, the situation was pretty much normal. The power of the Ottoman Turkish Sultan Suleiman the Magnificent cast a vast and terrifying shadow over Europe. The new empires of Safavid Persia and Mogul India were wealthy and cultured centers of civilization. Ming China was still by far the world's largest nation, busy working out the final parameters of traditional Chinese culture. Feudal Japan hovered on the edge of unification under the shoguns. Asia, in short, was thriving in the sixteenth century.

By the eighteenth, the picture looked very different. During this middle period of modern history, Asia could legitimately be described as losing ground, while Europe forged ahead.

This cultural retreat, or relative decline, took different forms in different parts of Asia during the 1600s and 1700s. The following pages will look first at predominantly Islamic West and South Asia—the Ottoman, Safavid, and Mogul empires—where the Muslim center of Asia failed at last and slid into decline. The chapter will then examine the Manchu conquest of China, the Tokugawa unification of Japan, and the long centuries of intensified isolation that subsequently enveloped both lands.

Throughout, emphasis must fall on the consequences of this decay and withdrawal of the great civilizations of the East. From this decline came the weakened and intensely conservative traditional Asia into which Westerners would finally force their way in large numbers in the nineteenth century. The imposition of the Western hegemony on the largest and most populous of continents was thus facilitated by the relative decline of the East during these centuries of the rise of the West.

The Tide Turns on the Golden Horn

Under Sultan Suleiman the Magnificent (1520–1566), the Turkish Empire had attained its greatest extent, stretching from the Persian Gulf to the Atlantic, from Hungary in the north to Egypt in the south. The wealth of the Ottomans was legendary, the efficiency of their government proverbial. And though the sultans at Istanbul made alliances with European rulers in the tangle of Renaissance power politics, the terror of the Turkish scimitar hung heavy over Europe as a whole.

Within five years of Suleiman's death, the situation began to change. The naval battle of Lepanto (1571), a great victory of Spanish and Italian galleys over the fleets of the Ottomans, effectively ended Turkish expansion in the Mediterranean. In the Balkans too, the Ottoman Empire would make few gains thereafter. In the east, the Ottomans faced the Safavid dynasty of Persia in a series of ultimately indecisive wars during the late 1500s and the earlier 1600s. On all sides, the Ottoman advance was blunted and turned. After one final expansive effort in the later seventeenth century, this halt to Turkish expansion turned into a disastrous retreat.

A series of energetic grand viziers of the Kiuprili family mounted the Ottoman Empire's last great offensives in Europe in the 1660s, 1670s, and 1680s. Turkish arms were victorious from Crete to Hungary, and in 1683 Muslim troops for the last time laid siege to Vienna, the capital of the Holy Roman Empire. But Vienna held. The siege was broken by a combined force of German and Polish troops led by the celebrated Polish king John Sobieski. Thereafter, the tide turned relentlessly against the once great power on the Golden Horn.

In the century following the failure of the last siege of Vienna, the Austrian Habsburgs and the Romanov czars of Russia proved more than a match for the Ottomans in eastern Europe. The Habsburgs took a substantial chunk of the northern Balkans, including Hungary and Transylvania, away from the Turks. The Russians, particularly under Catherine the Great in the later eighteenth century, pushed down to the northern shores of the Black Sea in the Crimea. They even forced the straits linking the Black and Mediterranean seas, bringing Istanbul itself temporarily within range of Russian naval guns. By 1800, Russia seemed quite capable of overwhelming Turkey entirely.

That she did not do so during the nineteenth century was due more to pressure from other European powers than to the dwindling strength of the Ottomans. Turkey was throughout the nineteenth century "the sick man of Europe," ghoulishly observed by Western powers waiting for their shares of the once vast Ottoman inheritance.

The internal decay of the Ottoman Empire was less spectacular but no less inexorable than her decline as a great power. The two were closely related, of course. Turkey's domestic conservatism and decline were reflected in her failure to keep up militarily with the advances of her powerful Western rivals. Turkey, whose big guns had once breached the walls of Constantinople, fell far behind in field artillery during the seventeenth and eighteenth centuries. Her fleets clung to old-fashioned ramming and boarding tactics long after Europeans had turned their naval vessels into floating gun platforms capable of demolishing their foes without ever boarding them at all. The famed Janissary troops, allowed to marry and mingle with ordinary citizens, soon lost their fighting edge and became a sort of Turkish Praetorian Guard, deeply involved in the court politics of Istanbul.

Indeed, corruption sapped the vigor of the entire Ottoman political system in the seventeenth and eighteenth centuries. Weak sultans more interested in enjoying than in running the empire surrendered authority to their grand viziers. Some of these chief ministers were effective rulers, but all of them used power to feather their own nests. *Begs* and *pashas* in the provinces and provincial cities followed this example. Military commanders who could no longer be rewarded with new conquests milked the sultan's own subjects instead. A regime envied in sixteenth-century Europe for efficiency and justice became by the nineteenth a byword for corruption.

Economic problems also afflicted the aging empire. There were some advances, notably the great increase in cash-crop agriculture and food production brought about by the introduction of corn and tobacco from the Americas. But manufacturing, dominated by a conservative guild system, did not keep up—a fatal mistake as the Industrial Revolution began in Europe. Fortunes were made in money lending and through political chicanery, but solid economic progress was neglected.

Division also beset the multinational Ottoman Empire. Various nationalities and religious groups made special arrangements with Istanbul. Greek Orthodox Christians, Jews, Armenians, and others were in effect ruled by their own authorities under the sultan. This tolerance, a virtue in the days of Suleiman, became a decided drawback as later sultans lost the respect of those they ruled.

By the early 1800s, the possibility of fragmentation of the empire was thus as real as that of Russian conquest. Russia had already declared herself official protector of the Christian subjects of the Ottomans. All the southern provinces, from Morocco to Egypt and Arabia, were autonomous or independent. Early in the nineteenth century, the Balkan states of Serbia and Greece successfully rebelled against their Turkish overlords.

The sun that rose over Istanbul still glinted on the masts and spars of the many ships thronging the Golden Horn, flooded the courts of splendid palaces, gilded the domes and minarets of ancient mosques. But the sultans were weak, European traders were many and rich, and the spirit of the Western Enlightenment was penetrating even this far east by the year 1800 of the Christian calendar.

Persian Cockpit

Safavid Persia had reached its apogee, as we have seen, slightly later than Ottoman Turkey, under Shah Abbas I (1571–1629). Abbas ruled an empire the size of present-day Iran, large enough to fill a sizable chunk of the western United States today. Under Abbas, the Safavids turned back both Ottoman and central Asian invasions. They also made their capital, Isfahan, one of the most beautiful cities in the world.

The century following Abbas's death, however, was not so splendid.

The seeds of Safavid decay were perhaps planted deep in the brilliant Persian dynasty from the beginning. The warrior tradition of *ghazi* princes smoldered always beneath the cultivated surfaces of beautiful Isfahan, finding violent expression in the many wars of the Safavid period. The militant Shiite spirit was central to the national identity of Safavid Persia from the days of the founder Ismail, but that spirit also made Shiite Persia an outlaw among the Sunnite majority of Muslim lands. The intrusion of Europeans, finally, was encouraged by even the great Abbas, who wanted their technological and military skills. But those same Western powers would contribute largely to the collapse of the empire into a cockpit of feuding peoples in the eighteenth and nineteenth centuries.

The long wars between the Shiite Safavids and the Sunnite Ottomans turned against Persia after Shah Abbas's death. His successors retired to their harems and the sophisticated pleasures of Isfahan. But persecution of Sunnite minorities in Persia still exploded from time to time. And the English and Portuguese who had competed for influence and trade in Persia were joined in the later seventeenth century by French, Dutch, Spanish, and Russians from north of the border.

In the early eighteenth century, a Sunnite rebellion in Afghanistan severed the eastern portions of the empire from Persia. In the 1720s, Afghan invaders overthrew the Safavids and precipitated an orgy of massacres and persecutions in Isfahan and elsewhere. Persian independence was restored by the militant Nadir Shah in the 1730s, and this great war leader soon overran both Afghanistan and northwestern India, compelling even the Indian Moguls to pay ransom. But Afghanistan soon produced its own great general, and the whole area of modern Iran, Afghanistan, and Pakistan sank into a welter of unending wars.

Moving dexterously around the fringes of the carnage, vying for influence and encouraging the combatants, were the advance guard of European imperialism. Europeans sold the guns and powder on which all sides depended. Russians pushed down from the north: there were Cossack raids in the 1660s, Peter the Great seized Persian territory in the 1720s, and a long competition with Britain for spheres of influence in Iran filled the following century. The British, meanwhile, pressed for Persian trade and considered influence at Isfahan essential for protecting their growing imperial involvement in India.

Shahs of Iran signed treaties, accepted subsidies and advisers, and continued their squabbles with their Afghan rivals on into the nineteenth century. What had once been a great empire, skillful at manipulating client princes, became herself increasingly a puppet of European powers.

Disintegration in Delhi

Akbar the Great (1542–1605), the most celebrated of the Mogul emperors, had ruled not only most of modern India but Pakistan, Bangladesh, and part of Afghanistan as well. As noted in Chapter 2, Akbar's toleration of other Indian faiths and his cultivation of Indian civilization made him popular with the majority of Hindu Indians as well as with his Muslim subjects.

After his death at the beginning of the seventeenth century, there was Muslim power in India still, but never a ruler as popular. And even the political power of Islam in India would disintegrate drastically in the eighteenth century.

The most powerful Mogul ruler of the 1600s was in fact the least popular of all the Moguls: Aurangzeb (1658–1707). Aurangzeb imprisoned his own father and thrust three brothers aside to seize the throne. He reigned long, sometimes cruelly, and generally intolerantly. He presecuted the Hindu majority, pulling down Hindu temples and making it increasingly difficult for any but Muslims to rise in his service. He carried on the military tradition of the Moguls by

The great seventeenth-century Mogul Aurangzeb looks appropriately militaristic in this Western impression. His efforts at economy in government and his vigorous reassertion of Islamic preeminence are not as apparent. (Library of Congress)

driving deep into the south, until at his death the Mogul realm encompassed almost the whole of the subcontinent.

Aurangzeb's long reign, contemporary with that of Louis XIV in Europe, was rendered illustrious in seventeenth-century eyes by these many victories. It was also unique in its effort to cut back on courtly magnificence and expenses. But the emperor's reputation for violence and unscrupulousness tarnished all the rest. A portrait of Aurangzeb shows a black beard, a hint of a smile, and large, liquid black eyes—a face more Indian than Muslim, and not at all brutal. The traditional history of the Indian countryside, however, attributes everything glorious and admired from these centuries to Akbar the Great, everything dark and terrible to the reign of Aurangzeb.

After 1700, disintegration advanced rapidly. The decay of Mogul power carried India, so seldom politically united, rapidly back to the more familiar plurality of feuding states. And from disintegration the subcontinent drifted more rapidly than any other part of the Muslim center into the orbit of the expanding West.

A prime center of discord even during Aurangzeb's time were the Marathas, the Hindu hill people of the Deccan plateau to the south. United by the famous Hindu leader Sivaji in the seventeenth century, the Marathas fought a long guerrilla war against the Moguls. Another center of Indian power lay among the Sikhs in the Northwest. A warrior people like the medieval Rajputs, the Sikhs rejected caste and priestly hierarchy, got along with Muslims, and soon had their own state in the Punjab.

Foreign pressure also mounted on the Moguls. Nadir Shah's Persian invasion in the 1730s resoundingly defeated Mogul armies and looted Delhi itself. Subsequent attacks by Afghan rulers further weakened the hold of the once mighty dynasty.

The greatest long-term threat, finally, came from the growing numbers of Europeans gathering in trading cities and isolated forts around the fringes of India. By the eighteenth century, the field had narrowed to the British and the French, and after 1763 the British, victorious in the Seven Years' War, were effectively alone in the field.

We have noticed the beginnings of Great Britain's Indian empire above. The British East India Company came to trade. Its officers became involved in princely politics in order to protect their interests. They ended by leading armies of *sepoy* Indian troops and signing political alliances with almost all the important *nabobs* (local governors) and independent *rajas* on the subcontinent.

In the 1790s the British crown assumed dual directorship with the company. By 1800 British dependencies stretched the length of the Ganges Valley, from the fringes of the Punjab to Bengal, and down the east coast to the southern tip of India.

The once mighty Moguls now had little more than formal claim on the allegiance of their governors and subordinate princes. Most Indian potentates now received British "advisers" at their courts, depended on British-officered *sepoy* regiments, and traded liberally in silks and cottons and spices, indigo and precious stones with Britain. The crown and the company in London still railed against political entanglements and costly wars. But in fact the company's "servants" had become the most powerful single force in India as the nineteenth century began.

THE FAR EAST TURNS INWARD

Cut Off from the Flow of History

The story of East Asia during the seventeenth and eighteenth centuries is rather different from that of the Muslim center of Eurasia. Both Manchu China and Tokugawa Japan were in many ways very successful dynasties. But China under her Manchu conquerors and Japan under the unifying Tokugawa shogunate both sought to isolate themselves from the outside world during this period. The result of their efforts to cut East Asia off from the flow of history was a slowing of social change and a relative decline by comparison with the dynamic culture of the West.

The next two sections will outline the Manchu conquest in the earlier 1600s and the following century and a half of stability but relative stagnation in China. The following sections will sketch the resurgence of centralized government in Japan under the Tokugawa shoguns around 1600 and the deliberate isolation of the island kingdom that followed. Throughout, the emphasis will fall on the turning inward of these two great civilizations in their last centuries of independent development.

The degree of East Asian isolation, as we shall see, was astonishingly complete. As late as the 1790s, when the British Empire already spanned the world, a British envoy to China was ferried upriver to Peking under a broad banner identifying him as a "Barbarian Bearing Tribute."[1] The Manchu emperor of that time, who was an extremely cultivated person, had only the haziest fairy-tale impression of Britain in the reign of George III as a sea kingdom somewhere far away to the west.

Manchu Banners

The Ming dynasty, which had replaced a regime of Mongolian conquerors in the fourteenth century, fell to a wave of Manchurian invaders in the seventeenth. The end of the Ming era was preceded by the familiar symptoms of dynastic decline: weak emperors, corruption at court and in the administration, drought, famine, and peasant rebellion. The Mandate of Heaven, China's equivalent of the divine right to rule, had clearly been withdrawn by the early 1600s.

Into this decaying order plunged the vigorous new Manchu armies from the north. Nurhachi (1559–1626), the founder of the Manchu state, had welded the Manchurian tribes into a powerful force, combining Chinese bureaucracy with his own system of military organization. The Manchu banner armies, named for the colors of their distinctive standards, were built on companies of three hundred men and included Mongol and Chinese units as well as Manchus. A total of sixteen bannerman armies—275 companies—participated in the invasion of China two decades after Nurhachi's death.

The conquest was prepared and led by two of Nurhachi's sons, Abahai and Dorgon, between the 1620s and the 1640s. Their success in this unlikely project—victory over a nation twenty times their size—was facilitated by a late-Ming peasant rebellion and by the collaboration of a Ming general. The last Ming emperor committed suicide in a capital beset by peasant rebels, and the Ming commander at the Great Wall opened the gates to the Manchu invaders. The Manchu, or Ch'ing ("Pure"), dynasty was formally proclaimed in 1644.

South China held out longer, as it had against the Mongols. Chinese generals carved out short-lived kingdoms for themselves in the south. Port cities and seagoing resistance forces fought to the end. But by the 1680s, all China was once again in the hands of invaders from the north. The Mandate of Heaven had passed, as it usually did even in this most stable of nations, in blood and violence.

The Ch'ing dynasty (1644–1912) was to be China's last. Autocratic and conservative in domestic affairs, the Manchus of the seventeenth and eighteenth centuries also brought growth, prosperity, and further expansion of China's already vast realm. It was only after 1800 that, with sickening suddenness, the decline began.

Two great and long-lived Manchu emperors divide the history of the century and a half between 1644 and 1800 between them: the K'ang-hsi emperor in the seventeenth century and the Ch'ien-lung in the eighteenth. Between them these two Chinese rulers outlived three Louis in France, the later Stuarts and the first three Georges in Britain, and almost the entire rise of the Hohenzollerns in Prussia. And their accomplishments were at least as great.

K'ang-hsi (1661–1722), the longest-reigning emperor in Chinese history, was the ideal monarch. A vigorous outdoorsman, hunter, and leader of armies, like his Manchu ancestors, he was also a Chinese scholar and intellectual and an administrator of endless industry and rigor. At the end of his sixty-year reign, the northern invaders were firmly seated on the throne of China.

K'ang-hsi ruled firmly and fairly, plowing through huge quantities of official reports daily. He preserved most of the Ming structure of government, pairing Chinese provincial governors with Manchu bannermen, combining continuity with the new leadership. He cut taxes and forbade further confiscation of Chinese lands by Manchus once pacification was complete.

As commander in chief of the armies, K'ang-hsi first completed the conquest of South China and then turned his attention to expanding Chinese power westward, into central Asia. He defeated the western

[1]Roy MacGregor-Hastie, *The Red Barbarians* (London: Pan Books, 1961), p. 11.

The ferocity of the Manchu onslaught, which carried them to mastery of seventeenth-century China, shows clearly in this picture. (New York Public Library Picture Collection)

Mongols, an ancient threat to China. He turned back the Russian Cossacks, point men for Russia's own expansion eastward to the Pacific. He imposed a pro-Chinese Dalai Lama in Tibet.

As a scholar, K'ang-hsi sponsored a famous dictionary, yet another gigantic encyclopedia, and an official history of the preceding dynasty. He patronized artists and philosophers. He had himself painted, surrounded by art objects, with a Chinese landscape painting and his own portrait on the wall behind him.

A contemporary of Aurangzeb in India and Louis XIV in Europe, Emperor K'ang-hsi combined the Mogul's military prowess with the Sun King's dedication to the art of governance. He has been called not only the longest-reigning but the most successful of Chinese emperors.

Ch'ien-lung (1735–1796) K'ang-hsi's grandson, led the Middle Kingdom to new levels of political strength, size, and population, prosperity and international power. Since many of the accomplishments of his reign represent the apogee of the dynasty, they will be developed at length in the survey of Ch'ing society that follows.

Ch'ien-lung's personal contribution was particularly visible in his magnificent style of life and his extensive foreign conquests. Under his direction, Manchu Chinese armies pushed westward, as they had in Han, T'ang, and Mongol times. Chinese sov-

ereignty was expanded once more across the wastes of central Asia as far as the towering Pamirs.

At home, prosperity and government revenues grew, so that Ch'ien-lung was able to live in the grand style. He built immense palaces and undertook magnificent royal progresses across the empire. His patronage of literature and learning produced a famous collection, *The Complete Library of Four Treasuries*, which amounted in the end to 36,000 volumes!

Ch'ien-lung's suspicious nature and absolutist bent led him to censor as well as to sponsor scholarly activity, and he suppressed any book he deemed anti-Manchu. But his splendid style cloaked a work schedule as relentless as K'ang-hsi's, beginning before dawn and exhausting his secretaries. Ch'ien-lung piously abdicated in 1796 rather than reign longer than his illustrious grandfather. But his powerful personality continued to dominate the government until death finally stilled his fierce energies in the last year of the century.

Dyarchy, Development, and the Beginning of Decline

The power of the Manchus, in numbers a small percentage of the population they had conquered, was imposed on China in a number of ways. Manchu garrisons were stationed strategically across the country.

Large tracts of land were set aside to provide revenues for the Ch'ing emperors and for Manchu bannermen. Manchus were forbidden to marry Chinese, Manchu women to bind their feet in the Chinese style. All Chinese men, by contrast, were required to shave all but a single braided pigtail from their heads, a symbol of acceptance of the overlordship of the Manchus, who wore their hair this way.

The political organization of China, however, has often been described as a dyarchy, a dual Chinese-Manchu government—and in many ways it looks more Chinese than Manchu. The trend toward royal absolutism, begun under the Mongols and the Ming, continued under the Ch'ing. Manchu emperors made all major decisions and many minor ones personally. But all important imperial bureaus were headed by two officials, one Manchu and one Chinese. Government boards were half Manchu and half Chinese in membership. As noted above, Chinese provincial governors were matched with Manchu governors-general.

Below the provincial level, however, all officials remained Chinese. Local magistrates and village headmen were chosen on the basis of local prestige, as in earlier periods. For the average peasant, to whom the Son of Heaven had always been a half-mythical being in a far-off capital, foreign rule can have made little difference.

One thing many must have noticed over most of the 1600s and 1700s, however, was the flourishing state of the economy under the Manchus.

Agriculture was basic, as it is to this day in China. New types of rice, improvements in irrigation and fertilization, and new crops such as corn and sweet potatoes boosted food production dramatically. Traditional handicraft industries grew steadily—pottery, silk, cotton, mining, and metalwork—practiced by ancient guilds in many parts of China. Domestic trade reached new highs, and foreign trade, though comparatively small, produced an inflow of gold and silver steady enough to warm the heart of a European mercantilist.

A further result of economic prosperity was a continuing growth in population, which probably doubled over these two centuries to approximately 300 million by 1800. Some of these teeming millions began to emigrate to Southeast Asia, the core of the overseas Chinese minorities of later centuries. Others, unable to leave, felt the growing pressure of population on even a burgeoning food supply. This Malthusian problem for all modern states was noticed by a Chinese scholar about the time that Parson Malthus detected it in 1790s Britain.

A final testimony to the success of the Ch'ing emperors during the 1600s and 1700s was the further

expansion of the empire. The Manchus brought Manchuria and its suzerainty over Korea with them to China. Once and for all they broke the power of the Mongols, the last of the great steppe nomads, by conquering Inner Mongolia and opening Outer Mongolia to Chinese commercial exploitation. They reconquered and finally incorporated the huge western lands of Sinkiang into the empire. They set up a protectorate over Tibet, garrisoned central Asia all the way to the Pamirs, and collected tribute from Vietnam, Burma, and other East and Southeast Asian states.

Yet in many ways even the greatest of the Manchus were inward-looking and conservative. As is so frequently the case, the seeds of their ultimate decline were there from the beginning.

To prove themselves more Chinese than the Chinese, the Manchu emperors encouraged the most conservative Confucianism. They stressed China's total self-sufficiency and supremacy, depicting their empire as the one truly civilized land in a barbarous world. Since they did not need the rest of the world, they did nothing to build a navy or a great merchant marine; the nation that had put huge fleets to sea in the fifteenth century was now left far behind in shipbuilding and naval development. Scholars and literatti also had no use for mechanical things, and so the nation that had invented printing, gunpowder, and the compass slid steadily further behind in industrial development also.

Contact with the West, reestablished under the later Mings, developed uncertainly and then declined under the Manchus. Jesuit missionaries were welcomed at court in the seventeenth century, mostly for their skills in Western arts and sciences. But later missionaries, who refused to compromise their opposition to Chinese traditional ancestor worship and the veneration of Confucius, were proscribed in the 1720s. Trade developed relatively freely in early Manchu times, but was narrowly limited to a section of the southern port of Canton in the later 1700s. Manchu emperors might enjoy learning to play exotic instruments such as the clavichord or dressing up a few court ladies in colorful Western costumes, but they saw little importance in European trade.

When the great decline in Manchu fortunes began around 1800, the Middle Kingdom would pay dearly for having ignored the chance to learn more valuable things from the West while there was time.

The Tokugawa Shoguns

The Japanese islands were much more open to foreign influences than China was in the early part of this period. In Japan also, a strong new dynasty came to power in the seventeenth century—not foreign conquerors but the unifying Tokugawa shoguns. But in Japan too, an increasingly conservative regime rejected foreign influences and turned inward over the 1600s and 1700s.

Japan, which had learned so much from China in centuries past, was initially much more willing than the Middle Kingdom to deal with the West. From this interaction came a transformation of Japanese feudalism and the reemergence of a strong government—which, paradoxically, proceeded to turn its back upon the West once more.

In the sixteenth century the wealthier Japanese barons, or *daimyo*, were glad to have Portuguese and later English, Dutch, and other merchants come with their goods. To attract the traders, some *daimyo* welcomed Jesuit and other missionaries, who were soon making more converts in Japan than in China. Most important of all in that war-torn age, Western muskets and cannon transformed the art of war in samurai Japan. Firearms gave the military edge to *daimyo* who could build companies of musketeers, artillery, and the huge new castles needed to resist these military innovations in the hands of others.

The suppression of feudal warfare and the political reunification that followed were the work of a series of three of these *daimyo* barons clever enough to exploit both the old feudal rules and the new military circumstances to their own advantage.

Their names were Nobunaga, Hideyoshi, and Tokugawa Ieyasu. These three men shared a knack for manipulating the new weapons with tactical daring. They were also masters of the traditional methods of feudal alliance-building through distribution of rewards, political marriages, and political intrigue. All three first moved to establish themselves as protector of the ceremonial emperor at the old capital at Kyoto, then turned to overcoming opposition from rival barons in the countryside.

Nobunaga (1534–1582) established a powerful *daimyo* alliance in the large central island of Honshu, moved on to Kyoto, and overthrew the Ashikaga shogunate, by then moribund and ripe for dispatching. Hideyoshi (1536–1598), a rude peasant who had risen to general's rank under Nobunaga, is usually considered the real unifier of Japan. Hideyoshi expanded Nobunaga's baronial connection to include all the chief *daimyo* in the island empire. He disarmed the peasantry, encouraged trade with the West, and dreamed megalomaniacal—and fruitless—dreams of conquering China itself. Tokugawa Ieyasu (r. 1603–1616), a vassal of Hideyoshi's, outfought all rivals for his master's legacy at the great battle of Sekigahara in 1600 and was officially named shogun three years later.

Under Ieyasu and his son and grandson, the Tokugawa shogunate was firmly established. They would wield power for the next two and a half centuries (1603–1868). Like the Manchu emperors of China, the Tokugawa shoguns were in many ways a very successful dynasty. But the Tokugawa, like the Manchus, made what became the fatal conservative error of trying to turn their backs upon the roaring tide of change.

Typical of this tendency was the great event of the immediate postcentralization period: the closing of Japan to Western influences.

By the early 1600s there were Portuguese, Spanish, English, and Dutch merchants in Japan. There were Jesuit and Franciscan missionaries and almost a third of a million Christian Japanese. There was much more interaction between the two cultures in Japan than in China: Jesuits learned the Zen tea ceremony, and fashionable Japanese wore crucifixes and smoked tobacco.

But the seventeenth-century Tokugawa shoguns grew suspicious of European imperialist ambitions. They began to see Christianity as a subversive ideology. Then official persecution set off a short-lived Japanese Christian revolt in one section of the islands. The government reacted with massive martyrdoms that destroyed all but a tiny underground remnant of Christianity in Japan.

Traders also became suspect. One Western trading power after another was expelled, until by the 1640s—a century after the first Portuguese had arrived—only a single Dutch trading post on an island in Nagasaki harbor remained to connect Japan with the Western world.

The fundamental conservatism of the Tokugawa shogunate extended to domestic as well as foreign affairs. Determined efforts were made throughout the seventeenth and eighteenth centuries to revive such traditional elements of Japanese culture as the samurai virtues, class structure, and the agrarian pattern of life.

The most famous such effort to turn the clock back was made by the eighteenth-century shogun Yoshimune (1716–1745). Yoshimune was a model of ancient Japanese rectitude. He issued many decrees on moral and social behavior and urged simplicity, decency, and the military code of the samurai upon his people. Yoshimune's economic reforms, intended to favor agriculture at the expense of trade, succeeded in triggering a major commercial depression, but this has not damaged his reputation as one of the most virtuous of the shoguns.

Division, Isolation, and the Character of Japan

The Tokugawa shogunate actually saw an odd amalgam during its first two centuries: an intensely conservative, still semifeudal political regime presiding over a booming urban, commercial economy. Out of this unlikely combination evolved the unique culture of Tokugawa Japan.

The political system of the Tokugawa shoguns was built on the feudal order out of which they had risen. Tokugawa "centralized feudalism" was a structure of power based on the huge landholdings of the shoguns and the substantial allotments of the puppet emperors and the shogun's vassal *daimyo*. The rest of society was fixed by law in a rigid system of classes—peasants forbidden to leave the land, samurai prohibited any but military or administrative careers. There was government support for the traditional agrarian economy. There was also repeated legislation against conspicuous consumption by people of the lower classes. The Tokugawa thus seemed totally dedicated to preserving old Japan in amber, an unchanging perfection in a changing world.

In fact, however, the Japanese islands were in the grip of rapid economic progress during these centuries. The resulting population growth, urban development, and cultural innovation had few points of contact with the conservative ideals of the Tokugawa shoguns.

Agriculture, encouraged by the government, developed steadily. Acreage under cultivation doubled under the impact of new fertilizers and seeds, double cropping, and other improvements in agricultural techniques. The increase in the amount of food available led in turn to considerable growth in population, from perhaps 18 million in 1600 to 30 million in the eighteenth century.

The growth of trade, though it was largely domestic, was even more spectacular, constituting a commercial revolution in Japan during the seventeenth century. Low taxes, a lack of government intervention, and the general lack of interest in business on the part of the country's feudal and Confucian rulers left merchants free to grow as fast as they could. Urban developement also contributed by concentrating large numbers of customers for merchants and artisans. Edo—later called Tokyo—reached a population of a million, and the commercial port of Osaka half that. The shoguns required the *daimyo* aristocracy to establish residences in Edo, and samurai collected there and in other cities, creating a growing demand for food, handicraft manufactures, and the luxury trades in particular.

Two geishas, *skilled and cultured Japanese courtesans of two centuries ago, go through their dressing ritual in this colored Japanese woodblock print by Kitagawawa Utamoro, a famous eighteenth-century artist. (The Metropolitan Museum of Art, Rogers Fund)*

Out of these transformations and tensions in an island kingdom largely cut off from the world, a distinctly Japanese national character evolved. Buddhist and bushido traditions, love for art and culture going back to Heian times, the success-worshiping values of the new commercial world, and the pleasures of urban life mingled in Tokugawa Japan. The result was a Japanese temperament combining aesthetic sensibility with a martial sense of duty, a compulsive determination to live up to ancient standards, and an intense drive for personal success.

It was a character that could cling doggedly for hundreds of years to the outdated feudal ideals of the Tokugawa—and then throw itself with equal passion into the modernization and Westernization of Japan in the later nineteenth century. In the seventeenth and eighteenth centuries, however, it was the past that prevailed as Japan turned inward once more to shape its own soul in isolation from the larger world.

CULTURES OF THE TWILIGHT

A Backward Glance

Only the narrowest Western vision could see cultural unity in the rich and varied civilizations of Asia. Even at the broadest stereotypical level, there is little similarity to be found among the crusading passions of Arabic Islam, the otherworldly acceptance of Hindu India, the scholarly humanism of the Confucian tradition, and the taut soldier's code of the samurai. The "Asia" that produced the Blue Mosque in Istanbul, Angkor Wat in Cambodia, and the Great Wall of China is surely more of a cultural smorgasbord than a unity.

During these centuries of decline and inward turning, however, a single note is struck again and again across the diverse cultures of the world's largest continent. It is a tone that may be described perhaps most simply as a backward glance.

The great cultures of the East were all firmly in place by early-modern times. They had evolved and changed since their foundations had first been laid down centuries or millennia before. But they were essentially accomplished by the seventeenth and eighteenth centuries. We speak of "traditional India," "traditional China" from then on, of civilizations whose main outlines are fixed and clear.

What remained was to comment on, to revive, to echo the great achievements of the past. In an Asia where the great centers of civilization were either crumbling away or withdrawing, that was precisely what happened.

New religions did not emerge—only sects. New art modeled itself upon old art, or otherwise reacted to the old masters. Philosophers were much more likely to be commentators on the ancient sages than original thinkers. The sciences were left with a shrug to the Westerners, who, as many Asians saw it, vulgarized everything they touched with the crudest of practical applications.

It was a culture of the twilight, thought and art conceived by peoples half conscious at least that their day was drawing to a close. A few examples of this culture of old Asia's waning centuries follow.

Muslims and Hindus Return to the Source

The Wahabi sect that emerged in the deserts of Arabia in the middle of the eighteenth century has at first glance little of a twilight feel about it. Flinty Arab fundamentalists, the Wahabis look more like Puritans building the new Jerusalem than a people at the end of an age. Their fundamentalist rigor was actually more than a backward glance: it was a wholehearted rush into the past, a pell-mell plunge back to Islam's beginnings.

The founder of the Wahabi sect, Muhammad ibn' Abdul-Wahab (1691–1787), preached a return to the teachings of the Koran and the Law, the most authentic Sunni traditions of the Prophet. Muslims, he declared, should live as Muhammad had taught them to, and nothing should come between the believer and submission to those fundamental teachings. With rigor worthy of a Martin Luther, Abdul-Wahab rejected all that had come since. The insights of Islam's golden age under the Arab caliphs, the mystical visions of the Sufis, all the accumulated wisdom of the Islamic community since Muhammad had to be rejected. Veneration of Muslim saints, broad interpretation of the Muslim Law, unsanctioned habits such as the drinking of wine—all were cast aside in that long, eager backward reach to the sources of Islam.

Deep in the desert fastnesses of Arabia, in the very area where the Prophet had once walked the earth, the Wahabis lived their vigorous, puritanical faith. Abdul-Wahab accepted the patronage of the ambitious house of Saud—the rulers of Saudi Arabia today—and Wahabism spread rapidly across the peninsula. Wahabis soon dominated both the Muslim holy cities of Mecca and Medina, and pilgrims carried word of the new sect back with them to all parts of the Islamic world.

An Egyptian invasion of Arabia put an end to the worldly expansion of the Wahabi movement. But the reputation and influence of the desert sect spread to pious Muslims as far away as Ottoman Turkey and even India. The Wahabis were *living* as Muslims had in the days of the Prophet! Forbidding as its puritanical rigor might be, this fundamentalist return to the source could not but be appealing in a bewildering time when history seemed incomprehensibly to have turned its back on the followers of Allah.

The Rajput painting of seventeenth- and eighteenth-century India, in its very different way, also cast that long, wistful backward glance.

The Rajput painters are normally considered artists in a popular tradition, to be contrasted with the sophisticated realism of the art of the Mogul courts. They actually worked at the courts of provincial princes in central India or in the foothills of the Himalayas. They painted many subjects in a variety of styles. But in both subject and style, there is once more that sense of turning back to the great traditions of the past.

Popular Rajput subjects, for instance, included the

heroic deeds of Rajput warriors in earlier centuries; passages from the ancient Indian epics, the *Mahabharata* and the *Ramayana;* and episodes from the timeless myths of Vishnu and Shiva. Rajput artists also painted scenes to illustrate musical modes and the many forms of love—but the latter at least was also a well-established Hindu tradition.

Style, essentially ahistorical, is a harder thing to read in historical terms, But there are elements of earlier schools in the work of most of these painters of the lesser courts. There is a refusal to change, to keep up with the first European influences creeping into the art of the great *rajas.* There is in the painting of one court in Rajastan, where the divine lovers Krishna and Radha were particularly revered, a twilight loveliness that transcends time and space, "a fragile elegance and a wan, neurasthenic refinement that are like an echo of the beauty of Ikhnaton's queen,"[2] the swan-necked Nefertiti,—doomed too, like the art of the Rajput princes.

Han Learning and Genroku Culture

Chinese thought and art had always managed a delicate balance of traditionalism and originality. Under the Manchus, culture seemed to career off to wild extremes, reacting with jarring extravagance to a powerfully felt sense of past greatness and present inadequacy.

Some aspects of Chinese culture continued largely as before. Confucius continued to be revered, sumptuous palaces to be built, immense quantities of traditional chinaware to be produced by government works for export. But scholarship exhibited the odd dichotomy indicated above: there was passion for "Han learning," the wisdom of two thousand years before, yet this same period saw a wave of literary detective work that actually challenged the authenticity of some of the most admired Confucian classics. Painters were divided into two rather different camps: the "orthodox," who followed stylistically in the footsteps of their predecessors, and the "individualists" and "eccentrics," who reacted violently against all earlier schools. Orthodox painters did beautiful work in traditions that went back to the Sung. The eccentrics produced wildly assymetrical or whimsical paintings drawn with blunted brushes or—in one case—even with bare hands!

Imitation, however, was probably more common than iconoclasm in this ambivalent preoccupation with the past. The most famous work of literature produced in Manchu times was also China's most loved novel, Ts'ao Hsüeh-ch'in's *Dream of the Red Chamber*. It is, characteristically, the story of a great family in decline. Generational conflicts, powerful female characters, and the intricate life of a traditional Chinese family combine against a background of social decay and profound Buddhist and Taoist devotion. *The Dream of the Red Chamber* thus offers a moving vision of yet another Eurasian culture of the twilight centuries.

Tokugawa Japanese culture has its aristocratic casting back to better times too. In particular the court of the figurehead emperor at Kyoto continued to develop a delicate sensibility that harked back centuries to Japan's medieval Heian culture. The shoguns trumpeted the virtues of more recent samurai times. But in Japan, almost uniquely, there was also a surge of originality and vigor under the Tokugawa. It appeared in the new commercial cities, especially in Edo and Osaka, and its finest flowering came in the half century around 1700. It is usually called Genroku culture.

Genroku culture blossomed most brilliantly in the urban subculture of playboys and prostitutes, popular entertainment, gambling, and bohemianism. It created *haiku* poetry, *kabuki* theater, and the Japanese print—an array of cultural innovation that would distinguish any age.

Haiku verse, with its deceptive simplicity—seventeen syllables arranged in three lines—deliberately leaves much to the reader's imagination. Typically a series of images drawn from nature is presented in order to stir up a unique complex of associations and echoes in the mind of each reader. Evocative, haunting, sometimes funny, *haiku* can stimulate a sense of spiritual depth as great as that of a misty Sung landscape. *Haiku* verse has tempted not only Japanese, but foreigners in many languages since.

Kabuki theater, which attracted wildly enthusiastic crowds in Tokugawa Edo, has proved less readily exportable. Begun by a troop of women actors and dancers in the early 1600s, *kabuki* evolved into a popular form of pageantry with gaudy costumes, dazzling scenery, and extravagant passions unleashed in traditional stylized movements. In time, male actors took over the productions. But the most admired of these actors were always the ones who, through a lifetime of training, specialized in playing the female parts!

The Japanese print, finally, is familiar to every Western admirer of the work of Toulouse-Lautrec, Degas, and others of the great nineteenth-century French precursors of modernist painting, who were profoundly influenced by the Japanese form. Done in four colors, these wood-block prints were the quintessence of Genroku culture. Beginning as illustra-

[2]Benjamin Rowland, *The Art and Architecture of India* (New York: Penguin Books, 1981), p. 350.

tions for "pillow books" (sex manuals), wood-block prints developed as pictures of famous courtesans, theatrical scenes, and representations of city life.

These eighteenth-century Japanese prints breathe the sophistication of the very unfeudal pleasure capitals of Tokugawa Japan.

SUMMARY

While Western power grew, the great empires of the East either declined or withdrew into isolation during the seventeenth, eighteenth, and early nineteenth centuries. For the first time, Asia lost the position of parity with or superiority to Europe that she had enjoyed throughout history.

In the Middle East, the Ottoman Empire ceased to be a threat to Europe, lost territory to Austria and Russia, and sank into political corruption and industrial decay. In Persia, the endless Shiite wars led to fragmentation, the successful secession of Afghanistan, and increasing British and Russian influence in Isfahan. Mogul India also felt the divisive force of religious difference—in this instance, Hindu revolts against Muslim persecution—and the pressure of growing European power, which climaxed in the ascendency of the British East India Company after the defeat of the French in 1763.

In East Asia, powerful new dynasties dominated both China and Japan in the seventeenth century. But both the Manchu emperors and the Tokugawa shoguns adopted isolationist policies toward the West which, in the long run, did not pay. The long-lived emperors K'ang-hsi and Ch'ien-lung led China to renewed power and still greater prosperity under the Manchus. But their intense Confucian conservatism and their rejection of Western influences left China ill prepared for the unprecedented Western onslaught that was to come in the nineteenth century.

The Tokugawa shogun Ieyasu, who seized power in 1600, brought an end to centuries of civil strife. He and his successors presided over a prosperous economy and a sophisticated urban culture. But the Tokugawas also preached conservative bushido traditions and expelled the Europeans who had found a foothold in their country.

In withdrawal or decay, Asia drew heavily on her past artistic and intellectual achievements during these centuries. Thus, Arab Muslims turned to Wahabi fundamentalism, and Rajput painters drew on India's ancient myths and epics for themes and subjects. Manchu Chinese culture went to extremes of conservatism and eccentricity. Only in Japan did cultural development take a dynamic new direction, in the sophisticated urban art and literature of Genroku culture.

SUGGESTED READING

BELLAH, R. N.   *Tokugawa Religion: The Values of Pre-Industrial Japan.* Glencoe, Ill.: Free Press, 1957. Religion and value systems in traditional Japan.

HABIB, I.   *Agrarian System of Mughal India, 1556–1707.* New York: Asia Publishing House, 1963. Agricultural land holding.

IRVINE, W.   *Later Mughals* (2 vols.). Calcutta: M. C. Sarkar and Sons, 1921–1922. Old, but still useful. For the completion of the story of the decline of the dynasty, see J. Sarkar's scholarly *Fall of the Mughal Empire* (4 vols.) (Calcutta: M. C. Sarkar, 1932–1950).

KAHN, H. L.   *Monarchy in the Emperor's Eyes: Image and Reality in the Ch'ien-lung Reign.* Cambridge, Mass.: Harvard University Press, 1971. Perhaps the greatest ruler of Manchu China.

KEENE, D.   *World Within Walls: Japanese Literature of the Pre-Modern Era, 1600–1867.* New York: Holt, Rinehart & Winston, 1976. Authoritative and elegantly written history of Japanese literature in the Tokugawa era. For haiku poetry, see H. G. Henderson, *An Introduction to Haiku* (Garden City, N.Y.: Doubleday, 1958).

KESSLER, L.   *K'ang-hsi and the Consolidation of Ch'ing Rule, 1661–1684.* Chicago: University of Chicago Press, 1976. See also R. B. Oxnam, *Ruling from Horseback: Manchu Politics in the Oboi Regency, 1661–1669* (Chicago: University of Chicago Press, 1975), on early Manchu government in conquered China.

LANE, R.   *Masters of the Japanese Print—Their World and Their Work.* Garden City, N.Y.: Doubleday, 1962. Japan's most imitated contribution to the graphic arts.

LEWIS, B.   "Some Reflections on the Decline of the Ottoman Empire," in C. M. Cipolla, ed., *The Economic Decline of Empires.* London: Methuen, 1970. Interesting reflections on the economic aspects of Ottoman decline.

MARUYAMA, M. *Studies in the Intellectual History of Tokugawa Japan*, trans. M. Hane. Princeton: Princeton University Press, 1974. A monument of Japanese scholarship.

METZGER, T. A. *Internal Organization of Ch'ing Bureaucracy*. Cambridge, Mass.: Harvard University Press, 1973. The final formulation of China's traditional administrative system.

QURESHI, I. H. *Administration of the Mughal Empire*. Karachi: University of Karachi Press, 1966. Scholarly description of India's last central government before the imposition of British rule.

SANSOM, G. *The Western World and Japan*. New York: Knopf, 1950. Includes the sixteenth-century period of initial penetration and the seventeenth-century expulsion of the Westerners. See also C. R. Boxer's *The Christian Century in Japan* (Berkeley: University of California Press, 1951).

SARKAR, J. *History of Aurangzib* (5 vols.). Calcutta: M. C. Sarkar, 1928. Old but irreplaceable piece of solid scholarship on the greatest of the later Moguls.

SAUNDERS, J. J. "The Problem of Islamic Decadence," *Journal of World History*, 7 (1963), 701–720. Consideration of the broad pattern of decline across the Muslim center.

SKINNER, G. W., ed. *The City in Late Imperial China*. Stanford, Cal.: Stanford University Press, 1977. Articles on urban development in traditional China.

SPEAR, P. *Twilight of the Mughals*. Cambridge: Cambridge University Press, 1951. The Mogul Indian Empire in the shadow of Western imperialism.

STOIANOVICH, T. "Factors in the Decline of Ottoman Society in the Balkans," *Slavic Review*, 21 (1962), 623–632. Failure of Ottoman rule in southeastern Europe.

TOTMAN, C. *Politics in the Tokugawa Bakafu, 1600–1843*. Cambridge, Mass.: Harvard University Press, 1967. Japanese politics from the reimposition of central authority to the eve of the Meiji reform.

TS'AO HSUEH-CHIN. *The Dream of the Red Chamber*, trans. and abridged by Chi-chen Wang. Garden City, N.Y.: Doubleday, 1929. China's most celebrated novel, and one of the richest and most sophisticated. A complete translation in five volumes by David Hawkes is now appearing under the title of *The Story of the Stone* (Baltimore: Penguin, 1973–   ).

Chapter · 10

THE AGE OF STEAM AND BALLOTS

AN AGE OF REVOLUTIONS

Breakthroughs

Europe in the nineteenth century has one of the least exciting images of any time and place. One thinks of frock coats and Queen Victoria. One imagines a world reeking of cultural smugness, moral hypocrisy, and overstuffed bad taste. Was this not the century that tried to deny sex, glorified imperialism, and prepared the way for the greatest war the world had ever seen? Much of the cultural history of the present century may be seen as a rejection of everything the preceding century stood for, a violent disowning of our most recent Western past.

It will not work. The nineteenth must, in fact, rank as one of the most important of all centuries, not only in Western history but in the crucial historical evolution from regional cultures through intercontinental empires to genuinely global history.

If we begin the historical nineteenth century a bit earlier, in the later 1700s, we see that the period stands out in two areas especially. It is the era that saw the evolution and dissemination of the new social ideologies spawned by the Enlightenment and the French Revolution. And it is the century of Europe's industrialization, beginning with the Industrial Revolution in Great Britain.

These two seminal trends originated in western Europe, especially in Britain and France, and spread slowly east, reaching Russia in full force only at the very end of the century. They became the most important Western exports to the rest of the world in the climactic New Imperialism of the later 1800s. They would also be the central shaping forces in the history of the twentieth-century world we live in. These two main currents—industrial development and ideologies—make the nineteenth century second only to our own in modern world history.

There will be room for a number of things in the following pages, from Napoleon and Bismarck to the most notorious prostitute in Paris and Sunday in the park with Seurat. But again and again we will find ourselves circling back through the French Revolution and the British Reform Bill, cartels and Karl Marx to these twin focuses of the century: industrialism and ideology, the steam engine and the ballot box.

Storming the Bastille

The Paris mob that attacked the Bastille on July 14, 1789, did not know that they were making history.

The Bastille had been built as a fort and converted to a prison, and was notorious as a place of incarceration for political offenders—Voltaire himself had once languished there. To the mob that surrounded its huge towers and creaking drawbridge that July morning, it was primarily a potential source of weapons to use against the royal troops who had been gathering in Paris over the past two weeks to control just such political violence as this.

A deputation from the crowd demanded the weapons and were refused. When some of the mob broke into the courtyard, they were fired on and scores were killed. When the governor of the prison finally yielded up the keys in return for guarantees of safety, he and a number of his officers were cut to pieces by the vengeful *sans-culottes*, the outraged rabble of Paris. Seven prisoners were freed: four forgers, two madmen, and a sex offender.

Next day the mob came again—to begin the dismantling of the Bastille itself. The prison was leveled, the keys sent to George Washington across the Atlantic in fraternal greetings. July Fourteenth became France's Fourth of July—her Independence Day.

The storming of the Bastille revealed the will of the French people to defy their ancient kings and take their political destinies in their own hands. Most important, however, it was a symbol—and ideological revolutions live on symbols. When word of the attack was carried to Louis XVI, he gasped, "It's a revolt!" "No, Sire," he was answered more gravely, "it is a revolution."[1] It is as a symbol of governmental tyranny and popular revolution that the Bastille has entered the language of modern ideological rebellion.

The French Revolution looms much larger in Western history than the American Revolution, which preceded it. The revolution in France, the greatest power in Europe, was the archetypal assault on the old order of kings, aristocrats, and priests that had prevailed in Europe since the Middle Ages. It introduced a cycle of revolt, Europe's Age of Revolutions, that would last for more than half a century, from 1789 through the Europe-wide Revolutions of 1848. Its causes, stages, and consequences therefore deserve a few pages here.

[1]Robert Ergang, *Europe from the Renaissance to Waterloo* (Boston: D.C. Heath, 1954), p. 657.

Crises

The complex causes of the French Revolution included some deep-seated social problems, subversive ideas, and a cluster of devastating political and economic crises.

Social discontent in France revolved around an anachronistic social structure. This social order gave special privileges to half a million aristocrats and churchmen, and denied them to 23 million members of the "third estate"—the rest of the population. Under this system, the urban poor languished in poverty and frequent hunger in city slums, free peasants grumbled at forced labor and other feudal survivals, and an increasingly aggressive and wealthy bourgeoisie resented the tax exemptions and unearned prestige of the nobility. The nobility clung to their feudal privileges and challenged both the absolute power wielded by the weak heirs of Louis XIV and the demands of the rising middle classes.

Even France's kings helped bring on the revolution. Louis XV lived for pleasure for most of his sixty-year reign and predicted with a sigh that after him would come the Deluge. Louis XVI, a well-meaning but weak-willed man, dithered through most of his fifteen years of power—and reaped the whirlwind.

The subversive literature of the Enlightenment further undermined the old order by creating a negative public image of the kings, aristocrats, and clergymen

The attack on the Bastille, July 14, 1789, France's Independence Day. The actual events of that day may not have been so dramatic, but the symbolic significance of the fall of this royal prison to a mob of angry Parisians was not lost on Europe. (Copyright Radio Times Hulton Picture Library)

who ran it. Voltaire and his colleagues depicted the clergy as worldly and bigoted, the aristocracy as foppish and feckless, and the monarchy itself as bearing ultimate responsibility for a society far gone in rot and decay. The French philosophes supported a Lockean notion of natural human rights which contrasted sharply with the traditional privileges claimed by the aristocracy and the church. The radical critique of the Enlightenment thus contributed significantly to the coming of the revolution.

In the late 1780s a series of linked economic and political crises swept France to the brink of revolution. Bad harvests and industrial depression sent mobs of bread rioters into the streets of French cities and gangs of hungry peasants roaming the countryside, burning and looting. At the same time, a financial crisis, rooted in military expenditures and in the tax exemptions of the nobility and the church, brought the government to the edge of bankruptcy. When all efforts at reform failed him, Louis XVI in desperation summoned an antique political assembly, the Estates General, to meet in the spring of 1789 and vote him the taxing power he needed to save the nation from economic and political collapse.

From that point on, things spiraled out of control. The representatives of the third estate—the 23 million—came up to the Estates General with long lists of popular grievances, shrugged off royal leading strings, and announced their intention to undertake a sweeping reformation of the state. The Paris mob stormed the Bastille. In the fall, another mob, composed mostly of Paris women, marched on Versailles demanding bread and returned with the royal family as virtual prisoners. In between these colorful scenes, the work of the revolution got under way.

The Violent Decade

This archetypal ideological revolution unfolded in four clearly definable stages over the violent decade, 1789–1799, that followed. The first and most creative phase of the French Revolution lasted for more than two years, 1789–1791. It produced France's bill of rights—the Declaration of the Rights of Man and the Citizen, including the celebrated trinity of Liberty, Equality, and Brotherhood. It formulated a written constitution replacing royal absolutism with limited constitutional monarchy. It saw the surrender of the feudal privileges of the nobility and the nationalizing of the French Catholic church and its vast wealth.

France was now roughly on a par with Britain across the Channel. For many enlightened French, this was quite far enough. But not for others, notably the Jacobin faction and their leader Maximilien de

Robespierre (1758–1794), a dedicated revolutionary known to his admirers as the Incorruptible. During the second stage of the revolution, the year of the constitutional monarchy (1791–1792), the revolt split into two main factions. The Jacobins and other extremists pushed for the establishment of a republic, while moderates such as the Girondins attempted instead to make the limited monarchy work.

Meanwhile, war hawks among the revolutionaries beat the drums for a great crusade to liberate all Europe from kings and priests. In so doing, they played into the hands of reactionary governments, who were looking for an excuse to extinguish the spirit of rebellion before it spread. In the spring of 1792, then, the Austrian Habsburgs led an invasion of France to rescue Louis XVI and his queen, Marie Antoinette, a Habsburg princess.

The third phase of the French Revolution was the notorious Reign of Terror (1792–1794). During this period of a little less than two years, Robespierre and the Jacobins ruled the beleaguered country through the Committee of Public Safety and the guillotine. Under Robespierre's ideologically impassioned rule, the king and queen were executed, the monarchy itself abolished. Many nobles were also guillotined and their lands confiscated. Attempts were made to abolish the church altogether. Considerable numbers of revolutionaries, too moderate or too anarchistically radical for the Jacobins, also died under the slanting blade.

The Jacobins also turned the tide of war against the Austrians and their allies. By declaring that the nation now belonged to its people, they mobilized modern nationalism for the first time. Huge revolutionary armies of enthusiastic volunteers drove the invaders out of France and even occupied the Netherlands and the Rhineland. The Committee mobilized all the resources, labor, and energies of the nation for this patriotic effort, which is thus sometimes seen as a precursor of the "total wars" of the twentieth century.

But the Square of the Revolution reeked with the blood of traitors, and even revolutionary Paris sickened of the carnage. In the summer of 1794, Robespierre and the Jacobin junta in their turn went under the knife, and the Reign of Terror was over.

The long, grimy final phase of the French Revolution was the rule of the Directory (1794–1799), a grubby period of ideological reaction and political opportunism. Genuine radicals were rooted out, while political careerists got rich. The war was prosecuted with zeal, not for the cause, but for loot, fame, and personal advancement. French armies led by one young general in particular won famous victories, first and most brilliantly in Italy, then still farther afield in Egypt. And when General Bonaparte returned from the Battle of the Pyramids, a cabal of Directory politicians tried to use him as a front for their own power.

The Man of Destiny

But Napoleon Bonaparte (1769–1821) had a vision of his own destiny. A coup in 1799 made Napoleon first consul of France. His armies and a seemingly unending string of victories over the great powers of Europe did the rest.

This one-time Corsican artillery officer had learned from brilliant French military innovators. He had risen rapidly in the wide-open revolutionary years, when careers were made by talent rather than by aristocratic names. Napoleon used the new light artillery brilliantly and maneuvered with great rapidity over the European roads built by generations of enlightened despots. He had the huge, now thoroughly seasoned armies of the French Revolution at his disposal. And he had a rare genius for military command that puts him on any short list of the greatest generals of all time.

For a decade and a half, Napoleon Bonaparte ruled a larger European empire than anyone since ancient Rome. He crowned himself emperor of the French in 1804. By 1810 he, his family, and his generals ruled directly or indirectly over a collection of states that stretched from Spain to the frontiers of Russia, from the English Channel to the toe of Italy. Wherever his armies went, furthermore, Napoleon spread the ideals of the French Revolution. At home he was France's enlightened despot at last, streamlining institutions and modernizing laws with military efficiency.

It looked almost as if Europe might find the unity she had enjoyed in Roman times, under a child of the French Revolution.

But Europe's old regime fought back tenaciously against the "Corsican upstart." Britain, safe on her islands, would not make terms. Napoleon's invasion of Russia in 1812 was a fiasco—his first major setback. He had beaten three coalitions of great powers, but in 1813 a fourth defeated him at Leipzig, in the epochal Battle of the Nations. Temporarily exiled from Europe in 1814, Napoleon returned the following year for the miraculous Hundred Days that ended in 1815 at Waterloo.

It was the end of a great adventure—and the beginning of something even greater. For the revolution and its general had seeded Europe with radical ideas, images, and memories that would bear startling fruit for much of the coming century.

Energy Revolutions

While the drama of the French Revolution and the epic of Napoleon were running their course across the Channel, events that would prove even more significant were taking place in Britain: the Industrial Revolution.

In the narrowest sense of the term, the Industrial Revolution was the transformation of European industrial production between 1760 and 1830. In a broader sense, the Industrial Revolution continues to this day, a long unfolding of new technologies from steam to petroleum to nuclear power, from the locomotive to the microchip. The nineteenth century, the steam-engine age, may look primitive from the perspective of our age of space exploration, electronics, and computer technology. But the technological breakthrough of the later 1700s was crucial to all that came afterwards.

To accomplish anything at all—to feed, clothe, house ourselves, to build a pyramid or a skyscraper, to read a book or play a tune—human beings must have access to one thing: *energy*. The amount of energy available to us for all purposes, however, is strictly limited by the sources of energy we have at our disposal. Three stages in the exploitation of energy may be distinguished.[2]

For most of our evolution as a species, it will be remembered, we were hunters and gatherers. Our Paleolithic ancestors depended entirely upon the animals and plants they could collect in the course of each day. If our accomplishments were limited over those endless generations, it was because we could in this way accumulate only enough energy to support a tiny population from day to day.

Around ten thousand years ago, in the Middle East, the Agricultural Revolution began. Our Neolithic forebears learned to cultivate grain, domesticate animals, and thus feed substantially larger populations. Cities and empires developed, with large classes freed from primary-energy gathering for more specialized tasks as priests and soldiers, merchants and craftspeople, artists and bureaucrats.

Nevertheless, the sources of energy at our disposal remained strictly biological, and a ceiling was thus placed on human achievement over the next ten thousand years, including the five millennia of recorded history. An acre of wheat could only support so many human beings, an acre of pasturage only so many bullocks to labor for their human masters.

Then, a mere two hundred years ago, came the Industrial Revolution. For the first time, nonbiological

[2]I follow here Carlo Cipolla, *The Economic History of World Population* (Baltimore: Penguin Books, 1982), chs. 1 and 2.

energy sources were exploited in substantial quantities. Coal came into widespread use first, then oil and its derivatives, then hydroelectric power, and finally nuclear energy in our own time. Such alternatives as solar and geothermal energy are still to be adequately developed.

The energy locked up in these sources was immensely, indeed incalculably greater than the energy in acres of wheat, laboring oxen, or toiling human backs. With this extra energy, we have doubled our life spans, redoubled our population over and over, and built the push-button world of skyscrapers and jetliners we live in today.

How did it happen—and why, out of all the centuries, did it happen when it did?

What All the World Desires to Have

Attempts to explain the Industrial Revolution of the later 1700s no longer focus on a single central factor such as inventions or investment capital. Instead, a complex combination seems necessary to explain so momentous an event. Commonly cited among the components of the chemical mix that made the Industrial Revolution possible are resources, labor, demand, capital, technology, and entrepreneurship.

Natural resources, especially coal and iron, were essential. So was a substantial labor force free from agricultural labor. An increased demand from a growing population is often cited, as is capital accumulation to pay the huge initial cost of tooling up for industrial production. Invention undoubtedly played a part, though in the more systematic form of an ongoing process of technological development. Perhaps most important, there was the role of the entrepreneur, the catalytic agent that brought all the other elements together, added a touch of factory management and marketing skills—and made the Industrial Revolution happen.

The cultural milieu within which this combination first developed was Great Britain in the 1760s. Britain had resources in the iron and coal of the Midlands "black country." She had surplus labor produced by the eighteenth-century Agricultural Revolution. She had immense amounts of capital from empire and trade, and a growing population to provide the requisite demand. She had a vigorous middle class, including both skilled technicians and aggressive entrepreneurs.

The process began in textile manufacturing, notably the new cotton industry, which was more willing to innovate than the older, more hidebound woolens business. In the cotton industry, small steam engines bred the factory system, embryonic assembly lines, and rapidly accelerating production. From tex-

tiles the new approach spread to heavy industry, transportation, and other central elements of the industrial economy. And from Great Britain the new technology spread to western Europe, North America, and on around the world. It is spreading still, its transforming effects greater even than the ideologies spawned by the French Revolution.

"Steam," they said in the nineteenth century, "is an Englishman." The importance of steam was summed up in a remark made by the well-known entrepreneur Matthew Boulton. Boulton had just finished showing a visitor around the Soho Manufactury, where he and James Watt produced the first industrial steam engines. "I sell here, Sir," Boulton told his guest, "what all the world desires to have—Power!"[3]

MAIN CURRENTS
OF THE CENTURY

Patterns

In the two central sections of this chapter, we will look at the complicated history of nineteenth-century Europe in two ways. The present section will survey some of the main currents of the century in Europe as a whole. The section that follows will go over the same period country by country, offering a cavalcade of European nations in what may have been Europe's golden age.

The overall patterns of the political and economic history of Europe will provide us with a skeleton upon which we can hang what follows.

The first half of the nineteenth century—once the French and Industrial revolutions are accounted for—is a short one, historically speaking. It covers the period from 1815 to 1849, from Waterloo to the mid-century revolts. In political terms, this was, in fact, Europe's Age of Revolutions, when Europe was as tormented by ideological revolt as the Third World has been since World War II.

At the time of Napoleon's defeat in 1814 and 1815, a great international conclave was held at Vienna to draw up a peace settlement after twenty years of Napoleonic wars. The goals of the Congress of Vienna, however, included not only a lasting peace but also a massive attempt to turn the historical clock back to the old regime, to the way things had been before 1789. To this end, pre-Napoleonic "legitimate" dynasties were restored to power, established churches

[3]H. W. Dickinson, *Matthew Boulton* (Cambridge: Cambridge University Press, 1937), p. 73.

were reestablished, and the old hereditary aristocrats were encouraged to reclaim their leading places in society everywhere. The primary architect of this Vienna settlement was the intensely conservative Austrian foreign minister, Prince Metternich. Metternich would lead the forces of European reaction for the next thirty-odd years.

You cannot, however, set history back like a clock. Reaction only bred more revolution—three and a half decades of it between 1815 and 1848.

The revolutions of the 1820s were largely on the southern and eastern fringes of the continent, in European backwaters such as Spain, the Italian states, Greece, and Russia. The revolutions of 1830, however, carried the spirit of revolutionary change into the heart of western Europe, to France again and to Belgium and a number of the German states as well as to Italy and elsewhere.

The revolutions of 1848–1849, finally, saw the great floodtide of the movement—and its ebb. The "springtime of the peoples" in 1848 saw rebellion in France, Austria, Prussia and other German states, various Italian states, and elsewhere. Another French king was overthrown in Paris. The Habsburg emperor and Metternich himself were driven from Vienna by a revolution spearheaded by students and workers. The pope was expelled from Rome by a revolutionary upheaval. "If someone had said, 'God has been driven from heaven and a republic proclaimed there,' " the Russian anarchist Bakunin remarked of those amazing days, "everyone would have believed it and no one would have been surprised."[4]

[4]P. H. Noyes, *Organization and Revolution: Working-Class Associations in the German Revolutions of 1848–1849* (Princeton: Princeton University Press, 1966), p. 57.

In 1849 the great tide turned. France got a new monarch to replace her deposed king, the Austrian emperor and the Roman pope returned, backed by bayonets, and the old order was apparently restored once more all across Europe.

Once again, however, pressures for change doggedly forced their way to the surface in Europe—peacefully this time, through continuing reform movements. And rulers, weary of revolutions, began to make concessions. By 1900 all the great powers except Russia had constitutions, elected legislatures, even bills of rights—and France was an established republic at last. Much more power remained in the hands of central and eastern European monarchs than was the case in western Europe. But the revolutionary agenda of the first half of the century had finally been achieved—through reform rather than revolution.

The second half of the century saw other major developments besides the victory of the ideals of the French Revolution, however.

Nationalist movements achieved amazing triumphs in the third quarter of the nineteenth century, which saw the creation of two new great powers in Europe. In 1859–1860, Italy was united at last under the king of Piedmont and the guiding hand of his prime minister, Count Cavour. In 1870–1871, the German Empire unified all the German states except Austria under the Prussian house of Hohenzollern. The new nation, immediately recognized as the greatest power in Europe, was a monument to the greatest diplomat of the century, Prussia's Otto von Bismarck.

The last quarter of the nineteenth century, finally, saw a diversity of trends. Socialism, labor unions, and other developments advanced the cause of Europe's industrial workers during these decades. But this pe-

Nineteenth Century Centers of Revolution in Europe

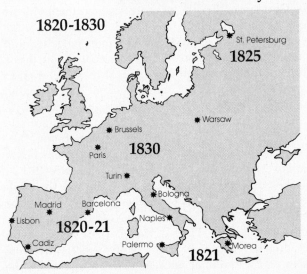

riod also saw the beginnings of the rise of big business as we know it today. In addition, this was the period of the climax of the New Imperialism and the firm establishment of Western hegemony over the world. It was also, however, the period that paved the way to World War I—the beginning of the end of Europe's global supremacy.

The nineteenth century was certainly one of Europe's greatest ages. International wars were few and brief within Europe itself. The Industrial Revolution made Europe richer than any people had ever been before. Political and social reform built toward the healthier, freer, more egalitarian if not necessarily happier Europe of today.

But golden ages are not placid ones, and the nineteenth century was, as this outline has tried to indicate, far more than waltzes and bustles, Victorian smugness, and tea in the afternoon.

An Age of Ideologies

It was, as indicated above, an age of ideological agitation unmatched by any in European history. It was, in fact, the century that saw the birth of all the revolutionary social ideas that have transformed the world in our own century.

A list of the radical seeds that were sown in the last century would have a distinctly contemporary ring to it. The first ideologically based student movement erupted in Germany just after 1815. The lifelong Italian freedom fighter Garibaldi pioneered the art of revolutionary guerrilla warfare in the 1830s, 1840s, and 1850s. The women's movement began to make significant numbers of converts in the second half of the century. The labor movement made substantial headway about this time also. The first stirrings of modern antiimperialism were felt in the colonies. And so on down a considerably longer list.

Three great ideological trends, however, informed most of these demands for change in nineteenth-century Europe, as they do in the twentieth-century world as a whole: liberalism, nationalism, and socialism.

Nineteenth-century political liberalism built on the ideas of the seventeenth-century English thinker John Locke and of French Enlightenment philosophes such as Montesquieu and Rousseau. Liberals believed in Lockean "natural rights" to liberty and equality. They further asserted Locke's contract theory of government—government by consent of the governed—as put into practice in revolutionary France and America. Liberals were thus militantly opposed to hereditary aristocracies, divine-right monarchies, and political oppression in all its forms. They demanded freedom of speech, the press, and religion, equality of economic opportunity and equality before the law, constitutional government, elected legislatures, bills of rights.

Liberalism had an economic dimension as well, however. Here liberals drew on the theories of Adam Smith, whose *Wealth of Nations* had come out in the revolutionary year 1776. Nineteenth-century liberals believed with Smith in natural laws governing the operation of the economy. These included the key law of supply and demand, which guaranteed that goods would be produced to meet any substantial demand, and that prices, wages, profits, and other aspects of the economy would best be regulated by natural market forces. Another basic liberal economic principle was the law of accumulation, which declared that the wealth of nations would grow steadily if supply and demand were allowed to operate freely. Liberal economists therefore opposed mercantilistic regulation of the economy and fought in particular for free trade—another of the great crusades of the first half of the century.

In some ways nationalism blazed even more brightly than liberalism across the nineteenth-century sky. Nineteenth-century nationalists built on the teachings of the eighteenth-century German cultural nationalists who preached the importance of each people's national spirit. They also drew on the model of the French Revolution, which had unleashed powerful patriotic energies, both in France and in nations conquered by Napoleon. Nationalists in the nineteenth century dedicated their energies to unifying divided peoples such as the Italians and the Germans. Or they labored to win national self-determination for oppressed minorities such as the eastern European, mostly Slavic peoples ruled by the Austrian, Russian, and Ottoman emperors. Later in the century, however, nationalism turned chauvinistic. It began to be used to justify the aggressive or expansionist policies of German or French or British governments in the eyes of their peoples.

Nationalists believed that common language and literature, history and custom welded a people into a larger whole—the nation. Some of them believed in a Folk Soul or Folk Spirit uniting a people spiritually. Many saw a national character that they shared with their fellow nationals: Frenchmen were naturally more civilized and artistic than other peoples, Germans more philosophical or scientific, Britons better at government and more practical, and so forth.

These apostles of nationality preached their patriotic creed in terms of native soil and blood—the black earth of Russia, for instance, or German or Anglo-Saxon blood. They expressed their loyalty with reverence for such concrete symbols as the national flag or the national anthem. They wept when the

French Tricolor or the British Union Jack passed by, and they sang the "Marseillaise," "Britannia Rules the Waves," or "Germany over All" with passion.

The last of the major isms to develop was socialism. Socialism could claim few antecedents in earlier centuries. Socialists sought a solution to a uniquely nineteenth-century problem, after all: the problem of widespread working-class poverty in the middle of the Industrial Revolution. The new industrial order was producing more goods and services than the world had ever seen before. Yet the laborers who worked in the factories and mines lived in slums, worked long hours under brutal conditions, and were subject to malnutrition, disease, and early death. The socialist solution to this very genuine problem was, quite simply, the transfer of the means of production—the new mines and mills, railroads, banks, and the rest—from private ownership to ownership by the workers themselves.

Several sorts of socialism emerged in the nineteenth century. Utopian socialists urged a rejection of the In-

Karl Marx, the most influential of all the nineteenth-century ideologues, does not look much like the prophet of World Revolution in this picture. Though the great global unheaval he foresaw never came, Marx's ideas have inspired revolutionaries around the world. (New York Public Library)

dustrial Revolution itself and a return to small-scale handicraft production, preferably in small communities in the healthy countryside. Inspired by prophets such as Charles Fourier, Utopians did, in fact, establish a number of socialist country communes—as their successors do, here and there, to this day.

The most influential socialist theorist, however, was clearly Karl Marx (1818–1883), some of whose followers came to call themselves communists in later years. Marx rejected Utopianism as naive. He preached a more violent creed of working-class revolution against the capitalist entrepreneurs and investors who owned the new technology.

According to Marx's widely influential theory, all history has been a chronicle of class struggles between patrician and plebeian, lord and serf, guild master and journeyman. The present class struggle between the proletarians (workers) and their capitalist bosses would lead to a great world revolution. This final class war would end class struggle forever by putting the means of production in the hands of the working people once and for all. In the little tract called *The Communist Manifesto*, which he and his lifelong collaborator Friedrich Engels wrote in 1848, Marx urged the workers of the world to unite, overthrow the bourgeois-capitalist order everywhere, and establish the workers' paradise. One consequence of Marx's appeal was the state-socialist, one-party nations of Eastern Europe today.

The form of socialism that has predominated in Western Europe, however, has been the more moderate type known as social-democratic or (in Great Britain) Fabian socialism. Social democrats drew some ideas from Marx, others from other socialist writers. But they firmly rejected revolution in favor of reform. Social democrats were more practical than the Utopians, more constitutionally minded than the revolutionary Marxists. They were willing to work with labor unions and liberal allies, using the free press and the ballot box to gain their ends. The socialist parties of Western Europe today are of this practical, reform-minded social-democratic sort.

Nineteenth-century ideologues of whatever stripe lived a hard life. Often censored, imprisoned, or driven into exile, they survived on dreams of coming revolutions and utopian futures. And though history seldom bore out their predictions in any detail, they did have a powerful impact on the history of their century—and of ours.

The First Developing Society

The economic development of preindustrial societies into modern, economically productive states has been high on the world's list of concerns since the new nations of Africa and Asia began to emerge after World War II. The first developing society, however, was Europe itself. And the European experience has influenced the development planning both of those who hold Europe up as a model and of those who reject the Western example totally.

The most striking elements in the continuing nineteenth-century evolution of the Industrial Revolution were the mid-century drive toward unrestricted freedom of competition and the countertrend of the later 1800s toward industrial combination—the startling phenomenon we call big business today.

The middle half of the nineteenth century, from the 1820s to the 1870s, was the heyday of free competition in the old-fashioned sense of the term. Liberal entrepreneurs persuaded many governments that mercantilistic regulation of the economy was a handicap rather than a help to the new technology of the Industrial Revolution. Free trade, freely negotiated contracts between capital and labor, and a decline in government regulation of all sorts resulted.

By mid-century, competition between rival nations, between old and new industries, between

countless small or middle-sized producers of the same good or service was widespread in Europe. Cloth making, coal mining, transportation all saw hundreds and even thousands of freely competing firms at work. "Competition," it was widely said, "is the life of trade and the law of progress."

In the last quarter of the century, however, there came a change. It was not a return to government regulation—that would not come on a large scale until the present century. It was rather the rigorous curtailment of free competition by businessmen themselves. These limits on competition were the result of large-scale business combination—the sort that American law would come to call "combination in restraint of trade."

The move toward monopoly combination that began in the 1870s was in part a defensive measure in the face of the sheer brutality of the fang-and-claw competition of the age. During the periodic depressions particularly, unregulated competition hurt all competitors and drove many into bankruptcy. Under such circumstances, many business leaders began to think that combination, not competition, might be the

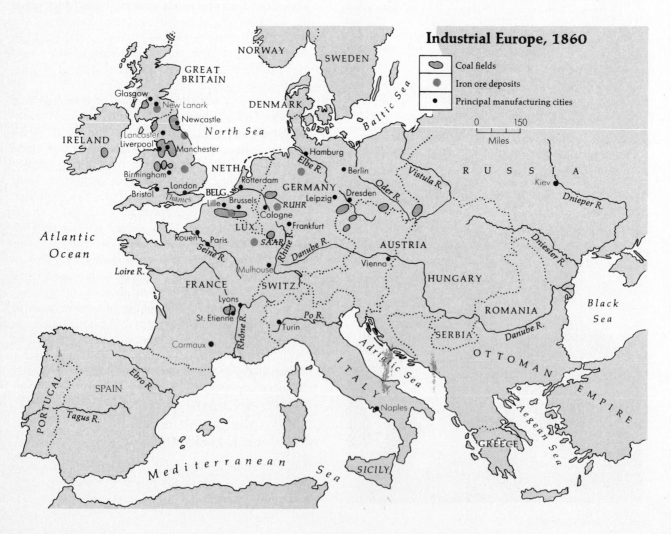

life of trade and even the law of survival. The result was the most amazing flower of nineteenth-century economic development: the rise of big business.

Some aggressive industrialists merged and bought out either competitors or related industries to produce giant new corporations. Thus Albert Krupp, the German steelmaker, bought up coal and iron mines, ore boats, and even user industries. When complete, the Krupp family's industrial empire included machine-tool plants, railcar manufactures, a shipyard, and the arms industries for which his descendants would be most famous.

Another form of combination did not go to the length of actual corporate merger, but simply resorted to working agreements called *cartels*. Cartels, which might be national or even international in scope, fixed prices, assigned quotas, or divided up the market in ways that effectively eliminated competition. A shipping cartel organized first in Britain, for instance, expanded to include major steamship lines in Germany, France, the Netherlands, and even Japan. This single group came close to setting ocean fares and freight rates on the sea lanes of the world.

This was the trend as the twentieth century got under way, and it has remained a main current of Western economic history since. Big business controls more of the Western world's economic activity today than big government ever has.

Slums and Bustles

The structure of society in an industrializing, increasingly ideological Europe of course differed in some striking ways from European society under the old regime. But there were notable similarities with the past as well. And there were indications of movement in directions that have a very familiar ring to citizens of our own century.

Over much of nineteenth-century Europe, the landed nobility remained the most prestigious class and the peasants—freeholders, laborers, even serfs—the most numerous. The medieval guilds at last expired, but many small shops remained, producing by hand everything from bread to shoes. Even the most progressive cities still had many more narrow, cobblestoned streets than modern boulevards, and any country lane still led to peasant villages.

The most noticeable new class in western Europe, and to an increasing extent in central Europe as well, was the new work force created by the Industrial

Gustave Doré, one of the best-known illustrators of the 1800s, here captures the grime, congestion, and pollution of a London slum. The working people of the great city are shown clustering in tiny back yards or leaning out of tenement windows to catch a breath of sooty air.

Revolution. The proletariat, as this group came to be called, was drawn in immense numbers to the new industrial cities by work in mills, mines, railway yards, and other elements of the new industrial society. Men, women, and children worked twelve- and fourteen-hour days and lived jammed into malodorous, unsanitary, disease-ridden slums. Frequently unemployed and normally underpaid and resentful, the proletariat was widely feared as a dangerous element in the population, social dynamite ticking toward an explosion.

The predominant class in western Europe, finally, consisted more and more of the industrial, commercial, and financial middle classes, who profited from the new industrial order. Britain was a "nation of shopkeepers" and proud of it. In France, the *haute bourgeoisie* of industrial and financial magnates pushed to the fore. Middle-class liberal politicians and journalists worked to advance the interests of this emergent elite. And the brownstone front in London and the Paris town house—the homes of the middle class—grew more and more crowded with the material possessions that were the sign and seal of their success.

Sheer numbers, finally, distinguished the society of nineteenth-century Europe as of so many other parts of the world. The accelerating population explosion turned the 200 million Europeans of the early 1800s into 450 million by 1914. Population growth seems to have been due, as usual, to a combination of causes: increased supplies of food, thanks to agricultural technology; younger marriages; the conquest of some diseases; and improvement in sanitation. Most of the new population flooded into the cities, and for the first time since the fall of the Roman Empire, cities of half a million, a million, and more appeared in Europe.

It was a contentious, crowded, vigorous society that took shape in that Europe of a century ago, a society many of whose problems would not be solved until our own time.

That Pedestal

The multiple conditions of women remained as diverse as ever, but there seems to have been a new twist: an image of womanhood that would prove a hard cross for subsequent generations of Western women to bear.

Peasant women still handled chores as well as housework and child rearing, and rallied to the fields at harvest time. Many poor girls and women, like many men, were personal servants or salespeople in shops or eating houses, and prostitution flourished in the mushrooming cities. Petty-bourgeois women often ran the shop, and aristocratic ladies supervised large households, as they had in past centuries.

Some new lines of work opened up for women, however. Female proletarians shared their husbands' grueling lives in the mills and even in the mines, perhaps suffering more for the lower wages they were paid. But a number of more respectable professions opened up to women, including positions as governesses, elementary schoolteachers, nurses (toward the end of the century), and, for the talented, writing. Novelists such as the three Brontë sisters and Jane Austen, George Eliot and George Sand, and poets such as Elizabeth Barrett Browning and Christina Georgina Rossetti established a place for women at the top of the world of letters.

In the latter part of the nineteenth century, the organized movement for female emancipation emerged in Europe. As early as the 1840s, Utopian socialists had preached female equality, and by mid-century some liberals also spoke up for political rights for women. During the later decades of the century, women in fact gained improved legal status: married women got control of their own property, for example, and divorce became easier. Contraception began to liberate some women from the burden of large families. Women began to be admitted to universities and to invade formerly all-male professions such as medicine. They were also increasingly prominent among radical and revolutionary groups in countries such as Russia and France. In England they organized a vigorous, sometimes violent campaign to get the right to vote—the "suffragette" campaign that finally led to women's suffrage after World War I. It was the first wave of a women's movement that still continues.

Most women of all classes, however, still married and reared children. And it was in the nineteenth century that this ancient women's profession acquired the special luster it was to enjoy for more than a hundred years thereafter, down to our own time. Middle-class women were even urged to do nothing else *but* serve as companions for their husbands and mothers for their children—both of which were now believed to be tasks requiring much tact, training, character, and intelligence. Women who aspired to the other professions just opening up to them were told that they were too "fine" for such crude masculine concerns as business, medicine, or politics.

They were, as the saying went, "put on a pedestal" to be worshiped by their men—who meantime went on running the world. The descent from this pedestal would require another psychic revolution in our own century.

A CAVALCADE OF NATIONS

Barricades or the Ballot Box?

The domestic history of Britain in the nineteenth century is usually presented as a chronicle of social and political reform. Queen Victoria (1837–1901) presided over a parliamentary government that was able to change with the times, to meet the needs of a rapidly evolving industrial society. Politicians of various persuasions, from the Liberal William Gladstone to the Conservative Benjamin Disraeli, both guided and responded to the wishes of a growing electorate to produce the model of a functioning nineteenth-century Western democracy—social change through the ballot box.

Parliamentary reform bills extending the right to vote to one group after another provided the skeleton of Britain's age of reform. The great Reform Bill of 1832 gave new industrial cities such as Manchester and Birmingham—and the industrial middle classes everywhere—representation in Parliament. Disraeli's reform bill of 1867 granted the suffrage to factory workers, Gladstone's bill of 1884 awarded it to farm laborers, and the 1918 bill climaxed the women's-suffrage movement by giving the vote to women.

Other reform measures included laws designed to render the new industrial system more livable. Laws regulating women's working conditions and child labor were passed, as were factory-safety acts and legislation limiting the length of the working day. Public education began in Britain in the later nineteenth century. During the years before the First World War, a Liberal government enacted such socialistic measures—as they then seemed—as the beginnings of public health service and old-age pensions.

There was tension, of course—the massive and sometimes violent demonstrations connected with the Reform Bill of 1832, the (failed) Chartist movement of the 1840s demanding universal manhood suffrage, and the women's campaign for the suffrage in the 1890s and early 1900s. But the system proved flexible and strong enough to contain and channel all such pressures. Change came comparatively peacefully, through the democratic process.

Social change came also to France, the other more liberal member of the great powers. But in France, change came as much through revolution as through reform.

Revolutionary barricades went up in Paris four times between the late 1700s and the later 1800s: in the great revolution of 1789, in 1830, in 1848, and in the destructive Paris Commune of 1871. New forms of government were established by force five times between 1815 and 1914: three monarchies—the restored Bourbons, the constitutional monarchy of Louis Philippe, and the empire of Louis Napoleon after 1848—and two republics, the Second and the Third, the latter lasting until 1940. Only the French civil service, a centralized structure of administration rationalized and strengthened by Napoleon I, provided basic continuity in government.

Political change thus came to France revolution by revolution. The restored Bourbons felt it expedient to grant France a constitution and a two-house legislature in 1814. Bourgeois voting and political predominance came with Louis Philippe, "the middle-class king," in 1830. Universal manhood suffrage made a brief appearance under the Second Republic, was permanently established by the Third in 1875. Women, however, did not vote till the 1940s. Other social reforms also lagged in the land that had given birth to the Enlightenment. But change did come, and nineteenth-century France saw no more revolutions after 1871.

Blood and Iron

The linked histories of the two central European great powers, Austria and Prussia, trace the story of a long power struggle with a dramatic resolution—the creation of the German Empire.

The Austrian Habsburgs had dominated the German states since the Middle Ages. The Prussian Hohenzollerns had been challenging that predominance since Frederick the Great's long feud with Empress Maria Theresa in the mid eighteenth century. In the nineteenth century, Prussia added to her efficient administration and her powerful army a dynamic, rapidly growing industrial machine and close economic relations with other industrializing North German states. Finally, shortly after the revolutions of 1848, the Prussian king William acquired a chief minister who was also the greatest diplomatic manipulator of his age: Otto von Bismarck.

Bismarck, a huge, powerfully built Junker with an incongruously high-pitched voice, was the architect of modern Germany. He was no ideological nationalist, but an old-fashioned royal minister, loyal to the interests of the house of Hohenzollern. He was also not the master planner of later legend. He was rather a brilliant opportunist and manipulator, playing his diplomatic cards as they fell and winning far more often than he lost.

Bismarck demonstrated the power of the Prussian army in the brief Danish War of 1863 and defeated Austria herself handily in the Austro-Prussian War of

1866. He then rallied all the rest of the German states in a war of revenge against their common enemy, the victorious Franco-Prussian War of 1870–1871. Intoxicated with their triumph over the French emperor Napoleon III, the German princes gathered in Louis XIV's great Hall of Mirrors at Versailles in the spring of 1871 to swear allegiance to the king of Prussia, now Emperor William I of the new German Empire.

Bismarck proceeded to guide the destinies of the new united Germany for the next twenty years. Austria, meanwhile, labored through a sea of troubles, political and otherwise.

Austria's besetting political problem between 1815 and 1914 was that of growing and conflicting nationalisms within her multinational empire. Inspired by ideologues to take their German, Italian, Hungarian, and various forms of Slavic background very seriously, the peoples ruled from Vienna demanded so much autonomy that in the wake of World War I the empire itself would be fragmented and destroyed.

Austria also industrialized in the nineteenth century, though not as impressively as Prussia or the new German Empire, which was second only to Great Britain among European industrial states by 1900. Austria and the new Germany both established elected legislatures, though each was elected by limited suffrage and neither had great power. But the central difference between them lay in their reactions to the new ideology of nationalism. The German Empire, however reluctantly, became the embodiment of Europe's most powerful national feeling, and prospered mightily. The Austrian Empire necessarily fought nationalism to the death—and perished thereby.

Garibaldi and the Cossacks

The new kingdom of Italy was a more or less pure and certainly enthusiastic product of the new nationalism. Divided like Germany into many small principalities since the Middle Ages, Italy after 1815—again like the German states—was dominated by Austria. For half a century, from the Congress of Vienna to the revolutions of 1848, Italian nationalists such as the ideologue Giuseppe Mazzini and the guerrilla leader Giuseppe Garibaldi worked to overthrow Italy's petty despots and expel the Austrian power that supported them.

Success, however, came only when the cause of Italian liberation and unification was taken up by Piedmont, the northernmost, most industrially developed, and most liberal of Italian states. Piedmont's prime minister, Count Camillo di Cavour, threw his boundless energies, his diplomatic skill, and his country's small but efficient army into the struggle in the 1850s. Cavour negotiated an alliance with France for a brief war against her ancient enemy, Austria. Behind this screen of military action in the north, well-organized rebellions in much of Italy and a brilliant campaign by Garibaldi in the south freed the peninsula of its Austrian puppet rulers. Then in a plebiscite the Italians voted for unification as a constitutional monarchy under the royal house of Piedmont.

If modern Italy was the creation of the new isms—nationalism, liberalism, industrialism—czarist Russia was the slowest of the powers to recognize these forces. The Russian Empire was the most determined hold-out against all the nineteenth-century ideologies, as well as the most underdeveloped industrially of all Europe's great powers. Despite the best that Peter and Catherine the Great had been able to do in the preceding century, Russia remained socially and economically backward. It had a minuscule middle class, a large serf population, and a medieval Russian Orthodox religion that had yet to come to terms with the Enlightenment, let alone Darwinian evolution.

Furthermore, because of the success of absolutist rulers such as Peter and Catherine, Russian autocracy was absolute. The czars depended on a horde of bureaucrats, a sinister secret police known as the Third Section, and regiments of Cossacks for riding down street demonstrations or punishing troublesome villages.

The history of Russia between 1815 and 1914 is a story of few and tentative concessions to modernity followed by brutal repression of "Westernizers" who sought reform or turned in desperation to revolution. The reforming czar Alexander II (1856–1881) abolished serfdom, instituted some local self-government, and undertook other, more modest reforms. But after his assassination—for not going far enough—repression was once more the order of the day. The Russia to which Marxism came at the end of the century was thus a land in which revolution seemed to many the only hope at all for change.

THE CLIMAX
OF EUROPEAN CULTURE

Moods: Romanticism and Materialism

It may seem foolhardy to label any period in the ongoing history of a living society as the climax of its cultural achievement. Surely there may be better yet to come? The nineteenth century was, however, the last period in which there flourished a distinctively *European* culture, free of major foreign influences, a model for colonial art and thought around the world. In this sense, at least, the life of the European spirit in the 1800s may be said to constitute the historic climax of European culture.

Two overarching world views dominated European cultural life during that century: romanticism and materialism. Romanticism flourished during the first half of the century, and enjoyed a revival in the late 1800s. Materialism predominated during the second half of the century.

These broad views of the world, or *Weltanschauungen*, were articulated less precisely than the ideologies were; they were more a matter of assumption, perspective, or attitude. But they did impart tone and feeling to the life of the Western mind. They determined public attitudes toward arts, sciences, ideologies, and indeed society itself. These sweeping world views may thus have been more important to European culture in this climactic period than more precisely expressed artistic insights or scientific theories.

The romantic movement, best known for its artistic expressions, was actually a broad-gauge cultural rebellion. Romantic poets, painters, composers, and other leaders of the movement certainly thought of it as an artistic revolt. It was a demand for movement, color, emotion in the arts, and a rejection of the rigidity and aridity of classicism. It was an enthusiasm for exotic new subject matter, from medieval knights and Renaissance adventurers to Turkish harems and simple peasant cottages. It was a call for freedom, the liberation of the romantic ego from the rules of the academies and the models of the ancients and the old masters.

It was also, however, the beginning of a broad sense of cultural alienation and of a sweeping rebellion against the tyranny of human reason itself. Both of these broader aspects of the romantic revolt have persisted down to our own time.

The romantics' feeling of alienation from the dull, crass bourgeois-philistine society they lived in was very powerful. It led them to turn from society to nature, to draw strength and solace from woods and flowers, from the Alps, the sea, the wild west wind. This romantic sense of alienation drove some artists to flee the West entirely, to explore North Africa, the Middle East, or even the South Seas. And many who

British artist J. M. W. Turner's Keelmen Heaving Coals by Moonlight *illustrates the nineteenth-century's rediscovery of light and color—concerns that would link romanticism with the modernist movement of the twentieth century. (National Gallery of Art, Washington, D.C. Widener Collection 1942)*

were not artists came to feel that they too were out of sympathy with their own time, strangers in their own land.

The romantic revolt against reason has become an even more fundamental part of Western consciousness. Romantics thought that the Enlightenment and the Scientific Revolution provided only thinly cerebral, emotionally unconvincing explanations for things. Since Plato and Aristotle, Western culture had defined humanity as the *rational* animal; now the romantics turned away from reason to glorify the emotions instead.

Love, beauty, suffering, human will, dreams, drugs, enthusiasm for such allegedly nonrational beings as peasants, savages, and children, a fascination with supernatural phenomena, mystic intuitions of God—nonrational elements flooded the romantic consciousness. "All theory, my friend, is gray," said Goethe's *Faust:* "but green is life's glad golden tree."[5] Wordsworth went even further in condemning human reason:

Our meddling intellect
Misshapes the beauteous forms of things;
We murder to dissect.[6]

The physical sciences, however, produced some notable advances in the 1800s. As new trends in the arts had fostered the romantic world view in the first half of the century, progress in the sciences encouraged the materialist *Weltanschauung* in the second half.

During this period scientists learned more than ever before about the nature of matter. The modern theory of the atomic and molecular structure of matter, the cellular construction of living matter, the germ theory of disease, Darwinian evolution, and much more first came to light at this time. The prestige of the sciences and the scientific method rose once again, especially after the appearance of Charles Darwin's epochal *Origin of Species* in 1859, as it had in the wake of Newton's *Principia* nearly two centuries before. And with science came materialism, which found more followers than ever before.

This was not the crude commercial materialism that delights in owning material possessions. It was the profounder philosophical materialism that denies the existence of anything *but* matter.

For this school of thought, God was a myth, the human soul an illusion, humanity itself simply a somewhat more complicated ape. Claiming to be realistic rather than sentimental, hard-boiled rather than tenderhearted, materialists turned from religion to science, from poetry to economics. They agreed with the ecstatic philosopher Friedrich Nietzsche that God was dead, and with Auguste Comte, the founder of modern sociology, that if there was anything left to worship, it was rational humanity itself.

Romanticism and materialism colored the thought of their respective half centuries. Early cultural nationalists were romantics, revolutionaries of the heart; Bismarck and Cavour, who unified their countries, were hard-boiled realists, manipulators of armies and masters of diplomatic chicanery. Utopian socialists were romantic, back-to-nature communards; Marx was an atheist, a materialist, and a worshiper at the shrine of hard economic facts.

Wordsworth's heart leaped up when he beheld a rainbow in the sky. Bazarov, the materialistic young antihero of Turgenev's *Fathers and Sons*, cuts up frogs for medical experiments.

Sunday in the Park

The arts in this divided age have one overwhelming thing in common: a fascination with the age itself, which fostered a longing to portray that age in words or pictures much as it really was.

Romantic painters, with their love for nature and for people who lived close to it, may have made their sowers and harvesters a bit more bronzed and husky, their countryside a little greener, their ocean bursting into spray a touch more sublime than nature managed. But John Constable surely got the farm wagons right in his *Hay Wain*, or Jean-François Millet the heave and strain of his laboring *Quarriers*. And if J.M.W. Turner's seascapes please us as abstract explosions of color, they also give a vivid impression of real sea and sky ablaze with sunset light.

The realist and even many impressionist and post-impressionist painters of the latter half of the century are more likely to show us around the city and the suburbs, the world of the triumphant bourgeoisie. One can wash up at the basin in front of the mirror in the morning with Mary Cassatt (*La Toilette*), spend Sunday in the park with Georges Seurat (*La Grande Jatte*), go dancing at the *Moulin de la Galette* with Auguste Renoir, the bourgeois artist par excellence, or visit the *Moulin Rouge* with the dwarfish nightclub painter Henri de Toulouse-Lautrec. One might end the evening with the urbane Édouard Manet, having a drink at *Bock's* and visiting the celebrated prostitute *Olympia*, her small body reclining a bit stiffly on the bed, an unconvincing flower over her left ear.

[5]Johann Wolfgang Goethe, *Faust, Part One*, trans. Philip Wayne (Baltimore: Penguin Books, 1949), p. 98.
[6]William Wordsworth, *The Thorn*, iii.

The prose and poetry of the nineteenth century also offer up the age in living, breathing, sometimes exhausting detail. Jane Austen's novels of English society bring the world of the country gentry convincingly before us, with their provincial balls and journeyings, their endless concern with property and marriage, family life, common sense, and human individuality. Charlotte Brontë's much-loved *Wuthering Heights* takes us deep into the labyrinthine twists and turns of two tormented human hearts, showing us two passionate lives led in a narrow North Country world of harsh winds and hardened souls.

The urban realities are there too, in the immense canvases of the century's fiction. The many socially realistic novels of Honoré de Balzac give us all Paris in the first half of the century, those of Émile Zola all France in the second half. We can visit the malodorous slums of London with Charles Dickens, explore the unfamiliar world of the Russian serfs in Ivan Turgenev's *Sportsman's Sketches*, or probe with the Norwegian dramatist Henrik Ibsen the corruption behind the frock coats, frilly bodices, and formal manners of the bourgeois drawing room.

When Balzac describes the boardinghouse where *Old Man Goriot* lives, we see every crack and knick-knack, we hear the very boardinghouse conversation over dinners a century and a half ago. When Zola takes us through *les Halles*, the vast, heaped, crowded, noisy food markets of old Paris, we can smell the rotting vegetables, see the bloom on the fruit that Paris housewives thumbed and dropped into their shopping bags a hundred years ago. Even the most Romantic poet of the nineteenth century had an eye for concrete detail that many a more modern writer might envy. Keats shows us summer woods as real as Balzac's boarding house as he wanders

> Through verdurous glooms and winding mossy ways . . .
> The murmurous haunt of flies on summer eves.[7]

The flies would never have been there in an Elizabethan sonnet; they might dominate the picture in a twentieth-century production. In the nineteenth, they were simply there, part of the richness of that European cultural climax.

[7]John Keats, "Ode to a Nightingale," in Arthur Quiller-Couch, ed., *The Oxford Book of English verse* (Oxford: Clavendon Press, 1939) p. 743.

SUMMARY

A century of radical change in Europe began in the later 1700s, with the French Revolution (1789–1799) and the Industrial Revolution, which got under way in England in the 1760s.

The French Revolution was rooted in the deep social dislocations of the old regime and in the radical social critique of the Enlightenment. The Revolution accelerated through a series of stages, which would be followed by later upheavals. Its most immediate outcome was the rise of Napoleon Bonaparte, the "man on horseback" who restored order and directed the new energies unleashed by the Revolution into the conquest of much of Europe. The key long-term consequence was the beginning of more than half a century of ideological revolutions in Europe.

The harnessing of steam power to work industrial machinery was at least as revolutionary an event. The Industrial Revolution, resulting from the coming together of a number of social, economic, and natural elements, put vast new energy sources at the disposal of the human race. The capacity to exploit these nonbiological forms of energy multiplied the economic output of the Western world many times over in the century that followed.

The main currents of nineteenth-century history flowed from these eighteenth-century beginnings. Between 1815 and 1848 Europe was swept by its age of revolutions, most of which failed but were followed by decades of reform. The third quarter of the century was highlighted by the unification of two new European great powers, Germany and Italy. The fourth quarter saw the rise of big business and of the labor movement and the resurgence of overseas empire building known as the New Imperialism.

It was an age of intensely felt revolutionary ideologies: liberalism, nationalism, socialism, and their offshoots. It spawned industrial corporations and cartels that dwarfed any earlier forms of economic organization. It was a century of expanding population, middle-class predominance, increasing pressure from the proletariat, and the birth of the modern women's movement.

The European nations related to these general trends in a variety of ways. Britain and France emerged as the most liberal of the European powers—the former through reform, the latter through successive revolutions. Bismarck unified Germany and saw her become an industrial colossus second only to Britain. Austria lost her preeminence in central Europe and much of her hold on her non-German national minorities. Italy, unified by dashing activists like Garibaldi and the shrewd Count Cavour, was more liberal but not as powerful as Germany was. Russia remained the most economically backward and politically autocratic of Europe's great powers.

The cultural history of nineteenth-century Europe was dominated by romanticism, originating in the arts, and by materialism, rooted in the progress of the sciences. Romantic alienation and materialistic atheism would spread further still in the twentieth century. The arts vividly reflected the social history of the age, from realistic fiction and romantic poetry to painting of all schools.

SUGGESTED READING

BARTLETT, C. J., ed. *Britain Pre-Eminent: Studies in British World Influence in the Nineteenth Century.* London: Macmillan, 1969. The unique position of Britain, mother of Parliaments and master of the world's largest empire, in the days when steam was an Englishman and Britannia ruled the waves.

BEALES, D. *The Risorgimento and the Unification of Italy.* New York: Barnes & Noble, 1971. Balanced survey of the nationalist movement in Italy and its consequences.

CIPOLLA, C. *The Economic History of World Population,* 6th ed. London: Penguin, 1975. Brief but brilliant account of the roots of modern achievement in basic energy sources.

COATES, W. H., and H. V. WHITE. *The Ordeal of Liberal Humanism.* New York: McGraw-Hill, 1969. European intellectual history in the nineteenth and twentieth centuries, organized around a liberal mainstream.

DOYLE, W. *Origins of the French Revolution.* Oxford: Oxford University Press, 1980. Good place to begin on the historical debate over causes of the great upheaval. See also R. W. Greenlaw, ed., *The Social Origins of the French Revolution: The Debate on the role of the Middle Classes* (Lexington, Mass.: Heath, 1975).

EISELEY, L. *Darwin's Century.* New York: Doubleday, 1958. The evolution of evolutionism. For its impact, see J. C. Greene, *The Death of Adam* (Ames, Iowa: University of Iowa Press, 1959).

FURST, L. *Romanticism in Perspective,* 2nd ed. Atlantic Highlands, N.J.: Humanities Press, 1979. Clear interpretative analysis, putting the movement in its historical setting. For a selection of representative writings, see H. Hugo, ed., *The Romantic Reader* (New York: Viking, 1975).

HEILBRONER, R. *The Worldly Philosophers,* 5th ed. New York: Touchstone, 1980. Eminently readable treatment of economists and economics in the tradition of Adam Smith.

KOHN, H. *Nationalism: Its Meaning and History,* rev. ed. New York: Van Nostrand, 1965. Concise summary of evolution and meanings of the most influential modern ideology. For a critical analysis, see B. C. Shafer, *Nationalism: Myth and Reality* (New York: Harcourt, Brace and World, 1955).

LANDES, D. S. *The Unbound Prometheus: Technological Change and Industrial Development in Western Europe from 1750 to the Present.* Cambridge: Cambridge University Press, 1969. The long view of the Industrial Revolution, convincingly presented. See also S. Pollard, *Peaceful Conquest: The Industrialization of Europe, 1760–1970* (New York: Oxford University Press, 1981).

LUKACS, G. *Essays on Realism,* trans. D. Fernbach. Cambridge, Mass.: MIT Press, 1983. Studies of the other main current of nineteenth-century art and thought, by an eminent Western Marxist.

MARX, K., and F. ENGELS. *Basic Writings on Politics and Philosophy.* Boston: Peter Smith, 1975. A good sample of the work of the founders of Marxism. For expert commentary, see G. Lichtheim, *Marxism: An Historical and Critical Study* (New York: Columbia University Press, 1982), or E. Wilson's less authoritative but extremely readable *To the Finland Station* (New York: Farrar, Straus & Giroux, 1972).

MARKHAM, F. *Napoleon.* New York: New American Library, 1963. Good life of the greatest general of modern times. For the debate over his intentions and accomplishments in the political sphere, see P. Geyl, *Napoleon, For and Against* (New Haven: Yale University Press, 1949).

MILL, J. S. *Essential Works of John Stuart Mill.* New York: Bantam Books, 1961. Includes important works of the quintessential nineteenth-century liberal. See also his *On the Subjection of Women* (Cambridge, Mass.: MIT Press, 1970).

PALMER, R. R. *The Age of the Democratic Revolution.* Princeton: Princeton University Press, 1980. Controversial but influential thesis of a wave of democratic revolutions sweeping across the Western world. See also J. Godechot, *France and the Atlantic Revolution of the Eighteenth Century, 1770–1799,* trans. H. R. Rowen (New York: Free Press, 1965).

PFLANZE, O. *Bismarck and the Development of Germany.* Princeton: Princeton University Press, 1963. Challenges older views; widely accepted.

POSTGATE, R. *Story of a Year: 1848.* Westport, Conn.: Greenwood, 1975. Colorful chronicle of the revolutionary year. On the significance of the "springtime of the peoples," see M. Kranzberg, ed., *1848: A Turning Point?* (Lexington, Mass.: Heath, 1959).

REYNAL, M. *The Nineteenth Century.* Geneva: Skira, 1951. European painting in the 1800s, beautifully illustrated.

RUDÉ, G. *The Crowd in History, 1730–1884.* Atlantic Highlands, N.J.: Humanities Press, 1981. Revealing analysis of the allegedly "faceless mob" by a pioneering student of revolutionary crowds.

TILLY, L. A., and J. W. SCOTT. *Women, Work, and Family.* New York: Holt, Rinehart & Winston, 1979. About women in England and France. On women in Germany, see J. C. Fout, *German Women in the Nineteenth Century: A Social History* (New York: Holmes and Meier, 1983). See also E. Riemer and J. Fout, eds., *European Women: A Documentary History, 1789–1945* (New York: Schocken, 1980).

Chapter · 11

FROM COLONIES TO COUNTRIES

YANKEE AMERICA

Changes

While Europe evolved astonishingly from the later eighteenth through the nineteenth century, the Europeanized New World across the Atlantic was in some ways even more dramatically transformed. The Americas had already changed drastically during the colonial period (roughly 1500–1800). During the century and a quarter after 1776, the former colonies would undergo as total a transformation in a half dozen generations as the world has ever seen.

Politically, this period saw what had once been English, Spanish, Portuguese, and other colonies become independent nations—the two countries of Canada and the United States in English-speaking North America and a score of new nations in Latin America to the south. Economically, almost all of these new countries were affected to some degree by the Industrial Revolution, and one among them—the United States—had developed the world's most dynamic industrial economy by 1900.

Demographically, the Western Hemisphere participated fully in the global population explosion, Europeans continuing to replace the original Amerindian population at an accelerating rate. Socially, there were also striking changes: the nineteenth century saw the destruction of surviving Indian societies, the freeing of Afro-American slaves, greatly increased social mobility for middle- and even some lower-class Americans, and the beginnings of the social emancipation of American women.

It was a time of great events and towering personalities. Revolution began the period, and wars studded its history, measuring the westward expansion of the United States and settling the frontiers of the new South American nations. Railways and telegraph lines began the unification of both continents, and modern cities like New York, Chicago, and San Francisco, Mexico City, Buenos Aires, and Rio de Janeiro mushroomed north and south. Names like Washington, Bolívar, San Martín, and Lincoln joined the world's short list of genuinely historic figures. A survey of these amazing changes fills the following pages.

From Sea to Shining Sea

From sea to shining sea, North America was a thinly settled continent during the period of European colonization. Most of the land, of course, was still inhabited primarily by Amerindian peoples during the colonial centuries. The Spanish claimed much of western North America and the Gulf Coast; the French, Canada and the Mississippi Valley; the Russians, the far Northwest. But a scattering of Spanish missions, French fur traders, and the odd Russian Cossack scarcely diluted the life of the indigenous population over most of the continent.

Only in one place were Europeans thick on the ground in the seventeenth and eighteenth centuries. In the English settlements along the east coast, European farms, villages, and cities steadily displaced the Indians who had lived there in 1600. Here on the Atlantic seaboard was born the expansive society that in the nineteenth century would sweep to the Pacific.

The thirteen English colonies differed from one another in important ways. The rocky New England hills of Massachusetts, Connecticut, and Rhode Island bred Puritan clergymen in the early days, flinty Yankee storekeepers and whaling captains in later centuries. The middle colonies, including bustling New York, New Jersey, and the Quaker haven of Pennsylvania, were the breadbasket of the colonies, producing grains such as wheat and barley. The balmier southern colonies, from Maryland and Virginia down through the Carolinas to Georgia, were the plantation territories, owned by debonair American equivalents of English country squires, worked by black slaves, and producing large cash crops of tobacco and rice for export.

But the thirteen colonies, penned in between the Appalachian Mountains and the sea, had important elements in common too. They had a large population, perhaps two and a half million by 1776—a third of the population of Great Britain itself. They also had a relatively homogeneous society, the Indians having been pushed westward out of English-settled areas, the African slaves thoroughly segregated in the southern plantations. It was in some ways a more prosperous society than that of Europe, thanks to the large amounts of land available for the taking. It was almost certainly a more mobile society, in which the ability to do a job came to count for more than family background. It was even a comparatively well educated culture, especially in the North, where the first European settlers had been dedicated Protestants, the "people of the Book."

Most important, perhaps, the thirteen English colonies were all used to a significant amount of self-government from the beginning. In Latin America, military commanders and royal officials dominated the *conquista* and the colonies. In English North America, by contrast, all the settlements had assemblies of freemen who debated and determined their own affairs. New England town meetings and colonial legislatures were part of the fabric of colonial life. Royal governors and mercantilistic regulations would run afoul of these colonial assemblies throughout the later colonial period. After 1776 this tradition of self-government would provide the model—and the experience—that would bring the world's largest republic into existence in the United States.

1776

The American Revolution may be seen a dozen different ways: as a patriotic struggle for freedom, as an economic revolt against mercantilism, as an ideological clash, as a theater of towering personalities, as part of a larger "age of democratic revolutions" around the North Atlantic, as the first of what would later come to be called national liberation struggles, and on and on. In a global perspective, the primary significance of the American Revolution is perhaps

George Washington presides over the last day's deliberations at the Constitutional Convention of 1787. The United States Constitution, built on European liberal ideas, became itself part of the evolving Western liberal tradition. (New York Public Library Picture Collection)

twofold. It revealed very early the fragility of the political structure of the European intercontinental empires. Its aftermath, however, demonstrated the tenacity of Western society, culture, and interrelations once the Western predominance was firmly established beyond the seas.

Even in retrospect, the Revolution seems to have come on with remarkable suddenness.

In 1763, Britain had won the Seven Years' War and stood mistress of the greatest of all the European overseas empires. The American colonies were the jewel of that empire—productive, populous, and full of promise. Almost immediately, however, the British government began an ill-considered series of mercantilist measures. These reforms were designed to increase government revenues from America after the expense of the recent war, much of which had been fought in defense of the colonies. They were also intended to tighten up London's hold on those cities, villages, and farms three thousand miles away.

Mercantilist economic regulation was not new, of course, and the measures did not seem extreme to the prime ministers who proposed them. Taxes on sugar and coffee and tea, stamp taxes on printed matter, and attempts to wipe out smuggling seemed legitimate enough in Britain—but they outraged the colonists. Decisions to quarter troops in the colonies and finally to reorganize colonial governments in order to destroy the power of their assemblies aroused violent opposition.

The colonies responded to a decade of such measures with a series of ingenious—and increasingly subversive—organizations of their own. They held colonial congresses and set up committees of correspondence to coordinate the activities of the colonial leadership. Some of them collected weapons and organized the riotous Sons of Liberty and the paramilitary Minutemen.

A roster of talented leaders emerged during those dozen years of crisis from 1763 to 1775. These included the aging but still witty Enlightenment intellectual Ben Franklin of Philadelphia, the passionate spokesman Sam Adams of Boston, and his determinedly anti-British cousin John Adams. The new colonial leadership also included a group of Virginia gentlemen, among them the orator Patrick Henry, the young lawyer Thomas Jefferson, and the most impressive of the Virginians, the planter and sometime soldier George Washington.

By the spring of 1775, subversive organization and mob violence had triggered military retaliation. Troops dispatched to seize arms caches in two villages west of Boston confronted colonial militia, and the shot heard round the world was fired on the village green at Lexington.

It was more than a year, however, before the leaders of the colonial revolt, assembled at the Second Continental Congress in Philadelphia, made the break official. On July 4, 1776, Jefferson's Declaration of Independence was formally promulgated, with its ringing Lockean assertion

> That all men are created equal, that they are endowed by their Creator with certain inalienable Rights, that among these are Life, Liberty, and the pursuit of Happiness.
> That to secure these rights, Governments are instituted among men, deriving their just powers from the consent of the governed. . . .

It is easy and normally sensible to take ringing political declarations with a generous pinch of salt. Still, there are times and places where basic ideas, widely held and passionately defended, do make a difference. A ninety-year-old veteran of the fighting around Lexington and Concord in 1775, asked some fifty years later about his motives in taking up arms that day, spoke with little of Jefferson's eloquence, but to much the same effect. "Young man," he said to his questioner, "what we meant in going for those redcoats was this: we always had governed ourselves, and we always meant to. They didn't mean we should."[1]

And so they fought. For six long years, ragtag regiments of summer soldiers fought armies of British regulars and Hessian mercenaries up and down the fifteen-hundred-mile strip of land, much of it still wilderness, between the Appalachian Mountains and the Atlantic. The colonial troops were ill trained, ill equipped, inexperienced, and given to desertion around harvest time. The Continental Congress could not supply their armies properly. Most of the colonial population was lukewarm or indifferent, and many were loyal to Great Britain. Freezing at Valley Forge, retreating from many defeats, the Revolution looked much less noble and romantic close up than it has in many a Fourth of July oration since.

But the British were an ocean away from home, the colonials frequently fighting in familiar fields and hills. There were some timely and heartening victories. The snowy midnight crossing of the Delaware to catch the Hessians unaware at Trenton is as much a part of American folklore as the grim winter at Valley Forge. Much more important was the surrender of "Gentleman Johnny" Burgoyne's army, invading from Canada, at Saratoga. On the strength of the Saratoga victory, Ben Franklin was able to negotiate the crucial French alliance that sent arms, money, and a

[1]George Brown Tindall, *America: A Narrative History* (New York: W. W. Norton, 1984), p. 203.

French expeditionary force commanded by the young Marquis de Lafayette to America.

Above all, perhaps, there was General George Washington (1732–1799). Six feet two, pale-skinned and blue-eyed, he looked good on a horse. He was a prudent man, not imaginative, but resolute once he had decided on action. This single-minded resolution, combined with a southern planter's reserve and a natural dignity, made Washington a perfect symbol for the cause he led, as later for the nation he governed.

Washington was no Napoleon: he seldom commanded ten thousand men (Napoleon could marshal hundreds of thousands), won few battles, and rather wore his enemies out by patience than out-generaled them. British problems and the French alliance were crucial to his final success. And yet when all is said and done, Washington kept armies in the field for six long years. And when the bands struck up at Yorktown in 1781, the song they played was "The World Turned Upside Down"—for it was a British army, the last of any size left in the colonies, that laid down its arms.

Novus Ordo Seclorum

The nation that evolved over the three quarters of a century after 1781 saw itself as a new beginning in human history. The great seal of the United States proclaimed a *novus ordo seclorum*, a "new ordering of the ages." In a global context, the rise of the United States of (North) America is perhaps better seen as a new surge of Western power—and as a main road toward the climax of the Western hegemony of the world in the twentieth century.

It was, in any event, a spectacular achievement. Three aspects of the growth of the United States between the Revolution and the Civil War will be examined here: the evolution of political democracy, economic growth, and imperial expansion across the continent.

The fruit and in many ways the most important political achievement of the new country was the United States Constitution, the oldest such document in the world today.

After a decade of groping for political stability under the wartime Articles of Confederation, the thirteen United States set a constitutional convention to work, again at Philadelphia, in 1787. Balancing the interests of large and small states, fear of tyranny against the need for unity, the Constitution created a strong yet flexible central government for the new republic.

Executive authority was put in the hands of an elected president with appointed officials and an army and navy at his disposal. Lawmaking power was vested in a two-house legislature balancing the claims of more and less populous states. There was an appointed but independent federal judiciary. The first ten amendments provided a Bill of Rights protecting the people against governmental encroachments on their liberties as citizens.

The power of this grudgingly accepted central government grew steadily in the hands of the men who filled the offices thus defined for the next few decades. Washington, the first president (1789–1797), brought immense prestige and even a modestly imperial style to the presidency. Alexander Hamilton, the first secretary of the Treasury, strengthened the crucial power of the government in financial matters, and John Marshall, chief justice of the Supreme Court from 1801 to 1835, emphasized the authority of federal laws over those of the states. The new national capital built at "Washington City" after the turn of the century and strong national leaders such as presidents Thomas Jefferson (1801–1808) and Andrew Jackson (1829–1836) also contributed to the power of the central government in the new country.

At the same time, however, the democratic base of the Republic grew apace. Major spokesmen for popular sovereignty included Jefferson, with his faith in the American "yeomanry," the solid landowning farmers he regarded as the backbone of the nation. A more rudely democratic spokesman was Andy Jackson. A westerner and one of the few heroes of the War of 1812, Jackson became a champion of the "common man," whether he owned land or not, and a vocal opponent of effete eastern aristocrats. Citizens of the expanding West generally carried the colonial enthusiasm for self-made men and opposition to inherited property and privilege to democratic extremes. In such a climate, taxpayer suffrage and even universal manhood suffrage spread rapidly, till almost all adult males could vote in America by 1850—decades earlier than in Europe.

There were limitations to all this political democratization, of course. Millions of black slaves and Native Americans had no part in the political process in the first half of the nineteenth century. The entire female half of the population would remain disfranchised throughout the 1800s. The democratic ideal, however, was firmly established. Its own logic—and rhetoric—would in time carry it to virtually universal application, in the United States as across the Western world.

Economic growth was also a striking feature of American history throughout the nineteenth century.

The United States had some distinct economic advantages over the Old World. These included free land in virtually unlimited quantities, which became available as rapidly as it could be taken from the sparsely distributed Indians. The U.S. also had at its disposal the unmeasurable natural resources of a continent that stretched westward for thousands of miles. Another advantage was a rapidly growing population, rising from less than 4 million at the time of the first census in 1790 to more than 30 million at the beginning of the Civil War—an eightfold multiplication in three and a half generations.

A final advantage, once more, was a relatively open and mobile society, in which it was comparatively easy to move from place to place or up and down the social scale. Particularly in the expanding American West, it was what you could *do*, not who you *were*, that counted. Most people did not make fortunes or rise from rags to riches. But there were enough poor-boy millionaires and shirttail western senators to make getting ahead a virtue and a genuine possibility in the United States.

The American economic "miracle," as similar surges elsewhere would be labeled in the twentieth century, was a jumble of lusty work songs and sharp dealings in land, of technological innovation and public-be-damned private enterprise. Its all-encompassing justification was, quite simply, success. That it had. From the Erie Canal boom to flush times in Alabama to the California gold rush, there seemed to be no end to opportunity for Americans.

To bumper crops and burgeoning mines, furthermore, was added the unprecedented eruption of the Industrial Revolution. Crossing the Atlantic from Britain almost as quickly as it crossed the Channel to Europe, the new potential for multiplied industrial production caught the U.S. at precisely the right moment in its accelerating economic growth. British investment capital, technology, and large numbers of European immigrants all made their contributions. The steam engine in the North brought an industrial boom to New England just as the cotton gin made cotton the king of the Southern agrarian economy.

Not everybody benefited, of course. Factory workers—women as well as men—were as likely to be exploited in the New World as in the Old. Black slaves were still slaves, however prosperous the cotton economy might be. Indians, dispossessed of their lands and pushed farther and farther westward, did not participate in the land boom. Immigrants, flowing in especially from Catholic Ireland and the revolution-torn German states, were as likely to be oppressed in northern mills as blacks were in the South or Indians in the West. Any significant trickle-down benefits would have to wait several generations for these segments of the population. But the growing wealth was there, and a fairer sharing would come, at least for some of these groups, in later generations.

This was, finally, the age that saw the beginning of a tremendous American imperial expansion. Westward "the star of empire," as the Manifest Destiny advocates called it, did inexorably move.

The new United States was ideally positioned for old-fashioned empire building in 1776. The most powerful political entity in North America, it had nothing between it and the Pacific but untended European colonies and weakened Indian confederations and tribal groupings. Through wars, cash payments, diplomatic maneuvers, and the irresistable westward push of population, the United States laid claim to all of North America south of Canada and north of the Rio Grande by the middle of the nineteenth century.

The Louisiana Purchase brought the huge middle swath of the continent into the Union in 1803. Texas, after it revolted from Mexico, was annexed to the United States in 1845. The Oregon Territory was secured through negotiation with Britain in 1846. California and most of the rest of the West were seized after the Mexican War in 1848. These, with smaller acquisitions in Florida and along the Mexican and Canadian borders and the purchase of Alaska from Russia in 1867, multiplied the size of the United States as its population and economic production grew.

Expansion was a heady tonic for the young nation. There was talk of further growth north and south, "from Panama to Hudson's Bay." President James Monroe's Doctrine (1823), originally proposed by the British to protect their commercial interests in Latin America, declared the entire Western Hemisphere closed to Old World colonization—but not, as it later turned out, to American imperialism south of the border. With American clippers racing to China in the 1840s and 1850s and Admiral Perry opening Japan to American influence in the mid 1850s, a global role for the new country seemed assured.

Then at mid-century, calamity struck the United States with the devastating fury of what seemed to Americans of those days the Lord's own terrible swift sword.

The High Tide at Gettysburg

The American Civil War (1861–1865) had been building for decades beneath the bustling enthusiasm of the new nation. The "irrepressible conflict" was rooted in part in the differing economic interests of the plantation South and the rapidly industrializing North. There was also a southern sense of decreasing political power as new western states undermined the influence of the region that had produced the "Virginia dynasty" of post-Revolutionary presidents. In the end, however, the central issues were the South's insistence on maintaining its "peculiar institution" of slavery even if it meant seceding from the Union—

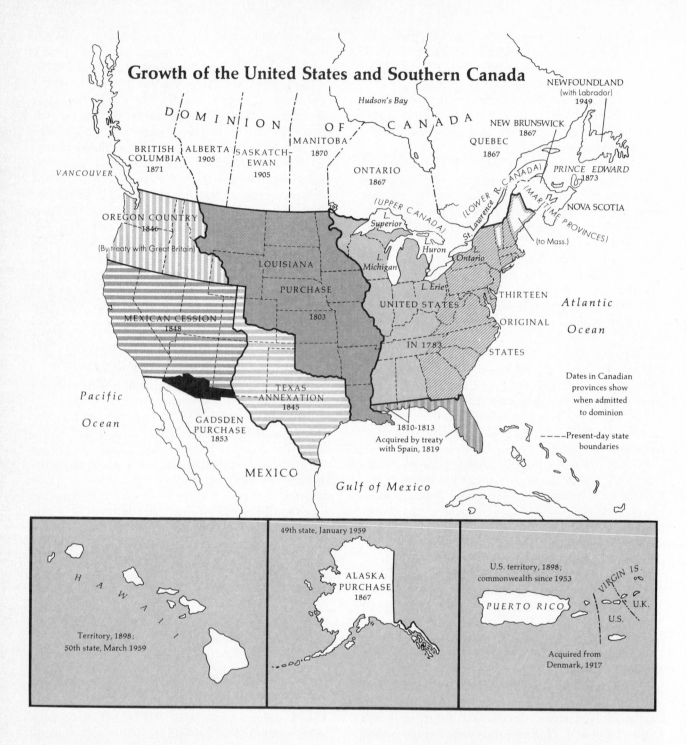

Growth of the United States and Southern Canada

NEWFOUNDLAND
(with Labrador)
1949

Hudson's Bay

D O M I N I O N   O F   C A N A D A

NEW BRUNSWICK
1867

QUEBEC
1867

MANITOBA
1870

BRITISH
COLUMBIA
1871

ALBERTA
1905

SASKATCH-
EWAN
1905

ONTARIO
1867

PRINCE EDWARD
1873

VANCOUVER

(UPPER CANADA)

(LOWER CANADA)

NOVA SCOTIA

L.
Superior

L.
Huron

L.
Michigan

L.
Ontario

St. Lawrence R.

(MARITIME PROVINCES)

(to Mass.)

OREGON COUNTRY
1846

(By treaty with Great Britain)

LOUISIANA

PURCHASE

1803

UNITED STATES

L. Erie

THIRTEEN

ORIGINAL

Atlantic

Ocean

MEXICAN CESSION
1848

IN 1783

STATES

Pacific

Ocean

TEXAS
ANNEXATION
1845

Dates in Canadian
provinces show
when admitted
to dominion

GADSDEN
PURCHASE
1853

1810-1813
Acquired by treaty
with Spain, 1819

- - - - Present-day state
boundaries

MEXICO

Gulf of Mexico

Territory, 1898;
50th state, March 1959

H
A
W
A
I
I

49th state, January 1959

ALASKA
PURCHASE
1867

U.S. territory, 1898;
commonwealth since 1953

PUERTO RICO

VIRGIN IS.

U.K.

U.S.

Acquired from
Denmark, 1917

and the North's determination that the Union must be preserved at all costs.

There were 4 million black slaves in the United States in 1860, mostly in the South and mostly field hands. But some were artisans or factory workers, and in Louisiana there was even a mulatto aristocracy set apart from both white and black. Slave importation had ended in 1808, but important elements of West African cultures had survived among the descendants of these forced African immigrants. Slaves were val-

uable property and hence not usually mistreated gratuitously. They were strong family people, hard workers, and nowhere near as given to rebellion as their contemporaries the Russian serfs. But they were slaves in a land that claimed to be free.

Antislavery abolitionist societies in the North crusaded for the total abolition of the peculiar institution in the decades before the Civil War. The underground railway smuggled runaway slaves north to Canada and freedom. Free-Soilers fought with rifles to keep new states such as Kansas free of slavery. Harriet Beecher Stowe's sociologically unconvincing but morally powerful *Uncle Tom's Cabin* moved the nation, and abolitionist John Brown's bloody raid on Harper's Ferry shocked it. Senators and congressmen thundered and maneuvered, seeking to avoid what to many seemed the ultimate catastrophe: southern secession from the Union.

But no crusade or compromise could cut the Gordian knot. The United States, said Abraham Lincoln, could not long endure half slave and half free. "The crimes of this guilty land," John Brown declared on the day he was hanged, "will never be purged away, but with blood."[2]

When Lincoln was elected president in 1860, the southern states began to secede and to organize themselves into the Confederate States of America. In the spring of 1861, southern troops fired on a U.S. fort on an island in Charleston harbor, South Carolina, and the Civil War was begun.

Both sides entered the war confident of victory. The Union under President Lincoln had three quarters of the free population, two thirds of the railways, four fifths of the industry, and most of the nation's wealth. The Confederacy under its hastily elected president, Jefferson Davis, had many of the most experienced military commanders, the patriotic and tactical advantage of fighting in defense of its own soil, and the powerful card of cotton exports, with which it hoped to win crucial support from European textile manufacturing nations such as Great Britain.

Southern generals did, in fact, more than compensate for superior northern numbers in the early years of the war. Robert E. Lee, "Stonewall" Jackson, and the brilliant cavalry commander J.E.B. "Jeb" Stuart repeatedly outmaneuvered and reversed northern advances. Later in the struggle, however, Lee met his match in generals such as the implacable Ulysses S. Grant and William Tecumseh Sherman. And the South, for all its dash and valor, never had a monopoly on courage.

Above all, the North had President Abraham Lincoln (1861–1865). Tall and gaunt and hopelessly ugly, his hair and beard ill combed and his eyes somber and hollow, Lincoln cut an unprepossessing figure in his stovepipe hat and habitual suit of solemn black. But he was a skillful manipulator of people and patronage, a speaker whose eloquence can move us still, and a man in whom confidence in his cause—the salvation of the Union—combined with an immense compassion for all who suffered in that time of national trial.

[2]Stephen B. Oates, *To Purge This Land with Blood: A Biography of John Brown* (New York: Harper & Row, Publishers, 1970), p. 351.

Abraham Lincoln, perhaps America's most admired president, is shown here in a photograph by famed Civil War photographer Mathew Brady. A shrewd politician beneath his legendary folksy stories, Lincoln presided over the costly effort that preserved the Union and freed the slaves. (Library of Congress)

The war Lincoln fought to a successful conclusion was the bloodiest in the history of the United States. The basic Union strategy was to blockade the South by sea and cut it off from the West before invading, destroying the southern armies, and ending the secession. Lee and the southern generals fought to defend territory and strove mightily to win victories—especially on northern soil—that might bring them foreign help. In the end, it was the northern strategy that worked.

Lee's greatest effort carried him as far north as Gettysburg, Pennsylvania, where in July of 1863 Pickett's famous charge carried across a long and bloody mile to the crest of Cemetery Ridge, to break at last in the acrid powder smoke and the crash of Union guns—and fall away. It was the high tide of the Confederacy—the high tide and the turn.

Ahead lay even bloodier battles in the West and South, and Sherman's notorious scorched-earth march southeast to Atlanta and then on to the sea. Ahead too was the awesome silence at Appomattox, where Lee laid down his arms in 1865—and the last shot, less than a week later, when a mad actor put a bullet through President Lincoln's brain.

Six hundred thousand men had died. The Union was preserved, the slaves freed. A nation "conceived in liberty and dedicated to the proposition that all men are created equal" had survived its most terrible ordeal.

The Gilded Age

The four decades between the Civil War and the emergence of political reformism at the end of the century were perhaps the grubbiest in the history of American politics. Economically, however, the nation boomed as never before. And U.S. expansive energies continued to manifest themselves, filling the American West and reaching out beyond the seas for a share of the world's trade and empire.

After the war to save the Union, the nation as a whole turned its back on political crusades and sank into a period of corruption and cynical disregard for the public welfare seldom matched in its history. Ineffectual presidents, state machines, big-city bosses, and legislators who cheerfully peddled their votes to big business dominated the political scene between Lincoln's death in 1865 and Teddy Roosevelt's accession in 1901.

In the South, the old white aristocracy soon reemerged. Blacks, freed without land, were reduced to sharecropping, working for landowners for a never sufficient share of the crops they grew. Hooded terrorists such as Ku Klux Klanners and a series of Jim Crow laws reduced blacks to second-class status at best, segregated, discriminated against, and denied even the basic right to vote.

Farmers' organizations did agitate for reform, and labor unions painfully took shape during the later nineteenth century. Some big-city bosses seem to have served the useful purpose of giving immigrants and other otherwise neglected citizens a bit of patronage in return for their votes. By and large, however, it was a dismal time politically.

Economically, however, the nation grew even faster than it had before the war. Resources were still seemingly limitless, and the population was doubling every quarter century. Vast amounts of capital were available, much of it from Europe, and technological advance was accelerating. What now amounted to a national faith in rags-to-riches entrepreneurship drove the nation to still greater efforts. Under such circumstances, the economic success of the continental republic was perhaps not surprising.

But it was certainly dazzling. In the decades after the Civil War, railroads stretched from sea to sea, till the U.S. had more miles of track than all Europe combined. The output of United States factories tripled from 1877 to 1892 alone. By the end of the century, the United States was both the world's leading agricultural producer and the world's leading manufacturer.

As in Europe, big business developed in the United States at this time. The railroads were the first huge corporations, hiring armies of workers and buying up great expanses of western lands. The names of financial giants such as J. Pierpont Morgan and industrial empire-builders such as Andrew Carnegie, the steel king, and John D. Rockefeller of Standard Oil became household words. Master organizers and employers of skilled managers, they learned to cut waste, buy and build in depressed times, and pyramid their holdings. Ruthless competitors, willing to use rebates, stock watering, and other shady or illegal devices, they became greater monopolists than their European contemporaries.

To muckraking reformers, the robber barons were symbols of monopoly capital and industrial exploitation. To admirers and would-be imitators, they were embodiments of what Americans were already thinking of as the American success story.

The climax of the westward expansion and the beginning of the nation's reach for empire overseas added to the sense of Yankee progress. It was a gaudy, giddy time, and they called it, if not a true golden age, at least a gilded one.

Cigars and Cuspidors

Socially speaking, the whole of the nineteenth century in the United States is perhaps best described by that most overworked of historical clichés, an age of contrasts.

Fourth of July speakers tirelessly reiterated that the great republic was the homeland of freedom, equality, opportunity, and hope. Equally impassioned—if rather less numerous—radicals pointed out that these great gifts were distributed quite unevenly among the classes, races, sexes, and other groups that made up the nation. And there was significant truth in both views.

The oldest Americans had essentially no share at all in the benefits of the new democratic-industrial state. Defeated in endless petty wars, betrayed by one broken treaty after another, Native Americans were chivied into "Indian territories" and "reservations" farther and farther west and on increasingly barren tracts of land. Here they lived according to what was left of their old ways, infected by whiskey and guns, tempted either to surrender to the lure of the conqueror's world or to rebel futilely against it.

Black Americans, still clustered very largely in the South, also had little or no part in American growth and self-government. They were the poorest citizens in the poorest part of the country, locked into subjugation before 1865 by slavery, afterwards by sharecropping, Klan terror, and Jim Crow laws. A few blacks, however, did move north to begin building a genuine black bourgeoisie in cities such as Chicago. Others began to construct a base for black advancement in the South itself through educational institutions such as Hampton Institute in Virginia and Tuskegee Institute in Georgia. A start was thus made, though in the nineteenth century it was no more than that.

Another frequently victimized group were the millions of new immigrants who poured into the country, primarily in search of economic opportunity but also to escape even more rigidly hierarchical societies in the Old World. Most of these newcomers were still Europeans, still mostly from northern and western Europe. Some, however, were East Asians, Chinese and Japanese, many recruited across the Pacific to help build the western end of the transcontinental railroad—while Irish immigrants built the eastern end.

Whether they came to lay rails, to farm the endless western plains opened up to homesteaders, or to practice European trades in the ghettos of eastern cities, the newest comers were likely to be cheated, exploited, and discriminated against. Clinging to fellow nationals in German or Irish neighborhoods, Chinatowns, or Scandinavian farming communities, they would typically require a couple of generations to achieve even an uneasy integration into their new country.

Farmers in the United States also had their share of problems in the latter part of the nineteenth century. Declining crop prices, unprotected markets, deflation, and mortgage debt ground them down year after year. Extortionate railway rates and an unfortunate surge of droughts, floods, and blizzards around 1890 added to their miseries. Many farmers were driven into bankruptcy, others into militant farmers' organizations such as the Grange or radical Populist politics. By the end of the century, Jefferson's yeomanry, the backbone of the nation, seemed to be lending an interested ear to very un-Jeffersonian agitators like "Sockless" Jerry Simpson, "Cyclone" Davis, and Mary E. Lease, who urged farmers to raise "less corn and more hell."

American labor also organized during the closing decades of the century, forming embattled unions, staging strikes that were often suppressed by hired strikebreakers or even the National Guard. The Industrial Revolution brought brutalizing social dislocation to American as to European labor: long hours, low pay, dangerous working conditions, and slums and company towns that further degraded workers. Waves of unemployment in the depressions of the last quarter of the century and helplessness before the economic and political power of the robber barons of the Gilded Age added to the bitterness of laboring people. Organizations such as the Knights of Labor and the American Federation of Labor and leaders such as the AFL's Samuel Gompers fought but lost a large number of strikes in the 1880s and 1890s. Genuine improvement for factory workers, as for farmers, lay two generations ahead, in the New Deal of the 1930s.

Women's lives, finally, were as varied in North American as in Europe. Recent research has reminded us of the brutal lives of women in New England mills in the earlier 1800s and in the sweatshops of New York's garment district around 1900. We have learned that pioneer women went west not only with their husbands and children, but on their own or as heads of families. Middle-class American women seem to have earned a particular reputation, especially toward the end of the century, for independence of mind and forthright strength of character. They toured Europe alone, or ran mission stations on isolated Pacific atolls. Europeans found them rather *too* independent; Asians found them inscrutable.

As in Europe, American women were likely to be involved in social causes, from the abolition of slavery to the emancipation of women themselves. They broke into the professions on this side of the Atlantic too, and were soon demanding the vote. There were many women writers in the United States, from Harriet Beecher Stowe before the Civil War to the reclusive poet Emily Dickinson and the great novelist Edith Wharton after it.

But American middle-class women also found themselves considered too fine and delicate for politics, business, science, and other careers deemed suitable only for the ruder clay and more rational heads of men. In America even more than in Europe, descending from this unsolicited pedestal would be a problem for the following century.

The later nineteenth century, the famous Gilded Age, belonged above all to the businessman—male, middle-class, and thoroughly in control. It was an era of whiskers, cigars, and cuspidors, solid bellies and gaudy waistcoats. Smoke-filled rooms brokered elections, and nothing cemented a sale like an aromatic Havana.

They weren't social reformers, and their notions of business ethics would scarcely pass muster in a civics class, then or now. But they were making the United States the richest country in the world—and at least some of that wealth, opportunity, and even political power would filter down to the rest of the nation in the century to come.

This perky river steamer symbolizes the economic enterprise that exploited every advantage the virtually untapped American continent offered, from minerals and fertile soil to great inland waterways. (National Gallery of Art, Washington, D.C. Edgar Wm. & Bernice Chrysler Garbisch 1953)

AMERICA SOUTH

Images

Latin America before it was *latina*—before the conquest—is to most people Aztecs and Incas. It is lost hearts in Tenochtitlán and the golden temples of Cuzco. Latin America in the colonial and early national period, from the *conquista* through the nineteenth century, is another and more confusing matter.

To most of us Latin America is, of course, still Indians: leathery, impassive faces and eyes with illimitable depths. The Spanish conquered the major centers of Amerindian population, and the *indio* element was thus much more prominent in Latin America than it ever was to the north. Middle and South America means colorful types of outdoorsmen too—usually associated with horses. It means Mexican *vaqueros* or Argentine gauchos, or the master of the hacienda, ramrod straight on horseback, inspecting his fields and herds. And Latin America is heroic geography still. It is the perfect aquamarine of the Caribbean, the green depths of the Amazon rain forest, the granite shoulders of the Andes, the long southward roll of the pampas.

It should kindle other images in our minds as well: whitewashed walls, ancient forts with rusted guns, baroque churches, splendid palaces. It should be bustling ports like Rio or Buenos Aires, as thronged with spars and smokestacks as London or Istanbul. It should be two names at least: Bolívar and San Mar-

tín, as different as fire and ice, as great as Washington and Lincoln.

It is to be hoped that the following pages will help put some of these and other images into all our heads.

Backwaters That Worked

The Iberian colonies in the Western Hemisphere were a century older and many times larger than the English colonies on the east coast of North America. Portugal's Brazilian colony alone, occupying half of South America, was almost as large as the United States is today. Spanish America included the rest of South America, the Central American isthmus and most of the Caribbean, Mexico and much of what is today California, Texas, and Florida, with the Southwest and the Gulf Coast in between. By contrast with Britain's compact strip of colonies—a fraction of the future United States—these continental expanses of colonial territory to the south must have strained any early-modern European government.

The population of colonial Latin America was also much more complex than that of the British colonies that would come to master North America. To the large numbers of Amerindians who survived the brutalities of the conquest, the victorious Europeans added masses of African slaves. The result was a tripartite population, like that of colonial North America but less rigidly segregated—caucasoid, mongoloid, and negroid mingling as they did nowhere else in the world.

This demographic pattern was further complicated by powerfully felt social divisions. There were, in the first place, two groups of Europeans. The peninsulars, primarily officials sent out from Spain or Portugal to govern the colonies, were the ruling elite in the colonial period. *Criollos*, European-descended Latin Americans born in the colonies, composed the provincial aristocracy of mine and plantation owners who would inherit power when the colonies broke free in the nineteenth century.

A final subdivision with a long future were the *mestizos*, Latin Americans of mixed racial background, descended primarily from European and Indian ancestors. This vigorous group belied every racial stereotype of the evils of "race mixing." Minor officials, petty tradesmen, and the like in colonial times, when they were discriminated against, they would emerge as the dominant cultural and political force in twentieth-century Latin America.

This vast expanse and complex population were administered through most of the colonial period in three colonial jurisdictions. These were the viceroyalty of New Spain (from California and Texas through Mexico to Central America), the viceroyalty of Peru (Spanish-speaking South America), and the Portuguese colony of Brazil. Viceroys, captains general, bishops, and other high-ranking officials were sent out from Spain and Portugal to govern, primarily in the interests of the crown. These men, many of whom were bureaucrats with little firsthand knowledge of the huge territories they administered, necessarily depended on local people and lower-ranking officials for the real work of running the colonies.

There were no town meetings or colonial assemblies to resist the authority of the Crown in Latin America, as there were in British North America. But there were the *audencias*, judicial boards whose numbers also served as advisers to viceroys and sometimes resisted misguided viceregal policies. At the local level there were small town councils usually dominated by the *criollo* elite. And there were local representatives of the Crown, minor officials often more interested in lining their own pockets than advancing any policies, royal or *criollo*.

This system, modeled on continental European absolutism and attempting to govern an area twice as large as all Europe put together, can be presented in a uniformly glum light. Top-ranking officials, who were sent out for short terms and whose primary allegiance was to the Crown, were too often stodgy bureaucrats uninterested in and ignorant of the colonies they ruled. Many of the local officials were extremely corrupt, and mercilessly exploited the conquered Amerindian villages under their jurisdiction. *Criollo* landowners and even Jesuit and other missions built their own little empires of wealth and power on the labor of large numbers of Indians or black slaves.

There is also the prevailing sense of the Latin American colonies being a cultural and social backwater during the seventeenth and eighteenth centuries. Spain and Portugal themselves had declined to second-rate powers after the sixteenth century; their colonies may be seen as the dusty provinces of decaying metropolises.

A more positive view of much of the colonial experience can also be taken, however. The neglect of the colonies by weakened and impoverished mother countries in the seventeenth century may be seen as a form of benign neglect that allowed local people to solve local problems. And in the eighteenth century, the Bourbon kings of Spain in particular embarked upon a campaign of enlightened reforms that had very positive effects. These included efforts at administrative, legal, and financial reform, as well as encouragement of agricultural and local industry and the building of churches and schools. Thanks at least in part to these manifestations of the spirit of the European Enlightenment, there seems to have been a surge of genuine prosperity toward the end of the colonial period, in the later eighteenth and early nineteenth centuries.

Colonial Latin America remained a sprawling region of isolated villages, backcountry plantations, and provincial cities. Sleepy plazas were ringed by dusty colonial baroque churches and palaces. Indians drowsed, *mestizos* hustled, and colonial gentlefolk in last year's European fashions strolled in the late-afternoon shade.

It was indeed a backwater. But in many ways it was a backwater that worked.

The Wars for Independence

Into this somnolent world on the far side of the Atlantic a new spirit intruded around 1800—the spirit of revolution.

Social, economic, and political resentments had been building up for centuries among a variety of colonial groups. Conquered Indians resented the conquest and all the subsequent oppression. Black slaves were never reconciled to slavery. *Mestizos*, cut off by prejudice from all other communities, envied the power of their fathers' European world and resented the oppression of their mothers' non-European people. *Criollos*, the chief builders of the colonial economy, saw no justice in the privileged social position and the political authority enjoyed by peninsular judges, bishops, military commanders, captains general, and viceroys.

Simón Bolívar, most famous of the liberators of Latin America. Something of the great freedom-fighter's dash and sense of drama comes through in this bust by Nicolas Veloz. (Library of Congress)

In the late eighteenth century, the subversive intellectual influences of the Enlightenment made themselves felt along with the enlightened reforms of the Bourbons. Satirical Voltairian attacks on foppish aristocrats and worldly churchmen applied as well in the New World as in the Old. Rousseauian talk of government by popular consent had as much appeal to colonials in South as in North America.

Then revolt broke out, in the 1770s in Britain's North American colonies and in the late 1780s in France itself. Under such circumstances, some sort of revolution in Latin America, where there were as many grounds for discontent as in either North America or Europe, is surely not surprising.

The most oppressed rebelled first—an Indian in South America and a black slave in the Caribbean.

Tupac Amaru, who claimed descent from the Incas, was Jesuit-educated and wealthy. Nevertheless, he led a 1780 revolt of the brutally exploited Indians of the Peruvian Andes that briefly liberated Bolivia and parts of Peru and Argentina. Toussaint L'Ouverture, grandson of an African king, was a Haitian slave who had made his own fortune. Inspired by the French Revolution, he launched a ten-year rebellion against the French planters in Haiti (1791–1801). Tu-

pac Amaru was captured and executed, many thousands of his followers slaughtered, his insurrection suppressed. Toussaint L'Ouverture freed Haiti but was betrayed to his enemies and died in a French prison. But the flame had been lit, in both South America and the Caribbean, and it would not go out.

Ironically, it was not the North American or French Revolution that triggered Latin America's fifteen years of revolutionary upheaval, but the great empire-builder Napoleon Bonaparte. Napoleon conquered Spain and Portugal in the early 1800s and put puppet kings on their thrones. Even royalists in the Latin American colonies turned against these usurping monarchs in Madrid and Lisbon.

Three major wars for independence ran their long and often bloody course between 1810 and 1824. There was a revolution in Mexico, pioneered by Father Hidalgo; another in northern South America, led by Simón Bolívar; and a third in southern South America, under the leadership of José de San Martín.

Mexican independence was declared in 1810 by a reforming village priest named Father Miguel Hidalgo y Costilla in the hamlet of Dolores, a hundred miles north of Mexico City. Hidalgo's Sunday sermon on September 16, 1810, before a congregation of poor *mestizos* and Indians gave the revolution its battle cry, the famous *grito de Dolores:* For Freedom and the Virgin of Guadalupe—Death to the Spaniards!

After this inspirational beginning, however, ill-armed and often poorly led hordes of Indians and *mestizos* made little headway against Spanish troops. Father Hidalgo himself was captured and shot. In 1820, however, a liberal revolution in Spain had the paradoxical effect of stimulating wealthy Mexican *criollos* to revolt—against the spreading infection of liberalism from the mother country! At their head was a rich and calculating man—and a formerly successful military commander *against* Hidalgo's rebellion—named Augustín de Iturbide. Iturbide joined the rebels he had once fought, and in 1821 he led a victorious coalition army into Mexico City. Mexico, and with it all of Central America, was liberated at last.

Simón Bolívar (1783–1830), the liberator of northern South America, was an eloquent, dramatic man with a flair for grand schemes and public triumphs. Born to wealthy parents in Caracas, raised by tutors steeped in Rousseau, well traveled in Napoleonic Europe, Bolívar felt himself destined for revolutionary leadership. A rare combination of intellectual and man of action, he was widely read in the Enlightenment and totally committed to freedom in all its forms. He freed his own slaves, promoted members of all classes and races, and tried to persuade his fellow *criollos* to distribute land to peasants and emancipate their slaves.

Bolívar's fifteen-year revolutionary career began with his participation in an abortive insurrection in Caracas in 1810, stimulated by the Napoleonic conquest of Spain. There followed a period of repeated setbacks and exiles in various Caribbean islands—including liberated Haiti. Victories began to come when Bolívar organized the interior of Venezuela and forged an alliance with the *llaneros*, the wild herders of the Venezuelan grasslands. He liberated neighboring Colombia first, then swung back to free Venezuela in 1821. Ecuador came next, and the three territories were thereupon united in the short-lived Republic of Gran Colombia.

Thereafter, Simón Bolívar presided over the freeing of Bolivia and Peru. But here the way had already been paved by the liberator of the south—San Martín.

José de San Martín (1778–1850) was a career military officer from Argentina, and a much quieter, more self-effacing man than the mercurial Bolívar. A tall, dark man, courteous and simple in his habits, he was a rigorous disciplinarian who cared for the welfare of his troops. He was also a skilled organizer and a general with a rare gift for grand strategy. He clearly ranks with Bolívar as one of the two great leaders of the Latin American revolutions.

Argentina had been in turmoil for years over the same sort of antimercantilist, free-trade issue that had agitated the North American colonies. Napoleon's invasion of Spain led leading citizens of Buenos Aires to declare their independence of the French emperor's puppet ruler in Madrid in 1810.

San Martín took service under the new regime and soon set to work on his grand strategy. The center of Spanish power in South America was in Peru, and San Martín proposed to attack that power base by a great flanking movement across the Andes and north through Chile. Practically single-handed, he organized a military expedition, led his Army of the Andes over the towering mountain barrier, and crushed the Spanish troops in Chile with a series of striking victories in 1817 and 1818. Thereafter he moved with greater caution north to Peru, maneuvered his way into Lima, and then sought an alliance with Bolívar for a final blow at the Spanish military in Peru.

A famous "meeting of the liberators" in Ecuador in 1822, however, revealed personal and political differences between the two men that were too great to bridge. San Martín therefore graciously stood aside, and it was Bolívar's troops who dealt Spanish arms in the Americas a final resounding defeat in the Battle of Ayacucho—Latin America's Yorktown—high in the Andes in 1824.

The independence of Brazil came much more quietly in 1822. The liberation of this largest of Latin American colonies occurred several years after the Portuguese royal family fled to Rio to escape Napoleon. During this period Brazil had gained valued rights, including the right whose denial by the Crown had exercised so many of the colonies—free trade. When an 1820 revolution in Lisbon threatened to countermand these new privileges, events were set in motion that brought full independence to Brazil with a minimum of violence. Alone among the new Latin American nations, Brazil was a constitutional monarchy—under the crown prince of the Portuguese ruling house—rather than a republic.

Paraguay and Uruguay, located between Brazil and Argentina, attained their freedom in a tangle of politics between their powerful neighbors. By 1824 all the Latin American states but a few small colonies around the Caribbean had won their independence. A saga of colonial revolt that began a half century before, in 1776, was ended.

The Reign of the Caudillos

The Latin American revolutions had been more protracted and much more costly in lives and property than the revolt of the thirteen colonies. It had been much closer to a social revolution, pitting *criollos* against peninsulars, and sometimes Indians and *mestizos* against the European power structure as a whole. But the result was no more a social transformation south of the Rio Grande than north of it.

Royal authority had been replaced by republican constitutions in most places, peninsular officials by a *criollo* ruling class, and mercantilistic regulation by free trade. But the basic economic and social structure of the region remained largely as it had been before, as we will see presently.

There were some political changes, however—not all of them for the best. There were, in the first place, a number of other wars and revolutions in the decades following the Wars of Independence. Some of these later conflicts led to major transfers of territory from one new state to another. Other clashes led to the fragmentation of some of the newly independent nations. Still others created a chronic political instability within the new countries.

Major Latin American wars of the nineteenth century included the lopsided struggle between the United States and Mexico (1846–1848), which cost Mexico 40 percent of her territory. Another such conflict was the Paraguayan War (1864–1870), in which Argentina, Brazil, and Uruguay ravaged Paraguay in a struggle that cost 300,000 lives. The War of the Pacific (1879–1883), finally, saw Chile emerge as a major power in Latin America by winning a nitrate-rich

Latin America, 1828
After the Wars
for Independence

MEXICO

REPUBLIC OF HAITI

UNITED PROVINCES
OF
CENTRAL AMERICA

PANAMA

Caracas

VENEZUELA

GREAT COLOMBIA

GUIANAS

Bogotá

Quito

Amazon R.

ECUADOR

EMPIRE OF BRAZIL

Lima

PERU

BOLIVIA

PARAGUAY

Rio de
Janeiro

CHILE

Santiago

URUGUAY

Buenos Aires

ARGENTINE
CONFEDERATION

0   1000   2000
Miles

northern region also claimed by Argentina and Bolivia.

Among the most important fragmentations of new nations was that of the United Provinces of Central America, which split into half a dozen Central American countries. Bolívar's Gran Colombia was divided into Venezuela, Colombia, and Ecuador. Uruguay also managed to make good its secession from southern Brazil.

Revolutions were common within the new nations of Latin America. Regionalism, which led to the Civil War in the United States, was equally prevalent in the new states to the south. There also, the hinterlands tended to resist the encroaching power of the industrializing cities. Such circumstances led to frequent civil wars and changes of government by force.

Central to this chronic political instability and endemic military conflict was a political phenomenon common almost everywhere in Latin America—the rise of *caudillismo*, the reign of the *caudillo*.

All these new countries had emerged from the Wars of Independence with constitutions, political parties, and civil liberties—at least on paper. In fact, however, political power usually devolved upon local strong men called *caudillos*. These backcountry mil-

itary chiefs seem frequently to have embodied traditional sources of authority in the countryside: they owned large estates, concluded marriage alliances, performed and received favors. But they also reflected the breakdown of central authority and the burgeoning power of the gun, which were among the by-products of the revolutions. *Caudillos* were above all commanders of military force and beneficiaries of the popular respect for courage and strength that was bred into these descendants of the conquistadores.

Most of the *caudillos* were thus local warlords who championed the autonomy of the regions against the centralizing efforts of the new national capitals. Sometimes, however, a *caudillo* would seize national power, bringing the violence and crudity of the backwoods to the center of national life. Examples included the dictatorship of Bolívar's lieutenant José Páez (1830–1848) in Venezuela after the liberator's death; the brutal regime of Manuel de Rosas (1829–1832) and his equally ruthless and Machiavellian wife, Dona Encarnación, in Argentina; and the inept rule of General Santa Anna in Mexico (1834–1855).

As military dictators, *caudillos* were frequently brutal; as country people, many of them were unlearned, even—in the eyes of more polished Latin Americans—barbarous. Secret police, organized mob violence, land confiscations, and executions were notorious adjuncts of many of these dictatorships. On the other hand, *caudillos* were sometimes quite popular with the poor. They shared the values and prejudices of peons and gauchos, and they saw to it that at least some of their patronage filtered down to the village level.

By the end of the century, however, *caudillo* rule was giving way to a new bourgeois class of progress-minded centralizers. These were the architects of the substantial economic advances of the end of the century, to which we now turn.

Haciendas and Dependency

Nineteenth-century Latin American economic history is normally divided around 1880. During the half century between independence in the 1820s and the 1870s, the typical Latin American country remained a hacienda economy of separate regions and *caudillo* politics. From the 1880s on, exports and foreign dependency increased, and with these economic changes the authority of central governments and port cities.

Through most of the century, then, the central Latin American economic institution remained the hacienda, the huge plantation or ranch operated by a *criollo* landowner with Indian, *mestizo*, or black labor. Slavery was abolished earlier in South than in

North America—as early as the 1810s and 1820s in Argentina, Mexico, and Central America. Throughout Latin America, however, Indian and *mestizo* workers remained peons, landless laborers bound by unending debt to their masters. The Wars of Independence brought little change to the life of the European-descended hacienda aristocracy, or to that of the laborers on West Indian sugar plantations, Argentine ranches and wheat fields, and Bolivian mines.

From the 1880s through the early decades of the twentieth century, however, foreign exports increased phenomenally. These exports were largely agricultural products and minerals: sugar, bananas, coffee, wheat, meat, and wool, as well as silver, copper, lead, and tin, all boomed as export products. Swelling profits from the sale of commodities like these stimulated great increases in foreign investment in Latin America and in Latin American imports of foreign manufactured goods. Argentina, Uruguay, and other progressive countries also used some of their earnings from exports for railways, roads, schools, and other reforms. Commodity exports looked to some like the road to progress for Latin America.

Actually, as recent scholarship has stressed, increases in exports also increased the dependency of Latin American countries on more developed nations—Britain especially in the nineteenth century, the United States in the twentieth. The nations of the south borrowed their capital and bought their manufactured goods overseas, while their own industrial production scarcely developed. The end of the century saw boom times for the merchants of port cities and for the landed producers of export products, but the average Latin American worker earned little more in 1900 than in 1800.

In politics too, it sometimes seemed as if the more things changed, the more they stayed the same. Regionalism declined, thanks to the new transportation and communications nets and to the increasing power of large cities. The local power of the *caudillo* thus diminished, and with the loss of his regional base the chances of his seizing national power also declined.

Yet military rule, political violence, and corruption remained almost as common after 1880 as before. The rough-and-ready *caudillo* was replaced by a spit-and-polish professional military officer—but the latter still felt an obligation to intervene in politics. The goals of the new juntas—Order and Progress—might have a more disinterested ring than the blatant self-aggrandizement of the *caudillo*, but civil government and civil liberties still failed to develop. Corruption at the lower levels of government, finally, remained as common in South as in North America in the later 1800s.

A Civilization Is Judged by Its Women

The social life of Latin American cities continued to be that of provincial Europeans, even after modern buildings and electric trolley lines made their appearance. For most of the century, *criollos* simply replaced peninsular Spanish or Portuguese aristocrats in the baroque palaces or churches around the plazas. Polished merchants or professional people or crude *caudillos* and their hangers-on were now the governors, judges, officials, and presidents. And Paris or London fashions, European plays only a year or two out of date still dominated the social and cultural life of urban elites.

The life of the backcountry hacienda went on as it always had. There was a big house with its self-sufficient workshops and stores, barns and corrals; villages of peons on poorer land up the hillside; and the endless acres of cropland or pasturage that belonged to the patrón, the patriarchal owner of the estate. The landed families all knew and married each other, in the way of country families everywhere. The villages had their own social integrity, based on shared labor and communal decision making. And there was frequently a personal bond between peon and patrón that transcended the peasant's eternal debt at the hacienda store—a relationship not rare in backcountry areas around the preindustrial world.

The condition of women in Latin America, finally, in some ways worsened in the century after independence. But there were the beginnings of more promising trends as well.

Colonial European standards continued to be urged on Latin American women in the nineteenth century. Religious piety, sexual chastity and fidelity, and will-less dependence on fathers or husbands were enjoined upon them from childhood. Domestic duties filled most of their adult lives, and laws passed by liberal bourgeois regimes sometimes actually increased the husband's power over his wife and her property.

In the later nineteenth century, however, some women escaped the seclusion of the household for work in the larger world. Admittedly, the work often turned out to be brutal sweatshop labor in the new factories of the Industrial Revolution. Few though these were, they were often glad to have women, who would work more cheaply.

A more promising direction was the increase in education for girls in some countries. In relatively progressive nations such as Mexico and Argentina, women began to find work as schoolteachers themselves.

There was even a nascent feminist movement in

Latin America in the last decades of the century. Women schoolteachers took the lead in organizing feminist societies and editing women's journals. Feminists worked diligently for the social and intellectual advancement of women, and tried to defend their sisters from economic exploitation.

One of the most famous Latin American writers—and a leading proponent of education for women—the Argentine Domingo Sarmiento, declared that "the level of civilization of a people can be judged by the social position of its women."[3] By that standard, Latin America was no more civilized than the rest of the world in the nineteenth century. But there were harbingers, at least, of things to come.

PROVINCIAL CULTURE

The Provinces of the Western World

The transformation of the Americas from colonies to countries was slower and more difficult in the cultural realm than in any other area of national development.

An armed revolt and paper constitution could bring political independence. Economic dependency on Europe might drag on, but at least the makers of economic policy now included Americans as well as their European trading partners. Enthusiasm for Old World ways and fashions might continue, but distinctively American social types, Yankee and *criollo*, began to take shape under the influence of New World conditions.

A distinctive American high culture, however, was very slow to develop. Both in the colonial era and during the first century of independence, the art, literature, and intellectual currents of the New World exhibited a character that may best be defined as provincial. American culture, North and South, was like that of a distant province of a more sophisticated metropolitan center. Europe was still the cultural heartland of the Western world; the Americas, culturally speaking, were its provinces.

The provincial nature of American culture during this transitional period came out in several ways. In part, the former colonies remained cultural colonies simply because much of their high culture was clearly derived from the artistic, literary, and intellectual life of Europe. Thus the Americas felt the impact of the eighteenth-century Enlightenment in late-colonial times and nineteenth-century European romanticism

[3]Benjamin Keen and Mark Wasserman, *A Short History of Latin America* (Dallas: Houghton Mifflin, 1980), p. 241.

in the early-national period, though the forms of both were modified to suit the New World cultural milieu.

American culture was also provincial in its lack of sophistication, and in an occasional air of backwoods crudity that was sometimes quite calculated but nonetheless reflected American realities. This seems to have been particularly true of North America, where a rich vein of "frontier culture" runs from Ben Franklin's *Almanac* and fur cap to Mark Twain's Mississippi days and Jack London's Yukon.

There is, finally, a provincialism that consists simply in a vigorously artistic anatomizing of what constituted the rather far-off and exotic provinces of the Western world. In seeking to understand themselves, Americans—perhaps South Americans especially—revealed a distant backwoods world to Europeans.

This world of Indians and gauchos, rain forests and pampas, mining camps and great rivers, was far stranger than any province of the old country, no matter how colorful and old-fashioned. New World intellectual concerns, with *caudillismo* or the "barbarism" of their own life, with transcendentalism or the abolition of slavery, were even more exotic. The books that brought this world and these concerns to vivid life were provincial simply in that their subject matter was the provinces of the considerably expanded Western world of the nineteenth century.

Let us look first at the provincial culture of the United States in the colonial era and the nineteenth century, and then at the cultural life of Latin America over the same period.

Song of Myself

The continuing cultural development between 1600 and 1900 of the new United States and the British colonies from which they were born was a striking combination of European influences and American originality. The influences, not surprisingly, were strongest during the colonial centuries; the originality emerged more strongly during the middle and later decades of the nineteenth century.

The most powerful cultural influence on the British colonies in the seventeenth century was the Calvinist Protestantism that had brought most of the New England settlers there in the first place. Puritan religiosity infused the simple white boxes and pointed steeples of New England churches, the passion of Cotton Mather's sermons, the lyrical intensity of Anne Bradstreet's poetry. This puritanical religious dimension might be partially transmuted into taut Yankee business sense in the next century—as it was among Puritans, Huguenots, and Dutch burghers in Europe. But moralism and religiosity remained important tonal elements in American culture in later centuries.

The most important eighteenth-century European influence all over the North American colonies was the Enlightenment. Benjamin Franklin was not the only colonist to embrace the new interest in science. The political ideas of the Enlightenment found an interested audience among the increasingly disgruntled colonists. John Locke's belief in natural rights and government based on a social contract, Montesquieu's theory of checks and balances in government, and other political beliefs of Europe's Age of Reason influenced the thinking of Franklin, Thomas Jefferson, the Adamses, and other architects of the new American nation.

Europe's Age of Revolutions in the first half of the nineteenth century was an age of fermenting ideas in the new United States. Abolitionism, the crusade against liquor, rights for women, the Mormons and other new sects, utopian socialism imported directly from Europe—all made converts in the U.S. These American social movements had a heavier religious and moralistic tone than the liberalism, nationalism, and socialism of the Old World. But these American ideological gropings also stirred passions and provided background at least for more radical enthusiasms to come.

The later nineteenth century, furthermore, saw more and more individuals and schools of thought whose work was unique, whose concerns were distinctly those of the far fringes of the Europeanized world. The two most strikingly American schools of thought were transcendentalism and pragmatism. Both originated in the intellectual center of the young United States, New England. But they illustrated two strikingly dissimilar aspects of the American mind.

Ralph Waldo Emerson, essayist, poet, and eager proponent of transcendentalism, urged confidence in our own instincts, an inner understanding that transcended reason, authority, even observation. William James, the philosopher who championed pragmatism the most ardently, declared that truth was really a matter of the *usefulness* of an idea, of its "cash value" to us. Emerson's view reflected the spiritual dimension of American thought, which went back to the Puritans, whereas James expressed the practical, this-worldly aspect of the American experience, with its emphasis on getting the job done.

Much of the cultural contribution of the young United States, however, was the work not of schools of thought such as transcendentalism or pragmatism, but of one-of-a-kind individuals.

There is much of the European romantic in the American poet and short-story writer Edgar Allan Poe and in the fiction writers Nathaniel Hawthorne and Herman Melville. Other aspects of their work, however, have few parallels in the Old World. In his obsession with death and beauty Poe exceeded most European romantics who held similar predilections. Hawthorne's flair for allegory and immersion in the New England past, Melville's combination of seafaring and symbolism have no obvious sources in Europe. "The Raven," *The Scarlet Letter*, and *Moby Dick* are all uniquely individual productions.

In the decades after the Civil War, novelist Henry James—William's brother—probed a uniquely American experience in novels such as *The Portrait of a Lady* and *The Ambassadors:* the rediscovery of Europe by Americans, who pitted their strength and provincial innocence against the Old World's sophistication and deeper knowledge of life. Mark Twain, meanwhile, went the other way, exploring the depths of the provinces in the small towns of the American South and West, and produced the novel Ernest Hemingway would call the best ever written by an American: *Huckleberry Finn*.

Among later nineteenth-century American poets, Emily Dickinson stands out in one way, Walt Whitman in another. Dickinson, living a reclusive life in a small New England town, never seeing either Europe or the Far West, came closer than anyone else of her time to capturing glints of the infinite in a few brief, crystalline lines. Walt Whitman, frequently hailed as America's greatest poet, celebrated the democratic heart of the nation and with equal fervor sang his "Song of Myself" in the lush, earthy, exultant lines of his *Leaves of Grass*.

Any attempt to characterize American thought and literature before 1900 would surely include moralism, from the Puritans to Hawthorne; humor, from Ben Franklin to Mark Twain; and interest in the special North American experience, from the rather unconvincing Indians of Longfellow's *Hiawatha* and Cooper's *Last of the Mohicans* to realist William Dean Howells's chronicle of a nineteenth-century robber baron, *The Rise of Silas Lapham*. But perhaps the outstanding feature of the culture of the new country was an almost exaggerated individualism, a democratic passion for common things that could find greatness in a runaway slave, a whaling ship, or a slant of light in a New England afternoon.

Gauchos and Indians

The culture of Latin America was also a self-consciously provincial one in these colonial and early-national periods.

The intellectual life of the Spanish and Portuguese colonies was in some ways more religious than that of the English-speaking colonies to the north. But it was a Counter-Reformation Catholic faith rather than a Protestant one, Jesuits its most ardent spokesmen instead of Puritan preachers. The hundreds of churches scattered over the southern continent were not simple New England boxes, but elaborately ornamental baroque cathedrals thick with marble and statuary, color and gilding and rich decoration. The greatest Latin American poet of the seventeenth century was a nun, Juana de La Cruz—who, like her Puritan counterpart Anne Bradstreet, was known as the Tenth Muse.

The Inquisition, busy in the New World as in the Old, seriously inhibited the spread of the Enlightenment in Latin America. The enlightened despotism of the Spanish Bourbons, however, did lead to an upsurge in scientific studies, particularly in Mexico. Mexico's famous School of Mines taught much more than that—geography and geology, astronomy, mathematics, and other sciences. Jesuits even labored to reconcile the rationalism and empiricism of Descartes, Bacon, and Newton with Catholic theology. On the historical side, an interest in the Indian past developed very early: missionary fathers and Indian informants were collaborating on chronicles of the Aztecs and Incas as early as the sixteenth century.

The nineteenth century saw a continuing approximation of the cultural history of the Old World unfolding in the new Spanish- and Portuguese-speaking nations. The romantic movement in particular stirred a parallel upheaval across the Atlantic. But Latin American romanticism had especially strong liberal-nationalist overtones. It also exhibited a powerful concern with such strictly Latin American matters as their conquistador and Indian past and the gauchos and *caudillos* of their own century. Mexico and the ABC countries of South America—Argentina, Brazil, and Chile—produced especially powerful literary and historical cultures in the 1800s.

Condemnation of their own Spanish ancestors was common among the Latin American writers and thinkers of the nineteenth century. The Chilean author Francisco Bilbao, writing under the influence of French liberal and socialist ideas, depicted the conquistadores as feudal Catholic holdovers from the Middle Ages. He saw these founding fathers as the source of the slavery, ignorance, and economic backwardness he detested in his own time.

The Indian past was also condemned as barbarous by some, particularly in Argentina. Others, however, especially in Brazil and Mexico, glorified the ancient Indian cultures, seeing them as their true American heritage. Thus in *Prophecy of Cuauhtémoc*, a poem of powerful romantic imagery, the Mexican Ignacio Rodriguez Galván summoned up the ghost of a martyred Aztec king to lead Mexico to new greatness.

Concerned more directly with present problems was the poetry and fiction of young liberal romantic writers who had been swept up in the opposition to the postindependence *caudillo* dictatorships. Esteban Echeverría, the moving spirit behind Argentine romanticism, was also a liberal and a utopian socialist who was driven into exile by the Rosas regime. Echeverría's grim little masterpiece, *The Slaughterhouse*, a realistic yet symbolically intended account of the torment and death of a young man of character and culture in a slaughterhouse reeking of carcasses, guts, and blood, characterized the Buenos Aires dictatorship.

Attitudes toward the lawless gaucho, *vaquero*, or *llanero* horsemen of the plains and the backcountry were more varied. Some, like the Argentine romantic leader Domingo Sarmiento, saw the gaucho as the base of *caudillo* power and a symbol of the nation's barbaric past. Others praised the gaucho as the symbol of a wild, free life that was being steadily undermined by the spread of bourgeois urban culture. José Hernandez's epic poem *The Gaucho Martin Fierro*, written in the racy language of the Argentine pampas and strongly influenced by gaucho folk songs, condemned officialdom, the military, and civilization generally and glorified the outlaw life of the vanishing gaucho breed.

Groping for a sense of national identity once national independence had been achieved, Latin American writers and thinkers, like their North American counterparts, turned defiantly to the exploration of their own frontier world. They approved of some aspects of what they saw—their Indian past, and frequently the fading gaucho present—and disapproved of others, such as the brutal *caudillo* dictatorships. Whatever their attitude, the result was a vivid depiction of these westernmost provinces of the Western world.

SUMMARY

During their first century of political independence, the new nations of the Western Hemisphere remained in many ways provinces of the Western world. Both North and South America moved toward a broader future. But both were still rooted in their colonial pasts during the nineteenth century.

The English colonists of eastern North America were

numerous, socially mobile, and accustomed to self-government. Attempts to tighten the mercantilistic ties that bound the colonies to the mother country led the generation of Washington, Jefferson, and the Adamses to break those ties entirely in the Revolutionary War (1776–1781). The new nation had its troubles, but strong early leadership and a flexible constitution, combined with the immense resources of the continent, led to a prosperous, increasingly democratic and territorially expansive first half century.

The Civil War (1860–1865) nearly tore the nation in half, but determined leadership by Lincoln and superior Northern firepower both saved the Union and freed the slaves. The last four decades of the century, however, were a gilded age of political corruption and disregard for the interests of farmers, blue-collar laborers, blacks, Indians, and immigrants. The latter half of the century nevertheless saw substantial additions to the nation's wealth and territory.

By contrast, the Latin American colonies of Spain and Portugal had a much larger admixture of Amerindians and a less rigidly segregated black African component. Colonial rule in Middle and South America permitted much less self-government; but during the later eighteenth century, Enlightenment reform brought many improvements and a surge of prosperity. The Wars of Independence began with ill-fated revolts by the most oppressed: blacks and Indians. Between 1810 and 1824, however, Bolívar in Venezuela, San Martín in Argentina, and the rebellion instigated by Father Hidalgo in Mexico liberated most of Latin America, and Brazil achieved its independence from Portugal.

The governments of the new Latin American republics, however, remained autocratic, though the new leaders were gun-toting local caudillos rather than appointed European administrators, and revolutions were far more common. Economically, the new countries were nearly as dependent on European capital, manufactured goods, and markets for their commodities as they had been as colonies. Prosperity and progressive reforms were found only in a few nations, such as Argentina and Uruguay.

Culturally, North and South America remained provincial in their involvement with European intellectual movements and in their concern with their own exotic provincial worlds of Amerindians and gauchos. North America did produce two original schools—transcendentalism and pragmatism—and a number of rugged individualists in literature. Latin American writers explored their colonial and precolonial past and their often rough frontier present, seeking a sense of national identity that would not emerge until the next century.

SUGGESTED READING

BREEN, T. H.   *Puritans and Adventurers: Change and Persistence in Early America*. New York: Oxford University Press, 1980. Society and settlement in colonial North America, especially Massachusetts and Virginia.

BROWNLEE, W. E.   *Dynamics of Ascent: A History of the American Economy*, 2nd ed. New York: Knopf, 1979. A good summary of recent views on the causes and course of American development. On industrial development in particular, see T. C. Cochran, *Frontiers of Change: Early Industrialism in America* (New York: Oxford University Press, 1981).

BURNS, E. B.   *The Poverty of Progress: Latin America in the Nineteenth Century*. Berkeley: University of California Press, 1980. Stimulating essay on the theme that economic advance was limited to Latin American elites, seldom trickling down to the masses.

FLEXNER, J. T.   *George Washington* (3 vols.). Boston: Little, Brown, 1968–1972. Standard account of the revolutionary commander and first president of the United States; makes him more interesting than most of the clichés about the father of his country.

FREYRE, G.   *The Mansions and the Shanties: The Making of Modern Brazil*, trans. H. de Onis. New York: Knopf, 1963. A classic study of Brazilian social and racial relations.

GENOVESE, E.   *Roll, Jordan, Roll: The World the Slaves Made*. New York: Random House, 1976. Perhaps the best of a number of important books debating the nature and consequences of black slavery in the United States. On the abolitionist movement, a good recent survey is J. B. Stewart, *Holy Warriors: The Abolitionists and American Slavery* (New York: Hill and Wang, 1976).

GERBI, A.   *The Dispute of the New World: The History of a Polemic, 1750–1900*, trans. J. Moyle. Pittsburgh: University of Pittsburgh Press, 1973. The Latin American defense against assertions that theirs was "merely" a provincial culture. For a suggestive comment on Latin America's search for identity, see E. B. Burns, "Themes for a World History: Latin America as a Source," *World History Bulletin*, 2, no. 2 (1984), 1–5.

HALPERIN-DONGHI, T.   *The Aftermath of Revolution in Latin America*. New York: Harper & Row, Pub., 1973. Newer views of Latin American history—particularly social and cultural—after the heroic days of the revolutions.

HARTZ, L. *The Founding of New Society: Studies in the History of the United States, Latin America, South Africa, Canada, and Australia.* New York: Harcourt, Brace, and World, 1964. Comparative evolution of new societies in the European intercontinental empires.

LANG, J. *Conquest and Commerce: Spain and England in the Americas.* New York: Academic Press, 1975. A comparative study of the empires of the two biggest winners in the New World.

LAVRIN, A., ed. *Latin American Women: Historical Perspectives.* Westport, Conn.: Greenwood Press, 1978. Includes accounts of women in the colonial period. See also C. R. Boxer, *Women in Iberian Expansion Overseas, 1415–1815* (New York: Oxford University Press, 1975).

LYNCH, J. *The Spanish-American Revolutions, 1808–1826.* New York: Norton, 1973. A thoroughly scholarly survey. On causal factors, see R. A. Humphreys and J. Lynch, eds., *The Origins of the Latin American Revolutions, 1808–1826* (New York: Knopf, 1965).

MASUR, G. *Simón Bolívar,* 2nd ed. Albuquerque: University of New Mexico Press, 1969. The best biography. On San Martín, see J. C. J. Metford's brief but still useful *San Martín the Liberator* (London: Longmans, Green, 1950).

MERK, F. *Manifest Destiny and Mission in American History.* New York: Knopf, 1963. The United States version of the Western world's imperialistic conviction of its right to rule and its global civilizing mission. See R. A. Billington, *Westward Expansion* (New York: Macmillan, 1974) and Merk's *History of the Westward Movement* (New York: Knopf, 1978) on the transcontinental conquest.

MIDDLEKAUFF, R. *The Glorious Cause: The American Revolution, 1763–1789.* New York: Oxford University Press, 1982. A good overview of the big picture. D. Higgenbotham, *The War of American Independence* (New York: Macmillan, 1971) focuses on military affairs. On the causes and significance of the revolution, see J. P. Greene, ed., *The Reinterpretation of the American Revolution* (New York: Harper & Row, Pub., 1968).

MILLER, P. *The New England Mind* (2 vols.). Cambridge, Mass.: Harvard University Press, 1983. A classic on the Puritan mentality. See also his *The Life of the Mind in America from the Revolution to the Civil War* (New York: Harcourt Brace Jovanovich, 1970) and, on antebellum American literature, F. O. Matthiessen's *American Renaissance* (New York: Oxford University Press, 1968). On post-Civil War cultural trends, including pragmatism, see B. Kuklick, *The Rise of American Philosophy* (New Haven: Yale University Press, 1977) and J. Martin, *Harvests of Change: American Literature, 1865–1914* (Englewood Cliffs, N.J.: Prentice-Hall, 1967).

NORTON, M. B. *Liberty's Daughters.* Boston: Little, Brown, 1980. Women's role in the American Revolution. For women's emancipation in the later nineteenth century, consult E. C. Dubois, *Feminism and Suffrage: The Emergence of an Independent Movement in America* (Ithaca: Cornell University Press, 1978).

OATES, S. B. *With Malice Toward None.* New York: Harper & Row, Pub., 1978. Recent life of Lincoln, the most enigmatic and internationally admired of American presidents.

PORTER, G. *The Rise of Big Business, 1860–1910.* Arlington Heights, Ill.: Harlan Davidson, 1973. Survey of the dynamic economic expansion of the Gilded Age. On business management in the age of entrepreneurship, see A. D. Chandler, *The Visible Hand: The Managerial Revolution in American Business* (Cambridge, Mass.: Harvard University Press, 1977). On the labor movement in the United States seen in the broadest context, see H. G. Gutman, *Work, Culture, and Society in Industrializing America* (New York: Random House, 1977).

RANDALL, J. G., and D. DONALD. *Civil War and Reconstruction,* 2nd ed. Boston: Little, Brown, 1973. Older, but perhaps still the best one-volume account. For a recent survey, see J. M. McPherson, *Ordeal by Fire* (New York: Knopf, 1982).

ROUT, L. B., JR. *The African Experience in Spanish America, 1502 to the Present Day.* Cambridge: Cambridge University Press, 1971. Has useful chapters on both the colonial and nineteenth-century periods. See also R. Mellafe, *Negro Slavery in Latin America* (Berkeley: University of California Press, 1975) for a survey of this phase of the black experience in Latin America.

STEIN, S. J., and B. H. STEIN. *The Colonial Heritage of Latin America.* London: Oxford University Press, 1970. Interpretive examination of colonial influences on later Latin American republics.

VAN DEUSEN, G. G. *The Jacksonian Era, 1828–1848.* New York: Harper & Row, Pub., 1959. An older but good summary. On Jackson, see R. V. Remini, *Andrew Jackson and the Course of American Empire* (New York: Harper & Row, Pub., 1977), *Andrew Jackson and the Course of American Freedom* (New York: Harper & Row, Pub., 1981), and *Andrew Jackson and the Course of American Democracy* (New York: Harper & Row, Pub., 1984).

WHITAKER, A. P., ed. *Latin America and the Enlightenment.* Ithaca, N.Y.: Cornell University Press, 1961. Cultural influences during colonial times. See also M. Picón-Salas, *A Cultural History of Spanish America from Conquest to Independence,* trans. I. Leonard (Berkeley: University of California Press, 1962), an eminently readable survey.

WOOD, G. S. *The Creation of the American Republic, 1776–1787.* New York: Norton, 1972. Frequently cited overview of the transformation of thirteen colonies into one nation.

Chapter · 12

THE CLIMAX OF THE GREAT CONQUEST

THE NATURE
OF THE NEW IMPERIALISM

Into the Heart of Darkness

The English poet Rudyard Kipling called it "the white man's burden." The Russian revolutionary socialist V. I. Lenin defined it as "the highest stage of capitalism." The distinguished Indian historian Kavalam Madhava Panikkar explained it as "the dominance of maritime power over the land masses." But Joseph Conrad, sea captain turned novelist, experienced it viscerally while nursing a rusty river steamer up the Congo into what he called the *Heart of Darkness:*

> Going up that river was like travelling back to the earliest beginnings of the world, when vegetation rioted on the earth and the big trees were kings. An empty stream, a great silence, an impenetrable forest. The air was warm, thick, heavy, sluggish . . . On silvery sand-banks hippos and alligators sunned themselves side by side.

And then:

> . . . houses on a hill, others with iron roofs, . . . A jetty projected into the river. . . .
> . . . A heavy and dull detonation shook the ground, a puff of smoke came out of the cliff. . . . They were building a railway.

Finally, halfway up the hill toward the company station:

> A slight clinking . . . made me turn my head. Six black men advanced in a file, toiling up the path. They walked erect and slow, balancing small baskets full of earth on their heads, and the clink kept time with their footsteps. . . . I could see every rib, the joints of their limbs were like knots in a rope; each had an iron collar on his neck, and all were connected together with a chain whose bights swung between them, rhythmically clinking.[1]

Sometimes it takes a novelist to capture the reality of things.

The great revival of Western expansion we call the New Imperialism, running from around 1870 to perhaps 1914, was one of the most astonishing aspects of nineteenth-century world history. The New Imperialism was particularly surprising because during most of the preceding hundred years, imperial expansion had been widely seen as a losing proposition by European statesmen. This feeling was generated by the loss of Europe's most highly developed colonies in the New World between the 1770s and the 1820s, when revolutions cost Britain, Spain, and Portugal their American colonies and France was prevailed upon to sell her substantial sweep of middle North America to the new United States. "Colonies," the philosophe and statesman Turgot declared in a famous aphorism, "are like fruits which cling to the tree only until they ripen."[2]

Still, large parts of the world either remained in European hands or were strongly influenced by European traders, missionaries, and others. For exam-

[1]Joseph Conrad, *Heart of Darkness* and *The Secret Sharer* (New York: New American Library, n.d.), pp. 102–3, 79, 80.

[2]F. Lee Benns, *European History Since 1870* (New York: Appleton-Century-Crofts, 1950), p. 13.

ple, there were British holdings in India and Canada and Britain's claims to Australia; the French West Indies and France's conquest of Algeria in 1830; and the Dutch settlements in South Africa and continuing Dutch preeminence in island Southeast Asia. For that matter, the former colonies in the Americas continued to be ruled by people of European descent and culture and remained closely bound commercially, socially, and intellectually to the Old World.

Then, around 1870, the Western peoples launched a startling new wave of imperial aggression against the rest of the world, an explosion of Western conquest that would dwarf the achievements of preceding centuries.

A Question of Motive

The causes of the New Imperialism have frequently been presented in the most simplistic and unconvincing way. The imperialists themselves claimed that Western colonialism was, in Kipling's phrase, "the white man's burden"—a moral obligation to spread the benefits of a "higher" Western civilization to a backward world. Particularly since the collapse of the European overseas empires after World War II, on the other hand, enemies of imperialism have depicted it as exploitation pure and simple, a cloak for Western capitalist looting of a helpless world. As with most major historical events, though, the New Imperialism seems to have been the product of a considerable variety of factors—economic, political, humanitarian, and even psychological.

As the exploitation theorists emphasize, economic causes played a large part in the new wave of overseas expansion. The Industrial Revolution created new and complex economic and technological demands that in many cases could best be met by the extension of European power into distant parts of the world. One of the most obvious of these needs was the demand for natural resources—many of them exotic commodities such as rubber, manganese, and oil—to feed into the vast hopper of the new industrial machine. There was also a demand for cheap labor, especially as European wages went up in the later nineteenth century. "Coolie labor" would work much more cheaply than unionized Western workers and was therefore hired in large quantities to extract, process, and ship the resources of far-off lands back to Europe.

Another economic motive for expansion was the need for colonial markets for the fantastic production of the newly industrializing West. The immense profits piling up in Europe, finally, sought new investment areas and often found them in the underdeveloped world. Building a trunk railway line across

Asia or Africa could bring in 30 percent interest on an investment, whereas a modest spur line in Europe returned less than five percent.

Political and military motives also played a part in empire building. The need for naval bases or coaling stations for the new steam navies and merchant marines could lead Western powers to seize key harbors or islands. Many strategic straits and strips of land with geopolitical value were targets for annexation. Political determination to outmaneuver a European rival could impel Western governments to acquire large territories having no detectable economic value at all.

Besides economic and political causes, humanitarian impulses—however wrongheaded some of them may look now—did in fact play a significant part in the New Imperialism. Protestant and Catholic missionaries thronged to the "mission fields" in Africa and Asia in unparalleled numbers. The flag often followed them, for governments were compelled by pious public opinion to support the spreaders of the Gospel in their good work.

Antislavery societies—formed after the Europeans themselves had given up slavery—urged Western governments to do whatever was necessary to suppress Arab slavers in the nineteenth century. And tidy-minded proconsuls of empire really did go out into what was for them the Heart of Darkness to spread European law, education, and medicine—as well as taxes and compulsory labor—south of the Sahara and east of Suez.

Finally, totally irrational psychological drives may have been at work beneath all of these expressed motives for imperial expansion. A simple but powerful sense of Western superiority, rooted in nineteenth-century progress, prosperity, and racist theories of the biological superiority of caucasoid humanity, was clearly part of the psychological equipment of most imperialists, for instance.

It has also been suggested that instinctive aggressiveness, revealed at home in a range of activities from sports to politics and business competition, may have helped cause imperialism. Europeans may have taken up arms against Zulus and Afghans for the pure primordial joy of "smashing 'em good." Even so simple a human psychological impulse as hero worship was perhaps better met by cavalry charges against the Apaches or skirmishes in the Khyber Pass than by portly politicians fighting election campaigns at home.

Political, economic, humanitarian, and psychological, the motives behind the New Imperialism were thus manifold. To all of these it might be well to add a final reminder that imperial conquest of other peoples is, after all, one of the great givens of history. A

Queen Victoria receives representatives of the King of Siam (Thailand). Such ceremonies of submission reached a climax at the Jubilee of 1887, when delegations from colonies and nations around the world paraded through London to honor the Queen on the fiftieth anniversary of her accession to the throne. (The Bettmann Archive, Inc.)

pattern of human behavior that can be traced back to the third millennium before Christ perhaps doesn't require too elaborate a scaffolding of explanation in our own day.

The World down the Barrel of a Maxim Gun

The awesome success of the New Imperialism probably requires more explanation than the motives for its undertaking. And here, at least, there is some agreement among the experts.

The new wave of Western aggression may have succeeded in part because of the powerful *esprit* of Western military forces, a total self-confidence generated by many triumphs and by the arrogant sense of racial superiority mentioned above. Another factor was almost certainly the greatly improved governmental organization and efficiency of post-Enlight-

enment Western administrative machinery. But the major cause of Western supremacy admits of little argument. Once again, the technology of the Industrial Revolution is at the heart of the matter.

Nineteenth-century European empire builders now faced Ashantis and Uzbeks with massed repeating-rifle fire. They confronted the junks and sampans of Eastern potentates with ironclad warships. They reduced the most impregnable strongholds of ancient kingdoms with heavy artillery and explosive shells. For a few brief decades a hundred years ago, the West had a technological advantage over the rest of the world that made her Foreign Legions and her thin red lines, her Marines and gunboats well nigh invincible.

There were many differences among cultures, as even the smuggest Victorian had to allow. But the difference that mattered, as a cynical commentator perceptively suggested, was that Western peoples had Maxim guns and other peoples didn't.

Forms of Control

To most people *empire* means colonies—something like the original thirteen American colonies, perhaps, with royal governors and redcoats. The New Imperialism, however, was a good deal more complicated than that. In fact it took several characteristic forms.

Some of the bastions of Western power overseas were colonies, of course. In a fully developed colony, European administrators set up centralized governmental structures in major cities. They also fanned out through the backcountry, scattering isolated "district officers" among the villages as agents of the new authority. European armies policed the newly acquired region. Marching up and down like Roman legions across Gaul, they often had to carry out several punitive expeditions before the new order was accepted.

A protectorate, by contrast, provided a form of control that was much less than total—and much less expensive. Here the key institution was the European *resident* or *adviser* to the local potentate. The traditional ruler accepted the advice of the European resident on any matter of concern to Europeans—trade, investment, missionary efforts, and the like. Otherwise, he ran his country in his own way. In return, the local sultan or shah or *raja* got financial aid, protection, and perhaps European support in his wars. The European resident was also supported by armed force, of course—commonly a naval squadron, which could patrol a large area and guarantee a number of protectorates.

The sphere of influence, finally, provided a still more diffuse and limited form of European control. The main objective here was almost always economic penetration. Western personnel took over a single institution—say, the customs service—or a limited area, such as a strip of land for a railway or the right to exploit mineral deposits. Spheres of influence commonly developed in regions where European rivals were evenly matched in strength; each would exercise an influence over an agreed-upon portion of the territory in question. The expense to European governments was minimal, the potential for exploitation and development often quite substantial.

There were, of course, many combinations of these three—colony, protectorate, sphere of influence—and bastard versions of each form. The internal imperialism to be discussed in a later section is not a matter of *overseas* empire building at all, but of absorbing neighboring peoples—a form of imperialism as old as civilization.

There are, finally, those who see any economic relationship in which one party gets the better of an-other—that is to say, most economic relationships—as forms of imperialism. This concept of informal imperialism will be discussed under the twentieth-century rubric of *neo-imperialism*—though, again, it is anything but new.

Let us turn now, however, to a chronicle of the final phase of the great conquest—the New Imperialism of the later nineteenth century.

AFRICA DISMEMBERED

First the Treaties, Then the Troops

The partitioning of nine tenths of the world's second largest continent among the colonial powers of Europe during the last quarter of the nineteenth century was a transfer of sovereignty to rank with the Iberian seizure of South and Central America in the sixteenth century or the Mongol conquest of much of Eurasia in the thirteenth. It was initially accomplished with minimal bloodshed, although holding the Africans in line, even for a few decades, sometimes turned out to be a very bloody business indeed.

The "scramble for Africa" by competing European powers was carried out by politicians and diplomats in Europe and by explorers, missionaries, military commanders, economic developers, and others in Africa itself.

Interest in the unknown interior of the "dark continent" was aroused initially by a handful of colorful individuals. Explorers poking about in search of the source of the Nile and other wonders kindled romantic enthusiasm at home. Increasing numbers of missionaries like Dr. Livingston carried Western religion and medicine into Africa and came back urging government intervention against the slavers.

In Europe, crowned heads and prime ministers began to concern themselves with Africa. Speeches were made about spreading the benefits of French civilization, defending Britain's lifeline to India, acquiring a "place in the sun" for Germany. There was public talk of developing the mineral wealth of inner Africa, suppressing the slave trade, expanding European commerce, and other issues. International conferences were held in Belgium (1876) and Berlin (1884) to lay down acceptable ground rules for carving up the continent.

On the African earth itself, it was first the treaties, then the troops. In the 1870s and 1880s, expeditions set out for the interior from the string of European settlements that had been scattered along the coasts since the heyday of the Old Imperialism. These hand-

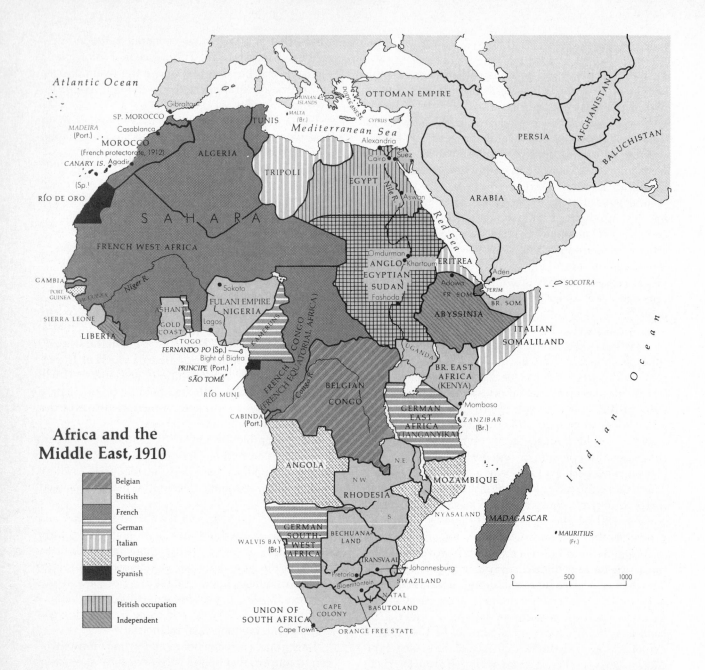

Africa and the Middle East, 1910

Belgian
British
French
German
Italian
Portuguese
Spanish

British occupation
Independent

fuls of government officials or agents for trading companies negotiated treaties with Muslim monarchs and paramount chiefs. In return for gifts, protection, and other benefits, African rulers thus accepted a European overlordship that many of them only partly understood.

The misunderstandings were thrashed out later, during the sometimes savage fighting of the 1890s and the early 1900s. The larger states of inner Africa resisted initial penetration. Other African peoples revolted later against the increasingly heavy hand of Western rule.

Rarely, however, was such resistance successful. The courage of the Africans was great, and their numbers often greater than those of the intruders. But a single Maxim machine gun could make numbers and courage suddenly irrelevant. From Egypt to the Cape, from the tree-studded grasslands of West Africa to the green hills of the East, Western organization, discipline, ruthlessness, and firepower carried the day.

The Indirect Imperialists

Great Britain's holdings in Africa comprised colonies and protectorates north, south, east, and west.

In North Africa, the Conservative prime minister Disraeli and the Liberal Gladstone between them established a British protectorate over Egypt, despite the bitter opposition of the French, who had just completed the Suez Canal on Egyptian territory.

Then trouble arose with a Muslim religious leader called the Mahdi farther up the Nile, and a famous British colonial officer known as "Chinese" Gordon was defeated and killed at Khartoum. British troops responded by pushing up the river, crushing the Mahdi's followers at the Battle of Omdurman, and establishing British authority in what became the Anglo-Egyptian Sudan.

In South Africa, the British faced two tenacious rivals: the Zulus, one of history's great warrior peoples, and the rugged Dutch settlers called Boers. Both were defeated, though at great cost. By 1914 Britain controlled the whole region, rich in gold, diamonds, and farmland. They divided it into the three colonies of Northern and Southern Rhodesia and the Union of South Africa.

On the Guinea Coast of West Africa, British colonies included Nigeria and the Gold Coast (Ghana today), isolated enclaves in the huge French-controlled bulge of West Africa. In East Africa, the British held what are today Uganda and Kenya, reaching from the Sudan to the coast. The western colonies were acquired by treaties with paramount chiefs, the eastern ones through British trading companies and a protectorate over the sultan of Zanzibar.

Almost everywhere in Africa, the British pursued a policy of indirect rule. They left traditional authorities in power at the local level, at least insofar as this was commensurate with British commercial interest and basic values. They intervened to maintain law and order and to support trading companies, railroad builders, and missionary activities. But local chiefs and *emirs* ruled in most matters and were even allowed to keep a substantial chunk of the taxes they collected to support the colonial regime.

An Extension of France Overseas

A very different policy was followed by the French in Africa. French colonies were concentrated in the Mediterranean Muslim lands of Tunisia, Algeria, and Morocco, in the great westward sweep of Saharan and Sudanic Africa, and on the huge East African island of Madagascar—twice the size of the British Isles. All were run as if they were provinces of the French nation.

French penetration of North Africa began as early as the 1830s with the bloody conquest of Algeria, due south of France across the Mediterranean. Tunisia was occupied late in the century at the urging of Jules Ferry, France's leading proponent of empire, and Morocco was made a protectorate after a tense dispute with Germany in the early 1900s. Meanwhile, French troops had pushed south across the Sahara, east along the Senegal River from the Atlantic, and north up the

Ceremonies celebrating the opening of the Suez Canal in Egypt in 1869, which provided a short route for shipping from Europe to Asia. Such monumental undertakings were major accomplishments of the new industrial technology—and of the New Imperialism. (The New York Public Library Picture Collection)

Niger into the Western Sudan. They overcame with considerable difficulty the prolonged resistance of Muslim rulers such as Samori, a Mande leader and heir of the great Mande Sudanic kingdoms of medieval and early-modern times. Madagascar, finally, proved a quagmire for the French. France's intrusion provoked violent revolts and a long pacification campaign, which climaxed in the deposition and exile of the last queen, Ranavalona III, and the declaration of a French colony in the late 1890s.

Because these areas were seized only after prolonged fighting and were ruled for some time by military commanders, a rigidly centralized system of government was established. All of French West Africa—an area roughly the size of the United States—was ruled by a single government in Dakar. French proconsuls did not negotiate with local chieftains or leave the largest share of government in their hands, as the British did. French officials regarded traditional local rulers as subordinates and summoned them to French offices to give them orders.

Arab children in North Africa would soon be memorizing French classical tragedy in their schools. Black Africans from the Western Sudan would be studying in Paris—all part of the effort to create an integrated empire that was in every sense an extension of France overseas.

Places in the Sun

The main area of British colonial control in Africa ran north and south in a broken strip from Cairo to the Cape of Good Hope. The primary French zone was the whole of northwestern Africa—the states of the Maghreb and of French West Africa and French Equatorial Africa, reaching from the Atlantic to the frontiers of the Anglo-Egyptian Sudan. Most of the rest of Africa beyond these two great blocks was soon absorbed by other European powers, jostling and shoving for their share of the dwindling continent. The most important of these other exploiters of Africa were Belgium, Germany, Portugal, and Italy.

The Belgian king Leopold hired the journalist-turned-explorer Henry Stanley to sign treaties with chiefs all across the dense rain forest of the Congo Basin in central Africa. This gigantic Belgian colony, almost ten times the size of Belgium itself, became a major copper producer—and a byword for colonial cruelty to native peoples.

Germany, filled with national pride and expansive vigor after the unification of 1870–1871, demanded its "place in the sun" rather late. But the new nation soon had three large colonies: Cameroons, at the hinge of West Africa; an East African territory that is today Tanzania; and a southern colony bordering South Africa and composed largely of desert—modern Namibia. The genocidal suppression of the Maji-Maji rebellion in Tanzania became another of the horror stories of the great conquest.

Portugal expanded ancient holdings into the two large colonies of Angola and Mozambique on opposite sides of the stem of South Africa. The new nation of Italy set out with much vigor but mixed success to acquire North African territories. She seized the desert sprawl of Libya between French Tunisia and British Egypt, and the northeastern strip of Somaliland on the Red Sea and the Indian Ocean. Italian efforts to conquer Ethiopia, however, met disaster when an Italian army was destroyed at Adowa by the Ethiopians early in the new century.

As the twentieth century began, then, only Ethiopia remained a truly independent African state. All the rest had come under the control, direct or indirect, of the relentlessly expanding West.

ASIA UNDER THE GUN

A Matter of Loans and Rights of Way

In Asia—the four fifths of Eurasia east of the Dardanelles—Europeans confronted a very different situation from that prevailing in Africa. The East, the original home of civilization, had for thousands of years been dominated by powerful Asian empires and complex urban societies. These Asian cultures had successfully resisted or effectively absorbed many invaders over the centuries.

Over much of the East, then, the more direct and brutal methods that had worked in Africa had less application. Military conquest and the establishment of a full-scale colonial administration did happen in Asia, but less often. More common was the protectorate, more common still the sphere of influence.

In Asia, imperialism was thus much less a matter of pith helmets and pacification campaigns. More often it was a dignified affair of bank loans or railway rights of way, of European officers retraining royal armies or European bureaucrats taking over crucial departments of someone else's government.

The gunboats were always there, patrolling the coasts of China or "opening up" Japan. There were savage struggles to hold India during the Mutiny of 1857 or to conquer chunks of mainland Southeast Asia. But much of the work of imposing the will of the West upon the East was done in meetings between Europeans themselves, in which they agreed to respect each others' "interests" in other peoples' countries.

There were fewer misunderstandings of the sort that might occur with a paramount chief in West Africa. Highly literate, if not always strong-willed, Asian sovereigns knew very well what they were getting into when a treaty was finally presented for their signature. There was simply very little that they could do about it. The benefits of a modernized army or a big loan were too great to be resisted. And the gunboats were still there.

Berlin to Baghdad

This was notably the pattern in the Middle East, where France and Germany, Russia and Britain all jockeyed for strategic position and long-range profits.

France was first into the Middle East, in the days of Napoleon's eastern campaign just before 1800. The French victory at the Battle of the Pyramids, which broke the once-feared Mamelukes, attracted respectful attention all across the aging Ottoman Empire. French stock—and interests—rose higher with the opening of the Suez Canal by a French company in 1869. The British pushed the French out of Egypt in the 1880s, but Paris simply turned further east, investing and building influence in Syria and Lebanon.

Germany developed a close relationship with the center of Ottoman power in Istanbul. German banks lent large sums to Turkey, and German officers worked to modernize the Turkish army. There were negotiations for a German consortium to build railroads in the Ottoman Empire. As the British talked of a Cape-to-Cairo line, the Germans dreamed of a Berlin-to-Baghdad railway with stops in Vienna and on the Golden Horn. Direct trade between the throbbing industrial heartland of Germany and the Far East via the Persian Gulf seemed a distinct possibility to William II, whose father had founded the German Empire in 1870, and who himself dreamed of a larger German empire overseas in the 1890s.

British and Russian imperial interests, finally, clashed in Iran and Afghanistan. These warring fragments of ancient Persia lay athwart the land route to British India—and along expanding Russia's southern frontier. Military commitments were therefore made by London and St. Petersburg to shahs and emirs in Teheran and Kabul. Russia continued to expand in central Asia, and Britain fought several Afghan Wars. Soon after 1900, however, an understanding between the two European powers dividing Iran into three spheres of influence: a Russian zone in the north, including Teheran and ancient Isfahan; a British zone in the south, dominating the Persian Gulf; and a large neutral zone in between.

Thus Western governmental efficiency and industrial development began to filter into the ancient Muslim center of Eurasia. With these influences, however, came increasing political and economic dependence on the West.

Empire East of Suez

The British in South Asia and the British and French in Southeast Asia were the primary participants in the great drive for more formal colonial empire east of Suez.

In British India, the subcontinent that constitutes the bulk of South Asia, imperialism took the form of the intensification and systematization of the British supremacy established there in the preceding century. This process was particularly accelerated by the Indian Mutiny of 1857.

The mutiny was a consequence of the increased British presence in India in the nineteenth century. Unpopular policies included the dispossession of some Indian princes of their states, campaigns by Christian missionaries against Hindu religious customs, and a tightening up of restrictions on the Indian officials in the employ of the British East India Company, which still ruled India under parliamentary supervision. The famous incident that triggered the great revolt by Indian troops, the greasing of cartridges with pig and cow grease, affronted the most ancient religious taboos of both Hindus and Muslims. In the resulting carnage, hundreds of British men, women, and children were slaughtered—as were thousands of Indians, whose villages were put to the torch by vengeful British soldiers.

After the suppression of the mutiny, the British government took over sole responsibility for governing almost the entire subcontinent. A number of small princedoms continued to exist on suffrance, but a royal viceroy and thousands of British civil servants henceforth guided the colony's destinies. Schools, railroads, harbor facilities were built, and serious attempts were made to root out such unacceptable religious practices as *suttee*, in which Hindu widows cremated themselves on the funeral pyres of their husbands as a display of devotion. India entered the twentieth century as the most glittering jewel in Queen Victoria's crown.

In Southeast Asia, Britain and France found themselves in uneasy competition as they established colonies on the western and eastern sides of the Indochinese peninsula. France pushed into Vietnam as early as the 1860s and subsequently established a protectorate over Cambodia and Laos. Expanding eastward from India, the British invaded and occupied Burma; other British expansionists pushed north from the key port of Singapore up the Malay Peninsula.

In the middle was Siam—Thailand today—the sole remaining independent state in mainland Southeast Asia. An agreement between Britain and France left Siam as a buffer between them. With the islands of today's Indonesia Dutch since the seventeenth century and the Philippines in American hands from 1900 on, Thailand remained, like Ethiopia in Africa, an isolated peak of independence in a sea of expanding European influence.

The Opening of Japan

Even East Asia, which had flourished so long in comparative isolation from the rest of Eurasia, was in the end sucked into the maelstrom of the New Imperialism. Ancient China became the largest victim yet of Western expansion. And Japan became the first major Asian convert to Western technology—and to Western-style imperialism.

The Meiji Restoration of 1868 was one of the decisive events of modern Japanese history. Its immediate cause was the shattering of Japan's traditional isolation by the West—in this case by the United States.

The Tokugawa shogunate, two and a half centuries old by the middle of the nineteenth century, was an institution—and a dynasty—on its last legs. The Tokugawa clan no longer produced strong leadership

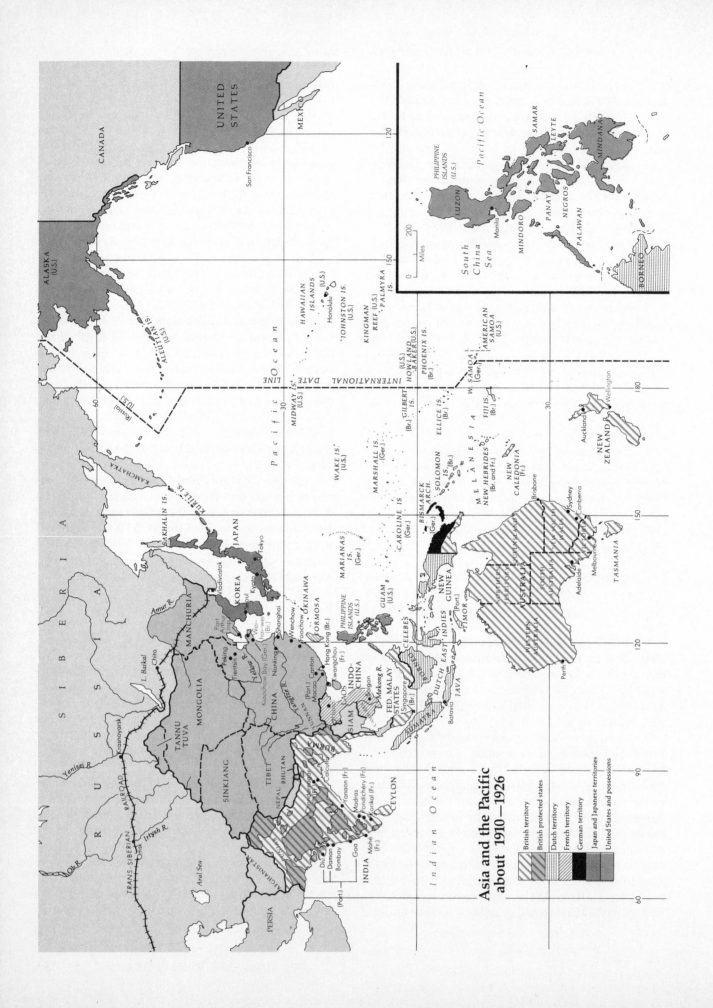

Asia and the Pacific about 1910–1926

British territory
British protected states
Dutch territory
French territory
German territory
Japan and Japanese territories
United States and possessions

CANADA

UNITED STATES

MEXICO

San Francisco

ALASKA (U.S.)

ALEUTIAN IS. (U.S.)

Pacific Ocean

HAWAIIAN ISLANDS (U.S.)
Honolulu
JOHNSTON IS. (U.S.)
KINGMAN REEF (U.S.)
PALMYRA

MIDWAY IS. (U.S.)

INTERNATIONAL DATE LINE

HOWLAND (U.S.)
BAKER IS. (U.S.)
PHOENIX IS. (Br.)

W. SAMOA (Ger.)
AMERICAN SAMOA (U.S.)

GILBERT IS. (Br.)
ELLICE IS. (Br.)
FIJI IS. (Br.)

WAKE IS. (U.S.)

MARSHALL IS. (Ger.)

CAROLINE IS. (Ger.)

SOLOMON IS. (Br.)
MELANESIA
NEW HEBRIDES (Br. and Fr.)
NEW CALEDONIA (Fr.)

BISMARCK ARCH. (Ger.)

NEW GUINEA

Brisbane
Sydney
Canberra

NORTHERN TERRITORY
QUEENSLAND
NEW SOUTH WALES
VICTORIA
Melbourne
Adelaide
SOUTH AUSTRALIA
WESTERN AUSTRALIA
AUSTRALIA
Perth
TASMANIA

Auckland
Wellington
NEW ZEALAND

KAMCHATKA

SAKHALIN IS.
KURILE IS.

JAPAN
Tokyo
Kyoto
Vladivostok
KOREA
Seoul
Port Arthur
Wei-hai-wei (Br.)
Dairen

MANCHURIA

Peking
Tientsin
Yellow R.
Nanking
Shanghai
Wenchow
Foochow
FORMOSA
OKINAWA

CHINA
Yangtze R.

Kiaochow Bay (Ger.)
Macao (Port.)
Canton
Kwangchou
Hong Kong (Br.)

PHILIPPINE ISLANDS (U.S.)
GUAM (U.S.)

SIBERIA

L. Baikal
Chita
Amur R.

MONGOLIA

TANNU TUVA

R U S S I A

Krasnoyarsk
Yenisei R.
TRANS-SIBERIAN RAILROAD
Omsk
Irtysh R.
Ob R.
Aral Sea

SINKIANG

TIBET

NEPAL
BHUTAN
BURMA

INDO-CHINA (Fr.)
LAOS
SIAM
ANNAM
Saigon
Mekong R.

CELEBES
BORNEO
DUTCH EAST INDIES
FED. MALAY STATES
Singapore (Br.)
SUMATRA
JAVA
Batavia
TIMOR (Port.)

AFGHANISTAN
PERSIA

INDIA
Delhi
Chandernagor (Fr.)
Calcutta
Yanaon (Fr.)
Madras
Pondichéry (Fr.)
Karikal (Fr.)
CEYLON
Diu (Port.)
Daman (Port.)
Bombay
Goa (Port.)
Mahé (Fr.)

Indian Ocean

Pacific Ocean

PHILIPPINE ISLANDS (U.S.)
LUZON
Manila
SAMAR
LEYTE
MINDORO
PANAY
NEGROS
PALAWAN
MINDANAO
South China Sea
BORNEO

Miles
200

capable of meeting crises decisively. Students of Japan's past had already begun to examine the traditional role allotted to the hereditary emperors, a position of religious and ceremonial importance but completely lacking in political power, and to speculate on restoring political authority to Japan's Son of Heaven.

It was at this point that an American fleet appeared. Commodore Matthew Perry arrived with a U.S. naval squadron, including three steam frigates, in 1853, instructed to "open" Japan to diplomatic and commercial exchange. The American ships with their massive artillery much impressed the Japanese. After months of bitter disputes in Japanese ruling circles, Japan signed her first unequal treaty with the United States—and soon after with other Western countries. By these treaties, she agreed to receive Western merchants and diplomats and to allow them special rights in Japan not to be granted Japanese in other countries.

In 1868, in the aftermath of these concessions, a group of outraged *daimyo* compelled the last shogun to resign—and passed political authority not to a new shogun but to the sixteen-year-old emperor, Mutsuhito. Known to history by his reign title—the Meiji ("Enlightened Rule") Emperor—Mutsuhito ruled Japan until his death in 1912 and saw her rise from victim to victor, from an isolated island nation in East Asia to world power.

The architects of the restoration of imperial power moved the imperial capital from old Kyoto to the shogun's former capital of Edo—renamed Tokyo—and set to work preparing Japan to resist Western penetration in an entirely new way. To this end, they engineered an amazing transformation of their country.

Like Peter the Great in eighteenth-century Russia, this nineteenth-century Japanese emperor and his allies consciously set out to Westernize their country from the top. Japanese students were sent abroad to learn, foreign experts brought to Japan to teach. Western methods of education and systems of transportation and communication were introduced. Industry, agriculture, banking were all modernized. Above all, Japan's military was updated, the old samurai class deposed, and a modern war machine created, from a steam navy to Western-style uniforms.

Forty years after Perry, Japan was ready to try her new power. In 1894–1895 Japan routed her ancient mentor, China, in the Sino-Japanese War. In 1904–1905 she decisively defeated one of the European great powers in the Russo-Japanese War—the first time in this age of the New Imperialism that a Western nation had lost to an Asian country.

From these victories Japan got Korea, the Liaotung Peninsula in North China—and a new status in the world. In the century that followed, she would play an expanding role as one of the great powers in the first age of global history.

The Triumph of the Western Barbarians

The destiny of China was final proof of how thoroughly the world was turned upside down by the unprecedented power and unappeasable drive for dominion exhibited by the modern West.

For more than two hundred years, European traders in the Middle Kingdom had been confined to a small section of the port of Canton and to the nearby Portuguese port of Macao, in South China. Jesuits might teach European painting styles or techniques of casting cannon in Peking, but they were not allowed to proselytize much for their faith. When a British ambassador showed up at the capital in the 1790s, he was graciously received and firmly turned away.

Then in the 1800s, Europeans seemed to burst into China from all directions, shattering her immemorial isolation forever.

China was brutally punished in four wars during the nineteenth century. Britain's Opium War (1839–1842) broke out over Chinese attempts to curb opium smuggling by Britain from her Indian colony into China. British naval activity, against which the Chinese could do little, compelled the emperor to sign the first of many unequal treaties. China was forced to open a number of other ports to Europeans and grant Britain her first slice of Chinese territory, the island of Hong Kong.

A second war (1856–1860), fought by the British and French against China, began with more naval action and climaxed with the temporary seizure of Peking itself. More "treaty ports" were opened up by the resulting agreements, and more diplomatic concessions made. The Japanese next humiliated China in the Sino-Japanese War, forcing her to open still more ports to the world and beginning a round of Chinese territorial concessions to foreign imperialist powers.

A final Western invasion, involving not only British and French forces but also United States, German, and Japanese troops, resulted from the Boxer Rebellion (1899–1900). This revolt was a desperate effort by mobs of Chinese peasants to destroy the by then ubiquitous Western presence in their country. The Boxers were summarily suppressed by a small international expeditionary force—which also brushed aside the Chinese army and took Peking again in the process.

This disastrous century for the ancient Middle Kingdom was made worse by violent civil discord.

British naval vessels bombarding Canton. This ancient port city in south China surrendered under a rain of shells and rockets—typical prelude to the extraction of unequal treaties from the helpless imperial government in Peking. (The Bettmann Archive, Inc.)

The terrible Taiping Rebellion of the 1850s and 1860s was inspired partly by traditional peasant discontents. But it was led by a Christian convert who mixed hazy Christian fundamentalism with Confucian social idealism—and ravaged the land for fifteen years.

At the highest level, China was also divided by the mounting Western pressure. Two factions of officials formed. There were those who favored following the Japanese road and learning modern methods from the West. There were others, including the indomitable Empress Tz'u-hsi, who clung to old methods and prayed to the old gods in this moment of crisis. By and large, the latter prevailed—with unfortunate results for China.

During the last sixty years of the century, then, the Chinese Empire was opened up with a vengeance to Western imperialism. China was forced to open her seacoasts and her great rivers to Western merchants, large areas of her hinterlands to Christian missionaries, and her capital to Western diplomats and embassies. She accepted the right of extraterritoriality: all these foreigners could live according to their own laws in China. She agreed to most-favored-nation clauses, which granted to all foreign countries every concession made to any one of them.

From the 1870s on, China surrendered her ancient claims to her tributary states in East and Southeast Asia: Vietnam to France, Burma to Britain, concessions in Sinkiang to Russia and in Korea to Japan. In the 1890s she gave up important slices of China proper to the outsiders: Canton to France, the Shantung Peninsula to Germany, the Liaotung Peninsula to Russia (later passed on to Japan), and coastal territories across from Liaotung and Hong Kong to Great Britain.

Europeans also secured rights to build railways, develop minerals, and otherwise exploit Chinese land. By 1900, Western troops were stationed in China to guard all these concessions, Western gunboats patrolled the coasts and rivers of China, and the Chinese customs service was run by an Irishman.

China's curse and China's preserver during much of this terrible time was the last of her great empresses, Tz'u-hsi (1835–1908). An imperial concubine who clawed her way to power in 1862 and ruled through a series of feckless males through most of her life, Tz'u-hsi was, practically speaking, the last of the Manchus.

In her later years especially, the Dowager Empress—the Old Buddha, as she was called behind her back—was a rigidly conservative, hopelessly superstitious, imperious old woman, determined to make no concessions to the ways of the Western barbarians. She suppressed efforts at reform, pinned much of her hope on a revival of the faithful scholarly bureaucracy, and even supported the Boxers.

Tz'u-hsi built all her hopes on China's immense past, and she lost. Had she been willing to learn, as the Japanese were, China might have been saved many of the humiliations of this century of the Western hegemony. On the other hand, a weaker person, less supremely confident in the rightness of all things Chinese, might well have presided over the destruction of the dynasty—perhaps of her country as a whole—half a century earlier.

Driven from her capital by Western armies as the Boxer Rebellion collapsed in a chaos of bloody reprisals in 1900, Tz'u-hsi survived to return to power and make final terms with her enemies. We have photographs of her surrounded by Western diplomatic wives, her aged face a mask of powder and paint, her clawlike fingers glittering with rings. Even in defeat she is the Old Buddha still, a grizzled hawk among doves.

INTERNAL IMPERIALISM

Pacifying, Settling, Civilizing

While Europeans partitioned Africa and imposed their will on Asia, another form of imperial expansion was coming to a climax also—the internal imperialism of Western nations whose territorial claims included large portions of the earth's surface still occupied by non-Western peoples. The pacifying, settling, and "civilizing" of such territories had, of course, begun with the first contact between Europeans and non-European peoples. But in several huge areas, this process reached a climax in the later nineteenth century.

Regions that thus came under definitive Western control in this climactic age of the New Imperialism included the Russian Far East, the American Far West, and the British continental colony of Australia. A number of similarities may be noted between these and other areas of internal colonization.

The first comers tended to be peoples from the fringes of the conquering society—mountain men in the American West, Cossacks in Siberia, beachcombers in Oceania. Traders and missionaries frequently followed, beginning the long job of transforming the material and spiritual lives of the peoples thus invaded. Then came farmers, driven by landhunger—American homesteaders, Russian peasants, Australian sheepherders—pushing the indigenous populations off their thinly settled lands.

Most of these native peoples were living at a much earlier stage of social evolution than their conquerors. Nomadic Amerindian hunters on the American Plains,

nomadic mongoloid pastoralists in much of Russian Asia, wandering Aborigine hunters and gatherers in the Australian Outback were thus overcome relatively easily.

The population of many of these native peoples fell drastically as a consequence of Western intrusion. Typically, these huge casualties were not the direct result of military action by the West. Maoris and Plains Indians, for instance, proved to be powerful antagonists. Genocidal declines in population were rather the result of Western diseases to which the natives had no immunities, and of starvation as they were driven from the lands where they had gained a livelihood.

Always, however, Western technology lay at the root of the destruction of these preurban peoples. Ships and railways, plows and barbed wire, and everywhere the increasingly devastating firepower of Western weapons destroyed not individual lives alone, but whole societies.

The Cossacks Are Coming

Russian eastward expansion across Eurasia paralleled the American westward movement. It was a slower and more deliberate advance, and one that covered even greater distances. But the result was the same: the imposition of a Europe-based culture upon the thinly scattered non-European populations who had once been masters of a substantial slice of the earth's surface.

Prior to 1500, the northern Eurasian steppe had been the homeland of the world's most extensive and formidable nomadic peoples. Semimilitarized, highly mobile, and frequently predatory in their attacks on the urban-imperial cultures to the south, these pastoral nomads were the most dangerous barbarians. The days of the great nomadic offensives in the West ended, however, with the Russian defeat of the Golden Horde in the fifteenth century. And from the sixteenth century on, the Russians themselves began to push relentlessly into central and East Asia.

The first Russians to cross the Ural Mountains—the traditional boundary of European Russia—were the Cossacks. These bands of free-living horseriders were seminomadic pastoralists themselves, as well as hunters, marauders, and sometime soldiers of the czar. Skilled navigators as well as horseriders, the Cossacks followed a network of rivers eastward across Siberia, reaching the Pacific shortly before 1650.

In 1689, a hundred years before the first British ambassador arrived in China, Russia signed a treaty with Manchu China delimiting their mutual frontier. Some Russian frontiersmen even crossed the Bering Strait to Alaska and worked their way down the Pa-

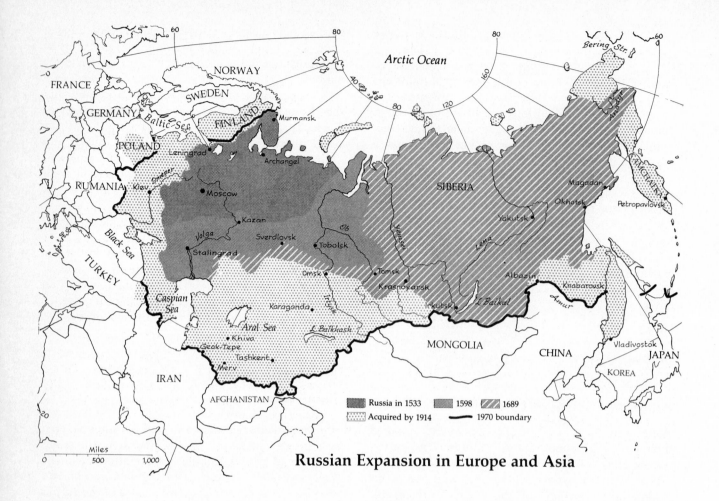

Russian Expansion in Europe and Asia

Russia in 1533   1598   1689
Acquired by 1914   1970 boundary

cific coast into California long before the United States existed to claim it.

Russia's eastward movement was punctuated by a series of southward thrusts toward her Asian rivals south of the steppes. In the eighteenth century, especially under Catherine the Great, Russian armies pushed south against the Ottoman Empire to the Black Sea. In the nineteenth century Russian troops fought their way into the mountainous Caucasus, between the Black and Caspian seas. They also overwhelmed the crumbling Muslim khanates of central Asia, east of the Caspian. In the Pacific Far East, Russia pressed south along the Amur River frontier with Manchuria, acquiring the site of her great Pacific port at Vladivostok.

Obtaining land, however, was not occupying it. Modern Russia expanded till it stretched for six thousand miles, a quarter of the way around the world. But most of this land was a vast frontier, only beginning to be settled by Russians in the nineteenth century.

The Cossacks had come in the seventeenth century as fur trappers and marauders. Traders, officials, and tax collectors soon followed, and a number of penal colonies were established in the wilderness. A few landowners took their serfs into western Siberia as early as the eighteenth century. In the nineteenth, increasing numbers of peasants moved east on their own, seeking free land to cultivate. After the emancipation of the serfs in 1861, peasants began to pour into the east. The opening of the Trans-Siberian Railway in the 1890s facilitated this migration. Three and a half million colonists took land in the east during the two decades before 1914.

The impact of Russian eastward migration was in many ways not as devastating as the American colonization of the West or the contemporary British occupation of Australia. Russians had known Turko-Mongol peoples for centuries and felt little racial superiority, and Russian peasants did not expect to live much better than Tatars or Mongols. There was none of the genocidal destruction of native societies that would mark the internal expansion of other continental nations.

Nevertheless, there were inevitable conflicts—and the subject peoples inevitably lost. Cossack depredations made the warning "The Cossacks are coming" feared by Mongol tribes all across Siberia, and official tribute-gathering was almost as burdensome. Tribal resistance to conquest would last for decades in the Caucasus Mountains, and central Asian nomads preyed on Russian caravans well into the nineteenth century. Russian Orthodox settlers hated and feared Islam in central Asia, and there were bitter feuds over irrigation water in those dry regions.

The czarist exploitation of the minority peoples of the empire was angrily condemned by the Bolshevik revolutionaries who took over Russia in 1917. But the work of Europeanization, begun in a haphazard way in czarist times, has continued in the Soviet Union to the present day.

The Trail of Tears

When the Europeans began to push their way into North America, there were perhaps a million Amerindians living north of the Rio Grande. Culturally speaking, they were far from homogeneous. In the varied environments of the northern continent, a variety of Native American cultures had been evolving for thousands of years. There were thus hundreds of different tribal societies, including nomadic hunters, agricultural villagers, and some few, like the Mound Builders or the Pueblo Indians, pushing to the edge of urbanization. During the colonial period itself,

loose confederacies east of the Mississippi bound tens of thousands of Indians for purposes of peace, war, and trade.

Almost all Indians, however, remained Stone Age tool makers. Most were organized primarily on the basis of clan and tribe. All were worshipers of animist gods, ghosts, and nature spirits. Like African animists, they frequently believed in a Great Spirit who was the author of all things.

The destruction of these societies took several hundred years. But the process accelerated significantly in the later eighteenth and the nineteenth centuries, reaching a climax during the American westward movement of the half century after the Civil War.

By 1776, the two and a half million English settlers on the east coast substantially outnumbered all the Indian nations on the continent—and their hostility to the Indians was well demonstrated. American land hunger and refusal to mix with the alien culture of the indigenous population thus set a juggernaut in motion. Rolling westward, the expanding United States dislocated, defeated, fragmented, and finally destroyed all the major Amerindian cultures from the Atlantic to the Pacific.

Disease, warfare with Europeans, and involvement in European wars had broken the back of the eastern Indian confederacies before 1800. Even the

Far from the world of gunboat diplomacy, the Amerindian population of the United States still lived much as their pre-Columbian ancestors had. But Western firepower easily shattered aboriginal societies like these around the world (Western History Collections, University of Oklahoma Library)

League of the Iroquois, which for two centuries had bound a half dozen large tribes into a loose but powerful unit capable of treating as an equal with Dutch, French, and English colonies, was divided and broken during the American Revolution.

After the Revolution came mounting pressure for Indian "removal" from all the lands east of the Mississippi. This was accomplished by force during the Jacksonian 1830s. Indians such as the Southern Cherokee were rounded up and headed west along the infamous Trail of Tears to Oklahoma, leaving many dead along the road to exile.

After 1865 the restless westward thrust of Americans—gold seekers and other miners, cattlemen, sheepherders, and farmers—shattered the buffalo-hunting Indian tribes of the Plains as they had the woodland confederacies of the East. Their weapons were technological and bureaucratic. Repeating rifles and pistols, railroads, barbed wire, and the steel plow defeated the nomadic "wild Indians" in the field.

The destruction of the Indian cultures was completed by treaties that were never kept, reservations that were always the worst land, exploitative Indian agents, land speculators, and other parasites. The final enemy of the Indian, ironically, turned out to be government reformers who claimed to be the friends of the "vanishing red man." It was these reformers who set out to introduce Indians to private property, modern education, and integration into American society—which meant the disintegration of their own.

The North American tribes had responded to the inexorable advance of the Europeans in many ingenious ways. The woodlands Indians acquired firearms, organized large confederations such as those of the Iroquois and the Creeks, and played the power game with the invaders as long as they could. Plains tribes such as the Cheyenne, the Sioux, and the Apache acquired the horse from the Spanish and became as mobile and fierce a nomadic people as any Mongol or Indo-European people of earlier centuries. Defeated once more by the cavalry and the virtual extermination of the buffalo herds upon which they subsisted, the demoralized Amerindian remnants took up religious movements like the Peyote Cult or the Ghost Dance, until even these were declared illegal.

The westward march of the frontier line, a measure of advance and expansion for most Americans, was a measure of the defeat and disintegration of Amerindian culture in North America. For the real first comers, it was all a Trail of Tears.

The Last Tasmanian

Other sparsely settled areas nominally controlled by Western peoples were also occupied and their indigenous populations subjugated in the course of the nineteenth century. Dutch and English settlers seeking land and gold pushed deeper into South Africa. Canadians moved westward across their even larger swath of North America, as their Yankee neighbors did. Latin Americans, especially in Mexico and the Andean regions, began to suck the withdrawn and silent Indian populations back into the economic life of the nation—meaning mostly peonage.

The most sweeping instance of Europeanization within a colony, however, came in Oceania, particularly on the continent of Australia and the large islands of New Zealand and Tasmania.

Oceania was the last part of the globe to be reached by the expanding peoples of the West. Explored in the eighteenth century and colonized in the nineteenth, the relatively simple societies of the far Pacific were quickly swept up in the cresting wave of the New Imperialism.

Whalers, sealers, traders, missionaries, and a variety of beachcombers and castaways moved among the thousands of South Pacific and Southeast Asian islands in the nineteenth century. Many were shocked at the customs of these paradise islanders, which in some societies included cannibalism, headhunting, and endemic warfare. But the Westerners brought their own afflictions: guns to intensify warfare, liquor, and, as everywhere, diseases to which Polynesians, Melanesians, and Micronesians had no immunities. These material misfortunes, plus Western government and European religion, slowly but surely undermined the integrated cultures of the South Seas.

In Australia and New Zealand, the process was more direct and violent.

Criminals came early to the Antipodes, as to Russian Siberia. A British penal colony was established at Botany Bay in New South Wales, southeastern Australia, in 1788. In the nineteenth century came sheepherders, cattle ranchers, and wheat farmers. Beginning at mid-century, a series of gold rushes began that once again drew adventurers and other dubious frontier types. Railway lines were built and Europeans spread into the arid Outback, the scantily watered interior of the continent.

There were perhaps 300,000 Aborigines scattered over the Outback, living by hunting and gathering, as the earliest humans had. Their technology was that of the Old Stone Age, their social organization based on the hunting band. They had neither clothes nor settled habitation, or indeed any substantial accumulation of worldly goods at all.

The aboriginal inhabitants were a nuisance to the frontier farmers, ranchers, and miners. Deprived of their own hunting grounds, they killed the ranchers' stock. To British settlers they seemed dirty, lazy, uninterested in acquiring European skills or in working for the newcomers.

The struggle was one-sided, seldom documented, and deadly for the Aborigines. They were driven off their lands by European sheep and cattle, killed by European diseases, the Border Police, the settlers themselves. The government finally herded them into "reserves," where some still live. Many more have joined the society of the conqueror.

The pattern in New Zealand differed in that the fiercely warlike Maoris made much more of a fight of it. In the face of increased demand for their land, they united under a single Maori king for the first time in their history. Around mid-century, settlers launched a series of wars aimed at destroying the emerging Maori polity before its strength grew. This they succeeded in doing, seizing vast acreages in the process. The Maori, like the American Plains Indians, took refuge in religious ecstasies—and slowly learned to adapt.

On the large island of Tasmania, off the coast of Australia, no adaptation was allowed. Tasmanians also fought the invaders, killing both herds and herdsmen. In 1830 a series of mass manhunts began, intended to exterminate the aboriginal population. Five hundred out of five thousand survived. The last of these native Tasmanians died in 1876.

The great conquest thus completed the destruction of the preurban peoples who once shared the world with the rest of us.

Populations may creep back upwards. In Australia today there are almost as many people who claim aboriginal descent as there were in 1800. There are at least half as many North American Indians as there were in Columbus's time. The Muslim peoples of Soviet Central Asia are actually among the fastest growing populations in the U.S.S.R.

What has gone are the cultures that these people once built for themselves. Destroyed by new governments, new religions, and new values, or preserved here and there in the amber of reservations, reserves, homelands, and other protected areas, these alternate ways of life are among the most striking casualties of the great Western conquest of the rest of the world.

SUMMARY

The resurgence of overseas empire building we call the New Imperialism brought almost all of Africa and large parts of Asia under Western domination, as well as immense tracts of Russia, North America, and Australia.

The motives of the New Imperialists were neither economic exploitation alone nor civilizing impulses pure and simple. The causal factors at work included a varying mixture of economic, political, humanitarian, and even psychological drives and interests. The elements that made possible so vast a conquest in the generation or two after 1870 included superior Western organization, esprit, and, above all, firepower. The resulting unprecedented global hegemony took several forms, including full-scale colonies, protectorates, and spheres of influence.

The "scramble for Africa" was the most dramatic theater of imperial expansion at the end of the nineteenth century. There European powers negotiated treaties with local chiefs and other rulers all over the continent, and frequently sent in troops later to enforce the new agreements. France's African colonies, mostly in West Africa, were tightly governed as extensions of metropolitan France. Britain's holdings in all parts of Africa were generally run on a system of delegated authority called indirect rule. Germany, Belgium, Italy, and other countries also seized parts of Africa.

In Asia the resistance of long-established and populous urban-imperial cultures was strong. As a result, protectorates and spheres of influence were more common, though there were important new colonies and some old ones as well. Among the areas that came under Western control were British India, German-dominated Turkey, and the British and French colonies on mainland Southeast Asia. Japan was also "opened" to Western trade and influence, and China became the hapless victim of European gunboat diplomacy from the Opium War to the Boxer Rebellion.

Control of areas already claimed by Western peoples often led to the destruction of indigenous pre-European cultures. Russian Siberia was less violently pacified than some other areas. The Amerindian peoples of the United States and the Australian Aborigines, however, were largely destroyed as independent societies.

By the turn of the century, then, the great conquest had reached its climax with a Western hegemony that was—for the first time in history—genuinely global in scope.

SUGGESTED READING

BAUMGART, W. *Imperialism.* New York: Oxford University Press, 1982. Comparative study of British and French forms of the New Imperialism. See also R. F. Betts, *Assimilation and Association in French Colonial Theory* (New York: Columbia University Press, 1961) and C. J. Lowe, *The Reluctant Imperialists* (London: Routledge & Kegan Paul, 1967) on British colonial policy.

BETTS, R. F., ed. *The Scramble for Africa.* Lexington, Mass.: Heath, 1972. A range of interpretations of the causes and nature of the New Imperialism in Africa.

—— *The False Dawn: European Imperialism in the Nineteenth Century.* Minneapolis: University of Minnesota Press, 1978. Authoritative overview.

DUIGNAN, P, and L. H. GANN. *Colonialism in Africa: The History and Politics of Colonialism.* Cambridge: Cambridge University Press, 1969. Thorough, detailed, and scholarly.

EDWARDES, M. *The West in Asia, 1815-1914.* New York: Putnam's, 1967. Useful survey of the New Imperialism in the East.

FAIRBANK, J. K. *Trade and Diplomacy on the China Coast: The Opening of the Treaty Ports.* Cambridge, Mass.: Harvard University Press, 1953. A classic example of gunboat diplomacy. See also F. Wakemen, *Strangers at the Gate: Social Disorder in South China* (Berkeley: University of California Press, 1966).

GORDON, D. C. *The Moment of Power.* Englewood Cliffs, N.J.: Prentice-Hall, 1970. An excellent analysis of Britain's imperial supremacy. See also P. Knaplund's fine textbook, *The British Empire, 1815-1939* (New York: Fertig, 1970).

HIBBERT, C. *The Great Mutiny: India 1857.* London: Penguin, 1980. The rebellion that shook the British hold on India—and ended by tightening that grip.

KINROSS, P. BALFOUR, LORD. *Between Two Seas.* London: Murray, 1969. One of the great enterprises of the New Imperialism—the building of the Suez Canal.

KIPLING, R. *Kim.* New York: Bantam Books and other editions. The teeming populations and many cultures of India move through the pages of Kipling's classic. For a grim and multilayered vision of European imperialists at work in Africa, see J. Conrad's famous *Heart of Darkness* (New York: Norton and other editions).

LANDES, D. S. *Bankers and Pashas.* Cambridge, Mass.: Harvard University Press, 1980. Good example of the subtler forms of the New Imperialism, here economic exploitation of Egypt by the French.

LUTZ, J. G., ed. *Christian Missions in China: Evangelists of What?* Boston: Heath, 1965. Range of views on the religious dimension of the New Imperialism.

MAY, E. *Imperial Democracy.* New York: Harper & Row, Pub., 1973. American imperialism. See also L. C. Gardner, W. LaFeber, and T. McCormick, *The Creation of the American Empire* (Chicago: Rand McNally, 1973), which gives some attention to revisionist emphasis on economic motives. On American westward expansion, see F. Merk, *History of the Western Movement* (New York: Knopf, 1978), and R. A. Billington, *Westward Expansion* (New York: Macmillan, 1974).

PRICE, A. G. *The Western Invasions of the Pacific and Its Continents: A Study of Moving Frontiers and Changing Landscapes, 1513-1958.* Oxford: Clarendon Press, 1963. A broad survey, with emphasis on the last two centuries.

ROBINSON, R., J. GALLAGHER, and A. DENNY. *Africa and the Victorians.* New York: St. Martin's Press, 1961. Stresses the degree of collaboration between imperialists and imperialized. On this controversial interpretation, see W. R. Louis, ed., *Imperialism: The Robinson and Gallagher Controversy* (New York: Franklin Watts, 1976).

TREADGOLD, D. W. *The Great Siberian Migration.* Princeton: Princeton University Press, 1957. Russia's eastward thrust as a popular movement, by a leading Russian historian. See also G. A. Lensen, ed., *Russia's Easward Expansion* (Englewood Cliffs, N.J.: Prentice-Hall, 1964) for readings on the history of Russia's drive toward the Pacific.

WINKS, R. W., ed. *The Age of Imperialism.* Englewood Cliffs, N.J.: Prentice-Hall, 1969. Good brief collection of source materials.

Chapter · 13

THE WORLD OF THE WESTERN HEGEMONY

WESTERNIZATION:
TOWARD A NEW WORLD ORDER

Global Reach

The New Imperialism had a much more important transforming influence on the rest of the world than the Old Imperialism had had. In many parts of the world, this second, more intense and penetrating wave of Western conquest inaugurated a process of social change sometimes called Westernization, sometimes simply modernization.

Distinctions can be drawn, but the overall pattern is evident, however we label it. The new and more pervasive Western presence led to the breakdown of many traditional cultural modes, forms of social organization, and patterns of belief. The advance of the West also stimulated the global adoption—and adaptation—of many economic, social, and political institutions, of ideological and technological forms derived from Western theory and practice.

This transformation would continue after the fall of the Western intercontinental empires. It would make a crucial contribution to the larger pattern of global exchange of goods, institutions, and ideas that would distinguish the twentieth century even more than the nineteenth. In itself, however, this great wave of Westernization that began in the later 1800s is an amazing historic development.

Many instances of far-reaching regional influences from a single dynamic center could be adduced as precedents. Islam had transformed cultures wherever it spread. The cultural weight of India had reshaped South and Southeast Asian societies. China's immense continuing presence had done the same throughout East Asia. But the global reach and the sheer rapidity of the Western impact resulting from the New Imperialism make Westernization a unique and awesome case.

Bright Lights and Gleaming Rails

Materially, the New Imperialism thrust its way into other people's cultures as the Old Imperialism seldom had. A European trading post on the shores of Africa or Asia, an isolated missionary or fur trapper in the Amazon rain forest or the Canadian wilderness could make a significant difference in the lives of other peoples. Increases in slave raiding or spice cultivation, the introduction of the iron ax or the horse were not negligible forces for social change. But the changes the new wave of Western intruders brought dwarfed all earlier material influences.

The makers of the New Imperialism exploited and developed colonial regions with unmatched thoroughness and intensity. They reaped harvests, tapped trees, dug mines, drilled for oil from Brazil to Borneo. They unrolled barbed wire, strung up telegraph lines, laid rails, constructed harbor facilities. They built processing plants and even manufacturing plants in the colonies to turn raw materials into something closer to the use objects the Europeans, the Americans, or their other customers wanted.

Westerners themselves came in increasing numbers. They came partly to administer and garrison the new colonies. But they also came to manage the new economies and to operate the new technology thus translated beyond the seas. They came as advisers to governments or businesses in old countries in the Middle East or new ones in Latin America. And wherever they came, more and more local people were hired to do the necessary physical labor of remodeling the world.

The material impact was vast, cumulative, and accelerating. Irreplaceable natural resources—Congo copper, Arab oil—began to be drained from the land. Patterns of agriculture were drastically changed. Cash crops replaced subsistence farming until populations that formerly fed themselves came to depend on imported food for sheer survival.

Local industries were ruined by the competition of cheap Western machine-made alternatives. The Indian cotton industry was the world's leader in the seventeenth century. It was driven to the brink of extinction by the cotton mills of Manchester and Birmingham in the nineteenth.

Native peoples were often uprooted and forced into new patterns of life. The bright lights of cities built by Europeans lured African villagers away from their old lives and into new ones that were often rootless and demoralizing. European laws were forced on local people by fiat of colonial administrators. European customs spread with the temptation of jobs and contracts that went to those who accepted European ways.

Everywhere, Western supremacy was flaunted in the shining new facilities—mines and factories, government houses, transportation networks—and the nice homes and private clubs of the European quar-

ters of town. Asians and Africans whose only contact with Westerners was to gawk at the viceroy's palace in passing, to scrub the floors of an engineer's home or take his children out to play could not help but be impressed.

Envious, resentful, filled with righteous wrath or a burning desire to live as these intruders did, the victims of this climactic phase of the great conquest were drawn as by a great magnet in directions their ancestors could not have imagined.

The World According to Newton, Darwin, and Marx

Intellectually and spiritually, the influence of the West on the rest of the world was perhaps even more astonishing.

Ancient traditional religions, systems of ethics, scientific ideas, political theories, and styles in art had mostly survived the Old Imperialism. Tolerant Eastern potentates had cheerfully added Christian priests to Muslim, Buddhist, and other holy men at their courts. Wandering missionaries had half-converted considerable numbers of "rice Christians," who were drawn to missions in time of famine and easily fitted Western divinities into their traditional pantheons.

But with the permeating impact of the New Imperialism, old systems of ideas and values began to

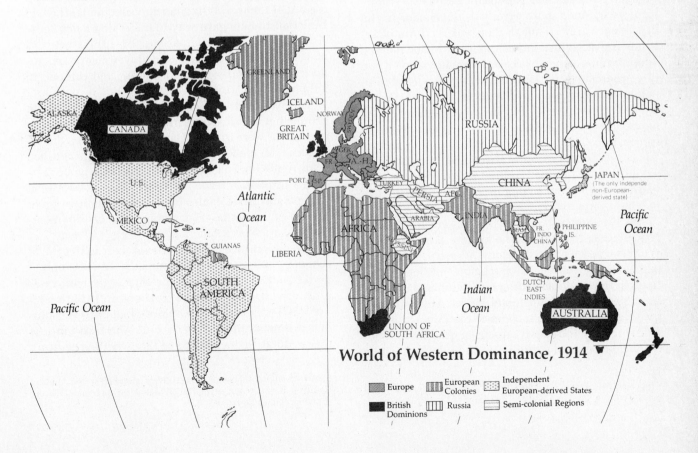

World of Western Dominance, 1914

Europe | European Colonies | Independent European-derived States
British Dominions | Russia | Semi-colonial Regions

melt away. It was the beginning of a process that continues today—a process that one authority has described as "the most totally pervasive example of what historians call cultural diffusion in the history of mankind."[1]

Some of the fundamental features of Western culture—in the intellectual sense of the term—thus spread around the world. European languages, for example, were so widely taught and accepted that they remain the languages of former colonial elites decades after independence. Thus, French still flourishes in what was once French West Africa, as English does in India.

Western Christianity spread more widely and deeply than ever before in Asia and Africa as unprecedented numbers of missionaries flooded the non-Western world. Much of the southern half of Africa is Christian today, and there are Christian enclaves from the Middle East to Southeast Asia. China was governed by a Christian—Chiang Kai-shek—in the earlier twentieth century, and the president of Tanzania since independence has been a Catholic, Julius Nyerere.

Perhaps more important, the new ideologies of nineteenth-century Europe were broadcast among non-European peoples.

European liberal beliefs were introduced slowly through the gradual democratization of at least some colonial governments. European nationalist notions were seized upon more eagerly as the clamor for independence grew. Though they took the form of antiimperialist agitation, colonial nationalism soon developed the same preoccupations with national culture, character, mission, and rights to self-determination that had animated nationalism in the West. Even European socialism, an ideology designed for industrially developed nations with large proletariats, spread to colonial dependencies as the new century advanced. Socialism, especially in its Marxist form, would thus be adapted to the needs of peasant populations in countries having little or no industrial sector, most importantly China.

But the most valuable of all Western intellectual contributions to the life of the world was undoubtedly Western science and technology. Western schools run by colonial governments or religious missions began to teach the world according to Newton and transmit technology on the Manchester model. Students from the colonies picked up such up-to-the-minute ideas as Darwinism or the relativistic social theories of modern sociologists and anthropologists in the universities

of their imperial masters—and found these notions as disturbing to their Buddhist or Hindu sensibilities as they were to Christian beliefs. Soon elites in other cultures everywhere were compromising traditional religious or philosophical beliefs in order to come to terms with the latest insights of the all-conquering West.

The spread of Western ideas, as well as Western material skills, would direct the course of non-Western development long after the Western structure of political power had been dismantled and the Western armies and administrators had retreated west of Suez. The pervasiveness of Western techniques and theories would make modernization a continuing feature of Third World history long after the great conquest had given way to the great liberation.

WESTERN PREDOMINANCE AND GLOBAL INTEGRATION

The Web of Trade

By the eve of the First World War—the historic end of the nineteenth century—the Industrial Revolution and the New Imperialism had combined to produce a genuinely integrated global economy for the first time in history. The exchange between Europe and the rest of the world that had appeared under the Old Imperialism now gave way to something much more elaborate and all-encompassing. By 1914 a network of commerce, communication, investment, and industrial development linked nations and colonies in all parts of the world.[2]

The web of trade was now centered not only in Europe but also in North America. The leading trading nations were Britain, Germany, the United States, France, the Netherlands, and Belgium. Established trade routes linked all the continents of the globe. The busiest arteries of trade, however, were not between Europe and her colonies but between the two great centers of industrial and commercial development, Europe and North America.

The importance of international trade in the global economy had also increased greatly. In 1800 only 3 percent of the gross national product of the world was exchanged beyond national frontiers. In 1914 the figure was 33 percent. Fully a third of all the goods produced flowed into the trade routes and sea lanes of the world at the beginning of the twentieth century.

[1]Paul Harrison, *Inside the Third World: The Anatomy of Poverty* (New York: Penguin Books, 1979), p. 48.

[2]These economic links can be effectively observed in the maps of Geoffrey Barraclough, ed., *The Times Atlas of World History* (London: Times Books, 1978).

Those routes had themselves improved unimaginably over the intervening century. For land transport, the railway had been invented during the interim and had rapidly eclipsed beasts of burden and vehicles drawn by animals as a conveyor of trade goods. By 1914 Europe and the United States were crisscrossed by a mesh of rail lines. Railroads had been built through the Alps and over the Andes, and transcontinental lines spanned the United States, Canada, and Russia.

The steamship had also all but replaced sailing vessels for most long hauls. Metal steamers with ten and twenty times the carrying capacity of earlier shipping now dominated the sea lanes of the globe. Key canals had been cut at Suez in 1869 and at Panama in 1914, so that ships could pass between Asia and Africa, or between the Americas, lopping hundreds of miles off their voyages.

A less visible but equally important force binding the peoples of the world into an increasingly integrated economy was the web of investment, again centered in Europe with a secondary center in the United States. Great Britain had twice the foreign investments of second-ranked France, with Germany, the Netherlands, and the U.S. following.

Britain's heaviest investments were, once more, not in her colonies but in the United States and the self-governing Dominion of Canada. Thereafter, the pound was deployed most widely in India, Australia, Latin America, and South Africa—a truly global reach. Most of France's smaller total was invested elsewhere in Europe, especially in Russia; lesser amounts of francs financed projects in North and South America, Sudanic Africa, and the Ottoman Empire. And so it went down the line, bankers in London and Paris, New York and Berlin financing much of the large-scale business activity of the world.

Final evidence of the economic ties that were binding the world as never before was the spread of the Industrial Revolution from its birthplace in Europe. During the later nineteenth and early twentieth centuries, the United States became the leading industrial producer, outdistancing even Britain and Germany. During this same period, Canada, Russia, and Japan also emerged as leading industrial nations, with India, Australia, and Argentina not far behind.

Much of this new industrial development was isolated in the nations in which it grew. The new industries in India and Argentina produced goods for export that had little effect on the lives of Indians and Argentinians. Nevertheless, it was a crucial first step toward the eventual industrialization of much of the globe.

This integrated world economy was clearly orchestrated and run by the West, in the interests of Western peoples. Frequently the new web of exchange, investment, and production warped the economies of non-Western nations. Many Latin countries and African colonies, for instance, became monocultural commodity producers, catering to the international market rather than to domestic needs. For good or ill, however—and there was plenty to lament about it—a global pattern was established that continues to the present day.

The Population Boom

The population explosion, which Parson Malthus had noticed at the end of the eighteenth century, was in full swing during the nineteenth. The growth and movement of population in the 1800s is another important dimension of the process of global integration stimulated by the Western hegemony of the world.

Statistics are still questionable or nonexistent for much of the world for this period, but informed estimates indicate a global population of 900 million at the beginning of the century, 1.65 billion at the end of it. In the broadest terms, a world population of considerably less than a billion around 1800 had advanced to well over a billion and a half by 1900.

Regional populations in 1900 ran roughly as follows: Asia, 935 million; Europe, 425 million; Africa, 120 million; North America, 100 million; South America, 45 million; and Australia, 5 million. In round terms, well over half the people in the world lived in Asia, another quarter inhabited Europe, and the remaining one fourth were scattered unevenly over the other four continents. The total Western share of world population, however, was growing: people of European descent accounted for about a fifth of the inhabitants of the globe in 1800, a round third in 1930.

Several of the reasons for the global population explosion are closely tied to the Industrial Revolution and the New Imperialism. In Europe and North America, technological improvements in agriculture, new jobs in industry, better plumbing, higher standards of cleanliness, and medical advances certainly contributed. Western industrial and agricultural enclaves in the colonial world also fed and provided jobs for more people, and thereby lengthened life spans. Population growth would accelerate in the non-Western world as food production and medical advances spread in the twentieth century, until by the late 1900s population itself would be one of the world's greatest problems.

There was also an unprecedented amount of population *movement* in the nineteenth century. A major flow of migrants took place from Europe to the other three Europe-dominated continents of North and South America and Australia. The new immigrants came sometimes for political or religious freedom, as in earlier centuries. They fled political repression after the Revolutions of 1848, and they sought to escape eastern European pogroms. More commonly, however, immigrants came for economic reasons. They came for cheap land, or to get rich quick in a gold rush, or simply because there were more opportunities to get ahead in the growing, less class-bound societies of Australia, Argentina, or the United States.

There were substantial movements of population from and to other continents, however. African slaves continued to be transported to the Americas into the nineteenth century, and to the Middle East via Arabia almost until the end of it. Emigrants from India continued their ancient drift down into Southeast Asia and Sri Lanka. But Indians also moved the other way, across the Indian Ocean to East Africa, where they came to outnumber European settlers, to dominate business, and probably to accumulate more money than even the Europeans.

Chinese, feeling the population pinch in that swollen country, spread both southwest into Southeast Asia and east across the Pacific to the western United States. These overseas Chinese became a powerful element in the business life of Southeast Asia and the Pacific, though in the United States many of them became manual laborers or opened small businesses in the segregated Chinatowns of American cities.

There was also considerable internal migration in the 1800s. Millions moved east across Siberia and west across the western part of the United States. Other millions migrated from one part of Europe to another, following the harvest or the shifting needs for industrial labor.

Migration from the countryside to the city, finally, was a central feature of the demographic history of the nineteenth century. The magnet, of course, was the insatiable demand of the new industries for factory hands, miners, transportation workers, and all the service personnel that the new urban environment required. Many of the new cities that resulted mushroomed out of nowhere, called into existence by mineral deposits, transportation hubs, market demands, or investment decisions in faraway board rooms.

These cities were soon more numerous and larger than the most impressive urban complexes of earlier ages. They were also as unsanitary, disease-ridden, and dangerous as any cities in history. Whole families crowded into a single room, entire tenement buildings shared a single toilet. Men, women, and children might suffer from malnutrition or, because all three groups participated in the labor force, from work-related ailments. Workers were often unemployed and sometimes violent. Huge fires were common, devouring miles of rickety tenements before they burned themselves out.

And still they came, drawn by jobs or rumors of jobs, by the bright lights of gas-lit streets, the excitement of the metropolis. Middle- and upper-class people shook their heads, wondering how human beings survived in the East Ends, the Left Banks, the Hell's Kitchens of the world. In fact, many were trapped, far from their home counties or their home countries. There were others, however, who wouldn't have gone back to the monotony of the provinces if you had paid them.

SUMMARY

Westernization—the restructuring of traditional non-Western societies along modern Western lines—became endemic in the new century as peoples around the world coveted Western material advantages. Non-Western peoples also absorbed the languages, religions, ideologies, and other cultural achievements that had originated in Europe. These trends would continue long after the political framework of Western imperialism collapsed half a century later.

The Western hegemony created by the overseas expansion that climaxed in the New Imperialism had a profound global impact. Global integration was advanced immeasurably by the creation of new or expanded intercontinental empires in the last decades of the nineteenth century. The economic demands of the Industrial Revolution now affected the whole world. Trade, investment, resource exploitation, labor allocation, and industrial development were all affected. The new styles of life that resulted also led to an unprecedented global population boom and to massive intercontinental migrations.

SUGGESTED READING

BARRACLOUGH, G., ed. *The Times Atlas of World History.* London: Times Books, 1978. Excellent graphic and cartographic coverage of the evolving global economy.

BARRATT-BROWN, M. *The Economics of Imperialism.* Harmondsworth: Penguin, 1974. A good place to begin on this aspect of intercontinental empire.

BLACK, C. E. *The Dynamics of Modernization.* New York: Harper & Row, Pub., 1966. Theoretical analysis of the transformation of traditional societies into modern ones.

CLARK, G. *The Balance Sheet of Imperialism: Facts and Figures on Colonies.* New York: Columbia University Press, 1936. Statistics on trade, migration, and other factors. See also the accompanying volume, *A Place in the Sun* (New York: Macmillan, 1936), which uses these statistics to consider the question: "Do colonies pay?"

COHEN, B. J. *The Question of Imperialism: The Political Economy of Dominance and Dependence.* New York: Basic Books, 1973. Economic relations in the colonial situation.

DARLING, F. C. *The Westernization of Asia.* Cambridge, Mass.: Schenkman, 1980. Transformations of South, Southeast, and East Asian cultures.

ETIENNE, M., and E. LEACOCK, eds. *Women and Colonization.* New York: Praeger, 1980. Anthropological analysis.

FEIS, H. *Europe, The World's Banker, 1870–1914.* New Haven: Yale University Press, 1934. Old but strong in its basic thesis and pre-World War I focus.

FIELDHOUSE, D. K. *Economics and Empire, 1830–1914.* Ithaca: Cornell University Press, 1973. Economic history of nineteenth-century imperialism.

GEERTZ, C., ed. *Old Societies and New States.* Glencoe, Ill.: Free Press, 1963. Anthropological perspectives.

HARRABIN, J. F. *Atlas of Empire.* New York: Knopf, 1937. The world of intercontinental empires just before the war that triggered their destruction.

LERNER, D. *The Passing of Traditional Society.* Glencoe, Ill.: Free Press, 1963. The change from the viewpoint of the colonized.

MANNONI, O. *Prospero and Caliban.* London: Methuen, 1964. Controversial psychohistorical analysis of settler and native reactions to their relationship.

MAUNIER, R. *The Sociology of Colonies,* trans. E. O. Lorimer. London: Routledge & Kegan Paul, 1949. Legal, racial, psychological aspects.

MEMMI, A. *The Colonizer and the Colonized,* trans. H. Greenfield. New York: Orion Press, 1965. Impact of the colonial experience on both settler and native.

OHLIN, B. *Interregional and International Trade.* Cambridge, Mass.: Harvard University Press, 1935. The world market as shaped by the New Imperialism.

Overview III

The World at War

Future historians may well consider the first half of the twentieth century to have been a step backward in the global drift of history.

The great wars and major revolutions that swept the globe between the early 1900s and mid-century pitted so many nations and peoples against each other—and against themselves—that it is hard to see the period as an advance in the global venture. The two world wars certainly seem to show the world at its most violently divided. The lengthy revolutions in some of the world's largest nations and the rise of cruelly authoritarian governments in many countries seem to reflect the inability of twentieth-century people to live together, even in well-established nations, without inflicting savage injuries on one another.

Yet these traumas, and the glimmerings of peace and material progress sandwiched here and there among them, were also in their way indications of a global future. Over those four or five decades, the major events, trends, achievements, and even disasters were, after all, increasingly global in scope. Even a cursory overview will reveal the extent to which the peoples of the world, once so isolated in their many cultures, had become thoroughly interdependent by the first half of the twentieth century, and historically involved with one another as never before.

World War I, fought mostly in Europe between European armies, was part of the ancient chronicle of continental rivalries that has darkened the history of that strife-torn region of the globe. But non-Europeans also fought in that war, and there were battles beyond the continent. Certainly the causes and consequences of the conflict were global in scale.

The economic history of the earlier part of the century focused still on booms and busts in Western stock markets, fields, and factories. But by the early 1900s, *Western* included North American and other European-settled regions too. The ties of empire, furthermore, linked the economic health of Africa, Asia, and Latin America to the prosperity of the 1920s and the Great Depression of the 1930s in Europe and America.

The earlier decades of the twentieth century also saw the longest and bloodiest ideological revolutions since the Reformation—and unlike those earlier European upheavals, these were global affairs. The Russian revolutionary transformation under Lenin and Stalin, the Chinese civil war that climaxed with Mao's victory, the long and bloody Mexican Revolution all served as models, inspirations, or warnings to whole regions. At least in part because of these revolutions, antiimperialist rebelliousness fermented in many parts of the globe.

The brutal decade of the 1930s was the age of ideological tyranny and aggression in Europe—the age of Hitler and Stalin. But it was also the decade of Japanese militarism and imperialism resurgent in the Far East, of continuing civil war in China, of Mussolini's invasion of Africa, and much more. The thirties were brutal years around the world, not just in the West.

World War II was beyond doubt a global conflict. Its theaters of war included Europe, Asia, Africa, and large sections of the Atlantic and Pacific oceans. Major combatants included great powers of all the inhabited continents except South America. No part of the globe escaped the conflagration unscathed.

It may seem perverse to cite the ruins that littered half the world in 1945 as evidence of the globalization of history. Yet this would seem to be exactly what the global rubble did, unhappily, demonstrate. Confronted with wave after wave of violence that girdled the globe, the survivors found it hard not to recognize, however ruefully, that they all lived on the same planet—that in the future what happened in one part of the world would have to be of concern to all the world's peoples.

Chapter · 14

1900 YESTERDAY

THE FADING CENTER

Turn of the Century

There will perhaps be some who read this book—and certainly some readers will have relatives—who can remember the turn of the present century. Even for those of us who cannot recall it, those years around 1900 may call up vivid, quaint, perhaps oddly comforting impressions.

That was the world of Sherlock Holmes, after all, of fogbound London and horse-drawn hansom cabs, of Queen Victoria and the Empire on Which the Sun Never Set. It was the *belle époque* of wicked gas-lit Paris, the cancan, and the Moulin Rouge. It was German officers and gentlemen strolling with their ladies on the Unter den Linden, music and rich desserts in old Vienna, and pleasantly scruffy young would-be revolutionaries passing out leaflets at factory gates in Moscow.

In other parts of the world too, "1900 yesterday"—as a popular song would later call it—also has a warm and nostalgic flavor. In the United States, the turn of the century is perhaps remembered most pleasantly as lemonade on the long front porch, with the music of a mandolin floating up a tree-lined street. But it was also glittering dinners at Delmonico's or the Waldorf, the smells and color and foreign babble of Hell's Kitchen, the last of the quick-triggered badmen slowly disappearing from the dusty western plains, and Teddy Roosevelt's toothy smile. South of the border, trolleys and electric wires were going up in Buenos Aires, and the gauchos were gone from the pampas. But Pancho Villa would soon be raiding across the Rio Grande; and José Martí, Cuba's most famous writer

and revolutionary, had just died fighting for Cuban freedom from Spain—and fearing a North American imperial predominance to come.

In Asia, the Dowager Empress Tz'u-hsi still ruled in China, the Meiji emperor in Japan. In the Middle Kingdom, the turn of the century calls up violent images of superstitious Boxers charging into Western machine guns in a frantic effort to fling the modern world bodily out of their ancient land. In Japan, by contrast, Tokyo's main street, the Ginza, looked like any European boulevard in 1900, all brick and gas lamps; Western clothing was required at court; and the Christian calendar was used in a Buddhist-Shinto state.

It was, in short, a changing world—as usual. But it was perhaps changing a bit more rapidly in 1900 yesterday than it ever had before.

By way of introduction to our own century, an overview of that turn-of-the-century world follows. We will look first at some of the independent nations of the globe during those years between the 1890s and the outbreak of the First World War in 1914. Thereafter we will survey that very substantial portion of the world that was not independent at all as the twentieth century began.

Lloyd George and Captain Dreyfus

Europe was still the center of a Westernizing world in 1900, the greatest concentration of political power, wealth, and military might on earth. The most prescient pundit or politician would have been astonished to be told that this European predominance, so long in the building, was almost over.

Within fifty years the European hegemony would

have faded. It would give way in the second half of this century to a world of superpowers and global blocs in which a divided Europe would play an important but no longer central part. In the 1890s, however, with what looked like half the exotic peoples of the earth paying homage to Queen Victoria, no one could have foreseen what was to come.

Some of Europe's half dozen great powers of 1900 were the same as those of 1800. Great Britain, France, and Russia were still territorially the nations they had been. Others differed drastically from their counterparts of a century before. Prussia had absorbed most of the German-speaking lands of the former Holy Roman Empire into the German Empire in 1871. Austria had lost these German territories and had had to share power with Magyar leaders in the Austro-Hungarian Dual Monarchy after 1867. And in 1860 the separate Italian states had found unity for the first time since ancient Rome, in the new nation of Italy. As the nineteenth century wound down and the twentieth began, all these nations had their share of problems.

British difficulties in the years around 1900 included the Boer War, continuing Irish agitation for home rule, an increasingly militant campaign for women's suffrage, and growing German economic and naval competition.

The revolt of the rugged Boer farmers in South Africa was eventually crushed, though it required the deployment of hundreds of thousands of British troops and the invention of the concentration camp, all of which cost the British severely in international esteem. A final solution to the long demand for self-government by the Irish Catholics—England's oldest colony—was deferred until after World War I. The same was true of the demand for the vote for women, which swelled into a national crusade under the leadership of Emmeline Pankhurst and her daughters in the 1890s. The dynamic industrial economy of the new German Empire, finally, was growing much more rapidly than Britain's; German goods were shouldering Britain's out of international markets; and the expansion of the German navy made British admirals yearly more nervous. About these problems, little or nothing could be done.

Not all of Great Britain's difficulties, however, were judiciously deferred or dealt with at such cost. In Britain, twenty years of primarily Conservative rule gave way in 1906 to a Liberal predominance in Parliament that was to carry through the First World War. The usual spate of reforms accompanied Liberal supremacy in the world's oldest parliamentary democracy. These reforms ranged from the beginnings of national health insurance and retirement benefits to constitutional limitation on the power of the hereditary House of Lords to veto legislation passed by the elected House of Commons. The most colorful politician of the Liberal period before World War I, the fiery Welsh orator David Lloyd George, even pushed through a government budget specifically aimed at redistribution of wealth from rich to poor through taxes on income and inheritance and other devices. To the liberal-minded, at least, the democratic parliamentary system seemed to be working well enough as the fatal summer of 1914 rose over the horizon.

France, just across the Channel, was in theory even more liberal than Britain. After all, the Third Republic, created in the aftermath of the fall of Emperor Napoleon III in the Franco-Prussian War, had dispensed with even a figurehead monarch. France was the only republic among the European great powers in 1900, and despite serious difficulties, she also seemed to be making democracy work.

Many of France's problems were the legacy of her past—of the century-long series of revolutionary upheavals since 1789 and her more recent humiliating defeat by the Germans in 1870. Politically, the nation was torn by feuds between defenders of the republic and those who longed for the good old days when kings, aristocrats, and priests still ruled French society. The famous Dreyfus case brought this conflict to a head during the later 1890s and the early 1900s. Captain Alfred Dreyfus, a Jewish army captain falsely accused of selling military secrets to the Germans, was finally exonerated, brought back from the Devil's Island penal colony, and even awarded the Legion of Honor. But the outcome came only after years of violent confrontations between liberals and republicans on the one hand, and virulently anti-Semetic supporters of the church, the aristocracy, and "the honor of the army" on the other.

France's industrial economy did not grow as rapidly as Germany's, but her overseas empire was much larger. French irridentist sentiment still demanded the recovery of the "lost provinces" of Alsace and Lorraine, taken by Germany in 1870. But no opportunity for a rematch with her powerful rival across the Rhine presented itself convincingly—until 1914.

The New Nations

Of the two new nations established in the second half of the nineteenth century, the German Empire fared notably better in many ways than the kingdom of Italy.

The shadow of Bismarck stretched across turn-of-the-century Germany, though the Iron Chancellor himself had been in uneasy retirement since 1890. The master diplomat of the second half of the century was widely recognized as the architect of the Hohenzollern German Empire. He had managed to preserve the nation's autocratic royal government while creating the most advanced system of social legislation in Europe. He had presided over the new Germany's remarkable surge of industrial growth and had quietly assembled the majority of her overseas colonies in Africa and Oceania. And he had managed to keep peace among the powers for twenty years in the bargain.

After Bismarck, what was there for Kaiser William II (1888–1918) to do? In fact, the young emperor who retired the great chancellor in 1890 accomplished little—but he did it very noisily indeed.

William II's public clamoring for a place in the imperial sun added few colonies to Germany's total. His aggressive naval buildup only made the British nervous enough to seek an anti-German alliance with France. German industrial growth continued with astonishing speed in the years before World War I, however. And it was a commonplace that the army of Bismarck and Frederick the Great was far and away the best in Europe.

The new Italy was more democratic than the new Germany, but it was never able to play a role in European affairs comparable to that of the powerful German Empire. Italy's economy was handicapped by poor agricultural land and industrial underdevelopment, especially in the south, and by an exploding population that put constant strain on the nation's limited productive capacities. Internationally, the newly unified country suffered a series of rebuffs and setbacks in these years. These misfortunes climaxed in her defeat by the Ethiopians at Adowa in 1896. A humiliating reverse for Italy's imperial aspirations, it was not erased in Italian minds by her seizure of the large Saharan colony of Libya in the early 1900s.

Nevertheless, political and social reforms did highlight Italy's history in the early twentieth century. The country's economic and international problems had bred all sorts of passionate ideological commitments, from socialism and anarchism to nationalism and imperialism. Italy's leading politician during the decade before the First World War, Giovanni Giolitti, manipulated these isms more than he shared them. But he was nevertheless responsible for a great expansion of the suffrage, encouragement of the labor movement, and a good deal of social legislation intended to alleviate the hard lot of the poor.

The Last of Their Lines

If the two new nations of Germany and Italy were a study in contrasts, the long-established Habsburg and Romanov monarchies of Austria-Hungary and Russia had much in common. Both Austria and Russia were ruled by well-meaning if not brilliant autocrats. Both were vast peasant states in which hereditary aristocrats still played a central role. Both had problems with minority nationalities, and neither was as developed industrially as it should have been. Both, finally, had an eye on the Balkan lands of the crumbling Ottoman Empire to the south. This rivalry would inexorably draw these two quite similar ancient states into a fatal face-down in 1914.

Emperor Francis Joseph (1848–1916), Europe's longest-reigning ruler after Queen Victoria, had little imagination but a great deal of experience and a strong sense of obligation to govern. His empire had really been two realms since 1867—an Austrian empire and a Hungarian kingdom, united by a common ruler. Austrian Germans and Hungarian Magyars were the majority populations of this polyglot medieval survival, but there were also millions of Czechs, Slovaks, Yugoslavs (including Serbs), Poles, Ukrainians, Rumanians, and others under Francis Joseph's rule. Many of these peoples had been inflamed by nationalistic zeal by dedicated nineteenth-century ideologues. Parading, demonstating, and disrupting imperial and provincial legislatures, these minority nationalities demanded the autonomy that in the end would pull the empire apart.

A prime source of the nationalistic virus in Austria-Hungary was the small neighboring Balkan state of Serbia. Freed from the Ottoman Empire in the later 1800s, the Serbs were eager to unite with fellow Yugoslavs in the Habsburg realm to form a Greater Serbia. Both the Serbs and the Austrians lusted after the Ottoman provinces of Bosnia and Herzegovina—Serbia for nationalistic reasons, Austria to frustrate these ambitions. When the Austrians annexed the provinces in 1908, the two countries came very close to war. Conflict was avoided, however—or, more accurately, postponed.

Nicholas II (1894–1917), czar of all the Russias, was that perennial downfall of embattled authoritarian regimes, a weak autocrat. Like Charles I in seventeenth-century England or Louis XVI in eighteenth-century France, the last of the czars meant well. But he did not like politics, and he left the country largely in the hands of rigorously authoritarian people such as Procurator Pobedonostsev, head of the holy synod of the Russian Orthodox church, and Minister of the Interior Plehve, head of the notorious Third Section, the czar's secret police. These officials, remembering all too vividly the assassination of the reforming emperor Alexander II in 1881, made no concessions to any ism. They dealt with popular discontent by sowing the land with police and secret agents and by suppressing strikes and student demonstrations with force. They also embarked upon a vigorous campaign to Russify the empire's minority nationalities—Finns and Poles, Baltic Germans, Jews, Armenians, and other conquered peoples.

Paradoxically, however, a major source of trouble was not the reactionary measures of Pobedonostsev and Plehve but the progressive industrializing policies of the czar's minister of finance, Sergius Witte. Witte encouraged industrial growth, mining, oil production, and the building of the Trans-Siberian Railway—and in so doing increased the size of Russia's discontented industrial work force considerably. Such progressive industrial policies, furthermore, did nothing to address the problems of the nation's peasant majority, who, though no longer serfs, still languished in poverty and ignorance as the century turned.

Internal repression and progress that was no progress combined with Russia's ignominious defeat in the Russo-Japanese War to trigger Russia's first twentieth-century rebellion—the Revolution of 1905. The widely hated Plehve was assassinated by a revolutionary terrorist in 1904. On Bloody Sunday in January 1905, a priest named Gapon led thousands of striking workers to the Winter Palace in St. Petersburg to plea for a constitution and better working conditions; they were met by withering rifle fire that killed hundreds in the snow. Within months, strikes paralyzed the economy, nationalistic and other riots flared, and there were even mutinies in the armed services.

Nicholas II responded with what looked like concessions. The October Manifesto promised more freedom and an elected legislative assembly. The assembly, called the Duma, actually met off and on during the decade between the Revolution of 1905 and World War I. In fact, however, the government emasculated both these reluctant concessions to the spirit of liberal reform. The manifesto was never treated as a binding constitution by the czar, and the powers of the Duma were limited so thoroughly that it never became a true Russian parliament. The little-known Russian revolutionary leader, V. I. Lenin, living in exile in Switzerland in 1905, declared grimly that the struggle against the czar was "only beginning."[1]

Turn-of-the-century rulers liked to sit for official portrait photographs, often surrounded by their families, as their predecessors had sat for portrait painters. A famous picture of Emperor Nicholas II and the Russian royal family shows only one smiling face, that of one of the czar's four daughters. The saddest faces of all are those of Alexandra, Nicholas's German empress, and of the imperial heir, Crown Prince Alexis, a tragic little boy afflicted with hemophilia, the shadow of death already draping his thin features.

With the sole exception of Queen Victoria, all the crowned heads mentioned in the last three sections had one unhappy characteristic in common. They were all the last of their lines. Though none of them would have believed it in 1900, Europe's long age of kings and queens had less than twenty years to run as the nineteenth century ended and the twentieth began.

EAST AND WEST

The Rough Rider, The Preacher's Son— and the Big Stick

Things looked better for the world's republics. Flourishing above all in the New World, elected governments, for all their limitations, had greater potential for survival than the European monarchies. The United States in particular enjoyed an impressive political renaissance in the decades around 1900. It was called Progressivism, and it was the first of the great waves of reform that would sweep across the United States during the twentieth century.

The Populist reform agitation of the 1890s, the militance of farmers, and the struggles of organized labor all contributed to the emergence of the Progressive movement. So did a fastidious genteel tradition of disgust at the crooked politics and vulgar greed of America's urban political bosses, corrupt legislators, and new-rich industrialists over the decades since the Civil War. A major source of the Progressive revolt, finally, was a turn-of-the-century surge of investigative reporting by journalists and popular historians called muckrakers. The muckrakers published blistering indictments of the methods and morals of the self-made millionaires of the Gilded Age, yesterday's "captains of industry," now dubbed "robber barons" in the popular press.

Beginning on the state and local levels, Progressive reform stressed increased democracy, challenges to political bosses and party machines, and greater efficiency in government. Progressives also emphasized regulation of big business through such measures as trust-busting—the breakup of corporations so big that they constituted "conspiracies in restraint of trade." The movement also sought some social legislation, including labor laws, tried to help the poor generally, and renewed the struggles for women's rights and "temperance," the outlawing of alcoholic beverages.

[1]Louis Fischer, *The Life of Lenin* (New York: Harper & Row, Publishers, 1964), p. 49.

Theodore Roosevelt and the Panama Canal—a triumph for TR's "big stick" imperialism. The drawing shows him complete with cowboy hat, "Teddy" bear, and the familiar features that made him a cartoonist's delight. (Library of Congress)

During the first two decades of the twentieth century the Progressive movement produced two of the most active and influential presidents in American history: the Republican Theodore Roosevelt (1901–1909) and the Democrat Woodrow Wilson (1913–1921).

They were two very different men. Moustached, big-toothed, roly-poly Roosevelt, the endlessly energetic exponent of vigor in all things, was a vivid personality. A self-made outdoorsman (he had been a sickly child), a national hero as leader of the Rough Riders in the Spanish-American War, and an aggressive reforming governor of New York, Teddy Roosevelt was one of the most popular of presidents. Woodrow Wilson, leaner and far less bumptious in style, a southern preacher's son and former reforming president of Princeton University, took a loftier moral tone. They ran against each other in the crucial election of 1912, Roosevelt preaching a more moderate New Nationalist version of progressivism, Wilson a more liberal New Freedom. Both were eloquent orators in their very different styles, both turned out to be skillful politicians, and both were pioneers of twentieth-century reform politics in America.

Roosevelt busted some trusts—including Standard Oil—regulated the worst abuses of the railroads, meat-packers, and others, and passed some legislation designed to improve working conditions in factories. He was an early conservationist, nationalizing large chunks of wilderness and other natural resources in order to save them from private developers for the nation as a whole. He was no radical, however, and his progressivism was directed rather toward equalizing competitive opportunities for all than toward government care for the unfortunate.

Wilson also began relatively conservatively. During his first term he reformed the tariff in the direction of free trade, stabilized the banking system by establishing regional Federal Reserve banks, and set the Federal Trade Commission to regulating interstate commerce. In 1916, however, he was caught up in a new surge of Progressive reform activity, including credit for farmers in need of loans, an eight-hour working day for factory hands, and other social legislation.

In general, the United States was more conservative in social reform than Europe was—and it still is. But Teddy Roosevelt, Woodrow Wilson, and the Progressives set the U.S. on a path of active government intervention on behalf of the governed that would lead most of the Western world to some form of the welfare state by the second half of the century.

The other side of the American coin in 1900 was the rise of American imperialism.

American overseas expansion was for many simply a natural extension of the continental expansion of the nineteenth century. Indeed the U.S. had already purchased Alaska from the Russians (1867) and taken over Hawaii from her last queen, annexing the islands in 1898. American traders had in fact been jostling Europeans in the "China market" on the far side of the Pacific for the better part of the preceding century.

The Spanish-American War of 1898, however, not only added the Philippines to the scattered Pacific holdings of the United States, it began several decades of aggressive U.S. intervention in the affairs of Middle America and the Caribbean. Teddy Roosevelt encouraged a Central American revolution and then acquired what became the Panama Canal Zone from the victorious revolutionaries in 1903. Woodrow Wilson intervened twice in the great Mexican Revolution that began in 1911. The U.S. Marines also landed to calm troubled regimes and make the Caribbean safer for foreign investors in Nicaragua, Haiti, and elsewhere.

Roosevelt called it the Big Stick; Wilson described it as instruction in democracy; critics labeled it Dollar Diplomacy.[2] In fact, the motives seem to have been a familiar Western imperialist mix of vested economic interests, a missionary zeal for spreading stable democratic government, strategic concerns, and a smug

[2]Teddy Roosevelt made the West African proverb, "Speak softly—and carry a big stick" one of his trademarks.

sense of cultural superiority. Imperial intervention by the United States, as by the other powers, kindled bitter resentment. The Philippines in particular, far from expressing gratitude for liberation from Spain, launched an insurrection against their new American rulers that took years to suppress and cost the United States as much in international approval—and self-esteem—as the Boer War did the British.

For Americans, then, the twentieth century began with a mixture of domestic reforms and foreign wars that would become familiar as the decades passed.

Beef, Bananas, Coffee, and Tin

In Latin America, the economic and political trends of the late nineteenth century reached a climax around 1900. Efforts at reform were much less pronounced than in North America, but then no comparable burst of imperial expansion was generated in the south. Altogether, Latin America was characterized much more by continuities with the 1800s than was the case north of the Rio Grande.

Economic dependency was perhaps the most striking carry-over from the nineteenth century. The Latin American republics continued to depend on the export of agricultural products—beef, wheat, coffee, bananas, and others—and of minerals such as nitrates, copper, tin, and oil to pay for their economic growth. These nations also depended on Europe and North America for imported manufactured goods and for capital to build the fine new streets of Mexico City, Buenos Aires, and Rio de Janeiro.

The results of development through economic dependency, recent scholarship suggests, were far from uniformly good. One obvious consequence was to strengthen the grip of the hacienda—which produced the raw materials for export—on the countryside, and the hold of the export merchants on the growing cities. By contrast, domestic industrial development languished, unable to compete with manufactured goods from Europe and the United States. Progress thus remained skin-deep, a matter of hacienda agriculture and industrial underdevelopment capped by shiny new cities, railroads, and other modern amenities and by imported luxuries for the wealthy few who could afford them.

The *mestizo* and Indian masses, in contrast, remained poor and illiterate. Deprived of their land by growing hacienda power, sucked into mono-cultural plantation labor or mining for export, many Latin Americans could no longer even feed themselves through subsistence farming.

It was a box into which other parts of the world were also sinking, and these regions would sink deeper as the twentieth century advanced. This global division of labor fostered by Western economic predominance was, in fact, to be one of the prime features of twentieth-century world history.

The histories of several of the major Latin American nations during the decades around 1900 illustrate these aspects of life in the other half of the hemisphere. Mexico in the north and the ABC countries of South America—Argentina, Brazil, and Chile—will all be glanced at briefly from this point of view.

Progress and Poverty

Mexico, ruled by the modernizing but brutal dictator Porfirio Díaz from 1876 to 1911, epitomized most of these turn-of-the-century trends. The Díaz dictatorship, which began as a popular constitutional regime, had by 1900 become government by and for large landowners, high churchmen, foreign investors, and growing numbers of generals and government officials. There were rewards, of course. British, United States, and other foreign capital and export profits, operating in the stable social environment produced by repression, had crisscrossed the nation with railroads and made Mexico the world's third largest oil producer and a leader in other mineral and agricultural products as well. But massive land grabs by speculators and hacienda owners, decline in production of ancient food staples such as maize and beans, and widespread peonage left the majority of Mexicans deep in poverty.

Elections were routinely rigged under Díaz, political opposition jailed, peasant discontent suppressed by backcountry policemen called *rurales*, and strikers attacked and even killed by troops. Government intellectuals called the *Científicos* ("Scientifics") pointed proudly to zooming production figures and insisted that economic strength must precede political democracy. As the century turned, however, there was growing opposition to the aging Díaz among peasants, proletarians, the liberal middle classes, and nationalistic opponents of foreign economic predominance. Mexico had little in the way of a progressive reform movement, but it would have its revolution—one of the most significant in Latin American history.

At the other end of Latin America, Argentina illustrated many of these same unhappy trends. But she also revealed the beginnings of both political freedom and radical agitation as the twentieth century began.

Argentina in 1900 was ruled not by a towering individual like Díaz, but by a loose political coalition called the Generation of 1880 (after the period when they came to power), or sometimes simply the Oligarchy. The Oligarchy meant—once more—government by wealthy landowners, export merchants, and foreign capital, especially British. Huge exports of meat and wheat from the rolling pampas made Buenos Aires a modern metropolis and built railways and processing plants. It also led to the usual expropriation of the Indians, land grabs, and peon labor. Argentina's economic boom, the wonder of the south, made her the most industrially developed nation in Latin America. But most of the new wealth stayed in Buenos Aires, where even the hacienda owners now moved to share in the good life.

Politically speaking, Argentina's Oligarchy was more flexible than the Díaz regime far to the north, and even intermittently liberal. In Argentina, undue church influence was curtailed, education was encouraged, labor unions were made legal, and some political dissent was even tolerated. The principal opposition was the so-called Radical party, really a rather moderate middle-class movement whose major achievement was to induce the Oligarchy to grant the nation universal manhood suffrage in 1912. But there were genuine radicals in Argentina too. Socialists and labor-union leaders, many of them European immigrants, were able to organize massive strikes and win a ten-hour-day law early in the 1900s.

Thanks to such piecemeal reforms, Argentina would escape anything like the revolutionary storm that was building in Mexico. And despite the problems of dependency, Argentina was one of the most industrially developed nations outside the Europe–North American axis as the century got under way.

Brazil, Argentina's enormous neighbor to the north, was as strikingly divided, economically, politically, and culturally, as any Latin American land in 1900.

Rio de Janeiro was being rebuilt around its perfect harbor and its trademark, Sugarloaf Mountain, into one of the most beautiful and modern cities in the world. Its new corporate offices, banks, and broad avenues matched anything in Europe or North America. The backlands, by contrast, were dark with the poverty of Indians and blacks who had been slaves until 1888, with the feudal power of great landowners, with rampant banditry and exotic religious cults that were sometimes cruelly suppressed for their radical social views.

The Brazilian monarchy, headed by a Portuguese prince, had been overthrown only in 1890. The alliance of landowners, businessmen, and progressive military officers who had engineered the coup had soon split, and power had fallen largely into the hands of the richest Brazilian landowners, the coffee planters. Brazil produced three quarters of the world's coffee in the early 1900s, and the coffee interests—with the help of foreign bankers—ruled the huge new republic in the decades before 1914.

Foreigners controlled the large banking, transportation, and export-trade businesses. Brazilians—including, however, many new immigrants—built a bustling light-industrial sector, particularly in textiles. In the mills, a Brazilian working class developed—again, composed largely of recent European immigrants. Among these workers, labor unions and socialist agitation began, despite police repression.

Chile, Argentina's long, string-bean neighbor across the Andes to the west, was the third of Latin America's ABC powers. Like the others, it was in many ways a textbook case of the common Latin American mix of progress and poverty.

Chile's economy was dominated by nitrate and copper production, mostly in the northern territories seized from Peru in the War of the Pacific in the early 1880s. The nitrate kings of the north, the owners of the railways, and other economic leaders were British; Germans were powerful in the south. An effort at government stimulation of a Chile-controlled industrial sector had ended with the overthrow of the would-be reformers in the 1890s. Thereafter, foreign capital and foreign influence continued unimpeded into the new century.

Politically, this was the period of Chile's parliamentary republic. Under this regime, the center of power was not in the presidential palace but in the Chilean legislature, where factions representing landowners, priests, business, and foreign interests managed the nation. It was a fundamentally conservative government, but a constitutional and parliamentary one. Growing numbers of factory workers and miners, labor organization, and the beginnings of socialist parties also exerted pressure for social reform. By the First World War, factory legislation had begun to be passed in Chile too.

One way to compare the development of North and South America at the beginning of the twentieth century would be to say that the southern equivalent of the U.S. Gilded Age of gaudy corruption and sometimes impressive economic growth continued unabated in Latin America after 1900. Certainly the southern republics had little to parallel the Progressive movement or the reform leadership of Roosevelt and Wilson in the early 1900s.

One might also point out that despite economic growth in some areas, Latin America had not by the turn of the century developed anything like the huge industrial machine of the United States. And it was this productive capacity that would enable the United States not only to escape European economic domination but to rival and then surpass Europe as an exploiter of economic opportunities in other lands—including Latin America—in the twentieth century.

Self-Strengthening That Failed

China around 1900 was at the depths of her century-long decline. It is hard to recognize, in that spectacle of late-Manchu decay, either the ancient empire of the East or the new China of the present day.

Following a disastrous series of mid-century conflicts—wars with Britain and France, the Taiping Rebellion—China had embarked upon a decades-long program of "self-strengthening." This rather desultory campaign, presided over by the immensely conservative Dowager Empress Tz'u-hsi (1835–1908), focused first on modernizing the Chinese military, then on encouraging the growth of merchant wealth in order to further strengthen the nation. The aim was to adopt a few Western techniques while retaining the essence of China's ancient civilization.

It had not worked. A new round of Western imperialism had seen Europeans seize control of a number of traditionally Chinese tributary states in the later nineteenth century and force concessions of leases and development rights to territories on the Chinese mainland. In 1895 Japan—which had flung itself much more wholeheartedly into Westernization—had humiliated China in the Sino-Japanese War. In 1900

The "Old Buddha," Dowager Empress Tz'u-hsi, symbol and sustainer of China's ancient civilization. Her defiance of changing times and Western power left China almost helpless at the turn of the century. (Library of Congress)

the Boxer Rebellion had brought Western armies back to Peking, with China's armies being swept aside once more in the process, and had left the nation saddled with a huge indemnity and even more Westerners.

At the beginning of the the twentieth century, then, China was filled with tumultuous dispute over more drastic reforms, about educational changes and constitutions, even about revolution. And now the debate focused on the core of the Chinese system: on the ancient Confucian administrative system that had served the nation so well for so long, and on the Manchu monarchy itself.

Tz'u-hsi's clawlike hand still moved to frustrate any reform that touched her own power. When the impressionable young Kuang-hsü emperor attempted the Hundred Days reform campaign after the Sino-Japanese War, she choked it off, executing some of the reformers and driving others into exile in Japan. When a constitution was actually drawn from her reluctant fingers after the Boxer debacle, she certainly had reservations as strong as any czar's about granting actual power to even quasi-democratic institutions.

Change, however, had to come to the battered Middle Kingdom. It would come only after Tz'u-hsi's death, when China was plunged into the longest revolution of the twentieth century, not to know peace again until 1949. And by that time, she would have yielded her customary primacy in East Asia to a much more enthusiastic Westernizer—the island kingdom of Japan.

The Most Powerful Nation in Asia

Japan at the turn of the century was a nation in rapid and vigorous transition. "Restore the Emperor and expel the Barbarian" had been the cry of the Meiji reformers of thirty years before.[3] The first objective had certainly been accomplished; but by 1900, Western "barbarian" influences were everywhere in the new Japan.

The Meiji Emperor (1867–1912), whose restoration to full power in 1868 had begun Japan's spectacular modern development, still ruled in 1900. Politically and economically, the land he ruled was a very different place from the Japan Commodore Perry had "opened" in the 1850s. And Japan's aggressively imperialistic foreign policy was already setting the expansionist pattern she would follow throughout the first half of the twentieth century.

Politically, Meiji Japan had developed a complex

[3]Ruth Benedict, *The Chrysanthemum and the Sword: Patterns of Japanese Culture* (Boston: Houghton Mifflin, 1946), p. 76.

constitutional structure that amounted to rule through the cooperation and competition of separate and often rivalrous elites. The emperor himself enjoyed great respect and the power to appoint officials up to and including the prime minister—though he customarily delegated this responsibility to a group of elder statesmen. The political parties of the Diet, the Japanese legislature, passed laws and voted on the budget in a very Western way, but had little of the power exercised by a European parliament, whose leader was also typically the political leader of the nation. The imperial bureaucracy, led by brilliant if conservative Tokyo Law School graduates, also had a good deal of authority in the nation. The army and the navy, finally, had great prestige because of their victories: the military had no civilian superiors in Japan except the emperor himself.

It was a complicated political system, one that could easily have evolved in more than one way. In the twentieth century it moved in two directions—toward military control in the first half of the century, toward democracy in the second half.

Economically, Japan was in the middle of a boom in 1900, and that surge of economic growth accelerated into the new century. Between 1900 and 1940, Japan's exports of raw materials would triple and her overseas sales of manufactured goods would multiply a dozen times. Her population would also explode once more, from 44 million in 1900 to 78 million in 1940, absorbing at least some of her economic gains. But the direction toward mushrooming growth was clear—and impressive.

The heart of Japan's expanding industrial, commercial, and financial economy was the small group of superrich business families known as the *zaibatsu*. These equivalents of the German Krupps or the American Rockefellers included such powerful industrial dynasties as the Mitsubishi, Mitsui, Kawasaki, and half a dozen other major firms.

Expanding to control a spectrum of ventures from mining and manufacturing to shipping and commerce, *zaibatsu* clans such as Mitsui and Mitsubishi may, in fact, have been the biggest privately owned corporations in the world. They made Japan's economic growth possible. They also had a powerful say in politics, thanks to close ties with the bureaucracy and—as in Europe and America—to substantial contributions to the campaign funds of political parties.

During the turn-of-the-century decades, finally, Japanese imperialism was a central factor in Far Eastern affairs. Japan's decisive victories over the world's two largest land empires—China in 1895 and Russia in 1905—astonished the world. Just as the United States regarded the Western Hemisphere as her bailiwick, so Japan clearly saw the Far East as her own back yard. It was not unlikely that these two dynamic, expansive nations on opposite sides of the Pacific would themselves come to blows sooner or later.

In 1900 the Western imperial powers tried with some success to limit Japan's gains from her initial victories. But there was no question that modernizing Japan was the most powerful nation in Asia—and no clear notion just how far she might go in the century just beginning.

THE WESTERN EMPIRES AND THE SPIRIT OF RESISTANCE

The View from Shepheard's Hotel

It is to the great Western intercontinental empires themselves, finally, that we must come at the end of this overview of the world at the beginning of the twentieth century.

Shepheard's Hotel in Cairo would have been the ideal place for a Westerner to sit and contemplate the world as the nineteenth century drew to a close. Cairo was centrally located—geographically in Africa, yet in local color and mood thoroughly east-of-Suez. It was also anomalous, like so much of the New Imperialism: nominally ruled by a *khedive* who was officially subject to the Ottoman sultan, turn-of-the-century Egypt was in fact governed by Lord Cromer, the British resident in Cairo. It was, finally, properly exotic and mysterious, thick with bazaars and mosques, a few miles' ride from the Pyramids.

The view from the terrace at Shepheard's—over a cold sherbet, say—would have been horses and carriages, pith helmets, starched frocks, and Western uniforms. For this most famous hotel in imperial Cairo faced the Ezbekiyeh Gardens in the heart of the European section. The imitation French architecture around the square, obsequious waiters in red sashes and *kepis*, urgent multilingual *dragomans* (guides or interpreters) eager to show you the wonders of the pharaonic past could give the Western tourist a lordly sense of being the master of all he surveyed. But there were only 25,000 Europeans in Cairo, and almost half a million Egyptians.

A short walk from the Ezbekiyeh would put one in the heart of the real Cairo, in all its exotic profusion. Arabs, Turks, Copts, water carriers, sherbet sellers, mule wagons, camels, *fellahin* in from the villages, bedouin in from the desert jostled and jeered and bargained and shouted. Shimmering silken robes mingled with the black gowns and veils of women, the *tarboosh* and the Syrian shawl. The streets were narrow and winding, with Arabesque latticing and carved gates, protruding second stories, whitewashed walls, narrow courtyards, and the clutter and din and clutching hands of the bazaars. At the end of every street, gleaming above the immense vitality of the city, rose the domes and minarets of a mosque.

This section will be concerned largely with what one could see from the terrace at Shepheard's, with the new world order the imperialists were building. But while we watch the changes come, we should remember that that other, older world was there all the time—and that it is there still.

The Resistance

The major intercontinental empires of a hundred years ago were among the most amazing human institutions ever constructed. Earlier empires—China, Rome, Persia, even the looser hegemonies of the Mongols and the Muslims—had grown over land, by gobbling up neighbors and turning them into provinces. The modern European empires grew over water, adding territories scattered over the globe. Over several centuries, then, a single European power could accumulate colonies in all parts of the world—Asia, Africa, the Americas, the islands of Oceania, and other places.

It is an astonishing picture, this world of the Western hegemony as it existed in 1900 yesterday. But it omits one crucial element, which must be included if the history of the world in the next century is to make any sense: resistance.

The rest of the world did not take kindly to the Western predominance. Even in the face of ironclads and Maxim guns, the other peoples of the globe resisted Western aggression. It was a disorganized, usually hopeless resistance, but it was a beginning. Within a long half century, it would emerge triumphant.

The colonial wars and revolts, the reform movements and embryonic nationalist groups of the late nineteenth and early twentieth centuries were of two types. We may call them traditional and progressive.

The large majority of these antiimperialist movements were traditionalist rebellions. They were rooted in ancient religions or long-established social structures and political loyalties. Such revolts could mobilize large numbers of ill-organized and poorly equipped native peoples against the new order of things imposed upon them from without. Almost always, they failed.

A few of these nineteenth-century movements, however, were the work of Westernized minorities in colonial areas. These people recognized the necessity of learning some of the organizational, technological, and military skills developed by the West if they were ever to expel the Westerners from their homelands. This approach was progressive not in any moral sense, but simply in that it reflected a determination to master the latest technical advances in order to use them against their inventors. It was an approach that had a much more successful future in the century that began in 1900.

There were prototypes for both these forms of resistance to Western imperialism as early as the 1850s. The Indian Mutiny was a traditionalist rebellion that resulted in an intensification of the British grip on India. The opening up of Japan in that same mid-century decade, however, set the Japanese on a crash course of modernization that enabled her not only to escape Western imperialism but to join the ranks of the imperialists by the end of the century.

A brief survey of some of the major revolts will at least give some idea of the variety and extent of the resistance even at the high tide of the great conquest.

Khartoum and the Little Big Horn

Continent by continent, it was a violent picture, a montage of fire and passion very different from anything the tourist would see over his cool sherbet on the terrace at Shepheard's.

In Africa the British faced a pair of rebellions in their Egyptian protectorate, the Mahdist movement in the Sudan in the 1880s and 1890s, and wars with the Zulus and the Matabele in South Africa and with the fierce Ashanti in the West African Gold Coast (today's Ghana) in 1900. The French had to deal with rebellions in Tunisia and Madagascar and with insurrections in French West Africa. These latter included a long resistance by the Mande, who in earlier centuries had built some of the most impressive kingdoms of the Western Sudan.

The Germans were challenged by indigenous peoples in almost all their African colonies after 1900. Their savage repression of the Maji-Maji revolt (1905–1907) in what is today Tanzania has lived as one of the most brutal assertions of Western supremacy. The Portuguese, the Belgians, and the Italians also confronted armed resistance in Africa in the late nineteenth and early twentieth centuries.

In Asia the British experienced determined opposition when they invaded Burma in the 1880s, and terrorism in both eastern and western India. The French met decades of armed defiance all over French Indochina. One of their most persistent opponents was the guerrilla Ham Nghi, who fought them from the colony's mountain spine in the 1880s. There were revolts against the Dutch in Java and Sumatra. A bitter guerrilla movement was directed against the American occupation of the Philippines at the turn of the century. The Boxer Rebellion of 1899–1900 in North China sought the destruction of all Westerners of whatever nationality in that country.

The final stages of United States and Russian continental expansion involved bitter fighting. Russian troops pushing south into the Caucasus faced decades of savage resistance from fierce mountaineers under Shamil, "destroyer of the unbeliever." There was a widespread revolt in Muslim central Asia against the Russian authorities as late as the First World War.

The expanding United States, as we noted above, faced recurrent resistance all across the North American continent and overseas as well. In the eastern United States, the most celebrated nineteenth-century fight was probably that of the Seminoles in Florida, who refused to take the Trail of Tears. In the West, the raids of the horseriding Plains Indians took decades to suppress. In the Philippines, the 1900 insurrection cost tens of thousands of Filipino lives.

Religion provided the impetus and inspiration for many of these resistance movements, including Islam in Africa, the Middle East, and Russia; Hinduism in India; the Ghost Dance among the American Plains Indians; and peasant polytheism in China. Other movements were tribal in origin, such as the resistance of the Mande, Ashanti, and Zulu people in Africa and that of the Moros in the Philippines. Sometimes traditionalist revolts fought doggedly in defense of traditional rulers, such as the emperors in Cambodia and Vietnam.

Modernizing or progressive rebellions were most common in Asia, where structured government, urban environments, and all the skills necessary for a changeover to Western ways already existed. Two of the most striking such modernization movements were the Persian Revolution of 1905 and the Young Turk revolt in 1908. Both were directed against antiquated indigenous governments that seemed likely to surrender their country to the Europeans. Both movements aimed, with some success, to modernize their nations sufficiently to withstand further Western aggression.

A peaceful modernizing movement with a long future was the Congress party, organized by professional people in India in 1885. In the next century Indian leaders such as Gandhi and Nehru would rise in this party and lead the country to independence after World War II. As we shall see, Mahatma Gandhi's nonviolent methods were rooted deep in Hindu traditions, but his goals included a great deal that was thoroughly Western.

With spears and machetes and rifles, with ancient prayers and traditional battle cries, they resisted. With what Western technology and bits of Western ideology they could muster, they strove to expel the foreigners. Homekeeping Europeans could shrug off such manifestations of discontent. It was not quite so easy for the soldiers of empire to ignore.

General "Chinese" Gordon and General George Custer had very little in common besides their unhappy fates. Gordon died at Khartoum in the Sudan at the hands of the Mahdi, Custer at the Little Big Horn in Montana, cut down by Sitting Bull's Sioux. Such victories for the resistance were rare. But the spirit of resistance was not.

SUMMARY

The world at the beginning of the present century was in the grip of rapid and accelerating change.

Europe was in its golden afternoon, still the most powerful continent in the world, but entering the century that would end that predominance. British problems included the Boer War in Africa, Irish demands for independence, German competition in the commercial world, and the suffragette movement at home. Nevertheless, Britain's parliamentary government continued to serve her well, and her empire was still the world's largest. France survived the Dreyfus case and the larger struggle between republican liberals and conservative supporters of an older social and political order.

The new Germany of Bismarck and William II was militarily master of the continent, had an advanced welfare system, and was rapidly overtaking the British industrially. The more liberal new nation of Italy, economically underdeveloped, nevertheless followed the path of reform in 1900. Conservative Austria and reactionary Russia both had huge backward peasant populations, militant minority nationalities, and conflicting interests in the Balkans. Russia experienced her first twentieth-century revolution as early as 1905, in the wake of her humiliating defeat by the Japanese.

Across the Atlantic, the United States experienced a great surge of political reform in the Progressive movement, led at the national level by the rival politicians Teddy Roosevelt and Woodrow Wilson. The United States also directed the expansionist drive of the preceding century overseas in its imperialist outreach of the Spanish-American War and Dollar Diplomacy.

South of the Rio Grande, the Latin American repub-

lics continued to be economically dependent on Europe—and increasingly on North America. Politically, autocratic regimes like that of Diáz in Mexico were common, though more flexible authoritarian governments like Argentina's Generation of 1880 or Chile's Parliamentary Republic were also to be found. Unlike most of the caudillos of the nineteenth century, these turn-of-the-century authoritarian governments often did bring basic if badly distributed progress to their countries. The result was a continent of contrasts as epitomized in Brazil, where modern cities and backwoods poverty were equally in evidence.

Beyond the Pacific, China seemed on the verge of collapse, while Japan was clearly on the rise in 1900. The Chinese Empire, battered by a mid-century round of wars and revolution, attempted only halfhearted modernization under Tz'u-hsi and lost more

territory and power to Europeans as a consequence. Japan, by contrast, had already developed a more efficient government, zaibatsu big business, a powerful military machine capable of defeating both China and Russia, and soaring imperialistic ambitions of her own.

The Western intercontinental empires were at their height in 1900. Britain and France had the largest, but older powers like Spain, Portugal, and the Netherlands still had overseas holdings, as did newcomers like Germany, Belgium, Italy, the United States, and Japan. However, the colonies were never willing victims, and rebellions were frequent. The revolts were normally crushed, but more progressive movements, learning from Western imperialists, were harbingers of things to come.

SUGGESTED READING

BEASLEY, W. G.   The Meiji Restoration. Stanford: Stanford University Press, 1973. Masterful study by a mature scholar. For an intriguing sociocultural study of the Meiji Restoration and its background, see H. D. Harootunian, Towards Restoration: The Growth of Political Consciousness in Tokugawa Japan (Berkeley: University of California Press, 1970).

CAMERON, M.   The Reform Movement in China, 1848–1912. Stanford: Stanford University Press, 1931. Old but still standard account of late Manchu attempts at reform.

CHAPMAN, G.   The Dreyfus Case: A Reassessment. Westport, Conn.: Greenwood, 1979. An able critique of France's great turn-of-the-century crisis.

COCHRAN, T., and W. MILLER.   The Age of Enterprise: A Social History of Industrial America. New York: Harper, 1961. Older but still recommended for coverage of big business in the age of the robber barons. See also E. Kirkland, Industry Comes of Age, 1860–1897 (New York: Holt, Rinehart & Winston, 1961), and F. L. Allen, The Big Change: America Transforms Itself, 1900–1950 (New York: Harper, 1962).

EKIRCH, A.   Progressivism in America. New York: New Viewpoints, 1974. Good survey of the American Progressive Movement. Equally solid is W. O'Neill, The Progressive Years (New York: Dodd, Mead, 1975).

EVANS, R.   The Feminists: Women's Emancipation Movements in Europe, America, and Australasia 1840–1920. New York: Barnes & Noble, 1977. Good comparative study.

HALE, O. J.   The Great Illusion, 1900–1914. New York: Harper & Row, Pub., 1971. Europe at the turn of the century—and on the eve of the Great War. See also B. Tuchman, The Proud Tower (New York: Bantam, 1972).

HARCAVE, S.   First Blood: The Russian Revolution of 1905. New York: Macmillan, 1964. The dress rehearsal for the revolutions of 1917.

HENDERSON, W. O.   The Rise of German Industrial Power, 1834–1914. Berkeley: University of California Press, 1975. Expert presentation of the economic growth that accompanied Germany's political unification and military achievements in the later nineteenth century. But see also L. L. Farrar, Jr., Arrogance and Anxiety: The Ambivalence of German Power, 1848–1914 (Iowa City: University of Iowa Press, 1981).

HUGHES, H. S.   Consciousness and Society: The Reorientation of European Social Thought, 1890–1930. New York: Random House, 1961. Perceptive interpretation of major shifts in the tone and content of European thinking after the turn of the century.

LAVRIN, A., ed.   Latin American Women: Historical Perspectives. Westport, Conn.: Greenwood, 1978. Essays including studies of this period.

LINK, A. S.   Woodrow Wilson and the Progressive Era. New York: Harper & Row, Pub., 1954. Authoritative account.

MAY, E.   Imperial Democracy: The Emergence of America as a Great Power. New York: Harcourt, Brace and World, 1961. Outline of America's surge to international prominence even before World War I.

MOWRY, G.   The Era of Theodore Roosevelt, 1900–1912. New York: Harper, 1958. Older but lucid overview of American politics at the beginning of the century. See also the extremely readable life of Roosevelt by J. M. Blum, The Republican Roosevelt (Cambridge, Mass.: Harvard University Press, 1954).

O'NEIL, W.   Everyone Was Brave: The Rise and Fall of Feminism in America. Chicago: Quadrangle Books, 1969. Widely commended summary of American feminism on the road to the suffrage amendment. For the women of the settlement-house movement in the nation's slums, see A. Davis, *American Heroine: Life and Legend of Jane Addams* (New York: Oxford University Press, 1973).

PURCELL, V. *The Boxer Uprising: A Background Study*. Cambridge: Cambridge University Press, 1963. Best book on the rebellion. See also the excellent article by F. Wakeman, Jr., on the recurring Chinese problem of peasant revolts, "Rebellion and Revolution: The Study of Popular Movements in Chinese History," *Journal of Asian Studies*, 36 (1977), 201–237.

SAFFORD, F. *The Ideal of the Practical: Columbia's Struggle to Form a Technical Elite*. Austin: University of Texas Press, 1976. Highly recommended study of this aspect of modernization.

SETON-WATSON, H. *The Decline of Imperial Russia, 1855–1914*. New York: Praeger, 1956. Knowledgeable history of Russia from reform to revolution.

SCHORSKE, C. E. *Fin-de-Siecle Vienna: Politics and Culture*. New York: Knopf, 1980. A crucial time and place for the evolution of modern culture, subtly evoked and analyzed.

TANNENBAUM, E. R. *1900: The Generation Before the Great War*. Garden City, N.Y.: Anchor Press, 1976. Well-illustrated book capturing the tenor of life on the eve of the "century of total war."

Chapter · 15

THE WAR TO END WAR

THE WORLD BEHIND
THE SHOTS AT SARAJEVO

The Terrorist

For many historians, the twentieth century began with two pistol shots on a sun-drenched, crowded street in the ancient Balkan city of Sarajevo. The man who pulled the trigger was a slightly built nineteen-year-old terrorist named Gavrilo Princip, an agent for a Slavic nationalist organization called Union or Death, popularly known as the Black Hand. The chief victim was the archduke Francis Ferdinand, heir to the throne of Austria-Hungary. The consequences of those two shots, fired on June 28, 1914, were the terrible guns of August, the beginning of the greatest war in human history up to that time.

Around that moment in Sarajevo—the excited crowds, the open cars approaching, the man with the plumed helmet and bemedaled chest, the woman in the wide summer hat—swirled a maelstrom of events, deeper causes, and incalculable consequences.

The Black Hand was centered in neighboring Serbia—the core of today's Yugoslavia—and was dedicated to the unification of all Yugoslav ("South Slav") peoples into what was then thought of as Greater Serbia. The prime enemy of Slavic unity, as Serbian nationalists saw it, was the Austro-Hungarian Empire. Hence the choice of the Habsburg heir as a symbolic victim. Hence also Austria's violent response to this act of terrorism: accusation, ultimatum, and, a month after the assassination, declaration of war upon Serbia.

Bad news for little Serbia, whose government probably had no part in the crime, and whose dreams of becoming the Prussia of South Slav unification were thus drastically reversed. But worse news for Europe as a whole—and disturbing news for the world at large.

The great powers of Europe in 1914 were locked into two opposing alliances. These treaty obligations were in some cases several decades old. The main coalitions were the Central Powers, Germany and Austria, on the one hand, and the *Entente* ("Understanding") or simply the Allies, comprising primarily Great Britain, France, and Russia, on the other. Established to keep the peace or to defend the legitimate interests of the members, these rival alliances were now to prove a deadly snare, sucking one power after another into a widening war that would quickly engulf all Europe.

Thus Serbia had a patron among the great powers, the Russia of Nicolas II, which announced that she would mobilize in support of her little Slavic brother. Habsburg Austria's strongest ally, William II's Germany, gave Vienna a diplomatic blank check, promising support for whatever action she took against Serbia. Tension thus mounted through July.

Russia's ally—and Germany's archenemy—France meanwhile seized the opportunity to put diplomatic pressure on Berlin. Britain hesitated, hoping to exercise a moderating influence on the increasingly belligerent powers. But when Germany's elaborate war plans led German armies to violate Belgian neutrality on their way into France, London honored its commitments to the *Entente* and declared war on the Central Powers. The guns of August thundered over the continent.

Bad news for Europe, but strange news also for a

larger world that had become used to the monolithic granite face of European mastery. For the peoples of the globe were now about to see that pale, enigmatic effigy of the world-conquering West cracked and fissured by the greatest war in history.

Gavrilo Princip's Browning revolver put a bullet into the Duchess Sophy's stomach and blew a gouting hole in the side of Archduke Francis Ferdinand's neck. But the terrorist of Sarajevo did a great deal more than kill the unhappy royal heir. His were truly shots heard and felt around the world.

One Thing You Can't Do with Bayonets

As is usual with such historic disasters, there were deeper causes for the First World War. Among those most often cited are rival nationalisms, economic competition, and militarism—what we call today an arms race.

Nationalism, perhaps the most powerful of the nineteenth-century European ideologies, had turned chauvinistic in the latter part of the last century. French patriots dreamed of revenge on Germany for France's humiliating defeat in the Franco-Prussian War of 1870. Russian nationalists aspired to a pan-Slavic sphere in eastern Europe—dominated by Russia, of course. And the tangled and conflicting nationalisms of the Balkans—Magyar, Czech, Slovak, Serbian, Greek, and others—had already kindled two brief Balkan Wars (1912–1913) before World War I even began. National feeling was thus a Europe-wide problem; when the war began, people danced in the streets of Paris and Berlin, Vienna and St. Petersburg.

The central economic rivalry in Europe at the beginning of the twentieth century was the competition between Europe's two leading industrial powers, Great Britain and the German Empire. Britain had first developed the new industrial-power sources and forms of economic organization of the Industrial Revolution in the later eighteenth century. For a hundred years, "Steam," as the popular saying went, was "an Englishman." After the unification of Germany in 1871, however, that nation's already formidable industrial potential had flowered astonishingly. By the turn of the century, Germany's dynamic new industrial plant was pushing past Britain's now antiquated technology to lead Europe in production. Such competition bred bad blood and lent a note of practical national interest to the patriotic fervor of nationalists on both sides.

Militarism was a problem long before nuclear weapons made atomic-age weaponry the transcendent national issue it has become. The new technology and the new wealth of the Industrial Revolution made huge, mechanized military machines affordable even in peacetime. Large military expenditures were soon being built into national budgets, millions of young men conscripted into national armies to be prepared for war if war should come.

Militarism gave special prominence to military leaders—to Germany's famous General Staff, for example, or to admirals in Britain. Arms races also inevitably developed. The most famous of these was the rivalry in fleet construction between a Germany eager for a slice of overseas empire and a Britain determined to maintain her naval preeminence over any conceivable foe. "All this," as a prominent historian of the period pointed out half a century ago, "was done in the name of peace, for it was argued that the best insurance against war was national preparedness."[1] In the end, however, Napoleon's shrewd remark that you can do anything with bayonets except sit on them proved more to the point than slogans about preparedness.

Conflict East of Suez

But there were still other sources of friction besides the fundamentally European conflicts created by alliances, nationalism, economic competition, and militarism. There was in addition a nexus of intercontinental issues created in large part by the colonial rivalries of the New Imperialism.

Some of the causes already cited were partially rooted in the renewed scramble for overseas territories after 1870. Chauvinistic nationalism fed on imperial conquest. Naval buildups were clearly related to establishing, maintaining, and defending empires beyond the seas.

Specifically colonial disputes made alliances between imperial rivals such as Britain and France (in Africa and Southeast Asia) and Britain and Russia (in Persia and Afghanistan) particularly difficult. But more divisive imperial competition developed in the early twentieth century between powers on opposite sides in 1914, and these colonial rivalries help to explain the feuds that led to war.

Germany and Britain, for instance, faced significant areas of conflict in both Africa and the Middle East. Britain objected to Germany's rapid establishment of colonies in Southwest Africa (Namibia today) and expecially in Tanganyika (Tanzania) in East Africa. The British were also made nervous by Germany's cultivation of the Ottoman Turkish sultan,

[1]F. Lee Benns, *European History since 1870* (New York: Appleton-Century-Crofts, 1938), p. 325.

seeing the German dream of a Berlin-to-Bagdad railway as a threat to Britain's lifeline to India at Suez. The British were especially incensed when William II sent an encouraging message to Britain's rebellious Afrikaner subjects in South Africa during the Boer War.

France's resentment of Germany, rooted in the Franco-Prussian War, was considerably exacerbated by German competition for Morocco. Disagreements over this remaining strip of North African coast produced the two Moroccan crises of 1905 and 1911. The French were also disturbed at the German development of a colony in the Cameroons, which thrust up into the solid block of French West and French Equatorial Africa.

Germany, for her part, grew increasingly angry over these same conflicts. German imperialists and militarists felt that the sprawling British imperial presence blocked German expansion around the world. They believed that France's victory—with British support—in the two Moroccan crises, climaxing in a French protectorate over the area, represented signal diplomatic defeats for Germany. These setbacks would have to be compensated for at the next opportunity.

Czarist Russia, the great power of eastern Europe, also had its share of frustrated imperial aspirations. Russia's ambitions to take control of the Turkish straits from the enfeebled Ottomans was of long standing. Russia felt an increasing need to control the entrance to the Black Sea, where lay Russia's only seaports not

closed by ice for a large part of the year. Here, however, Russia's ambitions conflicted with Germany's hopes for German predominance in Turkey.

The Balkan tinderbox itself was part of this larger, extra-European picture. The Balkans and the tensions that divided them were after all part of the legacy left by the decay of the once glorious Ottoman Empire. Russia's support of these new Slavic nations against their old Muslim overlord intensified the feeling that led Turkey to join the Germans and the Austrians in the Great War.

Conflicts south of the Mediterranean and east of Suez thus played their part in bringing on World War I. These areas, and regions still further afield, would be importantly involved in the war itself. And the world as a whole would be vitally affected by what Woodrow Wilson would call the War to End War.

HAMBURGER IN THE MUD OF FLANDERS FIELDS

1914–1918

The world has supped so full of horrors in this century that the "frightfulness" of the War of 1914–1918 may no longer shake us as it shook the generations who fought the Great War. It is perhaps hard for people who have grown used to the notion of a nuclear holocaust to empathize with a time that could still see

Casualties of the Great War. Millions were killed, millions more crippled, blinded, or shellshocked by the most terrible war in human history up to that time. (The Bettmann Archive, Inc.)

submarine warfare as cowardly piracy and machine guns and barbed wire as atrocities. We have gotten used to the grisly photographs of No-Man's-Land, and to disturbing verses written by young men who would soon become part of some forgotten battlefield.

As for the impact of the Great War on the world—the very phrase Lost Generation has become a cliché, and the Peace of Versailles has no more resonance than the Congress of Vienna. Nevertheless, an effort must be made to bring both the war and its consequences back to life. Both have left their marks upon all our lives.

The leaders were as varied a lot as the nations they led. The Allies were for the most part the democracies: Britian under the charismatic Welsh reformer David Lloyd George; France under the belligerently nationalistic Georges Clemenceau, sometimes called the Tiger; and the United States under the preacher's son turned Progressive reformer, Woodrow Wilson. But the Allies also included Russia, the most unrelentingly autocratic of the powers, under Nicholas II, and imperialistic Japan, thrusting her way to prominence in the Far East.

The key leaders of the Central Powers in 1914 were thorough autocrats, but were otherwise totally different. William II, the German emperor, was an aggressive expansionist who liked to pose, moustaches bristling, going over war maps with his generals. Aged Francis Joseph, the Austro-Hungarian emperor, was so opposed to war that he had to be tricked into signing the declaration of war against Serbia by a fake telegram reporting a Serbian invasion.

A traditional way to approach the war these men made is in terms of the great offensives that marked the coming of each new year. A list of some of the more famous of them may stir faint echoes of forgotten heroism. For there was heroism amid the horrors of the Great War.

There was, for instance, a race to Paris as a new generation of Germans strove to emulate their grandfathers' quick victory in 1870—and failed. There was a race to the sea, French and Germans striving to outflank each other until they reached the Channel and could go no further. There was the Gallipoli campaign of 1915, aimed at opening the Turkish straits into the Black Sea—the very name a symbol for futile loss of life.

There was the great German offensive at Verdun in 1916, when Frenchmen fell in unthinkable numbers for the ringing watchword "They shall not pass"—and the Germans did not. There was the colossal British offensive on the Somme, also in 1916, weeks of carnage that began with so many tens of thousands of British casualties in a twenty-four hour period that it has been described as the blackest day in the history of the British army. There was Caporetto in 1917, the debacle on the Italian front that was Hemingway's *Farewell to Arms*. There was the last great heave of the Kerensky offensive in Russia, again in 1917, which turned beaten Russian soldiers against their own officers, and against the politicians who had sent them off to the front once more.

After such offensives, all sides were exhausted and reeling by 1917. There were mutterings of peace in Austria and even in Germany. There were riots in Italian munitions factories, mutinies in ten divisions of the French army, and revolution in Russia. But 1917 was also a year of startling reversals and renewed hope for both sides, and these developments built toward the climactic battles of 1918.

A British naval blockade, imposed from the beginning of the war, led Germany to respond with something new—a massive submarine campaign against all shipping attempting to reach the British Isles. Both the blockade and the submarine campaign were having their effect by 1917. But the undersea war had an unfortunate side effect: it so outraged neutrals trying to trade with Britain that in 1917 it led Woodrow Wilson to bring the United States into the war on the Allied side—a major setback to German hopes of victory.

This pivotal year, however, also saw the abdication of the Russian czar, the subsequent seizure of power by the Bolsheviks, and their decision to pull battered Russia out of the war unilaterally. Thus if the Central Powers faced the long-run threat of huge American reinforcements, in the short run Germany could close down her eastern front and concentrate her forces for crushing offensives in the west.

This Generals Hindenburg and Ludendorff attempted to do in the summer of 1918. Three mighty German assaults hurled the Allies back dozens of miles and came as close to breaking through to Paris as Germany ever came. But France's Marshal Foch, enjoying for the first time a unified supreme command of the Allied armies, and reinforced by waves of fresh American troops, stemmed the German tide. As a cold, wet autumn settled over Europe, the war ground to a halt. An armistice was declared on November 11, 1918. The biggest, bloodiest, and, as it increasingly seemed to contemporaries, most pointless war in the history of the world was over.

No-Man's-Land

An analysis in terms of leaders and campaigns is traditional for great wars. But it is probably not the best approach to this one.

Studies of World War I have generally recognized it as a war of position rather than a war of movement.

In military terms, it was a war in which defensive capabilities outperformed offensive ones, so that neither side could achieve significant breakthroughs. In human terms, the result was trench warfare: four dehumanizing years of living and dying half buried in the earth, wet, cold, frightened, and bombarded by the most barbarically ingenious combinations of metal and chemicals the Western mind could invent.

This description applies best to the western front in France. Here the trench lines stretched from Switzerland to the English Channel and moved scarcely at all between late 1914 and early 1918. On the eastern front in Russia, the lines typically swayed back and forth, enormous Russian drives bogging down in a sea of casualties and finally reeling backward in defeat. In northern Italy too—after Italy joined the Allied cause in 1915—advances by one side were likely to be followed by regrouping and successful counterattacks by the other.

Everywhere, the machinery of modern warfare made its true potential felt for the first time in Europe. New weapons were flung into the fray one after another in hopes of achieving a breakthrough: submarines, tanks, airplanes, poison gas. But the most brutally efficient killers were the staples: repeating rifles, barbed wire and machine guns, artillery capable of lobbing explosive shells for miles and burying whole trenches full of soldiers when they hit. The "sacrifices" that patriotic orators liked to make speeches about were, as Hemingway said, "like the stockyards at Chicago if nothing was done with the meat except to bury it."[2] The war was a meat grinder, reducing generations of European youth to hamburger in the mud of Flanders fields.

The other great fact about the war was that it involved national commitment to an extent seldom even approached before. To keep millions of men fed, clothed, armed, and supplied with munitions sufficient for four years of firing at each other over hundreds of miles of front lines required an unparalleled effort by the populations involved. World War I thus became the first total war in history.

Governments took control of national economies as they had never dared do in peacetime. Government boards allocated raw materials, controlled transportation, regulated wages and prices, rationed food and other essentials. All able-bodied males were liable for conscription into the armed services. Many women went into the war plants to produce the shells and guns their husbands and sons would use.

New taxes, war loans, and a massive increase in the national debt of the warring countries were additional costs. A continual drain of food, fuel, clothing, and other essentials from the home front also resulted. Russians froze through icy northern winters, Germans went hungry, Austrians starved. Total war thus ravaged European economies even as it strengthened European governments.

This total mobilization of all the resources of great modern states was in its way as striking a feature of the Great War as the raking machine-gun fire and billowing clouds of mustard gas that turned European battlefields into no-man's-lands. And it would leave as long a legacy in battered economies and in governments with newfound powers.

War in the Larger World

"World War I," one historian of the great debacle has written, "was really a vast global enterprise—Europe became an enormous cauldron into which men and resources from Asia, Africa, and America were poured."[3] The First World War was, in fact, also fought outside of Europe, by peoples from other parts of the globe, and involved extra-European ambitions, resources, and conflicts that had little to do with an assassination at Sarajevo. These larger dimensions of the Great War must be surveyed briefly if the world-wide impact of the struggle is to be understood.

Global involvement in World War I took several forms. Germany had colonies, which of course became targets for the Allies, who controlled the oceans of the world. The Allies also drew upon their own overseas empires for military and support personnel. And important powers from as far away as the Middle East, the Far East, and North America became directly involved in the conflict. The First World War thus deserves its global label.

German colonies in East Asia, Oceania, and Africa were cut off from German reinforcement or support by British sea power, and most of them fell easily. The easternmost of the Allies, Japan, laid siege to Germany's base on the Shantung Peninsula of North China and soon captured it. British colonial forces from Australia and New Zealand rolled up German island holdings in Oceania. The Boers, who had fought Britain so recently, now led the imperial forces that overran German Southwest Africa, and Anglo-French colonial troops took Germany's West African possessions. Only in East Africa, in Tanganyika, did a skillful and prolonged German defense require years of fighting before a German colony was yielded to the Allies—in this case, Britain.

[2]Ernest Hemingway, *A Farewell to Arms* (New York: Scribner's, 1957), p. 185.

[3]Jack C. Roth, *World War I: Turning Point in Modern History: Essays on the Significance of the War* (New York: Alfred A. Knopf, 1967), p. 105.

Women at work in a British shipyard during World War I—evidence of the mobilization of an entire population to fight a modern "total war." These "feminine shipbuilders," according to the Illustrated London News, *were "praised for their industry and obedience." (Library of Congress)*

The European Allies, meanwhile, drew heavily upon their own overseas possessions to augment their forces in Europe. Large numbers of Indian troops fought in the British lines on the western front, and many Africans served in French armies. Both Chinese and Indochinese coolie labor worked behind the Allied lines in Europe in support of the war effort. The bloody Gallipoli campaign to open the Turkish straits was carried out almost entirely by Australian, New Zealand, Indian, and French colonial troops. Indian units also performed yeoman service for the British elsewhere in the Middle East.

The Germans thus lost their empire in the Great War. The British and the French, by contrast, profited immensely from theirs. Either way, colonial peoples far from Europe were significantly affected.

Lafayette, We Are Here

Besides these imperial contributions, the war drew in a number of independent non-European powers. Of these, Turkey, Japan, and the United States were the most importantly involved.

Germany's great influence in Istanbul and the long rivalry between the Ottoman Empire and Romanov Russia brought Turkey into the war on the side of the Central Powers in 1914. It was a disastrous miscalculation for the Ottomans. Turkish troops held heroically at Gallipoli. But British soldiers and rebellious Arab sheiks—urged on by the romantic British agent Lawrence of Arabia—chewed into the Ottoman Empire from the south. By war's end, this Middle Eastern campaign had detached large sections of Arabia, Palestine, and Mesopotamia from the dwindling Ottoman domain.

Japan also entered the war—on the Allied side—in 1914, and much more successfully than Turkey. The Japanese shrewdly exploited Allied support and European preoccupation on the other side of the world to advance their own imperial interests in the Far East, above all in China. After seizing Germany's bases in Shantung and on a Pacific island or two, Japan turned her attention to pressuring the new Chinese republic—established in 1911—into accepting what amounted to protectorate status under Japan! The Twenty-one Demands of 1915, which embodied this claim to imperial suzerainty, had little to do with the war, but they would be the basis for continuing Japanese pressure on China for decades to come.

The United States was the last and most important of the major extra-European participants to enter World War I. The U.S. had insisted on neutrality through the early years of the war, though she sold huge quantities of essential supplies to the Allied side. It was Germany's unrestricted submarine war on shipping destined for Allied shores, along with other manifestations of German resentment, that impelled President Wilson to declare war in 1917.

It was not till the spring and summer of 1918 that a significant number of American troops could be thrown into the struggle. They came at a propitious time, however, to help stem the climactic German offensives of 1918. And as the Germans slowly retreated that last fall of the war, the continuing arrival of fresh American troops undoubtedly helped to convince the German high command that the war was lost.

A famous cartoon of the time showed American doughboys debarking in France with the inspiring remark, "Lafayette, we are here!" There is little warrant for the notion that the United States was repaying a debt of honor that went back to the Revolutionary War when she sent her armies to Europe in 1918. If it was not a significant echo of the past, however, that first dispatch of American troops to western Europe was certainly a harbinger of things to come. American troops would be back for World War II and again for the Cold War. They are there today, guaranteeing the security of the Atlantic community of nations that has become the heart of the Western world.

SIGNIFICANT CONSEQUENCES, WESTERN AND WORLD

Ten Million Men

A German slogan in the First World War has a resonance of the Crusades of a simpler age: *Gott mit Uns*—God Is on Our Side. For their part, the Allies unleashed a flood of propaganda charging that the Central Powers were twentieth-century barbarians—the Hun come again to Europe—and claiming that the Allied struggle was a war to save civilization. Woodrow Wilson, widely hailed in war-weary Europe as a savior from beyond the seas, called it a "war to make the world safe for democracy" and even "the war to end war."

In the outcome, the Great War scarcely seemed to reflect any divine intent, did not make the world safe for either civilization or democracy, and certainly did not put an end to war. It did, however, have significant consequences, on both a European and a global level.

One thing the war produced on an awesome scale, of course, was casualties. At least ten million men in uniform were shot, bayonetted, poisoned, or blown to pieces, and perhaps half that many noncombatants died in the war zones. Millions more were hurt but not killed: Europe after the war was full of walking wounded—armless, legless, blinded, or broken-spirited men who could never seem to get their lives together again.

The numbers are numbing. During the worst periods of the war, for instance, the Russians took a quarter of a million casualties a month. The casualties in the battle of Verdun alone reached three quarters of a million; in the battle of the Somme they ran well over a million. Whole school classes of English, French, German, and other young men marched off to the front en masse. There, according to one eyewitness, they could look forward to about three more months of life. Statistics like these have shaped the twentieth century's attitude toward one of the most common of human occupations—the making of war—from that day to this.

A Smoldering Scar

Efforts to estimate the further impact of the war on Europe alone fill volumes. Diplomatically, politically, economically, and in many other ways, the Great War left a smoldering scar across the Continent.

Perhaps most obvious, the map of Europe was significantly altered by the war and by the peace the Allies imposed. All three of the great central and eastern European autocracies that began the war were gone by the end of it, the Romanovs toppled in 1917, the Hohenzollerns and the Habsburgs in 1918. Communists clung to power in Russia, and fledgling republics struggled to be born in Germany and Austria as the victorious Allies met in Paris to dictate peace terms. The peace treaties further modified the political map, recognizing the fragmentation of the Austro-Hungarian Empire and the independence of several minority nationalities who had seceded from the collapsing czarist Russian Empire. The result was a band of new or enlarged eastern European countries running from the Baltic Sea through Poland to the Balkans.

The terms imposed upon Germany by the Treaty of Versailles in 1919 left a bitter political legacy. Worked out in detail by platoons of technical experts, this and the other peace treaties, each dealing with a separate Central Power, reflected uneasy compromises among the three principal Allied war leaders: France's vengeful Clemenceau, Britain's pragmatic Lloyd George, and the perhaps unrealistically idealistic President Wilson. Most important, however, the Versailles Treaty reflected the determination of the British and the French to destroy the German power that had held all Europe in awe since Germany's unification half a century before.

The Versailles peace thus required Germany to acknowledge her "war guilt" publicly and imposed fantastic reparations, by which she was to pay for the war she had allegedly caused. The treaty compelled her to disarm so thoroughly that she would never again be a threat to her neighbors, stripped her of her overseas colonies, and generally strove to reduce the new German republic to a second- or third-class power. The Germans signed because they had to, seething inwardly at the injustice of the dictated peace. If the Allies had set out to provide Hitler with a list of causes upon which to build his career, they could not have done a better job.

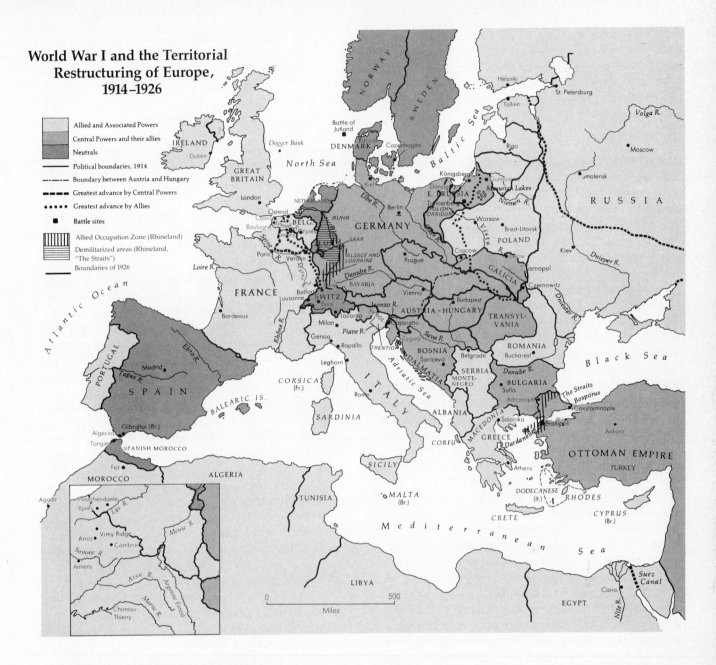

World War I and the Territorial Restructuring of Europe, 1914–1926

Allied and Associated Powers
Central Powers and their allies
Neutrals
—— Political boundaries, 1914
–·–·– Boundary between Austria and Hungary
▬▬▬ Greatest advance by Central Powers
•••• Greatest advance by Allies
■ Battle sites
Allied Occupation Zone (Rhineland)
Demilitarized areas (Rhineland, "The Straits")
Boundaries of 1926

More subtle social and economic changes also resulted from the war—not all of them as unpromising for the future as the diplomatic and political consequences sketched above.

Economically, the greatest change was that Europe was left deeply in debt. European investment capital had helped start other nations on the road to industrial development, so that much of the world was in Europe's debt in 1914. The enormous costs of the war, however, had absorbed all this foreign credit and had forced the combatants to borrow huge sums, particularly in the United States, to pay for supplies and war materiel. The Allies' war debts were, in fact, impossible to pay, like the reparations imposed on the

Central Powers, and the two would contribute to the disastrous economic fluctuations of the interwar period.

Some social groups, though, had done well because of the war. Skilled workers had earned good wages in defense plants. Women had taken a big step toward more flexible patterns of life through their work in war industries. In some places, as in England, women had been widely admired for their war service—British women got the vote on the strength of it.

Aristocrats and middle-class people in general, however, came out of the Great War shaken in status and self-confidence. Hailed as the pillars of the pre-war social order, these groups were now widely blamed for the war and all its horrors. The postwar militance of working-class people, plus the menacing power of the newly established Communist Russian power to the east, made many in Europe's ruling classes wonder how long their supremacy might last.

New Dominions

In the world at large, however, the First World War unleashed some wild new dreams indeed. There were new powers moving in the larger world after 1919, new aspirations and new institutions with a genuinely global focus. They were signposts toward a future that would have astonished the most prescient thinker only a few years before.

Expanded empires and emergent world powers were among the more striking larger consequences of the Great War. The peace settlements provided for yet more European protectorates and for colonial possessions enlarged by colonies confiscated from Germany in Africa and the Far East, and from the lands of the rebellious Arab princes of the former Ottoman Empire. Britain got Tanganyika; France acquired German West Africa; the Republic of South Africa received German Southwest Africa; and Japan got Shantung. The modern Middle East—with the crucial exception of Israel—came into being at this time, its southern tier of Arab states from Iraq through Syria and Lebanon to Palestine mostly under the control of Britain or France.

Even in this apparent display of imperial business-as-usual, however, there were differences. The new territories were not taken as of right, in the old way, but mandated to the care of European powers by a new international organization called the League of Nations. Some of these territories, at least, were intended for ultimate independence once they had been adequately "developed." The League at least seemed to be taking seriously some of the more idealistic New Imperialist rhetoric about civilizing missions and grooming for independence.

There was more than rhetoric that was new after 1919, however. Three rising world powers shouldered their way further into the international arena in the aftermath of the war. All three were influenced by Europe, and one was half European geographically, but all were part of an emerging global challenge to the established European hegemony of the world.

Japan, as noted above, had used the war to further advance her imperial ambitions in the Far East. She had seized Germany's Chinese holdings and after the war refused to return them to China. Japan's Twenty-one Demands on China, requiring changes in her government and policies that, if accepted, would have made her virtually a Japanese protectorate, did in fact gain some reluctant acceptance from Chinese officials. Japan used this measure of acquiescence as the basis for further aggression against China during the interwar years.

Militarily powerful and victorious in three consecutive wars—two of them involving European nations—Japan was also East Asia's most successful trading and manufacturing nation. By 1919 Japan had thus established the trajectory that would determine her rise to greatness over the rest of the century.

The new Union of Soviet Socialist Republics—still "Russia" to most people—looked much less like a winner in 1919. But the Soviet Union also had an astonishing future ahead of it.

Russia's non-European dimension—three quarters of her territory and much of her population were Asian—had been noted long before the twentieth century. The Bolshevik Revolution, however, put the country in the hands of militant ideological enemies of much that the rest of Europe stood for, from capitalism and democracy to imperial hegemony. The Russia of 1919, still bleeding from World War I, now swept by civil strife, seemed little threat to European predominance. But Joseph Stalin was already prowling in the wings, and the willingness of the Communists to use government power ruthlessly to build up the nation was already amply demonstrated. The Soviet Union too would play a global role in the emerging century.

The United States, finally, stepped definitively onto the stage of world history in World War I. Any attempts to hastily step off again would avail her nothing.

The richest nation in the world by the turn of the century, the United States emerged even richer from the war, thanks to European borrowing and to booming American war industries. The United States had also demonstrated in 1917 and 1918 that she could commit her youth to a major war if her interests and ideals were involved. America's President Wilson, whose idealistic Fourteen Points aimed to settle all the world's problems, was for a time hailed as a Messiah on both sides of the Atlantic.

Unaccountably to many, however, the U.S. drew back from the role thus thrust upon her in 1919. She refused even to join the League of Nations—Wilson's brainchild—and withdrew into fastidious isolation from the difficulties of the rest of the world. It would take another great war to propel the United States to the position of world leadership she would occupy during the second half of the century. But that direction too was laid down by the War of 1914–1918 and by America's part in it.

A Ferment of New Visions

There was, finally, a powerfully felt and growing hope for a larger and more just world order in 1919—one no longer dominated by European intercontinental empires.

Indians and Africans who had fought in Europe, Chinese and Southeast Asians who had served behind the lines went home with an image of the all-conquering Europeans that was rather different from the one they had once had. Woodrow Wilson's talk of "national self-determination of peoples," which had created the new nations of eastern Europe, seemed equally applicable to the colonies of Asia and Africa. V. I. Lenin's revolutionary charge that imperialism was a stage in the evolution of capitalist oppression had a great appeal to Westernized Asians particularly, as did his call for worldwide revolt. A ferment of new visions and new ideas, none of them conducive to continuing European predominance, was thus abroad in the world after the war.

Most impressive, perhaps, the peace conference at Paris, inspired and urged by Wilson, created a new international forum for such global aspirations: the League of Nations. Even after the United States rejected its own president's dream, the League seemed to point to a different worldwide order. Its Council of permanent and rotating members was empowered to plan for world peace and an end to aggression, by European empire-builders as well as by others. Its Assembly gave equal voting strength to all the nations of the world—and most of them were not European. The League of Nations was affiliated with other global organizations, such as the World Court, which also seemed a warning of things to come.

The League had little actual power and would founder after two difficult decades of existence. But it was a beginning, at least, toward recognition of a global system that could conceivably transcend even the interests of the great powers, European or otherwise.

The heritage of the worst of wars thus far was therefore not all danger and depression. The new powers, new visions, new institutions unleashed by that unprecedented conflict pointed down the generations to a wholly unexpected future for the world.

SUMMARY

World War I was triggered by the assassination of the heir to the Austrian throne by a Balkan terrorist. Larger causes, however, turned this local conflict into a global catastrophe. These deeper causes included entangling diplomatic alliances, nationalistic passions, economic competition, and massive military build-ups. Imperial rivalries also helped to create the conflicts of interest and the international tensions that led to World War I.

The Great War, as it was called, was the bloodiest in the history of the world up to that time. Major offensives by both the Allies—Britain, France, Russia, Italy, and later the United States—and the Central Powers—Germany and Austria—repeatedly failed. Trench warfare—a war of position featuring a horrifying array of new weapons, from planes and submarines to machine guns and poison gas—slaughtered millions in a four-year war of attrition. Total commitment was also required on the home front, where governments gained new powers, and economies were drained in the long struggle.

The war also involved non-European peoples. The German colonies overseas were lost, and the British and French colonies participated in the war. Turkey, Japan, and the United States also entered the war, the last two gaining significant imperial and economic benefits from their part in the struggle.

The results of World War I included 10 million dead and many millions more maimed or mentally shattered. Governments were toppled in Germany, Austria, and Russia, and resentments were kindled, especially among the Germans, that would have long-range repercussions. Economies were destabilized by Europe's immense war debts. Middle-class self-confidence was shaken, and the class conflicts seem to have intensified.

On the international scene, the British and French empires were strengthened, and the United States, the Soviet Union, and Japan emerged as world leaders. Perhaps most striking, the League of Nations was created—the first political organization to seek genuinely global participation, and a symbol at least of the growing globalization of history.

SUGGESTED READING

BAILEY, T. A. *Woodrow Wilson and the Lost Peace.* Chicago: Quadrangle Books, 1963. Wilson, Versailles, and the peace that paved the way for the next great war.

BALDWIN, H. *World War One.* New York: Harper & Row, Pub., 1962. Military history by a distinguished military analyst.

FALLS, C. B. *The Great War.* New York: Putnam, 1959. Well-constructed presentation by a gifted military historian.

FELDMAN, G. D. *The Army, Industry, and Labor in Germany, 1914–1918.* Princeton: Princeton University Press, 1966. The impact of total war on basic institutions on the home front. See in this connection M. Ferro, *The Great War, 1914–1918* (London: Routledge & Kegan Paul, 1973), stressing social and economic elements.

FUSSELL, P. *The Great War and Modern Memory.* New York: Oxford University Press, 1977. The literary image of World War I and its impact on modern consciousness.

GILBERT, F. *The End of the European Era, 1890 to the Present.* New York: Norton, 1979. Broad and detailed assertion of the view that European centrality in the world was destroyed by World War I. See also E. Fischer, *The Passing of the European Age* (Cambridge, Mass.: Harvard University Press, 1943).

HORNE, A. *The Price of Glory: Verdun, 1916.* London: Penguin, 1979. Detailed account of one of the great offensives that failed.

LAFORE, L. *The Long Fuse: An Interpretation of the Origins of World War I.* New York: Harper & Row, Pub., 1971. The causal chain, reaching back into the nineteenth century, that led to the first total war of the twentieth.

MARWICK, A. *War and Social Change in the Twentieth Century: A Comparative Study of Britain, France, Germany, Russia and the United States.* New York: St. Martin's Press, 1975. The transforming effect of both world wars on modern societies. See also J. Williams, *The Home Fronts: Britain, France, and Germany, 1914–1918* (London: Constable, 1972).

NICOLSON, H. *Peacemaking 1919.* Boston: Houghton Mifflin, 1933. A diplomatic history of Versailles by an expert.

REMARQUE, E. M. *All Quiet on the Western Front*, trans. A. W. Wheen. New York: Fawcett Crest, 1958. Vivid fictional evocation of trench warfare.

TUCHMAN, B. *The Guns of August.* New York: Macmillan, 1962. Moving narrative of the coming of the war.

WOHL, R. *The Generation of 1914.* Cambridge, Mass.: Harvard University Press, 1979. The ideas and attitudes of the generations that survived the war in Europe.

Chapter · 16

THE WEST BETWEEN THE WARS

DUBIOUS DIRECTIONS

Flappers and Fellahin

The stillness that settled over the battlefields of the Great War in November of 1918 triggered a variety of responses around the world. There was exultation in the streets of victorious nations, bitterness among the losers, dull indifference in the eyes of the maimed, the shell-shocked, the walking wounded. On one thing, however, there was general agreement: it was a different world after the war.

In the United States a new freedom emerged in the 1920s, projecting a vivid image of bobbed hair and short skirts, bathtub gin and wailing saxophones. In Europe young moderns got their new dances from across the Atlantic and daringly crossed the Channel by airplane. Older people imitated younger ones, and everybody seemed to drive fast cars.

This is an essentially middle-class image of the age, of course: Kansas farmers, Sicilian peasants, blue-collar workers at Ford's or Krupp's had no cars and would never fly in an airplane. But the prosperous bourgeoisie was the heart of Western society still, their life style glorified in magazines and films and admired by many who could not afford to share it. Their image reflects the ideal and much of the reality of the glossy new world of the West after the war.

Most of the rest of the world evidently did not share in this era of automobiles and airplanes that gave a hard-edged new meaning to that overworked adjective *modern*. As we have seen, there were shiny modern cities in South America, but Indians were still making pre-Columbian pottery in the jungles. Modern metropolises were emerging in Africa and the Middle East, but many Arabs were bedouin still, and village Africa was almost entirely intact south of the Sahara. People in Western business suits still swayed along in rickshas in Singapore and Shanghai, and Tokyo's handful of new earthquake-proof skyscrapers towered over a city of bamboo and paper. Yet change would come to these seemingly changeless regions too, just as it did to the Western world, between World Wars I and II.

It will take three chapters to survey the startling, sometimes horrifying trends of the 1920s and 1930s. The sections immediately following will outline the events of the Jazz Age and the Depression decade in the West. The next two chapters will deal with special features of the period in various parts of the globe: with the great revolutions that shook Russia, China, and other nations, and with the development of new forms of dictatorship in Germany, Japan, and elsewhere.

A typical American flapper might glory in change and newness, in art-deco modernity for its own sake. Egyptian *fellahin* laboring in the black earth along the Nile, as their ancestors had done since the beginning of history, might never have heard of the modern world at all. But time and change—not always for the better—would come to both of them between that stillness on the November battlefields of 1918 and the roar of Stukas rising into the dawn of September 1, 1939.

Twenties and Thirties—Boom and Bust?

It is hard to find two decades that seem to contrast more strikingly than the 1920s and the 1930s. The twenties were frivolity and fun; the thirties were a decade of agonizing social concerns, of taking stands and building brave new worlds. Most vividly, the twenties seem to mean prosperity, boom times; the thirties brought the Great Depression, the biggest economic bust in modern Western history.

On the economic side, however, the contrast seems in fact to have been rather less striking. This is particularly so when the two decades are examined from a global perspective.

The world as a whole seems to have suffered in the 1920s from a vast overproduction, a wartime buildup that could not find peacetime demand to sustain it. Commodity producers in Latin America and in the European colonies of Africa and Asia thus suffered from declining prices through much of the twenties. So did farmers in the United States, coal miners in Britain, and other primary producers within the West.

There were other economic problems as well. There was a postwar depression as hordes of demobilized soldiers swarmed into a job market that was already shrinking because of the end of wartime demand. Inflation soon followed in some parts of Europe, devouring the savings of middle-class citizens in Germany particularly.

Even the apparent prosperity of much of the population of the United States, Europe, and other Westernized lands such as Australia and Canada had an unreal quality about it. The United States, the world's most productive nation before the war, now her foremost trader and exporter of capital as well, was actually responsible for much of the apparent economic health elsewhere. The profits of booming American business, widely available to bolster flagging economies across the West, maintained a material well-being that was essentially artificial.

The central international role of the United States was illustrated most importantly in the nagging problems of reparations and war debt that haunted the twenties.

World War I had left even such prewar economic giants as Great Britain deeply in debt to the United States. To pay these war debts, all the Allies depended on the reparations payments from Germany prescribed by the Treaty of Versailles. But Germany, hard hit by the Great War, the inflation of the 1920s, the French occupation of the industrial Ruhr, and other problems, simply could not meet her reparations payments. To handle these obligations, Germany therefore borrowed heavily—from the United States!

Money thus flowed ponderously in a great circle, from the United States to Germany as loans, to the Allies as reparations, and thence back to the United States as war debts. It was a dubious procedure at best. When the American economy began to stagger, it would bring the economies of much of the world down in ruins.

The prosperity of the 1920s has thus been exaggerated in modern memory. The economic misery of the 1930s scarcely could be.

The world depression of 1929–1939 began with the collapse of the American stock market and was sustained by the long years of American economic paralysis that followed. American financiers, hard hit at home, soon cut back on their loans to Europe, putting the fragile structure of European prosperity also under pressure. The failure of Austria's central bank two years after the Wall Street crash triggered a similar wave of economic disaster across the Continent. As the depression deepened all across the West, finally, the commodity producers of the rest of the world began to feel the effects of the new poverty of their best customers. Prices of agricultural goods and raw materials, weak through the twenties, spiraled downward in the thirties. By the middle of that bleak decade, much of the world was thus locked in the grip of the Great Depression.

Political and economic leaders tried many expedients during the 1930s to reverse the spiral, prime the pump, get the laws of supply and demand working once more. In the end, paradoxically, it would take another world war to create sufficient demand to get the world economy moving again. In the meantime, as we will see below, the political and social repercussions of the Great Depression were felt all across the Western world.

The Age of Ford

Economic dislocation was thus a continuing feature of Western history between the wars, rather than a characteristic of the 1930s only. There were other areas also in which main trends carried on through these two apparently contrasting decades. One crucial aspect of Western life in which change would continue throughout the entire century was technological advance.

In every area, from industrial production, transportation, and communication to modern entertainment, the West and selected areas of the rest of the globe felt the impact of technological change throughout the 1920s and 1930s. The United States had become the recognized leader in many fields of technological development by this time, but the major nations of Europe were not far behind.

The rise of the twentieth century's two main sources of industrial energy, hydroelectric power and petroleum, had actually begun around the turn of the century. Electric lighting and electric-railway trains were common in the West by the twenties and thirties. Petroleum production, which had been only 20 million tons at the turn of the century, reached a quarter of a billion tons by the end of the thirties. Refined petroleum products powered ships, automobiles, and airplanes throughout the interwar years.

Technological improvement included key developments in both heavy industry and large-scale agriculture. The industrial assembly line, pioneered by Henry Ford, the American automobile manufacturer, was soon speeding up production in many other industries as well. In agriculture these decades were the age of the tractor. In the United States there were 160,000 tractors already at work in the fields in 1919; by 1939 there were a million and a half of them.

The central innovation in transportation during the twenties and thirties was, of course, the automobile. In Britain the number of cars in use multiplied twelve times between 1923 and 1938; in France, twenty times. And in the United States, forty times as many people had cars—almost 50 million of them—by the end of the 1930s as in the early 1920s, in spite of the depression! Railways remained important, airplanes rare except for military purposes. But the car was king of the road, retiring the working horse in city after city across the West after thousands of years of faithful service to humankind.

Communications, revolutionized by the telegraph in the nineteenth century, was revolutionized again by the telephone in the early part of the twentieth. But it was in the mass media of communications that the interwar decades saw major breakthroughs, particularly in the development of radio and film. Before World War I, radio was used primarily between ships at sea, where wireless communication was essential, and "moving pictures" were little more than an arcade game. Between 1920 and 1940, tens of millions of radio sets came into use in homes across America and Europe, and gaudy art-deco movie theaters blossomed in every city.

The impact of the automobile on the social life of the West, of the telephone on business and government, of radio and film on popular culture as well as in the hands of a Hitler or a Franklin Roosevelt is almost incalculable. And the takeoff time for all these social and technological revolutions was the period between the wars.

If the first half of the nineteenth century was the age of steam, then the early decades of the twentieth may well be described as the age of electricity—and Henry Ford.

Classes and Sexes

The Communists who seized power in Russia in 1917 confidently expected workers' revolts to follow in other countries—the world revolution Marx had predicted. Despite abortive starts in places as widely sep-

Ford motor cars, symbol of the new affluence of the 1920s, were produced by assembly-line methods that put them within reach of Americans of relatively modest means. (Ford Motor Company)

arated as Germany and China, this did not happen. Nevertheless, there was a good deal of talk about class conflict during the 1920s. And during the 1930s, such conflicts seemed to threaten the very fabric of Western society as never before.

There had, of course, been industrial violence before, particularly since the beginning of the Industrial Revolution. But with the Soviet Union intermittently championing proletarian revolt in the twenties, and then with the entire capitalist system apparently on the verge of collapse during the Great Depression of the thirties, socialist agitation and class consciousness reached new highs.

Deprivation and suffering among factory laborers, miners, transportation and construction workers, and others of the blue-collar labor force were in fact very great during the world depression. Unemployment, hunger, illness, a sense of injustice and oppression, and a willingness to respond with strikes, political organization, and even violence spread through working-class neighborhoods in many Western countries during the thirties.

Hitler in Germany, Roosevelt in the United States were able to defuse these class divisions in their very different ways. Other Western nations muddled through on a combination of the dole and worker hopelessness. But the tensions between the classes were certainly as great as they had ever been before, and greater than they have been since.

The conflict between the sexes, by contrast, seems to have been less of a public issue than before the war or in later decades. As we have seen, Western women had begun to demand legal, educational, economic, and political parity with men in the nineteenth century. They had made some progress, breaking into some male-dominated professions and crusading for social reforms, including women's rights. Early in the new century, women in some Western nations had secured the right to vote—in Australia and some Scandinavian countries shortly after 1900, in Britain, the United States, and Weimar Germany just after World War I. During the war, furthermore, many middle-class women had joined their poor sisters in working outside the home in war industries.

It was a heady era of progress for women on many fronts. But it drew to a close around 1920—the beginning of the period under consideration here.

Women's emancipation in the 1920s took such social and apparently frivolous forms as shorter skirts, cosmetics, public drinking and smoking. There was also an apparent increase in sexual freedom as women broke through the famous double standard, indulging in pre- or extramarital sex almost as casually as men did.

Most Western women, however, remained house-wives. Women were still effectively excluded from large-scale participation in traditionally male professions. And the new women voters did not vote as a block or put any significant number of women into office. The idealism of the women's movement seemed to have spent itself in the great effort for women's suffrage in the decades around 1900. For most of the rest of the first half of the twentieth century, other causes would preoccupy socially concerned women as well as men in the Western world.

A Dream of Peace

One of these causes during the 1920s and 1930s was the peace movement, as it subsequently came to be called. The dream of peace among nations had flickered before, of course, even in the frequently contentious West. The Roman peace was widely admired as one of Rome's greatest gifts to Europe. Medieval churchmen at least tried to negotiate occasional "truces of God" in a world of feudal violence. The humanist Erasmus, the philosopher Kant, and other modern thinkers had written tracts urging peace on heads of state. International meetings around 1900 had labored to create agencies such as the World Court that might defuse disputes between nations before they erupted in war.

The huge casualties and immense destructiveness of World War I, however, galvanized a much wider range of Western public opinion to attempt to prevent similar holocausts in the future. The greatest single achievement of those who dreamed that the First World War might really be the last war was, of course, the League of Nations. In addition, the 1920s saw a series of diplomatic agreements and disarmament conferences intended to prevent future wars.

The Locarno treaties of 1925, signed by most of the major European powers, tried to guarantee peace through agreements to negotiate all disputes. The Kellogg-Briand Pact of 1928, signed originally by the United States and France, then by more than twenty other countries, formally renounced war as an instrument of national policy. The League itself responded to some of the totalitarian aggressions of the 1930s with investigations and denunciations—though to little practical effect, as we shall see.

Disarmament negotiations focused on the world's navies, the preeminent long-range weapons systems in those days before B-1 bombers and ballistic missiles. Agreements were reached by the five major naval powers to freeze naval tonnage at a fixed ratio, to limit base strength, and even to scrap some "capital ships"—battleships and heavy cruisers. But discussions on limiting land forces bogged down throughout the 1920s in endless disputes concerning definitions of offensive weapons, methods of comparing various sorts of armies, and other matters too technical for any but a League subcommittee to understand.

The lay public had its say in the 1930s as some powers grew more bellicose, crises multiplied, and the chances of war mounted. Particularly in Britain and the United States, young people petitioned, argued, and demonstrated against war policies. Some even took the famous Oxford oath: under no circumstances would they take up arms to fight for their country. But the winds of war were already rising, and there were plenty of other young people in Germany, Japan, and elsewhere who were ready and eager to take up arms.

War did in fact come, in the fall of 1939, bringing an end to two decades of dubious directions and uncertain trumpets. The following section will look at the period a little more closely, in a regional and even a national focus. It will also illustrate more concretely some of the broad trends sketched above, the main currents of two decades that were building, whether people knew it or not, toward the biggest war of all.

WESTERN WORLDS

The Jazz Age

The United States in the 1920s was Jazz Age America. And thereby hangs a problem. How seriously can you take an age that is named for its popular music? At least the Renaissance was named for its serious culture! But the 1920s were fun times for many Americans, and perhaps it won't hurt to pay a little attention to fun once in a while. There were grimmer times coming.

Certainly there was little of profound significance to be found in the politics of the American twenties. The United States was run during that decade by three Republican presidents of no great distinction. The Harding administration after World War I was as scandal-ridden as that of Grant after the Civil War. Harding's successor, "Silent Cal" Coolidge, said little and did less. The third in the line, engineer and free-enterpriser Herbert Hoover, said he saw nothing but high hopes ahead for America—only months before the Crash of 1929. Like the Gilded Age, the twenties were not a great age of American democracy.

Most Americans couldn't have cared less. The enthusiasms of the Progressive Era had clearly run their course. Teddy Roosevelt and Woodrow Wilson, the war to make the world safe for democracy, and Wilson's last, most quixotic crusade, the League of Nations, were all consigned to the trash bin of history. "The business of America is business," the new breed

declared. It was okay to get rich again, and practically everybody seemed to be doing it.

There were weaknesses even in the American economy—the twenties were still hard times for farmers—but the overall economic trend was intoxicatingly upward. Per-capita income more than doubled between 1914 and 1929. Consumer luxuries such as wristwatches, washing machines, vacuum cleaners, and even automobiles became common. Technological advances such as the telephone, radio, phonograph, and movie were particularly widespread in America. Visitors from Europe were as impressed as Americans by the new opulence.

There were those who resisted the onward march of progress, of course. Fundamentalist Protestants defended established moral values and the "old-time religion." Intellectuals and literati sneered at the Babbits who ran America—doltish businessmen with little culture and less sensitivity, named for the central character in a novel by Sinclair Lewis. And many people lamented the passing of the front porch as a social center and its replacement by the automobile, symbol of freedom of youth, "petting parlors on wheels" to disapproving elders.

"Flaming youth," "modern youth," "the younger generation"—the young people of the American 1920s embodied all the vitality and foolishness of the decade. They drank too much, drove too fast, cut their hair and their skirts too short, invented endless fads and new dances every year. They adopted a brassy black style of popular music called jazz and took the gaudy, improvident life style of novelist Scott Fitzgerald and his glamorous wife Zelda as their ideal. For the giddy middle-class American youth of the 1920s, it was always New Year's Eve and no tomorrow.

New Deal, America!

Tomorrow came, of course—a morning-after like few in modern history—in the wake of the New York Stock Market crash of October 1929.

The causes of the Crash of '29 included unwarranted speculation, overcapitalized business ventures, shaky banks, lack of adequate government regulation, and plain fraud. The Great Depression that filled the next decade in America was rooted in deeper problems, however. Continuing hard times for farmers, miners, and others carried over from the twenties. Saturation of middle-class markets for big-ticket items such as autos and houses, a top-heavy income distribution that gave a third of the income to 5 percent of the population, and a "depression psychology" that paralyzed investment for years also contributed to the disaster.

The result was the terrible downward spiral of depression. Business bankruptcies threw people out of work. Unemployed people could not buy goods. More businesses thus closed, throwing yet more people into the ranks of the jobless. And so it went, spiraling down into a seemingly bottomless pit.

It is ancient history now, like scratchy old phonograph records or jittery black-and-white movies. But it was an unbelievable nightmare then.

"Brother, can you spare a dime?" Hoovervilles—tin-and-tarpaper shacks flung up on ash heaps at the edges of cities. Men wrapped in newspapers, sleeping on park benches. Holloweyed women and dirty-faced children watching the dry, dead earth of their farms blow away. Mugs of coffee, bowls of soup ladeled out by the Salvation Army to men who had once enjoyed hearty Sunday dinners and Sunday afternoon drives in the family Ford. Broken health, broken families, lives that started late or would never start up again. One and a half million Americans out of work in 1929. Thirteen million jobless in 1933.

Yet American democracy survived the decade. It was even strengthened in some ways, having used the crisis to pass some long overdue social legislation. Out of the Great Depression came the revival of the Progressive reform impulse we call the New Deal.

The survival expert who carried the nation through was an improbable upstate New York patroon with an aristocratic cigarette holder, a mellifluous voice, and a contagious certainty that "all we have to fear is fear itself"—and a man who could not get out of his wheelchair unaided. His name, perhaps the best-known in twentieth-century American politics, was Franklin Delano Roosevelt—FDR to headline writers everywhere. An unbeatable politician who was elected president four times—twice as many as any other—and who guided the nation through both the Great Depression and World War II, Franklin Roosevelt (1933–1945) stands with George Washington and Abraham Lincoln on the very shortest list of America's greatest presidents.

At Roosevelt's side throughout the presidential years was his wife, Eleanor, who thereafter became America's most admired woman in her own right. They made an unlikely couple at first glance. Franklin was a handsome, ambitious assistant secretary of the navy and an aggressive governor of New York—condemned to a wheelchair for life by a shattering attack of polio in 1921. Eleanor was plain and shy, the ugly-duckling daughter of an equally aristocratic family. Yet they forged one of the most effective political partnerships in U.S. history. Eleanor Roosevelt was FDR's eyes and ears, his physical presence where he could not go to hearten the people, and a militant champion of social causes.

Roosevelt was a man of action rather than an in-

These victims of the Great Depression might as easily be British or German as Americans. Even solid American family men were reduced to free food at public soup kitchens during the dark days of the global economic collapse. (Wide World Photos)

tellectual, and it was action that the nation wanted in 1933. "I pledge myself," he declared during his first campaign, "to a new deal for the American people. . . . This is more than a political campaign; it is a call to arms."[1] After three grinding years of waiting for the business cycle to turn up again, for the laws of supply and demand to pull the country out of the trough, Americans were finally ready for government involvement in the economy to a degree they had never tolerated before. The result was wave after wave of reform legislation through the 1930s—and a transformed America.

There was relief for the hungry, public-works projects for the unemployed, loans to help people keep their homes, regulation for Wall Street, insurance for banks, devaluation for the dollar. The Civilian Conservation Corps (CCC) and the Works Progress Administration (WPA) put hundreds of thousands of people to work on government-sponsored projects. The Agricultural Adjustment Act (AAA) raised farm incomes by encouraging cuts in production. The Tennessee Valley Authority (TVA) began the integrated development of an entire region of the country on the basis of cheap electricity and irrigation. The Wagner Act strengthened the bargaining position of labor unions as never before in America. Social Security at last brought national old-age pensions, begun decades before in Europe, to the United States.

The list of reforms, the blizzard of alphabet agencies went on and on. Some were failures; some were even declared unconstitutional. Enemies of the New Deal social revolution denounced FDR as a Caesar in the White House, and his ill-considered attempt to pack the Supreme Court with more sympathetic judges caused a national outcry. But the warm fireside-chat voice on the radio, the happy-warrior enthusiasm, the jokes and good-humored confidence, and the growing conviction among masses of forgotten Americans that Roosevelt had their interests at heart carried the day. The Roosevelt coalition of northern liberals, urban machines, and the solidly Democratic South, of workers, farmers, and black Americans carried all but half a dozen states in 1932, all but two in 1936.

Roosevelt's foreign-policy credentials were impeccably liberal also. He broke a conservative Republican front against the Bolsheviks by extending diplomatic recognition to the Soviet Union—and American businessmen as solid as Henry Ford were soon cheerfully trading with Communist Russia. FDR announced a new policy of nonintervention south of the border, a Good Neighbor Policy that at least looked

[1]James T. Patterson, *America in the Twentieth Century* (New York: Harcourt Brace Jovanovich, 1976), p. 158.

"Nothing to fear but fear itself!" Franklin and Eleanor Roosevelt seemed to embody a new self-confidence that many Americans found heartening even in the depths of the Depression. (UPI/Bettmann Newsphotos)

like a significant change from the days of Dollar Diplomacy and sending in the Marines.

Most important, by the end of the thirties Roosevelt was clearly aware of the international danger posed by the rise of aggressive totalitarian regimes in Germany, Italy, Japan, and elsewhere. His efforts to prepare Americans for the possibility of a new world war were handicapped by general disillusionment with the last one. But his estimate of Axis intentions would prove all too accurate as the decade ended.

Franklin Roosevelt could not stop the world depression—it took World War II to do that. But he carried America through it without recourse to totalitarian tyranny and with a renewed sense of national purpose and dignity. And he set the United States at last on the road other Western nations had already taken toward the welfare state—that precarious balance of capitalistic economy, democratic government, and socialist concern for the basic social and economic needs of the people.

Muddling Through

Europe never recovered the position of centrality she had enjoyed in the world before World War I. Europeans would still enjoy a standard of living as high as that of any people, and most western Europeans would preserve their democratic institutions. The European powers would cling to their overseas empires for another quarter century, until a second global conflict finally shook loose the European political hegemony of the globe. But the self-confident superiority of the Europeans was severely shaken by the biggest war so far, and by the political and economic experiences of the decade that followed.

Democratic governments and capitalist economies survived best in Britain and France, in Scandinavia (Norway, Sweden, and Denmark in particular), in the Low Countries (the Netherlands and Belgium), and in such isolated pockets as Switzerland and Czechoslovakia. In much of the rest of Europe, as we will see, very different tides were flowing. For now, however, it is the interwar experience of liberal capitalist western Europe that concerns us, particularly that of the two major western European powers, Britain and France.

Great Britain between the wars managed to muddle through. But her circumstances were sadly reduced, her imperial and commercial predominance undermined, and her empire increasingly unstable.

Economically, Britain had lost a quarter of her overseas trade and had been replaced as the greatest foreign investor by the booming United States. Her industrial plant, so vigorously challenged by Germany before the war, remained dated and slow to recover. British workers, particularly in badly depressed industries such as coal mining, were frequently on strike. The great miners' walkout of 1926 turned into the famous general strike of that year, shutting down almost the entire economy for ten days and leading to violent confrontations between blue-collar strikers and middle- and upper-class Englishmen fearful of Bolshevik plots.

When the Great Depression came in the 1930s, Britain handled it no better than other western European countries. The United Kingdom had no FDR to rally the nation against the rising tide of bankruptcies, layoffs, and poverty. A series of more or less ineffectual Conservative leaders cobbled together an array of half measures, from reluctant devaluation of the pound to an inadequate dole intended merely to keep the unemployed from starving. In the end, as elsewhere in the West, it was only World War II, with its booming war industries and military conscription, that put Britishers back to work.

Politically, Britain was dominated by a succession of unmemorable Conservative-party governments between 1919 and 1939. Perhaps the most important feature of British political life between the world wars, however, was the emergence of Labour—Britain's socialist party—as the Conservative party's major rival. The Liberals, meanwhile, declined to third-party status. It was a net shift to the left in British politics. But this shift, despite two Labour governments in the interwar period, would have little effect on Britain's national life until after World War II.

The British Empire also showed the strains of Britain's anomalous new position in the world. In India, an independence movement led by Mahatma Gandhi and the Congress party gained momentum. Closer to home, England's oldest colony, Ireland, was at last granted its freedom after a brief rebellion in 1916 and a bloody British struggle with the terrorists of the Irish Republican Army in the years around 1920. Northern Ireland, however, with its heavy Anglo-Protestant population, remained part of Britain—and a source of friction for decades thereafter.

A more positive adjustment to new realities was the creation of the British Commonwealth of Nations by the Act of Westminster in 1931. By this act, some of Britain's largest and oldest colonies, including Canada, Australia, and South Africa, gained complete political independence under the symbolic headship of the British crown, while still benefiting from "imperial preference" in trade.

Most of Britain's overseas territories remained colonies in 1931, including such giants as India. But a road to voluntary and mutually profitable association was opened by the Commonwealth, and dozens of former colonies have followed it since.

Maginot-Line Mentality

France, the other large democracy of western Europe, survived two even more undistinguished decades between the two wars. And here, as across the Channel, there was a sense of better times behind, of indecision and no clear line of movement into the future.

There were some advantages to being French. The world depression came late to France, and was not felt as fiercely. The braking effect of a substantial admixture of peasant farmers, old-fashioned artisans, and petty-bourgeois shopkeepers saved the French economy from the violent oscillation between 1920s boom and 1930s bust that looked so stark in America. The number of unemployed in France never much exceeded half a million, compared with three million in Britain.

Like Great Britain, the French republic had its first socialist government in the interwar years, in the 1930s. French socialism was as constitutional and committed to democracy as the British Labour party was. But the French Left was as fragmented as most democratic politics were in Europe, where the multiparty system prevailed. French socialist power thus depended on an alliance between two separate socialist parties and the French Communists, who at that time were committed to following Moscow's line. Only in the mid thirties, when Moscow urged all Communists to seek a united front with socialists and liberals, could the French Left form a coalition capable of holding power for even a brief time.

For most of these two decades, then, conservatives dominated French politics as they did politics in Britain. Right-wing splinters even flirted with totalitarianism in France. The far-right Cross of Fire veterans' party had a quasi-fascist image, including uniforms, extremist language, and an enthusiasm for street confrontation. But the Cross of Fire never really came close to power in that nation of peasants and shopkeepers.

French foreign policy in the 1920s and 1930s was also conservative and increasingly defensive in tone. France's overriding preoccupation was with the threat of revived German power across the Rhine and with the more distant menace of Bolshevism in eastern Europe. French leaders moved aggressively if imprudently in the 1920s, occupying the industrial Ruhr district in order to squeeze reparations payments out of Germany. The result was severe economic damage, to France as well as to Germany, and a negotiated settlement.

France also assembled a system of defensive military alliances, with Belgium against Germany and with Poland, Czechoslovakia, and others against Russia. In the thirties the French spent years and hundreds of millions of francs building an elaborate string of steel-and-concrete fortifications facing Germany—the notorious Maginot Line. While Hitler prepared to fight the next war with highly mobile panzer divisions, France braced itself to fight the last one over again in the grimly defensive spirit of Verdun.

This backward-looking, defensive, Maginot Line mentality in fact characterized much of French history between the wars. American tourists might enjoy Paris in the springtime, and there was still no better place to be an expatriate. But there was little sense of grandeur along the Seine, and no Napoleons in sight as France's next time of testing came on inexorably.

Capable of Coping

The United States and Europe were the heart of the Western World, as they would be throughout most of the twentieth century. But there were more Western worlds than one by this time. A look at two other areas of Western culture will therefore be necessary to complete this overview.

The nations of the British Commonwealth, scattered around the world geographically, were as much a part of this new, expanded twentieth-century West

as the United States was. Domestic autonomy had been granted to Canada, Australia, and New Zealand in the nineteenth century, to South Africa around 1900, soon after the Boer War, and to Ireland around 1920, following the Irish "troubles." The formal grant of independence and equality under the British crown in 1931 completed what had begun a century before—the creation of a British family of nations around the globe.

The nations of the Commonwealth were for the most part as democratic as any in the world, possessing representative legislatures, bills of rights, and lively traditions of political and social reform. South Africa, which contained a huge, totally disfranchised black majority, was the great exception to this tendency.

Economically, most of the Commonwealth countries had been outgrowing their original roles as suppliers of agricultural products and raw materials in return for manufactured goods from the mother country. They continued to produce large quantities of beef, wheat, mutton, wool, gold, diamonds, and other valuable materials. But the South African mining industries and Australian manufacturing grew apace, and Canada became one of the major manufacturing nations of the world during these decades.

All the nations of the British Commonwealth suffered in the world depression. But all survived it without draconian political measures, as they would survive World War II. For the most part, then, the Commonwealth countries entered the second half of the century as leading examples of successful Western nations, capable of coping with the worst this century could dish out.

Ardent Spokesmen for Ideals

The Latin American nations, like the Commonwealth countries, were in most ways as much a part of the Western World as the United States or Europe. Like the predominantly English-speaking nations of the British Commonwealth, this score of mostly Spanish- and Portuguese-speaking republics shared a dominant European heritage, here overlaid upon strong Amerindian and Afro-American traditions. Though Latin America escaped participation in both world wars, it was affected by them, by the depression, and—as we shall see in later chapters—by global trends toward revolution and authoritarian government in the interwar years.

By and large, the twenties were better times, the thirties considerably worse in Latin America, as for most of the Western World. Here, however, general trends stretching over both decades will be stressed.

It is easy to make a case for "no significant change"

over these years in Latin America. The backcountry, after all, still belonged to the haciendas, as it had since independence and before. National economies still depended heavily on commodity exports and imported capital. Even in the relatively peaceful and prosperous 1920s, authoritarian governments tended to manipulate or ignore democratic institutions. Yet there were changes, some of them of considerable long-range importance—and some clearly for the better.

Economically, a major change was the takeoff of a domestic manufacturing capacity in some of the more developed Latin American states. This change was partly the result of the high prices charged for North American and European manufactured goods. These prices were particularly hard for Latin Americans to pay during the depression, when the prices of their exports of agricultural products and raw materials shot down. All this led some Latin Americans to try to produce at home what they could not afford from abroad.

In part also, the building of new manufacturing plants and the nationalizing of foreign-owned extractive industries was a deliberate policy stimulated by national pride and by a growing awareness of Latin America's relative technological underdevelopment. The result, in any case, was genuine growth in consumer-goods manufacturing—notably in textiles—in Argentina, Brazil, and other nations, and of the oil industry in Mexico, Venezuela, and Andean states such as Peru.

Politically, there was also some striking evidence of progress between the wars, both in political performance and in ideals and social services.

Conservative and military elements did remain prominent in government during the period, but in the 1920s, at least, revolutionary seizures of power dwindled greatly. Some sectors of the civil service, such as the agencies dealing with public utilities and those concerned with irrigation projects, tended especially to be more modern and professional and less exploitative.

Outside groups pressured governments to enact reforms. Liberal, middle-class parties urged more democracy, as did students at Latin America's large universities. The growing working class, reinforced by a new influx of European immigrants bringing socialistic ideas and no tradition of subservience to Latin American establishments, demanded attention to the needs of working people. Furthermore, many Latin Americans of all classes, disturbed by the United States military interventions of the 1910s and 1920s, strongly resented foreign influences of all sorts in their countries.

Some genuine though limited progress resulted from the pressures generated by these new groups and by idealistic political impulses. Mexico and the ABC countries—Argentina, Brazil, and Chile—significantly expanded the role of their governments in providing social services for their people. Advanced labor codes regulating hours and conditions of work were passed in some countries. Even some of the more reactionary autocrats prided themselves on educational reforms. Mexico's nationalization of foreign oil wells in the 1930s exemplified a wave of government moves aimed at limiting foreign participation in Latin American economies.

Many of these reforms never reached the peons in the countryside, and others were never put into practice at all. Foreign capital continued to be needed, so that in the end, patriotic fervor frequently gave way to pragmatism, or to a desire for a share of the profits.

Nevertheless, much was accomplished. Domestically owned industries were at last beginning to grow, government's responsibility to the people was broadening, and twentieth-century social idealism had no more ardent spokesmen than in Latin America.

SUMMARY

The decades between the two world wars of this century are often contrasted. The 1920s are seen as the Jazz Age of prosperity, flappers, and fun; the 1930s, as the Depression decade, the red decade, the decade of unemployment, suffering, and ideological commitment. In fact, the two decades had much in common. Overproduction worldwide throughout the period led to poverty among commodity producers in both developed and underdeveloped societies. Technology further transformed the Western world, bringing widespread use of automobiles, telephones, electrical appliances, radios, and moving pictures.

Tensions increased between social classes, and the appeal of socialism reached a century-long high during the 1930s. The women's movement, however, languished or turned to new forms of social equality. Efforts to guarantee world peace included the League of Nations, a series of naval disarmament agreements, and student demonstrations.

A country-by-country survey of the West between the wars reveals a variety of national styles and developments. Politically, the United States in the 1920s was in a slump between strong presidents; economically, however, the United States sustained half the Western world. The depression decade in America was dominated by the powerful personality of Franklin D. Roosevelt and the New Deal. Britain muddled through both decades, surviving class tensions and massive unemployment, and even showing some of her old political flair in the establishment of the British Commonwealth of Nations. France was deeply conservative, building international alliances and the Maginot Line against foreign enemies, and escaping the worst of the depression because of her old-fashioned economy. In both Britain and France, however, socialist political parties chalked up their first national political victories.

The Commonwealth countries—especially Canada, Australia, and New Zealand—evolved as a loose family of self-governing nations. Their economies became increasingly independent, and Canada became one of the world's leading industrial nations. The Latin American republics also continued their development toward economic independence and revealed new tendencies toward political reform and social welfare. The depression, however, brought increased poverty and a resurgence of authoritarian regimes in Latin America.

SUGGESTED READING

ALLEN, F. L. *Only Yesterday*. New York: Harper & Row, Pub., 1972. Social and cultural trends of the twenties; lively reading.

BANNER, L. W. *Women in Modern America: A Brief History*. New York: Harcourt Brace Jovanovich, 1974. Brief but very readable history of American women and American attitudes toward women in the twentieth century. See also W. H. Chafe, *The American Woman: Her Changing Social, Economic, and Political Role, 1920–1970* (New York: Oxford University Press, 1972) for a scholarly survey.

BURNS, J. M. *Roosevelt: The Lion and the Fox*. New York: Harcourt Brace Jovanovich, 1970. Positive assessment of Franklin D. Roosevelt as leader and political tactician.

EYCK, E. *A History of the Weimar Republic* (2 vols.), trans. H. P. Hanson and R. G. L. Waite. Cambridge, Mass.: Harvard University Press, 1962—1963. Detailed, liberal in sympathies.

GREENE, N. *From Versailles to Vichy*. Arlington Heights, Ill.: Harlan Davidson, 1970. Complicated narrative of French political life from victory in World War I to defeat in World War II.

KINDLEBERGER, C. P. *The World in Depression, 1929–1939*. London: Allen Lane, 1973. The larger picture; good for Europe in particular.

MAIER, C. S. *Recasting Bourgeois Europe: Stabilization in France, Germany, and Italy in the Decade after World War I*. Princeton: Princeton University Press, 1975. Respected comparative study.

NUNN, F. M. *Chilean Politics, 1920–1931: The Honorable Role of the Armed Forces*. Albuquerque: University of New Mexico Press, 1970. Balanced and thorough study.

POTASH, R. A. *The Army and Politics in Argentina, 1928–1945*. Stanford: Stanford University Press, 1969. Compare the traditional power of the military with the equally traditional role played by students in politics, as illustrated in R. J. Walter, *Student Politics in Argentina: The University Reform and Its Effects, 1918–1964* (New York: Basic Books, 1968).

REES, G. *The Great Slump: Capitalism in Crisis*. New York: Harper & Row, Pub., 1971. The big picture of the depression. On the American stock market crash that triggered the global collapse, see J. K. Galbraith, *The Great Crash* (New York: Avon, 1980).

ROCK, D. *Politics in Argentina, 1890–1930: The Rise and Fall of Radicalism*. London: Cambridge University Press, 1975. The reforms and politics of the radical period.

SCHLESINGER, A. M. *The Age of Roosevelt*. Boston: Houghton Mifflin, 1957. Balanced but generally approving analysis of the New Deal. For a variety of views, see F. Freidel, ed., *The New Deal and the American People* (Englewood Cliffs, N.J.: Prentice-Hall, 1964).

SONTAG, R. *A Broken World, 1919–1939*. New York: Harper & Row, Pub., 1971. Excellent overview of this complex and many sided era.

TAYLOR, A. J. P. *English History, 1919–1945*. Oxford: Oxford University Press, 1965. Quick-witted and critical. For social history of the period, see R. Graves and A. Hodge, *The Long Weekend* (New York: Norton, 1963).

Chapter · 17

THE LONG REVOLUTIONS

THE MOST REVOLUTIONARY OF CENTURIES?

The Mystique of the Rebel

The twentieth century may well be the most rebellious of centuries. Certainly the rebel has become a stock figure of our times. We all know him—or her: young, committed to a great cause, challenging the established order of things. Some of us may in fact *be* this archetypal rebel, heading for the barricades once more.

The twentieth century did not, of course, invent rebellion, or even rebellion for a good cause. The literature and legendry of many peoples include versions of Jesse James or Robin Hood, stealing from the rich and giving to the poor. Ideological rebellions aiming at major social transformation go back to the eighteenth-century age of democratic revolutions in the West—back to the sixteenth century if you count the great wars of religion. But seldom have revolutions of all sorts played such a part in history—particularly in global history—as in the present century.

During the period between World Wars I and II, as we have seen, social and cultural revolutions transformed European and American life styles and even reached as far as Japan. Artistic rebels reshaped literature, painting, architecture, music. Popular Freudianism told sophisticated people that rebellion against inhibiting conventions was good for their emotional health. Young people rebelled against older people, women against the double standard. And all of these revolutions have continued since, becoming part of the fabric of our lives.

The major political and economic revolutions that will be dealt with below, however, have had a special place in history. These great revolutions of the first half of the twentieth century reached far beyond the Western world to set global history as a whole moving in new directions.

The Role of Ideology

The forms of rebellion—even of political revolt—are many and varied, and they are as old as history. As far back as our records run, there have been peasant rebellions, palace coups, civil wars between claimants to the same throne, feuds between factions within the same city. But the ideologically based revolution, inspired by new social ideas and envisioning a totally new social order, is a modern phenomenon.

There were slave revolts like that of Spartacus in ancient Rome. Peasant rebellions in China had a traditional social dimension, century after century. And there were numerous other instances. But the notion of seizing control of society by force and rebuilding it according to the theories of contemporary prophets has a very modern ring.

There are elements of ideological revolt in this sense in the English Civil War of the 1600s, a good deal of it in the American Revolution and particularly the French Revolution of the later 1700s. There was an epidemic of ideological revolution in Europe between 1815 and 1848. It was only in our own century, however, that revolution based on liberalism, nationalism, and socialism and their variants swept beyond the confines of the West into the larger world.

Of the major modern ideologies, liberalism has perhaps been the weakest in its impact on twentieth-century revolutionaries. Liberal convictions, political and economic, were most potent among rebels between 1776 and 1848. By 1900, many liberal objectives had been achieved in the West. Outside western Europe and America, demands for democracy and free trade often seemed less than central to the felt needs of insurrectionary peoples. The rhetoric of freedom was still widely heard, but it tended to mean something different to twentieth-century revolutionists around the world.

Nationalism, particularly in the form of antiimperialism, has been much more of a driving force behind the revolutions of this century. Resentment of foreign rule, or of foreign economic domination, has been the primary motive behind many popular struggles for independence since 1900. The European intercontinental empires would be shattered by nationalistic rebellion against foreign domination after World War II. Powerful currents of nationalistic feeling flowed also in the great Mexican and Chinese revolutions of the earlier twentieth century, to be dealt with below.

Marxist revolutionary socialism, however, has perhaps been more visible than any other ideology in the revolutions of the present century. This is in a way ironic, because Marxism was developed as a doctrine for rebellious proletariats in developed industrial countries, whereas most twentieth-century revolutions have come in preindustrial peasant countries such as Russia, China, and Mexico—the subjects of the present chapter. As a consequence, Marxist ideologues have had to do some recasting of theory to suit the needs of their preindustrial constituency (as in Mao's China) or have had to impose the new order in considerable part by force (as in Stalinist Russia). But Lenin's turn-of-the-century thesis that imperialism was an extension of capitalism overseas has appealed to revolutionary cadres around the world ever since.

The impact of ideology is much more complex than formulations such as "rebellions for a cause" might indicate. Like the religious motives of earlier times, ideological impulses are frequently mixed with other motives, from political ambition and social resentment to economic needs and desires. But the part played by visions of brave new worlds built on a bedrock of ideas has nonetheless been central. Liberals, nationalists, and socialists, whose influence on the West has been so great over the past two centuries, have been reshaping the world as well during the last hundred years.

How Long Is a Revolution?

Between 1911 and 1949, great ideological revolutions shook some of the largest nations in the world: Russia, the largest in territory; China, the largest in population; and Mexico, one of the largest on both counts in Latin America. During this same period between the wars, less violent but nonetheless ideologically based independence movements gathered force on the Indian subcontinent—second only to China in population—and in many parts of Africa, the second largest continent.

There would be many revolutions in the second half of the century as well, but these would tend to be in rather smaller corners of the globe, in places such as Vietnam, Algeria, and Cuba. These revolutions were significant because of their frequency, cropping up again and again around the globe in the decades after World War II. But the big revolutions came in the first half of this century, especially during the years between the wars.

The Russian, Chinese, and Mexican revolutions had much in common. They were based on Western ideologies and visions of social justice, and they anticipated a better social order. They became models for later generations of rebels in other parts of the world. But perhaps most impressive, they had *scale* in common.

They were fought over hundreds of thousands of square miles by millions of people. Their casualty totals dwarf those of the English, French, and American revolutions of earlier centuries. They changed the lives of hundreds of millions. And they dragged on, sometimes for decades, before a new social order was at last established, a new regime firmly in place.

For the historian, sheer length is perhaps the most striking feature. How long can a revolution be, after all, before it becomes a kind of violent social evolution, consuming whole generations in its quest for a brighter tomorrow?

There was heroism enough for any lover of courage in the face of terrible adversity. There were horrors to turn the sternest of us queasy at the unending violence. There was, finally, social change—though not always the change dreamed of by the founders, many of whom had long been in their graves when the consummation came.

The long revolutions of the years between the wars are historic monuments of our century. They have given us crusaders such as Madero and Gandhi, men of violence such as Pancho Villa, founders of new nations such as Lenin and Mao, transformers of whole societies such as Stalin. They gave the world new global powers—the Soviet Union and the People's Republic of China—and inspired the formation of new power blocs in Asia, Africa and Latin America.

Idealistic young rebels—and men and women of more ordinary clay—fell in hecatombs to bring these things to pass. The long revolutions are their monuments too—and their story.

SHAKING THE WORLD: RUSSIA, CHINA, MEXICO

The Hour of the Bolsheviks

Revolutionary tensions had been accumulating over the Russian centuries—in ancient Muscovy; during the time of Peter the Great; in 1825, when the Decembrists, the first Russian revolutionary movement, challenged the czar.

Russia was unique, even in relatively conservative and undeveloped eastern Europe. Its huge population of peasants, the eternally suffering *muzhiks*, were sunk in poverty and ignorance. Its fairy-tale aristocracy lived the life of the American antebellum South, of Versailles before the Bastille fell, with town mansions and vast estates, lavish balls, and sleigh bells jingling through the Russian night. Its divine-right emperor was a figure out of the Middle Ages, convinced that God had sent him to rule his people. And so he did, with the help of the largest and least efficient bureaucracy and the most notorious secret police in the Western world.

In the last century of czarist Russia's history, revolutionary rumblings had become endemic. Decembrist plotters, nihilist rioters, and Narodnik terrorists had all failed. Then, in the 1890s, this revolutionary tradition produced its final flower: the generation of Lenin.

It was a rebellious generation whose many voices demanded change of the new czar, Nicholas II. Local peasant disturbances were at a new high as the century turned. Workers in the growing numbers of factories and railway lines brought the industrial strike to Russia. Middle-class professional groups urged change less noisily. Students were demonstrating again. And underground, a tangle of feuding revolutionary groups demanded a more violent solution to the nation's long-standing problems.

There were two main revolutionary organizations, one of them divided into two factions. The older of the two major groups was the Social Revolutionary party—the SRs. Heirs of the Narodniks of the 1870s, they were convinced that the oppressed peasants would one day rise up to overthrow the man they still called the "dear father czar." The newer group, Russia's first Marxists, insisted that the new and still relatively small Russian industrial proletariat was the wave of the revolutionary future. This group called themselves the Social Democratic party, or SDs, though their revolutionary predilections made them very different from Social Democrats in western Europe.

The SDs split into two factions in the early 1900s:

the Mensheviks and the Bolsheviks, the "Minority" and "Majority" factions. The split was a matter of tactics, not goals. The Mensheviks urged a large, inclusive party that would take in supporters having a broad range of viewpoints and degrees of involvement in the cause. The Bolsheviks insisted on a relatively small, tightly knit party of disciplined, full-time revolutionaries. The leader of the Bolshevik wing was a man named Vladimir Ilich Ulyanov, known to history by his alias of Lenin.

Lenin (1870–1924) was a school administrator's son from the Volga region of eastern European Russia. A student demonstrator in his youth, he was an early convert to Marxism. His older brother had been hanged for plotting to assassinate the czar in the 1880s, and Lenin himself spent time in Siberia for organizing subversive "study groups" among Russian workers. With his wife and comrade, Krupskaya, he had in the 1890s followed the common path of nineteenth-century ideological revolutionaries of many persuasions—exile, first in Berlin and London, finally to Switzerland. There he lived, wrote, schemed, and organized through the opening years of the new century.

He was, said one who knew him, "a man of iron will, of indomitable energy, who combined a fanatical faith in the movement and the cause with no less faith in himself. . . . "[1] He looked old even in youth, with his rapidly receding hairline, broad forehead, narrow Tatar eyes, and small moustache. His fellows in the underground called him the Old Man, honored him for his skill in ideological debate, his strong will, and his twenty-four-hour-a-day commitment to his cause. Many followed him into the Bolshevik faction when the party split in 1903. They were still with him in 1917, when their hour came at last.

Masters of Russia

There is no question of the dedicated revolutionary zeal of Lenin and his colleagues. There is no doubt either, however, that they did not bring down the czar in 1917. World War I did that.

Lost wars stimulated domestic upheavals three times during the last sixty years of Romanov rule in Russia. The pounding Russia took on her own soil in the Crimean War of the 1850s kindled the nihilist rebelliousness—and led to the reforms—of the 1860s. Russia's humiliating defeat by Japan in 1905 led to the revolution of that year and to the political concessions that gave Russia her first legislative assembly, the Duma. In the same way, it was the terrible punishment Russia took in World War I that triggered

[1] Bertram D. Wolfe, *Three Who Made a Revolution: A Biographical History* (Boston: Beacon Press, 1948), p. 258.

Lenin orates to a Russian crowd in the darkest days of the civil war that followed the 1917 revolutions. Trotsky, intellectual and builder of the Red Army, stands at the base of the podium. (New York Public Library Picture Collection)

both the February and October revolutions of 1917. The Russian revolutionaries rode and to some degree guided the whirlwind. They did not conjure it up.

Romanov Russia's creaky economy, dilapidated administration, and military backwardness made her the least prepared of all the great powers to meet the challenges of total war in 1914. Her huge peasant armies were poorly led, trained, and equipped, their human-wave assaults costly and futile in a modern war. Russia's meager railway system and inefficient administration denied them supplies and kept casualties from getting back to medical help. Her cities, swollen with war workers, ran out of food, fuel, even housing in the long Russian winters.

The government of the last czar was a carnival of inefficiency and corruption. Nicholas II himself was at the front with the troops, further complicating the desperate efforts of his generals. Empress Alexandra, trying to preside at St. Petersburg, came increasingly under the influence of the "monk" Rasputin, whose ability to ease the suffering of her hemophiliac son Alexis, heir and hope of the dynasty, mesmerized her into thinking he had been sent by God to guide Russia's divine-right rulers in their hour of peril. In fact, Rasputin, an unscrupulous peasant faith healer almost totally ignorant of foreign affairs, devoted himself to debauchery, influence peddling, and promoting the fortunes of his equally unworthy cronies.

Under such external pressures, a government so thoroughly rotted within simply could not stand. Lenin was still in exile in Switzerland when it fell.

The February Revolution that brought down the czarist monarchy was guided by liberal Duma politicians and generals who recognized the hopelessness of the military situation. In the depths of that winter of 1916–1917, with mobs surging through the streets of the capital, this group went to Nicholas and persuaded him to abdicate for the good of the country. The nation, they said, would not follow him further.

Nicholas resigned, first in favor of his son, and then of his brother. But the momentum of the revolution quickly swept the Romanovs aside, and a republic was declared. The new provisional government of Duma leaders, basically liberal in composition, was headed by Alexander Kerensky, leader of a pro-labor party in the Duma. This regime, which ran Russia for less than a year, was the nation's one historic hope for Western-style democracy.

The great failing of the Kerensky government, however, was its inability to break radically enough with the past. Kerensky could not bring himself to take Russia out of the war that had already brought the Romanovs down. He launched one more vast offensive in the summer of 1917. When this last effort failed, the provisional government followed the czarist one into oblivion.

By this time, Lenin was back in Russia to pick up the pieces. The Bolshevik leader had hastened home after the fall of Nicholas II and devoted himself to organizing a second revolt against the "bourgeois liberal" Kerensky regime. An effort in June misfired. But in October, after the last military catastrophe, the time was ripe at last.

Beaten soldiers were streaming home that winter of 1917–1918, some of them mutinying, many bringing their rifles with them. The cities were hungry, cold, overcrowded, bitter. The provisional government was in disarray. The peasants were restless, the workers ready to strike.

The Bolsheviks were everywhere, plotting with the disaffected, haranguing mobs in the streets in order to intensify the disaffection. Lenin's bald head and short, choppy gestures became familiar in St. Petersburg. At this crucial juncture, the revolutionary who had devoted his life to Marxism had more sense than to try to explain the master's theories to the mob. "Land!" he shouted into the sea of upturned faces, land for the peasantry at last. "Bread!" for the starving cities. "Peace!" and an end to the hopeless carnage that the czar had bequeathed to Russia and that Kerensky, driven by miguided patriotism, had refused to reject. Land, bread, and peace did the job.

The fighting took place in the cities and was generally brief. Kerensky was driven from St. Petersburg into a long American exile. The walled Kremlin in Moscow fell after a bloodier battle. In other cities, Bolsheviks led workers' militias and squads of mutinous sailors from the Russian navy in quick seizures of power. The grip of the provisional government, never strong, was easily broken. The Bolshevik revolutionaries took their place, with Lenin at the head of the new government.

It was then that the Bolsheviks—soon renamed the Communists—showed what they were made of. For the great Bolshevik achievement lay not in seizing power but in holding on to it.

Through the late 1910s and early 1920s, the new Russian Communist government was beset by enemies on every side. So-called White Russian armies loyal to the czar took the field against the Reds. Subject nationalities—the Baltic states, Poland, and others—rebelled. Invading German armies forced a costly peace upon the new government. The newly independent Poles invaded Russia from the west, Russia's imperial rival Japan from the east. Allied forces—British, French, American—angry at Russia's separate peace and afraid of the Bolshevik virus, established beachheads in Russia and provided logistical support for her enemies. Thus surrounded and attacked from all sides, the Bolsheviks fought back with

an ingenuity, energy, and ruthlessness that finally carried the day.

Lenin threw a government together. He called for a constitutional convention, then dissolved it when peasant voters gave a majority to the SRs. He hastily nationalized large sectors of the Russian economy, less for doctrinaire reasons than to mobilize the nation's resources for civil war. And he jerry-built the first Red Army to fight it.

Lenin's right hand in the struggle was a relatively recent convert to bolshevism named Leon Trotsky. A thin, bespectacled, wild-haired intellectual, shrewd theoretician, and brilliant orator, Trotsky became the unlikely architect of the new Red Army. Roaring about Russia in his famous armored train, haranguing the troops or terrifying them by rigorous punishment for slackness or failure, Trotsky made a major contribution to the Bolshevik victory.

It was a costly triumph. The largest nation in Europe, already ravaged by the worst war in Western history, bled for more long years in the Russian Civil War. Red and White terrors rivaled each other in ferocity. Lenin himself was shot and badly wounded by an SR terrorist. Even the sailors, once the most dedicated of revolutionaries, rebelled at last, and Trotsky had to turn the Red Army on them in their turn.

The idealistic American journalist John Reed, who was in Russia in 1917, wrote a widely read account of the October Revolution called *Ten Days That Shook the World*. It took more like five years than ten days, and it was the retention rather than the seizing of power that earned the Bolsheviks their place in history. Nevertheless, they won. When Lenin, weakened by his immense exertions and his injury, died in 1924, the members of the renamed Communist party were the masters of Russia.

Beyond Their Wildest Dreams

After the immense strains of a decade of war and revolution, the 1920s saw a relaxation and a falling off of zeal in Russia—before the revolutionary drive was renewed once more in the Stalinist 1930s.

During the twenties, the Communist New Economic Policy actually represented a retreat on the economic front. Land was left in the hands of individual peasant proprietors; small businesses were left to entrepreneurs. Efforts to encourage revolution in other lands through the Communist International, or Comintern, had little success.

The great event of the twenties was a quiet power struggle in the Communist party after Lenin's death. And the winner was not one of the Old Man's close associates in prerevolutionary days—not even the

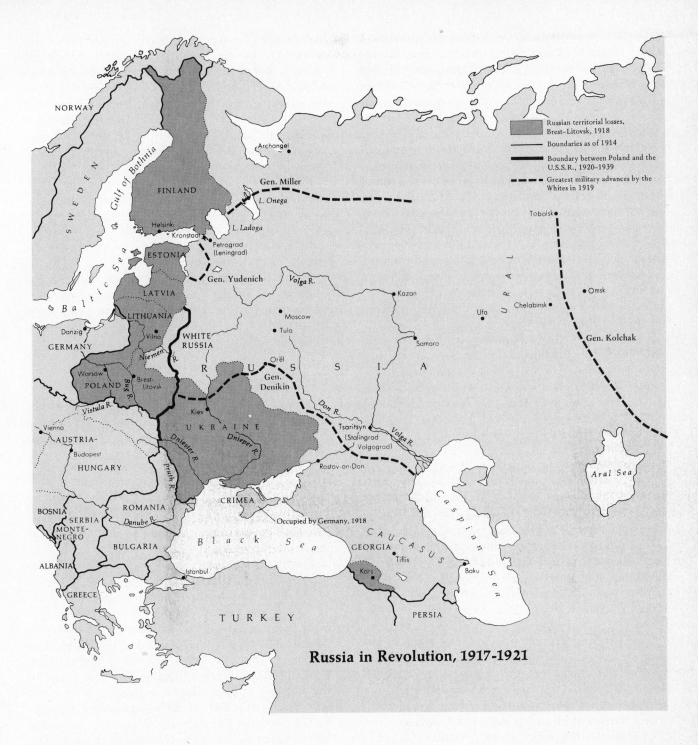

NORWAY

SWEDEN

Gulf of Bothnia

Archangel

Gen. Miller

FINLAND

L. Onega

Helsinki

L. Ladoga

Kronstadt

Baltic Sea

ESTONIA

Petrograd
(Leningrad)

Gen. Yudenich

Volga R.

Danzig

LATVIA

LITHUANIA

Vilna

WHITE
RUSSIA

Moscow

Kazan

Tobolsk

U R A L

Omsk

Chelabinsk

Ufa

Gen. Kolchak

GERMANY

Niemen R.

Tula

R   U   S   S   I   A

Warsaw

Vistula R.

POLAND

Bug R.

Brest-
Litovsk

Orël

Gen.
Denikin

Kiev

Don R.

Samara

Vienna

AUSTRIA-

Budapest

HUNGARY

UKRAINE

Dniester R.

Dnieper R.

Prut R.

Tsaritsyn
(Stalingrad
Volgograd)

Volga R.

Aral Sea

BOSNIA

SERBIA
MONTE-
NEGRO

ROMANIA

Danube R.

CRIMEA

Rostov-on-Don

Caspian Sea

BULGARIA

Occupied by Germany, 1918

Black   Sea

C A U C A S U S

GEORGIA

Tiflis

Baku

ALBANIA

GREECE

Istanbul

Kars

T U R K E Y

PERSIA

Russia in Revolution, 1917-1921

brilliant late convert Trotsky—but a stolid, hard-working Bolshevik from the south called Joseph Stalin.

Stalin—real name Dzhugashvili—was the son of a heavy-fisted cobbler from Georgia, in the bandit-haunted mountainous Caucasus region. After a brief seminary education he had become a convert to Marxism and a revolutionary organizer, preaching his new faith to railway workers and serving several terms in prison and in Siberia. While Lenin and Trotsky were arguing the party's future in Switzerland, Stalin was organizing "expropriations" at home—bank robberies to acquire funds for the party in Russia. Lenin never knew him well, added him to the party's Central Committee as an afterthought, and would no doubt have been astonished to learn that half a dozen years after his death, Stalin would be hailed everywhere as "the Lenin of today."

Stalin's rise to power was a triumph of political savvy, hard work, and the organization-man mentality. He was secretary of the Communist party in the twenties, and he made that post the real center of power in Russia. Running the party machine, he came to know its leaders—who the idealists were, who the opportunists, who needed what and how to get it. Neither a great Marxist theoretician nor a spellbinding orator, he had a much more valuable skill—a talent for manipulating power blocs. By the end of the decade Stalin ruled Russia. His rivals had either joined the chorus of support for "the Lenin of today" or, like Trotsky, were on their way to exile abroad.

As the 1930s came on, then, Stalin set out to win his own niche in history—by taking up the revolution once more. His chosen front was economic development, his method a series of Five-Year Plans for unprecedented economic growth in the most backward of the world's great powers.

Russia's long effort to catch up economically with western Europe had begun in Peter the Great's time two hundred years before. The reforming czar Alexander II in the 1860s and 1870s and turn-of-the-century financial minister Witte had nudged the process on. But World War I had shown how far behind Russia still was: she had been the first to collapse under the strains of modern, mechanized war. Feeling surrounded by capitalist enemies—especially after the Civil War, with its foreign interventions—the Communists had particular reason to strengthen the nation's economy. And Karl Marx seemed to show them the way: through government control, central planning, and collective effort, Communist Russia would succeed where czarist Russia had failed.

During the 1930s the first three Five-Year Plans did, in fact, transform and in key areas expand the Russian economy beyond the wildest dreams of Peter the Great. The Russian government assumed control of industry, agriculture, finance, and trade in the Soviet Union. Government planning commissions worked out schedules of growth for each region, each sector of the economy. Resources were allocated, quotas decreed for every sector, every factory and farm, every worker at his or her desk, lathe, or tractor.

In industry the results were spectacular. Great hydroelectric projects, huge dams, steel mills, tractor factories went up. Whole industrial complexes sprang from the empty steppes. Production goals were reached and surpassed. If there were questions about some of the statistics, the achievement was nonetheless genuine. In a capitalist world still reeling under the hammer blows of the Great Depression, Russia's achievement was particularly awesome.

Agriculture was collectivized under government control. Private farms were merged into large state farms owned by the government, or into farms run collectively by the peasants. Modern agricultural methods and centrally located government machine-tractor stations were introduced to improve production. The increased output was to be used to feed the industrial cities and sold abroad for vitally needed foreign capital. Advances on the agricultural front, however, were slower and much more costly than in the industrial sector, as we will see.

Nevertheless, as World War II came on, Stalin could claim convincingly to have carried Russia's long revolution to something of a climax. Communist-party rule was unquestioned in the vast one-party state, and state socialism had become a reality in the largest nation in the world.

What this transformation of society had cost the country will be deferred to the following chapter, which considers the rise of authoritarian government between the wars. For Stalin had also made Russia the largest totalitarian state in the world.

Viva Pancho!

The Mexican Revolution, a beacon in Latin America, was longer than the Russian Revolution and in some ways more complex than the Chinese. Like the Russian upheaval, the revolution in Mexico began with an abdication under pressure and ended with a massive attempt at a social transformation of the nation in the 1930s. In between, however—as in China—a host of conflicting leaders, armies, and parties competed for power in the bloodiest revolution in Latin American history.

Porfirio Díaz, Mexico's heavy-handed *caudillo* dictator for thirty-five years, was eighty years old in 1910. He had brought the country economic development in the usual Latin American way, through export sales of agricultural and mineral products, especially oil, which was controlled by British and American capitalists. But 90 percent of Mexico's *mestizos* and Indians were still desperately poor peons on the ranches or haciendas of a handful of wealthy landowners. Workers on the foreign-owned railways and in the mines and oil wells, which were becoming more numerous, were equally poverty-stricken. The population was 80 percent illiterate, miserably unhealthy, and kept in line by brutal rural police and federal troops.

Yet there was little opposition. A few middle-class liberals muttered about democracy. Workers occasionally struck and were suppressed. There were bandits in the hills. Otherwise the country was calm. The aging *caudillo*'s regime seemed impregnable.

Then in 1910 began a cycle of revolution that would last, in one form or another, for thirty years.

The first decade of revolt turned Mexico into a cauldron of violence. The next twenty years saw the establishment of a new revolutionary elite in power —and climaxed in a wave of social reform that paralleled and in some ways outdistanced the contemporary New Deal in the United States. At a time when much of Latin America was turning sharply to the right under a renewed surge of "personalist" dictatorships, Mexico's revolutionary achievement was remarkable indeed.

The names of most of the leaders who made this revolution—Madero, Villa, Zapata, Obregón, Cárdenas, and others—are not household worlds outside Latin America, as names such as Lenin, Stalin, and Mao have become. But the name of Cárdenas, at least, should surely be added to that list—though he stands closer in means and aims to Franklin Roosevelt than to Joseph Stalin.

Some of the rest of Mexico's revolutionary leaders, such as Zapata and Pancho Villa, have become popular folk heroes in Mexico. Others, such as General Huerta in the early years, were very much the ruffians that preacherly President Wilson across the border called them. But even the revolutionaries who succumbed to the temptations of power, such as the Northern Dynasty of presidents who ruled between 1915 and 1934, were at least efficient organizers who took some steps to help the Mexican masses.

The violent decade that took the lives of some two million Mexicans began almost casually with outbreaks of revolutionary activity against the aging Díaz in 1910. Three very different men led this diverse opposition. Francisco Madero was a slightly built, highly idealistic leader of middle-class reformers. In 1910 he broke the somnolence of Mexican politics by calling for free elections across the nation. Pancho Villa was a bandit chief from the north, a flamboyant incarnation of Mexican macho spirit and an instinctive cavalry leader. Villa led a motley horde of *vaqueros* (cowboys) in revolt in the large, arid northern province of Chihuahua. And Emiliano Zapata was a peasant horse and mule dealer in the mountainous southern province of Morelos. About this same time, he mobilized a guerrilla force to compel the redistribution of some of the local land among his long-suffering Indian and *mestizo* neighbors.

With pressure gathering on all sides, the long-pampered and inefficient Díaz regime suddenly showed its weakness. The government began to crumble. Porfirio Díaz himself abruptly packed up and left for Europe, and Mexico became a battleground for the violent forces thus unleashed.

There is no space here to follow the gaudy, bloody tale of the next decade—roughly 1910–1920—in any detail. The frail Madero was hailed as the Apostle of

Emiliano Zapata, champion of the peasants of southern Mexico. One of the most popular leaders of the Mexican Revolution, Zapata became a legend after his violent death. (Library of Congress)

Democracy, elected president, and murdered by survivors of the Díaz regime who still hoped to recover power. Zapata carried his "land to the peasants" crusade all the way to Mexico City, shared the limelight for a time with Villa, was forced back into Morelos, and finally was killed by troops under a flag of truce. Pancho Villa, after a colorful, bloody time of plundering, was driven back to his bailiwick in Chihuahua, took to killing gringos so as to precipitate U.S. intervention in the chaos, and had a fine time riding rings around General Pershing's expeditionary force. He was finally murdered by a personal enemy in the early 1920s. All three lived on as Mexican folk heroes; none had done much for Mexico.

Meanwhile, a succession of leaders from the dry, spacious northern provinces that abut the American Southwest came to the fore. This succession of powerful men, the Northern Dynasty, in time established a reasonably stable regime that at least preached some concern for the welfare of the Mexican people.

They were not saints. Perhaps the worst was General Huerta, a drunken warlord who briefly ran central Mexico from the bars and brothels of Mexico City. A self-aggrandizing politician from the old Díaz days named Carranza succeeded Huerta. Seeking popular support, Carranza at least left Mexico the Constitution of 1917, the most liberal in Latin America and a model for later revolutionaries throughout the southern half of the Western Hemisphere. This document promised land to the peasants; decent hours and wages as well as unions for workers; equal pay for women; and at least the possibility of nationalization of the property of the reactionary Mexican Catholic church and of exploitative foreign capitalists.

The United States intervened twice in this turmoil, in 1914 and 1916, to protect American lives and property and to teach Latin Americans how to choose leaders of a higher moral caliber, as Wilson unctuously put it.

During the 1920s and 1930s the Mexicans emerged from the bloodbath of the preceding decade and put together a remarkable compromise regime that realized some of the exalted promises of the Constitution of 1917.

Making the Revolution Work

The instrument that brought Mexico order out of chaos and some measure of social justice was a unifying, centralizing political party. Eventually known as the PRM, or Party of the Mexican Revolution, this organization combined all the nation's new leadership cadres—the military, the bureaucracy, businessmen and intellectuals, and now the labor unions and the peasantry—in a single structure that would run Mexico for the next fifty years.

It was essentially a one-party system, and more socialistic than anything ever seen north of the Rio Grande. But no less a democrat than Franklin Roosevelt was willing to declare a Good Neighbor Policy toward Cárdenas, the Mexican leader who carried the social revolution furthest in the 1930s.

The twenties saw two other leaders from northern Mexico—a one-armed, self-proclaimed socialist general named Obregón and his handpicked successor, the "Maximum Chief" Calles—lay down the party's basic structure and smother the last flames of revolution. These men organized the party and the basic PRM alliance of ruling elements. They made a beginning, at least, at land redistribution, supported some engagingly corrupt labor leaders against foreign business interests, and began a long and brutal struggle with the Mexican church. Too long in the saddle, these middle-aged revolutionaries also lined their own pockets in the process of rebuilding Mexico.

In 1934, however, the PRM leadership chose for the next president the last and most admired of all the leaders of Mexico's long revolution: Lázaro Cárdenas. Cárdenas was an Indian, young and vigorous, a tireless activist, and an instinctive politician. A friend to socialists, peasants, and workers, he was willing and able to defy the North American colossus and get away with it. He carried the revolutionary drive for social justice further than many believed possible.

Cárdenas was as much an organizer as he was an idealist. He kept the military on his side by letting generals alone—and won over the troops by military reforms. He earned the allegiance of much of the business community by supporting industrialization by Mexican rather than foreign investors. He replaced corrupt old revolutionaries with young radicals eager to make a social revolution of their own. He supported a huge new labor union and an even larger peasants' union, bringing new spokesmen for these groups into the PRM.

With this massive base of support, Cárdenas redistributed twice as much land to the tillers as all his predecessors had, some to private holders and some to collective farms. He supported workers' demands and raised their standard of living. He also supported Mexican entrepreneurs, who for the first time began to produce sufficient quantities of manufactured goods to break the ancient cycle of dependency on foreigners. And he astonished the world by nationalizing the American- and British-run oil industry, thus breaking the back of foreign exploitation of this key Mexican resource. Britain and the United States, preoccupied with the looming Nazi threat in Europe, bit the bullet.

There were failures, of course. The nationalized oil industry, deprived of foreign capital and technological know-how, almost expired in the early years. Mexico suffered throughout the period from a lack of technological skills, even as Mexican art became world-famous. And of course the PRM, for all its social conscience, continued to suppress any serious political opposition with a firm hand.

But when Cárdenas retired in 1940, Mexico was in crucial ways a different country from the Mexico of Porfirio Díaz. Its thirty-year revolution would be a banner and a beacon to many of the Latin American republics to the south.

The Legacy of Dr. Sun

The longest of all the long revolutions was the Chinese Revolution of 1911–1949, which began a few years before World War I and ended several years after World War II, in the hectic early years of the Cold War. These four decades include only the military phase of the longest revolution, leaving out the revolutionary transformation of Chinese society that followed the Communist victory of 1949. But these social and economic changes too were prepared by the forty years of political and military struggle to be traced here.

China's twentieth-century revolution—like all the movements to be dealt with in the remainder of this chapter—was triggered by contact with the West. In the case of China, it was the catastrophic encounter that ended the nineteenth century. It was Western victories that destroyed the Manchu dynasty by revealing its weakness. Westernized Chinese leaders fought the subsequent revolution, and their Western ideologies determined China's future direction. The victory of either of the nation's major factions, the Nationalists or the Communists, thus meant that China would join the modern world that first took shape under Western influences. There *was* no Confucian candidate!

The three great leaders of this long revolution were all world figures in their time: Dr. Sun, the founder, and Chiang and Mao, who fought for his legacy. In forty years, in a country the size of the continental United States and several times as populous, many other leaders rose and fell, many more rebellious banners were raised and struck down than can even be touched on here. But the central thread of Sun Yatsen's legacy and the long duel between Chiang Kaishek and Mao Tse-tung does give coherence and direction to the story of this longest and bloodiest of twentieth-century revolutions.

Bullied by foreign imperialists and deeply divided over how far to go in learning from the West in order to defeat the West, China was dissolving into a hopeless confusion of conflicting theories, ambitions, and factions as the present century began. The mandate of Heaven had clearly passed from the battered Manchus: but to whom?

Old realities and new influences collided in turn-of-the-century China. Established court politicians such as the military leader Yüan Shih-k'ai, powerful provincial generals, the perennially dangerous Chinese secret societies, and the eternally exploited, increasingly restless peasant masses would play important parts in the coming struggle, as such groups had in the past. New groups with equally important roles included the overseas Chinese community, many of them wealthy merchants scattered over Southeast Asia, the western Pacific, and even the United States; the growing numbers of Western-educated Chinese

students trained in Japan, Europe, or the United States, or at the new Chinese university in Peking; and the emerging Chinese proletariat, exploited products of the rapid industrialization of great Chinese cities such as Shanghai.

Among the better-educated of these groups, at least, Western ideas ranging from Darwinian evolution to nineteenth-century political ideologies circulated freely around 1900. Magazines and journals, clubs and discussion groups flourished, spreading the new ideas and debating their application to China's multiplying problems. Out of the tangle, two basic tendencies evolved: a reformist campaign for a constitutional monarchy, which reached even into court circles, and a revolutionary demand for a Chinese republic, which found support among radical students and insurrectionary organizations.

The reformers had their day first. In a final effort to save the Manchu dynasty, the Dowager Empress Tz'u-hsi uncharacteristically acquiesced in a series of changes in the old order that were far more drastic than any thus far. In the early years of the twentieth century, then, the nationwide system of Confucian civil-service examinations, which had served the empire for the better part of two thousand years, was abolished. Provincial legislative assemblies were introduced, and then a national assembly in Peking. Plans were laid for a gradual transition to a constitutional monarchy like those in Europe or Japan.

The result was to provide more issues for debate as the old Confucian-educated ruling class saw themselves being phased out, and new arenas to debate those issues—the new assemblies. Feuds broke out between the powerful Yüan Shih-k'ai and the regent for the three-year-old emperor who succeeded Tz'u-hsi in 1908. A rash of abortive popular insurrections made the weakness of the monarchy even clearer. By 1911, the hour of the republican revolutionaries had come.

Sun Yat-sen (1866–1925) was the best-known revolutionary proponent of a Chinese republic, both in China and abroad. Born of peasant stock near Canton, in the cosmopolitan south, he was a thoroughly Westernized Chinese. He had studied at a Christian mission school in Honolulu, read for his medical degree in the British colony of Hong Kong, established his first revolutionary organization in Westernized Japan. He had even made a special visit to his native hamlet to break the village idols, thereby symbolizing his rejection of the old China.

Sun had been to the United States and Europe and was well known among the wealthy overseas Chinese community. He had been involved in secret-society uprisings in South China. He had developed the charismatic personality and the ability to bring rival factions together that would earn him the title of Father of the Chinese Revolution.

Sun Yat-sen's legacy to those who followed him was also fully assembled by the time of the Revolution of 1911. That legacy took the form of his famous—and highly flexible—Three Principles of the People.

The Three Principles are usually stated as nationalism, democracy, and socialism. By nationalism Sun meant opposition to the Manchus as well as to Western imperialists. By democracy he intended democracy for all Chinese and constitutional government modeled in part on that of the United States. The socialist (more literally, "people's livelihood") plank was a rather undeveloped economic principle derived not from Marx or any other Western socialist but from the then-popular theories of the American land-tax crusader Henry George.

In the broadest sense, these three principles summed up all the European ideological development of the century following the French Revolution. These sweeping social ideals, suitably modified by a much longer indigenous tradition of social thought, would now begin the twentieth-century transformation of China.

Sun Yat-sen would work for the last fifteen years of his life (like Lenin, he died in his fifties) to make the Chinese republic a democractic reality. Generalissimo Chiang Kai-shek would become the maximum leader of China's Nationalist party through the 1920s, 1930s, and 1940s. Chairman Mao Tse-tung would organize and lead China's Communist party and would rule the nation through the 1950s and 1960s and into the 1970s. The Three Principles that were China's inheritance from Dr. Sun thus sum up much of the nation's history since.

Warlords and Student Rebels

The Republic came quickly. Within three years of Empress Tz'u-hsi's death in 1908, the demoralized empire finally collapsed in a welter of peasant rice riots, student agitation, army revolts, court intrigues, and revolutionary outbreaks led by Dr. Sun's own organization, the United League. Sun, like Lenin, was out of the country when the monarchy fell. After many abortive uprisings elsewhere in the nation, a local army revolt at Wuchang in the Yangtze Valley of central China in the fall of 1911 snowballed into a far-reaching repudiation of Manchu rule. Sun, who was in the United States rallying support for the cause, read about the revolution in a Denver newspaper. He hurried home in time to be proclaimed first president of the new Republic of China in January of 1912.

But the long revolution in China, like those in Russia and Mexico, rather began than ended with the collapse of the old regime. The diehard supporters of the old order, however, had their innings first.

Like Madero in Mexico, Sun was rather a symbol of the revolution than a ruler. Knowing that he had neither the power nor the support to govern a nation still sliding toward anarchy, he shrewdly used his new position to win to the republican cause the one man who could govern the country. Yüan Shih-k'ai was the most powerful survivor of the old order—court official, famous general and military reformer, currently prime minister of the constitutional monarchy still hanging on in Peking. In return for a promise of the presidency of the new republic, Yüan engineered the dissolution of the monarchy. In the spring of 1912 Sun stepped down and Yüan became the second president of the Chinese republic.

Yüan Shih-k'ai, however, was thoroughly a product of the old China. He accepted the newfangled foreign title—and at once began to intrigue to establish himself as first emperor of a new Chinese dynasty.

But the old order was finished in China. Sun opposed Yüan's plans; local rebellions again broke out, and some of the president's own generals refused to suppress them. With the outbreak of World War I in 1914, Japan further embarrased the new regime, first by seizing Germany's possessions in Chinese Shantung, then by imposing the notorious Twenty-one Demands on China's rulers.

These imperialistic demands included acceptance of Japanese political, military, and financial advisers, further economic penetration by Japan, and recognition of a paramount position for Japan in Manchuria and elsewhere in the north. Such concessions would have made the enormous continental empire little more than a protectorate of the island kingdom. Yüan, hoping for Japanese support for his dynastic ambitions, accepted most of the proposals—and turned the nation definitively against himself. His dream of an imperial restoration frustrated, Yüan died in 1916.

With the passing of the old order's strong man, China, as so often before in her long history, fell apart. A facade of republican government continued at Peking, but its authority was minimal. Military cliques claimed some power in North and in South China. Sun Yat-sen set to work to reorganize his faction, now dubbed the Kuomintang or Nationalist party. But real authority quickly fell into the hands of the local power brokers in the provinces, most of them military leaders with private armies who became known as warlords. Through the late teens and early twenties, the anarchy of the warlord era prevailed.

Chinese warlords, like the regional *caudillos* of nineteenth-century Latin America, were typically aggressive military commanders with strong and sometimes colorful personalities. Many were former generals or bandits, and they ruled their territories by force. Their armies were strengthened by modern weapons and by the mobility made available by railways and river steamers. They lived off the revenues of cities or seaports, by taxing or plundering the peasants, and sometimes on subsidies from foreign powers. They were quick to voice the new slogans about democracy, patriotism, and the people's welfare—and they were an unmitigated plague on the land.

But there was a new force too during this time—the Chinese student movement—and it grew in influence. These young products of the new school system, Westernized yet bitter enemies of Western exploitation of China, took seriously the ideological legacy that the warlords degraded. The students became the leaders in the hurricane of national outrage that exploded in the spring of 1919—the famous May Fourth Movement.

The May Fourth Movement was a nationwide wave of strikes and demonstrations against foreign exploitation—and the Chinese weakness that made such exploitation possible—launched by the students at Peking University. Triggered by the refusal of the Versailles Peace Conference to require the Japanese to return Shantung to China, the movement focused on a commemoration of Japan's Twenty-one Demands of five years before.

The student organizations were severely punished for their patriotic defiance of authority. But their cause triumphed. Workers' strikes, merchants' boycotts of Japanese goods, and public outrage drove the current cabinet in Peking to resign and forced the Chinese government to refuse to sign the Treaty of Versailles.

Students also took a leading role in China's New Culture Movement, a sweeping reassessment of the nation's ancient cultural heritage and a search for new directions for China. American pragmatist John Dewey, British pacifist and philosopher Bertrand Russell, Indian writer and Nobel laureate Rabindranath Tagore, and others toured the land lecturing to the new clubs and student groups. Chinese cultural and intellectual innovators of all sorts published in the new journals that spearheaded the New Culture Movement.

The most important new direction of the 1920s in China, however, was a turning away from Japanese, American, and other earlier influences and a new interest in Communist Russia. From postrevolutionary, pre-Stalinist Russia came antiimperialist assurances, political and military advisers, and the doctrines of Marx and Lenin. Marxism-Leninism explained imperialism in simple terms: it was a consequence of Western capitalism. Leninism offered the Bolshevik model of tightly knit organization and discipline in challenging the weak government in Peking and the foreign exploiters still present everywhere in China.

In 1920 a small group at Peking University began to study Marxism seriously. In 1921 the Chinese Communist party was organized at Shanghai. Among the organizers was a former Peking University student named Mao Tse-tung.

Chiang Kai-shek and the Bandits

Some Russian Communists were still working for the world revolution that had failed to materialize after World War I. They were realistic enough to realize, however, that the only group strong enough to pose a threat to the Chinese government in Peking was not the handful of Communists who organized in 1921, but Sun Yat-sen's Nationalist party, the Kuomintang. To the Nationalists, therefore, they offered no Marxism but instead practical help in organizing the Kuomintang as a disciplined Bolshevik-style party. The Russians also sent military advisers to retrain the Nationalist army under the superintendent of the Kuomintang military academy, a young officer named Chiang.

Chiang Kai-shek (1886–1975), a patriotic, ambitious soldier with training in both Japan and Russia, was soon carving out a central position of power for himself. Chiang's landlord background and the elitist military tradition of the samurai that he had absorbed in Japan had left him with little sympathy for either democracy or socialism. At the Whampoa Military Academy near Canton he trained a generation of officers to unify their country—and to support their teacher in the power struggles to come.

Sun Yat-sen died in 1925. The party he had founded continued to build its power in the south. Then in 1927 the Kuomintang armies, supported by Russian advisers and arms and led by Chiang Kaishek, moved out of South China in the long-awaited Northern Campaign to unify the nation. Scores of warlord armies capitulated or joined the host as it advanced. Propagandists spread out ahead of the troops, convincing many that Chiang was the man who could restore the one indisputable political necessity for peace and prosperity in China: unity.

Soon most of the country was his. The Peking government dithered, would fall the following year. Meanwhile, Chiang had what must have seemed a secondary problem to deal with: the divisive disagreements that kept cropping up between his Nationalist followers and the more recent Communist cadres in the Kuomintang.

The Chinese Communist party, founded largely as

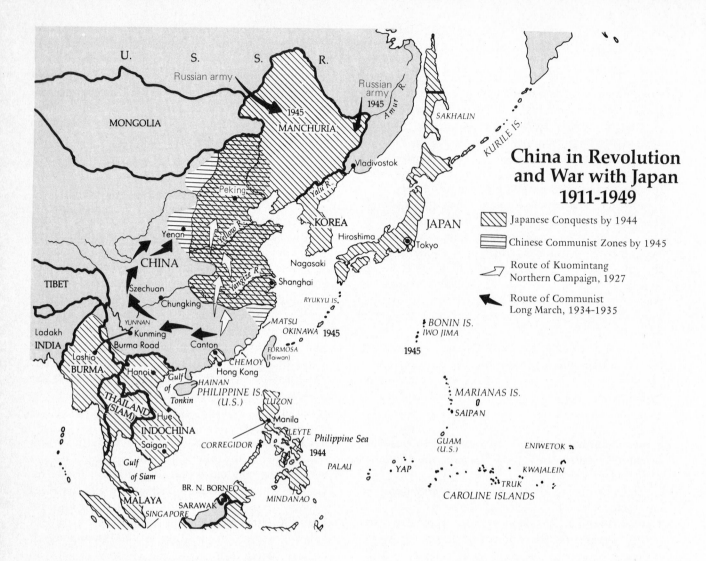

China in Revolution and War with Japan 1911-1949

	Japanese Conquests by 1944
	Chinese Communist Zones by 1945
	Route of Kuomintang Northern Campaign, 1927
	Route of Communist Long March, 1934-1935

a student group, had found many recruits among factory and railroad workers in rapidly industrializing cities such as Canton and Shanghai. Russian advisers, however, had urged the Chinese Communists to join the Nationalists in their drive to overthrow the Peking government. This they had done. But the alliance was purely one of convenience, and in 1927 the victorious Chiang Kai-shek decided to destroy these potential enemies within the Kuomintang.

He struck swiftly and without warning. Trapped in the cities where they had gathered to organize the workers, the Communist cadres were slaughtered. Their enclaves of proletarian support, isolated in that vast peasant country, were surrounded and crushed, and with them the Communist party in China. Or so it seemed.

Handfuls of the routed Reds escaped to the countryside, fled to the villages. Among the few who had already sought to organize the peasant masses was a now considerably more mature Mao Tse-tung (1893–1976). A man of peasant stock himself and a former

student Communist from Peking, he never forgot the devastating lesson of the debacle of 1927. In 1926 he had espoused the orthodox Marxist view that "the industrial proletariat is the leading force in our revolution"; but by 1928 he was pointing out that the communist cadres "have sprung from the agrarian revolution and are fighting for their own interests . . ."[2] No matter what Marx or Lenin said about the vanguard role of the industrial proletariat, in China it was the peasantry, with its incalculable numbers and ancient grievances, that would be the wave of the revolutionary future.

Chiang went on to capture Peking in 1928. Mao established a Communist base in the interior, in the hills of Kiangsi Province. Here, like Zapata in Mexico, he began to divide large estates among the peasants, to provide education and some health care, and

[2]Mao Tse-tung, *Mao Tse-tung: An Anthology of His Writings*, ed. Anne Freemantle (New York: New American Library, 1962), pp. 59, 90.

to teach a modified version of Marxist socialism. This Kiangsi Soviet became the model for the basic Maoist tactic thereafter—a tactic as old as guerrilla warfare—which he called "swimming in the peasant sea."

Chiang, established as head of the Chinese republic after 1928, tried to provide for the economic and social development of China too. He had married an American-educated woman named Soong Mei-ling, who, as Madame Chiang Kai-shek would become an immensely valuable voice for Chiang in the United States over the years. The Generalissimo, as the Western papers called him, thus acquired important American support. But he was also closely tied to Chinese banking families, and he depended on cronies and clients to help him run the country—all important political creditors to be repaid with favors and promotions.

The nation had been badly damaged by the warlord era, and now it faced an even graver foreign threat—a renewal of Japanese imperialist pressure in the 1930s. Thus surrounded by problems, China's foremost general nevertheless found time to launch a series of so-called antibandit campaigns to rout the Communists out of Kiangsi in the early thirties. Not till 1934 did Chiang succeed in dislodging Mao from his hills, and then only by completely surrounding the area and burning his way in through the villages.

Perhaps 100,000 Communists escaped the tightening noose. Led by Mao and his right-hand man Chou En-lai, the survivors of the shattered Kiangsi Soviet fled once more, this time north and west, pursued by the Nationalist armies. The perilous and costly year-long march that followed took them some 6000 meandering miles to a new sanctuary in the northern province of Shensi. Only a few thousand of them made it.

In Chinese Communist history, this is the Long March. The terrible casualties, the desperate river crossings, the frozen mountain passes that Mao's men and women moved through on their northern march have been immortalized in every art since the Communist victory in 1949. In the mid 1930s, however, as Mao and his remnant bands settled into the caves of their new Shensi base, ultimate victory must have looked very far away indeed.

Mao's Way

Chiang Kai-shek had failed to destroy the "Red bandits." But he had much worse problems in the 1930s. In 1931 the Japanese had seized the industrializing northern province of Manchuria. In 1937 they launched a major invasion of China proper. By 1939 most of eastern China was in their hands, and Chiang Kai-shek had retreated to the interior, to what became his wartime capital of Chungking.

Confronted with this massive foreign threat, many Nationalist leaders urged that the final destruction of Mao's Communists be postponed for the duration. The Communists themselves organized guerrilla warfare against the Japanese occupying forces in North China, thus strengthening their image as patriots. In a dramatic development, some of Chiang's own officers virtually kidnapped him and compelled him to sit down and negotiate a truce with the Communists so that both might concentrate on the war with Japan. Throughout the Second World War—1941–1945 in Asia—this uneasy armistice between the two rivals prevailed.

Chiang was China's recognized ruler, meeting in the larger Allied summit conferences with the rest of the Big Five—Roosevelt, Churchill, Stalin, and the Free French leader de Gaulle, most of whose country was also occupied by the enemy. Mao, meanwhile, built up his Red Army, strengthened his peasant support, and nicked away at the Japanese. Chiang failed to expel the invaders, and as his Chungking government grew more autocratic, corrupt, and inefficient, many Chinese who were not peasants began to wonder if Mao might not after all be a viable alternative to the Generalissimo.

When World War II ended in 1945, then, things at long last began to go Mao's way. In the last days of the war, the Soviet Union declared war on Japan and quickly liberated large chunks of North China. Though Stalin had not approved of Mao's peasant-based communism—had even apparently expelled Mao from the Communist International for a time—the Silent Man in the Kremlin now moved to help the Chinese Communists. Liberated territories and captured weapons were turned over to Mao's forces, not to Chiang's. Mao was left stronger than ever as the final confrontation approached.

As the later 1940s passed, furthermore, Chiang Kai-shek's American friends began to lose patience with him. Envoys from the United States demanded that he clean up the corruption in his government. Like his Russian advisers in the 1920s, his American mentors in the 1940s urged him to work with the Communists to unify the country.

Rivalries and suspicions that went back twenty years were not so easily erased, however. Within a couple of years after the defeat of Japan, clashes between Nationalist and Communist troops had escalated again to full-scale civil war. And this time Mao was on the offensive. Chiang's retreat into the South became a rout, and the roads were littered with abandoned American military hardware.

By 1949 Chiang had withdrawn from the main-

Chairman Mao. Dismissed as a ''Red bandit'' by Generalissimo Chiang Kai-shek, Mao Tse-tung ''swam in the peasant sea'' and defeated Chiang, to become the revolutionary ruler of the world's most populous nation. (UPI/Bettmann Newsphotos)

land altogether to the large offshore island of Taiwan (Formosa), where he was to survive as president of a Chinese mini-republic protected by an American fleet for the rest of his life. Mao, meanwhile, stood before a crowd of hundreds of thousands in Peking's T'ien-an Men Square to announce the new People's Republic of China—which he also would rule until his death.

Chiang's career was essentially over in 1949. But Mao's had only reached the halfway point. The great social revolution he would bring to China, the military clashes with India and the United States in Korea, the sometimes disastrous social experiments of his later years, and his immense reputation as a Third World revolutionary all lay in the future in 1949.

Mao's round, smiling face and slicked-back hair and the wart on his chin were unfamiliar to a world used to Chiang's handsome graying visage. But one thing, at least, became clear quite soon. China, after a half century of chaos, had found unity once more—

this time under a man who was as much a child of the twentieth century as he was a product of the ancient land he ruled.

THE REVOLT AGAINST THE WEST

A Gathering of Forces

Across the European intercontinental empires that sprawled over Asia and Africa, rebellious impulses also flickered and flared up during the two decades between the wars. They produced no great revolutions like those in Russia, China, and Mexico. But they did keep alive the spirit of resistance that had been born during the New Imperialism and that would bear fruit at last during the Great Liberation after World War II.

Most of the colonial struggles of the intervening period were not military insurrections, like the resistance of earlier decades. The peoples of Africa and Asia had learned that force was not the answer when dealing with Westerners, who were, for that time at least, the masters of the new technological warfare. Instead, the resistance tended to take political form within the institutional framework made available under colonial governments.

The new leaders of this simmering revolt against the West were now almost uniformly Western-educated. Most had studied in mission schools. Many had gone on for further training in Europe or America. They were people who knew the imperialists well, spoke their languages, and understood the rules of the political game as it was played by their colonial rulers. Many of them had also spent time in Western jails, but this too they were able to turn to their advantage as leaders of unfree peoples.

The Asian and African independence movements they led were for the most part at early stages of development during the 1920s and 1930s. They were preoccupied with such basics as defining goals, which might range from reform of the colonial administration through autonomy within the empire to complete independence. There was also the problem of gathering in adherents—not so easy when Western training had cut many leaders off from their own people. Finally, there was the matter of how best to organize for effective opposition. This last raised a number of very practical questions. Were study groups a good place to begin? Was it time to move on to a political party? Was terrorist activity necessary?

All the antiimperialist movements were primarily nationalist in content and tone. They drew heavily on the nationalist movements of nineteenth-century Europe for the basic idea of nationhood, but they were indigenous movements in terms of their characteristics, sought-after rights, and sense of destiny.

A detailed survey of these movements would yield nothing but a bewildering array of organizations, issues, small struggles won or lost. It is the slow gathering of forces we need to be aware of here in the colonial world, the preparation for the Great Liberation to come. With this in mind, we will trace in some detail the growth of one of the greatest of these movements—the Congress party of Gandhi's India—and attempt a few sweeping generalizations about the independence organizations among African peoples during this period.

The Great Soul of India

India during the early decades of the twentieth century was still the India of the Raj—the period of British supremacy—and the jewel in the crown of the British Empire. Ironically, if perhaps understandably, it was here that the most successful of anti-British independence movements evolved.

British rule had brought some distinct benefits to India. British engineers had built tens of thousands of miles of railroads, roads, and canals across the subcontinent, stimulating business activity and a new surge in the growth of India's traditionally bustling commercial middle classes. Pressured by Indian demands, the British took steps toward Indian self-government. Indians were admitted to higher positions in the colonial administration, including the English viceroy's advisory council. Provincial legislatures—elected by propertied elites—were introduced. Formal education was made available for more people than ever before, and Oxford and Cambridge were opened to the talented sons of India's *rajas* and urban wealth. There were attempts to improve public health in that huge and in places densely crowded stretch of Asia.

But British rule, for all its benefits, had cost Indians dearly. The new transportation networks, for instance, benefited the English economy more than the Indian, facilitating Britain's extraction of a third of India's raw materials and India's receipt of two fifths of her imports from Britain. The Western concept of private property, which undermined traditional family ownership and government claims on land, made some Indians very wealthy—and others poorer than they had ever been. Western education undermined India's traditional culture. Even Western health measures brought new problems by stimulating the disastrous population growth of twentieth-century India. And despite "steps toward" independence, genuine freedom still seemed very far away.

The Indian National Congress, or Congress party, had been organized in 1885 by a group of moderate middle-class reformers, mostly lawyers, teachers, and journalists. They had won important reforms from the British. At the same time, a Hindu renaissance of arts and letters had kindled a renewed pride among educated Indians. Around the turn of the century, a burst of nationalist violence that led to repressive measures by the British had further encouraged Indian nationalism and opposition to foreign rule.

But India still seemed an unlikely candidate for a popular nationalistic independence movement as World War I drew to a close. The isolation of her countless tiny villages, the traditional lines of social cleavage between the castes, the Hindu-Muslim split, the lack of a common language, and the great distance between the well-off, Western-educated leadership and the Indian masses looked like insuperable obstacles.

The man who bridged these gaps was Mohandas K. Gandhi (1869–1948), who became known to the world as Mahatma Gandhi, the Great Soul of India.

Raised by pious, well-to-do Hindu parents, young Gandhi was shipped off to London to study law. Isolated for years in a London slum, he pored over a potpourri of spiritual sources, from the ancient Hindu *Bhagavad-Gita* (Song of God) and the Christian Bible to nineteenth-century prophets such as Tolstoy and Thoreau. His first campaign for the oppressed came not in India but in South Africa, where he was sent as a young man by his Indian law firm. Here he took up the cause of the Indian contract laborers who worked as peons in the South African gold mines. The success of the peaceful protests he organized there brought him home to India to a hero's welcome from the Congress party.

Gandhi's message and methods were set from the time of his return during the First World War. Building upon the ancient Hindu principle of *ahimsa* (nonviolence), he organized a series of nonviolent demonstrations, first for reform in the administration of the Raj, then for Indian independence. He went repeatedly and peacefully to jail for his cause, frequently turning imprisonment into victory by embarking upon prolonged hunger strikes. As his reputation as a spiritual leader grew, he abandoned his Western clothing and life style entirely, dressed in a traditional Indian costume of homespun, and lived the life of a Hindu guru of an earlier age.

The principles he championed were an odd mix of ancient and modern. He urged a return to the simplest of ancient Indian ways of life. His campaign to get Indians to reject British manufactured cloth and

Mahatma Gandhi, Indian Congress party leader, shown here with his famous spinning wheel. Gandhi's unique blend of Western savvy and Indian spirituality made him the foremost leader of the independence movement in Britain's largest colony. (Library of Congress)

spin cotton at home on the old-fashioned spinning wheel put that homely implement on the Indian flag. At the same time, however, he was a firm believer in Western notions of human equality, rejecting India's traditional caste distinctions and preaching the equality of women with men. In Gandhi, then, the Indian National Congress found at last a leader who could bridge the many gaps that divided Indians and who could build a genuine sense of Indian national identity.

The English tongue—ironically—gave him the national language his country needed. His eclectic religious studies made it easy for him to work with Muslims as well as Hindus. His firm rejection of caste turned the lowest of the low from "untouchables" into "children of God," in Indian parlance. Above all, his common touch, his guru garb and manner, his endless traveling among the villages enabled him to bridge the immense abyss that separated the cosmopolitan Congress leaders, with their London-cut suits and lovely homes in Calcutta or Bombay, from the Indian masses in their uncountable mud-walled villages across the land.

Gandhi manipulated the foreign press with as much skill as he moved the hearts of other Indians. Colonial police and soldiers overreacted to nonvio-

lence—or to the riots that sometimes accompanied nonviolent demonstrations—and generated public support for Gandhi abroad, even in Britain. Viceroys learned to negotiate with him—when they were not locking him up. The bespectacled little brown man in white homespun became as familiar to newsreel watchers between the wars as FDR or Hitler. For many in the West as well as for hundreds of millions of Indians, Mahatma Gandhi stood out as the only living saint in a darkening world.

In the end, dealing with a basically democratic imperial power, Gandhi and his nonviolent protests prevailed. In 1947, in the antiimperialist aftermath of World War II, Great Britain let his people go.

Gandhi was shot in 1948 by an Indian fanatic who was outraged at the Mahatma's efforts to calm the terrible Hindu-Muslim rioting that accompanied independence. It was a violent death for a supremely nonviolent man. Nor was Mahatma Gandhi the last Indian leader who would fall victim to the religious differences that still divide that great nation.

Seedtime in Africa

The condition of colonial Africa between the world wars was quite different from that of India. Ten times the size of the subcontinent, Africa had only a little over half its population—less than 200 million people in 1940. Most of Africa remained less urbanized, less literate, less politically sophisticated, and less rich in roads, railways, and other modern facilities. Most of Africa also seemed much farther from independence than India under the Raj.

There were some signs of changing colonial attitudes during the 1920s and 1930s, however, which would work to the advantage of the second largest continent in its restless quest for freedom.

The upsurge of political idealism that accompanied the founding of the League of Nations and the peace and disarmament conferences of the interwar years affected colonial policies too, even in Africa. The German colonies—most of which were African—were turned over to the victors after World War I as mandates, territories to be governed as much in the interests of the indigenous peoples as for the colonizing Europeans, with regular reports required. Britain's policy of indirect rule through traditional local authorities evolved in the direction of a conscious policy of "preparing Africans for independence" at some admittedly hazy future date. French centralization, which envisaged no future separation of metropolitan France from her overseas territories, nevertheless welcomed African leaders to French educational institutions and political life, where they would obtain the skills they would later use against French rule.

In general, African colonies were more peaceful and produced more profits and taxes during these twenty years than at any time since their acquisition during the scramble for Africa at the end of the preceding century. Despite low commodity prices on the international market, there were revenues. Some of these were channeled into modest programs of economic development, health, and education. An air of relatively benevolent rule and an impression of slow but measurable advances along Western lines prevailed over much of Africa.

As in India, however, the impression was in many ways deceptive. Tensions were real, and the seeds—in some places, the fact—of militant revolt quite vigorously present.

Westerners saw Africa much as they did Latin America and much of Asia—as a source of raw materials. They utilized cheap African labor to siphon off the cotton of Egypt, the copper of the Congo (Zaire), and the gold of South Africa. They put black or Arab Africans to work on the farms of European settlers in East or South Africa, or along the Mediterranean shores of North Africa. The African middle class was much smaller than that of India, and Af-rican economic development proceeded much more slowly.

As for the "civilizing mission" of the colonizers and the preparation for independence that some claimed to be undertaking—there was, at best, much less evidence of it than in India. In all of French West Africa, an area the size of the United States, there were no more than eighty high schools; Nigeria was the only British African colony that boasted more than a dozen secondary schools. British indirect rule left local authority in the hands of traditional chiefs, but it did little to advance the few Western-educated Africans beyond clerk status in the colonial administration. French direct rule gave some Africans more power in the colonial government—but only those who were thoroughly transformed by total immersion in the French way of life.

Under these circumstances, then, antiimperialist sentiments, openly nationalist movements, and even a handful of armed resistance groups persisted in Africa between the wars.

Violent resistance was confined largely to North Africa. Here Islam's long feud with Christendom still simmered, leading to intermittent turbulence. Resistance by desert sheiks and tribes flared up during the 1920s, particularly in French Morocco and in Italy's new colony of Libya.

The Christian European predominance established in the Middle East and North Africa during the nineteenth century, meanwhile, stimulated a pan-Islamic cultural revival. Centered at the Al-Azhar University in Cairo, this intellectual revival of Islamic consciousness sent student militants back to their homelands all over Mediterranean and Sudanic Africa. In the 1930s these highly educated Muslim militants were organizing modern nationalist political parties to work for independence from the European rulers.

South of the Sahara, open independence movements were fewer, violence almost nonexistent.

African student organizations set up at British or French universities were a fertile source of dreams and plans for African independence, and the students would bring these dreams home with them. The pan-African ideal of African independence and unity, preached primarily by Afro-Americans such as the flamboyant Marcus Garvey and the scholar W.E.B. Du Bois also found eager converts among African students.

In Africa itself, reform-minded African nationalist organizations were set up in the British West African colonies of the Gold Coast (Ghana) and Nigeria, and in East Africa in Tanganyika (Tanzania). These groups typically made modest demands. But they used modern Western techniques of organization and newspaper journalism to spread their ideas among Africa's now growing urban populations.

In French West Africa, particularly in Senegal and the Ivory Coast, African politicians affiliated themselves with the more radical political parties of metropolitan France in order to work for colonial reform. In the 1930s they began to join the French Socialist and Communist parties and to dream even wilder dreams of autonomy and independence.

It was a comparatively quiet time in Africa south of the Sahara. But it was a deceptive calm. The students of the 1920s and 1930s—men such as Kwame Nkrumah, Jomo Kenyatta, Léopold Senghor, and others—would become the leaders of the great liberation movements of the tumultuous years after World War II.

Over Africa as a whole, in fact, it was seeding time, when ideas were planted and nurtured in some extraordinary young minds. The harvest would come with the Great Liberation of mid-century.

SUMMARY

The twentieth century may be the most revolutionary of centuries. Modern ideological revolutions—drawing on liberal, nationalist, revolutionary socialist, and anti-imperialist visions of a new social order—have been overthrowing governments around the world since before the First World War. The most impressive of these upheavals, however, involving millions of people and taking decades to run their course, sprang up in the first half of the century in Russia, Mexico, and China.

The Russian Revolution of 1917 came as the climax of a century of agitation against the political autocracy and economic underdevelopment of czarist Russia. It was the immense pressures of World War I on an underdeveloped country that overthrew the last Russian czar. Lenin and his Bolshevik cadres thus seized power in a crumbling nation with relative ease. But it was in retaining power that they revealed their true capacities, successfully turning back attacks by the forces of czarism, rival radical groups, rebellious minority nationalities, and foreign intervention during the civil war.

Lenin in his last years made some concessions to capitalism in order that Russia might recover from the war and the civil struggle. Stalin, however, worked his way into power in the late 1920s and plunged the nation into a new economic revolution in the 1930s. Heavy industry was vastly expanded under Communist state socialism. Agriculture was also largely collectivized, but production still dropped drastically due to peasant resistance to socialization.

Mexico also underwent a major revolution, beginning about 1910 and climaxing in the 1930s. The revolt against the Díaz regime began with the liberal bourgeois Madero movement and the popular insurrections of Villa and Zapata. The revolution expanded into a bloody nation-wide struggle that cost many lives and led to anarchic destruction. Under the Northern Dynasty of political leadership, however, progressive one-party rule was imposed on Mexico in the 1920s. And under the charismatic Indian leader Cárdenas in the 1930s, significant democratic and socialist reforms were achieved.

The Chinese Revolution was the largest and longest of them all, the military phase alone beginning before World War I and lasting until after World War II. China's ancient monarchy collapsed soon after the death of the autocratic empress Tz'u-hsi in 1908. The new Republic of China became little more than an arena in which rival political leaders and warlords struggled for power for the next forty years.

Dr. Sun Yat-sen left the feuding revolutionaries his Three Principles—nationalism, democracy, socialism—to guide them in the reconstruction of China. Of these, liberalism did not really take hold in the war-torn peasant nation. Nationalism was championed by Generalissimo Chiang Kai-shek, who succeeded Sun and ruled China from the late 1920s through the 1940s. Socialism, or "people's welfare," became Marxist state socialism in the hands of the Communist leader Mao Tse-tung. The struggle between Chiang and Mao, complicated by the Japanese invasion and by World War II, ended in 1949 with Chiang driven off the mainland to the island of Taiwan, and Mao triumphant in Peking.

Within the European empires, finally, resistance to Western hegemony laid the foundations for the future end of Western colonialism. The Congress party in India and the arrival of a new generation of Westernized African leadership both pointed toward liberation in later decades.

All three of these long revolutions provided models and inspiration for other upheavals around the world in the second half of the century.

SUGGESTED READING

ANTONIUS, G.   *The Arab Awakening*. New York: Capricorn, 1965. Standard, sympathetic account of the new aspirations triggered by World War I.

CHAMBERLIN, W. H.   *The Russian Revolution, 1917–1921*. New York: Grosset & Dunlap, 1965. An older but still standard account. See also E. H. Carr, *The Russian Revolution: From Lenin to Stalin* (New York: Free Press, 1979), by a leading authority; L. Schapiro, *The Russian Revolutions of 1917: The Origins of Modern Communism* (New York: Basic Books, 1984) for the nonspecialist reader; and the recent work by J. M. Thompson, *Revolutionary Russia, 1917* (New York: Scribner's, 1981).

CHI, H.   *Warlord Politics in China 1916–1928*. Stanford: Stanford University Press, 1976. One of a number of good descriptions of warlordism in China during this most recent of the huge nation's post-dynastic breakdowns.

CHOW, T.   *The May Fourth Movement: Intellectual Revolution in Modern China*. Stanford: Stanford University Press, 1967. Informed analysis of the intellectual upheaval that proved to be the seedbed of social action.

COCKCROFT, J.   *Intellectual Precursors of the Mexican Revolution, 1900–1913*. Austin: University of Texas Press, 1968. Another instance of intellectual dissent preceding action—a repeated pattern in the West since the Enlightenment.

DANIELS, R. V., ed.   *The Russian Revolution*. Englewood Cliffs, N.J.: Prentice-Hall, 1972. Sources on the revolution.

EASTMAN, L. E.   *The Abortive Revolution: China Under Nationalist Rule, 1927–1937*. Cambridge, Mass.: Harvard University Press, 1974. An essential study of the period of Chiang Kai-shek's domination of Chinese affairs.

ERIKSON, E.   *Gandhi's Truth*. New York: Norton, 1969. Psychohistorical examination of the Indian leader by a leading exponent of psychohistorical biography.

FITZPATRICK, S.   *The Russian Revolution 1917–1932*. New York: Oxford University Press, 1982. Recommended analytical overview, from the 1917 revolutions through the First Five-Year Plan.

HARRISON, J. P.   *The Long March to Power: A History of the Chinese Communist Party 1921–1972*. New York: Praeger, 1972. Richly detailed narrative of the rise of the Chinese Communists, up to and beyond victory in the Civil War.

HUTCHINS, F.   *The Illusion of Permanence*. Princeton: Princeton University Press, 1967. Britain's greatest imperialist illusion—the permanence of the Raj in India.

LIEUWEN, E.   *Mexican Militarism: The Political Rise and Fall of the Revolutionary Army, 1910–1940*. Albuquerque: University of New Mexico Press, 1973. Sociopolitical study of the makers of the Mexican Revolution.

PATTABHI SITARAMAYYA, B.   *History of the Indian National Congress* (2 vols.). Bombay: Padma Publications, 1946–1947. The party of Gandhi and Nehru, from its foundation.

REED, J.   *Ten Days that Shook the World*. New York: Random House, 1960. Gives a reporter's colorful view of the October Revolution.

SCHAPIRO, L.   *The Life of Lenin*. New York: Harper & Row, Pub., 1964. By a scholar with a broad background in both Russian history and the other ideological movements and leaders of the interwar years.

SHERIDAN, J. E.   *China in Disintegration: The Republican Era in Chinese History, 1912–1949*. New York: Free Press, 1975. Good survey of the whole course of the revolution, from the fall of the Manchus to the ascendency of Mao.

TANNENBAUM, F.   *Mexico: The Struggle for Peace and Bread*. New York: Knopf, 1950. The broad picture of social transformation since the revolution, seen in a pattern of alternating progress and setbacks.

UHALLY, S.   *Mao Tse-tung, a Critical Biography*. New York: New Viewpoints, 1975. Good life of one of the great revolutionaries of the twentieth century.

WOLFE, B. D.   *Three Who Made A Revolution*. Boston: Beacon Press, 1956. Lenin, Trotsky, and Stalin, underground and in exile, before 1917; readable and intriguing.

WILSON, D.   *The Long March, 1935: The Epic of Chinese Communism's Survival*. New York: Viking Press, 1972. Vigorous description of the most famous incident in the Chinese Revolution, Mao's retreat to the north in which the Communists won simply by surviving.

WOMACK, J.   *Zapata and the Mexican Revolution*. New York: Knopf, 1968. Perhaps the most admired of the Mexican revolutionary leaders, sympathetically portrayed.

Chapter · 18

THE BRUTAL YEARS

THE FLIGHT FROM FREEDOM

Redefining the Jackboot

In the mythology of our decades—the gay nineties, the flaming twenties, the rebellious sixties—the thirties are the depression decade, the red decade, the low, dishonest decade of appeasement. If we were painting them, the thirties would be gray, greasy storm clouds rolling in, with cracks of lightning advancing from a black horizon. It was a time when many of the best lacked all conviction, while the worst were full of passionate intensity.

The Great Depression accounted for much of the grimness of those years, of course: soup kitchens, bread lines, the dole. So did the continuing long revolutions in many parts of the world: nonviolent Indians clubbed into the dust, Chinese slaughtering Chinese on the endless Long March north. The advance of the second world war of the century across that numbing decade did its part to darken those years: Italian planes strafing Ethiopian roads, German bombers over Spanish villages, a baby screaming in the rubble of Shanghai after the Japanese planes had passed.

But there was an even more immediate source for the savage image of the decade. It was the political brutality of the new-style dictatorships that gave the thirties much of their tone and color in our collective memory. For this was the decade of Adolf Hitler and Joseph Stalin, of secret police, party purges, slave camps, death camps. Stalin's Iron Age, one author called it; others lamented—but did nothing to stop— the March of the Swastika. It did indeed seem like a reversion to an earlier, crueler time, a new iron age.

The brutal years did not begin in 1930. Mussolini's march on Rome, the Red and White terrors in Russia, street fighting in Germany went back to the 1920s. But the thirties were the climax, the decade that redefined the jackboot and seemed to put half the world into the hands of old-style authoritarian governments, a new wave of militarism, and—newest, most shiny-modern, and grisliest of all—the totalitarians.

The Liberal Faith Must Shut Up Its Temples

One of the most disturbing things about the upsurge of autocratic, authoritarian, and just plain tyrannical governments was that earlier twentieth-century people seemed to welcome them with open arms. It was not enough, some astute observers pointed out, to blame everything on the gangster mentalities at the top of many of the new regimes, or on the odious machinery of enforcement they commanded. Too many of the new dictators enjoyed widespread popular support among the peoples they tyrannized. There were too many cheering crowds lining the advance of Nazis or Fascists to power, too few tears shed for lost liberal institutions—it could not all be blamed on the Gestapo.

To many, it looked like what social psychologist Erich Fromm diagnosed as a flight from freedom. The nineteenth century had seen the steady advance of liberal political institutions across the Western world. The twentieth seemed to be witnessing a widespread rejection of freedom, a disillusionment with democracy. Confronted with economic and social challenges too great for its fragile new liberal institutions, the world seemed to be turning back to cruder, more brutal beliefs in blood and violence, in irresistible force and omnipotent leadership.

The difficulties of modernization or of recovery from the depression, it appeared, were too difficult to be handled by the majority votes of demoralized and battered peoples. The cult of the leader was the only answer. Let the SS, let the commissars, let the new samurai do it.

The new leaders themselves, not surprisingly, took up the theme with enthusiasm. From the bully pulpits of new authoritarian states around the world, they jeered at the decadence of democracy, the failure of capitalism, the physical weakness and moral corruption of the Western world. They contrasted the flabbiness and degeneracy of the liberal West with their own virility, discipline, and strength. "Today," Mussolini declared with total confidence, "the liberal faith must shut the doors of its deserted temples, deserted because the peoples of the world realize that its worship . . . will lead, as it has already led, to certain ruin."[1]

To liberal analyst and totalitarian critic alike, it looked very much, in the depths of the brutal years, as though liberalism was dead, authoritarianism and totalitarianism the wave of the future.

What Is Totalitarianism?

Not all the new dictatorships were of the sort normally described as totalitarian, but the most notorious and powerful of them were. It will therefore be worthwhile to spend a few paragraphs attempting to answer a rather subtle question: What exactly is totalitarianism?

This distinctive twentieth-century ism may be defined most simply as an attempt at total control of society by government. Totalitarian states have attempted to achieve this end by building on the commitment and discipline of ideologically based political parties. Totalitarian rulers have maintained their power over the less committed majorities of their people through two other instruments particularly well developed in our time: bureaucracy and technology.

The party, with its uniforms and parades, its access to power and the perquisites of office, its inspiring ideals and sense of driving purpose, brought many into the totalitarian fold. The omnipresent bureaucracy carried the power of the totalitarian state into the lives of all its citizens as never before. And technology, from propaganda to military police, from microphones to machine guns, was always there to deal with doubters and dissenters. The result was a regime

that tried to impose the will of new leaders and new elites, and the ideologies they preached, on whole populations. The new order subverted all other institutions and ideas, sucking all classes and groups, all ages and both sexes into the new Leviathan state.

A number of explanations have been offered for the rise of this new Leviathan. The economic, social, and political challenges of modernization, the strains of the Great Depression, the humiliations of imperial domination or military defeat certainly played a part. The sheer faceless power of the modern state with its endless hierarchies of officals, all of whom can claim that they were just following orders, helps to account for the iron grip of the system once it is established. The hypnotic grasp of modern ideologies, comparable to the power of religion in earlier centuries, surely underlies the new phenomenon—indeed distinguishes it most clearly from the authoritarian regimes of earlier centuries. And there have been some persuasive psychological explanations that seek to pinpoint a totalitarian personality, predisposed by family structure,

The totalitarians in their pride. Orchestration of public spectacles was a strong suit of the totalitarian leaders of the 1930s. (Library of Congress)

[1]Benito Mussolini, The Political and Social Doctrines of Fascism, trans. Jane Soames (London: Hogarth Press, 1933), p. 9.

child-rearing methods, and other distinctive cultural forms to accept, indeed to long for, autocratic control in society and the state.

Seen as a cast of mind rather than a form of government, totalitarianism involves total commitment to the cause, complete submergence of the individual in the group, unquestioning obedience to the authority of the party or the leader. From this sort of commitment, moral and emotional, comes a sense of inner harmony and collective strength. The petty ego of the individual, submerged in the larger whole of the group, swells with pride, strength, joy, disciplined purpose.

That is at least an attempt to understand the hearts that beat beneath the grim gray uniforms, the minds behind the fixed adoring eyes. Pettier matters, such as the arrogance of a uniform, a living wage in a depression-ridden country, and the career ladders open only to party members, perhaps help explain the lure of totalitarianism too.

So much for deeper explanations of the jackboot in the face. Now for a look at some historical realities.

AUTHORITY, DIRECTION, ORDER

Il Duce

The first totalitarian state was neither Hitler's nor Stalin's, but Benito Mussolini's Fascist Italy, which began to take shape when Mussolini came to power in 1922. *Il Duce*—the Leader—his Fascist party, and his reorganization of Italy along totalitarian lines became the models for later totalitarian and authoritarian regimes in the 1930s.

Mussolini began his career not as a right-winger but as a left-wing syndicalist before World War I. As such, he preached the syndicalist gospel, urging local socialist organization, mass revolution, and the subsequent abolition of the state—a far cry from the Fascist regime he would presently erect in Italy. After the war, however, Mussolini was caught up in Italian demands for "unredeemed" territories held by Austria and Yugoslavia. He changed his ideological stripes and became an ardent nationalist.

Mussolini organized the Fascist party in 1919 and was soon in full cry after his former socialist comrades. His strong-arm squads of militantly nationalistic war veterans, the black-shirted *squadristi*, were soon breaking up Socialist-party meetings, smashing left-wing presses, raiding the headquarters of industrial and agricultural unions. In so doing, Mussolini won the support of many factory owners and large landowners—the very people he had fought in the prewar years.

In 1921 and 1922, Italy's democratic constitutional monarchy went through a paralyzing governmental crisis. As would happen a decade later in Weimar Germany, no party or coalition of parties could form a government that could command a majority in the Italian legislature. Nobody, in short, was in charge in Rome.

During this tense period, the Fascist *squadristi* moved from attacking socialists and unions to seizing control of whole towns. When a Fascist march on Rome itself was announced, Italy's constitutional monarch, Victor Emmanuel III, capitulated and asked Mussolini to form a government.

Thereafter, through massive propaganda campaigns, roughly engineered electoral victories, constitutional "reforms," and an occasional assassination, Fascist power was institutionalized in Italy. Mussolini would be the Leader for the next twenty years, the senior if not the strongest of Europe's totalitarian rulers.

On the political side, totalitarianism in Italy meant the suppression of all rival parties and the submission of a single list of candidates—prepared by the Fascist leadership—to the voters. Elected officials of provinces and towns were abolished and replaced by appointed *podestàs*. Mussolini was given authority to make law by decree, and in time the legislature was abolished in its turn.

The Italian economy also came under at least nominal party control. An elaborate system of "syndicates" and "corporations" were set up, each representing labor, business management, and the government, each concerned with a particular branch of industry, agriculture, trade, finance, or the professions. This "corporative" economic system was run from the top. It forbade strikes and pushed steadily for higher production, and not incidentally for higher profits. Labor unions and free enterprise were alike suppressed as outmoded survivors of the liberal past. Tourists, however, were always pleased to see that in Fascist Italy the trains ran on time.

The rest of society also came under the more or less vigilant eye of the party. Politically untrustworthy individuals were taken up by the secret police and bundled off to the Lipari Islands off the coast of Sicily. The press was censored, education regulated, social and cultural organizations dominated by the Fascists. Children's and youth groups, from the Sons of the Wolf to the Young Fascists, were given their first uniforms and set to drilling at an early age. "Everything in the state," trumpeted Mussolini, "nothing outside the state, nothing against the state!"[2]

[2]F. Lee Benns and Mary Elizabeth Seldon, *Europe, 1914–1939* (New York: Appleton-Century-Crofts, 1965), p. 226.

Il Duce was a dictator much photographed, usually on balconies reviewing his troops or his Sons of the Wolf, unmistakable with his big jaw and increasingly solid belly. It has been suggested that he was not as massively in control as he seemed. His grab for political power in the twenties may have been almost forced upon him by the restless militance of his *squadristi* Black Shirts. The corporative economic organization, at its fullest development in the thirties, looks to some historians suspiciously like a front for big-business domination of the Italian economy.

Nevertheless, the model was established. Mussolini may have hit upon a profound political truth of those merciless years when he declared: "Never before have the nations thirsted for authority, direction, order as they do now."[3]

Why Democracy Failed

One of the greatest challenges of any attempt to deal with the Nazi period in German history is, quite simply, to explain how it could have happened. How could the Germans, best known in the nineteenth century for philosophy and music, then for science and industry—one of the most civilized of European peoples, in short—have produced the twelve-year Nazi nightmare? How could so many have gloried in it, defended the regime vigorously to foreigners who "didn't understand the *Führer*'s policies" even as the shattered glass of *Kristalnacht* tinkled in the streets?

The origins of Nazism are frequently traced to the notable success of autocracy in German history—and the equally notable failures of liberalism. It is a good place to start.

The rise of the Hohenzollern dynasty and of Hohenzollern Prussia to mastery of all Germany was rooted in such autocratic institutions of centralized state power as the Junker bureaucracy and the Prussian army. National heroes such as Frederick the Great and Bismarck had been strong men, wielders of "blood and iron" to advance the interests of the state. Liberalism, by contrast, had never really taken hold, even in the nineteenth century. The Student Union Movement of the early 1800s, the German contribution to the Europe-wide Revolutions of 1848, had dramatically failed in their objectives. So, as we will see directly, had Germany's third liberal experiment, the Weimar Republic of the 1920s. By 1933, then, liberalism meant weakness, authoritarianism strength to most Germans—and at that time, they desperately needed strength.

The debacle of World War I is another commonly

cited cause of the Nazi triumph in Germany. The failure of German arms was a terrible shock to the psyche of a people who had regarded themselves as the greatest power in Europe for fifty years, who had not lost a war since Napoleon's day. The manner of their defeat also—their armies still in the field, strangled by a British naval blockade, tricked by an armistice that somehow turned into an abject surrender—left many Germans feeling betrayed. The harsh Versailles peace terms, stripping Germany of lands, colonies, and military forces, and imposing huge reparations and the unspeakable war-guilt clause, outraged and embittered many Germans. Anyone who would denounce Versailles, give Germans a scapegoat for defeat, and promise victories to come could surely expect a great outpouring of support in Germany.

The political and economic problems of the Weimar Republic (1919–1933), which succeeded the defeated German Empire, also proved fertile breeding grounds for totalitarian sentiment.

In November of 1918, Kaiser William II was persuaded to abdicate for the good of the nation—as the Russian czar had been before him—by his own generals. Hindenburg and Ludendorff knew, if the German people didn't, that their armies could fight no more. The leading party in the Reichstag, the Social Democrats, thereupon took the lead in establishing a German republic.

The German Constitution adopted at Weimar in 1919 was, in fact, one of the most liberal in the world, providing for democracy, civil liberties, rights for women. It opened the way for a vigorous opposition press and the brilliant cultural life that distinguished Weimar Germany in the 1920s. The liberals and socialists who ruled through most of that decade were parliamentarians, labor leaders, and constitutional reformers.

Yet within fifteen years, political attacks from left and right and the economic buffeting of alternating inflation and depression had virtually paralyzed the new government—and opened the way for the rise of Adolf Hitler.

Political attacks from the left came first, with the rebellion of a Communist group called the Spartacists in 1919, followed by other abortive left-wing plots in the early 1920s. The Spartacists were suppressed, their leaders Rosa Luxemburg and Karl Liebknecht murdered while in custody. Right-wing attempts to seize power included an army revolt called the Kapp putsch and, in 1923, Hitler's futile Beer Hall putsch in Munich—which cost the Nazi leader no more than a few months in prison.

Through the rest of the decade, Communists, Nazis, and other political extremists organized para-

[3]Ibid.

military cadres and fought each other in the streets. Right-wing terrorists assassinated government officials—and generally got off with light sentences. The democratically elected government seemed helpless to do anything about it.

The economic ups and downs of the twenties and early thirties were equally disastrous for the new regime. Inflation unparalleled in modern times ravaged Germany in the early 1920s. The value of the German mark plunged from four to the dollar in 1914 to 4 billion to the dollar in 1923, wiping out the savings of Germany's once prosperous middle classes. After a brief respite, the Great Depression whipsawed the economy from the other side. Germany, hardest hit of all the European nations, had 6 million unemployed in the early 1930s.

The Nazis would promise peace in the streets and renewed prosperity, and although what they delivered was the peace and prosperity of the police state, many battered Germans would vote for them. For the Nazis did not seize power, as the Communists and Fascists had: they were voted into office.

Hitler's victory in 1933 climaxed a three-year political crisis, rooted in the Great Depression, that had made many Germans feel that democracy was unworkable in their country. The coalition of Social Democrats and centrist parties that ruled in 1930 fell apart over the problem of how to deal with the depression. Attempts to organize other coalitions of left- and right-wing parties in the Reichstag also failed, because of the refusal of Social Democrats to work with Communists and because of a similar rejection of the Nazis by old-fashioned German conservatives. Between 1930 and 1933, therefore, President von Hindenburg had to invoke emergency powers to govern at all, conferring authority on a series of conservative chancellors who had no majority support in the Reichstag.

Elections were held frequently during those three years, as those in goverment tried desperately to find a majority that could get the system working again. But the party that gained most rapidly as the depression deepened and the paralysis of democracy became clearer was the Weimar Republic's greatest enemy, Adolf Hitler and his National Socialist, or Nazi, party.

Who supported Hitler? Masses of statistics and elaborate theories have been advanced about the "people behind" the Nazi demagogue, but the point is still being argued. Students supported him noisily and gave him a thumping majority in university straw votes. Big business contributed to his war chest, but gave as much or more to other, more respectable conservative groups. Major support, however, seems to have come from lower-middle-class Germans—shop-keepers, civil servants, old-fashioned artisans—and from farmers; all these groups suffered from the depression. And a great ground swell of support came from embittered nationalists of all classes.

In large part, fear put Hitler in power. Fear of urban unemployment, of collapsing farm prices, of middle-class loss of status, of communism, of foreign humiliations, of governmental paralysis—all contributed to Hitler's meteoric rise. The convicted putschist of 1923 got 2.6 percent of the vote in 1928. In 1930 the Nazi total jumped to 18.3 percent. In 1933 the Nazis were the nation's most popular party, commanding 37.3 percent of the vote.

At the beginning of 1933, then, with Hitler clearly the nation's best vote-getter, the politicians around the aging Hindenburg persuaded him to appoint the Nazi leader chancellor of Germany. Like the politicos who made Napoleon first consul of France, they thought they could use the strident, vulgar little man with the ridiculous moustache for their own purposes.

Der Führer

Adolf Hitler (1889–1945) was not German but rather Austrian by birth. Failed art student, one-time Munich bohemian, wounded and decorated soldier in World War I, he had found his true career in the extremist politics of the Weimar Republic. He had joined a nationalist sliver group called the National Socialist German Workers party and had quickly come to dominate it, thanks to his fiery oratory and superpatriotic doctrines. The failure of the Beer Hall putsch in 1923 cost him some months in prison, but he spent the time assembling his credo in a famous book, *Mein Kampf* (*My Struggle*), and emerged as the idolized *Führer* (Leader) of the Nazi party.

Hitler preached German greatness, the superiority of Aryan or Teutonic racial stock, and the coming splendor of the Fatherland. He condemned the Versailles treaty, the Communists, and sometimes the very rich. He blamed Germany's troubles increasingly on the Jewish segment of the population, convenient targets of European persecution for centuries and a pathological fixation of Hitler's. He developed a high-pitched but electrifying speaking style and a natural flair for the dramatic—uniforms, swastika banners, night rallies, parades, marching songs. Once in power, he also demonstrated a knack for shrewd political tactics and ruthless manipulation of people.

During the first six months of 1933, the new chancellor made himself absolute ruler of Germany.

Hitler took advantage of an attempt to burn down the Reichstag building in Berlin, probably undertaken by a feebleminded Dutch Communist, to begin his assault on the structure of the Weimar Republic. Apparently genuinely fearful of a Communist power play, he suspended all civil liberties and arrested the German Communist leadership. Riding the crest of this victory, he held a quick election and won a Reichstag majority large enough to vote the chancellor special powers to make laws on his own authority for the next four years.

Thus strengthened, Hitler turned against the parties. He already had the Communists in jail. He now outlawed the Social Democrats, claiming they also were too far to the left. Then he talked all the other conservative and nationalist parties except the Nazis into dissolving voluntarily in order to promote unity on the right—in other words, to give the Nazis a free hand. Finally, in June of 1933, he purged his own party of potential rivals in the gory Night of the Long Knives, when his elite SS troopers seized and executed hundreds of Nazi and other leaders deemed undependable by the Leader.

During the rest of the decade Hitler made Nazi Germany into the archetypal totalitarian state. Political and economic institutions, religion, education, recreation, and all other aspects of national life came under the centralized control of the party and its *Führer*.

Totalitarian political structures quickly replaced those of Weimar democracy. All parties except the Nazis having been suppressed, the Reichstag became a rubber stamp for the Leader's decisions. The elected governors of the German states were replaced by appointed *Statthalters*. Everywhere, in provinces and towns, power passed into the hands of Nazi strong men called *Gauleiters*.

Totalitarian economic organization also evolved rapidly. In the 1920s Hitler had preached power to peasants, artisans, and shopkeepers, the traditional salt of the German earth. In the 1930s, however, he forged a monolithic alliance of big government and big business with which to run the German economy. Huge cartels were put in charge of industry and agriculture. Massive programs of public works (including the Autobahn highway system) and military rearmament (in defiance of the Versailles treaty) put much of the labor force back to work. At the same time, rigid controls were slapped on wages and prices, small businessmen lost operational control of their businesses, and labor unions were abolished.

The Nazi apparatus reached into every aspect of German life. The Protestant churches were merged into a single German Evangelical church under Nazi control; a concordat gave the party a say in the appointment of Catholic bishops and forbade priests to speak out on political issues. Nazi doctrines were taught in public schools while university professors were being discharged. Books were burned for presenting views the Nazis disapproved of. All professional, social, or cultural associations and clubs were politicized—Nazified—or abolished.

Young people were quickly enrolled in the Hitler Youth and the League of German Maidens, which replaced the traditional Boy and Girl Scout type of hiking and camping organization. Workers got free Strength-through-Joy vacations in the healthy countryside, which also strengthened them for future military service. Women were piously urged to stick to home and church—and produce children for the Fatherland.

Under Hitler's leadership Germany quickly pulled out of the depression, boosted production to new highs, and put almost everyone back to work. Hitler unilaterally rejected the Versailles treaty, rapidly built the most powerful army in Europe, and announced a new German empire—the Thousand-Year Reich. Germans stood tall again, proud of their country, contemptuous of the capitalist democracies still floundering in the depths of the Great Depression all around them.

The Final Solution

There was, of course, a price to be paid. The Germans brought their strong leadership, economic revival, and national pride at the expense of what must be a good candidate for the most brutal tyranny in European history.

Nazi propaganda glorified the leadership. Actually the Nazi elite seem to have been a heterogeneous group of adventurers and opportunists having few ideological or other principles and a strong attachment to showy wealth and conspicuous displays of power. Their military organization and early victories, their talk of commitment and building new worlds clothed them in a myth of efficiency, invincibility, and glamor that they did not deserve. In fact, the system seems to have survived as long as it did, not through monolithic unity and discipline, but on the basis of a rough balance of feuding factions—the Nazi apparatus versus the old bureaucracy, the *Führer*'s SS Corps versus the German army—and the clashing ambitions of individual Nazi leaders.

In the area of police repression, however, the Nazis were acknowledged masters.

The chief instruments of the Nazi terror were the *Schutzstaffel* (SS), the Leader's black-uniformed private troops, and the Gestapo, the Nazi secret police. The SS, originally Hitler's bodyguard, later an elite military force, were publicized as the perfect Aryans, blond, blue-eyed embodiments of Teutonic racial superiority. They purged the party for Hitler in the early

1930s and ran the concentration camps—the death camps—of the later 1930s and the 1940s. The Gestapo worked much more in the shadows, as a secret political police. It was they who made the after-midnight arrests and ran the most feared torture chambers since the days of the Spanish Inquisition.

Millions of human beings died in Hitler's concentration camps—political dissidents, resistance fighters from conquered countries, social misfits, "inferior" racial groups such as Slavs, gypsies, and, above all, Jews.

Hitler defined the Jewish "race" as the greatest threat to the German people, blaming them for their success in business and the professions, for Versailles, for the depression, and for weakening the blood of the German "master race" through "interracial" marriage. Once in power, Hitler passed discriminatory laws against them, expelling them from government service, confiscating their property, compelling many to emigrate. Riotous pogroms were organized against them, including *Kristalnacht*, the Night of the Broken Glass, when the windows of Jewish homes and businesses were shattered in cities all over Germany.

In the later 1930s Jews were herded into concentration camps. In the early 1940s the Final Solution to the Jewish problem got under way. This was the methodical extermination of the Jewish population of Germany and German-occupied Europe. This holocaust was undertaken at first rather haphazardly with machine guns. Then at camps like Dachau, Belsen, and Auschwitz, the process was systematized in specially constructed gas chambers, followed by cremation of the corpses. Six million Europeans of both sexes and all ages and conditions of life were worked, starved, stripped, gassed, robbed of rings and the gold in their teeth, and trundled off to the crematoria. It was almost certainly the largest deliberately instigated massacre in history.

Western people sometimes feel a certain superiority to other human beings. We shudder piously at the horrors of the Assyrian warfare state, at the piles of skulls the Mongols left in their wake, or the obsidian blades of the Aztecs lancing down. Whenever so tempted, we would perhaps do well to remember such Western atrocities as the fires of the Inquisition—and the gas chambers of the Final Solution.

Communism Comes to Russia

The sources of Stalinist totalitarianism in Soviet Russia reach further into the past than the roots of Nazi totalitarianism. But Communists tended to be more serious about their ideology than Nazis; hence there are ideological origins for Soviet totalitarianism too.

A mass grave at Belsen concentration camp. Victims of the totalitarian death camps were required to surrender their clothing and any remaining possessions before being shot or gassed. (UPI/Bettman Newsphotos)

As in Germany, finally, the historical circumstances of the 1930s helped to define the pattern of party dictatorship as it developed in Stalinist Russia.

Historically, relatively rigid authoritarianism went far back in Russian history—to Byzantine and Mongol models, to the heavy-handed rule of autocrats such as Ivan the Terrible in the sixteenth century and Peter the Great in the eighteenth. Even conservative nineteenth-century western Europeans were shocked at the absolute power of the czars, who ruled a vast peasant nation through a huge bureaucracy, secret police, and military repression, all justified by the traditional divine-right doctrines of the Russian Orthodox church. Some twentieth-century historians would see Communist Russia as little more than a continuation of this Russian autocracy, but with an even larger bureaucracy, a more efficient secret police, and Marxist dogma in place of Orthodox rationalizations of power.

But there were distinctive ideological sources of Stalinist tyranny too. Marx had had little to say about the political organization of the classless utopia of the future. But Lenin, seeking to impose discipline on disputatious Russian ideologues and ignorant proletarians, had developed the key political principles of the vanguard party and democratic centralism. Communists thus early came to believe that their party was the vanguard of the advancing proletariat—and that the workers themselves, unable to understand Marxist subtleties, must be brought to accept this party leadership through slogans and indoctrination. Bolshevik leaders came to believe also that ideological disputes within the party must in the end give way to discipline and obedience. Democratic debate within the party was all very well while policy was being hammered out. Thereafter, however, central authority must prevail, and all must close ranks behind the leaders.

Lenin dominated the party and the people by force of will and intellect, and by the sheer weight of his success. Stalin, lacking charisma or a brilliant record of revolutionary achievement, used the older political skills of manipulation and force. But Stalinist totalitarianism has been traced by many to the Leninist doctrine of democratic centralism.

The immense pressures of the 1930s also help to explain the regression of the Soviet Union to autocracy and terror under Stalin. The strains of the first Five-Year Plans, which attempted to achieve in a few years a level of economic development that had taken other nations much longer to accomplish, might alone account for draconian measures. The Communist fear of "capitalist encirclement" and especially of Hitler, who denounced international communism as he built up his own nation for war, impelled the Russian leadership to look for internal enemies and drive their people to work still harder.

To these external pressures we must add the desire of the party and its leader to increase their power. The Russian Communist party of the 1930s was no longer the scattering of underground or exiled revolutionaries living on dreams and ideology that it had been under Lenin. Stalin's party was a bureaucracy of *apparatchiks* ("machine men"), much less ideological and much more career-oriented. Stalin himself was the super *apparatchik*—a wooden oroter and a plodding thinker, but skilled at organizing and political maneuver. Aware of his limitations and of the greater brilliance of men such as Trotsky, he seems, especially in his later years, to have been a pathologically suspicious man as well.

The party wanted to increase its power, individual *apparatchiks* to advance their careers, by expanding Communist control into more and more areas of life. Stalin wanted to assure his own power and to eliminate potential rivals or enemies of his programs. And so, after the lull of the 1920s and the New Economic Policy came the Five-Year Plans—and the sweeping totalitarianization of Russian society.

Stalin's Iron Age

Like Nazism, Communism could boast of successes in the 1930s. As in Germany, unemployment was virtually eliminated as the state made work for every man and many women. Agriculture suffered severe setbacks, in part because of peasant resistance to collectivization. But at least the farms were collectivized and could now develop on a centralized, socialized basis. State-owned heavy industry grew rapidly, overall industrial production expanding at the phenomenal rate of 15 or 20 percent a year. Even allowing for doctored Stalinist statistics, it was an impressive achievement.

Western admirers who came to Russia in the 1930s to "see the future" were duly impressed by the new industrial cities, the huge dams and factories, the showcase Moscow subway with its dazzling cleanliness and its marble statues. They were sometimes even allowed a glimpse of beefy workers lolling on the pebbly beaches of the Black Sea as a reward for exceeding their quotas.

But there was more to Communism than the Moscow subway and Black Sea vacations, as there was more to Nazism than Autobahns and Strength through Joy. In some ways, Soviet totalitarianism made Hitler's version look like a ramshackle collection of compromises. Politically, economically, socially, culturally, the Communists either met less institutional resistance or were driven by ideological compulsions

Russian peasants march off to their newly collectivized fields in 1931, bearing a banner demanding the expropriation of the kulaks. Not all peasants responded this enthusiastically to Stalin's collectivization of agriculture (Wide World Photos)

to more sweeping measures. The total impact of the party on Russian life was commensurately greater.

Politically, party control was unquestioned from the moment Lenin dissolved the constitutional convention in 1918. Stalin gave the nation a shiny new constitution in the 1930s, and elections were held—but in a one-party state there was only a single list of candidates to vote for. And the Soviet Union was a one-party state: since the Communists were the vanguard of the people, what other party was needed? The real power structure was thus the highly autocratic one of the Communist party.

The economy under Stalin reversed Lenin's New Economic Policy. State planners now allocated resources and set quotas, government-appointed managers ran factories and the huge new farms, directed trade, transportation, and all other aspects of the economy. The small-time New Economic Policy entrepreneurs were squeezed out of business. Comparatively well off peasants, called *kulaks*, were expropriated outright, and almost all private farms were collectivized. Half the new collective farms were owned by the state; the others, collectively owned by the peasants who worked them, depended on the state for farm machinery and fertilizer and sold their crops to the state at fixed prices. Only tiny private plots and a few peasant markets remained outside governmental control.

Communists dominated the huge bureaucracy engendered by so much government involvement in the economy. Commissars shared command with military officers in the armed services. In any line of work, from science to the arts, Communist-party membership was the way to get ahead.

The Communists, as Marxists, were materialists—atheists in matters of religion—and the role of the Orthodox church as a pillar of the old order made it a natural target. Many churches were closed, atheism was taught in the schools, and museums of church abuses dotted the landscape. Education aimed at producing hardworking and obedient Soviet citizens, and courses on Marxism-Leninism were required. Communist children's and young people's organizations, beginning with the Young Octobrists and climaxing with the Komsomol, for people in their teens and twenties, filled the new generation with veneration for Marx, Lenin, and Stalin, "the Lenin of today."

As the 1930s advanced, the world outside began to become dimly aware of the human cost of Soviet achievements, and of the brutality of which this version of totalitarianism was capable.

The tip of the iceberg was the public "purge trials"

of leading Communists in the later 1930s. Once-revered party leaders, highly placed economic managers, famous generals were accused of crimes against the state. The charges included sabotaging the Five-Year Plans, plotting with Trotsky (then in exile overseas) or with capitalist foreign agents, voicing anti-party ideas, or simply failing to meet assigned quotas. More shocking still, the accused confessed to these crimes, some of which seemed very unlikely even to sympathetic Western observers, and were duly executed.

Only slowly did the more submerged depths of the Stalinist terror come out. The peasants, it gradually became clear, had resisted collectivization more vigorously than expected, burying their grain and slaughtering their animals rather than surrendering them to the collective. The *kulaks* among them had been sent off to labor camps in the Russian north, where many had died. Other peasants who resisted had had their grain dug up and carried off without compensation. This rigorous government response, coupled with bad weather and worse crops for a couple of years in the early thirties, had cost the lives of millions.

In the later thirties, the secret police added substantially to the human cost of Stalinism. Large numbers of less prominent people, charged with industrial sabotage, spying, or Trotskyite tendencies, were dealt with by the GPU (formerly the Cheka, later the NKVD, the KGB, and other secret police agencies) without benefit of public trials. For these officially defined enemies of the state, the knock on the door after midnight was followed by months of imprisonment without trial, rigorous interrogation, years of struggling to survive in a forced labor camp, or simply the well-known bullet in the back of the neck at the end of a long dark corridor. Tens of millions were sent off to work camps in Siberia or the Soviet arctic, and millions more were executed.

Stalin, who had none of Hitler's flair for the dramatic, made few public speeches. Western journalists called him the Silent Man in the Kremlin. But his machinery for destroying enemies of the state was at least as efficient as that of his archenemy ranting at him across the width of Poland.

Zaibatsu Liberalism

Japan, like Germany, moved from a period of troubled liberal government in the 1920s to one of strident nationalism, militarism, and renewed imperial expansion in the 1930s. If European-style totalitarianism did not develop in Japan, political tyranny and violence certainly did. The militarist Japan that joined the Axis alliance with Nazi Germany and Fascist Italy was no unworthy partner to those two totalitarian powers of the West.

From about the time of the First World War through the 1920s, the major political parties in the Japanese Diet enjoyed an enhanced share of political power among the complex system of elites that ran the country. Party leaders established close ties with leading bureaucrats and resisted rare imperial efforts to intervene in favor of one party or the other. The army and navy, though continuing to get large cuts of the budget for the mechanization of the armed forces, were generally prevented during the 1920s from undertaking further imperial adventures. The politicians in the Diet pursued policies of economic expansion instead, investing huge quantities of time and money in establishing close commercial ties with China.

Party power in the 1920s brought mixed results. From a liberal standpoint, laws providing for universal suffrage, legalized labor unions, and health insurance for factory workers were all to the good. The big businesses called *zaibatsu* made themselves felt in the Diet, however, producing crackdowns on radicals and government corruption.

Outside the Diet, military leaders and nationalists generally resented the unaggressive tone of Japan's politicians toward Europeans and Americans. And the peasant majority of Japanese, who did not share in *zaibatsu* prosperity during the 1920s, grew even more bitter when the World Depression of the 1930s further ate away at their already dwindling income. With little support from the liberal end of the spectrum and mounting unhappiness in such conservative quarters as the armed services, the peasants, and patriots generally, the political parties rapidly lost control in the thirties.

The Day of the Assassins

No single leader masterminded the military monopolization of power in Japan in the 1930s. The armed forces were frequently rivals with one another, and there were violent factional feuds within the leadership of the army itself. What happened was a tangled web of conflicting intrigues punctuated by outbursts of violence that left political-party rule a shambles, the nation in the grip of a wave of chauvinistic passion, and the army rampaging through China.

The decline of party influence began with the totally unauthorized seizure of most of Manchuria from China in 1931 by units of the Japanese army. The annexation was engineered by a cabal of young army officers who ignored civilian orders from Tokyo to cease and desist until their objective was accomplished. Brought to trial for insubordination, the officers were hailed as national heroes by many Japanese; like right-wing assassins in Weimar Germany, they got off with light sentences. The "liberated" areas, meanwhile, were reorganized as the Japanese puppet state of Manchukuo.

From this beginning at the start of the decade, Japanese military arrogance and power grew by leaps and bounds through the 1930s. Other superpatriotic young officers began to raid the headquarters of the political parties, to attack wealthy *zaibatsu* executives, and finally to assassinate important politicians, including the prime minister.

In 1936 a group of junior officers with hundreds of troops under their command seized downtown Tokyo itself, occupied government buildings, and murdered a number of prominent officials. The rebellion was quickly suppressed with the help of the navy, and one of the army factions was disgraced. But the military leadership as a whole was only strengthened, since civilian authorities thereafter lived in fear of a second and more successful military coup.

By and large, the Japanese people supported the military. The failure of civilian authorities to clean up corruption, cut ties with the *zaibatsu*, or substantially alleviate the suffering of masses of peasant farmers undercut their moral position. Many were glad to see military men emerge as the new political leaders. The average Japanese, after all, had little knowledge of left-wing radicalism and did not object when censorship, arrests, and other forms of persecution cut into radical ranks. The ideological void was easily filled by nationalistic propaganda and renewed assertions of absolute loyalty to the emperor.

Young Emperor Hirohito himself, ironically, had more than once stood up to the military. But by 1937, when another "incident" led to a full-scale Japanese invasion of China, there was nothing much even he could do to control the nation's new militaristic masters.

A Great Totalitarian Tide

Public attention focused on the major totalitarian and militaristic powers in the interwar years, particularly on Nazi Germany and Fascist Italy. But there were many other examples around the world of the disturbing flight from freedom that some critics noticed.

In Europe, many of the nations in the east and the south proved fertile ground for authoritarian regimes during these two decades. The Mediterranean peninsular states of Europe's southern fringe (Spain, Portugal, Italy, Greece) and the band of eastern European states from the Baltic (Estonia, Latvia, Lithuania) through Poland and Austria to the Balkans (Hungary, Rumania, Yugoslavia, and others) all flirted with or fell to authoritarian regimes.

Many of these were new countries, most of them poor and technologically underdeveloped. Almost all were dominated in 1920 by antiquated social groups and institutions—monarchies, established churches, landowning aristocracies. The strains of economic modernization, the poverty of both urban and peasant masses, the political demands of affluent middle classes, and the increasing appeal of various ideologies—liberalism, nationalism, and socialism, communism, and fascism—all contributed to tension and disorder in these areas.

In these unstable circumstances, the appeal of authority, direction, and order was obvious. The two groups who most vigorously exploited fear of anarchy or social revolution to create authoritarian regimes were military leaders and fascist ideologues. In some places, military strong men such as Marshall Pilsudski in Poland and Admiral Horthy in Hungary ruled with an iron hand. In other countries, uniformed proto-Fascist parties such as Rumania's Iron Guard or Austria's Fatherland Front broke heads, persecuted Jews, assassinated liberals.

In Latin America, the relatively good times of the 1920s turned definitively sour when the World Depression hit, drastically depressing the commodity prices on which the southern republics still depended heavily. In the early 1930s, more than half the twenty independent nations of Latin America responded to the resulting pressures with revolutions. The regimes that came to power followed a familiar pattern. Outside of Cárdenas's Mexico and a few other examples, military leaders, conservatives, and nationalists triumphed again and again.

The result for the major Latin American powers, such as Argentina and Brazil, was by no means uniformly bad economically. But the politics of the new regimes were almost always extremely undemocratic.

Thus Argentina's Radical party, which governed the country during the 1920s with policies that ranged from moderate to liberal, was overthrown by a military coup in 1930. The Conservative Republic, as the regime that ruled for the next dozen years is called, accelerated the growth of Argentine industry from small-scale workshops to much larger factories employing hundreds of workers. The new industry was capable of supplying much of the country's needs for manufactured goods without having to depend on foreign imports—a net gain for the economy.

Politically, however, democracy clearly lost ground under the Conservative Republic. The so-called *Con-*

cordancia, an alliance of militarists, nationalists, and conservatives, rigged elections and suppressed political opposition in Argentina as vigorously as any nineteenth-century *caudillo*.

Brazil's maximum leader for fifteeen years after he seized power in 1930, and again from 1951 to 1954, was the nationalistic military leader Getúlio Vargas. This long-lived dictator proved to be a skillful administrator who encouraged the growth of domestic industry and, most important, took great strides toward unifying the huge country under the central government in Rio de Janeiro. To accomplish this, Vargas both undermined the independent power of the separate Brazilian states and considerably expanded the functions of the central administration.

Besides these administrative reforms, however, Vargas frequently exercised dictatorial powers. He governed by censorship and decree, outlawed opposition political parties, and even deployed military force when necessary. Again, stability and progress were bought at the cost of stunted politcal liberties.

Some of the smaller Latin American states suffered from more brutal "personalist" dictators, building mass power on the traditional basis of personal fol-lowings and personal favors, during the hard times of the 1930s and beyond. The Somoza family seized power in Nicaragua in the mid thirties and were soon constructing a successful modern sector of the economy while savaging all political rivals. Rafael Trujillo did a brilliant job of modernizing the island republic of Santo Domingo—and turned it into the "dry guillotine" of the Caribbean in the process.

Across the world in the Middle East, much the same sort of procedure was noticeable. Modernizing autocrats such as the Pahlavi shahs of Iran might expand oil output and even sprinkle some schools and hospitals across the land. But political tyranny, extending to imprisonment, torture, and death for enemies of the authoritarian regime, was the perhaps exorbitant price the nation was asked to pay.

Everywhere during those gray, hard, often despairing years, democracy seemed like a lost cause. The strains of modernization, resurgent conservatism, the appeal of ideologies such as nationalism, and the impact of the World Depression proved too much for many fragile experiments in self-government. A great totalitarian tide seemed to be running in the world.

SUMMARY

While the liberal West struggled with its problems and while China and Mexico labored through their long revolutions, other nations succumbed to the totalitarian, militaristic, or otherwise authoritarian dictatorships of the brutal years. In the 1920s, 1930s, and 1940s, powerful and often cruel authoritarian regimes ruled in such major powers as Germany, Russia, Italy, and Japan, and in many smaller nations as well. The most powerful of these governments are often described as totalitarian, vesting total power in a single highly ideological party and appealing to the total commitment of party members to the cause, the movement, and its leader.

The prototype totalitarian state was Fascist Italy under Mussolini. Il Duce seized power from Italy's enfeebled liberal government in the 1920s. He created a regime characterized by one-party rule, economic centralization, and militarism.

Hitler's Nazi party rose to power in 1933, capitalizing on German resentment of the Versailles peace, disillusionment with democracy, and economic collapse. Once in power, Hitler, like Mussolini, suppressed free elections and free enterprise, and he remilitarized his country. He bailed the nation out of the depression with his public works and rearmament programs, and he unilaterally abrogated the Versailles Treaty. He also introduced Gestapo secret-police terror and SS death camps, massacring six million Jews and millions of others deemed biologically inferior to the "master race."

Stalin brought Communist party power to a climax in Russia in the 1930s. The new regime built on the czarist tradition of authoritarian rule, but developed the bureaucracy, the army, and the secret police far beyond czarist models. Stalin's party dictatorship did modernize much of the Russian economy and boost production dramatically. At the same time, however, Communist policy decisions and deliberate repressions cost the lives of millions of Russians—officially classified as enemies of the working class—in Stalinist work camps and prisons, or in the famines of the early 1930s.

In Japan, resentment of an unaggressive parliamentary regime and of zaibatsu big business allowed the militarists to dominate affairs in the 1930s. Through assassinations and the threat of a military coup, Japanese generals and admirals cowed civilian authorities into accepting increasingly nationalistic, imperialist, and reactionary policies.

A great authoritarian wave seemed to be sweeping over the world. One-party rule, military dictatorship, and other forms of autocratic government rose to power in many East European, South American, and Middle Eastern nations. Under the pressure of great economic and political problems, people seemed to be turning their backs on democracy.

SUGGESTED READING

ALLEN, W. S. *The Nazi Seizure of Power.* New York: Franklin Watts, 1973. Nazi rule comes to a single German town, a convincing microcosm of the nation.

BERGER, G. M. *Parties Out of Power in Japan: 1931–1941.* Princeton: Princeton University Press, 1977. Highly recommended survey of Japanese political history under militarist dominance in the 1930s.

BULLOCK, A. C. *Hitler: A Study in Tyranny.* New York: Harper & Row, Pub., 1964. Perhaps the best life of Hitler. See also J. C. Fest, *Hitler*, trans. R. and C. Winston (New York: Harcourt Brace Jovanovich, 1974).

CHAMBERLIN, W. H. *Russia's Iron Age* (2 vols.). Boston: Little, Brown, 1934. The trauma of the First Five-Year Plan, described by one who was there.

CONQUEST, R. *The Great Terror: Stalin's Purge of the Thirties.* New York: Collier, 1973. Causes, nature, and consequences of the Stalinist terror.

DANIELS, R. V. *The Stalin Revolution: Fulfillment or Betrayal of Communism?* Boston: Heath, 1965. Essays debating economic modernization, political terrorism, and other aspects of Stalin's impact on Russia.

FINER, H. *Mussolini's Italy.* Hamden, Conn.: Archon, 1974. Solid analysis by a political scientist.

FROMM, E. *Escape from Freedom.* New York: Farrar and Rinehart, 1941. Psychiatric diagnosis of Western humanity's fear of the responsibilities of freedom in the first half of the twentieth century.

HOLBORN, H., ed. *Republic to Reich: The Making of the Nazi Revolution.* New York: Pantheon, 1972. Crucial transition period from liberal democracy to totalitarian dictatorship.

KIRKPATRICK, I. *Mussolini: A Study in Power.* New York: Hawthorn Books, 1964. A diplomat's analysis, and the most detailed account of the first totalitarian.

MEINECKE, F. *The German Catastrophe.* Boston: Beacon, 1963. A renowned German historian's view of Germany's twelve years of totalitarianism.

MORRIS, I., ed. *Japan 1931–1945: Militarism, Fascism, Japanism?* Boston: Heath, 1963. Japanese "isms" during this age of authoritarian predominance.

NAGY-TALAVERA, N. M. *The Green Shirts and Others: A History of Fascism in Hungary and Rumania.* Stanford, Cal.: Hoover Institution, 1970. Fascism in Eastern Europe. See also H. Seton-Watson, *Eastern Europe Between the Wars, 1918–1941*, 3rd ed. (Hamden, Conn.: Archon, 1962).

NOLTE, E. *The Three Faces of Fascism*, trans. Leila Vennewitz. New York: Holt, Rinehart & Winston, 1966. Two places where fascism triumphed (Italy and Germany) and one where it failed (France); a complex and original appraisal. See the essays in H. A. Turner, Jr., ed., *Reappraisals of Fascism* (New York: Franklin Watts, 1975).

ROGGER, H. and E. WEBER, eds. *The European Right: A Historical Profile.* Berkeley: University of California Press, 1965. The rise of authoritarian right-wing parties across Europe, in a series of essays.

SOLZHENITSYN, A. I. *The Gulag Archipelago 1918–1956* (3 vols.), trans. T. P. Whitney. New York: Harper & Row, Pub., 1974–1978. Personal testimony of the labor camps and prisons of Stalinist Russia, collected by a leading Soviet exile novelist, who was there himself.

TANNENBAUM, E. R. *The Fascist Experience: Italian Society and Culture, 1922–1945.* New York: Basic Books, 1972. Life in a society dominated by the slogans and institutional structures of il Duce's regime.

TUCKER, R. C., ed. *Stalinism: Essays in Historical Interpretation.* New York: Norton, 1977. Essays by leading experts on the nature and significance of the Stalinist period.

ULAM, A. B. *Stalin: The Man and His Era.* New York: Viking Press, 1973. Stalin as a political manipulator. See also R. C. Tucker, *Stalin as Revolutionary* (New York: Norton, 1973), a much-debated psychohistorical portrait of the "silent man" in the Kremlin.

Chapter · 19

WORLD ON FIRE

THE CAUSAL CHAIN

On Land, on Sea, and in the Air . . .

It does not look like so much in the old news photographs, really. Moonscapes of ruins pall after awhile. Dead bodies on a beach are either a scattering of small dark blobs—from a distance—or, close up, an anonymous young face with its chin in the sand, helmet spilling forward, a tangle of expensive equipment, and perhaps one arm stretched out, fingers stiffening just short of an unused rifle.

Even smoke boiling up over St. Paul's, a bloodied German family stumbling from its ruins, or soldiers with odd-shaped hand grenades charging up what had been a street in Stalingrad are only pictures, after all. "Smoke Break in Malayan Jungles" or unshaven tankers in the Sahara, " 'Thumbs Up' after Rommel"—it all seems very far away somehow, as unreal as Verdun or Gettysburg. Or Agincourt or Jericho, for that matter.

Even at the time, it could sound a bit hysterical on the radio: "On land, on the sea, and in the air, we are hitting them, we are hitting them today. . . ." Or so low-key and understated as scarcely to merit the to-do, as in a letter from the front:

> What can one say about combat that has not been written time and time again. It is confusion, noise, but mostly hard work. . . . Then when one reaches some objective, one digs in, and so it starts all over again. . . . [1]

[1] Personal correspondence from John Calvin Kreamer to Ross Kreamer, Belgium, January 22, 1945.

What it was, quite simply, was the biggest war in human history.

It was a war of immense offensives, catastrophic defeats, stunning victories—all the adjectives are apposite. A war that saw whole armies annihilated in set-piece battles, nations toppling like tenpins in a few days, cities reduced to rubble too hot to touch in a few unthinkable hours. A war in which a single battlefront in Russia could stretch for 1800 miles—roughly the distance from New York City to the Rocky Mountains. A war in which uncountable millions of soldiers went slogging into the noise, the confusion, the hard work, the digging in and moving on . . . or not.

It was the biggest and most thoroughly global war in all the human venture. It was six years and a day of escalating carnage, from the German invasion of Poland on September 1, 1939, to the Japanese surrender on the battleship *Missouri* in Tokyo Bay on September 2, 1945.

On one of those days, the sergeant quoted above settled to a forest floor in Germany so naturally that the men behind him thought he had "seen something" and ducked for cover. A few minutes later the platoon commander crawled up to try to administer first aid, and died there. As, no doubt, did the men who killed them. As tens of millions of others did in the biggest war.

Building toward the Big One

Given what has been said about the nature of totalitarian governments, it is easy to see World War II as a splendid illustration of the "devil theory" of history—aggressive dictators on one side, democracies on the other. Certainly Germany, Italy, and Japan were aggressive, militaristic, and expansionist in the 1930s. On the other hand, Stalin's Russia was as totalitarian as Hitler's Germany, and "Uncle Joe" was on the Allied side. Britain still headed the largest empire in the history of the world in 1939. Even the United States, few as her holdings were outside the Continent, had made herself so unpopular meddling in the affairs of the Latin American republics that some of them would not side with the U.S. against the Nazis.

A related approach having much appeal because it seems to carry a message for our time is to see the cause of the war as Allied appeasement of Axis aggression. Again, there is much truth in this view, as will be apparent when we follow the grim sequence of crises down the thirties to the final confrontation over Poland in 1939. Yet this approach also is incomplete, for it does little to explain why the Axis powers were aggressive and expansionist in the first place.

Deeper, longer-range causes for the Second World War include the World Depression, the Versailles peace after World War I, and perhaps some deeply disturbing features of the global political order.

The Great Depression certainly accounted in significant part for Hitler's rise to power and for the decline of party government in Japan. Military expenditures were also a good way for Hitler and other totalitarian leaders to put people back to work in a hurry. Perhaps most important, however, the depression left the Western democracies badly weakened in the 1930s. Preoccupied by domestic problems, divided class against class by the new poverty, and unsure of their own future, democratic leaders found appeasement and the avoidance of confrontation as natural as aggressive rhetoric was to the heads of militarized totalitarian states.

Confrontations there were in plenty—and many of them went back to the unsatisfactory peace settlement signed at Versailles in 1919. The Versailles peace divided the great powers into two camps: the satisfied and the unsatisfied, the supporters of the settlement and those who demanded revisions. Britain, France, and the United States—to the extent that she involved herself at all—supported the treaty as signed. Germany, Italy, Japan, and the Soviet Union were among the major revisionists.

Germany and Russia had emerged from World War I as pariahs among the nations. Germany had been saddled with war guilt and reparations, stripped of her colonies and armies. Russia had lost large portions of czarist territory in the collapse of 1917–1918 and felt surrounded by capitalist enemies after the civil war that followed. Italy and Japan had seen their imperial ambitions frustrated by the Versailles settlement and by the diplomacy of the postwar period.

The revisionist powers, in the time-honored style of great powers, seized every opportunity to modify the settlement in their favor—and in so doing drew steadily closer to another great war.

There is, finally, the obvious, which it sometimes takes a certain amount of intellectual boldness to state:

> There is a larger view . . . according to which both [world] wars reflect fundamental shortcomings of a brilliant but flawed civilization that could not settle its differences without periodic blood baths. Nothing in the 1919 settlement had changed the basic division of . . . the world into separate sovereign states that recognized no higher authority than national interest. . . . Some would argue that until the state system is replaced by a world government, there can be no lasting peace.[2]

In a rapidly shrinking world, these differences would clash more frequently and more violently in the twentieth century than ever before. The state system itself and the system of international anarchy it generated would thus make world wars a more likely occurrence in our time than in any previous one.

Though they didn't know it, then, revisionist dictators demanding justice and defenders of the international status quo pointing to the sanctity of treaties, militarists and appeasers, aggressive politicians and peoples who were simply too busy with the depression to care about the international situation were all in their different ways building toward the big one.

Distant Thunder

A string of international crises led up to the final explosion. Each crisis pitted revisionists against defenders of the peace, authoritarian states against those that were at least less so. The result was a series of totalitarian and militaristic aggressions met with such tepid responses on the part of relatively democratic states as to give the word *appeasement* a bad taste ever since.

At first the confrontations seemed far off and exotic to the Western powers that still claimed to run the world. Japanese aggression in China, Italy's latest plunge into Ethiopia, even a civil war in Spain—land of bullfighters and sunny poverty—did not seem like central concerns to Western democracies struggling for their economic lives. Then it was much, much closer—but technical, still involving unfamiliar names and places: the Rhineland, *Anschluss*, the Sudetenland, the Polish corridor . . . And then the Panzers

[2]Robert O. Paxton, *Europe in the Twentieth Century* (New York: Harcourt Brace Jovanovich, 1975), p. 428.

were revving up their motors, the Stukas roaring into the dawn.

But at first it was distant thunder on a horizon half a world away. Japan in Asia, Italy in Africa first broke the peace so dubiously established in 1919.

Japan attacked China first in 1931, in Manchuria, and again, in an all-out invasion, in 1937. In both instances Japan's military leaders instigated the aggression while her own civilian government, the Chinese army, and the nations of the world did little but wring their hands in dismay.

Japan had been developing Manchuria, the old Manchu homeland northeast of the Great Wall, as a center of grain, coal, and iron production for decades. A campaign by Chiang Kai-shek to regain the political and economic initiative there, plus the revival of Russian power in the Far East under Stalin, aroused the concern of imperialistic Japanese fearful of losing their foothold in Manchuria. In 1931 a handful of Japanese officers stationed in the area staged an attempt to sabotage the Japanese-run railway and used it as an excuse to seize control of the whole region, rechristen it Manchukuo, and install a Manchu puppet there.

Reactions to this first major act of aggression on the decade-long road to World War II were illuminating. The Japanese officers used their trials for insubordination as platforms to explain their patriotic motives, and—as we have seen—were hailed as national heroes in many quarters. In the end it was the current prime minister and cabinet who resigned in disgrace. Chiang Kai-shek, preoccupied with his annual campaign against Mao's first base in Kiangsi, could do nothing. The League of Nations appointed a commission of inquiry. When the commission very mildly rapped Japan's knuckles over the incident, Japan simply withdrew from the League. She kept her new colony, and was soon expanding her influence into the neighboring provinces of China.

All-out invasion did not come until 1937. By that time Chiang had been compelled by popular opinion—and his own Kuomintang colleagues—to make common cause with Mao, now installed in Shensi, against Japanese power in the north. This united front, encouraged by the Soviet Union, threatened to reverse the Japanese expansionist drive. Another "incident," this one at the Marco Polo Bridge near Peking, gave Japan the excuse her generals sought for a full-scale invasion of China.

Over the next few years Japan's mechanized, highly trained and motivated army and navy dominated China's coasts, rivers, and harbors, occupied many of her cities, and conquered most of her east coast. Chiang Kai-shek's government, accompanied by large numbers of Chinese fleeing the sometimes savage behavior of the Japanese troops, retreated up the Yangtze Valley into the interior to establish a wartime capital at Chungking.

Chiang's scorched-earth policies as his troops retreated, Mao's guerrilla attacks, and the primitive logistics and transport systems in the interior of China soon turned the triumphant Japanese advance into a grim occupation. But despite strongly worded protests from the United States and some modest continuing Soviet aid, little was done for China. The United States, in fact, went on selling Japan such basic war materiel as iron and oil right up until 1941.

Italy invaded Ethiopia in 1935, halfway between Japan's aggression in Manchuria and her massive invasion of China proper. Confronted with Italy's African venture, the Western democracies once more reacted inadequately, and the aggressors carried the day.

Mussolini, the oldest of the totalitarian rulers, apparently felt that the younger generation of Fascists needed a great adventure, the party as a whole a new shot of glory. Italy also needed more space to resettle the growing numbers of the unemployed. And Ethiopia, which adjoined Italy's colonies in the Horn of Africa and was the last country on the continent without a colonial overlord, seemed a logical answer to his needs.

An incident between Italian and Ethiopian troops at an unused water hole on a disputed frontier gave Mussolini his excuse. The Ethiopian king, Haile Selassie, offered to submit the dispute to arbitration. Mussolini responded with shelling, aerial strafing, and mustard gas. The Ethiopians fought a gallant fight, but they could not match the weaponry of the civilizers from the north. By the spring of 1936, King Victor Emmanuel had been proclaimed emperor of Ethiopia.

The international outcry this time was considerably greater. The League of Nations voted economic sanctions against Italy, and the French and British governments worked through diplomatic channels. But the sanctions did not include oil, the one essential that, cut off, could have stopped Italy's war machine in its tracks. And the British and the French were still trying to keep Italy, their ally in World War I, from drifting into Hitler's orbit. So the aggressors rolled on.

To Die in Madrid

During the years 1936–1939, the Spanish civil war gave the self-proclaimed champions of liberty in the world another chance to stand up for freedom. Again, they left the field to the totalitarian powers. It was, by all accounts, the most heartrending lost cause of a decade that was littered with them.

Spain during the early thirties seemed to be going against the trend of that authoritarian decade—replacing a dictatorship with a budding democracy. In 1930 it had been a European backwater, afflicted by many of the problems of its former colonies overseas: arrogantly wealthy landlords and poverty-stricken peasants, a reactionary and influential Catholic church, and a military-officer caste habituated to interfering in government. In addition, a modest amount of industrial development had created a small, overworked, and underpaid proletariat, a happy hunting ground for anarchists, syndicalists, and communists. Regional nationalisms also flourished, particularly in Catalonia and among the Basques.

Conflicts among these groups had flared up in 1930 as the world depression added to the pressures building within the nation. In a few hectic months, both the most recent military dictator and then the monarchy itself were swept away. A shiny new Spanish republic thus set to work in 1931 to design itself a constitution and begin some desperately needed reforms.

Five years of rather modest social change—redistribution of some large estates among peasants, anticlerical legislation, autonomy for Catalonia—only deepened the divisions in Spanish society. A seesawing series of elections further divided the nation without determining who was to have power.

In July of 1936, then, a self-styled Nationalist movement headed by General Francisco Franco took up arms against the Spanish republic. Within a few weeks Franco had occupied half the country, the south and west. But the Republic held the capital of Madrid and the industrialized east, including Catalonia. For the next three years, the Spanish republic and the Nationalist rebels fought each other in a gory civil war that cost half a million lives. Symbolically, the Spanish civil war also became to many a political morality play, a struggle between good and evil for the soul of the Western world.

Franco's Nationalist coalition included militarists, landlords, strong Catholics, and Spanish nationalists. The Republic was supported by liberals, peasant anarchists, worker syndicalists, Catalonian nationalists, anticlericals, and communists. But it was the foreign friends of the Spanish contenders who determined all their destinies.

The liberal powers, Britain and France, trying to avoid escalation of a local conflict into a general war, urged noninvolvement and an embargo on arms shipments. Hitler and Mussolini, however, seeing a brother-in-arms in Franco, sent him tens of thousands of Italian troops and Germany's Condor Legion, the bombers of Guernica. Of the great powers, only the Soviet Union, fearful of German rearmament under

a militant anticommunist such as Hitler, sent advisers, money, and weapons to the republic.

Large numbers of idealistic young people, however, came to Spain as volunteers to fight for the Spanish republic and try to stop the further spread of fascist totalitarianism. They agreed with John Donne's warning quoted in Ernest Hemingway's novel of the Spanish civil war, *For Whom the Bell Tolls*, about the funeral bell tolling in Spain: "Never send to ask for whom the bell tolls: it tolls for thee." But the members of the International Brigade, the Abraham Lincoln Brigade, and the rest were going to fight in a lost cause; they were going, in the words of a film made long afterwards, *To Die in Madrid*.

Franco won. What was left of the volunteers, and many Spaniards too, fled across the Pyrenees. The bell went on tolling.

Hitler's War

Of all the totalitarian leaders, the most successful and in the end the destroyer of the peace was Adolf Hitler.

Having unilaterally revised the Versailles treaty and begun German rearmament on a vast scale, Hitler was soon demanding modifications of the territorial arrangements of central Europe. A passionate nationalist as well as a racist, he insisted that all German-speaking areas had a right to be reabsorbed into the new German Reich. He also talked about what he called *Lebensraum*—"living space"—for the dynamic and growing German people, meaning a resumption of Germany's historic tendency to push eastward, into the lands of the Slavs.

As steps toward these nationalistic goals, Hitler embarked on a series of aggressive moves in the heart of Europe, against Austria, Czechoslovakia, and Poland. As a preliminary step, however, he remilitarized the Rhineland in 1936.

This German frontier zone between Germany and France was to have remained free of troops so as to discourage border clashes between the two traditional enemies. But this also left Germany open to French invasion. In March 1936, Hitler therefore sent 35,000 German soldiers into the Rhineland, unilaterally revising an international agreement once more and materially strengthening his hand against the liberal Allies. It was his first international aggression. His armies were not ready for war, had apparently even been ordered to withdraw if confronted with force. But the French did not confront them, and the German troops stayed.

In March 1938 Hitler absorbed Austria into the Third Reich. Some of Austria's German-speaking population did, in fact, support what Hitler was doing across the border, and there was an aggressive Austrian Nazi party. Many other Austrians, however, wanted to maintain their historic independence, even of a Germany headed by the Austrian-born Hitler. Nevertheless, the German *Führer* browbeat Austria's leaders into accepting a Nazi chancellor, then dictated a "request" for German troops to "maintain order" in the shaken country. The German army marched in, to be greeted by cheering crowds, and the *Anschluss*—"unification"—of Germany and Austria was completed. Hitler now ruled a country of 80 million Germans—equal to the populations of Britain and France combined, and well over half the population of the United States.

In later 1938 and early 1939 he took over Czechoslovakia. Claiming that that country's German-speaking minority in the Czech Sudetenland was being mistreated, Hitler demanded the surrender of this territory to Germany. France and Russia both had treaty alliances with the Czechs, and Britain supported them publicly. But Hitler again blustered and threatened until the British and French leaders once more agreed to a settlement giving the Germans what they wanted. This final concession, agreed to by British prime minister Neville Chamberlain at Munich in September 1938, made the name of that city synonymous with the bankrupt policy of appeasement.

Most of Europe, however, heaved a sigh of relief: the dead of the First World War were only twenty years in their graves by that time, and many then living remembered. In March of 1939, meanwhile, German troops marched into Prague, and most of the rest of Czechoslovakia became a German protectorate.

In September 1939 Hitler moved against Poland, and Europe went to war again at last. Rectification of a dubious Polish-German frontier, the return of the German-speaking port of Danzig to Germany, and a German railway across the Polish corridor that separated Danzig from the Reich were the diplomatic demands that kindled this final crisis. In a broader perspective, the invasion of Poland looked very much like a continuation of the *Drang nach Osten*, Germany's historic drive into Slavic Eastern Europe.

By way of preparation, Hitler astonished Europe by negotiating a nonaggression treaty with his most vocal opponent—Joseph Stalin. The Nazi-Soviet Pact of August 1939 was a triumph of practical self-interest over ideology on both sides. It gave Hitler a free hand in Poland, and allowed Stalin further time to prepare for future conflict with his aggressive rival. A secret codicil also agreed on the division of Eastern Europe between them.

Britain and France had given ringing guarantees of Polish rights and territorial independence as the

A famous cartoonist's comment on the destruction of Poland in 1939 by her totalitarian neighbors. David Low's caricature of Hitler and Stalin shows the two former arch enemies greeting each other with a sardonic parody of the insults they had once exchanged so vigorously. (New York Public Library Collection)

crisis came to a head. Hitler, understandably, did not believe them. A week after the signing of the Hitler-Stalin Pact, German troops invaded Poland.

World War II had begun.

HOMAGE TO FIFTY MILLION

The First Global War

World War I had involved much of the world, one way or another, but most of the fighting had been in Europe, and most of the casualties and destruction were borne by Europeans. World War II, by contrast, was in every sense a truly global war—perhaps the first such conflict in world history.

The two great alliances of nations that confronted each other were clearly intercontinental. The major Axis powers were two European nations and one powerful Asian one: Germany, Italy, and Japan. Bound by a series of treaties in 1936 and 1937, including the Anti-Comintern Pact against the Soviet Union, the so-called Rome-Berlin-Tokyo Axis involved mutual recognition of one another's spheres of interest and future conquests in Europe and Asia.

The Allied Big Five—Britain, France, the Soviet Union, China, and the United States—included two purely European powers (though both had large overseas empires), one transcontinental Eurasian power, one purely Asian nation, and one North American state. Growing slowly from the Franco-British declarations of war on Germany in 1939 through the German invasion of Russia and the Japanese attack on the United States in 1941, this alliance was soon locked in combat with the Axis over much of the world.

Europe, Asia, North Africa, and Oceania were all major battlefields. The war was fought on many seas and islands, from the North Atlantic to the South Pacific, from Crete to Okinawa. Military planners—and armchair strategists at home—filled world maps with colored pins, and everybody learned to pronounce names they had never even seen before, let alone heard spoken over their radios.

The globe was thus divided into theaters of war where the two grand alliances battled for strategic islands, patches of desert, cities in the northern snows. The casualties and the destruction were spread around the globe much more widely than ever before. And when victory finally came, it centered in Berlin and Tokyo, two capitals on opposite sides of the world.

Blitzkrieg

World War I was a war of position: there was little change in the trench lines, and the armies swayed agonizingly back and forth, going nowhere. Generalities may suffice to give a sense of that terrible conflict. World War II, by contrast, was a war of movement: armies advanced hundreds of miles, fleets struck across even greater distances. Some narrative, then, will be necessary to give a proper sense of this story.

The war began with stunning Axis victories: Hitler's *Blitzkriegs* and the Phony War sandwiched in between.

The first *Blitzkrieg*—"lightning war"—struck into Poland in September of 1939. German motorized Panzer divisions rolled across the frontier, preceded by waves of bombing planes, at 5:00 A.M. on September 1. Western Poland was overrun in two weeks. Russia, Hitler's ally of one month, then stabbed into the hapless land between them, and Warsaw, Poland's last stronghold, fell before the month was over. It was Germany's first demonstration of what modern mechanized warfare could be like, not in defense, as in the First World War, but on the offense.

The so-called Phony War followed through the winter of 1939–1940. Russia, triumphant in Poland, turned next on her northern neighbor Finland. But her armies, which had just lost half their officer corps to the purge trials, became bogged down in a sideshow David-and-Goliath struggle with the Finns. The British and the French, meanwhile, finally declared war on Germany. With Poland gone, however, there

The German Army on the move. Tanks spearheaded Hitler's blitzkrieg *across Europe in the early years of the war. (Library of Congress)*

was little they could do to keep their pledge to defend her. Both western-European powers seemed content to defend themselves, the French in particular barricading themselves behind the steel-and-concrete ramparts of the Maginot Line. They were thoroughly prepared, thanks to massive military outlays during the 1930s, to fight the 1914 war over again. But that was not what was in the cards in 1940.

The reporters who had dubbed the winter lull the Phony War changed their tone when spring came, and with it another *Blitzkrieg*.

Hitler, seeking air and naval bases for himself and intending to cut Britain off from a prime source of foodstuffs, struck suddenly into Scandinavia in April 1940. In a plot so outrageous few thriller writers would attempt it, he dispatched "Trojan-horse" troop ships disguised as freighters and ore barges to pour Germans onto the docks in Denmark and Norway. Denmark, overwhelmed, capitulated. Norway fought—and lasted one month to the day.

The Low Countries came next. Determined to outflank the Maginot Line from the north—the Channel side—Hitler attacked the Netherlands, Belgium, and Luxembourg in May. While their troops flooded over the borders, the Germans made skillful use of paratroopers and brutal bombing of civilian centers to seize key cities well behind the lines. Little Luxem-

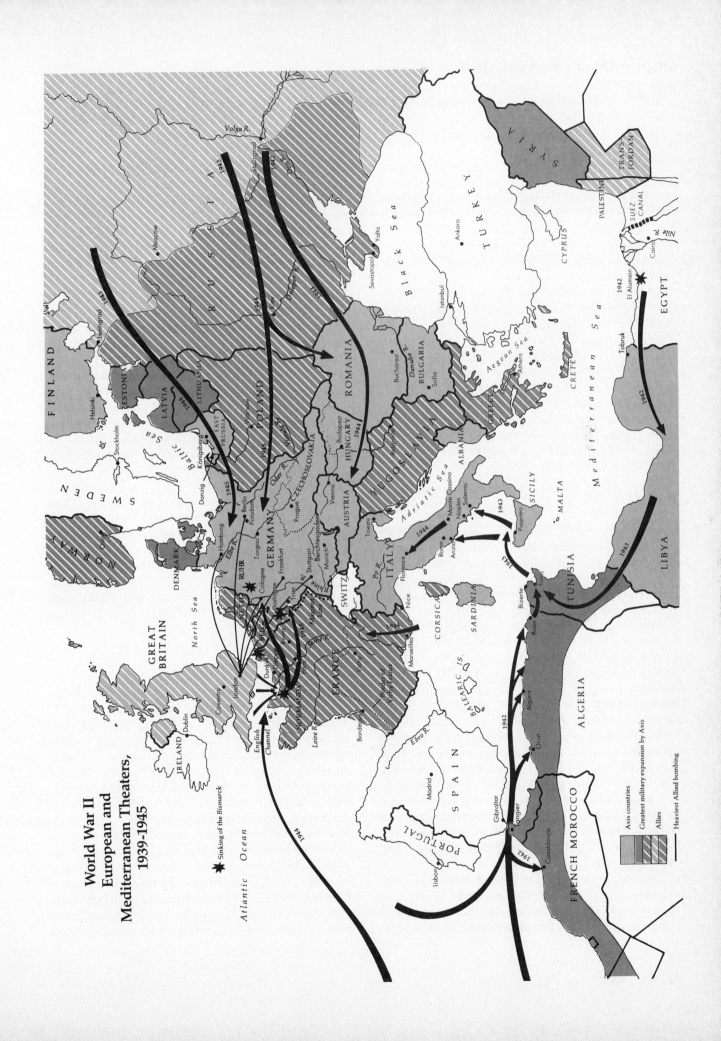

World War II European and Mediterranean Theaters, 1939-1945

★ Sinking of the Bismarck

Atlantic Ocean

FINLAND

NORWAY

SWEDEN

Helsinki

Stockholm

Oslo

RUSSIA

Volga R.

Moscow

Leningrad 1942

Stalingrad 1943

Don R.

ESTONIA

LATVIA

LITHUANIA

EAST PRUSSIA

Königsberg

Danzig

Dnieper R.

1944

Kiev

1941

POLAND

Warsaw

Vistula R.

1945

Oder R.

CZECHOSLOVAKIA

Prague

Berlin

Potsdam

Hamburg

Elbe R.

Torgau

GERMANY

RUHR

Cologne

Frankfurt

Stuttgart

Munich

Berchtesgaden

Maginot Line

Rhine

Nürnberg

1945

AUSTRIA

Vienna

HUNGARY

Budapest

1944

ROMANIA

Bucharest

Danube R.

BULGARIA

Sofia

YUGOSLAVIA

Belgrade

Trieste

Po R.

ITALY

Florence

Rome

Monte Cassino

Anzio

Naples

Salerno

1944

1943

Adriatic Sea

ALBANIA

GREECE

Athens

Aegean Sea

CRETE

Black Sea

Sevastopol

Yalta

Istanbul

Ankara

TURKEY

CYPRUS

SYRIA

TRANS-JORDAN

PALESTINE

SUEZ CANAL

Nile R.

Cairo

EGYPT

1942

El Alamein 1942

Tobruk

LIBYA

1943

Mediterranean Sea

MALTA

SICILY

Palermo

1943

SARDINIA

CORSICA

Bizerte

Bône

Tunis

TUNISIA

1943

BALEARIC IS.

Marseilles

1944

Nice

Border of Vichy France

Vichy

FRANCE

Bordeaux

Loire R.

Seine R.

NORMANDY

English Channel

Dunkirk

1945

BELGIUM

London

Coventry

Dublin

IRELAND

GREAT BRITAIN

North Sea

DENMARK

Rostock

Baltic Sea

SWITZ.

SPAIN

Madrid

Ebro R.

PORTUGAL

Lisbon

Gibraltar

Tangier

Oran

Algiers

1942

FRENCH MOROCCO

Casablanca

1942

ALGERIA

1944

GERMANY

Axis countries

Greatest military expansion by Axis

Allies

Heaviest Allied bombing

bourg fell in one day, the Netherlands lasted five. Belgium, bolstered by desperate French and British help, held out for two and a half weeks. But by the end of May she too had fallen.

In June, it was France's turn. But the British were thrust aside first.

The collapse of Belgium exposed the British Expeditionary Force on the Continent to disaster. Pressed back against the sea at Dunkirk in early June, the bulk of the British troops were evacuated with the help of a flotilla of private yachts and sailboats. But the "miracle" of Dunkirk was nonetheless a military disaster: the British had been hurled out of Europe.

The German armies, meantime, swung south and west around the end of the Maginot Line and drove for Paris—the great race they had been unable to win in the 1914 war. Before the month of June was out, gray-uniformed German infantrymen were goose-stepping up the Champs-Elysées. Hitler danced a little jig as he received the French surrender—in the same railway car where the Germans had been forced to accept the armistice of 1918.

More than half of France was occupied by the Germans for the remainder of the war. The rest of the country was governed by a puppet French government set up in the south.

Finest Hour

The next phase of the war, 1940–1941, saw the fighting still focused on the western end of Eurasia, in the Battle of Britain and the overrunning of eastern Europe. In this phase too the Axis was generally victorious, though not quite as uniformly as in the lightning thrusts of the preceding year.

Hitler turned his attention particularly to Britain in 1940 and 1941—and met his first setback. Like Napoleon before him, he abandoned plans to invade the British Isles directly because he lacked flat-bottomed barges to transport sufficient troops for the operation. He turned instead to the twentieth century's armory of new war machines—to planes and submarines.

He tried first to break the British by massive bombardment from the air, pounding cities such as Coventry and London with tons of high explosives in almost nightly air raids. Londoners slept in the subways and came up to smoke and ruin. But the Royal Air Force took an unexpectedly heavy toll of the attackers. The rolling oratory of the new prime minister, Winston Churchill, rallied the British people. And Britain did not surrender.

Thereafter the Germans settled down to a submarine siege of the islands, as in World War I. The goal was to cut Great Britain off from overseas supplies, either from the Commonwealth countries or in the form of increasing aid from the United States. For a while it looked very much as though that aim might be accomplished: during the first year after Dunkirk, the Germans sank 1400 merchant ships in Atlantic waters.

Still, the British did not yield—and the United States began to provide increasingly open support for the last fighting democracy left in Europe. Under a "lend-lease" arrangement Franklin Roosevelt negotiated an aid package that beefed up the British navy, and he announced that although he would not send American boys to fight overseas, the U.S. could and would become "the arsenal of democracy." In the summer of 1941 Roosevelt and Churchill met secretly at sea to sign an idealistic statement of mutual aims, the Atlantic Charter.

Frustrated in the West, the armies of the totalitarian powers were much more successful in eastern Europe. During 1940 and 1941, Hitler and Mussolini were mopping up the Balkans, Stalin the Baltic states.

Besides Finland and Poland, former czarist territories lost to Russia in World War I included the states of Estonia, Latvia, and Lithuania on the Baltic Sea. Stalin now seized his chance to reabsorb them into the Soviet Union. Hitler, meanwhile, with some help from Mussolini, overran the countries of the Balkan peninsula. Some—Hungary, Rumania, Bulgaria—were forced to join the Axis alliance. Others—Yugoslavia and Greece—were conquered, though bands of guerrillas remained active in the rugged mountains of both countries.

By the middle of 1941, after almost two years of fighting, the Axis tide was still at its flood. Then, in the latter half of 1941, Germany and Japan made their biggest mistakes of the war.

Barbarossa—and Tora! Tora! Tora!

In June 1941 Hitler launched his biggest offensive thus far—and made his largest error of judgment: the invasion of Russia. He seems to have been motivated by simmering disagreements over the spoils of war—especially the division of the Balkans, where Russia's interest went back to the pan-Slavism of the nineteenth century. The German ruler therefore decided on Operation Barbarossa. Named for the famous medieval German warrior-emperor, Barbarossa was planned as a quick campaign to break Russia as the German armies had so many others in those two years.

The invasion began in late June 1941, and in six months Hitler's armies had swept over half of European Russia. By December, German troops were fighting in the suburbs of both of Russia's historic capitals, Moscow and Leningrad (old St. Petersburg).

But neither city fell. Long supply lines, the slow

Soviet retreat that left only scorched earth behind, and the crushing cold of a Russian winter slowed Hitler's impetuous drive to a crawl, as they had Napoleon's in 1812. Meanwhile, the Soviet Union's newly built factories in and beyond the Ural Mountains farther to the east remained comparatively safe and productive, grinding out war materiel. And supplies from Britain and the United States began to arrive by sea, through Murmansk in the far north.

There were horrendous battles yet to come in Russia. But by the beginning of 1942, Hitler had reached his limits in the east, as he had in the west. Neither Britain on her tight little offshore islands nor Russia on her endless eastern plains would fall. And by that time a third great power was coming against him—the United States.

While Hitler was knifing into Russia, on the other side of the globe Japan was carrying Axis victories to a climax by overrunning almost all the Western colonies in the Far East during 1941 and 1942. In so doing, however, she made the other biggest Axis error of judgment: bringing the United States into the war.

Japanese imperialists and militarists, now thoroughly in charge of Emperor Hirohito's government, saw a golden opportunity for renewed empire building in the East while the Western imperial powers reeled from Hitler's blows. By the end of 1941, the Japanese had planned a coordinated series of attacks.

The first to be hit were the British colony of Hong Kong off the South China coast—and the two American colonies of the Philippine Islands in Southeast Asia and the Hawaiian Islands in the central Pacific.

Hawaii, too far away for invasion, was nevertheless hit first from the air so that the American Pacific fleet based there, at Pearl Harbor, could be destroyed. On a quiet Sunday morning—December 7, 1941—carrier-based Japanese planes swept in low over the islands. Shouting into their microphones the prearranged signal for success, *Tora! Tora! Tora!*—"Tiger! Tiger! Tiger!"—they zoomed along Battleship Row and inland over the airfield, raining down bombs. They sank eight battleships and ten other vessels, leaving the most powerful Western naval squadron in the Pacific dead and smoldering in the water.

Through the following winter and spring of 1942, Japanese forces conquered the American Philippines, British Hong Kong, Malaya and Burma, and much of the Dutch East Indies. They compelled the French to yield to them de facto control of French Indochina—Vietnam, Cambodia, Laos—and overran the last independent Asian kingdom, Thailand. In so doing they cut the famous Burma Road, the supply line from British India to China, and brought victory in the long Chinese struggle within sight at last.

The summer of forty-two was thus the high-water mark for Japan in Asia, just as Germany was reaching

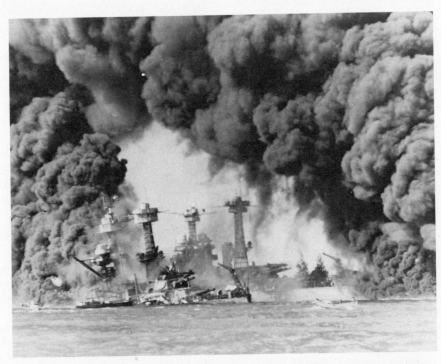

An American battleship sinks in the smoke and flame of Pearl Harbor on Sunday morning, December 7, 1941. The United States lost 2,400 men and most of her Pacific fleet in the Japanese surprise attack. (National Archives)

her limits in Europe. And Japan's error in attacking the United States was already beginning to show.

Counterattack

The years 1939 to 1941 were a period of almost unbroken Axis victories. From 1942 through 1945, the initiative shifted to the Allies, and with it the rising tide of victories.

In 1942 the United States, Britain, and the Soviet Union formed what Churchill, with eighteenth-century grandiloquence, called the Grand Alliance. France's government-in-exile under General de Gaulle and what remained of Chiang Kai-shek's China were lesser partners. The larger nations of the British Commonwealth joined them, and many other countries around the world found it prudent to cast their lot at least nominally with the Allied cause. The Big Three in particular—Roosevelt, Churchill, and Stalin—met repeatedly through the rest of the war to plan grand strategy and reaffirm their determination to make no terms with their adversaries, to accept only unconditional surrender.

The world's biggest industrial machine, that of the United States, now went into high gear. Factories and men, idle and rusting through the depression, went back to work with a rush. As in World War I, many women took jobs formerly held by men now absorbed by the armed forces. Huge quantities of war supplies were conveyed across the Atlantic to Britain and Russia in the teeth of the German submarines and planes.

In Europe, a massive coordinated air attack was launched against Germany. British and American bombers hit German bases, industrial complexes, and cities, the Americans by day and the British by night. In the Pacific, reinforcements arrived. British raiders began to strike back at the Japanese in the jungles of Southeast Asia. And the U.S. Navy began to raise and repair most of the shattered hulks the Japanese had left behind in Pearl Harbor.

The first major Allied victories, however, came on battlefields not even mentioned yet—in North Africa and Italy.

The deserts of North Africa had been the site of a seesaw tank war between the British under General Montgomery and the Germans under General Rommel, the celebrated Desert Fox, since 1940. The turning point of the struggle—and one of the turning points of the war—came in the Battle of El Alamein in the fall of 1942. Montgomery's victory here saved Egypt and the Suez Canal, Britain's lifeline to the east.

Thereafter the British drove the Germans and their Italian allies out of Egypt and pushed on into Libya,

Italy's major North African colony and an Axis stronghold in Africa. In the meantime, an Anglo-American force had landed in the French colonies of Morocco, Algeria, and Tunisia and easily overwhelmed the Germans and the collaborationist French forces there. By the spring of 1943, the last Axis armies in North Africa had surrendered.

Hitler had not only been stopped, he had been rolled back. And new Allied victories followed in Italy, later in 1943.

American and British forces leaped from North Africa across the narrow waist of the Mediterranean, first to the island of Sicily, off the toe of the Italian boot, and then to the mainland of Italy itself. The great southern metropolis of Naples fell in the summer of 1943. The impact of these combined defeats in Libya, Sicily, and southern Italy, furthermore, were sufficient to bring about the fall of Mussolini and the surrender of Italy in the autumn of that year.

The German armies in Italy fought on, and the battle for the peninsula turned into a grinding struggle that would drag on through the rest of the war. But one of the Axis powers, at least, had given up. And by the end of 1943, the war had turned against the Axis elsewhere as well.

The Biggest Fleet, the Longest Front

The years 1943 and 1944 were years of mounting pressure on the Axis, major breakthroughs for the Allies. In Europe these were the years of Stalingrad and D Day; in the Far East, the island-hopping war that brought American forces within reach of Japan.

The Battle of Stalingrad, like that of El Alamein, is generally considered a major turning point in the war. The Germans, unable to take either Leningrad in the north or Moscow in the center of European Russia in 1941, had swung south in 1942. They had aimed a great offensive at Russia's huge Baku oil fields and at Stalin's name-city on the Volga. Again, they reached the suburbs but never managed to take the city. The Russians defended Stalingrad street by street, house by house, room by room: "We have fought during fifteen days for a single house," a German officer recorded in his diary,

with mortars, grenades, machine guns and bayonets. Already by the third day fifty-four German corpses are strewn in the cellars, on the landings, and the staircases . . . . From story to story, faces black with sweat, we bombard each other with grenades in the middle of explosions, clouds of dust and heaps of morter . . . fragments of furniture and human beings. Ask any soldier what half an hour of hand-to-hand struggle means in such a fight.[3]

The Russian counteroffensive at Stalingrad ringed the German besiegers, lined up field artillery almost hub to hub, and pulverized the now trapped German forces. What remained of the German Sixth Army surrendered in February of 1943—a greater disaster than Dunkirk was to the British.

The Russians thereafter launched a series of tremendous offensives on the longest battlefront in a world at war. They attacked summer and winter, even in the Russian snows. By the spring of 1944, the last German forces were staggering out of Russia. Before the year was ended they had been driven out of Poland and the Balkans too, and most of eastern Europe had been overrun by Russian armies.

The spring of 1944 had worse news for Hitler in the west, however. In June of 1944 came D Day, the invasion of France.

The Russians had long been urging the opening of a "second front" that would take some of the German pressure off their own armies. On June 6, 1944, they got it, when Operation Overlord, under the overall command of American general Dwight Eisenhower, breached Hitler's Fortress Europe from the west. The largest invasion fleet in history—3200 warships, transports, and landing craft—crossed the Channel from Britain to materialize at dawn off the Normandy coasts. Within twenty-four hours they had put a quarter of a million American, British, and Canadian soldiers ashore, and the battle for western Europe had begun.

France and Belgium were liberated by the end of 1944, despite a powerful German counterattack in Belgium in the fall, the Battle of the Bulge on all the military maps. In spite of setbacks, then, United States and British troops opened 1945 camped on the Rhine, ready to invade Germany itself.

Hitting the Beaches

On the other side of the globe, where the world is mostly water, other landings on equally inhospitable shores were advancing the Allied cause in the Pacific. The Japanese offensive in the Pacific Ocean had actually ground to a halt as early as 1942—about the time of the critical German and Italian reversals at El Alamein and Stalingrad. In the east, it was the linked battles of the Coral Sea, Midway, and Guadalcanal that turned the tide.

[3]William L. Langer, et al., *Western Civilization*, vol. II (New York: American Heritage/Harper & Row Publishers, 1968), p. 789.

After their initial victories in Hawaii, Hong Kong, and Southeast Asia, the next likely Japanese targets were the big island of New Guinea and the thinly populated continent of Australia. When they began to move in this direction, from bases already seized in the Solomon Islands, American aid was rushed to these archipelagoes.

Here, in the beautifully named Coral Sea, between Australia and the Solomons, a United States naval force intercepted a large Japanese fleet in May 1942, and for the first time in the war won a major victory in this half of the world. In June the U.S. Navy met and defeated another big Japanese naval detachment, this one far to the north, approaching Midway Island, east of Hawaii. Both victories were won by the navy's carrier-based air arm—like Pearl Harbor itself, strong evidence of the crucial part air power would play in naval combat throughout the war.

There was, however, some bloody foot slogging left to do—in the jungles of Southeast Asia and on the islands of Oceania.

In Southeast Asia—the so-called China-Burma-India theater of war—Japanese military power was stretched to its thinnest. By overrunning Burma and cutting the Burma Road in 1942, Japan had temporarily severed the line that allowed supplies to reach beleaguered China, her original and always central target. But when Japanese forces pushed still further, into northeastern India, they were turned back by British, American, Indian, and other allied troops and forced off the subcontinent in 1943.

The war in this corner of the globe thereafter centered in the steaming jungles and precipitous mountains of Burma. Allied road builders carved a new highway through the rain forest while groups of irregulars with colorful names like Wingate's Raiders and Merrill's Marauders were keeping the Japanese off balance. Weakened by tropical diseases, mired in the monsoon rains, and handicapped by long and uncertain supply lines, the Japanese gradually gave ground. The British pushed east and south, capturing Rangoon and Mandalay and gradually retaking their former colony.

America's westward drive from island to island across Oceania began with the bloody Battle of Guadalcanal in the Solomons in the latter part of 1942. The first of many amphibious landings put U.S. Marines ashore on a jungle island defended by deeply entrenched and determined Japanese. Major air and sea battles roared overhead and in the surrounding waters, and the Japanese launched repeated counterattacks to recover lost ground. The back-and-forth struggle ended with United States forces in control, but it was a hard-won victory. Guadalcanal estab-

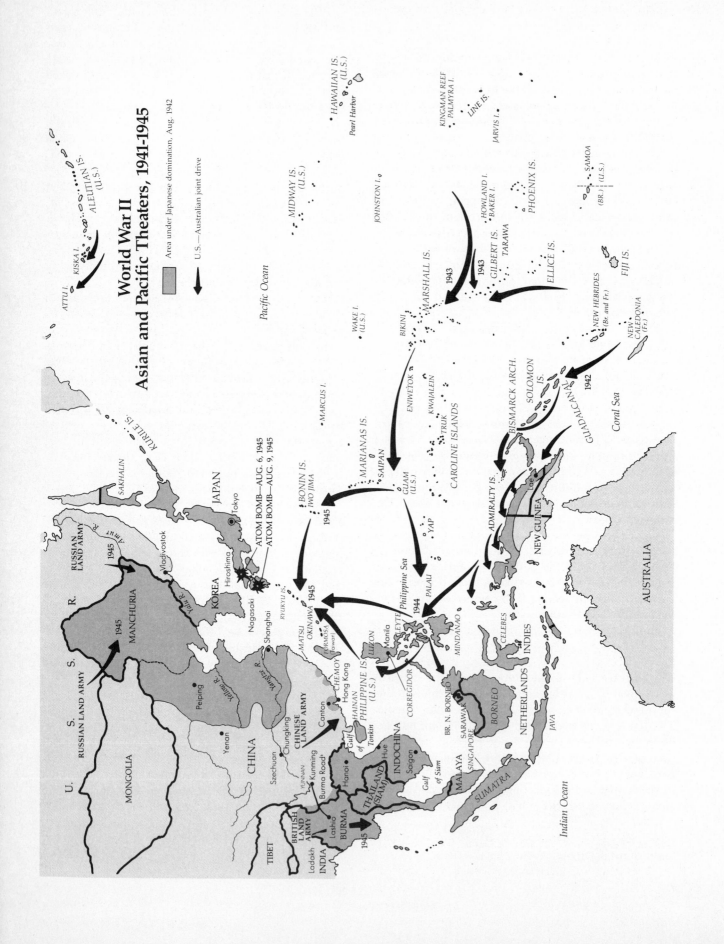

World War II
Asian and Pacific Theaters, 1941-1945

Area under Japanese domination, Aug. 1942

U.S.—Australian joint drive

Pacific Ocean

ALEUTIAN IS. (U.S.)

KISKA I.

ATTU I.

KURILE IS.

SAKHALIN

JAPAN

Tokyo

ATOM BOMB—AUG. 6, 1945
ATOM BOMB—AUG. 9, 1945

Hiroshima

Nagasaki

Shanghai

RYUKYU IS.

MATSU

OKINAWA 1945

FORMOSA

Taiwan

CHEMOY

Hong Kong

HAINAN

Canton

Gulf of Tonkin

PHILIPPINE IS. (U.S.)

CORREGIDOR

LUZON

Manila

LEYTE

Philippine Sea

1944

PALAU

YAP

MINDANAO

CELEBES

BORNEO

BR. N. BORNEO

SARAWAK

NETHERLANDS INDIES

JAVA

SUMATRA

MALAYA

SINGAPORE

Gulf of Siam

Saigon

INDOCHINA

Hue

Hanoi

THAILAND (SIAM)

BURMA

1945

Loshio

BRITISH LAND ARMY

Ladakh

INDIA

TIBET

Burma Road

Kunming

YUNNAN

CHINESE LAND ARMY

Chungking

Szechuan

CHINA

Yenan

Peiping

Yellow R.

Yangtze R.

MONGOLIA

U. S. S. R.

RUSSIAN LAND ARMY

1945

MANCHURIA

1945

Vladivostok

KOREA

Yalu R.

Amur R.

Sungari R.

Indian Ocean

AUSTRALIA

Coral Sea

NEW GUINEA

Lae

ADMIRALTY IS.

BISMARCK ARCH.

SOLOMON IS.

GUADALCANAL

1942

NEW HEBRIDES (Br. and Fr.)

NEW CALEDONIA (Fr.)

FIJI IS.

SAMOA (BR.) (U.S.)

PHOENIX IS.

ELLICE IS.

GILBERT IS.

TARAWA

HOWLAND I.

BAKER I.

1943

1943

MARSHALL IS.

KWAJALEN

ENIWETOK

TRUK

CAROLINE ISLANDS

GUAM (U.S.)

SAIPAN

MARIANAS IS.

BIKINI

WAKE I. (U.S.)

MARCUS I.

BONIN IS.

IWO JIMA

1945

JOHNSTON I.

MIDWAY IS. (U.S.)

HAWAIIAN IS. (U.S.)

Pearl Harbor

KINGMAN REEF

PALMYRA I.

LINE IS.

JARVIS I.

lished a pattern of bloody island campaigns that seldom varied thereafter.

The Americans in the South Pacific spent most of 1943 recovering from the losses sustained in the defeats and victories of the first year of the Pacific war, and in regrouping their forces for a major offensive. Then, with ships, planes, and U.S. Marines available in sufficient quantities, and General Douglas MacArthur in overall command, America launched a series of costly but successful amphibious attacks on the Japanese-held islands that formed the outer perimeter of her Asian empire. Through 1944 and 1945, coral atolls and jungle islands such as Tarawa, Saipan, Iwo Jima, and Okinawa became the sites of hard-fought United States victories. The Philippines were also invaded and retaken by MacArthur's troops.

Everywhere the Japanese fought with the courage of their samurai ancestors. But 1945 found American arms poised to attack the Japanese home islands themselves.

Flag on the Reichstag, Slow Roll on Tokyo Bay

Nineteen forty-five was the last year—the year of unconditional surrender.

In Europe, the Russian Red Army had driven German forces back out of eastern Europe, conquering Hitler's small Axis allies there and liberating the countries that had resisted him. In the latter effort they received important help from partisan leaders such as Marshal Tito in Yugoslavia.

The American, British, French, and allied forces, meanwhile, after containing the German counterattack in Belgium, pressed in on Germany from the west. The last line of defense, the so-called West Wall, was outflanked and breached, the Rhine was crossed at several places, and the Allies poured into Germany.

From the east, the Russians did the same. With Hitler's eastern European satellite states firmly in their hands, Soviet forces swept into eastern Germany. Under Marshal Zhukov, defender of Moscow and victor of Stalingrad, the Russians drove for Berlin. In the spring of 1945, Russian soldiers swarmed into the half-ruined capital of the Thousand-Year Reich.

Hitler, in his Berlin command bunker, hands shaking, face twitching as the thud of explosions shook his city, took poison. His body was burned by faithful officers. All across the country, battered German armies gave up. The unconditional surrender of all surviving German forces was signed a week after the fall of Berlin, on May 9, 1945—V–E Day, for Victory in Europe, in American parlance.

A famous photograph shows Russian soldiers plant-

Red flag over a gutted Berlin. Russian soldiers raised their banner over the Nazi capital in May 1945. (Sovfoto)

ing the red hammer-and-sickle banner of the Soviet Union high on a gutted tower of the German Reichstag. Below them, the wreckage that was left after years of American and British bombing fades into the smoke of the last battle of Berlin.

The fall of Japan was very different. It came after an exclusively aerial bombardment—a further graphic demonstration of the power of attack from the air.

From newly captured island bases, United States bombers began to visit the same sort of mass destruction on Japan that Europe, mainland Asia, and Oceania had already suffered. Through the first three quarters of 1945, high-explosive and incendiary bombs gutted large sections of Japanese cities, including Tokyo. Then in August, the war's most terrible secret weapon was deployed against two Japanese urban complexes, Hiroshima and Nagasaki. Atomic bombs destroyed most of both cities—in a matter of minutes. With the majority of her armed forces still intact and occupying foreign lands from Southeast Asia to China, Japan surrendered unconditionally to the Allies.

The surrender document was signed on the deck of the American battleship *Missouri*, anchored in Tokyo

The Japanese surrender on the deck of the American battleship Missouri *in Tokyo Bay in September, 1945. General McArthur stands at the microphone on the right. (Library of Congress)*

Bay, on September 2, 1945—V–J Day. There was no more than a gentle roll on the water, and the hands that signed the document were steady.

But one aspect of that scene was quite similar to the Berlin where the red flag fluttered. The city that ringed the harbor, like Hitler's shattered capital, was a bombed-out ruin as the biggest war drew to a close.

WHAT GOOD CAME OF IT AT LAST

Total War

World War II, even more than World War I, required a total commitment from the societies that fought it. To mobilize, equip, and support modern mechanized forces of millions of men, the great powers had to put immense political, social, and above all economic power into the hands of their central governments.

On the political side, this could mean significant increases in the authority of governing officials, even in democratic countries. Government censorship—or self-censorship by the press—of war news was universal, as were the combatants' propaganda campaigns to convince people on all sides that theirs was the righteous cause. Even in a country with an established tradition of civil liberties like the United States,

100,000 Americans of Japanese ancestry were interned for the duration on no better grounds than fear and racial prejudice. In Germany, it was after the beginning of the war that the systematic extermination of 6 million Jews and several million Slavs and other "inferior races" began.

Perhaps the most striking social consequence of the war, as in World War I, was the movement of large numbers of women out of the home and into war plants or even into the armed services themselves. In the United States alone, more than 200,000 women served in special units of the army, navy, marines, and Coast Guard, and 6 million worked in munitions factories. Some 40 percent of all American aircraft workers were women, a fact that permanently altered old-fashioned notions about the ability of women to acquire mechanical skills. Rosie the Riveter was a label that symbolized another step toward an equal place for women in the Western world.

The most striking area of increased government involvement in national life was, as in World War I, the economic sphere. Once more, governments allocated raw materials for war industries; regulated wages and prices; set labor policies, generally excluding strikes for the duration; and gave priorities to military production. For the totalitarian states, including the Soviet Union, this could make little difference to peoples already habituated to official control of the economy. Western nations that had hesitated even at some of the welfare legislation of earlier decades, however, were much more willing to accept a strong government role after this wartime experience.

In this total war, finally, civilian populations became military targets to a particularly high degree. For one thing, the sweeping conquests of World War II brought large populations under foreign rule. In a nationalistic age, this led to sizable resistance movements and guerrilla harassment—which in turn brought bloody reprisals against civilians by occupying troops.

More important, of course, the mechanical sinews of modern war were manufactured by civilian workers, who for this reason too became targets for the military. In an age of saturation bombing, these noncombatants also perished in large numbers.

Global Rubble

Not surprisingly, a total war fought with what were then the most up-to-date technological tools available produced vast ruin and unmatched casualty figures.

Years of fighting between huge armies in western Russia and in eastern China cost millions of lives. Large stretches of country were methodically denuded of human habitation, stripped of crops and flocks, emptied of human population. Everywhere, long experience of desperate combat led to a toughening of sensibilities. German soldiers routinely hung Russian civilians suspected of guerrilla activity. Japanese troops, brutally disciplined in their own army, were often savagely brutal to civilians. American troops in the Pacific turned flame throwers on dug-in Japanese soldiers simply as the most efficient way of getting them out.

But the most impressive material destruction, and the most astronomical casualty figures, came with the bombing of cities. Industrial cities, with their heavy concentration of defense plants, transportation junctures, and military facilities, were clearly essential to the enemy's war effort. It was also believed that a rain of destruction from the sky might break an opponent's will to fight on, thus hastening victory. As a result, lavish expenditures of money, scientific ingenuity, labor, and lives were poured into this key feature of the biggest of all wars.

The Japanese in China, the Italians in Ethiopia, and the Germans in Spain showed what could be done from the air before World War II properly got under way. In the early years of the war itself, German bombers began the practice of terror bombing in Warsaw, Amsterdam, Coventry, London. Late in the war, Hitler's last technological surprises, the V-1 and V-2 flying bombs, were still scattering more or less random havoc over Britain.

But as the war advanced, American and British bombing raids more than matched these German efforts. High explosives and incendiary bombs rained over German and Japanese cities. Terrible damage was done by the fire bombing of lightly built Japanese cities such as Tokyo, and even such solidly built metropolises as Hamburg were pounded to rubble by days of sometimes round-the-clock bombing. As many as 100,000 people may have died in a single incendiary raid on Tokyo; the notorious Dresden raid cost hundreds of thousands of lives in one night. And in a fraction of a second, in a single flash of light brighter than a thousand suns, Hiroshima was turned into as close an approximation of hell as twentieth-century humanity has thus far managed to achieve.

Total casualties in the greatest and most destructive of wars can only be estimated. Fifty million is an estimate frequently advanced.

A million is a hard number to comprehend. As an aid to the imagination, you might note that by the time it sees print, the book you hold in your hand will perhaps contain a quarter of a million words. Multiply that by four, and that again by fifty. Imagine each word as a small white cross on an endless field of green—the military cemeteries of Europe are me-

ticulously cared for—and you will be on your way to appreciating World War II.

Peace Not Yet

As in 1918, there was dancing in the streets in 1945. And as on that earlier occasion, the celebrations—where celebrations were in order—proved to be premature.

There was the wreckage to clean up, dislocated populations to resettle, defeated nations to occupy, shattered economies to rebuild. There was, in short, a large part of the world to raise from the ashes.

There were also new and unexpected problems to face. Across Asia and Africa in the postwar years there was an unexampled surge of demands for autonomy or independence. These demands were in considerable part stimulated—and the likelihood of their success increased—by the experience of World War II itself.

Even more unexpected was the almost immediate breakdown of the Grand Alliance that had defeated the Axis during the postwar period. First Europe and then much of the world was soon divided into two rapidly rearming camps, one headed by the greatest of Eurasian powers, the Soviet Union, the other by the North American colossus, the United States. The Cold War was under way—a global confrontation whose solution eludes us still today.

Peace was clearly not yet at hand in 1945, and the tensions and conflicts that surfaced then were of historic significance. World War II was, in fact, central to the history of the twentieth century. Its origins go back to the main currents of the first half of the century. Its consequences have in many ways dominated the history of the second half, as subsequent chapters will indicate.

A historical event, however, is more than the sum of its consequences. World War II was a chunk out of the lives of millions.

Some of the people in the old black-and-white photographs are still alive and can tell you about it. Solid burghers over a drink in a nice German living room will tell you how the thunder of the incoming planes shook the ground, how their numbers darkened the sun. A polite old man at the Ground Zero Arch in Hiroshima will explain for the millionth time what he was doing when it happened—and what happened then. Others—men, women, children—died soon after the old photographs were made: "Young Serviceman Celebrates the Night before His Ship Sails"; "Young Mother and Child Wait to Board the Train to Dachau." World War II is all their stories, their part in the unbelievable, sometimes unspeakable, human venture into history.

SUMMARY

World War II, the most terrible of all wars thus far, resulted from the usual tangle of causes. These included the dissatisfactions and ambitions of the more authoritarian powers—Germany, Japan, Italy, and Russia—and the weakness of the leaders of the liberal West—notably Britain, France, and the United States. Through the 1930s, a series of international crises in East Asia, North Africa, and several European countries built toward a final confrontation over Poland in 1939. Hitler's invasion of that country finally led Britain and France to declare war on Germany, beginning the second global conflict of the century.

The war began with a Nazi blitzkrieg of Poland, undertaken in alliance with Communist Russia. After a winter lull, Hitler launched a second series of lightning invasions, this time in western Europe, resulting in the defeat of France, Belgium, the Netherlands, and most of Scandinavia. German efforts to overwhelm Britain by air and submarine attacks failed, however, and had the effect of finally moving the United States to offer help to the last major democracy left in Europe.

The totalitarian alliance made two crucial errors in 1941. Hitler's armies invaded Russia, only to be stopped at the very outskirts of Moscow. The Japanese attacked the Pacific colonies of the battered Western powers, including those of the United States. The Soviet Union and the United States were thus brought into the war against the Axis powers.

The tide turned in favor of the Allies in 1942. In that year the British stopped the Germans short of the Suez Canal in Egypt, the Russians destroyed a besieging German army at Stalingrad, and the United States shattered two Japanese fleets in the Pacific and began to regain a foothold in the islands. Allied troops also invaded Italy, which became the first Axis power to surrender.

By 1944 the Russians were driving the Germans back across Europe, and the Japanese were in retreat in the Far East. A huge invasion fleet put American, British, and Canadian armies ashore in France. Hitler's Germany was crushed between advancing Russian and Anglo-American forces in 1945. In the Pacific, an American island-hopping campaign put their bombers within range of Japan, and two atomic bombs finally forced the last Axis partner to surrender in August of 1945.

The war had been a total war like World War I, and it produced vastly more ruins and tens of millions of casualties. It destroyed most of the totalitarian giants, but it did not eliminate international conflict from the world, as the Cold War was soon to show.

SUGGESTED READING

BERGAMINI, D. *Japan's Imperial Conspiracy*. New York: Morrow, 1971. Japanese expansionism in the Far East. See also A. Iriye, *After Imperialism: The Search for a New Order in the Far East, 1921–1931* (Cambridge, Mass.: Harvard University Press, 1965), and Y. C. Maxon, *Control of Japanese Foreign Policy: A Study of Civil-Military Rivalry, 1930–1945* (Berkeley: University of California Press, 1957).

BISHOP, E. *Their Finest Hour*. New York: Ballantine, 1968. Popular, well-illustrated story of the Battle of Britain.

CHURCHILL, W. S. *The Second World War* (6 vols.). Boston: Houghton Mifflin, 1948–1953. The war as it looked to the great war leader; resounding prose.

CRAIG, W. *Enemy at the Gates: The Battle of Stalingrad*. New York: E. P. Dutton, 1973. The bloody turning point in southern Russia.

DEAKIN, F. W. *The Brutal Friendship: Mussolini, Hitler, and the Fall of Italian Fascism*. London: Weidenfeld and Nicolson, 1962. Relations between the two most aggressive European totalitarians. On Hitler's relations with Japan, see J. M. Meskill, *Hitler and Japan: The Hollow Alliance* (New York: Atherton, 1966).

EISENHOWER, D. D. *Crusade in Europe*. New York: Da Capo, 1977. Military operations in Europe, as seen by the American commanding general.

FEIS, H. *Churchill, Roosevelt, Stalin*. Princeton: Princeton University Press, 1967. The Big Three, in a balanced presentation.

FLOWER, D., and J. REEVES, eds. *The Taste of Courage: The War, 1939–1945*. New York: Harper & Row, 1960. Vignettes and impressions. For images of battle in the Pacific, see D. Cogdon, ed., *Combat: The Pacific Theater—World War II* (New York: Dell, 1959).

HERSEY, J. *Hiroshima*. New York: Knopf, 1946. The famous book about the first atom bomb, as experienced by those who were under it. For a more typical example of the air war, see M. Caidin, *The Night Hamburg Died* (New York: Ballantine, 1960).

KEEGAN, J. *Six Armies in Normandy: From D-Day to the Liberation of Paris*. New York: Viking, 1982. Vivid account of three crucial months of fighting in France in the summer of 1944.

LEVIN, N.   *The Holocaust: The Destruction of European Jewry, 1933–1945*. New York: Crowell, 1968. Hitler's Jewish policy, escalating to the Final Solution. For a searing case study, see O. Friedrich's anatomy of the Auschwitz death camp, *The End of the World: A History* (New York: Coward, McCann and Geoghegan, 1982).

LIDDELL HART, B. H.   *History of the Second World War*. New York: Putnam's, 1970. Military history of the war by a famous military historian. See also P. Calvocoressi and G. Wint, *Total War: Causes and Course of the Second World War* (London: Allen Lane, 1972), hugely detailed and impressive.

MAUMONT, M.   *The Origins of the Second World War*. New Haven: Yale University Press, 1978. Diplomatic encounters along the road to war. A more controversial treatment is A. J. P. Taylor's *The Origins of the Second World War* (London: Hamish Hamilton, 1961), which contends that Hitler had no plan for war and apportions much of the blame on the British and French.

TAYLOR, T.   *Munich: The Price of Peace*. New York: Doubleday, 1979. Insightful examination of a diplomatic crisis whose resolution has become synonymous with appeasement. See also the broader scope of A. L. Rowse, *Appeasement: A Study in Political Decline* (New York: Norton, 1963).

THOMAS, H.   *The Spanish Civil War*, rev. ed. New York: Harper & Row, Pub., 1977. Perhaps the best account of this much discussed "little war."

TOLAND, J.   *The Rising Sun: The Decline and Fall of the Japanese Empire*. New York: Bantam, 1970. A Japanese perspective on the war.

WOHLSTETTER, R.   *Pearl Harbor: Warning and Decision*. Stanford: Stanford University Press, 1962. Convincing account of the much debated American disaster.

WRIGHT, G.   *The Ordeal of Total War, 1939–1945*. New York: Harper & Row, Pub., 1969. Excellent overview, with attention to the home front and to broader intellectual and social consequences.

Chapter · 20

A CULTURE AGAINST ITSELF

THE MODERN VIEW

Arts and Ideas under Global Headings

The cultural history of the first half of the twentieth century can be dealt with on a rather different basis from the arts and ideas of any earlier period. Such cultural developments will not be discussed here as primarily the products of regional trends or as the cultures of historic civilizations. Instead, we will look at the intellectual and aesthetic achievements of the period under global headings. We will examine what is perhaps the century's cultural mainstream—the fragmented intellectual vision and the modernist movement in the arts—from an intercontinental perspective, touching down in Europe, the Americas, and even Japan for important examples. We will look at the socially concerned art of the long revolutions and at the ideological culture of totalitarian movements wherever these trends surface: in Germany or Russia, Mexico, India, or Japan. In dealing with both modernism and commitment, we will find major instances emerging within a considerable variety of cultures.

The cultural innovations of the decades from the turn of the century to World War II will thus strikingly illustrate that globalization of history which is the most remarkable aspect of world history in our time.

A Disintegrating Vision

"No culture in the history of the world," a recent history of Western arts and literature declares, "has experienced either the extent or the intensity of change as that which the West has seen in our own century."[1] This is a sweeping but quite defensible summary of the high culture of the twentieth century. We may carry the characterization of the turbulence of art and thought in our time still further, however. We may legitimately describe ours as the best example we have of a civilization at war with itself, a culture that has turned sharply, and even violently, against its own most cherished ideals.

The Enlightenment of the eighteenth century and the political ideologies and broader cultural revolts of the nineteenth century all built toward this twentieth-century turmoil in the Western mind. The years between the world wars saw two major phases of this cultural revolution: the high-modernist moment in the arts in the 1920s and the anguished ideological tumult of the 1930s. Undergirding this tumult, however, was a disintegration and transformation of the primarily scientific world view that the Western world had been cultivating for the preceding three or four centuries. It is this disintegrating and changing scientific vision of the world to which we turn now.

Since the days of Copernicus and Newton in the sixteenth and seventeenth centuries, science had increasingly seemed to educated Western people to provide answers to the riddles of the universe that philosophy and religion had once attempted to explain. Around the turn of the twentieth century, however, scientists began to uncover evidence and to develop theories that brought much of the Newtonian world view into question. By the 1920s and 1930s, disturbing questions were being asked about the ul-

[1]Mary Ann Frese Witt, et al., *The Humanities: Cultural Roots and Continuities*, vol. II (Lexington, Mass.: D. C. Heath and Co., 1980), p. 231.

timate nature of matter, the validity of natural law, and the very possibility of scientific truth.

The distinctive qualities of matter had been clearly defined since the seventeenth century. Matter possessed mass and extension in space; it was solid, made of tiny concrete particles called atoms. But around 1900, the work of Marie Curie with radium—which disintegrated from matter into pure radiant energy—and the discovery of cosmic rays and X rays caused some scientists to question the solid materiality of all physical phenomena. The researches of H. A. Lorenz and of Ernest Rutherford and Niels Bohr showed that the allegedly solid atom was in fact composed largely of space between orbiting subatomic particles and their nucleus. In time, even these particles were discovered to be composed not of matter, as it had once been defined, but of pure charges of energy—a far cry from the materialist vision of the later nineteenth century.

Natural laws, the linchpins that had held the material world together since Newton, were also reinterpreted in disturbing ways in the decades after 1900. Evidence accumulated that exceptions to these alleg-

edly absolute principles were scattered throughout the natural world. These exceptions might be rare, and they might occur largely at the microscopic level. But they led scientists to think more and more that natural "laws" were really statistical probabilities rather than absolute truths binding on every particle of "matter" in the universe.

The very possibility of absolute truth, finally, was called into question during the 1920s. The absolute certainty of mathematics, the standard of truth since Plato's day, had been challenged by the formulation of the first non-Euclidean geometry in the nineteenth century. Pragmatic philosophy, developed in America by William James, declared that truth was a matter of usefulness: that the truth of an idea changed as its use-value changed from one time or situation to another. Cultural relativism, an approach evolved first by late-nineteenth-century anthropologists, suggested that even moral truths were relative matters, their validity being determined by the social needs and mores of a particular culture. What was right for a Fiji Islander might be a mortal sin for a Victorian English person—it was all relative.

The relativity of truth invaded pure science after the turn of the century with Albert Einstein's famous theory of relativity in physics. Einstein demonstrated that both space and time, the absolute givens of Newtonian physics, were in fact always relative rather than absolute. Einstein defined time as a form of perception rather than as something "out there." He saw that it was relative to the position of the observer, to his motion through space, and he even showed that it proceeds more slowly the more rapidly the "clock" that measured it moved through space. Space also, however, was far from fixed and absolute. The size of an object moving at velocities approaching the speed of light would actually decrease, whereas its mass would increase as the velocity did. Einstein's general theory of relativity, finally, redefined the universe as a whole as a four-dimensional continuum in which time and space were relative to each other— and in which the queasy layman might feel that he had nowhere solid left to stand.

Werner Heisenberg put the capstone on the confusion at the end of the 1920s by announcing in his notorious principle of indeterminacy that there were definable limits to human knowledge. Even the introduction of a scientific measuring instrument, Heisenberg asserted, would so alter the reality being measured that the complete truth about the behavior of even an electron could never be known.

Most of these doubts about the nature and validity of human understanding had to do with the far limits of scientific knowledge, with subatomic particles or speeds approximating the velocity of light. But such

Marie Curie, the French scientist whose exploration of the properties of radium challenged ancient assumptions about the nature of matter itself. (The Bettman Archive, Inc.)

doubts left the most enlightened Westerners questioning the omniscience of their own scientific gurus during the years between the wars.

Sex and Salivating Dogs

Even more controversial than the ideas of Einstein and Heisenberg were the theories of human nature proposed by psychologists such as the Russian Ivan Pavlov and the Austrian physician Sigmund Freud. Both conceived their fundamental notions around 1900, but it was not until the decades between the wars that their views began to have a powerful impact on the self-image of Western humanity.

Pavlov was the first proponent of the school of behaviorist psychology that came to dominate much of twentieth-century Western thinking about the human psyche. Working primarily with animals in his laboratories, Pavlov developed the concept of the conditioned reflex as the central explanation for human as well as other animal behavior. Discovering that animals could be conditioned by the positive or negative responses to their particular behaviors, he argued that accidental conditioning in a given social environment determines how all human beings behave.

Behaviorists actually came to believe that mental phenomena are little more than by-products of environmentally conditioned behavior, rather than the source of decisions that cause that behavior. Like dogs conditioned—in a famous experiment—to salivate at the sound of a dinner bell, the most complex human behavior patterns are products of material conditioning, and nothing more.

Freud's concept of the human mind was more complicated, and it left Westerners with even less of a sense of being masters of their fates. His emphasis on sexuality, childhood, the repression of our basic impulses, and the dominant role of the unconscious mind made him as controversial and influential a thinker as Marx during the interwar years.

For Freud the human psyche resembled an iceberg. The conscious portion of the mind is only the tip of the iceberg; the unconscious mind, nine tenths of the whole, is invisible beneath the surface. But it is the drift of that submerged nine tenths that determines where the visible tip will go. This unconscious mind beneath the surface is driven by what Freud called *libido*, primal psychic energy consisting originally of sexual desire—which thus becomes the central motivating force in human life.

Libidinal energy, Freud believed, is dammed up or repressed in childhood by painful encounters with reality or chastening authority. Repressed desire escapes, however, in socially sanctioned sexual activity, as sublimated creative energy, or as mental illness,

the form in which Freudian psychiatrists most frequently encountered it.

Again, the shock to Western rationality and morality was great. It had been bad enough to be told by Darwin that we are descended from apes, or by Pavlov that we are no better than salivating dogs. It was worse still to hear from Freud that animal instincts of which we are not even conscious govern all our lives!

The disintegration of scientific certainties dating back as far as Newton did not, of course, mean the end of the scientific world view. It was, in fact, the first step in the construction of a new science-based vision of the nature of things that was so important as to be commonly described as a second Scientific Revolution—to which we will turn in a later chapter. But the initial impact, like the first response to the Scientific Revolution of the sixteenth and seventeenth centuries, was one of resentment and bewilderment during these troubled decades between the wars.

The High-Modernist Moment

Art and literature, architecture and music also underwent some jolting changes during the early decades of the twentieth century. The origins of those swirling tides of artistic change that we call modernism may be traced back to the nineteenth century but they reached their first great flowering around World War I and in the 1920s.

Modernism, the major international artistic school of the twentieth century, was one of the great revolutions in the history of Western art. It began before the turn of the century, flowered between the wars, reached a climax and began its long decline after World War II. Like romanticism, modernism represented not only a revolt in the arts but a rebellion against the beliefs and values of Western society as a whole.

The insurrection in the arts began before the turn of the century in France with painters such as Paul Cézanne, Vincent van Gogh, and Paul Gauguin. These pioneers of modernism painted landscapes and still lifes, peasants, city streets, and South Sea islanders with directness, distortion, and an unacademic lack of realism and finish. Their simple figures and visible brushstrokes struck contemporaries as crude—and impressed most of the art world since as the genius of a new direction in artistic expression. By the early 1900s, painters such as the French *fauves* ("wild beasts") and the German expressionists were daubing their rude figures with bright or off-key colors that stunned generations raised on the perfection of Raphael or da Vinci.

Modernism, then, quickly gathered force as a re-

"The City from Greenwich Village," by the American painter John Sloan. Light, grit, and the realities of city life preoccupied this early twentieth-century artist, as they had Europeans of the later nineteenth century. Their break with exact representation and carefully concealed brush strokes paved the way for modernism. (National Gallery of Art, Washington, D.C. Gift of Helen Farr Sloan, 1970)

bellion against the old masters and the art-school academic training that the Renaissance had bequeathed to subsequent centuries. Renaissance naturalism, with its close study of anatomy, perspective, and nature, was replaced by a new passion for pure form. Modern artists took less and less interest in subject matter and gave themselves over wholeheartedly to exploring the formal elements of which all art is made: color, line, shape, volume, texture. They also glorified the quest itself; novelty, exploration, and innovation in the arts became ends in themselves. Originality in art, a cult since the romantics, became the high god of the modernists.

New schools of art thus proliferated during the early decades of the present century. Futurism in Italy and Russia came to terms with the speed and power of modern technology, worshiping at the shrine of the locomotive, the automobile, and the airplane. Cubism in France, led by the expatriate Spaniard Pablo Picasso, broke nature up into its component geometrical shapes and reassembled them in barely recognizable forms on the canvas. Surrealist artists such as Salvador Dali tried to liberate the Freudian unconscious by painting a dream world of sexually suggestive figures, melting clocks, and technicolor skies. Mavericks such as Paul Klee, Vasily Kandinsky, and Piet Mondrian abandoned subject matter com-

pletely, painting purely abstract patterns and brightly colored shapes that were dazzlingly decorative but totally without content.

Modernism raged happily through the arts. Architects such as Frank Lloyd Wright insisted that modern buildings should not imitate traditional Gothic or Greek styles but should follow function and integrate their structure into their natural surroundings. The twelve-tone scale invented by Arnold Schönberg revolutionized modern music, and Igor Stravinsky's *Firebird, Rite of Spring*, and other ballets scandalized Paris with their bizarre themes, staging, and rhythms, and their apparent abandonment of melody and harmony. The Bauhaus artistic community in Germany even revitalized the crafts, promoting a new awareness of modern materials through creations such as glass walls and tubular metal chairs.

Pablo Picasso (1881–1973), the king of modern art, was in his heyday between the wars. A lifelong experimenter—he lived into his nineties, changing every decade, sometimes every year—Picasso most disturbed the art world with his development of cubism before, during, and after World War I. Pictures such as *Les Demoiselles d'Avignon* and *Les Trois Musiciens* broke their subjects up into their component shapes, simplified these shapes into geometry, and then rearranged them for artistic effect, much as you might arrange flowers in a vase or rocks in a Japanese garden. Later cubists slapped paint on canvas with gay abandon, pasted on bits of linoleum or newsprint for textural effects, and generally played more freely and happily with reality than Western artists had ever done before.

Western literature went even further during the modernist era, rebelling not only against Western literary traditions but against Western society as well.

This endemic war between twentieth-century Western writers and society also had its roots in the nineteenth century. It built upon romantic bohemianism, which despised the vulgar philistinism of the middle classes, and on the nineteenth-century belief in art for art's sake rather than art as a means for conveying religious, patriotic, or other themes. Convinced that artists had a unique vocation, a higher calling than mere moneymaking, and that they must be true above all to their talent, modernist writers took up the cudgels against the twentieth century with an iconoclastic vigor that is hard to find in any other period.

The "best people" and leading institutions of Western society took a savage drubbing in the 1920s, as indeed they have pretty much ever since. Political corruption, commercial greed, the hollowness of patriotic slogans and organized religion, the emptiness of old-fashioned morality were all exposed to public contempt in the work of postwar experimental writers such as Marcel Proust, James Joyce, Franz Kafka,

The modernist trend away from subject matter and toward pure form seemed to have reached its apogee in geometrical abstracts like "Lozenge in Red, Yellow, and Blue" by Dutch painter Piet Mondrian. (National Gallery of Art, Washington, D.C. Gift of Herbert and Nannette Rothschild, 1971)

and T. S. Eliot, and even by such strong but fairly conventional stylists as Thomas Mann, Aldous Huxley, D. H. Lawrence, and Ernest Hemingway.

Writers also expressed their sense of artistic vocation—and their disinterest in a large readership—by a growing emphasis on self-expression as the point of art. This approach led in turn to a deliberate obscurity cultivated through the use of unfamiliar allusions, private symbols, and even foreign languages and references to details of the author's personal life that no reader would be likely to understand. Thus Eliot, perhaps the most famous Western poet of the century, was able to squeeze three languages and references to an Elizabethan dramatist, a French romantic poet, Dante, and the Hindu Upanishads into half a dozen lines of his poem *The Wasteland*.

The conviction that self-expression—rather than communication—was the point of literature led poets in particular to avoid narrative line, developed argument, or even sentence structure and syntax. The Italian futurist Filippo Marinetti hailed the poet's "entire freedom of images and analogies expressed by disjointed words and without the connecting wires of syntax" and illustrated his own thesis with lines of verse like these:

Sun gold billets dishes lead sky
Silk heat bed quilting purple blue[2]

Yet wonderful work could come from writers and artists working in these modernist modes. James Joyce's notorious novel *Ulysses* follows not a Greek hero but an ordinary Irish advertising solicitor through a single unexceptional day in Dublin, making that day emblematic of the whole of modern culture at its most various and dehumanizing. Picasso made use of cubist techniques to present the destruction of the Spanish town of *Guernica*, destroyed by Nazi bombers in the Spanish civil war, as a human tragedy. This caricatured vision of torn and lacerated flesh, with its broken fingers wrapped around a sword, its screaming horse, has a universality that no mere realist depiction of a bombed-out market town could muster.

THE CULTURE OF COMMITMENT

The Lost Generation

Much of the cultural life of the first half of the twentieth century, as we have seen, was rather more divorced from the historic trends of the times than

[2]David Perkins, *A History of Modern Poetry from the 1890s to the High Modernist Mode* (Cambridge, Mass.: Harvard University Press, 1976), pp. 308–309.

was Picasso's *Guernica*. The fragmented scientific world view, the modernist cult of pure form and self-expression had little connection with the world of Ford cars, Mao's Long March, or Mussolini's march on Rome.

But there was another side to the cultural life of the period that was clearly related to the main currents of our history. There was a culture of political commitment as well as a culture of disengagement.

In the West, the culture of commitment responded to such traumatic events as World War I, the depression, and the rise of totalitarianism. Elsewhere, it was a culture caught up in the long revolutions and the totalitarian ideologies of the century. Examples of each of these forms of politically and socially involved culture will be offered here.

It was World War I, to begin with, which fathered the notorious lost generation.

There was much that was frivolous about the postwar generation in Europe, America, and even far-off Japan, as we shall see in the next chapter. The "flaming youth" of the Jazz Age had their sexual emancipation, their passions for alcohol, jazz music, and a generally frenetic social life. Their "lostness" was defined in many ways. These included lost religious values, lost sociopolitical pieties connected with nationalism and liberalism, and what seemed to elders like plain laziness and lack of spunk. Spaghetti-spined postwar youth lounged and looked cynical, brooding on Erich Maria Remarque's *All Quiet on the Western Front* or Robert Graves's *Goodbye to All That*, reflecting on the emptiness of their lives and the hypocrisy of the eminent Victorians who had made the war happen.

Still, the 1920s produced an array of literary and artistic critiques of the age that clearly reflected a genuine sense of hollowness at the heart of the Western world. Marcel Proust's multivolume novel *Remembrance of Things Past* was, among other things, an acid exposé of life among the French upper and middle classes, high society and cafe society, in the decades before 1914. The American writer Ernest Hemingway ripped the lid off the bitter, alcohol-soaked life of the Lost Generation in his breakthrough novel, *The Sun Also Rises*, whose castrated hero and amoral heroine became symbols of what the war had done to its survivors.

The philosophically inclined could pore over Oswald Spengler's gloomily abstruse prophecy of the impending *Decline of the West*. And the American expatriate poet T. S. Eliot, living in London, provided his entire generation with the most vivid poetic evocation of its spiritual desolation in the most famous poem of the interwar years: *The Wasteland*. The symbols of Eliot's poem—the drowned Phoeni-

Norwegian artist Edvard Munch's "The Scream" is often seen as an expression of the spiritual anguish of the earlier twentieth century. (National Gallery of Art, Washington, D.C. Rosenwald Collection)

cian sailor, the dead man planted in the garden, the dry, dead land through which the poet travels—are all part of that spiritual desert where the generation of 1914 wandered in search of lost meanings and murdered dreams.

The Anguished Decade

The 1930s jolted some of the experimental artists of the 1920s into a confrontation with the social realities of their time. The new decade also generated new talents whose work was interwoven with an age of economic depression, ideological revolution, and totalitarian tyranny.

John Steinbeck provided the United States with its most disturbing vision of the Great Depression, particularly in *The Grapes of Wrath*, a moving evocation of dust-bowl drifters wandering westward in search of jobs that were not there. George Orwell, primarily a journalist and essayist (despite the great fame of his later novel *1984*), moved among Great Britain's down-and-out victims of the depression to write his painfully authentic *Road to Wigan Pier*.

André Malraux, novelist, art expert, resistance fighter in World War II and French minister of culture afterwards, began his career with searing novelistic descriptions of revolutionary struggle in China and Spain in *Man's Fate* and *Man's Hope*. Orwell and many other young idealists went off to the Spanish Civil War, the great European struggle against the totalitarianism of the 1930s. But Ernest Hemingway gave that lost liberal cause its most vivid literary depiction in *For Whom the Bell Tolls*, the story of a handful of Spanish guerrilla fighters and a lone American idealist confronting Franco's victorious war machine.

The confrontation with ideologically motivated political parties and the totalitarian regimes they built divided artists and writers in the West against each other—and sometimes against themselves. Few creative spirits in the liberal West had much to say in favor of right-wing totalitarianism—Fascism and Nazism—though the celebrated American modernist poet Ezra Pound did become an apologist for Mussolini's Italy. But Communist Russia, with its socialist roots and its apparent success at building Russia's economy up while capitalist economies were collapsing, won the sympathies of many Western social thinkers and writers.

Pablo Neruda, the Chilean poet who later won a Nobel prize, became a Communist in the aftermath of the Fascist victory in Spain. He divided the rest of his life in Latin America between poetry dedicated to the workers and the oppressed and to the political struggle to improve their lot. Arthur Koestler, a Communist through most of the 1930s, followed a more common pattern in quitting the party in disillusionment with Russian left-wing totalitarianism. His novel *Darkness at Noon* convincingly re-creates the mind of an "old Bolshevik," a veteran of Lenin's revolution who is languishing in one of Stalin's prisons, facing death at the hands of the Communist party to which he has given his life.

The political activists of the 1930s, like the lost generation of the 1920s, reflected the terrors and confusions of the still-young twentieth century as seen from a Western perspective. There were other perspectives on those decades, however; those of the revolutionaries and the builders of totalitarian states.

Self-Questioning, Self-Confident, Feuding or Locking Arms

In the tumultuous atmosphere of the long revolutions that swept China, Russia, Mexico, and other lands during the first half of the twentieth century, the arts also found new directions. The result was a distinctively revolutionary culture that excited many, both within and outside of the revolutionary lands that produced it.

Revolutionary culture, developing particularly in the 1920s and 1930s, was for the most part the product of a distinct mix of twentieth-century trends. Modernism inspired revolutionary artists with a new feeling of freedom to experiment with literary and artistic forms in order to better communicate their new visions of life in the brave new worlds they were building. The content of their work was usually provided by the ideologies that informed the various revolutions. Paradoxically, the artists of the new era frequently harked back to their national past for inspiration, strength, and even a sense of direction for the future.

These artists and thinkers within revolutionary movements or revolutionary regimes newly established brought a distinctive effervescence to the cultural life of the earlier twentieth century. Self-questioning or self-confident, feuding or locking arms, they brought their own vibrancy to the life of the mind and the arts. Rebelling against the establishment art and ideas of their various nations, they nevertheless enriched their national cultures with work of lasting value. From a global point of view, they vividly illustrate the revolutionary temper of our century at the deepest levels of thought and feeling.

Ferment, Earth Tones, and the Spirit of the River

Three examples of earlier-twentieth-century revolutionary culture will be touched on all too briefly here: the diverse culture flowerings that occurred in Russia, Mexico, and India.

Revolutionary culture, as we have loosely defined it above, flourished in Russia for no more than a decade, that of the 1920s. During this period of recovery from foreign and civil war, of the relatively uncentralized New Economic Policy and the search for a successor to Lenin, artists and writers were freer to experiment and innovate than at any subsequent time in Soviet Russian history.

The Communist party, of course, encouraged cultural work that praised workers and peasants and exposed the shortcomings of the old order. But "fellow travelers" in the arts, who did not always approve or disapprove of the proper things, were tolerated through most of the decade. And in the early years especially, literary and artistic methods could be as radically experimental as those of almost any western European avant garde. The result was a ferment of groups and schools and coteries in the Russian 1920s.

Symbolists and futurists from before the war; abstract painters and theatrical experimenters; groups such as the Serapion Brothers, who tried to create free of all ideological dictation; other groups such as the On Guard Group, which urged a strictly Marxist proletarian art—all mingled in the giddy pre-Stalin world of the twenties. Some of the work that resulted was essentially apolitical. The geometrical abstract art of Kasimir Malevich and others, for example, followed the most extreme Western artists in rejecting subject matter—and hence political messages as well. And poets such as Boris Pasternak, Anna Akhmatova, Osip Mendelstam, and the other Acmeists stuck essentially to humanistic themes in lyric verse of great beauty.

Many talented people were filled with genuine enthusiasm for the revolution in the early years. The futurist Vladimir Mayakovsky became virtually the poet laureate of the Russian Revolution. The symbolist poet Aleksandr Blok produced an evocative vision of the most violent days of the revolution in *The Twelve*, the lusty, sometimes brutal epic of a thoroughly human Red Guard platoon—led by the symbolic figure of Christ.

Theatrical reformers such as Vsevolod Meyerhold rejected the well-made plays and meticulously realistic productions for which prerevolutionary Russia had been famous, in favor of bare stages garnished with naked ladders, pulleys, and other gear, on which he mounted mass proletarian spectacles.

With the rise of Stalin to mastery of Russia in the thirties, the cultural ferment was quickly stilled. But for a time, at least, a genuinely revolutionary spirit had pervaded the art of Communist Russia.

In Mexico, painting was the predominant art in the remarkable renaissance that followed the revolution there. Revolutionary enthusiasms and PRM patronage exercised a rather more direct influence than was the case in the freewheeling Russian 1920s.

A militant "Indianism" infused much of this work. As part of their effort to elevate the long-oppressed Mexican peasantry, the Mexican revolutionary governments of the 1920s and 1930s celebrated the Indian as the most downtrodden of all prerevolutionary groups. The recent revolution itself, with its potential for Mexican spiritual rebirth, also offered vital subjects for Mexican art and literature. And the broadest human ideals, as epitomized in the rending experience of the revolution, captured the imagination of the new artists.

The most admired builders of Mexico's revolutionary culture between the wars were her internationally known trio of mural painters, José Orozco, David Siqueiros, and above all Diego Rivera. In huge modernistic paintings on the walls or ceilings of public buildings, these men celebrated the greatness of pre-Columbian Mexican culture and of the revolution, the nobility of the peasant and the factory worker, Mex-

ican patriotism and human achievement. Rivera's poetic, massively simplified, formally composed murals of *Earth and the Elements* and *Man in Four Aspects* (laborer, scientist, philosopher, rebel) bring years of training in European modernism to the service of the Mexican Revolution. Earth tones, simplifed forms, and sheer monumentality combine to give the ideals of the revolution the heroic stature its participants sought for them.

In India between the 1880s and the 1920s, continuing developments in Hinduism combined with a surge of Indian literary creativity to provide vigorous cultural support for the nationalistic political movement spearheaded by the Congress party.

On the religious side, traditional Hinduism was taught in seclusion by gurus such as Ramana Maharishi, who neither traveled nor wrote but instead instructed disciples at his isolated *ashram* in the south. Militants such as B. G. Tilak found support for aggressive political activism in the *Bhagavad-Gita*.

On the literary side, the Indian flowering grew through a fertile fusion of Indian and European elements. The influences of Western romanticism and realism contributed to the emergence of the modern novel and short story in India. Romantic and historical subjects persisted, but there was more attention than before to realistic description and modern psychological portraiture. Social problems, ranging from the caste system to the condition of women, became important subjects.

The leading light of this self-confident yet self-conscious Indian cultural revival was Rabindranath Tagore, whose Nobel Prize for literature in 1913 earned him worldwide renown. Tagore's poems, plays, stories, and novels were rooted in a deep love of his native Bengal, of the river Ganges that flows through it to the sea, and of the peasant villagers among whom he lived much of his life. His vision had a deep spiritual dimension as well, and he worked for both religious and secular education in India.

Rabindranath Tagore's global lecture tours in later life made him India's best-known man of letters. He embodied the fusion of ancient Hindu beliefs and Western influences that lay at the heart of the whole Indian nationalist movement, the fusion that would create the modern nation of India at mid-century.

Worshiping the Savage God

The totalitarian regimes of the interwar years—to turn finally to them—produced a great deal of propaganda art. In general, no one has had much to say for this ideological culture since Hitler, Stalin, Franco, Mussolini, and the rest passed to their rewards. But even these grim regimes could inspire a poet such as Mayakovski or filmmakers such as Riefenstahl and Eisenstein. And even the most self-serving of silly theories, the least convincing art of Communist or Nazi image makers, can tell us something, at least, of the self-images of these builders of the brutal years. This is who they thought they were—and it would perhaps be as well for us to know it.

The forms of totalitarian culture were as diverse as the cultural traditions from which these new and extreme forms of twentieth-century authoritarianism sprang. Yet there were some similarities too.

All totalitarian societies glorified leadership and leaders with an extravagance hard to match in the democracies. All had their elites—even the allegedly egalitarian Communists, for whom the party itself became a vanguard elite. Most had their "chosen people," a class, race, or nationality whose glorious destiny was the object of the exercise. Most had a strong sense also of a great enemy—the capitalists, the Jews—and of a coming battle between light and darkness. Against this fearful foe, in this critical moment in history, it was clearly imperative that the chosen stand together as an indestructible collective whole.

These are at least some of the common features that united these varied ideologies and the art they generated. To those swept away by totalitarian thought and feeling, they could be totally convincing. To those not as involved, those who could hear the measured tramp and smell the first drift of smoke from the camps, totalitarian culture was a return to barbarism. It worshiped what poet William Butler Yeats some forty years before had called the coming Savage God—what Christians had once called the Beast.

Totalitarian Gothic, Socialist Realism, and the Cult of the Samurai

Nazism was a jerry-built ideology, much of it thrown together to justify the new masters of Germany in an ideological age. But it did have roots in a major intellectual tradition. And there can be no question about its at least temporary power over German minds.

Nazi propagandists tirelessly preached the greatness of the *Führer*, the party elite, and the Aryan master race. They condemned Jews and the "Jewish principle" as the great enemy and justified any measure that might be necessary to defeat this foe. Hitler described his "struggle" as this great race war between the German master race and the Semitic subhumans.

All Germans, the Nazis admitted, might not share the physical features of their Aryan ancestors. Hitler himself was blue-eyed, but not blond, long-headed, or otherwise particularly Nordic in appearance. But all Germans, Nazi racial theory insisted, did share the superior character traits of Teutons: strength, courage, loyalty, discipline, as well as such poetic sentiments as love of children, the old German peasantry, and the German countryside.

Aryans were, in short, creatures of the emotions and in many ways true descendants of the German romantics. The Semitic spirit, by contrast, was characterized as hyper-intellectual and soulless. That spirit, incidentally, was not to be found just in people of Jewish descent. The Jewish spirit also infused such anti-Aryan groups and institutions as bourgeois democracy, Bolshevism, and Roman Catholicism.

Nazi art attempted to communicate this message with an eclectic array of romantic nineteenth-century and glossy modern imagery. Paintings of Hitler accoutered as a knight in shining armor, photographs of him accepting flowers from little girls in regional peasant costumes epitomized the romantic traits. The monolithic, square-pillared Nazi public buildings, sometimes described as "totalitarian gothic" by cynics, nevertheless projected the sense of strength and monumental power that was central to the Nazi self-image. Nazi regalia itself—the military uniforms, medals, weapons, the death's heads and lightning-shaped SS insignia, the flapping blood-red banners with the hooked-cross swastika emblem—all radiated the sense of barbaric strength the Nazis clung to.

The great party rallies were carefully staged so as to embody all these core qualities of Nazi totalitarianism. One, at least, has been preserved: the Nuremberg rally of 1934, which Leni Riefenstahl made into the artistically acclaimed *Triumph of the Will*. It is all there, living still on film: the Gothic architecture of the old city and the new Leader descending in a shiny modern airplane to his people. The blond, clean-cut Hitler youth, the little girls in peasant dresses, and the torchlight parade winding through old Nuremberg toward the stadium and the great moment. The klieg-lit rostrum and the hooked-cross banners, the *Führer* leaning toward them with his rising off-key rhetoric, his voice shaking with passion, eyes shining, fist slamming the podium. And the rigid military formations, rank on rank, listening in the darkness below and greeting every chopping point with right arms shooting up, voices rising in the rolling *Sieg heil!*—"Hail, victory!—of the Nazi salute.

A very different sort of totalitarian culture was cultivated with equal care in Stalinist Russia. Its ideological core lay in the much more theoretically developed ideas of Marxist revolutionary socialism, as adapted to Russian circumstances by Lenin. Its art was a conscious and calculated effort to project those ideas in the simplest, most traditionally realistic terms.

The ideological roots of Communism lay not in emotional romanticism but in the rational Enlightenment and in the "scientific laws of history" Marx claimed to have worked out in the middle of the nineteenth century. Russian Communists did not summon up the spirit of the barbaric tribal past, but looked to the classless utopia of the future. Communism, said Lenin, was Marxism plus hydroelectric power.

Lenin had explained the party's vanguard role in convincing detail. Communist party cadres were, by definition, the greatest experts on Marx's laws of progress through class conflict. As such, they were the natural leaders of the working people of Russia and the world in their revolutionary struggle. Under Stalin, the Communist elite asserted the latest party line as if it were religious dogma, and they used it to justify everything from the purge trials to the twists and turns of Soviet foreign policy.

Stalin's own ideas were few and pedestrianly expressed, but he did encourage one central contribution to the cultural life of Russia in the 1930s: the cult of his own personality. Stalin was praised in print and in public not only as the nation's maximum political leader and leading expert on Marxism-Leninism, but also as the final authority on everything from poetry to bricklaying. His picture was everywhere, his infallible wisdom trumpeted from party congresses to every schoolchild's "Stalin corner." Glorification of the leader was thus as much a central feature of Soviet as of Nazi totalitarianism in the 1930s.

Naturally, glorification of the working masses, the proletarians and peasants who were the chosen people of the Communist promised land, was another salient aspect of Soviet totalitarianism. And so, finally, was an ideologically unlikely emphasis on Russian nationalism. The need to generate enthusiasm for building up the national economy and preparing for the threatening war with Hitler's Germany accounts for this Communist effort to remind Russians of their past greatness. Thus, the long feud between socialist and nationalist ideologies was effectively transcended by the pressing historical realities of the 1930s.

The art and literature that embodied these concepts in the thirties went by the label of *socialist realism*. It was, as the Communist Union of Soviet writers declared, an art "saturated with the heroic struggle of the world proletariat and with the grandeur of the victory of socialism . . . reflecting the great wisdom and heroism of the Communist Party. . . ."[3]

[3]Gleb Struve, *Soviet Russian Literature 1917–1950* (Norman, Okla.: University of Oklahoma Press, 1951), p. 239.

Vast academic paintings of those days show brawny factory workers or bronzed farmers toiling for the socialist motherland, Lenin Speaking to the People, or heroic incidents from the Russian past. Formula novels, plays, and films glorified the achievements of "shock workers" (those who exceeded their quotas), the successful completion of great construction projects, and other achievements of the Five-Year Plans. Poetry and history celebrated Stalin, comparing him to past heroes such as Peter the Great, exaggerating his part in the Revolution of 1917, and praising his omniscience, activism, and many victories.

Even under the rigid restrictions of socialist realism, however, some impressive art could be produced. The internationally celebrated films of Sergei Eisenstein, in particular, grappled with the artistic problem of the collective hero posed by Communist doctrine with remarkable success. Eisenstein's masterwork of the 1920s, *Battleship Potemkin*, immortalized the 1905 naval mutiny that Communists saw as a forerunner of their own revolution. Art-film fanciers in the decadent West were soon lining up to revel in Eisenstein's surging crowd scenes and searing montage effects—the shattering cuts from cheering crowds to charging police, and then to the unforgettable close-ups—a baby carriage rolling down the wide cement stairs, a screaming face, broken glasses, blood gushing from an eye. Eisenstein's great historical film of the 1930s, *Alexander Nevski*, looked forward as well as back. He surrounded the medieval Russian prince with plenty of medieval Russians—the collective hero—and made his victory over the Teutonic Knights a stirring reminder of battles yet to come against the Germans.

No single-party rule developed in Japan in the 1930s, and hence no party line on culture. Nevertheless, there was a new direction in Japanese thought and feeling that commanded a growing consensus as the decade advanced.

The main trend in Japanese politics of the period is usually called militarism. It was also a form of nationalism, and there were increasingly strident imperialistic overtones and anti-Western feeling bubbling up. Japanese militarists, nationalists, and imperialists were united in their opposition to most of the gifts of the West to the new Japan: democracy, which seemed to boil down to a gaggle of conniving, compromising politicians in the Diet; the greedy capitalism of the *zaibatsu* tycoons; decadent Westernized cities such as Tokyo. They were in favor of the traditional Japanese peasantry, who were suffering grievously in the depression decade; Japan's traditional past, as opposed to her modernizing present; Japanese expansion overseas; the emperor; and the soldiers of the new Japan, heirs of her honored samurai tradition.

Out of this uneasiness and tension the militaristic cult of the samurai sprang. The Cherry Society of young army officers, organized in 1930, evoked in its very name the creed of the warrior of earlier centuries, as ready to die in battle as cherry blossoms are to fall from the tree. Dreams of martial heroism, passion for "the deed," dedication to personal honor, nation, and emperor, even a heroic fascination with self-slaughter as manifested in the traditional ritual of *seppuku* infused the activist military cadres of the thirties.

Their dreams of samurai glory led them to conspiracy and assassination. But their dedication also made them national heroes. Clearly, there were many in Japan who shared the young officers' immersion in the values of the Japanese past, the dreams of imperial greatness that led them into the greatest of wars.

SUMMARY

The cultural history of the first half of the twentieth century was determined less by the continuing evolution of regional cultures than by the global traumas of those decades. Western culture thus flourished from Europe to Australia, revolutionary and totalitarian ideas and arts in nations as widely scattered as Russia and Germany, Mexico and India.

The impact of World War I was particularly strong in the Western world. It produced a generation of young people, especially in Europe and America, who seemed to have lost all sense of values and direction. Intellectuals like T. S. Eliot saw the world after the war as a spiritual Wasteland.

Western culture went through a time of turmoil between the wars. The Western scientific world view became clouded as definitions of matter, natural law, and truth itself came into dispute. New views of human nature proposed by psychologists like Freud and Pavlov replaced a moral and rational human self-image with a view of humankind as the helpless puppet of irrational inner drives or conditioning circumstances.

Modernism in the arts challenged the traditional Western sense of beauty with a new emphasis on pure form, from Picasso's Cubism to distinctive forms of modern architecture. Modernist literature frequently attacked the most revered values and institutions of modern Western society. In the 1930s, finally, many artists became politically or socially committed, opposing Fascism or turning to Communism in the turbulence of the red decade.

Other concerns gripped artists and thinkers in lands swept by the long revolutions or overwhelmed by the totalitarian enthusiasms of the interwar years. Revolutionary arts flourished in countries like Russia and Mexico in the 1920s. Painters like Rivera celebrated Mexico's Indian roots, while film-makers like Eisenstein made the Russian people the heroes of her past history. Totalitarian culture also produced its own artistic trends, some of it as unadventurous as the Soviet propaganda art called socialist realism, some as melodramatic but effective as the carefully staged Nazi rallies. Intellectually, revolutionary and totalitarian thought was full of confidence at the very time that the liberal Western vision of things was fragmented and unsure.

SUGGESTED READING

ARNASON, H. H. *History of Modern Art,* 2nd ed. Englewood Cliffs, N.J.: Prentice-Hall, 1977. Well illustrated and well written history of modern art.

BORGES, J. L. *Labyrinths, Selected Stories, and Other Writings.* New York: New Directions, 1969. One of the first of the Latin American writers to win an international reputation with his enigmatic fiction.

CROSSMAN, R., ed. *The God that Failed.* New York: Bantam, 1950. An international array of authors, from Authur Koestler to Richard Wright, describe their emotional commitment to Marxism during the 1930s.

ELIOT, T. S. *The Waste Land and Other Poems.* New York: Harcourt, Brace, 1955. The poems that defined the cultural despair that underlay much of the frivolity of the 1920s.

ELLMANN, R., and C. FEIDELSON. *The Modern Tradition: Backgrounds of Modern Literature.* New York: Oxford University Press, 1965. Valuable collection of position papers on the modernist mode.

FEUER, L. S. *Einstein and the Generations of Science.* New York: Basic Books, 1974. A close look at the people and ideas that launched the twentieth-century surge in the sciences.

FREUD, S. *Civilization and Its Discontents*, trans. J. Strachey. New York: Norton, 1961. Psychoanalysis applied to the nature and problems of modern civilization.

GAMOW, G. *Thiry Years that Shook Physics*. Garden City, N.Y.: Anchor Books, 1966. A scientist and scientific popularizer on the "Second Scientific Revolution" of this century.

GAY, P. *Weimar Culture: The Outsider as Insider*. New York: Harper & Row, Pub., 1970. A brief, brilliant analysis of German culture in the 1920s—the glittering creativity and inner anxieties of a people on the eve of totalitarianism.

HEMINGWAY, E. *The Sun Also Rises*. New York: Scribner's, 1982. The voice of the disillusioned lost generation after World War I. See also his autobiographical essays, *A Movable Feast* (New York: Scribner's, 1983) on the expatriate writers of Paris in the 1920s.

HESS, T. B., and J. ASBERRY, eds. *Avant-Garde Art*. London: Macmillan, 1967. Essays on major movements in the arts from the turn of the century to the 1960s.

HULL, D. S. *Film in the Third Reich*. Berkeley: University of California Press, 1969. Stresses ties between ideology and art.

JOYCE, J. *Ulysses*. New York: Random House, 1967. The archetypal modernist novel, challenging both the ethical and aesthetic values of the time.

KAFKA, F. *The Penal Colony: Stories and Short Pieces, Including The Metamorphosis*. New York: Schocken Books, 1961. Good selection of the anguished short fictions of this distinctive twentieth-century spirit of the period between the wars.

LENIN, V. I. *Imperialism: The Highest Stage of Capitalism*. New York: International Publishers, n. d. One of the Russian revolutionary's most influential works.

RICHTER, H. *Dada: Art and Anti-Art*. London: Oxford University Press, 1965. An insider's view of the Dada-Surrealist revolt against traditional artistic standards.

SCHORSKE, C. E. *Fin-de-Siecle Vienna: Politics and Culture*. New York: Knopf, 1980. Central European culture at its most challenging and creative, imaginatively explored by a leading cultural historian.

SHATTUCK, R. *The Banquet Years: The Arts in France, 1885–1918*. Garden City, N.Y.: Doubleday, 1955. Vivid evocation of the Paris avant-garde at the turn of the century.

STERN, F. *The Politics of Cultural Despair: A Study in the Use of the Germanic Ideology*. Berkeley: University of California Press, 1961. Intellectual background to totalitarianism in Germany.

WOOLF, V. *To the Lighthouse*. New York: Harcourt Brace Jovanovich, 1964. Masterpiece by one of the giants of the high modernist period between the wars.

Overview IV

The Globalization of History

The twentieth century since the time of Christ—approximately the fifty-fifth since civilization was born in ancient Mesopotamia—is in some ways a climactic age. Our century has produced so many *most* and *biggest* things in the long human story: the most people, the longest lives, the biggest wars, the biggest cities, the most polluted environment, the most material wealth. The list of records is endless. From the perspective of the past, our century is certainly the climax of much that has gone before.

From the perspective of the future, however, ours may be seen as a century not of climaxes, but of beginnings.

There are innovations in science and technology, to be sure; we have almost come to expect them as a matter of course. But there have been beginnings also in major assaults on age-old social problems, from poverty to pestilence. There have been breakthroughs in mass culture, in large-scale social organization, and in much else. In our war-ravaged century, there has perhaps been a more widespread and serious commitment to peace than ever before.

Above all, ours is perhaps the first century of genuinely global history. Many aspects of the history of this second half of the century especially have shown the destinies of all peoples of the world to be inextricably bound up together.

The two great armed camps who have squared off against each other in the Cold War have been thoroughly intercontinental from the beginning. The Soviet Union, the leader of one side in the conflict, is the interregional power par excellence, sprawling across Europe and Asia. The United States, the leader of the other side, is the powerhouse of the Americas. Major Cold War confrontations have come in Europe, in Asia, in Latin America, in Africa—in every part of the world.

The Great Liberation of European colonies that followed World War II was as global as the intercontinental empires themselves had been. The result has been to create a new international bloc of nonaligned states, the Third World of developing nations. Again, it is a global designation for a reality that transcends any one region, continent, or cultural tradition.

The industrially developed "have" nations of the world are no longer limited to Europe, or even to Europe and North America. Fabulously rich oil sheikdoms, the evolving industrial powers of Japan and the East Asian rim, Australia, South Africa, the breakthrough ABC powers (Argentina, Brazil, Chile) and lesser success stories of Latin America all reveal the worldwide spread of technology and wealth.

The Third World, the world of village people and traditional cultures, has had its own global history since the liberation. Its problems of economic underdevelopment and dependence on industrial states, its oscillation between political instability and dictatorship, and its struggles with disease, illiteracy, overpopulation, famine, and new and old ways in conflict have been no respecters of boundaries or hemispheres.

In the latter part of the twentieth century, a truly global culture, bridging the gap between rich and poor nations, has begun to take shape for the first time in history. From American television to Indian religion, from Russian ballet to the wood carving of Africa and Oceania, the world today feasts at an unparalleled cultural smorgasbord, the foundation perhaps of the global civilization of tomorrow.

On the basis of this emerging planetary culture, finally, global organization has advanced at an extraordinary pace. From the Hague world-peace conferences around 1900 through the United Nations of 1945 to the thousands of global organizations, associations, and agreements that bind us all today, we have advanced to a point from which the dim outlines of a new world order are at least partially visible.

Tomorrow, then, will almost certainly be a global matter. We will either survive together, citizens of a slowly, no doubt painfully reorganizing globe, or we will perish with our planet. We will learn to live together in some sort of reasonably harmonious relationship, or we will expire together, starved by overpopulation or the exhaustion of our resources, choking on our own wastes or incinerated in a global firestorm of our mutual kindling.

Ours is thus a century of genuinely global history—with luck, the first of many. As such, it is rather a beginning than an end, a new dawn rather than a climax to history.

Chapter · 21

THE BALANCE OF TERROR

OUT OF THE ASHES

A Reddish-Brown Scar

Every American heard stories after the war. Personal anecdotes, newspaper editorials, vivid journalistic accounts—in those last pretelevision years—of what it was like "over there."

A six-foot man, a laconic U.S. Air Corps major said, could see from one side of Hamburg to the other. Graphic photographs showed what had once been the bustling modern Japanese city of Hiroshima, now

> four square miles of reddish-brown scar . . . range on range of collapsed city blocks, with here and there a crude sign erected on a pile of ashes and tiles ("Sister, where are you?" or "All safe and we live at Toyosaka"). . . . and in the streets a macabre traffic—hundreds of crumpled bicycles, shells of streetcars and automobiles, all halted in mid-motion.[1]

Some of the people who thought they were "all safe" were beginning to notice burns that did not heal, skin turning patchy, hair falling out.

Britain had "austerity"—more grim grey years of shortages and digging out of the ruins. In China, a renewal of the long civil war of the interwar years soon convulsed the land once more. From the Far East to Central Europe, hollow bellies and empty eyes told a common story of starvation, disease, and human misery.

The world was hungry for peace in 1945. Ironically, the settlement that followed led directly to a new conflict—the long and painful confrontation known as the Cold War.

The Peace Settlement

There was no great gathering of diplomats and heads of state to rearrange the world after World War II, as there had been at Vienna and Versailles after Europe's last two major military conflicts.

The Big Three met one last time later in 1945, at Potsdam in defeated Germany, but they were strangers already. Roosevelt was three months dead, and a feisty but not overly informed President Truman spoke for the United States. Winston Churchill was defeated for reelection in Britain during the conference itself, and Labour-party leader Clement Attlee brought a very different perspective to the meeting. Only Joseph Stalin had been there before.

The Grand Alliance, deprived of a common enemy, rapidly came apart at the seams. Peace treaties were signed with the lesser Axis partners, and eventually with Japan, but not with Germany. Some of the most important consequences of the war simply happened, evolving out of provisional or temporary military agreements that hardened into historic realities.

The territorial rearrangements that followed World War II were less complicated than those after World War I, but the dislocation of populations was much greater.

The chief postwar transfer of territory in Europe involved the westward shift of Poland's frontiers. This shift allowed Russia to keep her gains from the period of the Hitler-Stalin Pact and compensated Poland with a substantial slice of German territory. Even

[1]John Hersey, *Hiroshima* (New York: Bantam Books, 1959), p. 86.

more significant, however, was the division of Germany itself into four separate zones of military occupation. The American, British, and French zones coalesced into the German Federal Republic (West Germany), while the Russian zone evolved into the German Democratic Republic (East Germany). The two Germanies, allied to the rival power blocs of the United States and the Soviet Union, yet never dismissing the haunting possibility of reunification, would be key pieces in the jigsaw puzzle of postwar Europe.

Similarly tangled and unpremeditated territorial settlements occurred in the Far East. Russia declared war on Japan in the last days of World War II and quickly occupied Manchuria and the northern part of Korea. Manchuria was turned over to the Chinese Communist armies, who thus were strengthened for their final drive to power in China. Russia established a provisional government in the northern part of Korea, but the United States sponsored a new government in the liberated south as well. Once more, reconciliation between the two proved impossible, and the peninsula entered the postwar period as the two nations of North and South Korea. Within five years the United States would be plunged into a war in Korea, thanks to this division.

The war generated perhaps as many as 25 million refugees, perhaps half of them Germans expelled from the Slavic countries of Eastern Europe. Resettlement was undertaken by the victorious Allies through displaced-persons camps and through an International Refugee Organization. Frequently, however, the refugees themselves settled things with their feet, spreading outward in a great postwar diaspora to West Germany and Britain, the United States, the Commonwealth countries, Latin America, and Palestine.

The United States, finally, occupied Japan alone in 1945. The vigorous program of demilitarization and democratization that the United States embarked upon, coupled with Japan's rapid economic recovery, transformed that country in an amazingly short time. Here, at least, the postwar settlement led to an apparently stable and satisfying outcome.

Postwar Recovery

Economic recovery for the nations of Western Europe proceeded at first with agonizing slowness. The destructiveness of the war—not felt at first as any sort of advantage—and a series of harsh winters in the mid 1940s slowed things appreciably. The loss of important overseas markets to the United States during the war and the growing rift between the United States and the Soviet Union after the war also contributed to economic sluggishness at the outset. In 1948, however, at the urging of American secretary of state George Marshall, the nations of the West inaugurated a massive European Recovery Plan combining Euroean cooperation and self-help with substantial American aid.

Food, oil, coal, steel, farm equipment, trucks, electrical gear were soon pouring into Europe. The Europeans themselves negotiated an end to mutually destructive tariffs, balanced their budgets, brought inflation under control, and increased their share of

A man-made desert: the ruins of Nagasaki, Japan, destroyed by an American atomic bomb in August, 1945. The wreckage of many other great cities, leveled by more conventional explosives and incendiary bombs, littered Europe and Asia at the end of World War II. (UPI/Bettmann Newsphotos)

foreign trade. By the early 1950s, European production and commerce were surpassing prewar levels, and a model for continued economic cooperation had been created among the nations of Western Europe.

Two broad and somewhat contradictory currents informed the politics of Western Europe during the postwar years: the rejection of organized communism and the acceptance of socialist ideas and reforms.

Domestic communist parties enjoyed a temporary wave of popularity and electoral success in the years immediately after World War II. Their prestige was heightened by their important role in wartime resistance movements against Nazism, and postwar economic dislocation did, in fact, bring some votes to the far left. Thanks to vigorous campaigns by conservative leaders such as Charles de Gaulle of France and Alcide de Gasperi in Italy, however, the communists were defeated in key election campaigns. They soon lost the potential for power they had briefly enjoyed.

Socialist ideas, by contrast, continued to do well in Europe after the war. In Britain, the Labour Party under Attlee unceremoniously unseated the great war leader, Tory Winston Churchill, in 1945, and proceeded to nationalize large sections of the British economy, including coal mining, iron and steel production, and public transportation. In most Western European countries, government welfare programs were expanded significantly after the war, creating for the first time what British Labourites called cradle-to-the-grave security—the real birth of the modern welfare state.

In Eastern Europe, Russia played the central economic role filled by the United States in the west. There was, however, a basic difference; whereas the United States had grown richer during the war, the Soviet Union had been one of the most war-ravaged of the combatants. In the immediate aftermath of the war, the Soviets used Eastern Europe primarily as an economic resource for their own recovery. Not only East Germany but also Hitler's former allies in the Balkans were stripped of industrial and other resources. Close trade relationships were established and joint economic ventures set up, both of which tended to work to Russia's benefit. The Russians seemed to be trying hard to encourage most of Eastern Europe to depend on them for manufactured goods, while serving as their source of agricultural products and other commodities.

After Stalin's death in 1953, there was some backing away from too rigid an insistence on the Soviet model. Agricultural collectivization, for instance, was cut back in some places, never implemented in others. There was a new stress on consumer goods, in the allies as well as in the Soviet Union. Nevertheless, cut off by the Cold War from American aid and from lucrative exchange with the west, hampered by sometimes rigid ties to Russian needs, to Russian Marxism, and to the Russian economic model, the Soviet bloc did not achieve a significant level of prosperity until the 1960s.

China had been locked in a brutal war with Japan for eight years by 1945, and had been torn by civil war, as well as by intermittent Japanese intervention, through most of the preceding quarter of a century. Nor did the end of World War II signify an end to China's agony. Under American pressure Chiang Kai-shek might clink glasses with Mao Tse-tung for the photographers; but both men knew that their long duel was not finished. Recovery was thus not possible in China. The war was not over yet.

Recovery was quite possible, however, for China's great East Asian rival, Japan. Japan's war was definitely ended—and ended, as it turned out, in a way that opened the road to decades of even more impressive development for the most Westernized of Eastern nations. During the half dozen years of the American occupation that followed the surrender on Tokyo Bay, the democratic tendencies that had been submerged by militarism in the 1930s surfaced once more. As in Germany, this second exercise in representative government "took" as the first had not, and in a few years Japan became as stable a working democracy as any in the world.

The Japanese industrial economy also revived with remarkable rapidity, though her impressive economic development over the preceding century made this less surprising than the triumph of democratic institutions. The occupation also imposed some land reform, helping the most miserable of the peasant population, who had never shared in Japan's earlier modernization. By the early 1950s, then, Japan, like West Germany, was embarking on an economic miracle that would contribute substantially to the Western boom years that were coming.

The Nations United

A peace settlement of sorts had thus been made, and recovery from the war was underway before the end of the 1940s. Even more encouraging, a substantial step had been taken toward keeping the peace in the future: the organization of the United Nations.

The U.N. began as a war-time alliance against the Axis—a cause to which most of the world had nominally pledged itself by 1945. A United Nations Relief and Rehabilitation Administration was set up as early as 1943 to provide basic material necessities to liberated zones as the Allied armies advanced. At the Yalta Conference of the Big Three in early 1945, Roosevelt devoted much time to plans for a postwar United Nations Organization, which would both guarantee international peace and open up the world to freer economic exhange.

In the spring of 1945, with Germany and Italy defeated and Japan reeling, representatives of fifty countries met at San Francisco to design a new global organization to replace the League. The United Nations Organization, to be permanently headquartered in New York, was the result.

Like the League of Nations that preceded it, the United Nations had two central deliberative bodies to deal with major international issues, plus a number of special committees concerned with social, cultural, and humanitarian matters.

The most powerful element in the U.N. was the eleven-member Security Council. Five of its members were guaranteed permanent seats: the United States and the Soviet Union, the two most powerful countries in the world; Britain and France, holders of the world's largest empires; and China, the most populous country on earth. Each of these recognized great powers, furthermore, had the right to veto any item of business if it felt that its vital interests might be adversely affected. This special position of the great powers represented a realistic assessment of the fact that some nations *were* "more equal" than others. It was also necessary simply to get all the major powers into the organization.

The General Assembly grew in time to represent all the nations of the world. This larger body had less power than the Security Council. But it did provide an international forum in which the smallest country could air its grievances, and in which the collective feelings of the entire international community could be expressed by votes on large issues.

The U.N.'s many subagencies and committees concerned themselves with the social ills of the world at large. Under the broad umbrella of the Economic and Social Council were grouped such agencies as the World Health Organization, the United Nations Educational, Scientific, and Cultural Organization, the International Labor Organization, the International Trade Organization, and the Food and Agricultural Organization. In years to come these international bodies would mount campaigns to alleviate hunger, control major infectious diseases, bring literacy to the unlettered, and deal with a wide variety of problems.

As established in 1945, the U.N. was likely to be dominated by the United States, which could normally depend on the votes of her European allies and the Latin American countries, where American economic influence was strong. This situation would change over the years, as the Soviet Union acquired satellites of her own and as former colonial territories thronged into the U.N. with no predilection to support the Western powers who had once been their masters.

Global economic problems also preoccupied the Allies as World War II drew to a close. They held less formal, more specialized meetings in order to deal with some long-standing economic difficulties and to avoid some of the postwar economic dislocations that had afflicted the world after World War I.

Key decisions were reached at the Bretton Woods Conference, held in New Hampshire in 1944. Two long-lasting international economic organizations came out of this conference: the World Bank and the International Monetary Fund.

The World Bank—officially the International Bank for Reconstruction and Development—would supply loans to poor nations to help them develop their economies. The original function of the International Monetary Fund was to prevent drastic devaluation of major currencies. Later, however, it became essentially a lender of last resort to underdeveloped nations.

Like the United Nations, the Bretton Woods agreements originally did much for American interests. For the next quarter of a century, European currencies were pegged to the dollar at a highly favorable exchange rate. But Bretton Woods also stabilized key aspects of the international economy between the later 1940s and the early 1970s—a boon to all concerned.

Subsequent international compacts brought order to both Western and Eastern European economies —notably the Common Market in the West and COMECON in the East.

Regional improvements also surfaced during and after the war. During the war years Brazil, Argentina, and some of the other southern republics continued to build domestic industry beyond the small workshop stage. The mid 1940s saw the signing of a series of hemisphere-wide agreements at Mexico City, Rio de Janeiro, and Bogotá. These treaties created the Organization of American States, provided for mutual hemispheric defense, promised an end to intervention by one government in the internal affairs of any other, and encouraged economic collaboration and aid.

A WORLD DIVIDED STILL

The New Contestants

Peace after the biggest war was thus more or less established, recovery under way, and a new international organization created. But conflict was not yet banished from the earth. And even as these steps toward peace were being taken, the foundations of the Cold War were being laid down.

The leaders of the two new global alliances that emerged in the wake of World War II were the United States and the Soviet Union.

It is as easy to point out similarities between these two nations as it is to point out their differences. Both are huge nations, with large populations—250 million for the United States, 270 million for Russia—and vast natural resources. Most important, perhaps, both countries have been expanding throughout their modern history. Russia pushed eastward from the forests around Moscow and the Kievan steppes, America westward from her New England hills and tidewater South. Each had thus grown to a prodigious size and become the dominant power in half the globe—the United States in the New World, the Soviet Union in the Old.

Historic differences, however, are even more important. Russia's political tradition has historically been autocratic, from the legacy of the Byzantine emperors and Tatar khans, through the heavy-handed authoritarianism of Peter the Great, to the totalitarian regime of Joseph Stalin. Russia had the most autocratic royal government and the largest bureaucracy in Europe in the nineteenth century, long before communism came on the scene.

America's history, by contrast, has always included a strong element of representative government, from the colonial legislatures through the federal Constitution. In the nineteenth and twentieth centuries, the United States developed an increasingly democratic suffrage and a competitive party system. Americans are thus used to voting and to demanding their rights; Russians, to a strong hand on the helm.

The economic development of the two nations has also differed significantly. Americans have been a prosperous and in many ways a progressive people. Russia, by contrast, was technologically backward and economically underdeveloped through most of her modern history. Peter the Great's attempts to modernize his country were paralleled by Stalin's efforts two hundred years later.

One further historic difference should be cited: the deep roots of free enterprise in the United States and the Russian tradition of government intervention in the economy.

The United States inherited the western-European entrepreneurial pattern of economic development that went back to the commercial revolution of the medieval West. Free enterprise and large private corporations have dominated America's economic history.

Russia's commercial middle class, by contrast, has been small and comparatively undeveloped since commercial Novgorod gave way to czarist Moscow in Russia's late-medieval struggle for power. From Peter the Great to Stalin, therefore, Russia's economic growth has largely been the result of government initiatives, subsidies, and regulation. Like autocratic government and economic underdevelopment, government involvement in industry and commerce goes back a long way in Russia.

By the mid-twentieth century, finally, the Soviet Union and the United States had developed a number of conflicting national interests and attitudes that would contribute significantly to the shape of the Cold War.

Russian interests—under the czars as under the Communists—have for centuries included a need for warm-water ports which would give the world's largest nation commercial and naval access to the world's oceans. Russia has also had a history of feuding with the Germans that goes back to medieval wars with the Teutonic Knights and that climaxed with the two devastating German invasions of Russia during the first half of the present century. Any Russian government was therefore likely to feel a strong national interest in a weak Germany, an interest that the divided Germany and the string of puppet governments that came about in Eastern Europe after World War II satisfied admirably.

The United States, meanwhile, developed a historic set of strongly felt national interests of her own, most of them economic. From the beginning of United States history, New Englanders were traders, southern planters exporters. America's late-nineteenth-century foray into empire building fits this pattern to a considerable degree. The United States interventions in Latin America and the Dollar Diplomacy of the earlier twentieth century were also rooted in these crucial economic interests. So, almost certainly, was some portion of America's position in the Cold War.

It has also been suggested that Americans have tended more than most peoples to see themselves as a crusading nation with a message for the world. This tendency may be traced back to colonial New England, many of whose settlers came to build a Protestant New Jerusalem in America. The founding fathers of the American Revolution claimed to be building a *novus ordo seclorum*, a "new order of the ages." A sense of "manifest destiny" carried Americans across the continent in the nineteenth century, and they fought their global wars in the twentieth century to "make the world safe for democracy." The Cold War has thus been seen by many Americans not as a conflict of interests but as a morality play on a world stage.

An important aspect of Russia's attitude toward herself and her place in the world, by contrast, has been the notorious Russian inferiority complex. The Russians' sense of cultural inferiority went back to the days of Peter the Great. It was reinforced by the post–1917 fear of "capitalist encirclement." Cold War efforts by the United States to "contain" what she perceived as Russian ambitions by surrounding her with a ring of hostile alliances and bases only intensified this Russian sense of inferiority and persecution. It was a feeling that could lead her to strike out, or to cling doggedly to a course of action that was not always justifiable in purely practical terms of national interest.

The two most powerful countries in the world, maintaining sharply contrasting world views and possessing national interests that could easily bring them into conflict, thus faced each other across a prostrate Europe in 1945.

Jockeying for Position

Both the United States and the Soviet Union came out of World War II with substantial material gains: territorial gains for the Soviets, economic ones for the Americans. Both sought to expand these advantages during the immediate postwar years. In so doing, the two superpowers prepared the way for the decades of Cold War that followed.

Despite the heavy damage Russia sustained in the Second World War, her territorial rewards were very impressive indeed. For the first two years of the war, it will be recalled, Russia fought World War II on the German side. During this period, Russia acquired parts of Finland, the Baltic states of Estonia, Latvia, and Lithuania, a broad slice of eastern Poland, and some areas in the eastern Balkans, notably Bessarabia, a long-disputed section of eastern Rumania. All these areas were incorporated directly into the Soviet Union.

From 1941 on, Stalin fought on the side of the Allies against Hitler. Rolling back the German armies in 1944 and 1945, the Red Army occupied most of the rest of Eastern Europe. And Stalin made it clear to his major allies that he would insist upon "friendly" governments in countries located between Russia and Germany henceforth. In the case of Hitler's former satellites—Hungary, Rumania, Bulgaria, and of course Russian-occupied East Germany—the Western Allies could hardly object to the establishment of strongly pro-Russian governments. In countries where Communist guerrillas had led the resistance against the Germans—as in Yugoslavia and Albania—one could scarcely deny these partisans the right to set up governments that would be natural allies of the Soviet Union. In countries that had allied with the West but had been overrun by the Nazis—Poland and Czech-

oslovakia—the Russians proceeded more slowly, promising free elections but offering every aid to Communist candidates that the Red Army and the Russian security services could provide. The result, however, was the same: further expansion of the growing Russian sphere of influence in Eastern Europe.

American gains from the war were less obvious but just as real. As we have seen, these gains amounted to further improvement of America's already paramount economic position in the world. While European nations were blowing up each other's factories, the American industrial machine was revving up to fill the gap. By war's end, the United States gross national product had nearly tripled, whereas those of her European continental competitors had nose-dived. During the war, American enterprise had also pushed into markets and resource areas formerly controlled by Europeans in Latin America, the Middle East, and even Africa.

While the Marshall Plan was helping Europe to recover economically and compelling Europeans to begin serious economic integration, it was also benefiting the American economy. Aid took the form of American products, and this helped to carry the United States over the nervous period of conversion to peacetime production. Aid also enabled recovering Europe to buy necessary manufactured goods—again, mostly from the United States. Postwar economic settlements, finally, strengthened the dollar against European currencies, enabling American firms to invest very cheaply in European industry.

Altogether, American business came out of the war thriving. For a continuation of this trend, it was important that as much of the world as possible remain open to American enterprise after the war. Thus, as Russia swiftly established an Eastern European sphere of influence, the United States was pushing her way even into the older zones of Western European imperial hegemony elsewhere in the world. Russia was building closed zones of influence for herself, America pushing for an open world in which she expected to prosper. Out of the momentum generated by their respective World War II advances, then, came increasingly tense confrontations between the two superpowers.

The Lines Laid Down

Western objections to Russia's emerging sphere of influence became particularly loud only in the case of the two Eastern European states that had been among the most lamented victims of Hitler's aggression a decade earlier: Poland and Czechoslovakia.

In Poland a British-sponsored government-in-exile

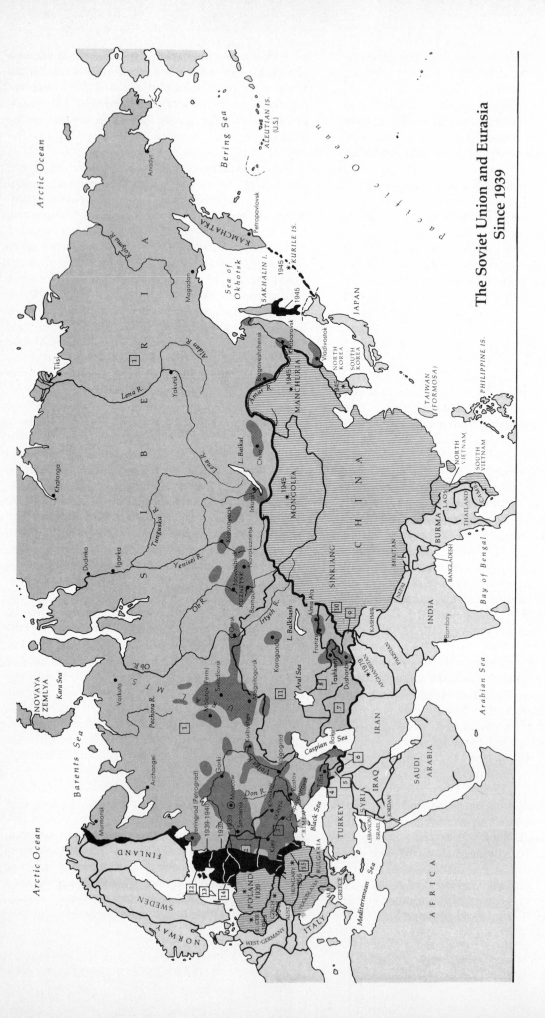

The Soviet Union and Eurasia Since 1939

SOVIET SOCIALIST REPUBLICS

1. Russian Soviet Federated Socialist Republic
2. White Russia
3. Ukraine

4. Georgia
5. Armenia
6. Azerbaidjan
7. Turkmenistan

8. Uzbekistan
9. Tadjikistan
10. Kirghiz Republic
11. Kazakh Republic

12. Estonia
13. Latvia
14. Lithuania
15. Moldavia

Areas annexed since 1940

Other communist countries

Industrial areas (in U.S.S.R.)

* Soviet interventions invasions, and occupations since 1939, excluding pursuit of German armies in World War II

was rudely shunted aside by a Moscow-sponsored one. Evidence accumulated that the Russians had also massacred thousands of aristocratic Polish army officers during the war. There were less substantiatable charges that the Red Army had deliberately halted its advance in order to allow a Warsaw rebellion by supporters of the "London Poles" to be crushed by the Germans.

The takeover in Czechoslovakia in 1948 was an open Communist coup. It involved the seizure of public buildings by Czech Communists, who thereby forced liberal president Eduard Beneš to cancel an impending election. And it climaxed with the "suicide" of the country's foreign minister, Jan Masaryk, while he was in the custody of the new regime.

The territorial division of Europe was rendered final by the division of Germany itself into two nations—the frontline states of the Cold War—in the heart of Central Europe. As we noted above, Germany had initially been divided simply for purposes of military occupation and administration into four zones—American, British, French, and Russian. Because of its importance, Berlin, located deep within the Russian sector, was also broken up into four military administrative districts. As the Western Allies and the Russians found it increasingly difficult to get along, these lines hardened. The Western zones were merged and eventually became the Federal Republic of Germany, one of the major Western powers. The Russian zone became the German Democratic Republic, the westernmost of the Soviet satellites. Berlin remained a zone of conflict and testing in the middle of East Germany.

As these events unfolded, the United States responded with a series of economic, diplomatic, and military moves of its own. The basic policy formulated in Washington was one of limiting Russian efforts to enlarge her influence or her new empire. As early as 1946, George Kennan, head of the U.S. State Department's policy-planning staff, had described America's policy toward the Soviet Union as "a long-term, patient, but firm and vigilant containment of Russian expansive tendencies. . . ."[2] The first result of this policy was to create a massive concentration of power, anchored in Europe but reaching around the globe, with which to counter Soviet expansive tendencies.

In 1947 President Truman enunciated a new diplomatic principle of American behavior, the Truman Doctrine. He promised United States help "to support free people who are resisting attempted subjugation by armed minorities or by outside pressures." He re-

ferred in the first instance to Greece and Turkey, both of which were fearful of Russian pressure from the north. By implication, however, the United States was offering aid to any government threatened by Communist rebels or Russian pressures anywhere in the world.

Two years later, in 1949, the key American military alliance came into existence: the North Atlantic Treaty Organization. The NATO treaty guaranteed mutual Western action against any further Russian expansion into Europe. It also stationed American troops permanently in Europe as part of a Western European NATO army in order to block any further Russian moves.

In later years the United States supported similar mutual security arrangements in the Middle East, in Southeast Asia, and elsewhere, all aimed at curtailing the further spread of Soviet power. American military bases in Europe, the Middle East, and East Asia brought Russia within range of American bombers, listening devices, and other forms of military pressure.

The Russians reacted by beefing up their own power in Eastern Europe. Economically, a series of bilateral treaties with her satellites was followed in 1949 by COMECON, an Eastern European equivalent of the Western European Common Market—which followed soon thereafter. Militarily, Russia expanded her army, hastened to develop an atomic bomb of her own, and in 1955 set up the East-bloc military alliance known as the Warsaw Pact to confront the Western NATO alliance.

What Churchill called an Iron Curtain thus divided Europe and the world in the middle of the twentieth century. With World War II barely into the history books, the globe was once more divided into two armed camps, the antagonists girding themselves for the complex, involuted struggle known, again in a Churchillian phrase, as the Cold War.

CONFRONTATIONS AROUND THE WORLD

Conflict in Central Europe

With the world divided once more, international confrontations were inevitable during the decades that followed World War II. The Cold War spawned conflicts in Europe and wars in Asia. It led to American intervention in Latin America and to Soviet repression of insurrectionary tendencies in Eastern Europe. More rarely—but even more dangerously—Cold War tensions led to facedowns between the two superpowers themselves.

[2]"The Sources of Soviet Conduct," *Foreign Affairs*, 25 (July 25, 1947), p. 566–582.

The "airlift" that broke the Berlin blockade of 1948. United States Air Force transport planes discharge cargos of flour, milk, and other supplies at Templehof airport in West Berlin. (Library of Congress)

In Europe, the first dramatic confrontation between the United States and the Soviet Union was the Berlin blockade of 1948–1949. This dangerous encounter grew out of a dispute over a currency reform introduced in the Western zones of occupied Berlin—part of a series of moves that the Russians interpreted as an effort to make Berlin a showcase for West German economic recovery. In hopes of forcing the Western Allies out of the old German capital entirely, the Russians closed all roads and railways across Russian-occupied East Germany into Berlin. The Allies, however, took up the challenge. They proceeded to supply the Western zones of the city entirely by air for almost a year, until the Russians ended their blockade. The Berlin airlift was widely hailed in the West as an indication of Western, and particularly American, resolution to resist any further expansion of Russian supremacy.

In 1961, however, the Russians stirred up a new crisis by building an amazing wall dividing the city of Berlin in half in order to close off an embarrassing and debilitating drain of illegal East German emigrants into booming West Germany. In the long run, the Berlin Wall became a propaganda victory for the West, looming as a dramatic symbol of the economic and political failures of the East. In the short run, however, America's inability to do anything about it looked like a distinct setback for the West.

By contrast, the Yugoslav defection from the Sta-

linist system represented a clear net loss to the new Russian East European empire. Heavy-handed Soviet efforts to reshape Yugoslavia economically and militarily in the image of Stalin's Russia had alienated the Yugoslav Communists. The expulsion of Marshall Tito, Yugoslavia's partisan hero and postwar ruler, from the ranks of international communism proved to be the straw that broke the Russo-Yugoslav alliance. The Yugoslav comrades responded by rallying around their leader. Tito became the chief international spokesman for the new doctrine of "many roads to socialism"—the view that each communist country should choose its own path to the classless society rather than blindly following the Russian model. For the next thirty years, Tito played a neutral role with consummate skill—accepting aid from Washington and Moscow alike—and enjoying an honored place among nonaligned Third World countries as well.

Rebellion in East Europe

On both sides of the Iron Curtain there were tensions, discontents, and occasional rumbles of insubordination over the years. When this happened, both Russian and American governments were capable of taking a firm stand with their allies and client states.

In Eastern Europe, continuing postwar poverty and the economic discontents that resulted from collectivization of agriculture, harsh industrial working conditions, and shortages of consumer goods all bred bitterness. This resentment focused on Russian exploitation of satellite economies and on the Russian presence generally. Nationalism also was a factor, impelling the peoples who had fought Ottoman Turks, Habsburg Austrians, and Hitler's Germany—not to mention each other—for a century and a half to turn against Stalinist Russia as well.

The first of a series of rebellions behind the Iron Curtain exploded in 1953 with demonstrations in Czechoslovakia against the Russian-supported government in Prague. In East Germany, a workers' revolt flared briefly, producing scores of deaths in the streets and hundreds of executions thereafter. Vivid photographs of German youths hurling rocks at Russian tanks symbolized to many Westerners the nature of the Eastern alliance.

In 1956, three years after Stalin's death, an anti-Stalinist reaction stimulated new challenges to Soviet control in Poland and Hungary, both nations with strong nationalistic and anti-Russian traditions. In both countries, the lead in demanding concessions was taken by anti-Stalinist Communists who had earlier been punished for defending national roads to the classless society. Wladyslav Gomulka in Poland, returned to power by noisy demonstrations, cut back on compulsory collectivization of peasant farms and on police repression, announced a new emphasis on consumer goods—and got away with it.

Hungary in 1956 went much farther—and didn't get away with it. Imre Nagy had attacked forced collectivization, police power, and shortages of consumer goods earlier in the fifties. Recalled to power by strikers, demonstrators, and rioters in October of 1956, he watched mobs topple Budapest's huge bronze statue of Stalin, tear down Russian flags, and attack secret policemen in the streets. He announced the withdrawal of Russian troops and a return to multiparty democracy.

The Russians responded with a massive military intervention. As many as 2500 tanks poured into the country, shelling thousands of buildings and killing several thousand Hungarians. Hundreds of thousands more fled abroad to exile.

The 1960s, which saw a surge of youthful dissent around the world, sparked discontent in Eastern Europe also. In 1970, Poles demonstrated against Gomulka, grown authoritarian in his later years, and forced his ouster. Rumanian Communists refused to lock their national economy into COMECON, the Soviet-centered Eastern European version of the Common Market. But the major anti-Russian revolt of the sixties was the Prague Spring in Czechoslovakia in 1968.

Sources of tension in Czechoslovakia, one of the

Stalin's head, broken from his toppled statue, lies in the streets of Budapest at the height of the Hungarian revolt of 1956. (UPI/Bettmann Newsphotos)

most highly developed industrial societies in Eastern Europe, included worker resentment of grinding industrial discipline. Equally important, however, were the demands of a new generation of technical experts and government administrators for the freedom to make decisions on a pragmatic basis rather than on the basis of party ideology. In 1968 a repressive older regime was replaced by a new Communist leadership headed by a more liberal party man, Alexander Dubcek. Dubcek cut back on police repression, abolished censorship, called for popular expressions of differing opinions, and unleashed a wave of popular demands for change, including multiparty democracy and withdrawal from the Warsaw Pact.

Russia responded with a military occupation of Czechoslovakia by half a million Russian and other Warsaw Pact troops. Dubcek and the new leadership were removed from power. Years of sedition trials followed that heady moment of rebellion in Prague in the spring of 1968, and more refugees crossed the frontiers.

A final major defiance of Soviet-sponsored Communist rule came in the 1980s—once more in Poland. In 1980 the Polish economy, with an unfavorable balance of trade and a huge debt to Western banks, was in especially bad condition. Polish workers compounded these problems by opposing new price hikes with an unprecedented series of strikes, plant occupations, and demands for a new labor union independent of the Communist party. Again a pressured party backed off, allowing not only an indepentent union—called Solidarity—but also more freedom of religion, an end to censorship, release of some political prisoners, and pay raises.

One reform that no Communist government seemed able to tolerate, however, was the existence of any strong center of power rivaling its own. In 1981, then, the Polish Communist party chose as its new head the tough general Wojciech Jaruzelski. And in December of that year, Jaruzelski abruptly imposed martial law on the country, smashed Solidarity, and arrested its leaders or drove them underground. No Russian intervention was required.

Revolution in Latin America

In Latin America, meanwhile, the postwar period saw a return to the sort of American intervention that had flourished in the first decades of the century. Peasants south of the Rio Grande had long lived with poverty and exploitation, both by their own landowners and military juntas and by the foreign businesses that drew substantial profits out of Central and South America. In the twentieth century, United States business replaced European enterprise as the primary developer—and exploiter—of Latin American countries. As a result, nationalistic anti-Yankee feeling erupted repeatedly over the decades following World War II.

The Central American republic of Guatemala offered a textbook case of this familiar Latin American syndrome. Dirt poor and dominated by the United Fruit Company, Guatemalans elected a reform-minded—and strongly anti-American—president named Jacobo Arbenz in 1952. Arbenz proceeded to redistribute land to peasants and to nationalize foreign holdings with minimal compensation—including hundreds of acres of United Fruit Company property. Worse yet from a Cold War perspective, there was a well-organized Communist party in Guatemala that cheered Arbenz on in his antiimperialist measures. The U.S. Central Intelligence Agency (CIA) thereupon sponsored and equipped a Guatemalan revolution against Arbenz. The president was overthrown, his Communist allies imprisoned and driven into the hills, and a Cold War victory quietly chalked up for the CIA.

Perhaps the most striking case of United States political intervention in the affairs of her Latin American neighbors during the Cold War, however, was Washington's long-running feud with Fidel Castro's Cuba—a Communist state and Soviet ally less than a hundred miles off the coast of the United States.

In 1959 Castro, a young Cuban lawyer turned revolutionary, led a ragged guerrilla movement to victory over the dictatorial pro-American government of Fulgencio Batista. Relations between Cuba and the United States soured rapidly after Castro's seizure of power. The new leader's rejection of Cuba's heavy economic dependence on the United States market for Cuban sugar, his nationalization of American industry and property, and his turn to the Soviet Union for trade and aid led to the ill-fated Bay of Pigs scheme. President Eisenhower began and Kennedy launched an invasion of Cuba by fifteen hundred CIA-trained Cuban exiles in the spring of 1961. Kennedy, however, refused to provide open air support for the covert operation, and Castro's popular support and military organization proved much stronger than expected. Almost all the invaders were captured, and no grass-roots rebellion emerged, as the CIA had believed it would.

The Cuban missile crisis later the following year (to be dealt with later) originated on the island but was carried on over Castro's head, as a military confrontation between the United States and the Soviet Union. Thereafter, affairs settled down to a long-term feud.

The United States imposed diplomatic nonrecognition and an economic boycott on Cuba, and persuaded most of the Organization of American States to go along with these measures for a number of years. Castro became active in the disputes which from time to time divided the leaders of international communism and the nonaligned nations. At the same time, however, Cuba served as a base for revolutionary attempts to overthrow governments in other Latin American countries. Some of these were notorious tyrannies, such as Nicaragua under the Somozas. Others, however, were progressive democracies, such as the Venezuela of Romulo Betancourt. The United States reacted by providing counterinsurgency training for threatened Latin American states and won a proxy victory of sorts when Castro's right-hand man, the charismatic Che Guevarra, was killed leading a guerrilla band in Bolivia in 1967.

A much discussed—if less decisive—instance of American interference was the covert support apparently given to the military revolt that overthrew Latin America's first elected Communist ruler, Salvador Allende, in Chile in 1973. Chile, one of the influential ABC powers of South America, was a functioning democracy with strong leftist parties, ongoing land-reform programs, and a good deal of socialized industry when Allende was elected president in 1970. By 1973

Fidel Castro in the Sierra Maestra. The Cuban guerrilla leader opposed not only the Batista dictatorship in his own country, but United States predominance in the Caribbean as well. (AP/Wide World Photos)

the Marxists' drive to give Chile state socialism by democratic means had brought economic chaos, a turmoil encouraged by official United States disapproval. In September of 1973 a military coup overthrew Allende, who died in an attack on the presidential palace, as did several thousand of his Chilean supporters. The Pinochet military regime that followed was widely condemned for brutal political repression.

The actual degree of United States involvement in Allende's overthrow remains disputed. The CIA does appear to have sent funds to "destabilize" the Communist government, particularly early in Allende's administration. The coup, however, was probably the work of the Chilean military officers who subsequently established themselves in power—a familiar enough political syndrome in Latin America.

A brief word, finally, should be said on the developing United States involvement in Central America in the early 1980s. This latest upsurge of political turbulence in Central America began in the later 1970s and reached a first climax with the overthrow of the Somoza dictatorship by the Sandinista rebels in Nicaragua in 1979. United States leaders at that time saw the new regime as a liberal one, likely to improve the lot of the peasantry without abandoning their newly won democracy. Washington therefore offered diplomatic recognition and even some aid to the Sandinistas.

In the early 1980s, however, the militantly anticommunist government of President Reagan saw the new Nicaragua in a very different light. By that time, too, circumstances had changed significantly in the area. There was an active guerrilla movement in neighboring El Salvador and a faction-torn Communist regime on the small Caribbean island of Grenada. Castro's Cuba seemed to be supporting the revolutions in all three small countries, and Reagan insisted that the Soviet Union was in fact behind it all.

Through the early 1980s, therefore, Reagan moved to extinguish the revolutionary fires that appeared to be building in Central America. The United States put heavy pressure on Cuba and Nicaragua to stop supporting the guerrillas in El Salvador. United States aid for El Salvador included substantial military support. The CIA organized an anti-Sandinista guerrilla movement of disaffected Nicaraguans and supported their efforts to topple the new regime. Then in 1984 the U.S. Marines seized Grenada, overthrowing the divided Communist government there and capturing or killing a number of Cuban engineers and military advisers in the process.

In the mid-1980s the United States continued to build up its military presence in El Salvador and neighboring Honduras and to provide help for an ill-concealed "covert" guerrilla war in Nicaragua. While a substantial body of American opinion apparently opposed any deeper involvement, the impetus of the Cold War threatened to carry the nation once more down the familiar road of intervention in Latin America.

War in Asia

Intermittent rebellions in East Europe and revolutions in Latin America thus punctuated the course of the Cold War during the years between the 1940s and the 1980s. The postwar decades also saw outbreaks of open warfare in China's ancient sphere of influence in East Asia.

Here China's long civil war came to an end in the late 1940s with victory for the Chinese Communists. Guerrillas challenged Western authority in Malaya and Burma, in the Dutch East Indies, and the Philippines in the years immediately after the war. There was a largely American war in Korea in the 1950s and a French struggle in her colony of Vietnam about the same time. In the 1960s the United States launched an escalating intervention in Vietnam that dragged on into the 1970s—when Russia in her turn felt it necessary to send an army into Afghanistan.

Many, indeed most of these struggles, were fundamentally antiimperialist rebellions, with or without a veneer of Marxist-Leninist rhetoric. The extent to which these wars were rooted in the Cold War, however, makes the Vietnamese and Korean struggles in particular part of the story of the protracted conflict between the two armed camps led by the United States and the Soviet Union.

The French Vietnamese struggle fits only tangentially into the broader pattern of Cold War conflict. The large majority of the Vietminh guerrillas who fought their former French overlords from shortly after World War II until 1954 were simply Vietnamese antiimperialists. But their leader, Ho Chi Minh, and many of his cadres were Marxists as well as antiimperialists, and the Communist government they established in North Vietnam was welcomed as a Russian ally.

The Korean War, by contrast, was clearly part of the larger Cold War picture. The ancient Korean nation, divided along the thirty-eighth parallel into American and Russian zones of liberation after World War II, had in less than five years evolved into two countries. Both Russia's ally in North Korea, Kim Il Sung, and America's protégé, Syngman Rhee, strongly favored reunification—each under his own rule, of course. It was North Korea that acted, invading South Korea in the spring of 1950.

There was no evidence of Russian instigation of the affair, but a North Korean victory could be seen as another gain for the Communist alliance headed by the Soviet Union. President Truman therefore responded by sending American occupation troops from Japan, under General MacArthur, to Rhee's aid. The American forces, however, were operating under United Nations auspices with modest contingents from other U.N. members in what was officially described not as a war but as a "police action"—all very typical of the increasingly involuted patterns of the Cold War.

Militarily, the Korean conflict turned into a seesaw struggle up and down the rugged peninsula. In the beginning the well-prepared and well-armed North Koreans almost drove the South Koreans and their American supporters into the sea. MacArthur then recovered, surprised the enemy with large amphibious landings behind North Korean lines, and drove the aggressors back across the thirty-eighth parallel. He did not stop there, however, but pushed on north, overrunning much of North Korea and pressing too close to the Chinese frontier along the Yalu River. The Chinese Communists therefore intervened in their turn, sending massive "volunteer" regiments across the Yalu to help the North Koreans—more Cold War deviousness. The front finally stabilized close to the

United States Marines advancing in Korea in 1951. The stalemated Korean War was much more a conventional struggle between regular armies than were the French and American Vietnam wars, in which guerrillas played an important part. (Library of Congress)

thirty-eighth parallel, where a truce was eventually signed in 1953—a nonpeace to end the nonwar in Korea.

Within a decade the United States was again drawn into a war in Asia, this time in Vietnam. The United States had declined to commit military force to help France keep her Vietnamese colony. However, Washington was willing to put a large military force into the field to prevent the overthrow of a pro-Western government in South Vietnam, as in South Korea. The outcome in Vietnam, however, was very different.

Within a few years of Ho Chi Minh's victory over France and his establishment in power in Hanoi, guerrillas appeared in the jungles of South Vietnam. Their goal was the overthrow of the Saigon government headed by the pro-French Ngo Dinh Diem and his ambitious family. Diem was undemocratic and authoritarian, and the initial guerrilla revolt seems to have been the work of South Vietnamese chafing under his rule.

The United States sent advisers and supplies to help Diem resist what American leaders saw as Communist imperialism. North Vietnam sent supplies and then troops to support the South Vietnamese guerrillas, and in time essentially assumed command of the war. Russia, and to a lesser extent China, supplied war materiel to North Vietnam.

The United States and North Vietnam, however, were involved far more deeply than other nations. By the later 1960s, the war had become primarily a contest between the North Vietnamese army and a half-million-man U.S. Expeditionary Force, each side with its own South Vietnamese auxiliaries. Several unpopular Saigon governments were overthrown with United States connivance. The Americans carried open warfare into the neighboring states of Cambodia and Laos, which North Vietnam had been using as supply routes to the south. The war cost perhaps a million lives and resulted in brutal devastation in the villages of Vietnam.

In the end, the unpopularity of the long war in the United States led to the withdrawal of its troops in 1973. In 1975 North Vietnamese armies overran the south, and soon thereafter South Vietnam was absorbed into a single unified Vietnam ruled from Hanoi, as in precolonial times.

In the broad perspective of Asian history, Vietnam's reemergence as an important second-level power in Southeast Asia was perhaps to be expected. From the point of view of the Cold War, however, the outcome was a clear setback for the West.

Besides Korea and Vietnam, a third major locus of Asian conflict clearly linked to the Cold War was Afghanistan. This mountainous, sparsely populated Middle Eastern land on Russia's southern frontier became the target of a major Russian military incursion at the end of the 1970s.

Afghanistan had experienced Russian incursions and influence for centuries. Most recently, a Russian-supported regime in Kabul had pushed modernization—and secularization—too far and too fast for the deeply conservative, notoriously combative Muslim tribes. By the end of the seventies, a village-based guerrilla revolt led by Muslim fundamentalists threatened to topple the pro-Russian government of Afghanistan. In a swift airborne assault late in 1979, Soviet troops occupied the capital and engineered a coup that left their own former client ruler in Kabul dead and a new and apparently more moderate pro-Russian leader in his stead.

The rebellion, however, remained to be crushed—no easy task in the mountains of Afghanistan. Like the American war in Vietnam, Russia's new Afghan war pitted modern firepower against guerrillas who swam in the peasant sea. Although between two and three million Afghans were driven into exile in Pakistan, this war also proved difficult for the superpower to win.

Confrontation between the Superpowers

The most dangerous conflict for the world has, of course, continued to be the Cold War confrontations between the United States and the Soviet Union. Armed with a nightmarish array of science-fiction weaponry, the two superpowers have repeatedly seemed to threaten the futures of all peoples with their willingness to risk "Mutually Assured Destruction" in defense of their conflicting interests and ideals. And the tensest of these threatened conflicts was almost certainly the Cuban missile crisis of 1962.

For most of the 1950s Stalin's successor, Nikita Khrushchev, and President Eisenhower managed to avoid major clashes, allowing their nations to recover from the tensions of the Stalin and Truman years. Then in 1960 the Russians shot down an American U-2 spy plane over the heart of the Soviet Union. When Eisenhower refused to apologize for this violation of Soviet air space, Khrushchev walked out of the United States-Russian summit meeting in Paris. It was the beginning of a very tense period in Russo-American relations.

President Kennedy came to office in 1961 with an image of youth and vigor and a campaign promise to end alleged Russian superiority in weapons development—the so-called missile gap. Kennedy's first year saw a jarring series of American setbacks. At a summit meeting in Vienna, Kennedy apparently failed to impress Khrushchev with his vigor and determination. The CIA-organized invasion of Fidel Castro's Cuba failed ignominiously as the invading Cuban exiles were mopped up on the beaches of the Bay of Pigs. And across the world in Berlin later that same year, the Berlin wall went up—a challenge that went unanswered. Kennedy was thus put in the position of having to prove that he could prevent the Russians from working their will in the world.

Kennedy's chance came the following year, in the Cuban missile crisis of October 1962. Khrushchev, it seems, was also under pressure at home to prove himself as tough with the Americans as Stalin had been. American missile strength was, in fact, rapidly outdistancing that of the Soviet Union in the early sixties, and the technological superiority of the West revealed by the U-2 rankled the Kremlin colleagues. Khrushchev therefore followed up the American humiliation at the Bay of Pigs by responding to Castro's pleas for more support by secretly stationing Russian missiles in Cuba plus bombers capable of striking the United States itself—only ninety miles away across the Florida straits.

When U-2 reconnaissance photos of Cuba revealed the new Soviet installations, Kennedy took the United States to the brink of war with Russia in order to get them out. The American president rallied the Organization of American States and as many Western European allies as he could, put the United States military on alert—nuclear bombers in the air, missiles ready to fire—and established a naval blockade around the island of Cuba. More Russian missiles were already on their way. Kennedy declared that they must be called back, and that those already in place must be removed or face American military action. Privately, he offered assurances that there would be no more invasions of Cuba, and even that some American missiles aimed at Russia would be redeployed elsewhere.

For a tense week, the world was on the edge. Then the Russians agreed to remove their weapons from the Western Hemisphere, and the crisis passed. But it left Soviet military leaders determined to overtake the United States in missiles and nuclear warheads—a goal they would achieve in the years that followed that most perilous of Cold War confrontations.

COLD WAR COMPLEXITIES

Coexistence and Détente

Over four decades, then, the Cold War has brought the world rebellions, revolutions, wars, and the threat of the ultimate confrontation between the superpowers. The Cold War has also, however, turned out to be much more subtle and complicated than a survey of these open clashes might suggest. The forms of conflict, the contending parties, even the terms of engagement and the goals sought grew immensely complex over the years.

One form the Cold War did *not* take was direct military engagement between the principals: the United States and the Soviet Union. There were proxy wars, as we have seen, involving American or Russian client states, revolutions supported by one side or the other, or other forms of conflict in which one or both superpowers became involved. There were near misses, most notably the Cuban-missile crisis, but so far, at least, the balance of nuclear terror has prevented military conflict between Russia and America.

There has, however, been a wide range of non-military contention between the two. There were propaganda broadsides aimed at their own people, at each other, and at "world opinion." There was espionage of all sorts, from the most sophisticated electronic gear to old-fashioned spying. There was intense technological and economic competition, ranging from the battle to see who could produce the most tungsten or toothbrushes to the race to the moon. And there was, of course, the unending arms race, to which we will turn presently.

Accompanying these varied forms of competition, however, were repeated attempts to improve relations between America and the Soviet Union. These efforts included a broad spectrum of political, economic, cultural, and military moves by the two sides. Under such rubrics as "coexistence" or *détente*, such

The United States and the Caribbean Since 1898

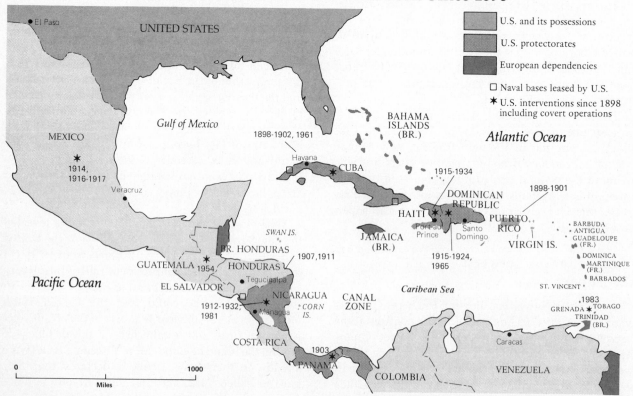

efforts provided a counterpoint of hope that the world might yet avoid a third global war in the twentieth century.

There were a number of summit meetings between the two states and a great many consultations between foreign ministers, ambassadors, and other lesser officials of the two governments. Direct electronic communications between the White House and the Kremlin were set up for easy and quick discussions when problems arose. Trade relations, while fluctuating with other aspects of the relationship, repeatedly provided a splendid opportunity for America to market her habitual agricultural overproduction and for the Soviet Union to import lifesaving quantities of grain during her periodic bad harvests. Western Europe also developed lucrative trade connections with Eastern Europe and Russia.

Cultural exhanges were another part of the long-term effort to improve international understanding. American audiences got a chance to see Russian ballet, famous since czarist times, and Russians enjoyed American jazz groups. Educational meetings of scientists and scholars from the two countries were frequent, as were exchanges at larger international meetings of all sorts.

Above all, agreements were negotiated limiting arms development in the two superstates—though this proved in the long run perhaps the most difficult problem of all for the two armed camps.

Polycentrism

Over the years after Stalin's death, the configurations of the two international alliances also changed. While leaders—and true believers—on both sides continued to talk about the "socialist camp" and the "free world" as if the lines were as clear and hard as they had been under Truman and Stalin, both sides, in fact, tended to fragment—and each side to intrigue for support on the other side of the Iron Curtain.

Thus Marshal Tito broke with Stalin in 1948 and took Yugoslavia out of the Soviet orbit. Little Albania, its mountain fastnesses even farther removed from Russia than Yugoslavia, also broke ideologically with Moscow—and found a new patron in Peking. Rumania, Czechoslovakia, Hungary, and other satellite countries often pushed for more trade with the West than Russia approved of. North Korea and North Vietnam, never satellites in the classical sense, apparently started their wars with their southern neighbors without either instigation or prior approval from Russia.

Most important, Mao's China broke with Russia in 1959–1960. Ideological differences partly explain the split. Mao's China saw itself in 1960 as more uncompromisingly Marxist than Russia under Khrushchev. A history of Russian imperialism in the Far East and continuing border disputes also help to account for the break. Soviet high-handedness, China's refusal to be treated like a junior partner, and, perhaps most important, the long frontier between thinly populated Russian Siberia and China's land-hungry hundreds of millions all contributed to the sudden chill between the Cold War partners.

The result was a great schism in the Communist world. Russia called home her technical advisers and canceled her aid programs to underdeveloped China. Trade between the two nations dwindled, border garrisons were beefed up. Moscow and Peking competed around the world for the allegiance of other Communist parties. Propaganda organs in both capitals dealt more harshly with each other than with the United States. Attempts to patch things up after Mao's death in 1976 eased the strain somewhat, but China's increasingly good relations with the United States—and her ancient sense of her own importance in the world—make any return to monolithic Russian leadership extremely unlikely.

On the Western side, Europe's rapid recovery from the war, as we noted in an earlier chapter, soon transformed the Western European countries from economic dependents of the United States to economic rivals. As a result, American allies felt increasingly free to develop independent foreign policies of their own, even toward Communist countries.

France under the strongly nationalistic de Gaulle, for example, broke with the North Atlantic Treaty Alliance and established its own nuclear strike force. The ultraconservative de Gaulle became one of the first Western leaders to trade freely with Communist China and Russia. West Germany, first under socialist chancellors like Willy Brandt and more recently under the conservative government of Helmut Kohl, explored avenues of rapprochement with East Germany and developed its own Russian policy, though without ever backing away from the crucial NATO alliance. The Western alliance, in short, became much looser than it was in the early years. It was always much freer than the Russian system, loose as that became in some ways.

The Race to Armageddon

Despite hopes for détente and weakening alliances, however, the United States and the Soviet Union continued the most dangerous form of Cold War competition throughout the postwar decades: the unending—even accelerating—arms race.

Popular discussion of the subject tends to distinguish between conventional and nuclear forces, as will the following paragraphs. In fact, however, the two are closely related. The West, for example, stressed the deployment of nuclear weapons where it could not muster the troop strength to win a conventional war—as in Western Europe, where they felt outnumbered and outgunned by the Warsaw Pact. In actual combat, however—as in Vietnam or Afghanistan—both superpowers preferred to commit their troops rather than to use nuclear weaponry—a decision only partially determined by the guerrilla tactics of the opposition.

The arms race began on the conventional side. In the 1940s the Red Army had overrun Eastern Europe. Under the North Atlantic Treaty Organization, the United States established a multinational Western European army, which included large American contingents, to guarantee her allies against any further Russian expansion. The Soviets responded in the 1950s with the Warsaw Pact and a Russian-led Eastern European army that, built with conscription, was soon larger than the NATO force.

The United States, meanwhile, had been seeking to counter Russia's massive land power in Europe by surrounding that country with a ring of American alliances and bases. After NATO in 1949 came the Southeast Asia Treaty Organization (SEATO) in 1954, the British-run Baghdad Pact in the Middle East in 1955, and its replacement, the Central Treaty Organization (CENTO) in 1959. By 1960 a total of 275 major United States bases were scattered through thirty countries around Russia's perimeter, from West Germany to Japan. The American Seventh Fleet patrolled the far Pacific, the Sixth Fleet the Mediterranean, and others the Indian Ocean, the North Atlantic, and most of the seven seas. Russia's advantages in Europe—still the heart of the conflict—were thus offset by a ring of United States bases and allies.

Increasingly, however, the two superpowers came to depend on a range of awesome new weapons involving nuclear warheads delivered by air. The aspect of the arms race that most terrified the world was the multiplication of these weapons and their potential for global destruction. The arms race was hectic, ever changing, and so expensive that it warped and drained the economies of both great powers.

The United States maintained its monopoly of the original Hiroshima atomic bomb—based on atomic fission rather than fusion—for only five years, until the Russians exploded their first test bomb in 1950. In 1952 the United States exploded the first H-bomb—the vastly more destructive hydrogen or thermonuclear bomb, based on fusion. The Russians tested their first H-bomb the following year.

Emphasis then shifted to delivery systems—ways of depositing these terrifying explosives on enemy mil-

itary installations and cities. By the mid 1950s American Strategic Air Command B-52 bombers had an intercontinental range, as did their Russian equivalents. The United States, however, had four times as many of these intercontinental bombers as the Russians did.

Then in 1957 the Russians tested the first long-range ballistic missile—a rocket-powered bomb that used its motor to establish a ballistic path and then followed this arching trajectory over thousands of miles to deliver a nuclear warhead without any airplane at all. The race to build intercontinental ballistic missiles was on. The United States rapidly overtook the Soviets in the field; by the time of the Cuban-missile crisis in 1962, America had more than four hundred targeted missiles to Russia's one hundred, as well as two thousand nuclear bombs to Russia's two hundred.

Through the 1960s the race went on. The United States pioneered in the arming of nuclear-powered submarines with nuclear missiles—an undersea force almost impossible to keep track of, and one soon emulated by the USSR. Other new devices included antiballistic missile systems (ABMs) intended to protect cities and missile installations from nuclear attack, and multiple independently targeted reentry vehicles (MIRVs), rockets that could carry several warheads instead of one.

In the 1970s and early 1980s came cruise missiles, which skimmed the treetops, thus slipping in under enemy radar detection systems. There was talk of using disease as a weapon, and of manufacturing neutron bombs that would cause very little damage while killing large numbers of people. Early in the 1980s President Reagan began to urge the development of a new defensive capability, using the potential of satellites, lasers, and other "Star Wars" weapons as an ultimate defense against surprise attack. But it was hard to imagine that any weapon could be truly "ultimate" in this seemingly unending competition.

International treaties were negotiated, and some signed, to control the escalating arms race. The first Nuclear Test Ban Treaty was signed by President Kennedy and Russia's Khrushchev in 1963. Two Strategic Arms Limitation Treaties (SALT I and SALT II) were signed in 1972 and 1979, though the second was never ratified by the U.S. Congress. In 1985 arms negotiations began again between the two superpowers, this time focusing on President Reagan's "Star Wars" initiative and on Russia's long arms build-up of the 1970s.

As in the disarmament discussions between World Wars I and II, there were technical disputes over definitions and equivalents, over what to count and how. Questions of verification of compliance also came up, and each side accused the other of violating agreements already in force. Since neither side was willing to give up a nuclear advantage, treaties were hard to negotiate. In the end, many years of dickering seemed to have done little to slow what to many began to look like a race to Armageddon.

SUMMARY

The shattered world that emerged from World War II recovered with surprising rapidity from the immense devastation of that global conflict.

Peace was patched together without a great international peace conference, but new divisions complicated the recovery picture. The falling-out of the victorious Allies left much of Europe and Asia divided between zones of American and Russian influence. Economic recovery came with surprising rapidity, especially to the Western nations, and the United Nations embodied a renewed commitment to international organization. But the Cold War brought conflict to the postwar world on a scale as global as the peace and the recovery.

Some aspects of the histories of the United States and the Soviet Union made rivalry between them likely if not inevitable. These two large and populous nations had different political traditions and patterns of economic development. They had differing interests and very different ideological points of view. The United States came out of World War II with a stronger global economic position than ever before, the Soviet

Union with a sphere of influence in East Europe. Each would feel impelled to defend its gains and to expand them where possible.

The Cold War involved economic and technological competition between the two superpowers. It led to rival military alliances and economic organizations. It impelled the United States to take covert action against revolutions in Latin America, Russia to employ direct military force to suppress rebellions in its satellites in East Europe. It sent American troops into Korea and Vietnam and Russian ones into Afghanistan. And it fueled an accelerating arms race which at least once, over Cuba in 1962, came close to plunging the world into nuclear war.

Efforts to achieve coexistence or détente continued, including trade agreements, summit meetings, and disarmament talks. The authority of both superpowers over their respective camps weakened, and each side sought to lure members of the other alliance into at least a neutral stance. But the unending, increasingly expensive, and unthinkably dangerous arms race between the two superpowers continued unabated.

SUGGESTED READING

BARNET, R. J. *The Giants: Russia and America.* New York: Simon & Schuster, 1977. The superpowers of the later twentieth century locked in global confrontation. See also A. Ulam, *The Rivals: America and Russia since World War II* (New York: Viking Press, 1972).

CALDWELL, L. T., and W. DIEBOLD, JR. *Soviet-American Relations in the 1980s: Superpower Politics and East-West Trade.* New York: McGraw-Hill, 1981. Recognizes the complexities.

CALVOCORESSI, P. *World Politics since 1945,* 4th ed. London: Longmans, 1982. Valuable overview.

DAVISON, W. P. *The Berlin Blockade.* Princeton: Princeton University Press, 1958. Anatomy of a crisis—arguably the most dangerous of the immediate postwar years.

DE PORTE, A. W. *Europe between the Superpowers: The Enduring Balance.* New Haven: Yale University Press, 1979. Valuable assessment of the European situation since 1945.

DINERSTEIN, H. S. *The Making of a Missile Crisis.* Baltimore: Johns Hopkins University Press, 1976. The Cuban missile crisis in perspective.

GADDIS, J. L. *Strategies of Containment.* New York: Oxford University Press, 1983. Balanced account of American policies in the Cold War.

GOULDEN, J. C. *Korea: The Untold Story.* New York: Times Books, 1982. Good survey. See also D. Rees, *Korea: The Limited War* (New York: St. Martin's Press, 1964).

GRAEBNER, N. A., ed. *The Cold War: Ideological Conflict or Power Struggle?* Lexington, Mass.: Heath, 1976. Excellent collection of contrasting views.

HALLE, L. J. *The Cold War as History.* New York: Harper & Row, Pub., 1971. Seeks historical perspective, as does J. Lukacs, *A History of the Cold War* (New York: Anchor, 1962).

HERRING, G. C. *America's Longest War: The United States and Vietnam, 1950–1975.* New York: Random House,

1979. Perhaps the best survey. Views critical of United States intervention include F. Fitzgerald, *Fire in the Lake: The Vietnamese and the Americans in Vietnam* (New York: Random House, 1973), and D. Halberstam, *The Best and the Brightest* (New York: Fawcett Crest, 1973).

HOROWITZ, D. *The Free World Colossus*, rev. ed. New York: Hill and Wang, 1971. Sees the United States as an actively counterrevolutionary force in the world, rather than as merely containing Soviet expansionism. Among those stressing American economic globalism are such revisionists as W. A. Williams, *The Tragedy of American Diplomacy*, 2nd ed. (New York: Dell Pub. Co., 1972). Accounts emphasizing Soviet expansive tendencies as a prime cause of the confrontation include H. Feis, *From Trust to Terror: The Onset of the Cold War, 1945–1950* (New York: Norton, 1970), and J. L. Gaddis, *The United States and the Origins of the Cold War, 1941–1947* (New York: Columbia University Press, 1972).

JOHNSON, H. *Bay of Pigs.* New York: Norton, 1964. The failure of the United States-sponsored effort to overthrow Castro.

KALDOR, M. *The Disintegrating West.* London: Allen Lane, 1978. Divisions in the Western camp. For essays on ideological divisions in the Communist camp, see W. Laqueur and L. Labedz, eds. *Polycentrism: The New Factor in International Communism* (New York: Praeger, 1962).

MOULTON, H. B. *From Superiority to Parity: The United States and the Strategic Arms Race, 1961–1972* (Westport, Conn.: Greenwood Press, 1973). Nuclear arms negotiations during the Kennedy-Johnson-Nixon years. For negotiations under Eisenhower, see R. A. Divine, *Blowing on the Wind: The Nuclear Test Ban Debate, 1954–1960* (New York: Oxford University Press, 1978).

SVITAK, I. *The Czechoslovak Experiment, 1968–1969.* New York: Columbia University Press, 1971. Events leading up to Soviet intervention in 1968.

ULAM, A. *Expansion and Coexistence: The History of Soviet Foreign Policy, 1917–1967*, 2nd ed. New York: Holt, Rinehart, 1974. Clear and concise analysis; perhaps the best single volume on the whole course of Soviet foreign policy from the revolution to the Cold War.

ZINNER, P. E. *Revolution in Hungary.* New York: Columbia University Press, 1962. The Hungarian revolt of 1956 and its suppression by the Russians.

Chapter · 22

THE GREAT LIBERATION

FREEDOM AND CONFLICT IN THE THIRD WORLD

Uhuru!

Sooner or later, the pattern was everywhere much the same. There would be parades, speeches, flags. There would always be soldiers, very spit-and-polish usually, and large, enthusiastic crowds. Quite commonly, since these were usually tropical countries, everybody would be perspiring freely.

The European speeches would come first, grave and measured, with talk of obligations discharged and of responsibilities and friendship to come. Then the pale faces would settle down at the back of the speakers' platform, and mongoloid or South Asian faces, negroid or Arab ones would take their places at the rostrum.

The climax was always the same. There would be the anthem of the European power, a salute to the old flag—British, French, Dutch, American—fluttering down the pole. Then guns would boom, and to the martial strains of some still unfamiliar national song a new flag, the symbol of a new nation, would rise into the blue.

Even a brief survey of the European empires that crumbled, the major new nations that emerged during the decades after World War II, will give some sense of the scope of this movement.

Great Britain granted independence to many of her colonies in Asia and Africa. In South Asia during the 1940s and 1950s, British India, Pakistan, and Ceylon (Sri Lanka) were liberated, as were Burma and Malaya in Southeast Asia. In the Middle East, British termination of the Palestine mandate led to the foundation of the new nation of Israel. In Africa, perhaps the most important British colonies to gain their freedom during the 1950s and 1960s were the Gold Coast (Ghana) and Nigeria in West Africa and Tanganyika (Tanzania) and Kenya in East Africa.

France, whose empire was second only to Britain's in size, more reluctantly liberated a number of territorial holdings in both Asia and Africa. In Asia, French Indochina—North and South Vietnam, Laos, and Cambodia—emerged from French rule as separate nations. In Africa, Algeria led the way to freedom, to be followed by all the colonies of French West and French Equatorial Africa.

Lesser Western imperial powers also surrendered their overseas colonies, usually unhappily. The Dutch East Indies, the Belgian Congo, and the American Philipines were all freed after the war. As late as the 1970s, some imperial holdouts in South Africa were at last liberated, including the large Portuguese colonies of Angola and Mozambique.

By the middle 1980s, only isolated enclaves of Western imperial control remained, usually by mutual consent, as in British Hong Kong. The major, much-resented exception is the powerful and wealthy state of South Africa, still governed by transplanted Europeans in spite of its large black African majority.

Otherwise, the Great Liberation dramatically transformed the global political picture. A total of ninety new countries emerged between the mid 1940s and the 1980s. Well over a billion people—a third of the earth's population—gained their independence of foreign rule.

Whatever the flags and ceremonies that heralded the emergence of each of these new nations, the magic

The British armed forces pull out of India. The modern buildings in the background were part of Britain's legacy to her huge colony. The departure of the troops was a product of the determination of former colonies everywhere to guide their own destinies. (Wide World Photos)

word "Freedom" was sure to crackle out over the microphones again and again, to be emphasized with pounding fists, to be repeated in all the jubilation that would fill the streets of the new capital on into the night. The Swahili word, used in various East African colonies, was *uhuru. Uhuru!* became a kind of symbol for what was granted—or taken—in these ceremonies repeated in one new country after another across Asia and Africa, particularly during the first two decades after the war.

Causes of the Great Liberation

World War II opened the floodgate of the Great Liberation in several ways. Most obviously, perhaps, the biggest of all wars seriously undermined the imperial vigor of the one-time *pukka sahibs* of the world. The war sapped the ability of some imperial powers to hold their empires in subjection any longer. Neither France nor the Netherlands, battered by Germany, could muster the power to maintain their former colonial ascendancy in the postwar world.

In other cases, this decline in imperial strength was really more a failure of will, or even an outright rejection of the whole imperial mystique. The British Labour party, sweeping into office on a postwar electoral tide, had for years opposed imperialism. The Labourites were only too happy to begin what the Conservative Winston Churchill had sworn he would never do—preside over the dismantling of the British Empire.

Even as World War II was weakening the colonial powers, it was encouraging their colonies to move against them. Perhaps it was the example of the Japanese, so easily overwhelming British, French, Dutch, and American troops from Hong Kong to the Dutch East Indies, that stirred the colonial peoples. The Japanese yoke did not prove to be any great improvement, but when they left, the Japanese sometimes left weapons behind—with suggestions for using them. When the Europeans reasserted their supremacy with rude force, their nothing-has-changed attitude further estranged their former subjects. This was the case, for example, in French Indochina—where it stirred the Vietnamese to rebellion almost at once.

The Second World War also produced a basic new set of power relations in the world—one that was essentially favorable to the independence of overseas colonies. The war had put global supremacy in the hands of the two superpowers. Despite their differences, neither the United States nor the Soviet Union aspired to old-fashioned overseas empires. Both of them, in fact, opposed such colonial holdings on ideological grounds.

Finally, there were new winds of opinion blowing over the world in the decades after World War II. Idealistic statements about freedom in wartime documents such as the Atlantic Charter of 1941 and the United Nations Charter in 1945 were expressions of a libertarian point of view that was generally hostile to the holding of colonial peoples in bondage. There was also a widespread practical conviction that, in the end, almost all colonies would have to have some kind of independence. Europeans might see autonomy as being generations away, but colonial leaders thought in terms of a few years at most. The difference was one of timing and method; the eventual achievement of freedom was inevitable.

Under such circumstances, then, it is not surprising that the great empires began to come apart almost as soon as World War II ended.

Patterns of Emancipation

The leaders of the various movements for colonial emancipation tended to be both Westernized and charismatic. As Western-educated people, they could deal effectively with their European rulers. The internationally known poet Léopold Senghor of French West Africa and Kwame Nkrumah of the British Gold Coast colony (today's Ghana), educated in France and in Britain and the United States, had no trouble talking to Westerners. As charismatic figures, flamboyant personalities such as Sukarno of the Dutch East Indies (Indonesia) and saintly ones such as Mahatma Gandhi in India could move their own people to action.

The strength of many colonial revolts also resided in powerful independence parties put together by the new colonial leadership. These intensely nationalistic organizations were strongly centralized in the person of the leader. They helped to overcome regional, religious, tribal, or other differences within the colony, to articulate common demands, and to mobilize mass support for challenges to colonial authority. After independence was achieved, however, these parties tended to become a stronger focus for loyalty than the new nation itself. In some places, they became the core of one-party government.

In some of the emerging nations, as we shall see, bitter and sometimes long-drawn-out revolutions were fought before independence was achieved. In general, however, a relatively low level of violence—by comparison, say, with the long revolutions of the interwar years—accompanied the Great Liberation. This was, in fact, a striking feature of the final disintegration of Europe's huge intercontinental empires.

A New Imperialism?

Violence, however, has not been absent from the Third World in recent decades. And there are those who suggest that imperialism also has not vanished with the collapse of the political empires of the Western Europeans.

Sources of conflict included the persistence of foreign economic exploitation of these former colonies in Africa and Asia even after the Western political presence was withdrawn. Another source of contention was to be found in precolonial claims and quarrels among Third World peoples themselves—old conflicts reemerging after emancipation. Much of the resulting bloodshed was from revolutionary violence within the new nations. But wars were fought between the new developing nations too, sometimes with a violence that matched that of the superpowers.

Throughout the postwar decades, there were great differences in wealth and material well-being between the less economically and technologically developed nations of the Third World and the wealthy industrial powers of North America, Europe, and Japan. The underdeveloped countries, many of them in the Southern Hemisphere, were thus immensely dependent on the developed countries of the north for trade, aid, and investment capital. This situation was extremely profitable for the developed nations, but this relationship often distorted the economies of less developed states, which had to produce what the wealthier nations wanted if they were to get the capital they needed for development.

This situation was often described—by its victims—as *neo-imperialism*, a new imperialism based entirely on economic hegemony. Lenin, after all, had defined the essence of earlier imperialism as "the highest stage of capitalism"—economic exploitation with a political and ideological superstructure. Third World radicals, whether they had read Lenin or not, often voiced this view in bitter attacks on foreign investors as exploiters of their countries, and on their own rulers and elites for doing business on a neoimperialistic basis.

Western multinational corporations, experts from the World Bank or the International Monetary Fund, and others might see development in terms of production statistics, expanding cities, and social and cultural modernization. Third World radicals identified with the peasantry and village culture and urged expenditures for social services rather than for industrialization or expanded exports. When their own ruling classes sided with—and profited from—neoimperialism, some radicals became revolutionaries. Violent revolts and bloody repressions often followed.

Revolutionaries of this sort might sound like communists to Western leaders, but the springs of their revolts were more often in the genuine differences between North and South than in the ideological disputes between East and West.

The Power of the Past

There were, however, other reasons for war and revolution that had little or nothing to do with neoimperialism. There were causes rooted deep in the past and vendettas that were still powerful enough to move people to violent action—and sometimes to draw in the great powers too.

China's sense of centrality in East Asia, for example, and the Iranian desire to reassert Persian primacy in the Middle East went back to a time when most European social organization was still based on the village and the clan. Tribal politics was still important in parts of black Africa and could lead to internecine conflict.

Perhaps most important, however, was the power of ancient religions, particularly the drive of a resurgent Islam. As many as a third of the member states of the United Nations could claim some degree of Muslim predominance. The postwar revival of that crusading faith contributed to clashes with other religions and ideologies from North Africa to Southeast Asia. The conflicts between Pakistan and India, the Iranian Revolution, and the long series of Arab-Israeli wars were all manifestations of this reborn spirit of *jihad* (holy war). Communists, Western powers, and Muslims of differing sects have all suffered at the hands of the new Muslim militance. And the lives of growing numbers of Muslims have been transformed by this resurgence of an ancient faith.

WINDS OF CHANGE IN AFRICA

Ghana and Algeria: Two Roads to Freedom

Africa, the second largest continent, was also the most completely colonized in 1945. Nor were the European imperialists who were established there in any hurry to grant the demands of independence movements in Africa. Most African colonies, however, were not much more than half a century old, having been seized during the scramble for Africa in the late 1800s. Vigorous campaigns for independence began to bear fruit in the middle 1950s, with the liberation of Ghana in West Africa. By the end of the 1970s, only the white-ruled Republic of South Africa remained in European hands.

Kwame Nkrumah, the leader of the emancipation movement in Britain's Gold Coast colony, was one of a brilliant postwar generation of African leaders that included Léopold Senghor and Sékou Touré in French West Africa, Jomo Kenyatta and Julius Nyerere in British East Africa, and Gamal Abdel Nasser in Egypt. Like them, Nkrumah was part of the new elite of Western-educated Africans, having lived and studied for years in both the United States and Britain.

The Gold Coast colony to which Nkrumah returned late in the 1940s was already agitated by economic tensions and antiimperialist sentiment. African farmers and workers believed they had not shared fairly in the war-stimulated boom in commodity prices. Strikes in the largest city, Accra, African boycotts of British goods, and criticism of the colonial administration were spreading. Turning his back on the older, more moderate African nationalist organization, Nkrumah set up his own Convention Peoples party (CPP) in 1949.

Nkrumah's CPP demanded drastic change—not administrative reforms in the colonial government but immediate independence—freedom now! Through the militant party newspaper in Accra, vigorous organizing in the villages, and his own charismatic personality, Nkrumah mobilized widespread support for the independence of the Gold Coast. Under this pressure, the British drastically accelerated plans for self-government, filling the colonial cabinet with Africans and holding elections for a parliament. In 1957 Nkrumah's labors were rewarded by independence for the Gold Coast—now renamed Ghana for the ancient West African empire—and by his election as first president of the new nation.

The other major British West African colony, Nigeria, achieved its independence three years later, and Britain's other West African colonies achieved their independence soon thereafter. The black star on Ghana's national flag, as magazines pointed out at the time, had been the morning star of African independence.

The Africans of the much larger West and North African territories controlled by France gained their freedom in two very different ways. The black African peoples of the Western Sudan and the Guinea Coast won independent statehood much as the British colonies did, through political organization and shrewdly applied political pressure, as did some of the North African Arab populations of French colonies. But in the North African territory of Algeria in particular, they had to fight for their freedom.

Most of French West and French Equatorial Africa was sun-bleached Sahara or tree-scattered Sudanic pastureland in 1945, thinly populated by Arab, Berber, or black-African peoples, almost empty of Europeans. The fertile Mediterranean shores to the north, however, had been supporting complex civilizations since ancient Carthage. Here in the Maghreb—Morocco, Algeria, Tunisia—French *colons* had been settling in large numbers for over a century, ever since the French conquest began in the 1830s. Here in the mid 1950s, within months of the end of their bloody Vietnam conflict, the French became embroiled in a second long and bloody colonial struggle—this one in Algeria.

Algeria was politically integrated into the mother

Africa Since 1950

Independent
French
Portuguese
Spanish

Member countries of the British Commonwealth

Member countries of the French Community

Dates indicate year of independence

Eritrea: united with Ethiopia in 1952

country across the Mediterranean. Many of her million or so French settlers had lived there for generations. But *colon* economic exploitation and political domination fanned the flames of antiimperialist resentment among the Arab and Berber majority of Algerians. In 1954 the National Liberation Front (FLN) began a campaign of terrorism and guerrilla struggle to oust the French. The French poured in 500,000 troops and resorted to bombing villages, stripping the countryside, and treating prisoners brutally. A *colon* vigilante force indulged in random violence, outdoing the FLN terrorists at their own game.

By the time the struggle ended in 1962, a million Algerian Arabs had been killed. France herself had been painfully divided. General de Gaulle, called back to power and granted virtually dictatorial powers to end the anarchy at home and the long war in Africa, proved himself more a statesman than a nationalist by acceding at last to Algerian demands for freedom.

Conflict in Kenya

East Africa differed from most of West Africa in that its fertile upland farm country had drawn much larger numbers of European settlers. These British farmers, who had taken over the best agricultural land from native Africans, resisted independence—and native rule—as vigorously as Algerian *colons* or the Afrikaners of South Africa did. And for some years after World War II, the British farmers in the Kenya colony especially continued to have their way.

Two strikingly dissimilar factors turned the tide against the settlers around 1960. One was an upsurge of terrorism by the Mau Mau, a secret society that sprang up within the dominant Kikuyu people of Kenya. The other was one man—Jomo Kenyatta, a Kikuyu with a London Ph.D., who became the leader of his people in their struggle.

Kenyatta's Kenya African National Union (KANU) party pushed vigorously for independence. The Mau Mau depredations, considerably exaggerated in the press, nevertheless led to many thousands of arrests, which further increased African resentment. Kenyatta had no connection with the superstitious Mau Mau, though he was imprisoned for refusing to disown them. Between them, however, these two quite different manifestations of Kikuyu power did convince the British to move more rapidly toward freedom for Kenya. In 1963 Kenya became an independent nation, the tall, impressive Jomo Kenyatta its first president.

Other British East African colonies also achieved their liberty in the 1960s. In many ways the most notable of these was Kenya's neighbor to the south, Tanganyika, which became the country of Tanzania under the young African Catholic socialist, Julius Nyerere. Outside of Kenya, however, *uhuru* came without violence. Agitation and organization by leaders such as Nyerere and Kenyatta prodded the colonial administration, and freedom came more rapidly on this side of Africa too.

Congo Crisis

The worst explosion of violence set off by independence movements in Africa south of the Sahara came in the immense central African colony of the Belgian Congo—the future country of Zaire.

The land of Joseph Conrad's *Heart of Darkness* was totally unprepared for freedom when it came with startling suddenness in 1960. The Belgians had lavished much time and money on developing the hugely profitable copper mines of the Congo's Katanga Province. But they had done almost nothing at all to educate an African elite, train African civil servants, or otherwise prepare residents of almost a million square miles of rain forest and bush villages for life in the modern world. At the first exploratory outburst of antiimperialist feeling in the Congo, the Belgian government turned its back on the whole imperial venture. Fearful of becoming mired in the sort of colonial warfare that had entangled the French, the

Jomo Kenyatta, leader of the Kenya independence movement, dominates a jubilant crowd with nothing more substantial than a ceremonial fly whisk. Like other leaders of African liberation struggles, Kenyatta combined Western training with charismatic popular appeal. (UPI/Bettmann Newsphotos)

Belgians announced the independence of the Congo colony and left the arena to the Africans.

An arena it was through the early 1960s, as Congolese and foreign elements battled for supremacy. The main contenders were Patrice Lumumba, a radical with a broad vision of national unity—and Communist connections; Moise Tshombe, suave ruler of Katanga Province—with close ties to Belgian mining interests; and General (then Colonel) Joseph Mobutu, the military strong man who came out on top in the end. Outside forces involved in the escalating Congolese chaos included the Belgians, who sent troops in to protect their nationals; the United Nations, which authorized several African members to send in armed forces to hold the country together; and various colorful and brutal white mercenary troops, who fought for the highest bidder.

The Congo crisis of 1960 revolved around Tshombe's attempt, supported by the Belgian mining combine, to detach the mineral-rich province of Katanga from the new country. To keep from losing this key source of national wealth, Lumumba, the nation's newly elected prime minister, called for help, first from the United Nations, then from the Soviet Union. At this point, however, a coup led by Colonel Mobutu overthrew Lumumba—and then turned him over to his archenemy Tshombe. Meanwhile, intertribal violence flared in many parts of the country as village people settled ancient rivalries with modern weapons.

In the end Lumumba was murdered, probably by

Katanga secessionists. Tshombe was overthrown in his turn, and the Katanga secession was ended by U.N. troops. General Mobutu emerged as the strongest of the strong men and ruler of the new country, which he renamed Zaire.

South Africa, Black and White

"The wind of change," British prime minister Harold Macmillan admitted during an African tour in 1960, "is blowing through this continent. . . . "[1] Those winds blew less briskly in southern Africa, however, than in any other part of the continent—indeed, than in almost any other part of the colonial world.

The liberation of the two Portuguese colonies of Angola and Mozambique was linked to the politics of their Portuguese masters. During the postwar years, Portugal was governed by the autocratic Salazar regime, which offered no concessions, either to liberalism at home or to antiimperialism in the colonies. It was only in 1974, when Salazar's equally autocratic successor was overthrown in Portugal, that Angola and Mozambique were granted their independence as well.

The two Rhodesias—named for the celebrated nineteenth-century British South African imperialist Cecil Rhodes—reached independence almost a decade and a half apart. Northern Rhodesia won independence as Zambia, ruled by its black African majority under mild-mannered Kenneth Kaunda, as early as the mid sixties. Southern Rhodesia, with its copper mines and determined English settler community, clung to minority white rule until the end of the seventies. It took an international boycott and a long struggle by two separate guerrilla groups—Robert Mugabe's Zimbabwe African People's Union and Joshua Nkomo's Zimbabwe African National Union—to win majority African rule in the new state of Zimbabwe in 1979.

But no amount of international pressure, guerrilla assault, or domestic resistance, seemed to shake the grip of European settlers in the Republic of South Africa. There the winds were blowing all the other way during the postwar decades, for this was the period that saw the imposition of the system of *apartheid* on South Africa.

The colonial and precolonial history of South Africa is a complex story of peoples, rights, and freedoms in conflict. Occupied by only a thin scattering of bushmanoid hunters and pastoralists and Bantu-speaking farmers in 1500, the southern tip of Africa

has since been overrun by successive waves of Zulu, Dutch, and British settlers, with admixtures of Southeast Asian slaves, Indian contract workers, and others.

Though British colonists have dominated the state economically in this century, the Dutch-descended Afrikaners have held political power. However, a great many more indigenous Africans live in South Africa than European-descended people of any description. The economic and political position of the black Africans, bushmanoid peoples, Indians, and other "colored" peoples has always been drastically inferior to that of the Europeans. But at the end of World War II the ruling Afrikaner Nationalist party set out to codify that inferiority in a system of discriminatory racial legislation reminiscent of the old Jim Crow laws in the American South.

Apartheid means "apartness," and the physical separation of the ethnic communities was clearly one purpose of the apartheid laws passed in the years around 1950. Europeans, black Africans, Asians, and others were to live in separate areas, be educated in separate schools, work at different jobs, find recreation in separate places. Marriages between Europeans and others were made illegal. Black Africans had to carry passes in white areas.

But it was, of course, more than a matter of separation. Black Africans were confined to the least productive lands, the least pleasant living places; they had the best jobs closed to them; they could not be elected to parliament. Apartheid meant separate and *unequal*, and all Africa knew it.

For decades after the imposition of apartheid, then, South Africa was caught up in a tragic, brutal confrontation, a struggle of guerrillas and counter-insurgency, of border raids and military incursions. South Africa was pitted against a handful of states on her borders—from Tanzania in the east to Angola in the west—all poor, many politically authoritarian. But South Africa faced a black continent that was ideologically as united against the racist regime in Pretoria as the Arab world was against Israel. And yet, like Israel, South Africa generally won.

South Africa's developed economy lured poverty-stricken neighboring black states such as Botswana and Mozambique into signing treaties with her. Her armies knifed repeatedly into the territories of more belligerent antagonists such as Angola, shooting up guerrilla camps in spite of Angola's Cuban garrisons. Foreign trade and investment from Western nations such as the United States kept South Africa rich and powerful—and provided jobs in industry for many black laborers, as Pretoria never tired of pointing out.

In the end, it did not seem possible for an apartheid regime to survive forever in a black continent.

[1]Speech of February 3, 1960, in *Vital Speeches of the Day* (March 11, 1960).

But an end did not appear to be in sight as the decades passed.

ASIA IN ARMS

The Arab World—and Israel

One of the most complex colonial situations was in the Middle East. There antiimperialist feeling and growing pan-Arab nationalism had led the British to give up control of Egypt and Iraq during the 1930s, though she retained control of the crucial Suez Canal. During World War II, Arab princes in the region established the Arab League, which, with British support, compelled the French to liberate Syria and Lebanon in the mid 1940s. In the 1950s, however, a nationalist revolt in Egypt overthrew the pro-British king of that country, and in 1956 the new military strong man, Gamal Abdel Nasser, nationalized the Suez Canal.

The most explosive colonial problem in the Middle East, however, had to do with the British mandate of Palestine and the emergence of the modern state of Israel. This strip of Arab land along the eastern end of the Mediterranean Sea, the site of the ancient Hebrew kingdom of David and Solomon, had been the focus of the Jewish nationalist movement called Zionism since the nineteenth century. Encouraged by a British statement of support during World War I, Jews had begun to emigrate from Europe to Palestine in the 1930s. After World War II, survivors of the Nazi holocaust poured into the British mandate, determined to establish a homeland.

The Arab population, strongly supported by the Arab League, resisted these incursions. As violence spread across Palestine, the British attempted to work out a compromise, and the new United Nations voted for a partition of the area between Arabs and Jews. In the spring of 1948, however, Jewish leaders in Palestine, citing the U.N. resolution and depending on strong American support, announced the formation of the new state of Israel. The surrounding nations of the Arab League at once declared war, determined to expel the Jewish immigrants and reclaim all Palestine for its Arab inhabitants.

The 1948 Arab-Israeli War, the first of a series, looked to be stacked in favor of the Arab countries. But the Arab princes competed among themselves and were not as familiar with modern weaponry as the Jewish immigrants from Europe and America were. The Israelis, fighting for their existence as a state, unified and determined, not only defended themselves but expanded beyond the U.N. partition line, creating an even larger Jewish nation for the Arabs to deal with.

For the surrounding Arab nations, Israel has been a bitter problem ever since. This problem has been considerably exacerbated by the large number of Muslim refugees—a million in 1948—who have not been absorbed by the neighboring Arab countries and continue to demand the return of Palestine.

The new nation of Israel has thus fought no less than five wars with the Muslim states surrounding her during the thirty-five years between 1948 and 1982. Militarily speaking, the earlier of these Arab-Israeli encounters were clear Israeli victories. More recent conflicts, however, have proved costly and have led to few detectable gains for Israel.

The 1948 war with which Israel's history began left the new nation larger than even her founders had expected. The 1956 war, fought by a secret alliance of Israel, Britian, and France against Nasser's Egypt over the Suez Canal, saw more Israeli military successes, though heavy international pressure forced the alliance to evacuate their conquests. The 1967 "Six Day War" was Israel's most smashing success, leading to the conquest of the large Sinai region from Egypt and the strategic Golan heights from Syria.

After the 1967 war, however, the leading role in the struggle against Israel was taken over by Palestinian refugee guerrilla organizations. Under the leadership of the Palestine Liberation Organization (PLO), the Palestinians stepped up border raids and terrorist attacks inside Israel. Israeli counterterrorist activities and harsh treatment of Arabs living within her borders cost her some international support from this time on.

Later Israeli wars were less successful. The 1973 "Yom Kippur War," so called because the Arabs attacked Israel on that Jewish holiday, led to Egyptian reconquest of part of the Sinai. Thereafter, peace initiatives by Egypt's new leader, Anwar Sadat, coupled with mediation by President Jimmy Carter, resulted in a peace treaty and the return of still more conquered territory.

Israel's invasion of Lebanon in 1982, finally, did result in defeats for both Syria and the PLO. But Israel's effort to establish a strong client regime in Beirut failed, and she eventually withdrew from Lebanon with little but a tarnished image to show for this latest of her long series of wars with her Muslim neighbors.

Middle Eastern Tangle

Despite postwar Pan-Arab sentiment, the Muslim rulers of the Middle East proved to be among the more contentious of the world's leaders. Domestic discord further aggravated the tensions and sporadic violence that made the region one of the world's hot spots.

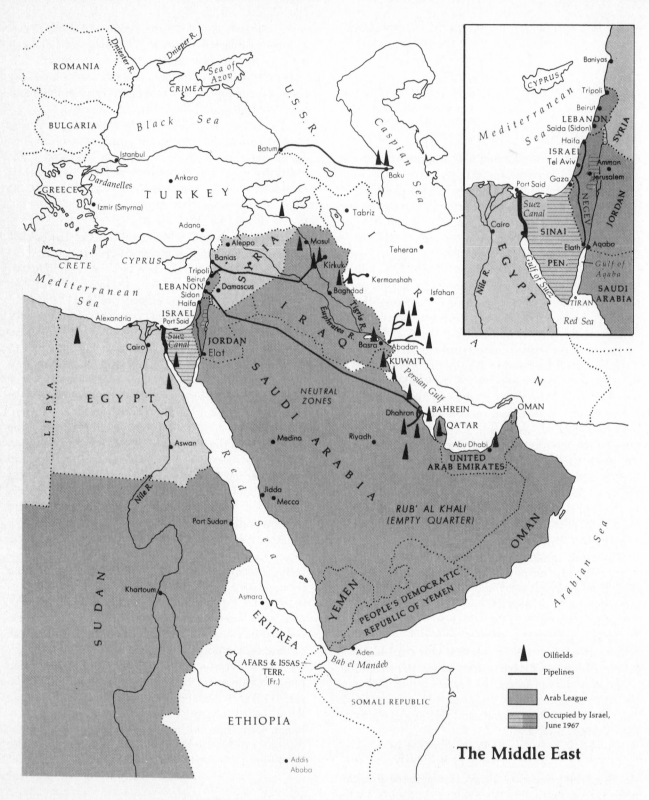

The Middle East

Legend:
- ▲ Oilfields
- — Pipelines
- ▨ Arab League
- ▤ Occupied by Israel, June 1967

One center of turmoil in recent years has been Iran, heir of past Persian greatness and of the most militant of Islamic traditions, the Shiite sect.

Iran had been divided into British and Russian zones of influence as late as World War II, and Russia had attempted after the war to reach out for paramount influence through a strong local Communist party and the presence of the Red Army in the north. The main result of this effort, however, was to drive the shah of Iran firmly into the arms of the West. A strongly nationalist premier named Muhammad Mossadegh attempted to seize control of the nation's Western-run oil industry, but was overthrown by a coup engineered by the American CIA.

For the next quarter of a century Iran was an American ally, ruled by a modernizing shah who spent his oil money to build up his country to something of its ancient preeminence in the Middle East. He left to his notorious secret police the suppression of both radical opposition and resurgent Islam. In 1979 it was the Muslim *mullahs* who pulled him down, mobilizing huge crowds of militant demonstrators to demand the shah's overthrow and to welcome an exiled spiritual leader, the Ayatollah Ruhollah Khomeini, in his place.

Militant Shiite followers of the Ayatollah, like the *Kizilbashi* supporters of Shah Ismail in the sixteenth century, were soon running the nation and shaking up the Middle East. Following Khomeini's dictum that "the legislative power in Islam is limited to God alone," the *mullah* leaders purged both American sympathizers and Russian-leaning Marxists.[2] The Ayatollah's supporters embarked upon a national effort to build an "Islamic republic," a theocracy operating according to the religious and social principles of the Koran and Islamic Law. Women appearing in public were veiled once more, and religious minorities and leftist students alike suffered under the new regime.

In 1980 the new government confronted the United States when a group of Muslim student militants seized the American embassy and held it—and its personnel—for a year of increasing tension.

The Ayatollah's militance disturbed a number of Arab powers almost as much as it did the United States. Khomeini, like Persian Shiites of earlier centuries, talked extravagantly of unleashing a *jihad*, or holy war, against the "corrupt" Sunni states around him. The particularly pious Sunni state of Saudi Arabia, keeper of the holy places at Mecca and Medina, was much disturbed.

But it was Iran's neighbor Iraq that responded with force to the Ayatollah's challenge. This Muslim nation, which also used the Persian Gulf to export large quantities of oil, was run by the Ba'athist Party—dedicated to Arab socialism, heavily dependent on an alliance with the Soviet Union, and ruled by a tough military man, Saddam Hussein. Iraq's strike into revolutionary Iran late in 1980 at first promised a quick success, thanks to superior equipment and military leadership. But the invasion bogged down in a human

---

²Ruhollah Khomeini, *Islamic Government*, in Nikki R. Keddie, *Roots of Revolution: An Interpretive History of Modern Iran* (New Haven: Yale University Press, 1981), p. 207.

sea of fanatics willing to die for the Ayatollah's *jihad*. The war dragged on for years, shifting back to Iraqi territory and escalating to involve attacks by both sides on shipping in the Gulf—a threat to the world's oil supply that gave Western powers a special stake in the conflict.

The Subcontinent Divided

Conflict along religious lines also haunted the subcontinent of India during and after her liberation from British rule. After independence, differences between Hindus and Muslims led to a long series of disputes between the new nations of India and Pakistan.

The Indian Congress party, led by Mahatma Gandhi and Jawaharlal Nehru, had spearheaded the struggle for Indian independence during the interwar years. Gandhi and the Congress party, however, were Hindus, spokesmen primarily for India's 350 million practitioners of that faith. But there were 100 million Muslims in India too. The chief spokesman for this huge minority was Muhammad Ali Jinnah, head of the colony's Muslim League.

When the newly elected British Labour government began to negotiate the final liberation of the subcontinent, bitterness between Hindus and Muslims was wildly inflamed. Rioting flared, civil war threatened, and in the end the huge colony was partitioned. Two nations, Hindu India and Muslim Pakistan, thus came into existence in 1947.

Freedom, however, only exacerbated the rioting between the two religious communities. Some 15 million Hindu and Muslim refugees abandoned their villages and headed for the new frontiers. More than half a million died violently or by starvation and exposure on the road. Gandhi himself was assassinated by a Hindu extremist who hated the Mahatma for his efforts to curb violence between Muslims and Hindus.

During the following decades, three wars were fought between the two new nations. Two were over the lovely, high-mountain northwestern Indian province of Kashmir, whose population has a Muslim majority. Despite these wars of 1947–1948 and 1965–1966, the area remains disputed.

A third clash, in 1971, was over the isolated northeastern territory of East Pakistan. This portion of divided Pakistan, almost entirely surrounded by Bengal India, felt exploited and oppressed by the central government in West Pakistan. East Pakistan finally rebelled and, with Indian help, founded the independent state of Bangladesh. During the prewar repression and the conflict itself, casualties mounted over the million mark, and 10 million refugees fled into India.

Pandit Nehru, Leader of India's Congress party, speaks before a women's organization in Bombay. His wife, Kamala (seated), shares the platform as she shared his struggle, including arrest and imprisonment in the cause. (Library of Congress)

War in Southeast Asia

Religion counted for less, politics for more in the struggles for independence—and after independence—in East and Southeast Asia. Ceylon achieved independence in 1948 as the new island nation of Sri Lanka with minimal difficulties. Burma, however, freed the same year, was at once faced by revolts led by two distinct groups of Communist guerrillas and by various ethnic minorities, struggles that would drag on for years.

The Malay Peninsula faced both Communist-led revolts and ethnic rivalries so serious that independence there was postponed for a decade. British troops stayed on until the Communist guerrillas were defeated. Ethnic and cultural differences between the Malay peoples of the peninsula and the overseas Chinese majority in the great commercial center of Singapore proved harder to deal with. In the late 1950s the colonial union between the two areas was therefore dissolved, and once more there were two nations where one colony had been: the country of Malaya and the immensely prosperous little city-state of Singapore.

By far the bloodiest struggle for independence in Asia—and the most violent aftermath—was that in French Indochina. As we discussed in Chapter 21, this conflict between French armies numbering up to half a million and Vietnamese guerrilla forces under Ho Chi Minh dragged on from 1945 until 1954, producing large casualties for the Vietnamese—and defeat for the French.

Ho Chi Minh, the Mao of Southeast Asia, was a Vietnamese nationalist, a Communist, and a militant antiimperialist. In 1945 Ho had declared the independence of Vietnam as soon as the Japanese left. The French, however, had no intention of surrendering their colonies, and French colonial authorities broke up Ho's provisional government, reestablished the old order, and prepared to suppress any terrorist activities that might result.

Ho and his right-hand man, General Giap, led a determined guerrilla struggle for most of the next decade. Like Mao's troops in China during the interwar years, Ho's soldiers were farmers by day, fighters by night. The paddies, the jungles, and the mountains were Ho's real country, the cities the true centers of French control. In 1954 the French finally tried to break the stalemate by luring Ho's guerrillas out into the open with a prize too rich to ignore: the powerful, isolated French fortress of Dien Bien Phu. The guerrillas took the bait, but they came with prudence, skill, and artillery. They surrounded Dien Bien Phu and crushed it.

That same year, at a peace conference in Geneva, the French let Indochina go. Ho Chi Minh, however, was deprived of the full spoils of victory. He got only North Vietnam. South Vietnam, Cambodia, and Laos—the other subdivisions of French Indochina—were freed under their own governments, and the Saigon government remained a center of Western influence. The seeds of future struggle—including America's Vietnam War—were thus sown by the peace settlement that got the French out of Southeast Asia at last.

The Middle Kingdom Once More

In the struggle for predominance in East Asia, China had to face—and accept—the challenge of one spectacular rival. As the dust of World War II and the Chinese civil war settled, Japan, the third wealthiest nation in the world after the two superpowers, was the dynamo of the Far East. But Japan's imperialistic ambitions seemed to have expired with the samurai spirit in the smoke of the war. She depended on her United States allies for protection against her great Far Eastern rival, Russia. The Japanese undertook few foreign-policy initiatives not having to do with foreign trade, and concentrated most of their formidable energies on technology and business.

The People's Republic of China, by contrast, concerned itself from the moment of Mao's victory with reestablishing the Middle Kingdoms's ancient frontiers and old influence, at least insofar as circumstances allowed. Most of China's energies also went into domestic affairs: the staggering task of bringing something resembling a modern quality of life to one quarter of the world's population. But Mao and his successors also found time to remind their neighbors that the old imperial giant was still there.

In 1950, the year after winning control of China, Mao sent the Chinese Red Army to occupy the high, thinly populated plateau of Tibet—a Chinese domain for centuries before the Europeans came. Manchuria, Inner Mongolia, and other large areas were also firmly incorporated into the new China. In 1962 China fought a brief border war with India to readjust some mutual frontiers in the Himalayas; similar disputes were settled peacefully with Burma, Nepal, and Pakistan.

A major continuing territorial dispute was with China's former Communist ally, the Soviet Union, over the region along the Amur River border northeast of Peking. A crucial sticking point in China's relations with the United States was America's support for the Chinese Nationalist regime on Taiwan, an an-

cient part of China that in Chinese thinking had to be reabsorbed sooner or later into the Middle Kingdom. And in 1984 Britain negotiated the return of her colony of Hong Kong, the rich gateway to South China, to Chinese sovereignty by the 1990s.

One of the cornerstones of China's foreign policy, in short, had nothing to do with ideology, but simply to do with reestablishing her own imperial position in the Far East. China's involvement with Korea and Vietnam, two peoples who had in earlier centuries been her most successful satellite cultures outside of Japan, illustrated this basic Chinese concern.

In both these countries, as we have seen, China supported northern Communist regimes in wars against large American armies in league with governments established in the south of the two peninsulas. But in both cases China's concern was modified by the fact that both Vietnam and Korea were much closer to Russia than to their former overlords in Peking. Only in this complex context of past Chinese preeminence and present Russo-Chinese rivalry can China's ambiguous role in the Korean and Vietnamese conflicts be understood.

China had no part in North Korea's invasion of South Korea, and she did not intervene in the struggle until American troops pushed too close to China's own frontier along the Yalu River. Then, probably preferring a small Korean neighbor to an outpost of American power, Peking entered the war, pushed the Americans back as far as the former frontier with South Korea, and let it go at that.

During America's long struggle on the Indochinese peninsula, China did supply North Vietnam with some aid. But Ho Chi Minh depended primarily on Russia for war materiel, and Chinese support was apparently always lukewarm.

Indeed, once the North Vietnamese had won their war, China seems to have taken alarm—and understandably so. In 1975, while South Vietnam fell to the North Vietnamese, Cambodia and Laos were also overrun by their own Communist-led guerrillas. In 1977 Cambodia (renamed Kampuchea and ruled by the brutal Khmer Rouge regime) tumbled into a new civil war—and was then overrun by North Vietnamese troops. Laos also quickly came within Hanoi's orbit. North Vietnam thus came to control a larger part of the Indochinese peninsula than ever before—and to present a formidable challenge on China's southern frontier.

In 1978, then, the People's Republic of China seized upon the mistreatment of overseas Chinese in Vietnam as a cause for conflict and sent a "punitive" expedition across Vietnam's northern border. The ancient rivalry between the two thus flamed into the open once again. The brief incursion also demonstrated that China could attack a Russian client state in Asia with impunity. The short Chinese incursion into Vietnam thus served as one more reminder of China's historic primacy in East Asia.

SUMMARY

The decades after World War II saw the collapse of the vast intercontinental empires constructed by Europeans over the preceding five centuries.

The causes of this collapse included the resentment against foreign domination and economic exploitation that had been building for generations in the colonies. These feelings were strengthened by the encouraging spectacle of Japanese victories over Westerners, by European weakness of will and resources after the war, by the fact that both the United States and the Soviet Union opposed old-fashioned territorial imperialism.

The great liberation that followed the war was violent in some places, as in Vietnam and Algeria; it was relatively peaceful elsewhere, as in most British colonies. A third of the world's population thus gained political independence. Asia and Africa thereafter joined Latin America in the vast bloc of politically free but economically underdeveloped countries known as the Third World.

The freedom struggles of the new nations were followed by other conflicts on the two largest continents. Some of these conflicts were traceable to the economic dependency of poor nations on rich ones. Others went back to precolonial political or religious rivalries that reasserted themselves after the passing of the colonial era.

In the Middle East, Israel fought a long series of wars with her Arab neighbors. Muslim militance and the rivalry of Middle Eastern rulers led to a number of armed clashes. In Asia, Hindu India and Muslim Pakistan fought repeatedly. And in East Asia, China reasserted her primacy by limited interventions in Korea and Vietnam, as well as by the occupation of Tibet and continuing disputes with the Soviet Union over their mutual frontier.

Black Africa, repeatedly shaken by coups and revolutions, was spared many international wars. Around the borders of white-controlled South Africa, however, guerrilla struggles flared up repeatedly over the years.

SUGGESTED READING

BURKE, S. M. *Mainsprings of Indian and Pakistani Foreign Policies.* Minneapolis: University of Minnesota Press, 1974. Authoritative. See also his *Pakistan's Foreign Policy: An Historical Analysis* (London: Oxford University Press, 1973), and W. A. Wilcox, *India and Pakistan* (New York: Foreign Policy Association, 1967).

CHANG, P. *Beijing, Hanoi, and the Overseas Chinese.* Berkeley: University of California Press, 1982. Brief monograph on the clash between the two Asian Communist powers that followed North Vietnam's victory over South Vietnam.

CROSS, C. *The Fall of the British Empire, 1918–1968.* London: Hodder and Stoughton, 1968. Sweeping overview of the decline of the largest of the overseas empires.

DUPUY, T. N. *Elusive Victory: The Arab-Israeli Wars, 1947–1974.* New York: Harper & Row, Pub., 1978. Comprehensive, detailed survey, excluding only the Lebanon incursion of the early 1980s. On efforts to make peace, see M. A. Friedlander, *Sadat and Begin: The Domestic Politics of Peace-Making* (Boulder, Colo.: Westview Press, 1983).

EMERSON, R. *From Empire to Nation: The Rise of Self-Assertion of Asian and African Peoples.* Cambridge: Cambridge University Press, 1960. Excellent overview of the Great Liberation from the colonial perspective.

FAIRBANK, J. K. *The United States and China,* 3rd ed. Cambridge, Mass.: Harvard University Press, 1971. An expert summary of relations between the oldest of the industrially underdeveloped nations and this century's leading industrial power.

GILIOMEE, H., and R. ELPHICK, eds. *The Shaping of South African Society.* Capetown: Longmans, 1979. Essays on the complexities of South Africa's situation. On two crucial elements in the problem, see J. Suckling, et al., *The Economic Factor of External Investment in South Africa* (London: Africa Publications Trust, 1975). See also J. W. Johnson, *How Long Will South Africa Survive?* (London: Macmillan, 1977), and on the larger ramifications of the situation, C. Legum, *The West's Crisis in Southern Africa* (New York: Africana, 1978).

HUNTINGTON, S. P. *Political Order in Changing Societies.* New Haven: Yale University Press, 1969. Broad analysis.

KAHIN, G. M., ed. *Governments and Politics of Southeast Asia*. Ithaca: Cornell University Press, 1964. Triumphs and troubles of the Great Liberation in this corner of Asia. On the Japanese influence, particularly strong here, see W. H. Elsbree, *Japan's Role in Southeast Asian Nationalist Movements, 1940–1945* (Cambridge, Mass.: Harvard University Press, 1953).

KEDDIE, N. R. *Religion and Politics in Iran: Sh'ism from Quietism to Revolution*. New Haven: Yale University Press, 1983. Religious background to the overthrow of the shah and the resulting tumult in the Middle East. See also his *Roots of Revolution: An Interpretive History of Modern Iran* (New Haven: Yale University Press, 1981).

LEGUM, C., et al. *Africa in the 1980s: A Continent in Crisis*. New York: McGraw-Hill, 1979. Outlines some possibilities, including projections in international relations and economic dependency.

LENCZOWSKI, G., ed. *The Political Awakening in the Middle East*. Englewood Cliffs, N.J.: Prentice-Hall, 1970. Nationalism and anti-imperialism in the ancient Muslim center of the Old World. For the life of an outstanding liberation leader in the region, see J. Lacoutre, *Nasser* (New York: Knopf, 1973).

MENON, V. P. *The Transfer of Power in India*. Princeton: Princeton University Press, 1957. A scholarly account. See also M. Edwardes, *The Last Years of British India* (Cleveland: World Pub. Co., 1964).

QUANDT, W. B., F. JABBER, and A. M. LESCH. *The Politics of Palestinian Nationalism*. Berkeley: University of California, 1975. On this vexing question of a homeland for the Palestinian refugees, see also views strongly critical of Israel, including E. W. Said, *The Question of Palestine* (New York: Random House, 1980) and N. Chomsky, *The Fateful Triangle: The United States, Israel, and the Palestinians* (Boston: South End Press, 1983).

SHARABI, H. B. *Nationalism and Revolution in the Arab World*. New York: Van Nostrand, 1966. A central feature of the Arab awakening.

SNYDER, L. L. *The New Nationalism*. Ithaca: Cornell University Press. Crucial aspect of the anti-imperial revolt all across the Third World.

THOMAS, H. *Suez*. New York: Harper & Row, Pub., 1967. One of a number of accounts of what has been described as the last gasp of old-style Western imperialism.

WALLERSTEIN, I. *Africa: The Politics of Independence*. New York: Random House, 1963. Good on the liberation of Africa. See also A. A. Mazrui, *Protest and Power in Black Africa* (London: Oxford University Press, 1972), and V. LeVine, *Political Leadership in Africa* (Stanford: Hoover Institution, 1967), on the postemancipation elites, shaped by the liberation struggle.

Chapter · 23

THE SKYSCRAPER AGE

342

THE GLOBAL NORTH

Cityscape

The cover of the *New York Times Magazine* shows a man in a hard hat sitting on an orange girder, his feet dangling into space. Far enough below to dim its outlines, dull its hue, is the top of the nearest skyscraper. Beyond and still farther below, block after block, mile after mile, the vertical world of New York City spreads under a glistening haze.

It is a world of narrow man-made canyons, of concrete and brick, glass and asphalt, jammed with cars, streaming with millions of people. It is a world so new that a word has had to be coined to describe representations of it: not a landscape, but a cityscape. It is a world built by human hands—by the hands of men in hard hats—whose skyline is dominated by the imperial splendor of the skyscraper.

The drawbacks of city life are not to be ignored, indeed cannot be ignored by anyone who lives there. The daily devouring of irreplaceable resources, from petroleum products to aluminum cans, by a city of several millions boggles the imagination. So do the mountains and sluices of waste the modern city generates, and the pollution darkening the waters around it, thickening the air above it. The millions themselves—double-digit millions of people now, in metropolises such as Tokyo and Mexico City—put their own immense strain on the system. They require food, housing, schools, jobs, police protection, garbage collection, care for children, care for the growing numbers of the elderly.

Yet the role of the urban complex remains central. The twentieth-century metropolis, with its concentric rings of suburbs and its links by rail and road and air with other cities, is as much the core of the modern industrial state as the walled city was of the urban-imperial state of ancient times. The uniquely vertical skyline of the twentieth-century city—originating in the United States, found today on every continent—is an instantly recognized symbol of the technologically based wealth and power of the global North today.

Modern cities are to be seen in every part of the world, but they cluster most thickly in the Northern Hemisphere, more particularly in the north temperate zone—in North America, Europe, and East Asia, especially Japan. Urban culture and the power and affluence that go with it are thus heavily concentrated in what has recently come to be known as the global North, in contrast with the less affluent, less urbanized, warmer lands of the South.

Both the so-called First World and Second World— the American and Russian zones, sometimes called the West and the East, respectively—are parts of the global North in terms of technological development. The towers of the Manhattan skyline, the rank on rank of housing blocks marching out a main road in Moscow, alike represent the ascendancy of the wealth, power, and technological ingenuity of the northern reaches of the world in our time.

High Tech

The secret of it, of course, is techology, the harnessing of new power sources to do the world's work. Begun in Europe two hundred years ago, it has seemingly burst all bounds in our own century. Technological progress, since World War II especially, has made

The skyscrapers of Manhattan dwarf towers of earlier centuries. Built for the most part by great business corporations, these many-storied structures were as typical of the twentieth century as the palaces and temples of earlier centuries were of their times. (Wide World Photos)

marvels ordinary, miracles everyday occurrences in the developed nations of North America, Europe, Australia, and Japan, and in the modern urban enclaves of Latin American, Africa, and Asia.

Much of the technological progress made by the North, beginning in the 1950s, manifested itself in improved—or at least interestingly varied—lives for large segments of the population. This was particularly so in the West, where consumer demand still had a central role in determining what got developed and manufactured. From basics such as air conditioning and frozen foods to frivolities such as stereo equipment, video recorders, and electronic arcade games, the buying public has gotten its share of the latest technology in capitalist countries.

Much of the applied science of the age, however, was the preserve of the specialist or the large institutional user, from government and big business to the general hospital and the airline. In these areas, East-bloc countries, especially the Soviet Union, contributed importantly to the science fiction world in which we all lived. From space exploration to medical technology to nuclear weaponry and delivery systems, Russian applied science put them among the world leaders in the postwar decades.

The peoples of the global North thus created a dazzling new material culture for themselves during the third quarter of the twentieth century. Thousands of later-twentieth-century people walked around with remarkable artificial limbs or electronic pacemakers regulating the beating of their hearts. Decent hygiene, diet, exercise, wonder drugs, and hospital tech-

nology doubled the human life span. In industry and government, steady progress in computer technology, robotics, electronics, biological engineering, and energy science continued to reshape the world around us.

In the decades after World War II, regularly scheduled jumbo jets linked the cities of the world, till there was virtually no place more than a day away from anywhere else, and millions flew the friendly skies of the world every year. Artificial satellites orbited the earth, beeping back a spectrum of information ranging from hourly weather reports to newscasts from the other side of the world—straight to the home television screens of countless viewers.

In 1961 the Russian cosmonaut Yuri Gagarin became the first human being to orbit the earth in an artificial satellite. In 1969 an American, Neil Armstrong, became the first to set foot on the moon. In the mid 1970s Russian spacecraft landed on Venus and American ones sent back vivid photographs from the surface of Mars. The peoples of planet earth grew quite blasé about angle shots of the rings of Saturn and fly-bys of the moons of Jupiter. For the developed nations of the North, at least, it seemed as if even the sky was no longer the limit.

The Helicopter Economy

The economies of the nations of the North also exhibited a tendency to rise at an unprecedented rate during these decades after World War II.

The free-enterprise nations of the West did do a

certain amount of nationalizing of major industries, from transportation to steel, during the postwar years. But they retained a solid core of privately capitalized corporations, and with them the stimulus of competition as an incentive to produce and sell. By and large, it worked very well for them, providing an engine of economic growth that flooded the Western world with goods and services.

The Western capitalist economy was no longer the fang-and-claw economic jungle of the nineteenth century. The major corporations themselves imposed order—and controlled competition—as efficiently as any medieval city guild in a wide variety of fields, from oil and automobiles to air travel and fast foods. Government regulated the conduct of business—everything from environmentally polluting by-products to employment practices. Western governments also provided support and direction for industry, agriculture, export trade, and other sectors of the economy by measures ranging from tightening or loosening credit to guiding industry into areas having a strong export future—and sharing the cost of research and development.

Such economic "fine tuning" helped. So did the advantages of cheap immigrant labor and raw materials from the global South. The result was an economic boom of unprecedented proportions through the 1960s and into the 1970s.

In 1973, however, and again in 1979, the oil producers' international cartel, OPEC, drastically hiked the price of petroleum, the single most important source of energy for Western industry. Meanwhile, particularly in North America and Europe, labor costs had been rising steadily while labor productivity declined (as much because of antiquated machinery as of labor practices). Economic feuds between members of the European Economic Community and between the United States and Japan intensified. In the 1970s and early 1980s these and other factors combined to produce the deepest recession since the Great Depression of the 1930s.

Recovery led by the United States came in the middle 1980s. There were some questions about the long-term vitality of the economic revival, especially if the largely voluntary agreements regulating international trade were to be replaced by a wave of nationalistic protectionism. But the graph lines were slanting upward once again, and though unemployment was still high, there seemed to be grounds for hope.

In the East bloc, the Soviets continued to chalk up impressive advances in gross production totals and heavy industry, outstripping the United States in some areas. East Germany and some other satellite states also developed powerful industrial sectors. There was also more integration between the economies of East and West than looked likely in the early days of the Cold War.

Nevertheless, consumer goods remained harder to come by in the East bloc than in the West. One major East-bloc economy, that of Poland, deeply in debt to Western banks, all but collapsed at the beginning of the eighties. The overall picture was still one of less abundance east of the Iron Curtain than west of it.

Both capitalist and Communist economies in the later twentieth century aimed at perpetual growth, at steadily rising statistics of production in all possible fields. The numbers rose more sharply in the West, though the rise was punctuated by some sudden falls. Both were "helicopter economies"—rising as economic production had never risen before, but requiring considerable fine tuning (in the West) or central planning (in the East) to stay aloft.

A One-Class World?

The distribution of the good things, however, remained a problem for the nations of the North in the later twentieth century, as it had since the beginning of the Industrial Revolution. Capitalist countries preached equality of opportunity rather than economic parity for all people. Because of the great prosperity of the West over most of the time since World War II, the majority of the citizens of its countries enjoyed a vastly improved standard of living. By the 1960s, cars, television sets, decent housing, paid vacations, and other perquisites of the new wealth were commonplace.

In addition, capitalist countries generally supplied a safety net of public services for all, paid for by tax money. It included such welfare measures as unemployment insurance, public health care, old-age or retirement benefits, and many more.

Even among these postwar "people of plenty," however, there were striking economic disparities. Women, ethnic minorities, immigrant workers, among others were all paid less than other segments of the population. Some even slipped through the welfare state's safety net and suffered grievously during economic downturns, particularly during the great recession of the later 1970s and early 1980s.

At the other end of the economic scale there were people as wealthy as any Gilded Age tycoon. In fact, governments often left money in the hands of the rich in order to encourage them to invest it productively in the economy—the sort of investment psychology on which capitalism had grown since the nineteenth century. Both the very poor and the very rich were minorities. There were substantial gradations in between, and no real economic equality likely, at least in the near future.

The most successful demonstrator during the turbulent American 1960s was Dr. Martin Luther King. He is shown here with his wife, Coretta King, and other leaders of the black civil rights struggle in the United States, marching on Montgomery, Alabama, in 1965. (UPI/Bettmann Newsphotos)

The Communist Eastern European countries had made an outright commitment to economic equality, at least in Marxist theory. But slogans such as "From each according to his ability, to each according to his need" had a rather utopian ring in the real world of the Soviet bloc. In the Soviet Union itself, even before World War II, the state had adopted piecework, quotas, and other incentives to production that set successful "shock workers" off from the rest of the work force.

In the early postwar years the Yugoslav heretic Milovan Djilas declared in print that a "new class" of party leaders, government bureaucrats, industrial managers, scientists, generals, and others had come to dominate Communist society.[1] The new elite, like the old capitalist one, garnered a larger share of the material rewards than less exalted comrades ever could. The gap between rich and poor might be less in Eastern-bloc nations, but so was the overall standard of living. And there were still classes—on both sides of the Iron Curtain.

Youthquake

In the twentieth century it became apparent that there were other important subgroups in society be-

sides the classes and castes, religious sects and ethnic groups whose interaction was such an important part of the history of most peoples. In particular, two biologically based subdivisions of the world's cultures thrust their way into popular consciousness: young people and women.

The revolt of the younger generation—the youthquake of the 1960s, as clever journalists called it—highlighted the emergence of youth as a force in history. But the development of a distinct twentieth-century youth culture went back very far, at least to the 1920s.

The subculture of the young transcended national boundaries, class lines, and most other traditional divisions in the societies of the global North. It was a subculture with its own shifting kaleidoscope of manners and mores, its endlessly new clothing styles, haircuts, dances, music, drugs and fads, folk heroes, and other enthusiasms. It was a consuming society, supporting whole industries from blue jeans to phonograph records. It was also frequently a culturally rebellious group, rejecting the values and beliefs of older generations, determined to "do their own thing."

In the 1960s the youth culture turned political. The youth revolt of the sixties took many forms. Young people in Japan opposed their government's conservative policies and the military alliance with the United States. In America they mobilized for educational re-

[1]Milovan Djilas, *The New Class: An Analysis of the Communist System* (New York: Praeger, 1957).

form, for civil rights for black Americans, against poverty, and against America's role in the Vietnam War. In Western Europe it was educational reform, ban-the-bomb, Yankee-Go-Home; in East Europe, it was demands for an end to secret-police terror, for democracy, for more consumer goods—and Russky-Go-Home!

The demonstrations, marches, sit-ins, occasional violence, and general noise of the youth movements of the sixties were unprecedented in scale. Nor were they without effect. Youth movements helped shape the history of those years, from the Chinese Cultural Revolution to the American withdrawal from Vietnam, from more relaxed social mores to more rigorous regulation of industrial pollution.

Long Way, Baby?

During the postwar decades, many women once more took up the crusading spirit of the turn-of-the century women's suffrage movement—this time primarily in the economic sphere. Again, the results were striking.

In the immediate aftermath of World War II, "Rosy the Riveter" seemed to be content to return to the older patterns of life as wife and mother. What came to be called the feminine mystique praised these time-honored social roles, as it urged longer dresses, frillier fashions, and a more feminine image on the female half of the population.

The turmoil of the 1960s, however, stirred the women's movement to life again. In the following decade, women's organizations such as the National Organization for Women (NOW) in the United States began a campaign to overcome the remaining forms of discrimination against women.

Women in the 1970s ran for and won election to political office in unprecedented numbers. Strong women in many lines of work became role models for younger ones. All forms of social deprecation were firmly rejected, women opened their own doors, paid their share of the tab, used their own surnames after marriage, and expected to be called Ms.

The main thrust of the revitalized women's movement, however, was economic. Women demanded equal pay for equal work, promotion of more women to executive levels in business, larger representation in the ranks of the professions. In some of these areas, at least, they seemed to be making progress in the 1970s and 1980s. More than half the married women in the United States worked outside the home, and it was no longer difficult to find successful women as role models in all spheres of life.

In Eastern Europe, women had been integrated into the economy for decades, a measure as much of the need for labor as of ideological commitment. Child care for working women was almost universally available. Some professions were thoroughly integrated: most of the doctors in the Soviet Union were women.

In other ways, however, women in the Soviet bloc seemed to be trailing behind their sisters on the other side of the Iron Curtain. The male sense of superiority had apparently not withered in the Communist world. Women were expected to do a day's work at the factory or office and then come home and get supper for the family—a practice that seemed to be declining in emancipated circles in the West. And there were as few women in top spots in the societies of the East bloc as there were in the West.

Women in the eighties could thus give only a qualified Yes to the cigarette advertisements that asked if they hadn't come "a long way, baby," since 1900. There was still a long way to go.

Problems of Prosperity

By the standards of the global South, Europeans, Americans, Japanese were all "American millionaires"—and should have been the happiest of peoples. This was not, however, the case. The peoples of the global North actually seemed to derive a perverse pleasure from reminding themselves of their own failings. And they did, in fact, have their share of problems.

In their work lives, Britons or Russians might see themselves as unproductive and even cynical about a good day's work; Americans, as conformists trapped in a meaningless rat race to an unfulfilling future in the suburbs; Japanese, as obsequious dependents clinging to the skirts of the big companies that were mothers and fathers to them all. At home, European males were still heavy-handed and paternalistic, and American two-career families were breaking apart under the pull of diverging ambitions.

Russians drank too much vodka, French people too much wine, Americans too much scotch or beer—and some added drugs to the list of destructive intoxicants. Contagious diseases, the diseases of poverty, were largely conquered in the North—but cancer and heart disease, the diseases of age and high-pressure living, flourished. Mental illness filled half the hospital beds in some developed countries.

The inevitable exhaustion of raw materials and the pollution of air and water were widely discussed problems. High crime rates, auto accidents slaughtering tens of thousands every year, and other difficulties abounded. The list of problems could go on—as could reminders that many of the fortunate citizens of the global North were quite free of all or most of them. But the general point was clear to the most optimistic social critic of the period. The species that could send space probes beyond the planets could not keep its hands off a pack of cigarettes plainly labeled "injurious to your health."

Utopia was not yet in sight, even for the richest people in history.

THE STRATEGIES OF PROGRESS

Power Structures

There were two sorts of political power structure in the North during the decades after World War II. There were important similarities between them, as social scientists often pointed out. But the differences were real too—and important enough to have generated the most dangerous conflict of the postwar period, the Cold War between East and West in the global North.

The most striking similarity was that governments on both sides of the Iron Curtain were performing a great many more services for the governed than governments ever had before. Even in the free-enterprise West, public education, health care, housing, paved roads, streetlights, water and sewers, public transportation, police and fire protection, mail delivery, and a thousand more amenities of modern life were provided by national, state or provincial, and local governments. In the state-socialist countries of the East bloc, nationalized economies and central planning meant that all the office staffs of Western private business were government employees too—making big government even bigger.

Complaints about bureaucratic inefficiency were endemic on both sides. In the West there was an additional drumfire of complaint that government was offering services the people didn't need, shouldn't have, or should provide for themselves. Communist governments, at least in the satellites, sometimes abandoned unproductive collectivized agriculture, and conservative governments in the West turned inefficient nationalized industries back to the private sector, or even cut back on welfare.

Nevertheless, the vast structure of bureaucratic power—and the services it provided—tended to survive all such attacks. East or West, it was an integral part of the structure of Northern prosperity, and one not likely to go away.

Capitalist and Communist thus had a basic pyramid of bureaucratic power in common. The significant political difference between them, however, lay in the degree to which the citizens were free of and could regulate the behavior of that power structure.

Western democratic governments came in several varieties. There were multiparty systems, common in Western Europe, in which coalitions of parties governed. There were also two-party versions, especially in English-speaking countries, in which two major parties competed for office.

Looked at another way, there were parliamentary and presidential systems. In the parliamentary pattern, modeled on the British House of Commons, executive and legislative power were merged, the prime minister and his cabinet representing the majority party—or coalition of parties—in the elected legislature. A presidential system, such as the varied versions to be found in the United States and France, put much more authority in the hands of a chief executive, who was elected separately and who could be of a different political party from the legislative branch.

All Western democracies, however, had two things in common: elected rulers and civil liberties. Periodic elections required political leadership to account to the people for its stewardship. Civil rights limited political repression and prescribed the basic freedom to complain about the way things were going. In combination, the freedom to speak one's mind and the requirement that politicians stand for periodic reelection gave the governed at least some control over their governments.

One-party states, especially those infused with a strong ideological component, put power in the hands of a single, usually autocratically run party. With the destruction of most of the fascist states in the Second World War, almost all the surviving one-party states of the North were communist—the Soviet Union and her East European allies.

In communist countries, dispute over public policy was confined to party members, especially to those in the upper echelons. Elections were held, but since the ballot contained only the names of party-approved candidates, there was little genuine choice and very little public check on the policies and politics of their rulers.

These politically authoritarian systems were strengthened by the lack of most of the civil liberties valued in the West. Freedom of the press, of speech, of the right to organize politically was seldom to be found east of the Iron Curtain. In Russia the brutal repressiveness of the Stalin years seemed to recede after his death in 1953. But dissidents were still routinely exiled to the provinces or incarcerated—sometimes in insane asylums, on the grounds that serious opposition to life in the workers' paradise must indicate serious mental disorder.

A survey of these varied strategies for progress in the global North follows.

American Epoch

The United States, between her victory in World War II and the middle of the 1980s, was the world's wealthiest and most powerful nation. Both of her chief defeated foes, West Germany and Japan, as well as the once-predominant imperial powers of Western Europe, Britain and France, accepted America's leadership in the postwar period. Much of the rest of the earth fed the hoppers of her industry with their raw materials, filled her treasuries with trade or investment profits, or accepted her largesse in return for political or military commitments of one sort or another.

A distinguished historian called it the American Epoch.[2] Europeans talked about the *Pax Americana*—the American Peace—and complained about American economic predominance and the "Cocacolazation" of their ancient cultures. American influence was certainly greater than it had ever been before.

American political history during the latter part of the twentieth century breaks down into decades. There were the tense Truman years immediately after

[2]Arthur S. Link, *American Epoch: A History of the United States since the 1890s* (New York: Alfred A. Knopf, 1955).

the war, and the conservative and prosperous Eisenhower 1950s. There were the colorful sixties, the turbulent, reforming, affluent Kennedy–Johnson years. There were the economically depressed, self-interested seventies, a time of less distinguished presidents. And there were the half-done eighties, the Reagan years, which tried to turn the country back to Eisenhower conservatism with a degree of success that startled American liberals.

The United States had no ruins to dig out of after World War II and only a few hundred thousand war dead to mourn—a measure of the fury of the war elsewhere. She had the most powerful army in the world, a two-ocean navy, and sole possession of the most devastating weapon ever devised, the atomic bomb.

America's industrial economy was by far the most productive in history, and her agricultural sector would soon learn that it could feed half the globe. With Europe and Japan temporarily out of the running, the whole world was open to American exports and overseas investments. Her democratic government was stable, even if Republicans did some chafing under the long Democratic control of the federal government by the late Franklin Roosevelt.

Roosevelt's successor, bustling, sharp-tongued Harry Truman (1945–1952), was to all appearances

American liberal hopes at the beginning of the 1960s were embodied in the "Camelot" image of President John Kennedy and his elegant wife, Jacqueline. Kennedy's short term in office, characterized as much by youthful style as by legislative substance, was ended by an assassin's bullet in 1963. (Library of Congress)

a very ordinary hack politician from Missouri, chosen as vice-president merely to balance the ticket, now suddenly confronted with some of the most critical decisions in American history. But Truman managed the early years of the Cold War with vigor. He pushed on with the New Deal program, stressing full employment, higher wages, government subsidized public housing, more social security, aid to education, even a new campaign for civil rights for black Americans. And when in 1948 he ran for a second term on this expanded New Deal platform, he astonished everyone by winning.

The international tensions of the Truman years, however, generated domestic divisions as well—most disturbingly the wave of anticommunist witch hunting dominated by the powerful personality of Senator Joseph McCarthy.

The Communist victory in China, the Korean War, the speed with which the Russians built an atomic bomb, and allegations that spies had sold United States atomic secrets to the Soviets all contributed to this burst of witch hunting and scapegoating in the early fifties. Senator McCarthy, generally condemned since as a demagogue seeking to advance his own career, seized upon the theory of an all-powerful "international Communist conspiracy" to explain a wide range of disturbing phenomena, from the New Deal to the Cold War.

McCarthy's wild charges ruined careers and smeared reputations, especially in the foreign service, with accusations of Communist sympathies or affiliation. United States courts convicted a handful of Russian agents, and two government employees, Julius and Ethel Rosenberg, were executed for giving atomic secrets to Russia. In general, however, McCarthy and his allies offered little evidence to support their charges. In the hysteria of the time, charges were enough.

McCarthy finally overreached himself by claiming that the U.S. Army was full of reds. Censured by the Senate, he faded from the political scene while the fires he had kindled expired in the calmer atmosphere of the Eisenhower years.

Dwight Eisenhower (1952–1960), the first Republican president since the New Deal, was a broad-faced Kansan who had become famous as the commanding general of the Allied armies in Europe in World War II. He knew very little about politics, preferred playing golf to reading position papers, and depended heavily on his cabinet, a body dominated by conservative big businessmen.

Nevertheless, as a self-styled progressive Republican, Eisenhower legitimized the New Deal by simply not moving to repeal it. He even made a few modest

contributions himself, expanding social security and committing the country to the Eisenhower highway program, which in subsequent years crisscrossed three million miles of America with superhighways. During Eisenhower's second term he reluctantly sent troops into Arkansas to enforce a crucial 1954 Supreme Court decision requiring racial integration of American schools. Here, and in the 1956 Montgomery, Alabama, bus boycott led by the young Reverend Martin Luther King, began what would become the most successful crusade of the decade of crusading that followed.

The 1960s combined the social excitement of the 1920s and the political commitment of the 1930s in the most tumultuous American decade of the century on the domestic scene. Two Democratic presidents presided: Kennedy as inspiration, Johnson as technician. But much of the demand for change welled up from below, particularly from the most rebellious younger generations in American history.

John Kennedy (1960–1963) was a handsome young Irish-American millionaire from Boston, the first Catholic president, and the embodiment of the youth and energy that America seemed to want in 1960. In fact, he accomplished little, at least in domestic affairs. He combined a tax cut and a little Keynesian fine tuning of the economy to produce a new boom after a late-Eisenhower recession. He committed the United States to a race with the Russians to put the first human being on the moon. But his more substantive reforms were stalled by a conservative Congress, and he had neither the patience nor the political know-how to push them through.

Then in the fall of 1963 Kennedy was shot by a neurotic young man named Oswald. The new president, Lyndon Johnson (1963–1968), had all the political skills Kennedy lacked, and he used the national grief over the assassination to propel a final flood of New Deal–style reforms through the Congress and into law.

Medical insurance for elderly Americans, aid to education, public housing, aid for rural poor whites in Appalachia, aid for depressed, often largely black inner cities, and a hundred lesser reforms were passed. So was the most sweeping civil-rights bill in United States history, an act that outlawed racial discrimination in all public places, in employment, and in other aspects of American life.

Domestic reform was Johnson's strong suit; his major contribution to American foreign policy was the disastrous involvement in Vietnam. As a reformer, however, Lyndon Johnson's administration was the real climax of the New Deal wave of social change begun thirty years before.

Much of the excitement of the American 1960s, however, was the work of the demonstrators and agitators, most of them youthful, who swarmed the streets of the nation. Young Americans demanded a freer, more human educational system, further relaxation of already relaxed sexual mores, freer use of drugs other than alcohol, and other youth-oriented changes. In addition, a host of ad hoc youth organizations launched campaigns against unequal treatment for black Americans, against the "pockets of poverty" still left in affluent America, and against the Vietnam War.

Martin Luther King spearheaded the civil-rights struggle for black Americans. He won a Nobel Peace Prize for his efforts, as well as a whole series of changes in law and practice, particularly in the South. Lyndon Johnson declared a War on Poverty, but his efforts to eradicate it fell short of success. And by 1968 two of the three candidates for the Democratic presidential nomination, including John Kennedy's younger brother Robert, were converted to the cause of peace in Vietnam—which, ironically, was finally achieved under the Republican, Richard Nixon, who was elected.

Over these two very different decades, it should be stressed, the United States flourished economically as never before in its—or anybody else's—history. The gross national product was valued at something over $200 billion in 1945; by 1970 it was pushing the trillion-dollar mark, a fivefold increase. The United States in 1970 had 6 percent of the world's population—and reputedly consumed well over half the world's production.

Things changed during the demoralized and depressed 1970s. The United States withdrawal from Vietnam, followed by the Communist victory there, shook American self-confidence badly. The Arab oil-price hikes of the seventies staggered the economies of all nations, including that of the United States. And the political debacle of Richard Nixon left the country reeling and adrift by the middle of the decade.

Republican President Nixon (1968–1974), former vice-president under Eisenhower and an established anti-communist politician, succeeded Johnson at the end of the sixties. Nixon's foreign-policy record was impressive, including the revival of American relations with China. But his overreaction to massive, sometimes violent political demonstrations led him to countenance a series of undercover schemes that violated the civil rights of the governed. In the end, he, his vice-president, and a number of his cabinet members and other key officials resigned under fire, many of them serving prison terms as well.

Of Presidents Gerald Ford (Republican) and

The conservative resurgence of the 1980s was personified in the United States by President Ronald Reagan. Here "the great communicator" makes a forceful point without losing the geniality that made him so successful a campaigner. (Pete Souza, The White House)

Jimmy Carter (Democrat), little need to be said except that both were honest. But the deepest recession of the postwar period continued during their presidencies, and foreign affairs did not go well. In 1980 a former actor and two-term governor of California named Ronald Reagan was elected president—the most conservative man to serve in the White House in fifty years.

Reagan tried to repeal large chunks of the liberal legislation of the preceding half century. His goals were to save money by cutting welfare and to cut taxes putting more money in people's pockets to stimulate national economic recovery. Unfortunately, he also launched the most expensive armament program in United States history, pyramiding the national debt to a point where it threatened to abort the recovery that came on with a rush in the middle of the eighties. Reagan's religious supporters, calling themselves the Moral Majority, preached vehemently against such manifestations of the social spirit of the sixties as sex without marriage and legal abortion, and to urge more religious emphasis in the schools.

Ronald Reagan was re-elected by a landslide in 1984. Some Democrats dismissed the victory as a personal one for the popular president. Conservative Republicans, however, claimed a major shift in America's political climate—their way. How this conservative resurgence would fare was a problem for the later 1980s and beyond. America was not, however, alone in this conservative turn, as we shall see in later sections.

The Soviet Achievement

The Soviet Union emerged as the second most powerful and productive nation in the world during the second half of the twentieth century. Politically, however, the Russia of the post-Stalin decades remained repressive, a huge one-party state whose sheer stability was perhaps her greatest political achievement.

Joseph Stalin had ended his life in a new wave of state terror, rapidly refilling the prisons and work camps after the heroic fervor of the Great Patriotic War. His passing left no one capable of filling his shoes. But two strong personalities did rise above the sea of faceless *apparatchiks* to guide the nation through the next three decades: Nikita Khrushchev (1956–1964) and Leonid Brezhnev (1964–1982).

Both Khrushchev and Brezhnev were older men, party men, products of the Stalinist pyramid of power established as early as the 1920s. Both shared final authority with influential colleagues during their rule, and both depended on the machinery of the state and the Communist party. Both, finally, had to face the same recurring problems with the United States and the Eastern European satellites, agriculture, consumer goods, and Soviet dissidents.

But there were differences between both the men and their regimes. And the Soviet Union, for all its seeming monolithic sameness, did have a domestic history in the 1950s, 1960s, and 1970s.

Nikita Khrushchev's major political achievement was destalinization, the famous Russian Thaw of the middle 1950s. Soon after Stalin's death in 1953, the current head of the secret police was unceremoniously executed. Soon most of the vast secret-police-operated forced-labor camps, the notorious Gulag, were closing down.

In 1956 Khrushchev, by then recognized as the winner of the almost bloodless struggle for power that followed Stalin's passing, read a famous "secret speech" to the Communist leadership. In it he denounced Stalin's personality cult and blamed the purges, the camps, the pounding Russia had taken early in World War II, and other misfortunes on the late Great Leader.

The Thaw did not last long. A few books, such as Alexander Solzhenytsin's labor-camp novel *One Day in the Life of Ivan Denisovitch*, ripped the lid off the brutality of earlier years. Then the government clamped on the censorship again, and dissidents were soon being harassed and imprisoned once more. But their numbers were far fewer now, and the great fear engendered during Stalin's Iron Age would not recur.

Other things did not go as well for Khrushchev. His campaign to deal with Russia's perennially flagging agricultural production by opening vast tracts of virgin Siberian lands to the plow did not solve the problem. The spirit of the Thaw spread to the satellites and triggered a revolt in Hungary in 1956. Khrushchev had to send in the tanks, thereby undermining his—and Russia's—new liberal image. He built up Russia's nuclear-missile armory from a small beginning, but he was still so far behind the United States that he had to back down to Kennedy over the Cuban-missile crisis of 1962. In 1964, reeling from the split with China, the retreat before American power, and another bad harvest, Khrushchev was quietly and painlessly forced to retire by his colleagues in the Kremlin.

He was replaced by what looked like a presiding duo, Alexei Kosygin as premier and Leonid Brezhnev as secretary of the Russian Communist party. But the heavy-set, heavy-browed, stolid Brezhnev was clearly the senior man, and the pallid, bespectacled Kosygin, who had always been a highly skilled technocrat, settled into the background and continued that role.

Brezhnev handled problems with a methodical pragmatism. He dealt with a bad harvest by buying American grain, with a lack of high tech by contracting with French and Italian companies to build him a plant in Russia. He had no use for dissenters, sent some to labor camps, some to jail, some into exile, where they could regale their hosts with the evils of the Soviet system to their hearts' content.

Brezhnev did, however, build up the nation's nuclear arsenal till it rivaled America's. He expanded the conventional armed forces in Europe and on the Chinese frontier in the East. He met rebelliousness in Czechoslovakia in 1968, reacting as Khrushchev had in Hungary—by sending in troops. He even indulged in an uncharacteristic foreign adventure or two, including Russia's long, drawn-out intervention in Afghanistan.

Overall, however, Brezhnev kept things on an even keel. He established détente with American president Nixon that lasted through most of the 1970s. His failing health in the early 1980s and eventual demise in 1982 seemed to end an era of predictability and stability in Russo-American relations that might well be missed.

Two old men from the Khrushchev-Brezhnev generation succeeded them briefly in the early 1980s. The accession of the relatively young, vigorous, and thoroughly informed Mikhail Gorbachev in 1985, however, seemed like a real turning point in Russian history. At age 54, Gorbachev could look forward to many years in which to guide the development of his country.

There was, however, more to Russian history from the 1950s through the 1970s than Communist party

Mikhail Gorbachev, who took the helm in Moscow in 1985, reflected a new, more sophisticated style of Soviet leadership. Even Britain's arch-conservative Margaret Thatcher thought she could "do business" with Gorbachev. (Reuters/Bettmann Newsphotos)

continued to rise throughout the succeeding decades, taking a leading part in the first probes of the universe beyond our planet.

Japan and Germany: The Miracle Years

Japan emerged in the postwar decades as the most productive nation in the world after the United States and the Soviet Union. There were those who even suggested that by the turn of the century she would be a lot closer to Number One than Number Three.

Democratic political institutions established during the American occupation guided Japan's destinies effectively. The conservative Liberal Democratic party won most elections, despite vigorous opposition led by the Socialist party. Neither violent student demonstrations in the 1960s nor some nasty Liberal Democratic political scandals in the 1970s put any serious strain on the system.

Economically, Japan boomed. The economic miracle of her recovery from the war was only the beginning. The Japanese were early leaders in a system of government guidance of business firms into profitable export markets. This system—sometimes wryly called Japan, Incorporated—plus a hardworking and loyal work force, a frugal population willing to save and reinvest, and the sheer energy and drive of the people made the island nation a tough competitor for the older exporting nations.

In the 1980s millions of automobiles clogged Japan's own roads, virtually everyone had a television set, and her bullet trains were a world's wonder. Tokyo was larger than New York and had a worse smog problem than Los Angeles.

Japan had her problems. These included the need to import almost all her natural resources, an extremely serious pollution problem, and repeated requests from her trading partners for "voluntary" limits on Japanese exports—a serious difficulty for a country that prospered by trade. But Japan's remarkable postwar success augured well for an equally thriving future.

West Germany, the other major loser in World War II, was also soon back among the leaders. She became the most successful economic performer among Western European nations, and a notably successful democracy as well.

Forged from the Western zones of occupation, the Federal Republic of Germany had most of the population and resources of the prewar Reich. With a new capital at Bonn, she soon revived the democratic spirit of Weimar without its deep divisions and weaknesses. She was fortunate too in her leading statesmen in the early decades. The conservative Christian Democratic chancellor Konrad Adenauer, former

politics. There was an intriguing range of economic and technological problems—and impressive Soviet achievements in both areas.

Agriculture remained the nation's largest economic bottleneck, requiring the labors of up to half of Russia's work force (compared with 5 to 10 percent in the West). Partly because of peasant inefficiency and recalcitrance in the face of compulsory collectivization, partly because of several bad harvests, inadequate grain supplies required the Soviets to buy large amounts of grain overseas in the middle 1970s and again around 1980. Most Russians, however, ate solid meals and dressed quite decently, if not in Western European style.

As in the Stalinist years, the Russia of Khrushchev and Brezhnev did best on big government-run projects. The Soviet Union forged ahead in heavy industry, replacing the United States as the world's leading producer of steel, coal, and oil. Most impressively, the Soviet Union pioneered in space exploration. A Russian was the first into space in an orbiting earth satellite in 1961. And if the United States won the race to the moon, Soviet rockets, satellites, and spaceships

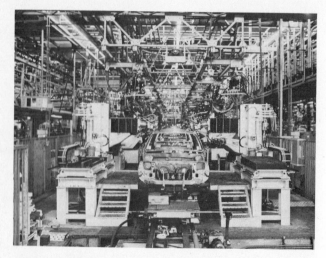

Japan's emergence as one of the most productive industrial nations in the world is clearly illustrated in this robot-run Japanese factory. "Japan, Incorporated" was at the cutting edge of technological development in many fields in the 1980s. (© Michal Heron 1982)

anti-Nazi mayor of Cologne, guided her through her first fifteen years with skill and dignity. The first of several prominent Social Democratic chancellors, Willy Brandt, who made his reputation as mayor of West Berlin, eased tensions with the Soviet bloc and kept the door open for future reunification with East Germany.

The Federal Republic's economic miracle startled the world even before Japan's. It was built on billions of dollars of Marshall Plan aid, millions of German refugees from Eastern Europe and "guest workers" from other countries, and on the proverbial hard work and technical skills of the German people as a whole. The architect of the achievement was Adenauer's free-enterprise economic minister Ludwig Erhard, but there was a good deal of judicious government support for the upwardly mobile economy too.

West Germany, like Japan, had a serious problem in her lack of oil, and as a result her economy was shaken by the global recession of the 1970s and early 1980s. Long-range difficulties such as the dream of reunification with East Germany might loom in her future. Overall, however, the Federal Republic of Germany, like Japan, was one of the pillars of the Western world in the mid 1980s.

The New Europe

Both Britain and France had some wrenching readjustments to make after the war. The loss of the two largest intercontinental empires, the loss of primacy in international affairs to the United States and the Soviet Union, and the dawning realization that their defeated foes, Germany and Japan, were rapidly

outdistancing them economically were not easy blows to absorb over the postwar decades. Both nations, however, played major roles in the formation of a new Europe during the third quarter of the twentieth century.

Britain, under Labour leader Clement Attlee, led postwar Western Europe into the comprehensive system of social services known as the welfare state. Expanded unemployment insurance, old-age pensions, public-housing estates, raw new middle-class universities, and above all the much-debated British public health service provided cradle-to-grave security for Britons. Soon all Western European nations had similar systems of social welfare for their citizens.

Another fundamental change in postwar Western Europe was a much larger role for government in the direction of a national economy—a trend in which France took an early lead. This system involved nationalization of leading banks, insurance companies, utilities, and mines on the one hand, and a deliberate policy of channeling investment into strong private industries in order to direct economic development on the other. Other European nations used other methods, but everywhere the new "welfare capitalism" included government participation in economic development on a scale unprecedented in capitalist countries.

The world recession of the 1970s and early 1980s hurt the Western European countries also. Interestingly enough, it was Great Britain, which had led Europe into the welfare state thirty years before, that now set a new trend—toward conservative retrenchment.

Tory leader Margaret Thatcher, first elected prime minister in 1979, faced her very substantial industrial problems with a strongly conservative program. She cut back on services, turned some nationalized industries back to the private sector, and accepted massive unemployment in order to trim Britain's labor bill and make her internationally competitive again. How successful Thatcher's approach would be remained uncertain in the middle 1980s. But by that time the Iron Lady was not alone in her conservative crusade. The United States, West Germany, Canada, and other nations had joined in the rightward drift of the eighties. Even France's new Socialist president, François Mitterand, after a renewed burst of nationalization and expanded services, had to turn to a Thatcher-style austerity in the middle of the decade.

Even in depressed times, however, life remained materially far better for Western Europeans than for most of the world's peoples.

Politically, all Eastern European states remained one-party authoritarian regimes, ruled by their Communist parties. Any talk of multiparty democracy on the Western European model—as in Hungary in the 1950s and Czechoslovakia in the 1960s—led to rapid Soviet military intervention. The growth of the Polish labor union, Solidarity, into a potential rival of Poland's Communist-party apparatus led to a rigorous crackdown by the Polish military. A more liberal political order, in short, did not look likely soon.

Economically, however, the Eastern European countries began to grow more prosperous in the 1960s. The heavy sacrifices demanded of their peoples to help Russia recover from the war and then to begin their own industrialization, at last began to pay off some two decades after World War II.

Eastern Europe did not reach the levels of productivity or per-capita income achieved in Western Europe. But industrial productivity did rise, and consumer goods did appear in more profusion, especially in the cities. Cafés were jammed, and expensive blue jeans and even motorbikes and cars became part of the urban scene in the East as in the West. Relative prosperity, and the demand for more of it, became central features of society in this corner of the global North too.

Peoples of Plenty

Scattered around the world, mostly in the global North, there were other nations, smaller in size or population, whose inhabitants were also among the twentieth-century's peoples of plenty. Most of these affluent countries were European, or were nations dominated by European-descended populations.

Some of these smaller rich nations had higher per capita incomes than the United States. Switzerland, a world banking center, and Sweden, one of Europe's most highly developed welfare states, had almost literally no poor people at all. Sweden in particular was also known for its extensive foreign aid to less developed peoples.

In North America, Canada had been a major industrial power for much of the century. The huge northern nation depended heavily on trade, especially on massive agricultural exports to China and Russia. She also traded extensively with, and imported capital from, her even wealthier neighbor to the south, the United States.

Australia, the other continental nation of the older Commonwealth, encouraged immigration and foreign investment, especially from the United States and Britain, developed her mineral resources, and inaugurated major water projects to irrigate her arid Outback. Australia also took a leading part in the economic life of East and Southeast Asia.

Israel received large amounts of foreign aid from the United States and West Germany. She also benefited from the latest Western technology and from a highly skilled and motivated population, including many immigrants from Europe and America. She thus became far and away the most developed nation in the Middle East, featuring an economic growth rate of over 10 percent annually throughout her early decades.

Israelis might complain about a three-digit inflation rate, Britons about years of crippling unemployment, Americans about a crushing national debt, but few citizens of these developed industrial states would have traded places with the peoples of the global South.

SUMMARY

The material achievements of what is sometimes called the global North—the developed nations of Europe, North America, Japan, and other areas—were truly spectacular during the later decades of the twentieth century. High technology was the secret, a continuation of the Industrial Revolution that produced a range of marvels from frozen foods and television to space science and nuclear weapons. Free enterprise—with some government fine-tuning—produced more goods and services for Western peoples than any people had ever enjoyed. State socialism in communist countries was less spectacularly successful, but it still fed and clothed the citizenry better than they had ever been before.

Social inequalities remained on both sides of the Iron Curtain, but government safety nets, in the form of social welfare programs, saw to it that most people were adequately provided for. During the 1960s and 1970s, demands for more equal treatment were heard from both young people and women, while black Americans in particular fought for and won constitutional rights and greater opportunities. Even the developed countries faced a variety of problems, from alcoholism and automobile accidents to dwindling resources and pollution, that made it clear that paradise was not yet just around the corner.

Progress was the goal of the governments and peoples of the global North on both sides of the Iron Curtain. Western countries favored democratic governments, communist ones regimes that still included many features of the totalitarian governments of the 1930s. Both, however, had large bureaucracies that performed many services for the governed—and took a commensurate cut of the gross national product.

The United States was the predominant power in the world of the later twentieth century, enjoying prosperity much of the time and consuming a substantial portion of the produce of the world at large. Political stability prevailed, whether under liberal administrations such as those of Truman, Kennedy, and Johnson, or under conservative regimes such as those of Eisenhower, Nixon, and Reagan.

In Russia, the world's second most productive industrial nation, much less of the gross national product reached the consuming public than in the United States. Solid party men like Khrushchev and Brezh-

nev dominated the nation politically. Japan was number three in productivity during these decades and successfully challenged even the United States in high-tech development.

In Europe, Germany loomed as the richest nation, carrying on in its prewar tradition of industrial skill. Britain and France pioneered such advances as the welfare state and European economic integration. The nations of East Europe began to grow economically in the 1960s and increasingly sought closer economic ties with their more advanced neighbors in the West. Other highly developed nations, not all of them in the geographical north, included Canada, Australia, and Israel.

SUGGESTED READING

BEER, S. H.   *British Politics in the Collectivist Age.* New York: Knopf, 1965. British institutions in the age of the welfare state. For an illuminating comparison of the oldest and youngest industrial powers, see R. P. Dore, *British Factory, Japanese Factory* (Berkeley: University of California Press, 1973).

BIALER, S.   *Stalin's Successors: Leadership, Stability, and Change in the Soviet Union.* New York: Cambridge University Press, 1980. Important, especially on the Brezhnev years. On Khrushchev, see a perceptive Russian analysis by R. A. Medvedev and J. A. Medvedev, *Khrushchev: The Years in Power* (New York: Columbia University Press, 1976). On voices of dissent in the still strongly authoritarian Soviet state, see A. Rothberg, *The Heirs of Stalin: Dissidence and the Soviet Regime, 1953–1970* (Ithaca: Cornell University Press, 1972).

BROOKS, J.   *The Great Leap: The Last Twenty-five Years in America.* New York: Harper & Row, Pub., 1966. Economic advances in the United States in the postwar decades. On America's postwar affluence, see D. Potter, *People of Plenty: Economic Abundance and the American Character* (Chicago: University of Chicago Press, 1954), and J. K. Galbraith, *The Affluent Society* (Boston: Houghton Mifflin, 1960).

CARRÉ, J. J., et al.   *French Economic Growth.* Stanford: Stanford University Press, 1976. Government central planning in a developed capitalist state. For France's greatest surge of unrest since World War II, see E. B. Brown, *Protest in Paris: Anatomy of a Revolt* (Morristown, N.J.: General Learning Press, 1974) on the archetypal 1968 youth rebellion.

CHAFE, W. H.   *The American Woman: Her Changing Social, Economic, and Political Roles, 1920–1970.* New York: Oxford University Press, 1974. Good survey of the period between the suffrage movement at the beginning of the century and the renewed militance of the 1970s. On the latter, see J. Freeman, *The Politics of Women's Liberation* (New York: Longman's, 1975).

CHILDS, M.   *Sweden: The Middle Way.* New Haven: Yale University Press, 1961. Democratic welfare-state socialism in Western Europe.

DAHRENDORF, R.   *Society and Democracy in Germany.* Garden City, N.Y.: Doubleday, 1969. West German society after democracy finally took hold. See also M. Dönhoff, *Foe into Friend: The Makers of the New Germany from Konrad Adenauer to Helmut Schmidt* (London: Weidenfeld and Nicolson, 1982), tracing the range of democratic leadership, from conservative to socialist, in postwar Germany. On Germany's postwar "economic miracle," see H. C. Wallich, *Mainsprings of the German Revival* (New Haven: Yale University Press, 1955).

FEJTO, F.   *A History of the People's Democracies: Eastern Europe Since Stalin,* trans. D. Weissbort. New York: Praeger, 1971. The nations of the Soviet sphere of influence in all their diversity.

HARRINGTON, M.   *The Other America.* Baltimore: Penguin, 1981. The rediscovery of poverty in the richest country in the world; a signpost toward the social legislation of the Kennedy-Johnson years. On the problems of postwar affluence in America, see W. H. Whyte, *The Organization Man* (New York: Simon & Schuster, 1956). On women trapped in the suburbs and their own self-image, see B. Friedan, *The Feminine Mystique* (New York: Norton, 1963).

HEIDENHEIMER, A. J., H. HEDO, and C. T. ADAMS.   *Comparative Public Polich: The Politics of Social Choice in Europe and America.* New York: St. Martin's Press, 1975. Draws distinctions between the social policies of these two major centers of democratic capitalist society.

IKE, N.   *Japanese Politics: Patron-Client Democracy.* New York: Knopf, 1972. Postwar political structure. See also N. Thayer, *How the Conservatives Rule Japan* (Princeton: Princeton University Press, 1969), on the long conservative tenure of power. On the impact of the postwar American occupation of Japan, see K. Kawai, *Japan's American Interlude* (Chicago: University of Chicago Press, 1960), and H. Passin, *The Legacy of the Occupation—Japan* (New York: Columbia University Press, 1968).

KITZINGER, U. *The Politics and Economics of European Integration.* New York: Praeger, 1963. Subtle explanation of problems and opportunities for greater continental integration in the postwar world. See also, L. N. Lindberg and S. A. Scheingold, *Europe's Would-Be Polity* (Englewood Cliffs, N.J.: Prentice-Hall, 1970) and C. Friedrich, *Europe—an Emergent Nation?* (New York: Harper & Row, Pub., 1969).

LAPIDUS, G. W. *Women, Work, and Family in the Soviet Union.* New York: M. E. Sharpe, 1982. Contrasts significant female contribution in the workplace with continuing inequality elsewhere in society. For a comparative study, see A. Heitlinger, *Women and State Socialism: Sex Inequality in the Soviet Union and Czechoslovakia* (London: Macmillan, 1979).

LAQUEUR, W. *Europe since Hitler.* London: Penguin, 1982. Survey by a leading European historian. See also his *A Continent Astray: Europe, 1970–1978* (New York: Oxford University Press, 1979). On Europe's postwar resurgence, see R. Mayne, *The Recovery of Europe, 1945–1973* (Garden City, N.Y.: Anchor Press, 1973).

LEWIS, A. *Portrait of a Decade: The Second American Revolution.* New York: Random House, 1964. Narrative of the American civil rights movement, by a reporter who covered it. See also the life of the movement's charismatic leader in D. Lewis, *King: A Critical Biography* (New York: Praeger, 1970). On other aspects of the tumultuous 1960s in America, see M. Dickstein's counter-culturally oriented *Gates of Eden: American Culture in the Sixties* (New York: Basic Books, 1977), and L. M. Baskir and W. A. Straves, *Change and Circumstance: The Draft, the War, and the Vietnam Generation* (New York: Knopf, 1978), on the antiwar movement.

MOORE, B., JR. *Soviet Politics: The Dilemma of Power.* New York: Sharpe, 1977. Theory and practice of government in the world's oldest communist state. For an observant and sympathetic journalist's view of life in the Soviet Union, see M. Binyon, *Life in Russia* (New York: Pantheon, 1983).

MOWAT, R. C. *Creating the European Community.* New York: Barnes & Noble, 1973. The forging of Europe's unexampled economic institutions in the years after World War II. See also M. M. Postan, *An Economic History of Western Europe, 1945–1964* (London: Methuen, 1967), and Kitzinger, above.

OPHULS, W. *Ecology and the Politics of Scarcity.* San Franciso: Freeman, 1979. Ecological concern in the United States, a nation more concerned than most about saving the environment.

PATRICK, H., and H. ROSOVSKY, eds. *Asia's New Giant: How the Japanese Economy Works.* Washington: Brookings Institution, 1976. Articles on Japan's economic challenge to the older developed nations. See also H. Patrick and L. Meisner, eds., *Japanese Industrialization and Its Social Consequences* (Berkeley: University of California Press, 1976).

REISCHAUER, E. O. *The Japanese.* Cambridge, Mass.: Belknap Press, 1977. By the leading authority and former United States ambassador to Japan. For the new urban culture and its contrast with traditional Japanese life, see R. P. Dore, *City Life in Japan* (Berkeley: University of California Press, 1958).

SCHLESINGER, A. M., JR. *A Thousand Days.* Boston: Houghton Mifflin, 1965. The Kennedy years in the United States, by a historian who also served in the government. On the social legislation of the Kennedy-Johnson years, see G. Steiner, *State of Welfare* (Washington: Brookings Institution, 1971) and P. Marris and M. Rein, *Dilemmas of Social Reform* (Chicago: University of Chicago Press, 1982).

SULLEROT, E. *Women, Society, and Change.* New York: McGraw-Hill, 1971. Women in Western Europe after World War II. For comparisons between the British and American women's movements, see O. Banks, *Faces of Feminism* (New York: St. Martin's Press, 1982). For comparisons across the Iron Curtain, see H. G. Shaffer, *Women in the Two Germanies* (New York: Pergamon Press, 1981).

Chapter · 24

THE GLOBAL VILLAGE IN FERMENT

THE GLOBAL SOUTH

Village People

A Third World village is a cock crowing while it is still dark outside, or perhaps a *muezzin* calling to predawn prayers. It is close-set houses made of wattle and daub, clay brick, roughly whitewashed plaster over stone, roofs of thatch, palm leaves, tile, or tin. It is hard-packed earthen paths and streets, bare feet, sandals, a bike or two. It is water from a village well, vegetables from the back garden, chickens underfoot, goats, sheep, perhaps a sacred cow wandering at will.

It is dirt under your fingernails, in the cracks of your skin, sunshine, insects, and a sore back by noon. It is women gossiping as they slap wet clothes against the rocks in a stream and lay them out on the grass to dry. It is kids in school uniforms hopping off the school bus at the crossroads, books swinging in straps or satchels, and racing into town. It is dried-up old people without teeth, kids with untreated umbilical hernias, overworked young women ready to drop at the end of the day, young men away in the city, working.

It is dust, heat, the noise of someone banging on metal, a single open-fronted shop, perhaps with a refrigerator in back, flies crawling over the corn flakes in an open jar. It is domestic squabbles over cooking oil when the government lets the price go up, and bad news on the radio again, with anxious faces listening.

Village people are three quarters of the human race, three out of the four billions of us who swarm over this planet today. They live mostly in Asia, Africa, and Latin America—the three continents of the global South, the world south of the north temperate zone. They are for the most part non-Western peoples, dwellers in hot lands who wear clothing unlike that worn by Americans, Europeans, or the average Japanese.

There are important exceptions: underdeveloped China is not in the geographic south, fully developed Australia is. But by and large, the global South is where village people live.

They may live in an ancient civilization like that of India or China, temporarily relegated to the unfamiliar category of "backward" or "underdeveloped" by the West's sudden leap ahead in industrial technology a mere two centuries ago.

They may be citizens of the same nation, such as Ghana or Tanzania, building from scratch, only decades old, even its name a recent acquisition, all its uncertain history still ahead.

They may be residents of a middle-level developing country such as Venezuela or Mexico, with resources and some industry to give them the long-run hope of an industrialized future, with regular elections and a land-reform program.

Plenty of books will tell you about their problems: overpopulation, disease, malnutrition, unemployment, illiteracy, one-crop economies, political authoritarianism or instability or both, swollen cities, dying traditional village cultures. It is harder to get a handle on the vitality of many Third World countries. You get a sense of that, perhaps, from watching a West African market woman sail regally through the market-day tumult with a fantastic array of things balanced on the tray on her brightly kerchiefed head. Or from the peanuts you buy in India—wrapped in a page covered with quadratic equations, torn from a child's exercise book.

The pages that follow will deal mostly with the many problems and the sometimes erratic course of Third World history over the two or three decades since most of these countries gained their independence. But it would be well to remember the human lives that compose those histories, the human vitality that in the long run is surely the best hope for all the village peoples of the globe.

Back to Basics

Marshall McLuhan, the media expert, applied the term *global village* to the peoples of the world, linked by television and other media of communication into a single worldwide community. The term seems equally appropriate, however, for the village peoples of the globe, who despite all cultural differences are united by even more compelling hopes and problems.

The most all-encompassing of these problems is poverty. The poverty of the have-not nations is not simply a lack of cars, television sets, or flush toilets. Poverty in the Third World means shantytowns full of the unemployed—and no work in the villages either. It means malaria, cholera, typhoid, sleeping sickness, leprosy, hookworm—all the plagues of the Old Testament still killing children and crippling their elders today. It means malnutrition even in a decent year. If the crop is bad or nonexistent in arid India or the Sahel countries along the southern fringe of the Sahara, it means swollen bellies, matchstick arms, death under the blowing dust.

Dealing with such fundamental problems requires meeting such basic needs as enough food, drinkable water, access to some sort of clinic. It means selling birth control to people for whom children are a duty, a source of free labor, and the only available old-age insurance. After these needs, the newer nations must find funds for education, roads, capital investment in industrial or agricultural projects that might give their people hope for a better way of life somewhere far down the road.

The basic economic problems of the global South are those we have seen evolving for over a century, first in Latin America and then in the colonial world during the period of the New Imperialism. They are problems rooted in the basic inequality of North and South, and in the global division of labor—and wealth—this inequality has fostered.

The traditional way of acquiring money to pay for development was through the export of what Third World countries had to sell: raw materials or agricultural products. The new nations thus joined Latin America as commodity exporters, shipping overseas vast quantities of coffee, tea, sugar, bananas, copra, palm oil, wheat, beef, cotton, rubber, oil, copper, iron, uranium, bauxite.

When the prices for these products of the southern earth were high. the South did passably well—and invested commensurately in new projects. When the prices went down in the world markets, the new countries suffered commensurately. Commodity prices, furthermore, were frequently determined not by Third World producers, but by speculators in First World countries or by what Second World governments were willing to pay. Desperate for foreign exchange, the countries of the global South often cut back even on subsistence agriculture in order to put more land into export crops—and hence had to import food. The result was a very serious set of export-related problems.

A second major category of difficulty was the sort of dependency syndrome that had afflicted Latin America for so long. Third World countries in general depended on other nations for both manufactured goods and energy—meaning mostly oil. Again, a crucial factor in the economic development of the global South was beyond their control, in the hands of oil sheiks and European or American or Japanese manufacturers.

A third fundamental problem for developing nations followed directly from those of commodity exports and dependency. This was the huge debt that many countries in the South incurred, particularly over the last two decades, because the other way to capitalize development projects was to borrow the money. This many Third World countries did, negotiating loans from major European or North American banks and from such international agencies as the World Bank and the International Monetary Fund. When these loans began to come due, the countries of the South found commodity prices still low, the cost of dependency for oil and essential manufactured goods still high. Many of them could not pay the loans or even make interest payments on them—unless they borrowed more money.

In the middle 1980s, the downward slide at least seemed to be slowing. Banks with large outstanding loans to Third World countries preferred to extend these loans—at increased interest, of course—rather than absorb the huge losses of a default. Energy prices settled somewhat as a global petroleum glut developed. But the best the South could expect from such modest improvements was an equally modest easing of the pressure. The road to renewed economic growth seemed long indeed.

The Challenge of the New, the Pull of an Older Life

The rapid pace of social change in the present century has given all cultures future shock, the jolting confrontation with the unfamiliar and the new. In the Third World, however, the differences between the traditional and the modern, between the way things were done in Dad's day and the way Junior wants to do them, could be infinitely greater than they were in the developed world. Relations between rich and poor, between young and old, between men and women were all affected. So were the special Third World problems of relations between foreigner and native, between the Westernized and the unreconstructed in their own populations.

Economic differences and dependencies involving the large landholders or wealthy merchants and their less affluent fellow citizens of course existed in the non-European world long before the Europeans came. Imperial exploitation sometimes enhanced these differences by making the large landowners or merchant princes even richer. But political liberation in most cases did nothing to bridge the gap between the landed magnate and the field hand, the export merchant and the stevedore.

Indeed, independence often added a new elite: the political leaders and party chiefs who had freed their country and felt that, as no less a democrat than Andrew Jackson would have it, "to the victors belong the spoils." There were mitigating factors. In countries where social revolutionaries were in power, as in China and North Vietnam, ideological constraints limited the wealth of the new rulers. In African countries, the new big men normally felt a traditional responsibility to share their wealth with their large extended families in the villages. Nevertheless, many Third World politicians became some of the world's gaudiest grafters, wallowing in flashy suits and big imported cars while their countries sank deeper into poverty.

The conflict of generations was also exacerbated in the slowly modernizing countries of the Third World. A first priority for many new nations was Westernized education that would teach the young the skills they would need to transform their countries in years to come. An unhappy by-product of such educations, however, was to turn young people with education thoroughly against the old life. Preferring the modern material and cultural life to which they felt entitled as their country's new elite, they sometimes turned their backs on their elders and their villages entirely. Compelled to return and do government work in the backwoods, they longed for the city and a return to "civilization."

Women also grew discontented, perhaps for more convincing reasons, in the decades after independence. Traditional societies everywhere had regulated the lives of women even more rigorously than European or American societies had. Women's work—like men's—was clearly defined. In some cultures, as in the Islamic world or Hindu India, women were cut off from male society and from public life generally. In the developing world, furthermore, women were often "the poorest of the poor,"[1] traditionally exploited economically by fathers and husbands, often left to feed the family when their men went off to the city to work.

None of these patterns would give ground easily. Some of the new efforts at economic development even made women's lives harder. Aid for African development, for example, frequently went to traditionally male labor. Education, when it was offered in the villages, was normally taken advantage of by men rather than by women.

To these social problems must be added a whole complex of difficulties revolving around the continued economic, technological, and cultural dependency on the nations of the developed North. Foreign technical experts had to stay on in former colonies to keep what Western technology there was running, and to build more. But they were understandably resented. Westernized elites among the indigenous population also created problems—indeed embodied them in their own persons. A child of the old traditional order, the Westernized non-Westerner was a sometimes tragic figure, torn between the tastes and values of the new world he wanted his country to join and the deep roots of his people in an older life.

The physical image of the contrast between old and new in the global South in the later twentieth century was the Third World city—and its surrounding shantytown.

Urban migration, the key to the modernization process in Europe and America in the nineteenth century, reached crisis proportions in Asia, Africa, and Latin America in the later twentieth. Driven by the lack of land and jobs in the rural areas, drawn by dreams of the high life or by a realistic awareness that education, health care, and job opportunities were concentrated in the city, peasants poured into Third World cities in the millions every year.

[1]Paul Harrison, *Inside the Third World: The Anatomy of Poverty* (New York: Penguin Books, 1979), pp. 438–439.

Caracas, Venezuela, capital of one of the most developed of the Third World countries. The common pattern of urban growth is clear: a shanty town in the foreground, with the high-rise towers of a modern city against the mountains beyond. (Owen Franken/Stock, Boston)

In the downtown city centers, foreign business outlets and domestically owned emporiums glistened with modernity. But the new immigrant from the country would never find his niche in this glittering world of the city center. His world would be the shantytown.

The majority of those who migrated to the city got no jobs, and the few who did worked as manual laborers, street hawkers, or something less respectable. Still whole families of them came, finding a square of littered earth to call their own in shantytown, and hanging on, hoping that their streetwise, half-educated children would at least find a toehold in the modern world.

THE POLITICS OF DEVELOPMENT

Party Men, Military Men, and Rebels in the Streets

The new nations of Africa and Asia, like the older Third World countries of Latin America, tended to alternate between authoritarian regimes and revolutionary upheaval. The authoritarian governments were normally either one-party systems or rule by military strong men.

A one-party regime would often emerge soon after independence, built on the loyalty of the people to the party that had won the colony its independence. Frequently, however, this party of national liberation would, with the passage of time, no longer deserve the people's support. Failure of some grand schemes for development was often the cause of this loss of popular support, but flagrant corruption and high living—considered unsuitable in a tribune of the people—was an even stronger source of disillusionment.

At this point, a military cabal would usually make use of the other major institution that could command disciplined support—the army—to overthrow the party in power. Such military juntas might, or might not, prove more honest, but they generally lacked the skills needed to run a civilian government, let alone the economic and technical knowledge necessary for nation building. Thus the country was often no more likely to progress under the military than under one-party rule.

The one-party states with the most capacity for staying in power were those ruled by socialist or communist parties. Such regimes also had their liabilities. They sometimes turned to ideologically justified but impractical policies, subsidizing benefits for their people that the country was not yet rich enough to afford. Such countries also frequently had to face the hostility of powerful capitalist nations like the United States.

A small number of democratic governments

emerged in the Third World. A more common alternative to authoritarianism, however, was revolution; coups and rebellions, guerrilla wars in the back country and terrorism in the cities were widespread across the underdeveloped world. The two great Cold War adversaries also frequently provided moral or material support for the contestants—the United States most commonly for military regimes or the rare democracy, the Soviet Union for one-party governments or guerrilla movements. This outside involvement further complicated Third World politics.

The world grew used to media reports of corruption, military dictatorship, single-party authoritarianism, guerrilla attacks, and "death-squad" repression in the global South. In mitigation, it should be pointed out that these really are very new nations, most of them dating only from the period since World War II. Poverty also might account for many of the difficulties, a poverty rooted in a global economy largely beyond the control of Third World nations.

Underlying all these political gropings for direction, there did seem to be a fundamental concern: a search for a viable strategy of economic development, for the modernization of these premodern peoples. Politics throughout the global South was thus fundamentally the politics of development. It is this thread which will unite most of the examples cited below.

The Thoughts of Chairman Mao

China's domestic history after the end of her long civil war in 1949 was determined by the Communist party leaders who won that war. For the first quarter century of that period, this meant rule by the leader of the Chinese Revolution, Mao Tse-tung, or in his later years by the group of revolutionary ideologues who gathered around his iron-willed wife, Chiang Ch'ing. Throughout the years from mid-century to the middle 1970s, Mao's round, smiling face and receding black hairline, Mao's "thoughts" in the famous little red book, and Mao's revolutionary legend dominated Chinese life even more than Stalin's personality cult had towered over Russia in his heyday. Mao's policies and those of his associates, however, seemed to follow a rather more spontaneous course than Stalin's had, with sometimes disastrous results.

The Chinese Communist party and a wide variety of other mass organizations—from the All-China Federation of Trade Unions to the Young Communist League and the All-China Federation of Democratic Women—gave the Communist leadership an unparalleled capacity to mobilize China's hundreds of millions for mass action. Harsher measures were also used to control the nation. Ideological dissenters were given

peasant labor that would proletarianize their thinking. Hundreds of thousands, as Mao himself admitted, were "liquidated" in the early years, and more hundreds of thousands, as his successors charged, died during the Cultural Revolution later on. Most of the time, however, a combination of persuasion and party control was adequate to move the world's largest nation along the paths laid out for it by its new rulers.

Those paths could take some colorful turns as they followed the sometimes erratic thoughts of Chairman Mao and the more modest insights of those who followed him. Early land reforms were soon followed by loose collectivization of agriculture on large peasant-owned farms. Nationalization of heavy industry and government Five-Year Plans followed the familiar Russian model. But in the later 1950s Mao announced a Great Leap Forward involving tightly organized communal farms and small-scale backyard industry on the local level. Peasant discontent with the loss of their private plots and with the compulsory group living, plus a series of bad harvests, led to a pulling back from some of the extremes of this Maoist reform.

During the later 1960s, however, the aging Mao decreed a new campaign, the so-called Great Proletarian Cultural Revolution, which came very close to shaking the system to pieces. Mao, his young wife—film actress Chiang Ch'ing—and their allies in Peking apparently felt that the People's Republic was drifting away from its ideological roots, settling into old bureaucratic ways, and losing its revolutionary zeal. The Cultural Revolution mobilized millions of young people in the new Red Guard units to denounce bureaucrats, compel self-criticism by any and all–up to and including Mao's old comrades in the top leadership—and to reassert the primacy of Marxist-Maoist thought.

The result was a reign of terror that had nearly paralyzed the country by 1968. Large numbers were hounded to death by local vigilantes or killed in clashes between rival factions, including rival gangs of Red Guards. In the end, the Chinese Red Army had to be called upon to regain control.

In the long run, however, pragmatism won the day. By the early 1970s, practical men such as Mao's old colleague Chou En-lai had even arranged a rapprochement between China and Richard Nixon's America. And after Mao's death in 1976, the pragmatists seized power under another old revolutionary—and victim of the Cultural Revolution—Deng Xiaoping. Under the diminutive but bustling Deng, the new leadership actually brought to trial and convicted Mao's widow and her allies, the now condemned Gang of Four, for the excesses of the Cultural Revolution and the follies of the Great Leap Forward.

China had broken her close relationship with the Soviet Union as early as 1959–1960. After the middle 1970s the pragmatic new leaders sought closer economic ties with Western nations, including the United States and Japan, in order to help modernize China. Here and there, capitalist-sounding incentives were introduced to encourage increased production, though no major revisions in the centralized economy seemed to be contemplated. In a country that had been habituated to a considerable degree of centralization for more than two thousand years, centralized economic planning seemed a natural way to go.

And genuine progress was made during the decades of Communist rule. In overall production, China ranked with the leading Western European nations (though still far below the United States, the Soviet Union, and Japan) by the mid 1970s. The People's Republic was able to feed her one billion citizens, and her cities were sprucer, her domestic industry developing. Public education was much wider, public health was improved, and a rigorous birth-control program was introduced to deal with what was perhaps the nation's number one problem, massive overpopulation.

Perhaps most important of all, China in the eighties was ruled by Chinese, not by foreigners, as many would have expected at the turn of the century. China's place in the future seemed sure to be a prominent one.

Father and Daughter in India

India too was her own mistress once more from the late 1940s on, and she made progress under the leadership of a strong national party and charismatic leadership. But there were crucial differences between the two Asian giants. India's economic growth was somewhat slower, but her politics were democratic, her charismatic leaders elected by those they ruled.

The Republic of India was governed for most of the four decades after independence in 1947 by a "dynasty" of father and daughter: first by Gandhi's disciple Pandit Nehru, from 1947 till his death in 1964, then by Nehru's daughter Indira Gandhi (no relation to the Mahatma) from 1966 until her assassination in 1984. Their problems were many, their successes striking in this context of endless difficulties.

India, seldom united over her long history, had to be welded into a nation before it could be governed. Institutionally, at least, Nehru accomplished this by compelling all the surviving *rajas* of the so-called princely states to accept absorption into the new country. Mrs. Gandhi had the harder task of melding the subcontinent's many peoples, languages, tradi-

tions, and religions into some approximation of a citizenry. This she at least began to do by a combination of personal appeal, political manipulation, and occasional use of force.

Attempts to develop the country economically encountered similar difficulties. The Indians tried a wide variety of methods to encourage development, from Five-Year Plans to foreign investment, from foreign aid (from both Russia and America) to the agricultural technology of the Green Revolution. In overall production, India achieved a respectable rank somewhere between that of the leading Western and Eastern European nations.

The best efforts of Nehru and Gandhi, however, repeatedly foundered on India's greatest problem: her burgeoning population. As Nehru said, it has been necessary for India to run very hard simply to keep up with the needs of the millions who are added to her citizen body every year. The country thus remained a sprawling land of poverty-stricken and in many cases illiterate villages, and the gap between those masses and the wealthy residents of Calcutta or Bombay was perhaps even greater in the 1980s than it was in the 1940s.

Politically, however, the nation managed to preserve a flexible democratic system. There was a short period of "emergency dictatorship" by Indira Gandhi in the 1970s. There were periods of anarchic violence triggered by ancient religious differences, most notably the conflicts between Hindus and Muslims in the 1940s and those between Hindus and the movement for Sikh autonomy that cost Mrs. Gandhi her life in 1984. Rajiv Gandhi succeeded his mother by the largest majority in Indian political history—further evidence that this vast land of many faiths and peoples deserved its title of "the world's most populous democracy."

Success in East Asia, Turbulence in Islam

The string of nations curving down the eastern end of Eurasia into mainland Southeast Asia provided one of the success stories of Third World history. Taiwan, Hong Kong, Singapore, and to a lesser extent the two Koreas all became productive and relatively prosperous new nations of the underdeveloped world.

Still supporting substantial numbers of extremely poor people, these small countries combined cheap labor with foreign capital, domestic drive with ingenuity, to build up light industry and commerce in order to give them a competitive leg up on the rest of Asia. Their growing economic clout combined with Japan's leading place in the world economy and with China's incalculable potential to make East Asia probably the most rapidly developing section of the Third World.

Islamic militance and the dark gleam of oil determined the history of a wide swath of Asia and North Africa in recent decades. Politically speaking, the Muslim nations followed different paths. Some, like Iran under the shah and the oil-rich giant Saudi Arabia, remained anachronistic absolute monarchies in the later twentieth century. Others became military dictatorships, like Pakistan, Iraq, and the Libya of Colonel Kaddafi. A few have found solutions that defy classification. Egypt, for example, was dominated for decades by a series of former military men of great charisma and political skill, above all Gamal Abdel Nasser and Anwar Sadat.

The vast reservoirs of oil that stretch from Iran to the far end of the Sahara gave these recently emancipated sheiks and colonels a powerful new economic role in the world. They used some of their wealth to feud with each other or with their non-Muslim neighbors ranging from Israel to India. Much of it went into lavish living and foreign investments—the petrodollars that flooded the banks of the West. Some of their oil wealth, however, did go into providing agricultural projects, education, health care, decent roads, and housing for the scanty populations of these mostly arid lands.

Islamic religious fervor was at a new high in the postwar years; this dynamic element kindled some sensational violence. Indonesian Muslim fundamentalists, encouraged by the Indonesian army, rose in righteous indignation against local Communist cadres and their atheistic gospel, slaughtering hundreds of thousands of them in 1965. In Iran, the Muslim followers of the Ayatollah Ruhollah Khomeini overthrew their autocratic modernizing shah in 1979. Soon they had instituted a religious reign of terror of their own, decimating student radicals and religious minorities alike and holding the U.S. Embassy and its personnel hostage for a year in the early 1980s.

But Islamic fundamentalism also made a positive contribution to the lives of these Muslim peoples. After a century and a half of disarray and confusion as their empires crumbled and Christian rulers imposed an alien order on their lives, Muslims could once more command a respected place in the world. And if oil money brought material well-being into the lives of some Arabs, renewed Islamic faith gave meaning to the spiritual lives of many more.

Black Africa's Struggle

In Africa south of the Sahara, political instability and autocratic one-party or military rule alternated in a bewildering kaleidoscope, punctuated by bloody flashes of rebellion. Economically, some of these countries prospered on a combination of commodity exports and foreign aid and investment; others seemed to settle deeper into poverty.

For black Africa, life after the Great Liberation was a struggle in many ways more difficult than the victorious fight for independence had been. In French-speaking West Africa, for instance, close economic relations with France enabled such liberation leaders as Félix Houphouët-Boigny of the Ivory Coast and Senegal's Léopold Senghor to lead their new nations to relative prosperity. There were paved roads there, bright lights, marketplaces full to bursting, and new skyscrapers in the great African cities of Abidjan and Dakar. But landlocked inner African Sahel states such as Mali, Niger, and Chad remained dusty, poverty-ridden backwaters.

In the former colonies of British East Africa, two of the continent's best-known liberation leaders, Jomo Kenyatta of Kenya and Julius Nyerere of Tanzania, provided an interesting contrast in development styles. Kenyatta opened his doors to Western capital, while Nyerere preached self-reliance and socialism—and got aid from European socialist countries and China. Kenya, with a considerable colonial head start in development, grew more rapidly, building some industry and an East African metropolitan center in Nai-

Apartheid in South Africa, clearly labeled here both in English and Afrikans. The daily humiliation imposed by the last vestige of Western imperialism in Africa met increasing resistance by the 1980s. (United Nations Photo 151609)

robi. Nyerere's Tanzania provided water, food, some education and health care for his people first—and was on the edge of bankruptcy as the 1980s advanced.

African countries generally were among those hardest hit by declining world prices for the commodities they produced and rising costs for things they consumed—particularly oil—during the 1970s. Terrible famine added to the travail of a number of African nations in the 1970s and 1980s. Drought, government mismanagement, devastating civil wars, and the spread of the desert into areas bordering the Sahara all contributed to the disaster. In Ethiopia, the Sahal countries, and elsewhere, hundreds of thousands died and whole districts were depopulated by starvation.

The greatest struggle of all persisted in the Republic of South Africa, whose all-white government continued through the postwar decades to deny her black majority more than a token share of power.

Blacks organized to demand equal treatment during the postwar period, particularly after the implementation of apartheid policies in the early 1950s. But demonstrations and strikes were suppressed, sometimes violently, as in the Sharpeville massacre of 1960 in which scores of Africans were shot down. White radicals who called for racial compromise were placed under house arrest. Black resisters were imprisoned, among them Nobel Peace Prize winner Albert Luthuli; some, like student leader Steve Biko, died under suspicious circumstances while in custody.

South Africa tried separate-but-equal segregation of blacks in so-called homelands—but the territories assigned to the blacks were generally poor lands that were economically dependent on surrounding white South Africa. In the early 1980s the republic took steps toward allowing some non-Europeans a modest part in the political process. But black terrorism had by that time been added to the unpalatable mix, and there seemed to be no way out of the impasse.

The Venceremos Spirit in Latin America

The Latin American nations were also engulfed in struggles of many kinds during the later decades of the twentieth century. Efforts at accelerated economic development, governmental reform, and even social revolution were all prominent parts of their postwar history. The Cuban slogan, *Venceremos!*—"We Shall Overcome!"—summarizes much of the spirit, if not always the results of this Latin American ferment.

Development became an all-devouring passion south of the Rio Grande in the decades after World War II. In its name, poor people supported and mid-

dle-class businessmen frequently tolerated strong governments of left or right that promised development in return for submission to authoritarian rule. Central planning, import-substitution industries, diversification of industrial and agricultural production, continued construction of such essential infrastructures as the new postwar highway systems—all contributed to Latin American economic growth. In some places social services proliferated, though the gulf between rich and poor still remained great in the southern republics.

The 1960s were the boom times. By the early 1970s two large Latin American nations, Brazil and Mexico, ranked with some European countries in overall production. Even in these successful cases, however, poverty remained endemic in the villages where most Latin Americans lived. This poverty of the domestic market choked off the boom in the 1970s and 1980s.

Economic failures stimulated an increasingly radical ideological opposition to the status quo in Middle and South America. This new revolutionary spirit flourished particularly among university students inspired by Fidel Castro's Cuban Revolution, among some Catholic priests preaching a new gospel of social reform called liberation theology, and among radicalized peons and urban workers. The resulting wave of radical agitation and revolutionary activity ranged from university strikes to urban terrorism to guerrilla warfare. It led to the election of Marxist presidents in Guatemala and Chile and to renewed bitterness toward North American and European influence. It also led to a strong countercurrent of reaction, which in several cases was at least as violent as the radical wave that had called it forth.

An early manifestation of the new demand for change was the decade-long personal dictatorship of Juan and Eva Peron (1946–1955) in Argentina. Peron drew his support from the growing Argentine urban working class, the *descamisados* ("shirtless ones"), whom he gave higher wages, social services, and retirement benefits. The magnetic Evita, a former actress, worked for women's emancipation and services for the poor. The Perons, however, also rigged elections, feuded with the Catholic church, and tended to ignore the problems of the peasantry. Three years after Evita's death in 1952, Peron was overthrown by the military.

The most flamboyant and infuential revolution in the region during this period, however, was that led by Fidel Castro in Cuba. During his quarter-century of rule in the island country, Castro ran a one-party Communist government. But though many middle-class Cubans fled, the peasant population remained loyal to the revolution, and in many ways benefited from it.

Economic growth was not exuberant under the *Venceremos* regime. Early efforts to diversify the country's one-crop sugar economy did not succeed, and Castro came to depend on selling sugar to Russia, as his predecessor Batista had on selling it to the United States. A United States-sponsored economic boycott further stunted Cuba's development.

Despite this lack of economic growth, Castro forged ahead with the most elaborate set of social services offered by any of the southern American republics. He built public housing and schools for the poor, and provided health care and retirement pensions. A weak economy and impressive social services were thus combined, thanks to substantial economic aid from Russia.

The most recent surge of revolutionary social experimentation in Latin America occurred in the Central American republic of Nicaragua. Here the brutal Somoza dictatorship was overthrown in 1979 in a bloody insurrection that involved practically every social class and political faction. The victorious revolutionary regime, called the Sandinistas (after a martyred revolutionary leader) represented a range of anti-Somoza views, from socialist and middle-class liberal to the liberation theology of some of the priests who took part. A variety of changes were instituted in the early 1980s, from socialization of important parts of the productive economy to literacy and public-health campaigns.

Like most revolutionary juntas, however, the Sandinistas had a low tolerance for political opposition. And by accepting help and encouragement from Cuba and Russia, they incurred the enmity of the militantly anticommunist Reagan administration in the United States. Charges that the Sandinistas were supporting a guerrilla movement in neighboring El Salvador led Washington to organize an anti-Sandinista partisan force inside Nicaragua. This constituted a further drag on an economy that was already being asked to support new social services for Nicaraguans.

A regional revolution that attracted fewer headlines was the resurgence of democratic government in many Latin American nations during the later 1970s and the 1980s. Where authoritarian regimes, frequently military dictatorships, prevailed in the 1950s, elected civilian governments came to power in the 1980s. Older democracies like Mexico and Venezuela were thus joined by the largest South American countries, Argentina and Brazil, as the military gave way to civilian leadership.

While some critics pointed out that democracy had come and gone in Latin America before, others warned that without major economic improvements, political reforms might not change the lives of many Latin Americans. But the surprising fact remained that there were only a handful of military dictatorships left in South America in 1985.

SUMMARY

The prosperity, political stability, and high-tech modernity of the global North in the later twentieth century contrasts strikingly with the serious political, economic, and technological problems of the nations of the global South during these same years.

The Third World countries of Asia, Africa, and Latin America cover large tracts of the globe where the agricultural village is still the basic unit of social organization. The South faced such basic problems as lack of adequate food, medical care, and education for exploding populations. In addition, Third World countries felt a strong need to develop economically in order to achieve the urban-industrial prosperity enjoyed by the nations of the North. Efforts to achieve these ends, however, have trapped the global South in economic dependency on the North and have led to cruel suffering when commodity prices, loans, and foreign aid from the North declined.

Conflicts between the traditional world of the village and the new urban world also threatened Asians, Af-

ricans, and Latin Americans with the same sort of painful cultural uprooting that afflicted Western peoples when the Industrial Revolution first spread in the preceding century. And many Third World people who did come up from the villages to join the modern world of the city ended up in shantytowns, the slums that ring the new metropolises from Caracas to Hong Kong.

The problems were the same, but the patterns of response varied from one region of the Third World to another.

Many of the countries of the South were one-party governments or military dictatorships, and revolutions and coups were common on all three Third World continents. Even China, with its ancient tradition of central government, was shaken by the social experiments of Chairman Mao and other Communist leaders, including such abortive efforts as the Great Leap Forward and the Cultural Revolution. India, under Nehru and his daughter, Indira

Gandhi, managed to preserve that nation's democratic institutions while struggling with her immense economic, demographic, and religious problems. Some of the greatest Third World success stories came in East Asia, where smaller countries like Hong Kong and Singapore followed the Japanese pattern of competitive capitalist modernization.

A broad swath of Muslim countries, from Iran to North Africa, developed rapidly on the basis of oil wealth, though the gap between rich and poor remained substantial, even in the relatively small populations of these nations. Much of Africa south of the Sahara struggled with considerably more limited resources and much greater dependency on world commodity prices, bank loans, and international aid. In Latin America, finally, similar economic problems led to a number of revolutions, from Cuba to Nicaragua, which sought state socialist solutions to the difficulties of development.

SUGGESTED READING

BAIROCH, P. *The Economic Development of the Third World since 1900.* London: Methuen, 1975. From colonialism to postimperial dependencies.

BARNET, R. J., and R. E. MULLER. *Global Reach.* New York: Simon & Schuster, 1974. The role of multinational corporations in shaping the economies of developing countries. See on this same subject, the United Nations report, *Transnational Corporations in World Development: A Re-examination* (New York: UN Commission on Transnational Corporations, 1978).

BRANDT, W. *North-South: A Program for Survival.* Cambridge, Mass.: MIT Press, 1980. Urges major changes in the distribution of global wealth. See also A. Fishlow, *Rich and Poor Nations in the World Economy* (New York: McGraw-Hill, 1979), a summary of different dependencies.

BREESE, G., ed. *The City in Newly Developing Countries.* Englewood Cliffs, N.J.: Prentice-Hall, 1972. A number of valuable essays on the problems of rapid urbanization in the underdeveloped world. See also M. P. Todaro, *Internal Migration in Developing Countries* (Geneva: International Labor Office, 1976) for more on causes of country-to-city migration.

CHENERY, H., et al. *Redistribution with Growth.* London: Oxford University Press, 1974. The case for combining social justice with economic development. See also I. Adelman and C. T. Morris, *Economic Growth and Social Equity in Developing Countries* (Stanford: Stanford University Press, 1973).

CONGDON, R. F. *Introduction to Appropriate Technology.* Emmaus: Rodale Press, 1977. Small-scale, locally rooted technology seen as more appropriate for developing nations than the mass-production technology of developed nations. On other Third World solutions to Third World problems, see V. Djukanovic and E. P. Mach, *Alternative Approaches to Meeting Basic Health Needs in Developing Countries* (Geneva: World Health Organization, 1975), and E. Faure, et al., *Learning to Be* (Paris: UN Educational, Scientific, and Cultural Organization, 1972) on education.

ELLIOTT, C. *Patterns of Poverty in the Third World.* New York: Praeger, 1975. Survey of the basic problem of the world's newer nations. See also G. Myrdal's impressive work, *The Challenge of World Poverty* (London: Allen Lane, 1970).

FINER, S. E. *The Man on Horseback.* London: Pall Mall Press, 1962. Military takeovers in the Third World. On the political corruption of many civilian governments among the new nations, see J. Nye, "Corruption and Political Development," *American Political Science Review*, 61 (1967), 417–427.

GOODE, W. J. *World Revolution and Family Patterns.* New York: Free Press, 1970. Crumbling of traditional family structures in modernizing Third World countries.

GOTT, R. *Rural Guerrillas in Latin America*, rev. ed. Harmondsworth, England: Penguin, 1973. One of many studies on the guerrilla activity common in developing nations.

HARRISON, P. *Inside the Third World*, 2nd ed. Harmondsworth, England: Penguin, 1981. Insightful and vivid first-hand reportage by a well-traveled journalist. See also his *The Third World Tomorrow* (Harmondsworth, England: Penguin, 1980), on potential solutions for Third World problems.

KAMARCK, A. *The Tropics and Economic Development.* Baltimore: Johns Hopkins Press, 1976. Analyzes the agricultural, nutritional, medical, and related problems of developing countries. See also D. Grigg, *The Harsh Lands* (New York: Macmillan, 1970).

LEGUM, C., et al. *Africa in the 1980s: A Continent in Crisis.* New York: McGraw-Hill, 1979. Problems of independent Africa in its third decade.

LEWIS, O. *Children of Sanchez.* New York: Random House, 1966. Vivid, if controversial, account of the culture of poverty. See also his *Five Families* (New York: Basic Books, 1959).

LLOYD, P. C. *Africa in Social Change*, rev. ed. Harmondsworth, England: Penguin, 1972. Village life in Africa. For a darker vision of village life in Latin America, see F. Julião, *Cambão—The Yoke* (Harmondsworth, England: Penguin, 1972).

PALMER, I. *Food and the New Agricultural Technology.* Geneva: UN Research Institute for Social Development, 1972. The Green Revolution—and its unintended side effects. See also his *The Social and Economic Implications of Large-Scale Introduction of New Varieties of Foodgrain* (Geneva: UN Research Institute for Social Development, 1974), and L. Brown, *Seeds of Change* (New York: Praeger, 1970).

RUTHENBERG, H.   *Farming Systems in the Tropics*, 2nd ed. Oxford: Clarendon Press, 1976. Survey and analysis of traditional agricultural methods in many developing nations. On land redistribution to peasant farmers, see the UN Food and Agriculture Organization's *Progress in Land Reform, 6th Report* (New York: United Nations, 1976). On less tractable ecological problems, like deforestation and desertifica-tion, see E. Eckholm, *Losing Ground* (New York: Norton, 1975).

STANFORD, Q. H.   *The World's Population*. London: Oxford University Press, 1972. Trends and problems of a world where population growth continues to put pressure on the food supply. For papers reflecting differences between the First and Third Worlds on the significance and solutions of the population explosion, see *The Population Debate* (2 vols.) (New York: UN Department of Economic and Social Affairs, 1975).

Chapter · 25

PLANETARY CULTURE

THE MIND OF HUMANKIND

Our Minds Begin to Mesh

In dealing with the cultural history of the first half of the twentieth century, we noticed that the arts and ideas of those decades no longer broke down primarily by region or historic civilization. Both of the main cultural trends of the period made most sense when analyzed under global headings. Thus we looked at modernism from Paris to Tokyo, at ideological or committed art as practiced by revolutionaries, totalitarian regimes, Western liberals, and artists in search of their roots from Mexico to India.

In looking at the intellectual and artistic life of still more recent world history, we move even further toward a global perspective. We will attempt to survey the mind of humankind as a whole. We will examine the inner life of the species as it moves for the first time toward some common ground of understanding, some commonly accepted forms of expression and communication. This would seem to be a difficult thing to do, given the deep-rooted cultural differences, the economic and political conflicts between East and West, North and South. Yet there is some evidence for the beginnings of just such a global culture.

In the present century, and particularly in the second half of it, ideas of various sorts, artistic trends for the elite and for the mass audience have, in fact, begun to surge across regional and cultural boundaries as never before. Especially in religion and science, and in the realms of international ideology and that cool pragmatism which is its opposite, the same beliefs and feelings may today be found in many parts of the world. The same is true of the arts, from high modernism to mass-appeal television. Our minds have begun to mesh, a genuinely planetary culture to emerge on this battered globe.

The following pages, then, will outline some of these convergences of beliefs, some trends in the arts with an intercontinental range.

The Faiths of Our Fathers

To begin with the obvious, the established world religions have by no means faded away in our century. Some attention has been paid to the Islamic revival in recent chapters because of its impact on world affairs, especially in the Middle East. The Muslim faith still meets the spiritual needs of many millions, particularly in Asia and Africa. Buddhism is also still a vital force from Southeast Asia to Japan. Hinduism reaches the other way, from Southeast Asia up to its original home in India.

Christianity has the widest geographical dispersion today, dominating Europe, North and South America, and Australia, and still boasting some substantial enclaves in Africa and Asia. Of the major forms of the Christian faith, Catholicism predominates in southern Europe and South America and is the leading single denomination even in North America. Protestant sects prevail in northern Europe, North America, and elsewhere. Christian, Islamic, and other religious minorities are even to be found in the officially atheistic Communist countries running from Eastern Europe across the Eurasian sprawl of Russia to the Pacific.

When we factor in such spectacular demonstrations of religious concern as the immense audiences of radio and television preachers, the intermittent spread of cultism among the young, and the perennial appeal of various forms of mysticism and supernatural phenomena, there does seem to be evidence for a basic and widespread human hunger for spiritual understanding.

The resilience of religious faith and the new ease with which religions pass from one culture and one continent to another make religious belief still a global force today.

Global Ideologies

The most highly touted substitute for religion in our century has been ideology. The major ideologies—liberalism, socialism, nationalism, and their various forms and offshoots—have had a global appeal in recent times.

The liberal faith and liberal institutions have more than once been dismissed as doomed in the present century—notably by the totalitarians in the 1930s and by liberals themselves in the 1960s and 1970s. Only a small minority of the world's countries are in fact liberal democracies, and half the citizens of an old established democracy such as the United States do not bother to vote. Nevertheless, it was the totalitarian nations of Nazi Germany and Fascist Italy that went down to crashing defeat in the biggest of wars, not the liberal powers of America and Britain. And the simple fact that peoples as vigorous, successful, and forward-looking as the West Germans and the Japanese became enthusiastic converts to democratic institutions after World War II would seem to indicate that liberalism still has something to offer the world.

The favorite of the world's intellectuals for most of the time since World War II has, however, generally been some form of socialism. Totalitarian Marxism has of course prevailed in Communist countries. An eclectic mix of socialism and liberalism often called social democracy has flourished in many Western European and other developed countries. The apparent relevance of Lenin's writing on imperialism to the problems of former colonies has made revolutionary Marxism appealing to many Third World leaders.

The most intensely and widely felt of all ideologies is, however, also the most divisive: nationalism in all its forms. National feeling still seems to be easily kindled in even the most blasé older nations. Among the new countries that have emerged since mid-century, nationalism is in many cases even more intense. Cultural nationalism, militant chauvinism, "pan" movements (pan Africanism, pan-Arabism), and other aspects of this powerful sense of primary allegiance to the nation-state are to be found on all continents in the second half of the twentieth century.

Liberals, socialists, and nationalists have frequently disagreed, at least about priorities. Yet it is quite possible to be, for instance, a patriotic social democrat, combining moderate versions of all three views. And conservatives of all stripes have learned to share their countries with the whole range of ideologies, something that would have seemed impossible half a dozen generations ago.

Widely distributed around the world as they are, the modern ideologies link people of diverse backgrounds in all parts of the globe. They constitute another form of belief that acts as a unifying force on a global scale.

Quantum Physics and Social Engineering

Certainly modern science, the belief system of educated people everywhere, also performs this linking function. The physical sciences, and to a lesser extent the social sciences, have in fact become common intellectual currency East and West, North and South. And unlike religions and ideologies, the sciences do not foster differences of opinion sufficiently strong to counter their unifying impact.

In the course of the present century, the mathematical and biological sciences have become the core of modern education everywhere, and applied science the key to social and economic modernization around the world. Educated people in many lands have thus acquired a fundamentally scientific vision of a world of subatomic particles and radiant energy melting into one another, an expanding universe of uncountable stars and galaxies. The new views of life as a biological slime infesting the crust of planet earth and of human beings as clever primates has spread far beyond the West.

Not only did non-Western people accept these ideas, they soon began to contribute to them. Darwin and Einstein, like Copernicus and Galileo, were Europeans. But in our century laboratories and universities in Japan and China and India were soon publishing their scientific discoveries too. They also began to apply them, as illustrated by Japan's position in high-tech industry and the nuclear bombs developed by both China and India.

The social sciences have a less universal range, but they have also found increasing acceptance around the globe as explanations for the way we are—for the way human society works and the ways that, with a little "social engineering," it can be made to work.

Thus, while Western capitalist countries try to fine tune their economies according to the ideas of John Maynard Keynes, development economics has become a subject of vital interest in the new, underde-

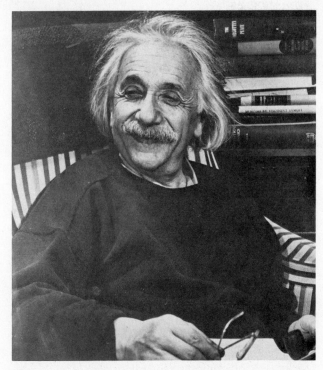

Albert Einstein, the most famous genius of the "Second Scientific Revolution." The man whose theory of gravitation upset Newton's and who introduced relativity into the exact sciences looks understandably pleased with himself. (The Bettmann Archive, Inc.)

veloped nations. The sociological study of classes and their conflicts, under Marxist or other auspices, has permeated all the social sciences on both sides of the Iron Curtain. Anthropology, originally developed as the study of preurban non-Western cultures, continues to flourish, and there are more and more contributions from anthropologists outside the Western world.

For social scientists, national frontiers and cultural barriers have disappeared, leaving the world at large a happy hunting ground for new insights into the social behavior and institutional organization of humanity.

Neither Marx nor Jesus

The latter part of the twentieth century, finally, has seen the global spread of an intellectual attitude that has never enjoyed as broad an acceptance as it does today. The new view favors limited intellectual goals and social aspirations over intellectual absolutes and exalted utopian visions of the future. It considers itself realistic, practical—and above all, perhaps, *pragmatic.*

The prevailing pragmatism of the later twentieth century has seldom been codified, and its main tenets have a largely negative ring. There are few gods in its pantheon, and divine prescriptions are seldom con-

sulted in the formulation of its policies. In this view, all social rules and ethical imperatives are *relative*— valid only for the time and culture that generated them. Knowledge is necessarily limited to statistical probabilities, even in the hard sciences. Art is not a revelation of timeless beauty but a matter of current fashion or self-expression, sometimes hardly distinguishable from therapy. And so on through all the eternal verities held by the older cultures of the world.

But this has been seen by its enemies as a spiritually thin and emotionally unsatisfying view of the world. Its supporters answer that at least it is cost-effective. An idea, the new pragmatists would say, is valid today if it works today, and we need not worry too much about what Confucius, Christ, or Karl Marx would have said about it.

East and West, North and South, people in charge of getting things done seem increasingly to share this view. If private agricultural plots and incentive wages in factories will boost production, then socialist idealism must give ground, even in Communist Eastern Europe. If government involvement in business helps Japan Incorporated to move successfully into world markets, than perhaps American capitalism can sacrifice some free-enterprise principles in the interests of expanded exports. American and European banks might be the very incarnation of imperialism-as-the-highest-stage-of-capitalism—but if a developing country needs a loan, a compromise with imperialism can be arranged.

Bureaucrats, business leaders, and managers everywhere seem to be willing to sacrifice metaphysical depth for practicality and efficiency. It is an attitude shared by people as disparate as the post-Stalin leadership in Russia, the post-Mao leadership in China, the "neither-Marx-nor-Jesus" philosophers in Paris, and union heads and top management alike in the United States.

The new pragmatism is one more in the series of large ideas that between them appear to be pulling the world toward a greater degree of intellectual harmony than ever before. Common concerns and commonly felt problems, if not uniform solutions, seem increasingly to point toward a single global cast of mind in centuries to come.

PLANETARY CULTURE

A Smorgasbord of Culture

Although shared ideas can help to hold a culture together, art is often as important a social cement.

Christian and Muslim ideas, for instance, certainly

unified Christian and Muslim culture during the Middle Ages. But cathedral imagery in stone and glass and the poetry of the Koran also helped to shape the common consciousness of members of each of these international communities. In the twentieth century, some important trends in the arts may in the long run help to forge an even larger sense of global cultural unity.

The global art scene in our century has in some ways become an aesthetic smorgasbord, where the art lover picks and chooses among a bewildering array of international cultural fare. One year Latin American novels are the particular vogue; the next year it may be ancient Chinese bronzes or a wave of enthusiasm for the new Australian films. All are made available to large numbers of people, thanks to translations, television specials, and your neighborhood movie theater.

In this profusion of art from many times and lands, however, some features that make for genuine cultural unity may be detected. The following pages will suggest that the later twentieth century has seen the peoples of the world drawn closer together by three trends in the arts of our time: a broader international audience for the folk arts of many lands, the spread of modernism as an international style for elites everywhere, and the often deplored but culturally unifying taste of the world's mass audiences for some forms of popular art in our time.

Folk Art Goes Cosmopolitan

The arts around the world displayed a tendency toward convergence and the beginnings of some sort of genuinely global taste in the later twentieth century. Traditional art and propaganda art, high modernism and the least exalted levels of popular television drama or illustrated magazine art all exhibited these trends toward common patterns of development. There were increasing similarities of taste and response across a variety of cultures around the world.

Traditional arts would seem at first glance the least likely to contain such a global dimension. Artistic traditions, after all, are typically the defining features of separate regional cultures. From patterns on pots to styles of temple building, traditional styles have historically distinguished one culture from another, heightening each people's sense of its own uniqueness. Styles in African masks, the folk dances of various Soviet socialist republics, Andean textiles, Appalachian folk tales—all are cultural products that—it is often suggested—only a native can completely appreciate.

As it happens, however, the present century has

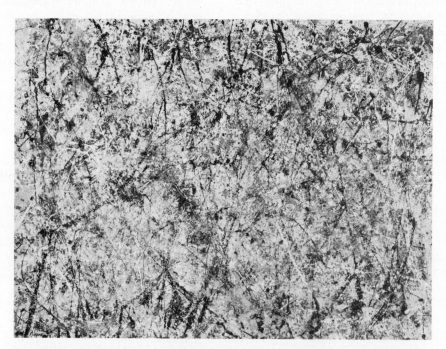

Jackson Pollock's "Number 1, 1950 (Lavender Mist)" is a prime example of the abstract expressionist painting of the New York school. Modernism enjoyed perhaps its last great flowering in the United States after World War II. (National Gallery of Art, Washington, D.C. Alisa Mellon Bruce Fund 1976)

seen a steadily growing appreciation for the traditional arts of all peoples. Interest in other peoples' cultural traditions spans an astonishing range today, from arts as demanding as Japanese Kabuki theater to those as accessible as African drumming and Cossack dances.

This international smorgasbord of traditional art has had its limitations and weaknesses. The very popularity of foreign culture could lead to the proliferation of "airport art"—mass-produced copies of authentic village art intended to separate tourists from their travelers checks. Even the most sensitive non-native, furthermore, is unlikely to grasp the full social and spiritual significance of traditional art removed from its place in a living culture and hung like a trophy on a museum wall.

On the other hand, interest in other peoples' traditional art forms did mark a very considerable broadening of the world's taste. When whole museums were dedicated to "primitive" art, when sophisticates from New York, Paris, Berlin, New Delhi, Tokyo, or Mexico City could look at one another's traditional art with some understanding and with genuine admiration, the world's peoples were clearly closer to mutual respect than they had been before.

Shapes and Contours

The true high-international style of the twentieth century—particularly since the Second World War—has been modernism. As we have seen, modernism originated in Europe late in the last century. As early as the years between the wars, however, non-European writers such as the Argentine Jorge Luis Borges and the Japanese painter Togo Seiji were producing widely admired work in the modernist vein. In the decades since World War II, the modernist determination to break with all Western cultural tradition has made the modernist style both acceptable and accessible to peoples around the world.

Modernism's reduction of art to its fundamental formal elements, of humanity to its basic drives, makes modernist work uniquely comprehensible as a purely aesthetic or human experience. Borges's labyrinths and mirrors, like Samuel Beckett's characters isolated in a surrealist dreamscape, are as culture-free as art can be. Even the colorful Latin American atmosphere of a book such as Gabriel Garcia Marquez's *One Hundred Years of Solitude* is universalized by the "magical realist" quality of his writing. Experimental art, it seems, is truly free of cultural limitations—and hence is the ideal international style.

Above all, modernist architecture has traveled with ease and appropriateness around the globe during the post–World War II years. Developed especially by European architects such as Mies van der Rohe or le Corbusier, these distinctively twentieth-century styles of building are based on exploiting the possibilities of new building materials and modes of construction: reinforced concrete, glass, steel, plastics, the high-rise block, and the geodesic dome. The result is a vocabulary of basic shapes and sweeping contours that is as free of associations with any particular culture as any art could be.

Modernist techniques and styles have thus been ap-

Eero Saarinen's Trans-World Airlines terminal at Kennedy Airport in New York looks about to take off for outer space itself. Modern building materials freed modernist architects from pillars, arches, and other structural devices typical of earlier centuries. (Courtesy TWA)

plied with equal success to public buildings and business blocks, hotels and universities in many countries. Whole national capitals for countries as culturally diverse as Brazil, Arabia, and India have been built in the modernist mode. A roughly representational mural on a local theme, a decorative band of Aztec hieroglyphics or Arabic script seems to be enough to make modernist architecture fit into any tradition around the world.

"Dallas" Dubbed in Greek

Modernism has in a sense been *the* first global style, the intercontinental style par excellence. But it has also been high culture, an art for elites. People with education, money, and power stay in modernist hotels, work in modernist commercial, cultural, or government buildings, read Borges and Beckett, and cover their living-room walls with abstract expressionist art. Recent years, however, have seen the birth of an international popular culture as well.

Popular arts having an international appeal are perhaps most noticeably those of music and film. Jazz, blues, and other forms of Afro-American music had a global appeal between the two world wars, as did such Latin American dances as the samba, the conga, and the rhumba. American rock 'n' roll, West Indian reggae, and the performances of intercontinental superstars such as the British Beatles and Rolling Stones continued this tradition of internationally adored popular music. A group hadn't "arrived" until it had toured Australia, and hotel musicians in Communist Yugoslavia were belting out international favorites such as "Itsy-Bitsy Teeny-Weeny Yellow Polka-dot Bikini" in the depths of the Cold War Years.

Perhaps the most dazzlingly successful form of popular art internationally, however, has been film. The movies of Hollywood's dream factories also go back to the interwar years in their popularity, and it is a popularity that continues to this day. Worldwide taste for American television—also a film medium, of course—has been overwhelming. Despite the ideological objections of some governments, despite the clucking of people with higher sensibilities in many lands, popular audiences around the world have taken enthusiastically to American television series.

The taste for Western film is not a passion for things Western as much as it is for things *modern*. American television has the urban feel and the smell of money, the violence, slickness, professional precision, and glitter of the century itself. The world of series such as "Dallas" is the dream of all the world—an unrealistic fantasy of a global Texas symbolized by the gleaming new skyscrapers and fabulous wealth of that quintessentially twentieth-century city. "Dallas" is the Skyscraper Age incarnate. No wonder the boy who grabs your bags in Bombay or Buenos Aires will sport a T-shirt emblazoned with magic name, and the bar on the corner in Karystos will be showing the program dubbed in Greek.

A Harmony of Feelings and Beliefs

Can we look forward, then—with varying degrees of enthusiasm, depending on our views—to a world in which a single common culture serves as the cement for a global society? All we can say with any certainty is that it is a possibility, and that we have gone some distance down that road already.

Five centuries ago, the great regional centers of the globe were virtually closed books to one another. China was half mythical to Europeans, all the rest of the earth barbarians to the Chinese. The New World was as unknown to the Old World as Eurasia was to the peoples of the high Andes or the Valley of Mexico. Even one century ago, only a few sons of Asian princes studied in Europe, a handful of Western scholars pored over Sanskrit or Arabic texts, and almost no one cared about preliterate cultures enough to attempt to understand the arts and ideas of the world's preurban populations.

Today's picture, comparatively speaking, is one of massive cultural interaction on all levels. And these exchanges of ideas, images, music, emotional attitudes, and mystical inspirations can scarcely help but draw the peoples of the world closer together. To know an Arab or an American may not be to love him, but it is at least to *know* him better than we ever have before.

Other currents of our times are also pushing us toward greater intercontinental harmony, as will be emphasized in the next chapter. Political agreements, economic relationships, and the shining links of modern technology also seem to be impelling us to recognize that we do, after all, live on a single planet. But ideas and artistic developments also have their part to play in this slow convergence.

Rigid uniformity of outlook or aesthetic expression is probably unlikely—thank goodness, many will say. Complex regional societies, even individual nations, have in the past nourished quite a range of subcultures. Still, some of the widest disparities among the varied cultures of the world do seem to be fading, and some universal tastes and enthusiasms manifesting themselves. The result may well be enough of a harmony of feeling and belief to enable us all to live together on our common planet with a minimum of social discord—somewhere down the road.

SUMMARY

The cultural history of the world in this second half of the twentieth century has revealed, even more than that of the first half, the global drift of our times.

Intellectually, educated people in many parts of the world came to share a handful of basic ideas and points of view. A few genuinely world religions, including Christianity and Islam, continued to dominate the spiritual lives of millions on several continents. The social ideologies developed in the West, notably liberalism, a variety of nationalisms, and Marxist socialism, guided the thought and action of leaders and elites in many parts of the globe.

The modern scientific world view was as widely accepted among educated Africans and Asians as by educated Europeans and Americans by the late twentieth century. And a pragmatic concern with utilitarian ideas that would get the job done increasingly found advocates in a world of technocrats more interested in results than in religious or ideological absolutes.

The arts also had an intercontinental dimension. In an age of jet transport and home television, citizens of developed nations and great cities everywhere had access to a cultural smorgasbord of the arts of all nations. Folk art, once so narrowly limited in appeal to the particular folk that produced it, now found an audience on stages and in museums far from its point of origin. The largely formal aesthetic appeal of modernism made this the quintessentially international style of the century. And a global popular art grew up, with a range of forms running from rock music to television drama.

A truly planetary culture, in short, seemed to be at least a possibility as the twentieth century drew toward a close.

SUGGESTED READING

ACHEBE, C. *Things Fall Apart*. New York: Heinemann, 1981. A disturbing novel of the new Africa by a leading African writer.

ARNASON, H. H. *History of Modern Art*. New York, Abrams, 1969. The arts of the twentieth century, including the postwar period.

BARRETT, W. *Irrational Man: A Study in Exsistential Philosophy*. Garden City, N.Y.: Doubleday, 1958. Origins and cultural impact of existentialism, from Kierkegaard to Sartre. For selections expertly introduced by a philosopher, see W. Kaufmann, ed., *Existentialism from Dostoyevsky to Sartre* (New York: New American Library, 1956).

BECKETT, S. *Waiting for Godot*. New York: Grove, 1954. Perhaps the most famous of the absurdist plays of the post-World War II period. On Beckett, Pinter, and others of this school, see M. Esslin, *The Theatre of the Absurd* (Garden City, N.Y.: Doubleday, 1961).

CAGE, J. *Silence*. Cambridge, Mass.: MIT Press, 1969. Collected works of the Zen-influenced inventor of silent music and the unplanned artistic "happening."

CROUZET, M. *The European Renaissance since 1945*. New York: Harcourt Brace Jovanovich, 1970. Cultural revival rooted in social progress. See also S. Hoffmann and P. Kitromilidos, *Culture and Society in Contemporary Europe* (London: Allen and Unwin, 1981) for the intellectual scene in the early 1980s.

ELLISON, R. *Invisible Man*. New York: Random House, 1972. Being black in America; a classic.

GARCÍA MÁRQUEZ, G. *One Hundred Years of Solitude*, trans. G. Rabassa. New York: Harper & Row, Pub., 1970. Epic of the Latin American backlands, written in the neosurrealist "magical realist" style of many postwar Latin American writers. On this Latin American literary renaissance, see D. F. Gallagher, *Modern Latin American Literature* (New York: Oxford University Press, 1973).

GRASS, G. *The Tin Drum*, trans. R. Manheim. New York: Random House, 1971. One of the leading postwar German writers looks back scathingly at his country's experience in this century.

KUHN, T. *The Structures of Scientific Revolutions*. Chicago: University of Chicago Press, 1962. Valuable insight into the workings of the scientific mind in a century that has learned more about the material world than any other.

LABEDZ, L. *Revisionism: Essays on the History of Marxist Ideas*. New York: Praeger, 1962. The permutations of Marxist ideas in the twentieth century; Russian, Western, revisionist, Third World and other varieties.

MCLUHAN, M. *Understanding Media: The Extensions of Man*. New York: McGraw-Hill, 1965. Once-fashionable book with some shrewd insights on print and electronic media despite the pop prose.

MISHIMA, Y. *The Temple of the Golden Pavilion*, trans. I. Morris. New York: Putnum, 1981. Passionate and profound novel built around the destruction of Kyoto's Golden Pavilion after World War II. For Japan's literary flowering since 1945, see H. Hibbett, ed., *Contemporary Japanese Literature: An Anthology of Fiction, Film, and Other Writing since 1945* (New York: Knopf, 1977).

PASTERNAK, B.   *Dr. Zhivago.* New York: Ballantine, 1981. An epic of ordinary people—and one poet—caught up in the Russian Revolution.

SANDLER, I.   *The Triumph of American Painting.* New York: Praeger, 1970. Abstract expressionism and the "New York School" after World War II.

SARTRE, J.-P.   *No Exit and Three Other Plays.* New York: Random House, 1955. The emotional impact of existentialism, especially the postwar French variety, is best absorbed through Sartre's theater or the novels of A. Camus. See also Camus, *The Plague*, trans. G. Stuart (New York: Modern Library, 1948). For a personal close-up of the Paris intelligentsia after the war, see S. de Beauvoir, *The Mandarins*, trans. L. M. Friedman (New York: Meridian Books, 1960).

SCHILLER, H.   *Communication and Cultural Domination.* New York: International Arts and Sciences Press, 1976. The "cultural imperialism" thesis of Western cultural influence as a form of aggression. See also J. Tunstall, *The Media Are American* (London: Constable, 1977), a critical analysis of the impact of America's mass media on the Third World.

SENGHOR, L.   *Nocturnes*, trans. C. Wake and J. Reed. New York: Okpaku Communications, 1971. West Africa's poet of "blackness" and a major voice in twentieth-century poetry.

STROMBERG, R. N.   *After Everything: Western Intellectual History since 1945.* New York: St. Martin's Press, 1975. Critical analysis of the trends of our times.

WILSON, E. O.   *On Human Nature.* Cambridge, Mass.: Harvard University Press, 1978. Most accessible presentation of the sociobiological emphasis on the genetic (rather than environmental) sources of human behavior. On the dispute, see A. L. Caplan, ed., *The Sociobiology Debate* (New York: Harper & Row, Pub., 1978).

Chapter · 26

THE GLOBAL DRIFT

TECHNOLOGICAL LINKAGES AND ECONOMIC INTERDEPENDENCE

Utopia Now

One of the fundamental clichés of our times—clearly illustrated in both this and the preceding chapter—is that this world grows smaller every year. One of the great utopian dreams of our blood-soaked century is that we will one day recognize that we are all citizens of this same planet and start trying to live like it.

But are these only clichés and utopian dreams? There are, in fact, several ways in which the drift toward one world has already gone considerably farther than the sharing of ideas and attitudes. The development of modern technology, for instance, has shrunk our world drastically, making all parts of it accessible in hours, information from anywhere available in seconds. The growth of economic interdependence has also linked our fates, making what a Middle Eastern sheik decides to do of crucial importance to ordinary citizens in America or Japan. In addition, the peoples of the globe have begun to organize themselves on a world scale in many areas of human endeavor.

We have spent a good deal of time reviewing the differences that sunder the world's peoples one from another. Conflicts between nations and alliances of nations, between colonizers and colonized, between East and West, North and South have defined the history of our century. Beneath divisions and conflicts, however, other trends and currents have also been flowing in the twentieth century—trends toward ma-

terial links and interdependence, toward supranational organization, toward cultural understanding, if not homogeneity. This global drift is the subject of this chapter.

Strapping the Continents

Five hundred years ago Western technology—borrowing heavily from other peoples—achieved an unequaled capacity to cross the oceans of the globe in force. European sailing ships—floating gun platforms with the latest navigational instruments and a unique cut to their canvas—quickly made Europeans rulers of the seas and gave them a unique access to all other continents and peoples.

In the nineteenth century the age of steam and telegraphy strapped continents across with rail lines, bound one continent to another with steamships, and laid down undersea cables that provided almost instantaneous communication around the world. Intercontinental empires flourished as never before. Economic interdependence grew apace. Technological progress thus made a true world order possible for the first time.

Throughout the present century technology has continued to make such a global order easier to attain. The supertanker of today dwarfs the steamships of the turn of the century—which were already ten or twenty times the size of their sail-driven predecessors. Automobiles, buses, trucks, and trains that travel more than a hundred miles an hour have revolutionized land transport in this century. And the air, penetrated only in dreams by our ancestors, has been successfully and massively invaded in the twentieth century. Electronic communications have also been updated dramatically by devices ranging from telephones and radio to television, the computer terminal, and the communications satellite.

Today, millions fly back and forth across the Atlantic between Europe and the Americas every year. Everyone in the West knows what the Great Wall of China looks like, and many in the Third World have at least a hazy idea about the New York skyline. Media expert Marshall McLuhan once said that the world was turning into a "global village," as familiar to us all as the woods and fields around the smallest county town were to its inhabitants only a century ago.

Machine Skills and Industrial Discipline

Applied science and technology have already made ours "one world" in some important ways. The cultures of all the rich nations, and even the urban cultures of less affluent societies, are one—at least in their common dependence on advanced technology. The peoples of many countries thus share a common technological sophistication, styles of life based on machines, and attitudes of mind inculcated by this common technological culture. The "gentlemen of Japan" who watched Admiral Perry land in the 1850s had almost nothing in common with their American visitors. Today, descendants of those first Americans travellers to Japan may buy their automobile or television sets from that country. They may even find that Japanese children play better baseball than their own kids do!

The cultures of the less developed nations also have more in common today, thanks to the worldwide spread of modern industrial technology. Third World people who move from the more traditional back-country into urban areas will find themselves sucked into technologically sophisticated styles of life. Machine skills, industrial discipline, and the bright lights downtown will be enough to make an African lathe operator very much like a Chinese lathe operator in Singapore.

Even the large numbers of citizens of the Third World who stay in their villages will find themselves depending on industrial technology in many ways. From plastic buckets to the school bus, from the community radio to store-bought clothes, they will feel the impact of a larger word. That first contact may well set them on the road toward still deeper involvement in the larger technological society of the world.

If we all do move further toward one world, then,

industrial technology will have played a key part in bringing it about.

The Merry-Go-Round of Money

Money, any cynic or economic historian will tell you, makes the world go round. The economic historian, at least, will probably feel that if the world is moving toward a higher degree of unity, that unity will be fundamentally economic in nature.

The gleam of gold was clearly one of the prime motives of the Old Imperialism that established the first intercontinental hegemonies five centuries ago. It was gold and silver and pearls, fish and tobacco, spices and silks and tea, slaves and brazilwood that filled the royal treasuries, earned dividends for the companies—and sent new generations of conquerors and factors out in search of expanded global dominion.

The economic dimension of the New Imperialism of the nineteenth century was obvious even to contemporaries. Western needs for raw materials and markets, for investment opportunities and cheap labor were certainly among the prime causal factors. The first intercontinental political institutions, then, reached their highest development on a foundation of economic relationships.

The "cocacolazation of the world," as the spread of American influence was sometimes called, reached even to China—here in the most literal sense. Coke is also on sale in the Soviet Union. (The Coca-Cola Company)

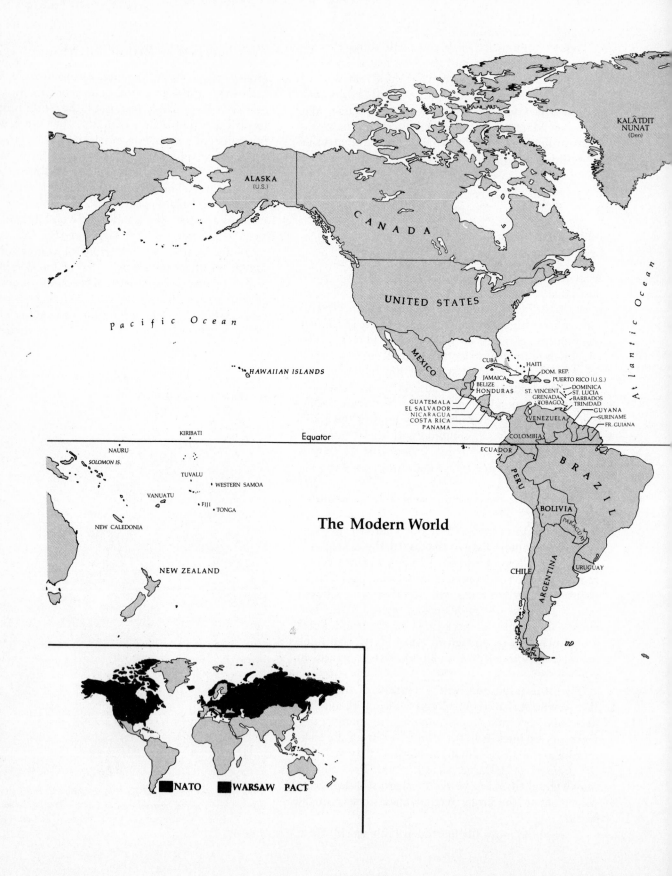

Pacific Ocean

Atlantic Ocean

KALÂTDIT
NUNAT
(Den)

ALASKA
(U.S.)

C A N A D A

UNITED STATES

MEXICO

HAWAIIAN ISLANDS

CUBA
JAMAICA
BELIZE
HONDURAS
HAITI
DOM. REP.
PUERTO RICO (U.S.)
DOMINICA
ST. VINCENT
ST. LUCIA
GRENADA
BARBADOS
TOBAGO
TRINIDAD
GUATEMALA
EL SALVADOR
NICARAGUA
COSTA RICA
PANAMA
VENEZUELA
GUYANA
SURINAME
FR. GUIANA
COLOMBIA

KIRIBATI

Equator

ECUADOR

NAURU
SOLOMON IS.
TUVALU
WESTERN SAMOA
VANUATU
FIJI
TONGA
NEW CALEDONIA

PERU
B R A Z I L
BOLIVIA
PARAGUAY

The Modern World

NEW ZEALAND

CHILE
ARGENTINA
URUGUAY

■ NATO   ■ WARSAW PACT

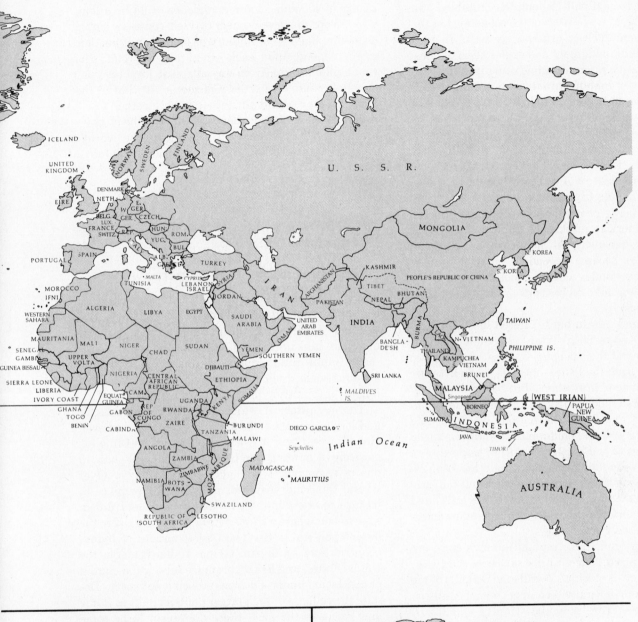

ICELAND

UNITED
KINGDOM

NORWAY

SWEDEN

FINLAND

U. S. S. R.

DENMARK
NETH.
EIRE
BELG.
LUX.
FRANCE
SWITZ.
W. GER.
E. GER.
CZECH.
HUN.
ROM.
YUG.
BUL.
ALB.

MONGOLIA

N. KOREA
S. KOREA

PORTUGAL
SPAIN
ITALY
GREECE
TURKEY

MALTA
TUNISIA
CYPRUS
LEBANON
ISRAEL
SYRIA
JORDAN
IRAN

KASHMIR
AFGHANISTAN
TIBET
NEPAL
BHUTAN

PEOPLE'S REPUBLIC OF CHINA

TAIWAN

MOROCCO
IFNI
WESTERN
SAHARA
ALGERIA
LIBYA
EGYPT
SAUDI
ARABIA
UNITED
ARAB
EMIRATES
OMAN
PAKISTAN
INDIA
BURMA
N. VIETNAM
PHILIPPINE IS.

MAURITANIA
MALI
NIGER
CHAD
SUDAN
YEMEN
SOUTHERN YEMEN
BANGLA-
DESH
THAILAND
KAMPUCHEA
S. VIETNAM
BRUNEI

SENEGAL
GAMBIA
GUINEA BISSAU
UPPER
VOLTA
NIGERIA
CENTRAL
AFRICAN
REPUBLIC
DJIBOUTI
ETHIOPIA
SRI LANKA
MALAYSIA
Singapore

SIERRA LEONE
LIBERIA
IVORY COAST
EQUAT.
GUINEA
CAM.
UGANDA
KENYA
SOMALIA
MALDIVES
IS.
BORNEO
(WEST IRIAN)

GHANA
TOGO
BENIN
GABON
REP.
OF
CONGO
RWANDA
SUMATRA
INDONESIA
PAPUA
NEW
GUINEA

CABINDA
ZAIRE
BURUNDI
TANZANIA
DIEGO GARCIA
JAVA
TIMOR

ANGOLA
MALAWI
Seychelles
Indian Ocean

ZAMBIA
MOZAMBIQUE
MADAGASCAR
MAURITIUS

NAMIBIA
ZIMBABWE
BOTS-
WANA
SWAZILAND

AUSTRALIA

REPUBLIC OF
SOUTH AFRICA
LESOTHO

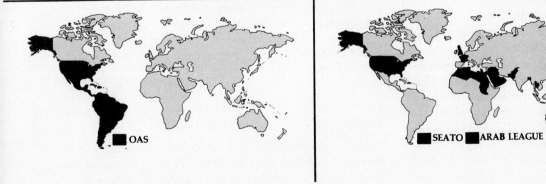

■ OAS

■ SEATO ■ ARAB LEAGUE

If world empires contributed substantially to the globalization of history, economic ties were thus evidently central to this phase of our evolution toward a more unified society.

When the formal political empires crumbled after World War II, as we have seen, the economic ties that underlay them did not crumble as well. In some places, Western investment and exploitation of cheap labor overseas, Western draining of natural resources and dumping of manufactured goods in Third World markets have even accelerated since the Great Liberation.

In the twentieth as in earlier centuries, furthermore, imperial economic ties worked both ways, making each side increasingly dependent upon the other. If Europeans or Americans bought copper or coffee or oil or jute from a former colony, that commodity-producing people became dependent on European or American markets and on the prices set in those markets far away. At the same time, however, the purchasers became dependent on their sources. Developed economies could sometimes prove extremely vulnerable to oil boycotts or high commodity prices overseas.

When large Western banks offered substantial development loans to Third World governments, those governments and their peoples—whose labor must in the end pay back the loans—mortgaged their future to foreign financial institutions. But the banks also incurred a massive dependency. The default of loans large enough to help whole nations develop could shake the biggest bank, could put the entire financial underpinnings of the Western world in jeopardy.

A mutual economic dependency had thus been established among the nations of the world. It had created not only the rival economic interests of buyer and seller, lender and borrower, but some common interests as well—such as survival.

In the short run, these mutual interests were not always recognized. The oil-price shocks of the 1970s, the financial crisis of Third World loan defaults of the mid 1980s were generally seen as economic conflicts, in which there were potential winners and losers. Western nations cut their consumption of oil and tried to squeeze higher interest rates out of debtor nations who had borrowed more than they could pay.

Yet in both cases there was some common sense, some awareness that these problems were mutual. The West did need the oil, the oil producers, a stable Western economy in which to invest their petrodollars. Third World debtor nations did need more loans in the future, and Western banks had no desire to absorb the unthinkable losses that would ensue if they declared these loans uncollectible. In the end it was a game nobody could win—unless both sides won.

Awareness of the common economic catastrophes that could result from failure to recognize mutual interests seemed to grow as the twentieth century entered its closing decades. Simple recognition of the reality of economic interdependence could be a long step toward the development of a self-conscious global economy. Such a community of getters and spenders might depend upon each other to get through the rough patches, not from any altruistic impulses, but simply because all parties realized at last that in the long run they would all sink or swim together.

Economic interdependence, then, may be as powerful a force as technology in bringing the world's peoples closer together, in converting an arena into a community.

WORLD ORGANIZATION

From Hunting Band to Superpower

It is also possible that humanity may drift closer in this unprecedented global venture than technological ties and global economic interdependence. For humans are also organizing animals, and we have already begun in this century to organize ourselves on a world scale as never before in history. How far might this tendency take us in centuries to come?

There is historical evidence of a drift toward larger and larger organizations and more regional and even global institutions. A world population consisting exclusively of hunting bands did, after all, give way to one of somewhat larger agricultural villages. Over several thousand years this new order gave place in its turn to one dominated by city-states, and this in time to one where nation-states and empires were the largest political units. The largest nations of today, countries such as Russia, China, India, Canada, the United States, and Brazil, organize substantial chunks of continents under a central ordering authority. Despite the collapse of such larger political units as Rome and Persia in the past, there does seem to be some indication of social evolution at work.

Against this background, then, let us look at the recent tendency toward international and even supranational structures.

Transcending the Nation-State

Effective international organization on anything resembling a global scale had to wait until the nineteenth century. At that time, a series of technical organizations were set up to deal with problems common to many nations or to provide international institutions where they were obviously necessary. Such groups included the International Telegraphic Union in 1865, the Universal Postal Union of 1874, and patent, copyright, and other international unions from the 1870s on. Organizations relating to peace and war between nations were also established, notably the International Red Cross in 1864 and the World Court (Permanent Court of Arbitration) set up by the First Hague Conference in 1899.

The twentieth century, and particularly its second half, has seen two major attempts at global organization intended to keep the peace and to deal with problems common to a number of peoples. The League of Nations, founded after World War I, and the United Nations, growing out of World War II, represent the most ambitious efforts thus far at global organization. Even the U.N., however, should be seen as only the apex of a pyramid of regional and global institutions that affect all our lives.

Europe alone boasts an elaborate structure of regional organizations—in some cases two such structures, one for Western Europe, one for the East bloc. Besides the two military alliances, NATO and the Warsaw Pact, there are the Western European Common Market and its Eastern equivalent, COMECON. The West also boasts the European Coal Community, the European Steel Community, and EURATOM, the European Atomic Energy Community. These latter are true supranational rather than merely international organizations, since they have some power to control aspects of the policy of their members, to innovate and direct the development of the nations, rather than simply carrying out their wishes.

Other important regional organizations include the Organization of American States, the Central American Common Market, the Latin American Free Trade Association, the Organization of African Unity, the Organization of Petroleum Exporting Countries, as well as the regular meetings of the heads of state of nonaligned countries, the economic summits that bring together the leaders of the half dozen most developed Western nations, and so on.

Global organizations associated with or grouped around the United Nations, finally, include the Food and Agricultural Organization, the World Health Organization, the United Nations Educational, Scientific, and Cultural Organization, the World Bank (International Bank for Reconstruction and Development), and the International Monetary Fund, as well as such holdovers from earlier years as the World Court and the International Labor Organization. At the top of this bewildering array of world organizations stands the United Nations, with its Security Council for the great powers and its General Assembly for all the nearly two hundred smaller nations of the world.

The story of these twentieth-century attempts at organizing our world on a scale that transcends the nation-state is one of continual expansion, and of expansion in more ways than one. International associations have certainly grown in number, from a handful of multilateral organizations and compacts at the turn of the century to thousands today. Originally centering in Europe, they have spread to Asia, Africa, and the Americas, as the names of some of the regional groups listed above indicate. The staffs and activities of such institutions have also expanded and become more truly international. From small numbers of administrators, most of them European or American working in Europe or the United States, these staffs have grown to thousands and tens of thousands, drawn from all parts of the world and working on all continents.

The world thus already has an international bureaucracy in place, attempting to do for international problems what the civil services of the nations do for their own peoples. These international administrators still depend totally on the nations, particularly the great powers, for the funding and support to do their work. Nevertheless, they may have an important part to play in our common future.

Private Sector International

The world is thus meshed in a net of international and supranational regional and global organizations, associations, unions, communities, compacts, agreements. But there are an even larger number of global and regional associations that have nothing to do with nation-states or governments. These are the organizations of private groups of all sorts that link people through a common pursuit or interest or help them to carry out a common line of endeavor.

Such organizations bind the world in myriad ways. Examples from the bulky *Yearbook of International Organizations* include associations of business people, such as the European Liaison Committee for Machine Tool Importers; of laborers, such as the Arab Federation of Transport Workers; and of professional people, including such specialized groups as the World Association of Veterinary Microbiologists, Immunologists, and Specialists in Infectious Diseases.

There are international organizations dedicated to sport, such as the Asian Basketball Association; to culture, such as the International Institute of Comparative Musical Studies; and to good causes, such as the International Peace Research Association, the Latin American Council for Adult Education, and the International Temperance Association. For young people with an urge to get involved, there are the World Council of Young Men's Service Clubs—and the International Federation of Liberal and Radical Youth.

The private sector, in short, is as internationalized as the governments of the world are becoming. Business leaders, sports enthusiasts, do-gooders are all used to operating on a global level, aware of the larger world beyond their national frontiers. Many of these groups are small and of limited impact on the nations or the world. But there are twenty thousand such organizations listed in the latest issue of the *Yearbook*—and the number is growing.

THE GLOBE ENCOMPASSED

Global Elites

Conversation between two businessmen, overheard in a bar in New Delhi:

"How's the wife?"

"Oh, very well. And Sally?"

Pictures of growing children pass from hand to hand. Compliments are exchanged. Another round is ordered.

It is a conversation scarcely worth noticing. Except that one of the two men is American, the other Japanese. They first met in Panama, where their respective firms were engaged in construction projects. They are engineers, experts in earthquake-proof construction, in New Delhi for an international conference on earthquake engineering.

"Please give my regards to your wife."

"And mine to Mrs. Takahira."

The names were not Sally or Takahira, but the rest of the conversation was quite real. And the two men themselves represent a very important group in the world today—the new global elite.

There are a number of such elites, actually. Engineers and scientists, managers and business executives, representatives of governments and of international agencies are among the most important. They include such people as the Ford technicians who set up assembly lines in the Soviet Union in the 1930s, the Russian technicians in Cuba in the 1960s, and the Cuban technicians in Africa today. Jet-hopping around the world, rebuilding the world in the image of our century, they contribute enormously to the sense any traveler must feel of one world in the making.

There are also strictly national elites who are cast so thoroughly in an international mold that they constitute a force for international solidarity without ever crossing a national frontier. In their Western-style

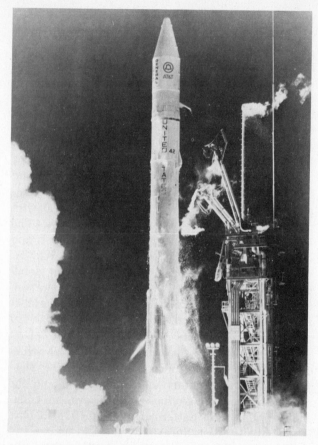

An American Telephone and Telegraph communications satellite is lofted into space by a NASA rocket. Technology linked all the continents as the twentieth century drew to a close. (A. T. & T. Co., Photo/Graphics Center)

business suits or their American-style shirt sleeves, sharing a common body of technical training, managerial skills, problems of government or business, career-mindedness, greed, or humanitarian dedication, they are much more alike than any of their ancestors could have been.

Likeness does not guarantee harmony among peoples. But contacts and common interests among elites surely make international tolerance and understanding that much more likely in the future.

Global Encounters

The same is quite likely true of the immensely expanded number of encounters between peoples in the past century. Such international encounters between ordinary citizens of different countries take many forms. We think first perhaps of tourists, traveling easily in Europe or America, or being the first in their group to fly to China. But large numbers of migrant laborers—"guest workers"—live for years in foreign countries now as well. Business people of many nations, like the two engineers in the preceding section, are routinely assigned to distant lands. American or Russian military personnel may be stationed anywhere from Korea to Afghanistan to their respective Germanies.

Students throng to foreign universities, and young backpacking wanderers travel the dusty roads of everywhere by foot and bus. Members of the Peace Corps settle into the villages of Africa or South America to help local people build a school or learn to grow a new strain of corn. There are even missionaries of many faiths out there still, offering medicine as much as missionary faith, many of them spending more of their lives among peoples of other lands than at home.

Such close contacts with other peoples dwarf any previous contacts between the continents. To know your neighbors is not necessarily to love them, of course, and culture shock or resentment of intrusive foreign ways are common early reactions in such people-to-people encounters. But many who are fortunate enough to meet and live with others come to feel that, although their own ways are clearly better, there is something to be learned from the rest of the world too.

Global Problems

Little more need be said about the great problems of our era, many of which have obvious international ramifications. Population growth may be a greater

One world, seen from space. Keeping the globe intact is the greatest single challenge facing the generations that will carry the human venture into the twentieth-first century. (NASA)

problem for Third World countries, pollution primarily a threat to the industrially developed nations. Nuclear power plants do not look like a menace to Third World countries that do not have any such plants, or any likelihood of acquiring them in the foreseeable future. Economic dependency, famine, disease, and illiteracy, by contrast, are much more obvious difficulties for Africa and South America than for Europe or North America.

Nevertheless, we do all share the same planet, and a problem for one region or type of nation can easily become a problem for all. A hungry, frustrated, angry Third World would clearly be a global problem. Pollution that damages the earth's atmosphere affects all peoples. Accidental—or deliberate—discharge of atomic radiation into the air would affect us all, regardless of political alignment or level of economic development.

Such problems, in short, are problems for *all* of us. We all have an interest in seeing them solved with minimal damage to our common world. It is another link that binds us as citizens of planet earth.

That Global Drift

A central thesis of this book has been that we are living today in the first age of truly global history. Beneath the turbulence of our times, we may discern a drift toward a new world order. The global interdependence, organizations, elites, and people-to-people encounters mentioned above, the possibilities of planetary culture, and the certainty of planetary problems are all evidence that such a glacially slow but inexorable drift is in fact in motion.

In a perverse way, the very tumult of our age might be adduced as evidence that such a new world order is taking shape. Social chaos has not infrequently preceded—indeed, motivated—the emergence of new social orders. Out of the ancient struggle between Upper and Lower Egypt emerged a pharaonic unity that prevailed for most of the next three thousand years. From China's centuries-long Warring States Period came the Ch'in-Han unification of the Chinese Empire, the oldest civilization existing today. The chaotic European Dark Ages preceded the synthesis of the High Middle Ages, a time of cultural, if not political, unity.

We should perhaps stress variety here, since the global drift of our times—if such there be—may well lead to something resembling a balance of powers sharing a common culture, rather than to a unitary structure of government. The common culture of Europe, of Latin America, or of the Muslim center of Eurasia might come closer to what awaits us on a global scale than the examples of the United States or the unitary Chinese Empire of history.

Should a new and larger planetary order be in the making, it would be grounds, at least, for hope. We might yet avoid the global disaster that many today see as the most likely conclusion to the conflicts and confrontations that divide our world.

SUMMARY

In the later twentieth century, a broad historical drift toward one world was detectable in a variety of fields. Technologically, economically, politically, and in many other ways, the peoples of the world were bound up with one another as they had never been before.

Technologically, the trends of past centuries continued into the twentieth, binding the globe with rapid transportation and instant communication. Shared machine skills and common acceptance of industrial discipline also made people on all continents more alike than they had ever been.

Economically, the nations of the world found themselves more mutually dependent than ever before. It was becoming apparent by the 1980s that even the global North and South had fundamental economic interests in common. A Third World nation's debt was as much a problem for the creditor bank as for the debtor government.

Most strikingly, perhaps, global organizations proliferated in the second half of the twentieth century. Superstates and international treaties and associations bound millions. Private organizations and special-interest associations linked people to their fellow human beings in other nations, regions, and continents.

Other common elements in the world of the 1980s were further evidence of this global drift. These included global elites, who often had much in common based on their common functions at the top of the bureaucratic-industrial world; the increasing frequency of encounters between people from different cultures; and the common problems shared by all people on this shrinking globe.

SUGGESTED READING

BARNET, R. J. *Global Reach: The Power of the Multinational Corporations.* New York: Simon & Schuster, 1974. The multinational corporation as a key factor in the world economy.

BELL, D. *The Coming of Post-Industrial Society.* New York: Basic Books, 1976. Future social trends, as understood by an eminent sociologist.

BUGINCOURT, J. "A New Colonialism," *Development Forum* 5 (1977). Critical treatment of Western tourism in the Third World.

CERVENKA, Z. *The Unfinished Quest for Unity: Africa and the OAU.* London: Friedman, 1977. Good example of a major regional organization with more potential for unity than is commonly assumed. On the original impetus for African togetherness, see I. Geiss, *The Pan-African Movement* (London: Methuen, 1974).

CHAUDHURI, N. *The Continent of Circe.* Bombay: Jaico Pub. Co., 1966. The mind-set of Westernized elites in Third World countries.

CONNELLY, P., and R. PEARLMAN. *The Politics of Scarcity.* New York: Oxford University Press, 1976. Discusses Third World commodity producers' cartels, another important organizing force in the evolving global economy. See also R. J. Barnet, *The Lean Years: The Politics of the Age of Scarcity* (New York: Simon & Schuster, 1980).

DIAZ-ALEJANDRO, C. F. "North-South Relations: The Economic Component," *International Organization,* 29 (Winter 1975), 213–241. The broad picture of this central aspect of the often painful ties that bind developed and underdeveloped countries.

FOSTER, G. M. *Traditional Cultures and the Impact of Technological Change.* New York: Harper & Row, Pub., 1963. The homogenizing impact of modern technology around the world. For an important regional example, see S. Langdon, "Technology Transfer by Multinational Corporations in Africa: Effects on the Economy," *African Development,* 2, no. 2 (1977), 95–114.

HERMAN, B. *The Optimal International Division of Labor.* Geneva: International Labor Organization, 1975. One important form of global interdependence is explored here.

LASSERRE-BIGORRY, J. H. *General Survey of Present-Day International Migration for Employment.* Geneva: International Labor Office, 1975. Summary of migrant labor patterns around the world—a more potent force for global unity than tourism or other casual travel.

LUARD, E. *A History of the United Nations*. London: Macmillan, 1982. Deals with the earlier years of the most promising international political organization to date.

MEAD, M., ed. *Cultural Patterns and Technical Change*. New York: New American Library, 1955. A distinguished and concerned anthropologist gives her view of the impact of modernizing technology on the diversity of cultures.

ROSTOW, W. W. *The World Economy: History and Prospect*. Austin: University of Texas Press, 1978. A well-known developmental economist looks ahead to the global future.

WALLERSTEIN, I. *The Capitalist World-Economy*. Cambridge: Cambridge University Press, 1979. Economic predominance as a global force.

Index

Congo River, 60, 174
Congress of Vienna, 138–39
Congress Party, 255–56, 337
Conquistadores, 75, 92–93, 96
Conrad, Joseph, 174
Conservatism, modern Western, 136–39,
    145–46, 166, 23–36, 265, 350–51, 353–
    54
Conservative Party, 235, 354
Constable, John, 148
Constantinople, 12, 30–32 (See also Instan-
    bul)
Constitutional monarchy, 110–11, 136
Constitution of 1917, 248
Constitution (US), 154, 156
Containment policy, 315, 324
Continental Congress, 155
Cook, James, 94
Coolidge, Calvin, 232
Copernicus, Nicolaus, 114
Copper, 76, 180, 207–8, 333–34
Coral Sea, 285
Cortez, Hernando, 93, 95–96
Cossacks, 122, 125, 185–86
Counter-Reformation, 23–25, 92, 169–70
Crimean War, 242
Criollos, 163–65
Cromwell, Oliver, 111
Cromwell, Thomas, 16
Cross of Fire Party, 236
Crusades, 31
Cuba, 96, 318–19, 321–22, 324, 366–67
Cuban missile crisis, 318, 321–22, 324
Cultural diffusion, 192, 194
Cultural evolution, 74
Cultural pluralism, 8
Cultural Revolution, 363
Curie, Marie, 294
Cuzco, 74, 76
Czars, 242–43
Czechoslovakia, 236, 279, 313–14, 317, 323

Da Gama, Vasco, 92–93, 95
Daimyo, 50, 127–28, 183
Dakar, 179, 365
"Dallas," 376
Danzig, 279
Darkness at Noon, 299
Darwin, Charles, 148
David, 18–19
Davis, Jefferson, 159
D Day, 285
Decameron, 20
Decembrists, 242
Declaration of Independence, 155
Declaration of the Rights of Man, 136
Decline of the West, 298
Defoe, Daniel, 116–17
De Gaulle, Charles, 310, 323, 332
Delhi, 35, 39
Delhi Sultanate, 35
Democracy, 139, 145, 156, 203–8, 222, 236–
    37, 348, 364, 367
Democratic Party, 206, 234, 350–51
Demoiselles d'Avignon, 296
Demonstrations, political, 255, 346–47, 351
Deng Xiaoping, 363
Denmark, 11, 280
Dependency, economic, 166–67, 207–8, 360–
    61

Depression, Great, 228–29, 231–37, 261,
    265, 270, 276
Détente, 322–23
Díaz, Porfirio, 207, 246–47
Dickens, Charles, 149
Dickinson, Emily, 161
Diem, Ngo Dinh, 320
Dien Bien Phu, 338
Diet, 210, 270, 302
Directory, 136–37
Disarmament negotiations, 231–32, 324–25
Discovery, Age of, 93–94
Disraeli, Benjamin, 145, 178
Divine Faith, 36
Divine right, 14
Djilas, Milovan, 346
Dorgon, 124
Drake, Francis, 17, 98
Dream of Han Tan, 52
Dream of the Red Chamber, 130
Dreyfus, Alfred, 203
Dubcek, Alexander, 317
DuBois, W. E. B., 257
Duma, 205, 242–43
Dunkirk, 282
Dupleix, Joseph, 98–99
Dutch, 16, 22–24, 93–94, 96–98, 127
Dutch East India Company, 97, 283, 330
Dutch East Indies, 211, 328
Dutch Empire, 96–97, 175, 179, 181, 328–
    29
Dutch Revolt, 16, 24
Dyarchy, 125–26
Dynastic cycle, 44–45

Earth and the Elements, 300
East Germany (German Democratic Repub-
    lic), 309, 313, 315, 317, 323
Echeverría, Esteban, 170
Economic growth, 156–57, 160–62, 167, 203,
    207–8, 210, 228–29, 232, 237, 246, 266,
    268, 270, 309–10, 312–13, 344–45, 366–
    67
Economic interdependence, 381–84
Ecuador, 73, 165–166
Edo, 128, 130, 183 (See also Tokyo)
Egypt, 30, 32–33, 121–22, 178, 180, 210–11,
    284, 335
Einstein, Albert, 294, 372–73
Eisenhower, Dwight, 285, 321, 349–50
Eisenstein, Sergei, 302
El Alamein, 284
Eliot, T. S., 297–98
Elizabeth I, 14, 16–18, 98
El Salvador, 139, 367
Emerson, Ralph Waldo, 169
Empires, 3–4, 87–89, 211 (See also Imperi-
    alism, Western, and individual em-
    pires)
Encyclopedia (Chinese), 52
Encyclopedia (French), 115
Energy, 137–38
Engels, Friederich, 141
England, 11, 14–18 (See also Britain)
English Revolution, 24–25, 106, 110–11, 240
Enlightened despots, 107–9, 163 (See also in-
    dividual rulers)
Enlightenment, 105, 107, 115–17, 135–36,
    164, 168–70

Entente, 216
Entrepreneurs, 138
Erasmus, Desiderius, 18
Erhard, Ludwig, 354
Essays, 20
Estates General, 14, 110, 136
Este, Isabella d', 13–14
Estonia, 282
Ethiopia, 180, 277, 366
Eunuchs, 46
Eurasia, 7–8, 120
EURATOM, 385
Europe, 2–4, 7, 9–26, 32–33, 43, 81, 89, 91–
    102, 104–17, 120, 134–49, 202–5, 216–
    25, 234–35, 275–89
    Eastern Europe, 271, 285, 310, 316–18,
        354–55
    Western Europe, 138–39, 309–10, 323,
        353–55
Europeans, 4, 11, 48, 62, 161, 196
Ewuare, 60
Extraterritoriality, 184
Eyck, Jan and Hubert, 19

Faerie Queene, 20
Farmers, 160–61, 188–89, 205, 224, 229–30
    (See also Agriculture, Peasants)
Fascism, 262–64
Fascist Party, 263–64
Fatehpur Sikri, 39–40
Fatherland Front, 271
February Revolution, 243
Ferdinand, 14–15
Ferry, Jules, 179
Feudalism, 50–51, 128
Ficino, Marsilio, 13
Finland, 280
Firebird, 296
Fitzgerald, Scott, 232
Five Year Plans, 246, 268–70
Florence, 12–13
Foch, Marshal Ferdinand, 219
Folk art, 374–75
Forbidden, City, 45
Ford, Henry, 230, 234
For Whom the Bell Tolls, 299
Fourteen Points, 224–25
France, 10–15, 22–25, 105–7, 109–11, 139,
    145–46, 155–56, 203, 216–22, 224, 235–
    36, 277–79, 282, 285, 310–11, 323, 354
Francis I, 14–15
Francis Ferdinand, 216–17
Francis Joseph, 204, 219
Franco, Francisco, 278
Franco-Prussian War, 146
Franklin, Benjamin, 155–56, 168–69
Frederick II the Great, 108
Frederick William, the Great Elector, 107–
    8
Free trade, 142
French, 93–94, 97–98, 123, 179, 321, 328–
    29
French East India Company, 97–99
French Empire, 97–99, 153, 174–75, 179–81,
    224, 257–58, 320, 328–29, 331–32, 335,
    338–39
French Equatorial Africa, 180, 328, 331
French Indochina, 211, 283, 338–39
French Revolution, 134–37, 140, 240
French West Africa, 179, 257–58, 328, 330–
    31

Freud, Sigmund, 295
Fugger family, 12
Führer, 262, 264, 266

Gagarin, Yuri, 344
Galilei, Galileo, 114
Gallipoli, 219, 221
Galván, Ignacio Rodriguez, 170
Gandhi, Indira, 364
Gandhi, Mohandas, 5, 212, 241, 255–56, 337
Gandhi, Rajiv, 364
Ganges, 35, 123, 300
Gapon, Father, 205
García Marques, Gabriel, 375
Gargantua and Pantagruel, 20
Garibaldi, Giuseppe, 140, 146
Gaucho Martin Fierro, 170
Gauchos, 162, 170
Gaughin, Paul, 295
Gauleiters, 266
General Assembly (UN), 311
General Strike, 235
Generation of 1880, 207–8
Geneva, 22
Gentileschi, Artemisia, 13
German Empire, 139, 145–46, 180–81, 217–18, 222–24
German Southwest Africa, 217, 220 (*See also* Namibia)
Germany, 11–12, 20–22, 106–8, 139, 145–46, 203–4, 216–22, 224, 264–67, 275–76, 278–89, 301, 308–9, 312, 315 (*See also* Prussia, East Germany, West Germany)
Gestapo, 266–67
Gettysburg, 159
Ghana, 330–31 (*See also* Gold Coast)
Ghana, Old, 58
Ghazis, 31, 122
Ghost dance, 188, 212
Gilded Age, 160–61, 205
Giolitti, Giovanni, 204
Gladstone, William, 145, 178
Globalization of history, 370–88
Goa, 95–96
Gold, 12, 92, 100–101, 110, 179, 236
Gold Coast, 179, 211, 257, 330–31 (*See also* Ghana, Old)
Golden Horde, 185
Golden Horn, 31, 121–22
Gompers, Samuel, 161
Gomulka, Wladislav, 317
Good Hope, Cape of, 2
Good Neighbor Policy, 234
Gorbachev, Mikhail, 352–53
Gordon, General Charles "Chinese," 179
Government economic planning, 246, 288, 348
GPU, 270
Gran Colombia, 165–66
Grande Jatte, La, 148
Grant, General Ulysses S., 159
Grapes of Wrath, 298
Great Leap Forward, 363
Great Wall of China, 49
Greece, 18, 20, 33, 122, 282
Grenada, 319
Guadalcanal, 285–86
Guatemala, 70, 318, 366–67
Guernica, 297

Guerrillas, 146, 318–21, 332–33, 363, 366–67
Guest workers, 386–87
Guevarra, Che, 318
Guinea Coast, 8, 56, 59–60, 179
Gunboat diplomacy, 180

Habsburg dynasty, 15, 106, 108, 121, 136, 139, 222
Haciendas, 166–67
Hafiz of Shiraz, 38
Hagia Sophia, 40
Haiku poetry, 130
Haile Selassie, 277
Haiti, 164, 206
Hamilton, Alexander, 156
Hamlet, 20
Ham Nghi, 211
Hampton Institute, 161
Han learning, 130
Hanlin Academy, 51–52
Hanoi, 49
Hanseatic League, 12
Harding, Warren, 232
Hawaii, 283, 285
Hawthorne, Nathaniel, 169
Hay Wain, 148
Heart of Darkness, 174
Heian culture, 50, 130
Heisenberg, Werner, 294
Hemingway, Ernest, 169, 278, 298–99
Henry, Patrick, 155
Henry IV, 15, 110
Henry VII, 14, 16
Henry VIII, 14, 16
Hernandez, José, 170
Hidalgo, Father, 164
Hideyoshi, 127
Himalayas, 35
Hindenburg, Paul von, 219, 264–65
Hinduism, 129–30, 181, 212, 255–56, 300
Hindus, 36, 122, 181, 364
Hirohito, 271, 283
Hiroshima, 287, 289, 308
Hitler, Adolf, 222, 230, 236, 262, 264–68, 270, 276–87, 301
Hitler Youth, 266
Ho Chi Minh, 320, 338–39
Hohenzollern dynasty, 106–8, 145–46, 204, 222, 264
Holmes, Sherlock, 202
Holy Roman Empire, 11, 15, 21–22, 33, 106–8 (*See also* Austria, Austria-Hungary)
Honduras, 70
Hong Kong, 183–84, 283, 339, 364
Honshu, 49
Hoover, Herbert, 232
Horn, Cape, 2
Horthy, Admiral Nicholas, 271
Houphouët-Boigny, Félix, 365
Howells, William Dean, 169
Huckleberry Finn, 169
Huerta, Victorino, 247–48
Huguenots, 15–16, 22–24
Huitzilopochtli, 71, 74–75
Humanism, 18
Hungary, 33–34, 121, 271, 282, 313, 317, 323
Hunting and gathering, 4, 80–83, 85, 137
Hus, Jan, 21
Hussein, Saddam, 337

Hydroelectric power, 230, 234, 246
Hydrogen bomb, 324

Ibsen, Henrik, 149
Ideology, 3–5, 139–41, 193–94, 240–41, 246, 250, 252, 262–63, 299–303, 372
Ieyasu, 127
Ife, 63–64
Ilkhans, 31, 38
Imams, 34, 337
Immigrants, 157, 161, 186–89, 195–96, 237, 334
Imperialism, Western, 4–5, 45–46, 87–88, 92–93, 120, 122–23, 126–27, 206–7, 251
Old Imperialism, 91–102, 122–23, 126–27, 153–55, 162–63
New Imperialism, 140, 157, 174–96, 210–12, 217–18, 224–25, 254–58, 328–40
Inca highway, 76
Incas, 4, 8, 73–74, 76–77, 93, 96
Incendiary bombs, 289
India, 4, 28, 35–37, 95–99, 120, 122–23, 129–30, 181, 235, 255–56, 300, 331, 337–39, 364
Indian Mutiny, 181, 211
Indian Ocean, 4, 8, 33, 95–96
Indians, 196, 221, 334
Indians, American (*See* Amerindians, Native Americans)
Indirect rule, 179, 257
Indochina, 181 (*See also* French Indochina, individual countries)
Indonesia, 181, 365 (*See also* Dutch East Indies)
Industrialization, 217, 229–30, 237, 246, 268–71, 363–66, 380–81 (*See also* Technology)
Inflation, 12, 265, 345
Inquisition, 15, 25
International bureaucracy, 385–86
International Monetary Fund, 5, 311, 385
International organizations, 306, 310–11, 384–86 (*See also* specific organizations)
International Telegraphic Union, 385
Iran, 33, 181, 272, 336–37, 365 (*See also* Persia)
Iraq, 33, 337, 365 (*See also* Mesopotamia)
Ireland, 235–36
Irish, 203
Iron Guard, 271
Isabella, Queen, 14–15, 92
Isfahan, 35, 40, 122
Islam, 7, 28–40, 58, 62–63, 87, 122–23, 129, 212, 257, 335–37, 364–65, 371
Shiites, 34, 122, 336–37
Sunnites, 34, 122, 337
Islamic empires, 7, 31–37
Islamic fundamentalism, 365
Ismail, 33–34
Israel, 33, 335, 355
Istanbul, 32–33, 39–40, 121–22
Italian Empire, 180
Italy, 11–15, 18–20, 107, 139, 146, 204, 263–64, 275–79, 284
Iturbide, Augustín de, 164
Ivan IV the Terrible, 108–9
Ivory Coast, 258, 365
Iwo Jima, 287

Jackson, Andrew, 156, 188
Jacobins, 136

Jahan, 40
James, Henry, 169
James, William, 169, 294
Janissary Corps, 33, 121
Japan, 5, 7–8, 43, 49–53, 88, 99, 120, 126–
    28, 130–31, 181–83, 209–11, 220–21,
    244, 250, 270–71, 275–77, 279–80, 282–
    83, 285–89, 302–3, 309–10, 329, 339,
    353
Japanese, 253, 271, 288
Japanese prints, 128, 130–31
Jaruzelski, Wojciech, 318
Java, 97
Jazz Age, 228, 231–32, 298
Jefferson, Thomas, 155–56, 169
Jerusalem, 31
Jesuits, 23, 48, 169–70
Jews, 15, 265–67, 335
Jinnah, Muhammad Ali, 337
Joan of Arc, 14
John III Sobieski, 121
Johnson, Lyndon, 349–50
Joint stock companies, 12
Jordan, 33
Joseph II, 107–8
Joyce, James, 297
Juana de la Cruz, 170
Justices of the Peace, 16

Kabuki theater, 130
Kabul, 181, 321
Kaddafi, Maummar, 365
Kafka, Franz, 297
Kamakura shogunate, 50
Kampuchea, 339
K'ang-hsi, 124–25
Karanga, 61–62
Kashmir, 39–40, 337
Katanga province, 333–34
Kaunda, Kenneth, 334
Keats, John, 149
Kellogg-Briand Pact, 231
Kennan, George, 315
Kennedy, John, 321–22, 349–50
Kenya, 179, 332–33, 365–66
Kenyatta, Jomo, 258, 333, 365–66
Kepler, Johannes, 114
Kerensky, Alexander, 219, 243–44
Kerensky offensive, 219
Keynes, John Maynard, 372–73
Khmer Rouge, 339
Khomeini, Ruhollah, 337, 365
Khrushchev, Nikita, 321–22, 352–53
Kiangsi Soviet, 253
Kikuyu, 333
Kim Il Sung, 320
King Lear, 20
King, Martin Luther, 346, 350–51
Kipling, Rudyard, 174–75
Kiuprili family, 121
Kizilbashi, 33–35
Koestler, Arthur, 299
Kohl, Helmut, 323
Kongo, 60–61
Koran, 28, 39
Korea, 43, 48–49, 126, 183–84, 309, 339 (See
    also North Korea, South Korea)
Korean War, 320, 339
Kremlin, 246, 253, 270
Krishna, 130
Kristalnacht, 264, 267

Krupp, Albert, 143
Kulaks, 269–70
Kuomintang Party, 249–53, 277
Kyoto, 49, 127, 130

Labor, industrial, 138, 143–44, 157, 161, 248
Labor unions, 139–40, 161, 208, 234, 263,
    266, 318, 355
Labour Party, 235, 310, 329, 337, 354
Lafayette, Marquis de, 156
Laos, 181, 283, 321, 339
Last Supper, 19
Latvia, 282
Laura, Sonnets to, 20
Lawrence, T. E., 221
League of Nations, 5, 224–25, 231, 277, 385
League of the Iroquois, 188, 257
Lease, Mary E., 161
Leaves of Grass, 169
Lebanon, 33, 180, 335
Lebensraum, 278
Le dynasty, 49
Lee, General Robert E., 159
Lenin, Vladimir Ilich, 174, 205, 225, 241–
    45, 251, 268, 302
Leningrad, 282, 284 (See also St. Petersburg)
Leninism, 242, 244, 251, 268–69, 302 (See
    also Marxism)
Leo X, 21–22
Leonardo da Vinci, 19
Leopold II, 180
Lepanto, 16, 121
Lexington, 155
Liaotung peninsula, 183–84
Liberal Democratic Party, 353
Liberalism, 139–40, 145, 194, 240–41, 250,
    261–62, 264, 278, 372
Liberal Party, 145, 203, 235
Liberals, 264, 266
Libya, 33, 180, 204, 257, 284, 365
Liebknecht, Karl, 264
Lincoln, Abraham, 159
Ling Meng-ch'i, 52
Lithuania, 282
Livingston, Dr. David, 177
Llaneros, 165
Lloyd George, David, 203, 219, 222
Locarno treaties, 231
Locke, John, 115–16, 136, 140, 169
London, 11–12, 143, 176, 255, 282
Long March, 253
Lorenz, H. A., 294
Lost Generation, 297–98
Louis XI, 14–15
Louis XIV, 97–98, 105–7, 109–11
Louis XVI, 135–36
Louisiana Purchase, 157
L'Ouverture, Toussaint, 164
Louvois, Marquis de, 110
Low Countries, 235, 280–82 (See also indi-
    vidual countries)
Loyola, Ignatius, 23
Lumumba, Patrice, 333–34
Luther, Martin, 21–22
Lutheranism, 22
Luthuli, Albert, 366
Luxembourg, 280–82
Luxembourg, Rosa, 264

Macao, 95
MacArthur, Douglas, 287, 320

Machiavelli, Niccolo, 18
Machine guns, 220
Machu Picchu, 76
MacMillan, Harold, 334
Madagascar, 179, 211
Madero, Francisco, 241, 247
Madras, 98–99
Madrid, 278
Magellan, Ferdinand, 2, 4, 93
Maginot Line, 236, 280–82
Mahabharata, 130
Mahdi, the, 179
Maji-Maji Rebellion, 180, 211
Malacca, 95
Malaya, 181, 283, 338
Mali, 58, 365
Malraux, André, 299
Mamelukes, 32
Manchu banners, 49, 124
Manchu (Ch'ing) dynasty, 124–26, 209,
    248–53
Manchuria, 43, 49, 124, 126, 186, 253, 270–
    71, 277, 309, 339
Manchus, 48–49, 120, 123–26
Mandarins, 46, 209
Mandate of Heaven, 44, 124, 249
Mandates, 224, 257
Mande, 58, 179, 211–12
Manet, Édouard, 148
Man in Four Elements, 300
Man's Fate, 299
Man's Hope, 299
Maoism, 363
Maoris, 185, 189
Mao Tse-tung, 241, 249, 251–54, 277, 323,
    339, 363–64
Marathas, 123
Maria Theresa, 107–8
Marie Antoinette, 136
Marines, US, 206, 285, 287, 319
Marinetti, Filippo, 297
Marlowe, Christopher, 20
Marshall, John, 156
Marshall Plan, 309–10, 313
Martí, José, 202
Marx, Karl, 4–5, 141, 230–31
Marxism, 141, 241–42, 246, 268–69, 300,
    302, 372
    Marxism-Leninism, 251, 268
Masaryk, Jan, 315
Masks, African, 64–65
Massachusetts, 153
Materialism, 148
Mather, Cotton, 168
Mau Mau, 333
Mayans, 70
May Fourth Movement, 251
Mayakovsky, Vladimir, 300
Mazzini, Giuseppe, 4–5, 146
Mbanza, 60
McCarthy, Joseph, 350
Mecca, 28, 40
Medici family, 12–13, 21
Medici, Lorenzo de', 13
Mediterranean Sea, 10–11, 32–33, 179
Meiji Emperor, 183, 209–10
Meiji Restoration, 181–83
Mein Kampf, 265
Melville, Herman, 169
Mercantilism, 97, 110, 140, 155, 165
Merchants, 11, 92–93, 96–97, 111–12
Mesoamerica (See Americas, Middle Amer-
    ica)

Mesopotamia, 32, (*See also* Iraq)
Mestizos, 163–65, 207, 246–48
Metternich, Prince Klemens von, 139
Mexican Revolution, 206, 241, 246–48
Mexican-US War, 157, 175
Mexico, 8, 68, 70–72, 93, 96, 163–64, 166–67, 170, 206–8, 246–48, 300, 366–67
Mexico City, 164, 247–48, 343
Meyerhold, Vsevelod, 300
Michelangelo Buonarroti, 13, 18–19
Middle Ages, 12, 14
Middle Classes, 11, 92–93, 96–97, 111–14, 116–17, 138, 144, 223–24, 228–30, 255, 257, 265, 297, 345–46
Middle East, 3, 5, 28, 30–33, 37, 180–81, 224, 335–37
Midway, 285
Mihrab, 40
Militarism, 270–71, 302–3 (*See also* Arms races)
Military rule, 167, 270–72, 362–63, 367 (See also *Caudillos*, Warlords)
Millet, Jean-François, 148
Ming dynasty, 4, 45–53, 120, 124
Missiles, nuclear, 321–24, 352
Missionaries, Christian, 36, 48, 51, 92–93, 97, 126–27, 163, 175, 183–84, 193–94
Mississippi River, 93–94, 97, 99
Mitsubishi family, 210
Mitsui family, 210
Mitterand, François, 354
Mobutu, Joseph, 333–34
Moby Dick, 169
Mochica, 73
Moctezuma I, 71
Moctezuma II, 71–72, 96
Modernism, 293, 295–97, 374–75
Mogul dynasty, 4, 30, 35–37, 39–40, 98, 120, 122–23
Mohacs, 34
Molière, Jean Baptiste, 116
Mona Lisa, 19
Monarchies, 14–18, 31–37, 44–45, 50, 58, 60–61, 105–11, 121, 126–27 (*See also* Absolutism, Constitutional monarchy, Enlightened despots)
Mondrian, Piet, 296–97
Money, 12, 92, 100–101, 195, 265, 311, 313, 381, 384
Mongolia, 43, 45, 126, 339
Mongols, 12, 31, 44–45, 81–82, 87, 124–25, 186
Monkey, 52
Monks, Christian, 21
Monopolies, 12, 110, 142, 160
Monroe Doctrine, 157
Montaigne, Michel de, 20
Montesquieu, Baron Charles de, 116, 169
Montgomery, General Bernard, 284
Moors, 15
Morelos, 247
Morgan, J. Pierpont, 160
Moroccan crises, 218
Morocco, 59, 179, 218, 257, 284, 331
Moscow, 244, 268, 282, 284, 343
Mosques, 40
Mosque of Shah Abbas, 40
Mosque of Shah Suleiman, 40
Mossadegh, Muhammad, 336–37
Most-favored-nation treaties, 184
Moulin Rouge, 148
Moving pictures, 230, 376
Mozambique, 180, 334

Mugabe, Robert, 334
Muhammad the Prophet, 28–29, 129
Muhammad II the Conqueror, 31–32
Mukden, 49
Munch, Edvard, 298
Munich, 279
Muslim center, 28, 30–31, 37–40, 43, 101, 120–23, 181
Muslim Law, 28–30
Muslim League, 337
Muslims, 7, 28–31, 35–37, 121–23, 129, 181, 185–86, 211, 255–56, 321, 335–37, 364–65
Mussolini, Benito, 262–64, 277–78
Mutsuhito (*See* Meiji Emperor)

Nadir, Shah, 122
Nagasaki, 287, 309
Nagy, Imre, 317
Namibia, 180 (*See also* German Southwest Africa)
Napoleon I, 136–38, 156, 164–65, 180
Napoleon III, 145, 203
Napoleonic Empire, 137, 164
Narodniks, 242
Nasser, Gamal Abdel, 335, 365
Nationalism, 139–41, 145–46, 194, 204–5, 217, 241, 250–51, 270–71, 278, 302–3, 317–19, 372
National Liberation Front, 332
Native Americans, 156–57, 160, 185, 187–88 (*See also* Amerindians)
Navigation, 91–92
Nazi Party, 261, 264–67
Nazism, 265–66, 301
Nazi-Soviet Pact, 279, 308
Nehru, Jawaharlal, 337–38, 364
Neoimperialism, 330, 360
Neruda, Pablo, 299
Netherlands, 11–13, 15–16, 96–98, 107, 110–12, 280–82
Netzahualcoyotl, 71
New Culture Movement, 251
New Deal, 233–34, 350
New Economic Policy, 244, 269
New England, 23, 98, 153–54
New Guinea, 285
New Monarchs, 14–18
Newton, Isaac, 105, 114, 148
New World, 8, 15, 68–70, (*See also* Americas)
New York, 97, 154, 311, 343–44
New Zealand, 188–89, 220, 236
Nicaragua, 206, 272, 318–19
Nicholas II, 204–5, 219, 242–44
Nietzsche, Friedrich, 148
Nigeria, 257
Niger River, 179
Ninety-Five Theses, 21–22
Nixon, Richard, 351, 363
Nkrumah, Kwame, 258, 330–31
Nobunaga, 127
No drama, 53
Nomads, 4, 81–82
Normandy, 285
North, global, 343–55
North Atlantic Treaty Organization, 315, 324
Northern Dynasty, 247–48
Northern Rhodesia, 179, 334 (*See also* Zambia)

North Korea, 309, 320, 339, 364
North Vietnam, 320–21, 338–39
Norway, 11, 280
Nuclear Test Ban Treaty, 324
Nuclear war, 5, 323–25, 387–88
Nuremberg, 262
Nurhachi, 49, 124
Nyerere, Julius, 333, 365–66

Obregón, Alvaro, 248
Oceania, 84–85, 94, 188, 285–86
October Manifesto, 205
October Revolution, 244
Oil, 5, 229–30, 248, 365
Okinawa, 287
Oklahoma, 188
Old Man Goriot, 149
Olympia, 148
Omar Khayyám, 37–39
Omdurman, 179
One Day in the Life of Ivan Denisovich, 352
One Hundred Years of Solitude, 375
One-party states, 348, 362–63
Opium War, 183
Oregon Territory, 157
Organization of African Unity, 385
Organization of American States, 311, 318, 385
Organization of Petroleum Exporting Countries, 5, 385
Origin of Species, 148
Orozco, José, 300
Orwell, George, 298–99
Osman (Othman), 31
Ottoman Empire, 7, 11, 30–34, 38–40, 120–22, 204, 210, 218, 221 (*See also* Turkey)
Ottoman Turks, 12, 30–34

Pachacuti Inca, 73
Pacific Ocean, 2, 84–85, 285–86
Paéz, José, 166
Pahlavi dynasty, 272, 337
Pakistan, 321, 337, 365
Palestine, 221, 335
Palestine Liberation Front, 335
Pan-Africanism, 257, 385
Panama Canal, 206
Pan-Arabism, 335
Panikkar, K. M., 174
Pankhurst, Emmeline, 203
Paraguay, 165
Paraguayan War, 165
Paris, 12, 99, 136, 219, 236, 282
Parlements, 14, 110
Parliament, 16–17, 110–11, 145, 348
Parliamentary Republic, 208
Party of the Mexican Revolution, 247–48
Pashas, 33
Pasternak, Boris, 300
Pastoral peoples, 4, 81–88
Paul III, 23–24
Pavlov, Ivan, 295
Pearl Harbor, 283
Peasants, 11, 22, 37, 48, 108–9, 113, 146, 166–67, 241–42, 246–48, 252–53, 268–70
Peasants War, 24
Peking, 45, 124, 183, 250–52, 254, 277
Peninsulars, 163, 165

Pennsylvania, 154
Peron, Eva, 366
Peron, Juan, 366
Perry, Commodore Matthew, 157, 183
Pershing, General John J., 247
Persia, 7, 33–35, 38–40, 120, 122, 212, 217, 331 (*See also* Iran)
Persian Gulf, 34, 181, 337
Persian miniatures, 38–39
Personalist dictators, 247, 271–72
Peru, 8, 72–74, 76–77, 93, 96, 163–65
Peter I the Great, 107–9, 122, 246
Petrarch, Francesco, 18, 20
Philadelphia, 155–56
Philip II, 14–16
Philippine Insurrection, 207, 211–12
Philippine Islands, 2, 181, 207, 283, 287
Philosophes, 114–16, 135–36
Phony War, 280
Picasso, Pablo, 296–97
Piedmont, 139, 146
Pilsudski, Marshal Josef, 271
Pitt, William, 99
Pizarro, Francisco, 93, 96
Plains Indians, 188
Plehve, Vyacheslav, 204–5
Poe, Edgar Allan, 169
Poland, 11, 107, 222, 236, 244, 270–71, 279–80, 308, 313–14, 317
Poliziano, Angelo, 13
Pollock, Jackson, 374
Pollution, 5
Polycentrism, 323
Pope, Alexander, 116
Popes, 12, 16, 21–25, 139
Popular art, 376
Population, 5, 101, 113, 126, 128, 138, 144, 157, 162–63, 195–96, 364
Population Explosion, 5, 12, 153, 195
Populism, 205
Portugal, 11, 92–93, 95–96, 107, 163, 165, 334
Portuguese, 60, 64, 92–93, 95–96
Portuguese Empire, 95–96, 163, 165, 174, 180, 334
Potsdam conference, 308
Poverty and underdevelopment, 360
Pragmatism, 169, 364, 373
Prague, 279, 317
Precious Ships, 45–46
Presbyterianism, 22
Pretoria, 334
Preurban peoples, 8, 80–85 (*See also* Hunting and gathering, Nomads, Pastoral peoples)
Prince, The, 18
Princip, Gavrillo, 216–17
Progressivism, 205–6, 232
Proletariat (See Labor, industrial)
Prophecy of Cuauhtémoc, 170
Protectorates, 177, 180
Protestants, 154
Proust, Marcel, 297–98
Prussia, 106–8, 145–46 (*See also* Germany)
Ptolemy, 114
Pueblo culture, 82
Purge trials, 269–70
Puritanism, 23–25, 111, 168

Qadis, 30–31, 33
Quebec, 97, 99
Quetzalcóatl, 70

Rabelais, François, 20
Racine, Jean, 116
Racism, 265–67
Radio, 230
Railroads, 143, 160, 181, 186, 195, 229–30, 380
Rajas, 35–36, 97
Rajputs, 36, 39, 129–30
Ramayana, 130
Rambouillet, Madame de, 117
Ranavalona III, 179
Rasputin, 243
Reagan, Ronald, 319, 351, 367
Recession of 1970s and 1980s, 345
Red Army, 244
Reformation, 10, 15–17, 20–25, 92
Reform Bill of 1832, 145
Refugees, 309, 335, 337
Regionalism, 157–58, 166
Reichstag, 265–66, 287
Reign of Terror, 136
Relativism, cultural, 294
Relativity, theory of, 294
Religion, 3, 20–25, 28, 30, 33–35, 64–65, 92, 121, 193–94, 371–72 (*See also* specific faiths)
Remarque, Erich Maria, 298
Rembrandt van Rijn, 116
Remembrance of Things Past, 298
Renaissance, 10, 12–15, 18–20, 114, 116
Renoir, Auguste, 148
Reparations, 222
Republican Party, 206, 232, 350–51
Revolutions, 15–17, 139, 154, 163–66, 199–200, 240–54 (See also individual revolutions by country)
Revolutions of 1848, 139, 196, 264
Rhineland, 278
Richard III, 16
Richelieu, Cardinal, 110
Riefenstahl, Leni, 301
Rio de Janeiro, 162, 165, 208, 272
Rise of Silas Lapham, 169
Rivera, Diego, 300
Road to Wigan Pier, 298
Robespierre, Maximilien de, 136
Robinson Crusoe, 116–17
Rockefeller, John D., 160
Rock 'n' Roll, 376
Romance of the Three Kingdoms, 52
Romanov dynasty, 106–9, 121–22, 222, 242–43
Romanticism, 146–48, 168–70
Rome, 18–21, 139, 263
Romeo and Juliet, 20
Rommel, General Erwin, 284
Roosevelt, Eleanor, 233–34
Roosevelt, Franklin, 233–34, 248, 282, 284, 308, 310–11
Roosevelt, Theodore, 206
Rosas, Encarnación, 166
Rosas, Manuel de, 166, 170
Rousseau, Jean-Jacques, 115
Rubaiyat, 38–39
Rubens, Peter Paul, 19
Rumania, 33, 271, 282, 313, 317, 323
Russia, 11, 32–33, 106–9, 121–22, 139, 146, 204–5, 216–20, 222, 224–25, 267–70, (*See also* Soviet Union)
Russian Empire, 181, 185–87, 217–18
Russian expansionism, 108–9, 121–22, 185–87, 212, 313

Russian Revolution, 241–46
Russians, 122
Russo-Japanese War, 183–242
Rutherford, Ernest, 294

Saarinen, Eero, 375
Sadat, Anwar, 335, 365
Sadi of Shiraz, 38
Safavid dynasty, 7, 30, 33–35, 39, 120–22
Sahara Desert, 56, 179
Sahel states, 365–66 (*See also* individual states)
Saladin, 31
Salazar, Antonio de, 334
Salon, the, 117
Samori, 179
Samurai, 50–51, 127, 130, 302
Sandinistas, 319, 367
San Martín, José, 162, 164–65
Santa Anna, Antonio de, 166
Santo Domingo, 272
Sarajevo, 216–17
Sarmiento, Domingo, 168, 170
Satellites, artificial, 344, 386
Saudis, 129, 365
Savonarola, Girolamo, 21
Scandinavia, 11, 235 (*See also* individual countries)
Scarlet Letter, 169
School of Mines, 169
Schutzstaffel (SS), 266–67
Science, modern, 19, 114–15, 194, 293–97, 372–73
Scientific Revolution, 19, 114–15, 194
Scotland, 22
Scream, The, 298
Security Council (UN), 311
Seiji, Togo, 375
Sekigahara, 127
Self-strengthening campaign, 209
Selim the Grim, 32
Seljuk Turks, 30–31, 38
Seminoles, 212
Senegal, 258
Senegal River, 179
Senghor, Léopold, 258, 330, 365
Seoul, 49
Sepoys, 123
Serbia, 122, 204, 216 (*See also* Yogoslavia)
Seurat, Georges, 148
Seven Years War, 98–99, 107–8
Shahs, 33–34, 337
Shakespeare, William, 16, 20
Shamil, 212
Shanghai, 251–52
Shantung, 184, 220
Sharpville massacre, 366
Shensi Soviet, 253, 277
Sherman, General William Tecumseh, 159
Shintoism, 52
Ships, 45–46, 91–92, 176, 184, 195, 203, 231, 283, 285, 380
Shiva, 130
Shoguns, 50, 127–28, 130
Siberia, 185–87, 270, 323
Sicily, 284
Sidney, Sir Philip, 20
Sikhs, 123, 364
Silver, 12
Singapore, 338, 364

Wang Yang-ming, 52
War debts, 223
Warlords, 250–51
War of the Pacific, 165–66, 208
Warsaw Pact, 315, 317, 324
Wars of Independence, 163–65
Wars of religion, 15–17, 24–25
Wars of the Roses, 16
Washington, D.C., 156
Washington, George, 99, 154–56
Wasteland, The, 297–98
Waterloo, 136
Watt, James, 138
Weapons, 31, 35, 51, 92, 94, 121, 127, 177, 188, 220, 223–25, 288–89
Weimar Republic, 222, 229, 231, 264–66, 271
Welfare state, 310, 354
Westernization, 183–84, 192–96, 207–10, 212, 249, 254–58
Western Sudan, 56, 58–59, 179
Western World, 4–5, 10–11, 126
West Germany (Federal Republic of Germany), 309, 315, 323, 353–54
Westminster, Act of, 235
Whitman, Walt, 169
William I, 145–46
William II, 204, 218–19, 264

William of Orange, 110–11
Wilson, Woodrow, 206, 218–19, 221–22, 232, 247
Witte, Sergius, 205
Wittenberg, 21–22
Wolsey, Cardinal, 16
Women, 13, 37, 48, 62, 113–14, 128, 130, 144, 161, 167, 220–21, 223, 228, 231, 284, 288, 347, 361
Women's Movement, 140, 144, 167–68, 207, 231, 347
Women's suffrage, 144–45, 203, 231
Wordsworth, William, 148
World Bank, 5, 311, 385
World Court, 231, 385
World market, 4, 101, 194–95, 381–84
World War I, 216–25, 228–29, 231, 242–44, 250, 263–64
World War II, 222, 234, 275–89, 308–11, 313–15, 329–30
Wright, Frank Lloyd, 296
Wuthering Heights, 149
Wycliffe, John, 21

Yalta conference, 310–11

Yangtze River, 46, 250, 277
Yi Song-gye, 48–49
Yorktown, 156
Yoshimune, 127
Yoshitsune, 53
Young Turks, 212
Youth, 232, 346–47, 361
Youth movements, 346–47, 351
Yüan Shih-k'ai, 249–50
Yugoslavia, 33, 282, 287, 316 (*See also* Serbia)
Yung-lo, 44–46, 52

Zaibatsu, 210, 270–71
Zaire, 334
Zambia, 334 (*See also* Northern Rhodesia)
Zanzibar, 179
Zapata Emiliano, 247
Zhukov, Marshal Gregory, 287
Zimbabwe, 334 (*See also* Southern Rhodesia)
Zimbabwe, Great, 60–61
Zionism, 335
Zola, Émile, 149
Zulus, 179, 211–12, 334